REA

OVERSIZE

Y0-ABQ-932

MISSING STORIES

An Oral History of Ethnic and Minority Groups in Utah

MISSING

STORIES

Leslie G. Kelen
and Eileen Hallet Stone

UNIVERSITY OF UTAH PRESS   Salt Lake City

The US WEST Foundation is proud to sponsor publication of
Missing Stories: An Oral History of Eight Ethnic and Minority Groups in Utah.

The Utah Centennial Series

Library of Congress Catalog-in-Publication Data
Kelen, Leslie G., 1949–
    Missing stories : an oral history of eight ethnic and minority
groups in Utah / Leslie G. Kelen and Eileen Hallett Stone.
        p. cm. — (The Utah centennial series ; v. 8)
    ISBN 0-87480-516-3 (alk. paper)
    1. Minorities—Utah—History—Anecdotes. 2. Utah—History—
Anecdotes. 3. Oral history. I. Stone, Eileen Hallett, 1943–   .
II. Title. III. Series.
F835.A1K45 1996
979.2'004—dc20   96-43382

Drága Apukámnak—to my dear father—Alex Kelen
    July 18, 1911—March 28, 1996
for teaching me to listen and to ask questions,
    and to the members of
the Klein, Roth, Weisz, and Schonfeld families,
    murdered in the Shoah.
May your names always be remembered.

—Leslie Kelen

To my mother who got me started with her observations,
for Adam who lived as long as he could,
and to Daniel who steps into each day with natural definition.

—Eileen Hallet Stone

There is something to be told about us for the telling of which we all wait. In our unwilling ignorance we hurry to listen to stories of old human life, new human life, fancied human life, avid of something to while away the time of unanswered curiosity. We know we are explainable, and not explained. Many of the lesser things concerning us have been told, but the greater things have not been told; and nothing can fill their place. Whatever we learn of what is not ourselves . . . will likewise leave the emptiness an emptiness. Until the missing story of ourseves is told, nothing besides told can suffice us: We shall go on quietly craving it.

—From *The Telling* by Laura (Riding) Jackson

CONTENTS

ACKNOWLEDGMENTS

We thank the Utah Humanities Council, the Kennecott Corporation, the Herbert I. and Elsa B. Michael Foundation, American Express, Mervyn's, and John and Vera Eccles for providing funds to complete the first phase of the Ethnic and Minority Oral History and Photography Projects. We also thank Shirley Reed, Rabbi Eric Silver, Joel Shapiro, Pastor France Davis, Judge Raymond Uno, and Alice Kasai for guiding us in our initial series of interviews in the Ute, Jewish, African-American, and Japanese communities; and we thank Ed Kim, Dr. Anand Yang, Dr. Philip Notarianni, Constantine Skedros, Penelope Koulouris, Dr. Bill Gonzalez, Reuben Jimenez, and Robert Archuleta for similarly guiding us in interviews in the Chinese, Italian, Greek, and Hispano-Chicano communities.

We acknowledge our deep debt to Maestro Maurice Abravanel, Joseph Rosenblatt, Ellen Furgis, John Florez, Ernest D. Mariani, Nick Vidalakis, Dr. Gregory Thompson, President Chase Peterson, the board of the Oral History Institute, the Greek Orthodox Community of Salt Lake City, and the George S. and Dolores Dore Eccles Foundation, for helping us establish the Ethnic and Minority Documentary Archive at the University of Utah and for providing the funds to complete this manuscript.

We pay special tribute to Richard Dorman Ligh, grantwriter; Robert Doherty, historian; Sandra Telford Fuller, interviewer, writer, fund-raiser, and editor; Tim Funk, consultant; Doris Mason, OHI board Secretary; Hugh Pinnock, advisor; Mr. and Mrs. John Mitchell, patrons; Helen Papanikolas, historian, consultant, and editor; Darrell A. Gardner, Sr., advisor; Penny Sampinos, field coordinator; Carolyn Bennion, transcriber and editor; Mitsugi Kasai, translator; Dorcas Nakao, translater and typist; Kent Miles, photographer; Joyce Kelen, Leslie's supporter and loving partner; and Randy Silverman, Eileen's *mein geliebte*. They embarked on this journey during its chaotic, early days and stayed on board long enough to steer the vessel to a safe harbor.

Finally, we acknowledge the generous contributions of our informants in the state's Ute, African-American, Jewish, Chinese, Italian, Greek, Japanese, and Hispano-Chicano Communities. What power and beauty this book contains is due to their skills as narrators. What errors of omission or commission exist are, of course, our own.

PREFACE

When in the spring of 1982 we received funds from the Utah Humanities Council to carry out an ethnic and minority oral history project, we had little idea of the complex long-term endeavor we were about to begin. We had proposed a one-year project to the council, in which we would conduct interviews with senior citizens and community leaders in Salt Lake City's Ute, African-American, Jewish, Chinese, Italian, Japanese, Greek, and Chicano-Hispano communities "to create a documentary portrait of ethnicity in Utah before it was too late"—before the elderly (who were the repositories of their community's formative experiences) passed away. We had envisioned taping 120 interviews, then shaping the interview contents into a book. Approximately eight years and 689 interviews later, we completed the project; four years after that, we finished the manuscript.[1]

In retrospect, it is clear that undertaking this project was akin to opening the lid of Pandora's notorious little box: We were beset with challenges from the start. The communities we targeted proved more factionalized and multifaceted than we supposed; interviews took longer to tape than planned; published community histories were only moderately effective in establishing backgrounds on which to build interviews; and our interview methods themselves had to be honed over time to be effective. In addition, as we discarded our early assumptions about the communities we were studying, we came to realize that we were not merely building on previous historiographic foundations; we were shaping essential community experiences from scratch.

We quickly learned, for instance, that although the city's Jewish community boasted a recently "merged" congregation, consisting of members of former Conservative and Reform synagogues, the union had not healed the long-

---

1. The figure "689" represents the total number of interviews we conducted with 352 informants.

standing religious and cultural differences that had divided the community early in the twentieth century and had kept it divided for nearly six decades. We also came to understand that the city's African-American community was densely "layered" in its makeup. From the slaves who accompanied the Mormon vanguard of 1847 to the professionals who entered the state during the civil rights era and beyond, black families had arrived in at least four distinct migrations. And while the religious and political activities of the African-American community created an image of unity, individual speech was unmistakably inflected, representing people's diverse backgrounds and histories.

Further complicating our work was our realization that the communities we were studying had not, as communities, come to terms with recent events and experiences. Sharply conflicting accounts were offered of how communities developed, how much discrimination people faced, and how they had dealt with such difficulties. These earnest and profoundly diverging testimonies compelled us to take the time to listen, investigate, and report. Our one-year project thus grew into a two-year project; our two-year project (after we added a photodocumentary component) became a four-year effort; and our four-year effort (once we decided to develop a statewide portrait of ethnicity) became an eight-year endeavor.

What kept us on track during those years and allowed us to move forward with vigor and purpose was our steadily growing realization that we were telling a new story in a new way. The eight communities, representing our state's oldest, largest, and most culturally viable racial and ethnic groups, had never before been depicted in a single volume; and the history of non-Mormon ethnic and minority groups in Utah had never before been told from the bottom up—from the perspectives, that is, of its average citizens. Formal histories, narrating late nineteenth and early twentieth century ethnic experiences, had laid a solid academic groundwork, but the voices and lives of ethnic people had never found their way into Utah consciousness. The small communities that are the basis for this book (according to the 1990 census, only the Chicano-Hispano community contained more than one percent of the state's population) appeared unessential to the state's public life. Even our informants occasionally echoed this belief. If you want "real" ethnic stories, they would insist, interview in New York, or Chicago, or California, where massive ethnic enclaves exist. What stories, after all, could Utah's tiny ethnic groups relate that would prove vital to understanding our state? What could these voices tell us that we don't already know?

What the voices told us—singularly and collectively—was the story of how individuals and families fared and how communities were settled, developed, and maintained throughout the years 1920–1986; they shared accounts of parents and grandparents who endured the ordeal of losing aboriginal lands to whites or who made transcontinental, transpacific, and transatlantic voyages "to come to a new land"; they recalled the arduous task of sustaining families and earning livelihoods on reservation allotments, in mining towns, on small farms, and in growing cities; they shared stories of catastrophes and triumphs, many of which had acquired mythic stature within their communities; they described the lifestyles of parents and grandparents, evoking ancient customs brought over from the Old World or founded in the New World; they enumerated folk remedies for illnesses and problems ranging from chest colds to childbirth; they celebrated parents and relatives who could foretell the future, decode the meaning of dreams, and cure the evil eye; and they remembered loves, losses, longings, predictions, predilections, admonishments, formal and informal teachings, and counsel that carried over from one generation to the next.

Our informants confided their mixed emotions over relinquishing or modifying traditional customs and establishing bicultural lifestyles, which they accomplished by keeping tenuous footholds in each world or by learning to make inner adjustments to balance the scales between losses and gains. They confided personal choices that took them down one road rather than another; identified terrible personal setbacks that could *not* be rectified and shocking losses that could. They described native cosmologies that were both startlingly foreign conceptions and excitingly familiar renderings of ancient world maps, and they shared their hardships and their accomplishments in unique, culturally modulated tones, syntax, imagery, anecdotes, and wit.

What they showed us was the courage and vision needed to build businesses and careers that sometimes exceeded parents' wildest immigrant dreams and the strength and steadfastness necessary to combat the racism that has so profoundly marked the twentieth century. What they confessed was their rage at being stereotyped, mistreated, overlooked, and undervalued and what it took to work through tribal councils and such organizations as the National Association for the Advancement of Colored People, the Japanese American Citizens League, and the Spanish-speaking Organization for Community, Integrity and Opportunity to articulate grievances and redress wrongs. They taught us that cultural and ethnic boundaries are real, that customs and rituals—though attenuated and altered by time—persist and must be honored, and that the way to celebrate our common humanity is through acknowledging our differences. In all, these voices colored a familiar landscape with previously unknown tales, portraying dense clusters of lives that were missing from our textbooks, guidebooks, and map books.

Presented here is the story we taped and molded into book form. To "tell" this story, we combed through more than twenty thousand pages of transcript and, in a real sense, reexperienced the project as it existed on paper. For, as long as the documentary work was under way, we could not come to terms with what we had done. Once we stopped photographing and interviewing (and surrendered the immodest hope of ever truly "completing" the project), we were able to confront what we had amassed and determine what to do with it. It was a frightening and daunting task, because we knew the interviews we selected would have to stand not only for what *we* did but also for what our informants told us.

To incorporate as much interview content into the book as possible, we initially tried to tell each community's story chronologically. We selected first the interviews with the oldest informants and then steadily built toward younger people and more recent events. Although some measure of this concept persisted throughout the entire editing process, we found we could not maintain the format in each chapter. Interviews are extended conversations between people that sometimes produce powerful self-portraits and sometimes community analysis. Forcing interviews to serve a chronological model blurred these distinctions.

After running into several cul-de-sacs, we decided the foremost criterion for including an interview *had* to be literary. An interview had to offer a dramatic and believable account of a life. Next, we would allow a community's strongest interviews to suggest the shape of the chapter. We would not impose any a priori design and choose interviews to fit it. And finally, as much as possible, we would arrange the interviews to reveal both the broad trajectory of a community's history and the dialogue within a community that described its struggle for identity and accounted for the vitality of its communal life. In the chapters about the Ute and Jewish communities, for instance, meeting this criterion meant interspersing interview excerpts among full accounts and proceeding from a relatively contemporary perspective into the past, then coming forward again; in the chapters about the Greek and Japanese communities, we used an extended prologue to highlight the different sensibilities of first- and second-generation community members; and in the chapters about the African-American and Chicano-Hispano communities, we emphasized the struggle for civil rights while adhering to the chronological principle.

We selected material from twenty-five percent of our informants, (88 out of 352) to create *Missing Stories.* Many splendid interviews were, consequently, left out of this book. Most omitted accounts did not fit into or enhance a particular chapter's narrative. In some instances, though, we included interviews with people who had lived on the margins of their community and left out interviews with prominent community members. Our choice was not meant to insult the prominent or to ennoble the obscure. We simply sought to portray a community's entire range of sensibility and experience.

A small number of the interviews we selected were nearly fully usable in transcript form. In the majority of cases, however, to bring an informant's story into focus, we deleted content, shifted paragraphs, and added transitions. In "in-depth interviews," which often ran to several hundred pages of transcript, we selected one story or several from many vivid accounts. We tried to choose stories that both revealed an individual's character and evoked central community experience. We approached each chapter in the book—each community's narrative—as if it were a book in itself. Every chapter, as a result, has a formal beginning (sometimes a prologue), a broad middle, and a definite denouement (occasionally an epilogue). Aware that each community has its own unmistakable speaking style, we scrupulously strove to present this unconscious music. In addition, midway through the four-year editing process, we asked ethnic historians to contribute prefaces to each chapter. We felt these prefaces were necessary to provide formal historical contexts to the interviews and to orient the general reader to the unique historical and cultural dimensions out of which each person spoke.

Finally, *Missing Stories* is meant to be read on several levels at once. The first and most apparent is the historical: As a dramatization of non-Mormon ethnic and minority life in Utah, this book aims to provide the story that, until now, has only been alluded to by Utah historians. The second level of significance reflects the personal, the psychological. Here, we refer to the quest for identity —the journey toward spiritual development—which is recounted by a few informants in each community. Although all of the stories extend historical content, that is not their exclusive virtue. By teaching us what it *feels* like to live as a member of a specific ethnic community while deepening our understanding of how human beings face and overcome adversity, these tales add to the precious vocabulary by which we give shape and meaning to our lives. Finally, *Missing Stories* is the cumulative revelation of our multicultural past and present. This story identifies where we came from, suggests where we are headed, and illuminates the cultural and experiential resources that inform our lives. As we approach the end of the millennia, perhaps we can finally admit to ourselves that we cannot comprehend the drama and richness of our lives until we realize that *this* story is *our* story—the story of the American experience itself.

LESLIE G. KELEN AND EILEEN HALLET STONE

INTRODUCTION

Helen Papanikolas

This is not a book of scholarly history. It is a book of voices, voices of speakers who desperately want us to know how life was for them and their forebears in Utah, this once-Indian, then Mormon land of desert and mountainous terrain. For decades, Mormon people of North European heritage did not hear these other voices, not even those of the indigenous Native-Americans. Nor did they listen to the African-Americans, both slave and free, who had come to Utah with the Mormon pioneers.

The settlers uprooted the sage and rabbitbrush, planted fields, dug irrigation canals, grazed sheep and cattle, searched for coal and ore, and proselytized within the nation and abroad. As other peoples came to Utah, not as converts to the fledgling church but to "earn their bread," as they said in their various languages, their voices, too, did not find their way into its history and left it impoverished, unfinished. Before their voices became ghostly though, their children heard them. The children garnered their own experiences together with their people's communal and familial memories, and they now speak to us in this unique volume. We are touched and surprised by insights into pain, cruelty, indifference, love, and perseverance. We learn what was previously unknown. The invisible threads of memory become starkly alive.

Generations after Mormon settlement, a Native-American might not know of the incursions of white settlers and profiteers into Indian land throughout the nation. He might never have heard of the dusty-robed fathers, Domínguez and Escalante who trudged through their Indians' Utah domain, or heard the gunfire of mountain men and fur trappers, or seen the covered wagons winding through the land, their strange occupants building shelters, leveling the alluvial earth, destroying the seeds and small animals that had sustained his people. He might not have witnessed his people in ceremonial finery dancing to their gods, as Indians did elsewhere, entreating them to stop the relentless encroaching onto their ancestral land. He remembers, though, his grandfather's prophetic words that the whites would outnumber them. They would fight and get what they were after.

The speaker knows this is true. Communal memory tells him so. His people had lost their land to white settlers and were shunted onto reservations, where their fishing and hunting were curtailed. There they were left to subsist on beans, salt, sugar, and meat doled out to them by government agencies. On their reservations they knew nothing of the great burst of industrialization that seized the country in the latter part of the nineteenth century, that brought millions of immigrants to build branch railroad lines, change narrow to standard gauge rails, man factories, dig coal and ore and transport them to mills and smelters.

As the destiny of the Native-Americans had been decided by Mormon colonization, the fate of emigrants and immigrants in Utah was determined by the transcontinental railroad. The joining of the Central Pacific and Union Pacific railroads in Promontory, Utah, in 1869, was a catalyst to industrialization. Brigham Young denounced the railroad tent towns that attracted gamblers and transient women as "sinks of pollution," but the Mormon kingdom on earth was not to remain in wishful isolation. As homestead laws were drawing Americans and immigrants to the Midwest and West, the joining of the railroads brought Utah Territory tardily toward industrialization and capitalism.

The transcontinental railroad put an end to transporting coal and ore by mules and horses. The immense mineral deposits within the Wasatch Range could now be profitably delivered to eastern furnaces. New techniques had been found to extract copper from the ore that had enticed earlier gold and silver entrepreneurs to Bingham Canyon. Silver was being mined in the Tintic area; and in eastern Utah Territory railroad workers for Denver and Rio Grande Western Railroad uncovered rich bituminous coal veins while cutting through Price Canyon to reach Salt Lake City.

A vanguard of immigrant labor agents and foreign-language newspapers energetically made industries' demands known. Ships steamed back and forth bringing the famed "wretched refuse" seeking escape from pogroms, vendettas, and the traditional poverty of their countries. Except for the Jews, they came as sojourners who intended to trade their physical strength for American wages and return to their native lands.

The immigrants were subjected to intense discrimination, a reaction to fears that they would "mongrelize" the "white" race and destroy American life as the founding fathers had envisioned it. Americans formed mobs to prevent the newcomers from finding work and killed with impunity. Eleven Italians were lynched in New Orleans in 1891. Immigrant neighborhoods were torched; a spectacular fire destroyed several blocks of South Omaha's Greek district in 1909.

Still, the cry for laborers, the "cheap labor" industrialists sought, grew as mines, mills, and smelters multiplied. Villagers came in a deluge. In the first decade of the 1900s, six million immigrants entered the country's ports. Labor agents sent men of all nationalities to work in eastern factories, often as strikebreakers. Many South Slavs (later to be called Yugoslavs) traveled westward to the anthracite mines in Pennsylvania; others went to the Iron Mountain district of Minnesota. Italians laid brick in eastern cities, shoveled coal into giant furnaces of the Gary, Indiana, steel mills, sawed trees in the Northwest, and worked on railroad gangs. Greeks blasted and shoveled coal and ore throughout the Intermountain West and made up large railroad gangs in the Midwest and West. Japanese worked mainly on section gangs and on the West Coast as farm laborers. Notwithstanding emancipation, African-Americans continued to do the menial labor of the nation. Jews worked in factories and small shops and sold clothing, shoes, and notions from pushcarts. Syrians and Lebanese later followed the same route to independence.

The life of industrial workers in Utah was similar to that in the nation as a whole. An added element faced the Utah newcomers, however. They found themselves living in a theocracy the Latter-day Saints' leaders envisioned. They were not of the "blood of Israel," not people of the Book of Mormon. They arrived, though, with personal, familial, and communal memories. These memories helped to sustain them in the harsh new land. Their experiences, often wretched, sometimes joyful, would in turn become memories that would be passed on to their children and to their grandchildren.

The earliest sojourners were the Chinese remnants of the thousands who had laid rails for the Central Pacific railroad. Their pick work on the portals and walls of Carbon County, Utah, coal mines had been called "beautiful to behold." But after an insidious campaign against the Chinese, called the Yellow Peril, aroused the country, Chinese throughout Utah joined their compatriots in their flight to the relative safety of Chinatowns on the East and West coasts. A few Chinese remained to run laundries, work in restaurants, and carry water to workers in mining towns.

Irish laborers and their "Cousin Jacks," English and Welsh immigrants, rushed to replace the Chinese in the mines. When they went on strike, Finns and Italians arrived and replaced them. Strikebreaking was often the fateful expediency that brought new immigrants to Utah.

Not all people in Utah received the benefits of its transition from an agrarian to an industrial society. One group of American Indians living in a remote desert area, for instance, who had been hired to work on a railroad gang were summarily sent back to their reservation when Italians arrived. Blacks were hired as "water boys" in mines and cleaned engines in roundhouse railyards. Those more fortunate worked as porters and waiters on railroad cars. Neither Native-Americans, African-Americans, nor Mexicans, who began arriving to escape the Mexican Revolution of 1910-1920, shared in the comparative prosperity of Utah's workers. Balkan, Mediterranean, and Asian immigrants accepted long hours, poor working and living conditions, and low wages, considering steady work a great good fortune.

In Salt Lake City, Ogden, the mining camps of Carbon County, the copper town of Bingham, the mill and smelter towns of Magna, Murray, Midvale, and, later, Tooele, workers congregated in neighborhoods with their own kind. A few ventured to provide imported foods of their cultures; others opened cafés and barber, shoe repair, and tailoring shops. The immigrants began to establish houses of worship, coffeehouses, tongs, and lodges. The American born called these rudimentary neighborhoods Greek Towns, Little Italy and Wop Towns, Jap Towns, and Bohunk Towns. Small clusters of houses for African American railyard workers were referred to as Nigger Towns. In Salt Lake City, Jews lived in the area of Ninth South and Main Street, not far from their shops. An anomaly were the Jews who lived in the Clarion agricultural colony of 1910 near Gunnison, Utah, the disastrous attempt of eastern Jewish philanthropists to send slum-dwelling Jews to learn farming in the West.

In their enclaves the immigrants felt safe. They knew nothing about the long fight for Utah's statehood. They could not read the local newspapers that reported on the federal government's barring of Mormon officials from taking seats in Congress. They heard, of course, of Mormon polygamy. That the Mormon's practiced polygamy strengthened the immigrants' view that they were living among a strange people. Those from the Balkans and the Mediterranean, whose people had lived for centuries under Turkish rule and knew that Muslim law allowed a man to have four wives, were especially affronted by polygamy.

The immigrants congregated in neighborhood coffeehouses, boarding-houses, tongs, and lodges to debate the religious and political events of their homelands. Their nationalism was unsettling to Americans. Except for the Japanese, the immigrants had come from countries that had struggled under foreign conquerors for centuries. The American and French revolutions had inspired their forebears to fight for their own eventual liberation. The immigrants' extreme nationalism alone would provoke the Americans to a burgeoning nativism.

Although hostility toward them grew unabated, the immigrants found life in America, even with its discrimination and blatant restrictions, far more promising than in their homelands. They prolonged their stay in America and brought over women, the picture brides of the immigrant era. The brides were told to leave behind the hand-dyed, woven blankets and handiwork they had worked on since childhood. America, their future husbands wrote, had better, machine-made items. Often the first meeting of the future bride and groom involved a struggle by one or both to conceal their dismay. It was not unusual for the exchanged photographs not to resemble the living persons they supposedly represented.

The brides became young matriarchs. Many took in boarders to help with buying property or opening stores in the future. They planted and irrigated gardens, baked bread in outdoor earth ovens, prepared the pastries and liqueurs of hospitality. Into this milieu of ethnic neighborhoods, a generation of immigrant American children were born. Here began the childhood experiences that would become memory and finally the adult voices that speak to us in this book. The enclaves were replicas of the native villages. The extended families the immigrants had known in those villages had to be replaced by a strong dependence on customs, such as godparenthood, that gave them cohesiveness and assured them that their children would be cared for if death or illness invaded their homes. Old World religious and ceremonial customs, midwives, folk healers, dream explainers, priests in black robes, Buddhist priests in Shinto dress, rabbis, cafés and stores selling a great variety of imported foods, and foreign-language newspapers were the province for the immigrants and their children.

Death hovered over the immigrant towns. Mine, mill, and smelter accidents and coal mine explosions punctuated the pages of the mine inspectors' and coal mine inspectors' reports. The largest losses occurred in the Winter Quarters Mine in 1900 when 200 men died, 62 of them Finns, and in Castle Gate Mine Number Two in 1924 when 171 miners, 49 of them Greek, were killed. The orphans did not know how many miners were killed; they simply knew their fathers and others in their neighborhood were dead. They heard their mothers keening at the sides of open caskets, saw them praying for the dead at their icons, crucifixes, or altars, and watched them prepare memorial foods. Wherever they went, these children were set apart in their black-dyed clothes. They became, at a cataclysmic burst, not only children of disparaged immigrants but fatherless as well.

Outside their noisy, busy neighborhoods, all immigrant children were stigmatized by hurtful attitudes, some brought on by events of which they were ignorant. They knew, though, their effects. First, they were the children of aliens whom inflammatory newspaper articles and demagogic oratory accused of coming to this country "to take over." Americans were especially hostile to the immigrants for sending money back to their families instead of keeping it in the country. Second, the children's fathers had been Americanized to the extent that they were drawn into workers' movements, which were condemned as despicable and un-American. They participated in strikes: in the Carbon County coal fields in the early 1900s, in a Murray smelter in 1909, in Carbon County in 1911, and in Bingham Canyon in 1912, the latter a devastating strike called by the Western Federation of Miners that brought almost all immigrant miners into the union. Third, their families responded instantly to Europe's entrance into World War I, each group siding with its native country's loyalties. Americans were unpleasantly surprised at their great concern for the countries of their birth.

As the war expanded, drawing more countries into either the side of the Great Powers or the side of the Allies, antiforeign feelings raced through the United States. When America entered the war in April 1917, a frenzy against all immigrants overran the nation. Two near-lynchings of Utah Greeks occurred in that year. The Greeks were saved by the prompt arrival of their armed countrymen. The immigrants were expected to volunteer to fight in the war, and when they did not, nativism exploded. Why was it that two hundred Utah Greeks returned to their country to fight against the Turks in the Balkan Wars of 1912–1913 yet were reluctant to fight for the country that gave them work? They were "dogs biting the hand that fed them," newspapers reported.

Soon immigrants began to volunteer or appear for induction, even though most were not U.S. citizens. Newspapers praised immigrants who volunteered and castigated those who sought exemption. Compounding the precarious position of the immigrants were the factions within them. The Serbs resented being called up while the Croats were exempt because they could be fighting against their own people of the Austro-Hungary Empire. When the war ended, animosity against the immigrants was kept alive under American Legion leadership. Legislation was enacted to restrict further entry into the country; the Palmer raids led to the deportation of many true and purported Communists; and in Utah, laws were passed forcing immigrants into a compulsory education program, though they were taken seriously only by the Japanese.

In the middle of the anti-immigrant conflict, the Carbon County coal mines joined in the national coal strike of 1922. Immigrant miners, many with their first citizenship papers, joined the strike. Some were army veterans who had been awarded citizenship for World War I service. (Japanese army veterans, though, had been rejected as citizens.) When one of their striking countrymen was killed by a deputy sheriff, the Greek miners became fanatic strike leaders.

The immigrants' strike participation, on top of their initial reluctance to appear for army induction, brought the hostility of Americans to new heights. The immigrants did not perceive how events had brought them to such a precarious state and were incapable of explaining the Americans' hatred to their fearful children. "It's because we are foreigners," they said.

All signs of clinging to native-country customs were derided as evidence that immigrants were incapable of becoming true Americans. "Like oil and water, they don't mix" was a common expression. The Greeks were disparaged for their Greek schools, coffeehouses, and fraternal organizations; the Italians and the people later to be called Yugoslavs were derided for their aggressive labor activity and lodges. Jews were labeled with ancient derogatory epithets. Mexicans who had fled the 1910–1920 Mexican Revolution and had entered the state as strikebreakers in Bingham later were able to find only the most arduous labor on railroad gangs, on road crews, and in mines, if they could find work at all. The Japanese felt the utmost discrimination. The 1922 Cable Act took American citizenship away from American-born Japanese women who had married Issei (Japanese born men). The Japanese found themselves in the position of the Chinese under the Exclusion Act of 1882. Japanese immigrant children learned early that the children of "Americans" and of people of North European heritage were looked upon more favorably than they.

The anti-immigrant campaigns culminated in the 1924 Ku Klux Klan attacks. Immigrants and their children saw white-robed Klan members march down Salt Lake City, Helper, and Magna streets and watched crosses burning on Salt Lake's Ensign peak, on Bingham and Helper mountainsides, and near the Magna graveyard. Stories of Klan attacks bombarded the children's ears. Immigrants who had married American women were most vulnerable— crosses burned in front of their businesses, women clerks and waitresses working for immigrants were threatened. In Helper, the Klan invaded stores, rampaged through them, and forced American women employees to their houses. A child watching a cross burning at night was forever wounded in spirit.

The anti-immigrant campaign resulted in the 1924 immigration restriction laws, which drastically cut the number of southern European, Balkan, and Middle-Eastern immigrants allowed to enter the country.

All through these turbulent years, the children of the immigrants were straddling two cultures. Those whose fathers had been killed in mine explosions and other industrial accidents experienced disastrous poverty, but others had moved out of the towns during the prosperity of the 1920s into middle-class neighborhoods. As we read the words of all these children in this book, we see that two overriding forces fashioned their lives: their relations with their immigrant parents and the intense discrimination against them as "aliens" within the "American" world. Inside their homes, they were immersed in their parents' religious practices, language, customs, and nationalism. Japanese, Jews, and Greeks held classes that children attended in addition to public school. When parents spoke of "our" country, "our" people, "our" history, the children heard the words with divided loyalties; they knew their parents were not speaking of America but of countries thousands of miles away that they had never seen.

Outside their towns, the children lived another life: American school, the English language, and allegiance to the American flag. They were caught in the ambivalence of knowing their roots were good and of knowing the American denigration of them. Immigrant children were constantly wary of what each day would bring. Taunts and fights on school grounds were regular occurrences. What child could read a schoolmate's letter in the local paper asking that Greeks and "Japs" not be hired in the mines without feeling tainted in some unexplainable way. In Tooele, petitions were circulated demanding that immigrant sons be barred from the high school football team. Only the coach's threat to resign deterred the school board. Three of the players, Joe Rinaldi, Dan Savich, and George Melinkovich, who later was an All-American at Notre Dame, went on to play professional ball. In the early 1930s, in both the Cyprus and Carbon County high schools, parents and teachers wanted assurances that their daughters would not be kissed by "foreigners" in the schools' play productions. Immigrant children were constantly on the alert to defend themselves.

Although they were at best patronized, the children of Balkan and Mediterranean immigrants were saved from the glaring overt racism directed at Asians, African-Americans, and Native-Americans. Minority speakers in this book recall that in theaters they were sent to the balconies; almost all restaurants refused them service; and real estate clauses prohibited them from buying houses in certain areas.

Girls and women of all age groups were further restricted by their peoples' codes. Far from white contact in their closed communities, Native- American and African-American girls continued their traditional ways. Immigrant girls, however, who attended American schools, watched movies, and listened to radios, saw starkly how their lives differed from those of girls outside their ethnic groups. Sons had fewer restrictions placed upon them by their elders, but daughters were constantly watched. They had to return home immediately at the close of school; they were not allowed to attend school dances; at ethnic communal functions they were careful to appear well bred because alert eyes were scrutinizing their demeanor. Daughters were raised to follow all the old-country customs of hospitality, deportment, and respect for elders.

The first immigrant daughters born in America often were taken out of school when the compulsory age limit of sixteen was reached to become brides in arranged marriages. Education for girls was unimportant to the first immigrants, and young women who continued their education beyond high school were few. Several voices in this book tell us of wanting more education, but it was reserved for their brothers, not for them. The American custom of dating was an amazement and abhorrence to the immigrants. How uncaring Americans were, they said, about their daughters' virginity. The voices in the stories that follow recall the old-country mores that had shadowed girls' and women's existence.

Except for a brief recession in the early 1920s, the immigrants became part of the post-war prosperity. With their extreme frugality, their new prosperity gave immigrants the opportunity to leave labor for business. The decade was financially good for them. But the stock market crash of 1929 signaled the beginning of the decade-long 1930s Depression and created a desolation of unemployment and ruined hopes. Mines closed or worked half-shift; sheepman lost their flocks to banks; and Utah's immigrant population declined as families moved to California hoping to find work with compatriots. During the Depression Mexicans were arbitrarily treated. Many were sent back to Mexico, among them naturalized citizens of the United States. For Native-Americans, suffering on the reservations became acute until some federal aid began in 1933. Still, Native-Americans were denied work offered to others under the Works Progress Administration, the WPA. African-American looked to their churches for the meager help available. They lived the old dictum "Last hired, first fired."

A great number of immigrants became politicized during President Franklin D. Roosevelt's New Deal programs and began voting, often for the first time, as ardent Democrats. Talk of return to their economically devastated native countries languished. The promises of higher education for their sons proved elusive, and many law-abiding immigrant parents joined Americans in bootlegging to raise the necessary funds.

During the Depression, American-born children of Japanese immigrants actively began fighting for their civil rights. The Japanese American Citizens

League succeeded in lobbying for a bill that amended the 1922 Cable Act, and American citizenship was restored to Japanese-American women who had married Issei. American citizenship was also granted to seven hundred World War I Issei veterans.

The Depression was conquered by the nation's entering World War II against Germany, Italy, and Japan. The war also brought mobility to the immigrants' children. Sons and some daughters entered the armed services and later benefited from the GI Bill that provided veterans with an opportunity for higher education. Yet Japanese community leaders were placed in internment camps, and West Coast Japanese and their American-born children were sent to relocation camps—Utah's was called Topaz. Utah's depleted number of Hispanics grew immediately, supplying labor for the war effort in federal depots and supplying workers to Bingham Canyon and Carbon County mines. African-Americans were recruited to serve on trains and work in railyards.

World War II ended the great epoch of immigration into the country. The second generation of immigrant families had become adults; they dropped many Old World customs, particularly those associated with death, and increasingly married into the "American" community.

The immigrants and their children shared in the postwar prosperity. War and work experiences gave the nation's and Utah's minority population the impetus to overcome injustices. Several Hispanic organizations, associated with the Mexican consul in Salt Lake City, were formed for cultural and social activities. Organizations that formed later stressed the problems of Mexican-Americans in an Anglo society, problems that persist because Mexican immigration continues and the need and desire for accommodation to American life never ceases. Blacks have long worked through the formidable National Association for the Advancement of Colored People, the NAACP. Native Americans have also formed organizations, but they face today the most difficult struggles of all the minority groups. These various groups are ever alert to force compliance to the 1964 federal legislation that struck down discrimination against minorities in housing, public accommodations, and businesses. Their struggle continues unceasingly because discrimination, overt and covert, has deep roots in Utah, as it does elsewhere. Many minority children are inadequately educated. Their rate of unemployment is high. They seek escape from despair in alcohol and drugs.

In the 1970s several sociologists argued that there was no such entity as ethnicity; it had vanished. In 1996 it is plain that although their native language has been lost by the third generation, cultural traits are passed on from parents to children, and this diversity gives a uniqueness to American life and to Utah in particular. The grandchildren of immigrants in Utah are reminded of their origins when they hear of attempts to retain Mormon dominance. Yet from most of the stories in this book we become aware of the educational and economic progress achieved by the children and grandchildren of many immigrants—progress that would have forever eluded them if their people had remained in their native countries. When Native-Americans, African Americans, and Hispanics also reach this plateau, we can truly say we are a good people.

Although neighborhoods in Utah exist where African-Americans and Hispanics predominate, the Little Italys, "Bohunk," Greek, and "Jap" Towns are gone. The early matriarchs and patriarchs are dead now. It is their children's turn to face the unknown. It is our good fortune that their voices have not yet been stilled and that their inimitable experiences will find their way into Utah history.

The speakers in this book tell us of those early neighborhoods and the hostile world that formed them. Anger, fear, and incomprehension have weakened for some over time. More often, the voices speak of hard-working parents—parents from the old country, on the reservation, in segregated neighborhoods. They retell incidents that give intuitive understanding of their parents and of communal character. We hear proverbs of ancient wisdom, vestiges of the many proverbs once heard.

The speakers had nearly forgotten much of their forebears' experience in Mormon country, but in talking about their lives, memories emerged. As they increasingly thought about long-ago incidents, forces, and perceptions, the invisible threads of memory became ropes connecting them to their people. One senses that the memories helped the speakers examine and assess their lives, helped them find new or renewed pride in the people from whom they came.

In their voices we hear a nostalgia for what once was, a sadness for the loss of language and custom; we hear an elegiac tone. We are grateful for those voices and to the editors who struggled to bring them to us honestly and poignantly.

BOOK ONE
UTE COMMUNITY

PREFACE

Kathryn A. McKay and Larry Cesspooch

This is Ute country. The people of this land, the Nuche, have lived here hundreds, perhaps thousands, of years. They have power from dreams, solitary journeys, and hardships. They have community based on kinship ties and ceremonies such as the Bear Dance, and they are blessed though visions of Sun Dancers. Nuche created strategies for living in this country of desert sinks and mile-high mountains, of plateaus and carved-out canyons, in this country that shimmers in dry heat, parches out except along the rivers, the seeps, and the oases, and transforms from greens to browns to golds to whites through the seasons. Nuche knew how to tan deerskin white, which became a famous trade item, when to gather chokecherries, and from all directions how to walk to Bear's Ears Mountain. And they had the words to tell the stories of jack rabbit and geese and coyote.

Nuche once occupied most of the mountain regions of what is now Colorado, most of Utah, and part of southern Wyoming and northern New Mexico. Speaking a language of the Southern Numic branch of Uto-Aztecan, the *Nuche* are linguistically related to the indigenous peoples of Mexico. The English label "Ute" is a shortening of the earlier name *Utah,* which was taken from the New Mexican Spanish word *Yuta.* The origin of this Spanish name is unknown, but it is probably a loanword from another Indian group who gave that name to the *Nuche.*

Organized in small family groups, *Nuche* traveled with the seasons. They went to high mountains in the summer, living by hunting small and big game animals and birds, fishing, and gathering a variety of berries, nuts, seeds, and plants. In the fall they traveled back into sheltered foothill valleys or the edge of the deserts. Hunting, fishing, and gathering sites were not owned; access was communal and granted to all. Some *Nuche* raised crops along stream alluvials. Some *Nuche* transformed themselves into horse-based cultures after horses came into the region in about 1660. Some *Nuche* followed buffalo herds onto the Great Plains, and some went to Taos Pueblo to trade.

Nuche society was, and is, centered on family—extended family in which kinship ties are respected and maintained. Resources were to be shared communally. *Nuche* leadership was not hierarchical. Every person in the family had certain roles, some gender specific, some age specific. Grandparents raised children and kept the histories. Children and old people helped adult women care for crops planted along waterways, gather berries, roots, and nuts in season, and process all for eating. Men fished the rivers and streams, set snares to catch small animals and birds, and joined forces to hunt deer. Group activities were directed by leaders only to the extent that the activity needed such supervision. Men and women who had spiritual powers, success in hunting, or skills in tanning and basketmaking were respected and consulted.

Groups of families often spent winters together in certain areas. These loosely structured groups came to be known as bands—and after 1850, they were considered to make up the Ute tribe. Totaling upward of ten thousand people, these bands included, among others, the Mouache band of the region around the Sangre de Cristo and San Juan mountain ranges and the Capota band of the San Luis Valley. The Mouache and Capota are nowadays land-based at the Southern Ute Reservation, which has its headquarters at Ignacio, Colorado. The Weeminuche, who traveled the Dolores River Valley, are now land-based at White Mesa, south of Blanding, Utah, and at the Ute Mountain Ute Reservation, which has its headquarters at Towaoc, Colorado.

Another group, Uinta-ats, lived in and around the Uinta Mountains. They and descendants of the Cumumbas of the Weber River Valley, the Pah Vants of the Fish Lake area, the Sheberetch of the southern Utah canyons, the San Pitch of that valley, and the Tumpanawach, or Timpanogos, of the Utah Lake region came to be called the Uintah band. The Parianuche of the Colorado River Valley and the Yamparikas of the Yampa River Valley came to be called the White River Utes. They and the Tabeguache, or Uncompahgre, of the northern San Juans were forced to join Utah-based *Nuche* in the Uintah Basin, and the three bands came to be called the Northern Utes. The Northern Utes today are based at the Uintah-Oray Reservation, with its headquarters at Fort Duchesne, Utah.

Non-Indian intruders came into *Nuche* country beginning in the sixteenth century—Francisco Coronado came in 1540, after hearing stories of the legendary rich cities of Quivera. Spaniards arranged treaties with the *Nuche,* the first in 1670. In the mid-eighteenth century, the *Nuche* and other peoples—Navajo, Comanche, Apache, Pawnee—had shifting alliances with one another as the Spaniards and French vied for influence in the Southwest and Great Plains. In 1776 two Catholic fathers, Dominguez and Escalante, followed stories, journals, Indian trails, and *Nuche* guides into the Green River and Utah Lake regions.

In the first half of the nineteenth century, stories of streams full of marketable beavers provoked fur traders—English from Canada, Americans from Missouri, and French and Spanish from New Mexico—to establish trade relations with the *Nuche* and further involve them in a market economy. The Old

Spanish Trail, opened in 1829, crossed the lands of Capota, Weeminuche, Tumpanawach, and Pah Vant. Some *Nuche*, such as Wakara, a leader of the Tumpanawach in military affairs, prospered by demanding tribute from travelers along the trail. But the trading posts established on *Nuche* lands became centers of prostitution and drunkenness.

In the 1840s, guided by stories from fur traders and explorers such as J. C. Fremont, a large community of Anglo-Americans established what was to become a permanent settlement on the edge of *Nuche* country in the Great Salt Lake Valley. These people were members of a new American religion—the Church of Jesus Christ of Latter-day Saints (LDS). The Mormons, as they were called, came to actualize their own narrative of creating a literal Kingdom of God on earth. But the earth they chose was already storied, already understood, already occupied by *Nuche*.

The intruders carried childhood diseases, such as measles, whooping cough, and smallpox, which came to kill ninety percent of the peoples of the Americas—who had no immunities to these microbes. During the first winter the Mormon settlers spent in *Nuche* country, measles spread quickly among the *Nuche* who visited them. The Mormons buried thirty-six *Nuche* in one grave alone.

Unlike the *Nuche,* the intruders had neither the knowledge nor the skills to live on this land. The land was not theirs; they had to change the land into what they could understand, into what would support their economies and institutions. These changes destroyed the grasses that supported the game herds, deteriorated mountain watersheds, which has since caused periodic flooding, and turned fish, trees, beavers, canyons, and wildflowers into marketable commodities. Ironically, these changes so drastically transformed the environment that it may not be sustainable in the twenty-first century.

The intruders followed a religion of domination—humans dominating all other creatures, Christians dominating all other believers—and thus felt justified in taking the land and denigrating its inhabitants. The Judeo-Christian story of creation is a story of human beings being flung from the light and beauty of the Garden to the dark and ugliness of the earth, which humans must control to survive. In contrast, most indigenous Americans tell creation stories of human beings coming out of darkness into the light and beauty of the earth, to which they are tied by spiritual relationships that are expressed through ceremonies. The *Nuche* say that human beings came out of a bag that coyote mischievously opened while *Sinauve* (the Creator) was away. Thus, the intruders and the natives conceived of the basic relations of humans and their environs in profoundly contradictory ways.

Yet, the Mormons believed they had a unique understanding of the indigenous peoples. The Book of Mormon was supposedly written for the Indians in particular, to help them regain their alleged true identity as descendants from the House of Israel. The Mormons were eager to proselytize among the indigenous peoples, to redeem them from their "history of apostasy." However, the Mormons were also as willing as other intruders to appropriate land

and resources for their own purpose. Keith Parry described these two con-flicting Mormon orientations to the peoples of the Great Basin as a "mission-ary" orientation, which fused condescension with altruism, and a "pioneer" orientation, which conceived the indigenous peoples as rivals.[1] Certainly there are Mormon stories about Indian friendships, conversions, marriages, and adoptions. But there are many more about Indian savagery, "moral inferior-ity," and stupidity.

Profound differences between the intruders and the natives also existed in the ways information was transmitted. Not only were their economies, philosophies, theologies, and societies different, but so were the very means of conveying information about these institutions. The intruders had a visual communication tradition, in which ideas were expressed through sight sym-bols. The intruders "knew" only what was mapped, written, photographed, or computed, not what was told, sung, danced, or visioned. As the intruders came to control not only this land but the knowing about this land and the history of this land, the stories, songs, and ceremonies of the indigenous peoples were discounted.

Yet, even in the written materials evidence exists of the misunderstandings, conflicts, and frustrations that are the legacy of the intrusion of non-Indians. Examples are the several treaties negotiated between the intruders and the *Nuche,* some involving trade agreements, some involving promises of peace, and others concerning land transfers. Evidence also exists that these negotia-tions were kept more faithfully by the *Nuche* than by the intruders.

One such document is the order decreed by Brigham Young early in 1850 to kill all the male Indians in Utah Valley, sparing women and children if they "behaved" themselves. Another is the executive order (made in 1861) by which President Abraham Lincoln set aside the Uintah Valley as a reservation for the Indians of Utah—the Mormons had requested this reservation as an Indian removal area and a buffer zone between themselves and non-Mormons settling to the east. The Uintah Reservation was only a remnant, and a forlorn remnant, of *Nuche* land. It could not possibly provide all the hunting, fishing, gathering, and agricultural practices that sustained the *Nuche*. As a result, the *Nuche* were forced into dependency on the intruders.

Still another document highlighting the conflicts between the *Nuche* and non-Indians is the Ute Agreement of 1880, by which the *Nuche* in Colorado were forced to move to Utah after White River Utes rebelled and killed their obsessive Indian agent Nathan Meeker, who was determined to force Indian compliance to Euro-American ways. Not only White River Utes but also Uncompahgre Utes were forced at gunpoint to the Uintah and Uncompahgre reservations (the latter established by executive order in 1882).

Other documents record the presence of the U.S. Ninth Cavalry of African-American soldiers on the Uintah Reservation in 1886, the soldiers were sent there to establish Fort Duchesne to "discipline and control" the *Nuche*. They record the refusal of *Nuche* to send their children away to school, particularly after the measles epidemic of 1901. They record the 1906 protest of *Nuche* spiritual leader Red Cap against the opening of the reservation to non-Indians—a protest that involved several hundred *Nuche* walking and riding to South Dakota, hoping to establish a league of the northern tribes against the federal government.

Documents also describe the shifting status of the *Nuche* under the intruders' legal systems. Under Spanish and Mexican law, the native peoples were citizens of Mexico. Under U.S. law, citizenship for all indigenous Americans was not established until 1924. Utah laws forbidding native peoples from participating in state elections were not overturned by the U.S. Supreme Court until the 1950s. People having fifty percent or less Ute blood (the so-called mixed-bloods) were terminated by the federal government from the membership rolls of the Uintah and Ouray Tribe in 1961 as the government's first step toward ending the relationship established by law and treaty between the federal government and all Utah *Nuche*. The Ute Distribution Corporation (UDC) was set up to handle and distribute twenty-seven percent of the tribe's undividable assets to the mixed-bloods. Some mixed-bloods sold their shares to non-Indians, who are still today receiving a portion of the tribe's assets.

In the twentieth century, the *Nuche* acquired a reputation of being "the rich Utes." They were among the first native peoples to win awards of claims against the United States for unlawful and unfair land takings. Several million dollars were awarded to the *Nuche* in 1911, 1933, 1950, 1961, and 1981. These funds were placed in trust and held by the Bureau of Indian Affairs. Much of the money went to irrigation, housing, and education projects. Some went to individuals in paternalistic programs that involved the approval of federal officials. With the introduction of such programs, however, there suddenly appeared on the reservations car and appliance salesmen and bogus investment schemes.

Trust funds received for lands taken continue to be a major portion of the annual operating budget used by the tribe to support its many services and projects. The Ute Indian tribe draws from the interest generated by these trust funds to establish its operating budget. These funds are not welfare payments, but are compensation for land and resources taken from the *Nuche*.

In the 1970s courts ruled that the *Nuche* owned significant historical water rights, a valuable asset in an arid region in which water is at a premium. The Uintah and Ouray Tribe deferred its water rights (as first user) to the state of Utah for twenty years in return for promised water projects. Unfortunately, those projects have not been developed. The unjust manipulation of Indian water rights in the Central Utah Water Project is evidenced in many documents.

In 1985 the U.S. Tenth Circuit Court ruled that the language of the 1905 congressional act opening unallotted reservation lands to the public domain was not evidence of congressional intent to diminish the Uintah Reservation. The ruling affirmed the *Nuche's* efforts to assert tribal jurisdiction over reservation lands, and the decision offered the *Nuche* possibilities for a measured sovereignty on these lands, leaving them free to determine their own internal affairs. However, the cities and counties of the Uintah Basin and the state of Utah continued to oppose *Nuche* tribal sovereignty in court. Finally, in 1994 the U.S. Supreme Court, in a seven to two vote, ruled that the language of the 1902 and 1905 acts had indeed expressed the intention of Congress to terminate the reservation status of the unallotted lands; tribal jurisdiction was declared not to extend over the 1861 reservation.

In the twentieth century the living standard of the *Nuche* has improved. The population, which had been plummeting since the eighteenth century, has risen. Life expectancy has also risen. Tribal and federal efforts have been made to transform the reservation from an island of rural poverty to the homeland that had been promised. However, the scarcity of gainful employment and the imposed marginality of the *Nuche* to Euro-American society have made this transformation problematic. Among the *Nuche* alcohol and drug use, suicide, and homicide have continued to increase. The majority of *Nuche* left the reservation looking for jobs and education, some as participants in the federal Relocation Program, most as part of a larger shift of rural populations to urban centers. Many relocatees have returned, however, realizing how difficult it is to maintain their culture in these urban centers.

Intruders, some with the best intentions, deliberately and methodically stripped the *Nuche* of their land, culture, and language. Many *Nuche,* some with the best intentions, let their *Nuche* ways go. There is a gap between the older generations, who remember the old ways, and the younger generations, fewer and fewer of whom even speak the language. Some *Nuche* know and understand their culture. They have retained it within their families. Many more struggle to figure out how to continue to be *Nuche* while being separated from traditional beliefs, homelands, and ceremonies. Much determination exists among *Nuche* to maintain and protect the spirituality that infuses their culture. The ceremonies continue to be held; the sacred places continue to be used. For many *Nuche,* it is this spiritualness that most defines their identity.

Documents tell part of the history of the *Nuche* and the intruders—a history of misunderstandings, mistakes, and misinformation—but they do not tell all of that history. The rest is in the stories—stories of the supernatural, of ceremonies, and past ways—that define cultural identities and in the personal narratives that tell of the struggle to make sense of change, frustration, alienation, and hope. The following stories are told by persons willing to explore the question of what it means to be *Nuche*. The stories are spiritual autobiographies and personal ethnographies. They are revealing of self, culture, and community.

It is impossible to reconstruct all of the emotions, ponderings, gestures, and fabric of individual lives. Stories are only partial reconstructions and vary with each new telling. But the power of stories, as Edward M. Bruner has noted, is that they give meaning to the present and enable us to see the present as part of a set of relationships involving the constituted past and future.

These stories are told by survivors, persons of creativity and intelligence who have the ability to communicate across cultures. They give hints of contradictory and multifarious experiences and glimpses of *Nuche* ways and ideas that inform the experiences. As we all struggle to create conversations of stories told, stories heard, and stories taken into account, these stories matter. We have asked *Nuche* to speak to us. We must behave properly and listen.

NOTE

1. Parry, Keith, " 'To Raise These People Up.' An Examination of a Mormon Mission to an Indian Community as an Agent of Social Change" (Ph.D. Diss., University of Rochester, 1972).

Julius Murray. *Kent Miles*

Lester Chapoose. *Kent Miles*

THE UTE LANGUAGE CONFERENCE

In 1981, the Ute Tribe's Division of Education received grant funds to create an experimental bilingual program in an elementary school near Fort Duchesne. Aimed at reviving the Ute language, which had fallen into considerable disuse on the reservation, the program was the tribe's initial effort to take an active role in creating curricula for the education of Ute children. In the fall of 1983, while struggling to acquire funds to maintain the program, the education division held its first Ute Language Conference at the Bottle Hollow Motel in Fort Duchesne. The purpose of the conference was to review the program's achievements during its first three years of operation and to examine the deep threat to the traditional Ute lifestyle it was trying to redress. The following is an edited version of Forrest Cuch's introductory remarks to the participants. Forrest Cuch was the director of the division at the time of the conference.[1]

The reason we have called this conference is to share ideas about the Ute language and what we have done over the past three years [in our program]. The real reason is that our language is being challenged. And by language, I mean our traditional beliefs. They are being challenged like they've never been challenged before, because they're being challenged by our own people. Our own people are starting to disregard the value of these traditions. When that kind of thing starts to happen, the spirit of a culture will die and along with it young people who believe in themselves. They too will begin to die.

We started this language conference late this morning. They call that "Indian time." My research indicates that that's really a misinterpretation. Because my research indicates that our people were really very punctual. For most white people, where they got the idea of Indians always being late is that our people in general took a long time when it came to making an important decision. It might be a couple of days or a couple of weeks. But when the decision was made, it was made. When we entered into a treaty with the United States government that treaty was sacred. It meant a lot. What that means to me is that my people valued honesty and integrity.

With the loss of our language and our traditions, I ask: What is going to happen to honesty and integrity? I think this question has been answered over the last few years. We are starting to see a lot more corruption in tribal government. We are starting to see a general increase in suffering among the people, increased alcohol and drug abuse, not to mention the suicide rate. Meantime, we have more money than we've ever had before.[2] So money has not been the answer. Never has been. But I think education in the Ute belief system, our traditional ways, is.

When our kids lose the language, they forget who they are and where they come from. When that happens, it's like cutting the spirit out of a young child. It's breaking the spirit. And it hurts. At a general council meeting—some of you might have been there—a young girl stood up and said, "I can't speak my language, and it hurts." And she started crying. That's how painful it is. We are talking about a serious thing here. When the Tribal Council [members], the leaders we elect, no longer respect or value Ute language and our traditions, and demonstrate that by eliminating Ute language programs, that's a real serious message. That indicates that we no longer want to be Ute people. That indicates that we've sold out our race and our traditions. That also means that, for the most part, our people are ashamed of who they are. They believe the worst that the dominant culture has to say about them. They believe it. That's what it means. It means we've lost our spirit. We've lost our honesty and integrity. It means we are lost as a nation. I see it here. I see a whole lot of suffering. Young people who are lost. I've been out there, went to college, did everything I was supposed to do, and I was still lost. I was still confused, crazy, until I came home. Then I started another education process, getting to know myself and my people.

The old people used to tell the young people, "It is good to go to school and get an education." But they did not mean for them to give themselves away. So let's be very careful here. We send our kids to school, and we have to think about what we want them to accomplish. Do we want them twenty years from now to walk into the house with a suit and tie, short hair, packing a briefcase and interested in making money only? Do we want them to deny their brown skin, deny their language, disrespect the family? Do you want them to say, "I'm a white man"? Take a look at that, because there are a lot of people walking around that are brown on the outside and white on the inside. . . .

But, you see, it's not their fault. It's not their fault. The public school system is set up that way. It's set up to produce white people, not Indian people. But there is a way. There is a way. You can take what the dominant culture has to offer in education, [but] not all of it. You take only that which will benefit you. And you take the best of our culture and our traditions, and you keep them, and you take off. That's what I'm suggesting. It can be done. It can be done.

We've got to stay away from extremes. Either/or. We're not either for or against education. That's not the issue. We are for some things in education and against some things in education that do not allow our children to feel good about themselves. Kids can't learn unless they feel good about themselves. You can be sitting in school, and if you feel a lot of pain inside, don't know who you are or if you belong, don't feel adequate, it's going to be difficult to learn. That's my interpretation of this conference. It's to share [our experiences], but also to remember what we are really here for. It's to retain our true identity and our spirit.

JENSEN JACK, 56, WHITE RIVER ELDER, SUN DANCE CHIEF, AND MEDICINE MAN

If things don't seem right to my eyes, I ask the Healer for a blessing. I talk to him to help me, to clear that blurry thing away from me. I don't want nothing [to] happen to my mind. I want clear thinking, clear understanding. That's what I say when I pray. I want to be right with other people. I care for people. I love people. That's what I say in that talk to this man that we look for. But [this man], he's here. We don't have to look for him. He is here. Right today. Listening. I got his heart. So have you. It's [the] spirit's heart. His eye is looking right through us. We see things for him. 'Cause we're living. That's what I know about this. That's the way I believe.

RUBY BLACK, 48, CHAIRPERSON, UTE TRIBAL COUNCIL (1977–1980)

The first woman elected chairperson of the Ute Tribal Council, Ruby Black was considered a grassroots-style leader by the tribe and a formidable, fractious, and unpredictable adversary by local whites. The director of the Ute Tribal Museum and the tribe's official historian, Clifford Duncan, characterized her as a "traditional person and a traditional leader," one who was not "easily led by the white man's halter."

Ruby Black is a small, moon-faced woman with dark skin and shoulder-length, jet-black hair. She laughs easily and is unimpressed by formal titles. The interview with her was conducted at the tribally owned Bottle Hollow Motel at the conclusion of the language conference.

From what my mother tells me, I was born here in Fort Duchesne at the old hospital. The year was 1935, and she called me Ruby Katie Atwine. Later I got married and got the name Black, and now I'm known as Ruby Katie Atwine Black. I was named after the nurse that delivered me. Her name was Ruby Crumble, one of the [mixed-blood] people that was once on the roll.[3] So that's how I got my name. Katie was my grandmother's—my dad's mom's—name. She was a sister to Andrew Frank, a known leader of the Uintahs at one time. And Jim Atwine was my dad's uncle, and he was a known leader of the tribe, too. So I feel proud to be a Ute Indian, because of my ancestry.

The older people, when they talk to me, they say, "You've come from a people that have talked for the tribe and have talked for the reservation. It's only right that you speak and we listen." That's what the older people tell me. It's something good to hold on to. It kind of makes me feel good about what I'm saying. So when I go to say something, I really think about it. I don't want to say something just to be saying something. Keeping in mind that these people believe what I say, I've got to say what is true.

My dad used to tell me, "Think about what you're going to say. Then, if you've got time, think about how it's going to affect the people. Don't just say it." In the Indian way he is saying, "Follow your words. Follow [them] good. Guide your words. Hear in your mind what you're saying, so that people will know and comprehend what you're talking about—git it, you know. If you don't, you're just talking out of air and it's got no meaning. It's got no help to it." That's what my dad used to say. He used to be an interpreter for the tribe, and I wanted to be an interpreter, too.

I grew up here most of my life. My dad was a member of the Native-American church, and I was brought up to believe in the spiritual ways of that church.[4] I believe their values are good because they don't knock anybody down. They don't say there are things you shouldn't do; they don't say there are certain people you've got to associate with. The teachings say you're a person and that man or woman next to you is another human being. Respect him for what he is, not for what you want him to be. Accept him for what he is, whether he's got faults or not, because he's only human. "Never judge, because it's not for you," the teachings say. "The only one that can judge people is the Creator." So I don't judge. I accept people. I like to talk and laugh. They call me little niece or little cousin or sister. In [the] Indian way, we like to relate to each other as sisters or brothers, even if we're kind of distant cousins, you know. That's the way it goes.

Now, my dad, he was a giant of a man. He was very tough and tall. I always say one of my sons takes after my dad. His name is Bishop Black, and people can't believe he's the youngest boy of my children, but he is. My oldest son is small. Bishop towers over him. And that's the way I picture my father—tall and handsome. I was proud of him, and I'll always remember him that way: big and husky and smart.

My dad worked for the Bureau [of Indian Affairs] Police for a long, long time. Then he worked as a night watchman in the area. He was on the Tribal Council for a long time, too, representing the Uintah band. (I represented the White River band, because my mom was a White River.) And my dad interpreted. I remember right here in Fort Duchesne, there was a house right in the middle of it. They used to have meetings right in that place, then they'd feed the people after the meeting. Some white people would come that wanted to talk to the tribe, or the attorney used to come. Then my father would interpret and I was proud, even prouder because he understood and spoke English.

What amazed me was that people were quiet. They would sit and listen. And I'd look and think, my dad's got everybody's attention. They really want to know what he is talking about. If they missed something, they'd always ask him. When he said that word, what did he mean? Then he'd have to explain. It put real big pride in my heart when I used to see him standing up there interpreting for the tribe, whether it was into English or into Ute.

And I'll tell you, long before I got in the council, my dad told me—and it has proven to be evident—[how] the white man is. He said, "He'll play a word game. He'll tell you what he thinks you want to hear or what he wants to hear, what sounds good to him, hoping you'll get it just the way he presents it." He said, "Listen for it. Sit and listen. And think about what he's talking about. What is he really saying? Then throw it back to him. Ask him, 'I don't really understand what you're talking about. Could you explain a little further?' That way, he's going to tell you what he really means. But if you don't do that, you're going to get something you didn't bargain for. Even if you [think you] understand, say, 'I'm sorry but I don't understand what you're talking about.' Or throw it back to him and say, 'Is this what I hear you saying?' That way, you'll get a lot out of it."

My dad was a smart man. And a lot of people knew that. Even today, they say he was a smart man. But he never displayed it in a big way. When he spoke, all right, he said what he needed to say. That's the way he was. But he was usually reserved in a very special way. And that makes me proud, too. So I bless the day the good Lord put him here on this earth to be my father. And I bless the day cupid went and got into my dad's heart with my mom's arrow.

When I was growing up, we were a traditional family. We followed the old ways. Like when you're on your woman's business—my mother used to say "your woman business"—you'd have to stay in for all that time.⁵ You didn't go among the people. It's not right. And that's the way my mother used to do with us. We had to tell her it was time, and she'd say, "All right, your house is ready." And she made a little house for us or pitched a tent outside the house. Or when we moved down here [to Fort Duchesne], my mom put us in one corner of a room. We never went to school, and she made sure we never went out. She went to the school and told them, "My daughter is not coming because of a certain reason . . . ," and the school understood.

When I was bringing up my kids, the school stopped understanding. They'd be pig-headed. They wouldn't agree to excuse my girls. So I told them, "If they have to be in school, I don't want them involved in sports or anything. I want them to be by themselves." Still, they didn't listen. So I told my daughter[s], "Just be careful what you're doing, that's all." Because there was nothing we could do about it. . . .

When we had our babies, we had to be away from people, too. So my mother would lock us up, and our men had to stay out of that room for thirty days. That's the way it had to be. And Mom made sure we went along with it, because after we had our babies, she'd come stay with us. [Laughs] She cared. And she told us certain things. We were not supposed to put our hands in our hair either during our woman's business or after a baby. Even the men didn't put their hands in their hair, and you don't wash your hair [out] until you're all through. Then you washed everything off and you're all right. . . .

Now, Indians never showed affection by putting their arm around you. My dad never put his arm around us. Yet, inside, I knew he loved us, he cared for us, because he done things for us. If I felt like it, I'd go over and sit by him, lean on him. And he'd stroke my hair. He never hugged me or anything. But he showed his affection when he touched my hair, stroked it, or when he'd call me by my Indian name. My father had boys, but he never raised them. They all died as infants. So he just had us five girls to cope with. And every now and then he'd also say a word that describes, you know, "my girls." The word actually meant my children. He'd say that—"*Du-wutch-oon*"—and we knew he loved us.

There were other women on the council before me. But I was the first woman to be a chairperson for this tribe. It was an honor. Of course, to get in, I campaigned like everybody else. I went to homes that I knew had large families. My mom came along with me, and my sister and some cousins helped. My effort caught on, so I got in. My victory came at a good time, because my kids were grown. Larry was married, Gary was working, and the youngest was fourteen, so I really didn't have anybody to worry about. I could be concerned about the tribe—try to put into use some of what my father taught me. And I did.

One of the big concerns I had was about a dam they were going to build up in the Uintah Mountains, above White Rocks. The people were opposed to it. When I was out amongst them, I heard them talk about it. Many of them were complaining about it. But did the council [then in office] listen? No, they didn't. So I went in feeling I knew what the people wanted.

When I got in, I started asking the CUP [Central Utah Project] people about it. What is it you're trying to do? What is the tribe going to get out of it aside from a dam and the water being backed up? What safety measures are you using? What will happen if the dam breaks? Who is going to pay for those lives? What will this bring the tribe aside from water rights in that dam? It may be good that we save and dam our water so it won't just run down the whole country, but to me personally and a lot of other people, there was a danger. Then the other councilmen along with me started talking about the fact that the tribe won't really get any benefit from this dam because we are not farmers. The only farmers around here were non-Indians, and it would be to their advantage.

A lot of our people said, "The land changes from year to year. If you put a dam there and it changes, it's going to put a crack in it." Even today at springtime, the Indians that live around White Rocks will say, "Hear the roar. The mountain is stretching, and the land moves." If you go to the mountains all the time—and I love the mountains—you'll notice it. One year you're there, and the next year you go something is different. There's a crack in the face of a wall or something you noticed the year before is gone. It may be [due to] erosion or weather, but [either way] it's change.

The other concern I had was [the town of] Roosevelt wanting to buy the water called Big Springs. They were after that because it's pure artesian water, a natural spring, and it comes right out of the hills. They wanted to tap that so it'll run from there to White Rocks and clear down through Roosevelt. The council was going to sell that water. But a lot of the old-time tribal members didn't want that to happen because that's spiritual water. Big Springs is where they get the water that comes into the Sun Dance before the dancers go out. That water has spiritual meaning. It's been blessed by the Creator. That's the way the Indians believe.[6]

So selling it didn't seem right. But what the city engineers were telling these council members that went along with it was, "We're not going to tap it where it comes out of the mountain. We're going to run our pipes way down below." Now, that's good. It *sounds* good. But I said, "How can you do that when you put chlorine in the water? You won't put it way down there. It don't seem right, it doesn't sound right. What's the original plan?" The engineer, who was presenting to us, looked at me and said, "What original plan?" I said, "I'm sure you had an original plan long before you approached the tribe." He looked at me and went, "Where did you hear about that?" I said, "Nowhere." And I hadn't. But I had in mind what my father said—they were telling us what they thought we'd go along with 'cause we're new on the council and don't know any better. When they brought that plan out, they didn't have the pipes below Big Springs. [They were] right on the spring itself. If we'd okayed it, it would have plugged up that whole thing.

So I said, "No way. That spring belongs to my people, and I want to keep it that way." They [the Ute people] appreciated that. They also appreciated us not going along with the water project. They felt safe. It's not that they didn't want to share the water; it wasn't dams per se, it was just dams up here. So we said "No dams" because we knew the land changes and we didn't want it to change on us and see ourselves going down the river.

We stopped those developments. But there are other changes you can't guard against. A long time ago, you know, Indian ways survived because the Indians didn't really get themselves into this rat race. They were by themselves, not knowing what the neighbors over there were doing, or other tribes, or the white man. They did what they did, year after year, and survived that way. Nowadays, that's not possible. You can't isolate yourself and be a Ute in the old way. You can't go back to living in tepees or wickiups. Yet you want to be a Ute and still retain your culture, your Indianness, just to be proud of yourself.

But how do you do that? While I was chairperson, teachers often asked me to go into the schools to speak about Indian ways. I'd tell the kids that life's changed on the reservation. I'd tell them the way it was, the way it is. "It's not a nice world," I'd say. "But education is important. You've got to learn. Don't just read because you're supposed to. Read and know what you're reading about. What are the words in the story really telling you? Think about those things."

What made them laugh, though, these little seventh and eighth graders, was when I'd tell them, "Whatever kind of life you want, make it good. If you want to be the best drunk there is in the whole Uintah Basin, make the best of it." They'd laugh. I'd tell them, "If you want to be a ditch digger, be a good ditch digger. Even a ditch digger has got to know how far he's got to go and how wide it's got to be." They'd sit there and laugh and say, "I don't want to be a drunk, I don't want to be a ditch digger. I want to be a lawyer, doctor." Big things. I'd tell them what I told my own kids when they were growing. "That's big ideas. Right now, grow little. Just start out and climb up. You've got a lot of time in your life, a lot of years ahead of you. It's not going to be over tomorrow. It's only going to be over for you tomorrow if you end it. So make your world the way you want to."

LESTER CHAPOOSE, 49, CHAIRMAN, UTE TRIBAL COUNCIL
(1974–1977, 1981–1984, 1985–1989)

A heavyset, affable man with short hair, dark skin, and an unflappable temperament, Lester Matt Chapoose was born in Fort Duchesne, Utah, on December 1, 1937. A graduate of the University of Utah, where he received his B.A. degree in political science, he was the spur behind the tribe's intense, controversial, and ultimately short-lived economic development effort in the mid-1970s and early 1980s.

We drove down from Salt Lake City in the fall of 1986 and met Chapoose in front of the tribally owned Bottle Hollow Motel and Convention Center. Due to financial setbacks, the motel was closed. We left our cars in the empty parking lot, walked over to one of the motel's unheated offices, and there, bundled in our winter coats and shivering, we conversed for three hours.

Chapoose spoke candidly about the tribe's multifaceted problems and his impatience with leaders who blame the tribe's misfortunes on whites. He emphasized education and employment as the keys to overcoming the tribe's obstacles. As for his role on the Tribal Council, he characterized himself as a negotiator. "I have no animosity towards the non-Indians in the community. I work as well with the Tribal Council as with the County Commission. I think there's an awful lot of room for the tribe and the non-Indian community to get together on issues that concern us both."

The first three years of my education was at this old Ballard School, about halfway between Fort Duchesne and Roosevelt, on the right-hand side of the road. I was the only Indian kid in the whole class, but I never had any problems with that. I wasn't outstanding by any means, but I wasn't dumb, either. I had great respect for authority. They used to make us recite the Pledge of Allegiance and teach us various things of a patriotic nature. So I grew up with the red, white, and blue almost draped around my shoulders. And I was quite proud. Even though there was nobody at home to help me, I did my work the best I could. I don't know, all of my life it just come to me: Education was something that could pull me out of where I was at. And that's what I was doing, you know, trying to get myself in a better situation, to a better place.

Indians were not affluent when I was coming up. But their value systems

JULIUS MURRAY, SR., 79,
UINTAH ELDER AND MEDICINE MAN

My grandfather was more or less a mountain man. He knew all of the big-wigs, like Kit Carson and Jim Bridger, because he'd done a lot of guiding, helping, showing people how to survive within this country that had never been explored too much. I was very, very close to him. I traveled a lot with him. And he taught me and told me many things.

He said whites would settle and take over the West, and the Indian people would lose much of their holdings. That would be one of the things the white man will take. "The white man will make agreements and treaties," he said, "that won't mean nothing. This isn't right, but that's the white man's way of life. That's the way they live. They will outnumber you. They will fight you. They will kill you, slaughter you, punish you, but they'll get what they're after. So in order to survive when you get down to where you can't [physically] resist anymore, you'll have to make some other way to ward it off." It happened just as he said.

were in accord with the traditional Indian values—taking care of one another, helping one another. If an Indian child needed a home, for whatever reason, someone on the reservation would take him in. Whether they were related or not, they would take him in. But now, not even their extended families will take them in. When I was growing up, the extended family was a working group. My cousins, my aunt, and different people didn't live too far from where we did. We visited one another, constantly. You don't see that nowadays. Today, people are out to take care of themselves.

Seekits was my grandmother on my mother's side. She didn't have a first or last name. In Indian society, the grandparents did a lot of parenting. In my case, my grandmother took care of me for the first six years of my life, which was when she passed away. After that, my mother assumed responsibility. When I knew my grandmother, she was a rancher. She had cattle, a little farm, and was a very resilient, strong-willed person. One of the things she stressed—as did all the older Indians—always stressed this—was education. She encouraged me all the time. Since she didn't know how to speak English, I became bilingual.

My father passed away the year I was born, so I never had the opportunity to see him or his family. The elderly people remember him as being a spokesman for the tribe. Today, when some of them disagree with a position I take, they'll come up and tell me straight out that my dad would not have done that. My dad had a lot of respect. I guess I've been trying to prove to everybody that I'm just as good as he was or better. [Chuckles]

I grew up in an agrarian-type society. A lot of people had ranches, small cattle operations, farms, and were a little more self-reliant than most people are today. They did things—probably because they had to or it wouldn't get done. And people were scattered all over the reservation. Now, everybody's living in Fort Duchesne, Randlett, and White Rocks. We've urbanized to some extent.

When my grandmother sold her land to the tribe, we moved to Fort Duchesne—[into] a place they called Little Chicago. All it really was then was shacks that you could throw up in a day or two. After Grandmother passed away, my mother, my brother, my sister, and my stepdad and I spent a few winters there. For years, every summer when the fruit harvest was going to begin, a farmer from Utah Valley used to come out and take a load of us to pick fruit. I have a son that's twelve years old. He's never picked anything in his life. But we did. We picked tomatoes, potatoes, anything that was available. After the summer, my parents would bring me back to the old Uintah Indian school. That's the way life was. Most people were on their own [financially], and they were surviving. And in some respects they were better off.

In the early '50s, the Judgement Funds for the Ute Tribe came in. I don't know just how many millions of dollars it was, but I recall distinctly the day that came about. They give them each a thousand dollars. It was the first payment they ever received.[7] I was going to school at White Rocks then. I must have been about thirteen or fourteen, and I had a thousand. Everybody had a thousand dollars, but children didn't see the money. It seems to me that since those Judgement Funds became accessible, people began to act different. They became more dependent on that money than on trying to work for a living. Those funds were the beginning of our trouble. That first thousand dollars must have cleaned out all the car lots in town—because that's the first thing people bought. They also bought things they never had before: radios, clothes, appliances. . . .

In addition to the money problem, alcohol was the second thing on the reservation to hurt us. Until 1955, the state of Utah would not allow Indians to drink. They couldn't be served in a bar; they couldn't go into a liquor store. But in the early '50s, Colorado changed their liquor laws and permitted Indians to drink. There used to be a town—Artesia, Colorado—it was sixty miles from here. By this time, these Indians had cars, so they'd go to Artesia, fill up with their wines and liquors, and bring them back across state lines. They devised many ingenious ways to transport their stuff, because the highway patrol weren't fools. They knew that anytime they saw an Indian coming from Colorado he had liquor with him. So Indians started going through Ouray, hitting all the back roads.

When I was about thirteen, I started driving people over. Since they were going to be drinking going over and drinking going back, they always needed a sober driver. A lot of times I took them just for the ride, but I'd end up getting drunk with them after we got back. I was only thirteen and I was drinking heavily, more than I should. I still went to school and did pretty good. But I drank a lot. And that's the real reason I didn't get anywhere in high school.

So two weeks after I turned seventeen, I joined the navy. I didn't care what branch of the service I went into. I just wanted to be on my own and not be a burden to my family. Since the navy recruiter was the first to open that morning, I went there. I stayed in Fort Douglas for two or three days and then went to the Great Lakes, where I completed my training. After that, I was stationed in San Diego for four or five years.

I never did miss this place when I was gone. I missed my parents, but even then I seldom wrote letters. I was by myself, you see. I was where I wanted to be, doing what I wanted to do, and being what I wanted to be. That's all that mattered.

In 1959, I got discharged. I was twenty-two. I came home for two weeks, then went right back to California. I didn't have work lined up, but I figured having an honorable discharge and service training, I probably wouldn't have problems. But I couldn't find a job. If I ever felt insignificant, it was when I was walking around Los Angeles looking for work during the day and sleeping in parks and in vacant buildings at night. I survived by working temporary labor. I also started going to the Indian bars on Third and Main. If you wanted to meet anybody or you needed company, you'd go to the Ritz or the Columbine. On Saturday nights, they were full of Indians. And those bars were just like the society we had here before the money come in. Since everybody knew it was hard for a person just off the reservation to make it, they'd band together and help each other out.

I went like that for a year, then I came home and signed up for the Relocation Program, where the BIA [Bureau of Indian Affairs] sends you off to different places to help you find employment.[8] They found me some temporary work in Los Angeles, so I went back. I liked it there, I guess, but you had to be pretty dang tough to survive. You couldn't take any shit from anybody, and you didn't give anybody a bad time—unless you wanted to go out and really get hurt. And that's the way it was. It was no picnic there for anybody that didn't belong.

I stayed in LA until about 1963, when I finally decided to go back to school and get into accounting. I got on the GI Bill and eventually enrolled at Southern Utah State College and went for a bachelor's degree in accounting. It was a two-year college then. By the time I left, I had taken every business class they had to offer. In 1966, I transferred to the University of Utah [to complete my degree], but everything suddenly fell apart. I started drinking heavily, dropped out of school, and went back to my old job in LA. It wasn't until 1970 that I got on my feet again and returned to school. . . .

Now, the second time around, I did well. I got involved with the Grand Central stores. They placed me in their executive development program, in their Accounting Department. So I felt like I was going places. And I stayed pretty clean. I didn't want to screw up the job, because that's what I was shooting for. It was no easy thing working those long hours, but it was a prestigious position for a person like me. It was a turning point in my life. If I was good enough to be accepted in that program, I had to be a better person than

I had been. So I slowed up on my drinking and became serious. I was on the verge of graduating when the Ute Tribal Council offered me an accounting job on the reservation.

I had a hard time deciding if I wanted to go back to the reservation. But I guess I had some desire to return. Maybe it was the desire to see if I could make a contribution to change the reservation with the knowledge I had. Maybe I wanted an opportunity to see if I could do that. But that decision was the first step in my trek back. For a hundred dollars a week, I started work in the Accounting Department. Within a short time, I was hired as an administrative officer, because they needed someone who knew budgeting and could talk Indian. I stayed there for a year. Then the Business Committee elections came about—that was in 1973. Out of curiosity, rather than for political reasons, I threw my hat in the ring, and I'll be darned if I didn't win—even if only by four votes.

Now, during my first term on the council, I became a controversial figure, because a lot of things happened, particularly with regard to economic development. The Bottle Hollow Motel was built, the tannery was built, the bowling alley was built, and Ute Fabricating. Working closely with the Business Committee, I pushed economic development measures hard, because there had been no available employment on the reservation.[9] We subsidized the tannery and Ute Fabricating by about half a million dollars each. That cost the tribe a million dollars. We lost some money [in the process]. But we generated business well over the million we put in, and we employed in excess of one hundred people. So, by the end of my first term, in 1977, we had an unemployment rate of fourteen percent, and that is low when compared to today's seventy percent.

But a lot of people didn't approve of our program or the fact that the key people running our organizations were non-Indians. So I was defeated in my reelection bid. In 1977, a group of Indians who didn't know how to run businesses came in. A bunch of backward Indians, in other words. The first thing this new Tribal Council did was Indianize the operations I had. They did away with my resource guy—put an Indian guy in his place. Then they closed up the tannery and Ute Fabricating. And rather than investing our monies in tribally owned enterprises, they gave these funds directly to the people through monthly payments. Today, we have no employment, but we are getting three hundred dollars per month. And it's costing the tribe an arm and a leg. . . .[10] Yet there are mineral and human resources on this reservation that can be developed. The only thing we're tapping is oil—hydrocarbons—and that just can't last.

Now, I'm not the easiest person to get along with on this [presently elected] council. If people want a handout, I'm probably the person that's most likely to say no. So it surprised me that I beat Ruby Black in 1981 and won again in 1985. So this is my third term. And right now, and on into the future, given our rate of unemployment, the number-one priority on the reservation has to be employment. That's definitely number one.

My other priority is youth development. I'd like to see the tribe allocate more money for that. I say that because my son is twelve years old, and I take care of his needs. Which is as it should be. But I'm only one parent. There are many parents on this reservation who neglect their children's education. They don't encourage their kids to stay in school. They leave it to the tribe. And the tribe can't do it.

These kids are confronted by many social problems. For the most part, we don't have a big drug problem on this reservation. But we do have a big alcohol problem. You don't find people dying from old age anymore. People are dying as a result of alcohol.

I'm going to be forty-nine years old in December, and I feel very fortunate to have lived as long as I have. Especially when I see young people maybe ten and twenty years younger than me passing away. I don't drink at home anymore. I don't even drink around the reservation. I don't do it because I don't want my son to think it's all right. But it makes me upset to see kids whose parents are drinking excessively. These young ones don't have much of a future. Today, Indian kids are barely graduating from high school. Their marks aren't high enough for them to get into college. If they tried to go to the University of Utah, they'd never make it past the first year. They're unprepared.

Yet we continue to spend an awful lot of money on alcohol programs for adults, and I disagree with that [allocation] from a philosophical standpoint. My idea is that if we're going to do anything to affect this alcohol problem, we'd better do it before they get to that point. So I'd like to see the efforts of our Social Services Department put on preparing these young kids to stay in the schools. We can't do much about them old folks that's passed that stage. We've got to keep them alive somehow, but it's the younger ones that concern me. They're going to have to sit here when I'm gone, and I don't want to leave this chair to somebody that don't know what's going on.

So those are my priorities. But I don't have any more authority than any other member of this council. I can vote, I can conduct meetings, but that's it. On other reservations the tribal chairman has more power. But not here. I had a good council when I started. Since then, the council members have been pretty much polarized. We're not working together for the common good. Everybody has his own idea on what he wants. Anytime I make a proposal, the chances of that passing are only about twenty-five percent. [*Laughs*] I've worked under these conditions for the last five years. This year, though, I'm hoping the new faces on the council will back me up. If not, I might decide to get out of this. Because if I'm not able to accomplish anything, I shouldn't be here. There's no two ways about it.

Postscript: Lester Chapoose died in Salt Lake City on June 6, 1990.

JASON CUCH, 66, WHITE RIVER ELDER

One of the things I enjoyed about my grandparents was that they talked about how one should behave. They had a psychology, it seems to me, a way of handling things, built into them. For example, if you pointed at anybody that was crippled they would say, "Don't point at that person. You could very well be that way." They would make sure what they were saying came across by adding, "That man who's got his finger cut off, that's what happened to him after he pointed at somebody." Or they would say, "Don't point at the rainbow. That person pointed at the rainbow, and the rainbow cut his finger off." Things like that stuck with you. You made sure you never pointed at anything.

Another thing they would say was, "Don't step over anyone. It will shorten his life." They'd say, "See that little guy over there. That's probably what happened to him. So don't step over your brothers or sisters." They had a way of saying, "If you do this, this is going to happen." I noted the good reasoning behind these things. What they said had a lot of influence on me.

The other thing was that they really cared for me. So I enjoyed the stories they told me, especially about Big Foot. They called him *See-hans*. My grandparents would visit us at my father's house, and after supper we'd sit down and ask Grandma to tell us a little story. We'd all sit in a circle and listen. I remember she said, "You guys be quiet. Quit making noise. We're going to tell you a story about what happened to one boy who was rowdy and loud. This bogeyman cut an opening in his tent, pulled the boy out, stuck him in a basket, then walked off with him because he heard him making noise."

The old folks taught us to behave through these stories. And what made it

DARRELL GARDNER, 56?, TRADITIONAL UTE CRAFTSMAN AND SWEAT LODGE KEEPER

The auto accident that killed Darrell Gardner's eldest son altered the course of Darrell's life. An accomplished painter and traditional Indian craftsman, he walked away from his secular identity in his late forties and began to live the life of a medicine man.

Darrell Gardner was born in Price, Utah, on December 20, 1931 or 1932. He is not sure of the year. His mother was Caucasian. His father was a Colorado Ute raised by a Mexican family. The interview with him took place at his cabin in Farm Creek, which is situated along the northern border of the reservation. The one-room cabin, which faces the house trailer where his wife and the youngest of his fifteen children sleep, was the scene of a joyous chaos. Deer, bobcat, and a bear hide were draped over a rocker. A massive, brown buffalo head stared back from the wall. Utensils and Indian artifacts hung from nails. Herbs and Indian tobacco were in pouches on the lone dresser. An unassuming, articulate man, Gardner sat on the edge of his bed and spoke softly.

I've gone back to the blanket, I guess. That's what they say. Because I've been on the other side, seen that other side, and have come back to this.

special was the fact that you lived in a one-room house that was your kitchen, your living room, your bedroom. A family of four—you wonder how they got along in it. But the old ones had ways of communicating and keeping control of the whole family in that one room. In the old days, you didn't talk back. You behaved, and if you had something to say, they would listen to you and answer you.

I remember my grandfather lived in a cabin he built himself. It had a dirt roof and a dirt floor, and it was comfortable during the winter. Three or four months before winter set in, my grandparents would prepare. They would go up to the mountains and pick choke-cherries and currants and dry them and make fruit patties, which they would later mix with flour and water to make a gravy and then serve with meat. In April, the garlic would start growing. They'd get out there and dig it up before the sheep got it. They would pick a lot of garlic. There was also a leaf they ate that had a garlic taste—only sweeter—and that grew along the banks of water. You twisted it up into a ball and ate it with your food.

I remember the Bureau [of Indian Affairs] had a clinic in White Rocks. Most of the time, though, our people preferred using medicine men. At that time we had quite a number on the reservation. I was treated when I was a kid. I had dropsy. The medicine woman who treated me said my body was consumed with liquid. Every time I'd pinch my body anywhere, it would remain [pinched]. She said, "Your body is just filled with liquid."

These medicine men and women were important to us. We respected them. They had what you'd call X-ray vision. They could visualize what was wrong with you. If it was a broken bone, they would say, "I can see where it is broken." That's how powerful they were.

Maybe that's what I did. But the old way is a good way. I can't forget it. I wasn't meant to forget it. And I can't let my people forget it. If they don't want to listen, that's up to them. The only thing I can do in my sweats is make an example for these younger kids.[11] They can look two ways. They can see people out there drinking and killing themselves, and they can see this other way, the old way.

Our prayer circle has two roads. It's just like everything else. For every force, there is a counterforce. That's nature's way. We let these little kids see that. Maybe they'll choose the good way. All of us fall off the good road—we call it the red road—sometimes. But we got to encourage these kids to get back on and stay there. We can only do so much, but we got to do the best we can. Because every time we lose one of them [young] people, we're all diminished by it. And right now, we lose them two or three a week from drinking and drugs.

My mother's name was Evelyn Wiseman. My father was called Ramon Gonzales. He was raised by Mexicans in Colorado. At the time I was born, my dad was the disciplinarian down at the Indian school. Then he ran off with another woman. So my mother brought me up here in Farm Creek.

Darrell and Colleen Gardner.
Kent Miles

When I was fifteen, I joined the service. I had to go in, because I got in some trouble. I stole some fish from the hatchery and they caught me. They fined me twenty-five dollars, and we didn't have twenty-five dollars. So I had to join just to get out of paying that. I told them I was eighteen. I was big for my age, I guess. [*Chuckles*] They put me in the marines and sent me to Korea just as the war broke out.

Now, you can't walk through that mud there without being changed. You come back with a little bit of that stuck to your feet. I'd like to forget it sometimes. But once you've seen the ugliness of human beings—of what people will do to others—it sticks in your craw. There is no getting rid of it.

Indians have a sixth sense, I guess, like an animal. If you're up on a hill looking at deer, and they don't know you're around, they somehow can tell. They get nervous. I remember—I was just a kid, a runner, a reconnaissance man, and I could feel somebody was watching me. I could feel the hair on the back of my neck coming up. I tried to tell my sergeant. He said, "You've got some imagination." Then we started getting shot at. The next time I said it, he paid attention.

I learned quite a bit out there, I guess, but when I came back I felt my world was changing. When I was a kid, we could go riding horses down through this grass. [And] anytime we'd come by somebody's house when it was suppertime, they'd say, "Come in and eat." No kid ever went hungry. Now, if you go down there at dinnertime, they'll close the door. . . .

After Korea, I stayed in these hills for a while. I got married. I made a living trapping beavers, catching bobcats, selling the hides. Then the government sent us to Denver, on relocation. They said it was to get us away from the reservation because there weren't jobs around. But they pushed us out too fast. No one could get jobs. See, they sent these people out to compete with people that's lived that way all their life, and our people couldn't do it. It just didn't work. Everybody who left came back. It messed up a lot of people. They came back feeling like they're less than they were. A lot of them started drinking.

Here, they were men. They done their things—they hunted. But if there's a job out there and there's a white man and an Indian, we know damn well who is going to get the job. They're not going to take the dark one. So they got whatever was left over. Well, you go back to your family and say, "I got this job for two dollars an hour." Your kid looks at you and says, "My friend at school, his dad makes ten dollars an hour." So it took their pride from them. They said, "Hell with it," and went out and got drunk. . . .

We came back too, after Denver, but there was nothing here. I couldn't earn a living. If I had a ranch, I might have had a chance. But Indians aren't ranchers. They're not farmers. Digging things up is woman's work. It's degrading. They won't do it. They can hunt and fish and trap. They're damn good at that. But when they try something else and they are no good at it, it makes them look small.

I stayed here for a while, then I went down to Salt Lake, and for fifteen years, I "adapted." I had two businesses of my own, then I went to work for KUTV [Channel 2]. When they hired me, they thought I was an Indian from India. [*Chuckles*] I worked from the bottom up. I did anything and everything. Went all the way from errand boy to floor director. But my girl was hit by a car there—twice. The first time, we let it go. But the next time, it ran right over her and broke her up. That's when I said, "The hell with it." I loaded my family up and come home. They tried to hire me back. They even sent Bill Marcroft [a local sportscaster] out to find me. He went to the tribe and asked if they knew me. They said "Yeah." He asked [them], "Where does he live?" "Up there." They pointed to these hills and wouldn't tell him where. They thought he was a bill collector, I guess. [*Laughs*]

After I came back, I started drinking. I became an alcoholic. There was nothing else to do [here], and everybody was doing it. That was the main problem. Everybody was doing it. Finally, though, I quit. After my boy wrecked his car and killed himself, I quit. . . .

See, me and him were drinking that night—and he went out to get some more. It was so senseless, so useless. He was not only my son, but my buddy.

And he was gone. I couldn't let his death go. There had to be some good that came from it. It *couldn't* just happen and nothing good comes out of it. I figured—if I stopped drinking and started doing some good, doing my job and helping people the way I was supposed to, this will be the one good thing that comes out of it.

Running sweats has been with me all my life, you see. There are certain things that's happened to me ever since I was a kid to give me the impression that that's the line I was supposed to take. But I wasn't taking it, and it damn near ruined me.

I remember, when I was about nine or ten, I was walking over these hills one night, coming back from my sister's house. I sat down on a hill to look at this little valley, and the whole world turned blue, a brilliant, neon blue. I looked at my hands . . . and they were blue. The rocks were blue. The earth was blue. And there was something in me that made me cry. It's hard to explain the feeling. It was just some of the power the Creator gave me as I look back on it now, that power that is so much greater than anything else in the universe. And it touched my heart and my soul. And it was reflecting on my spirit, telling me I had a job to do.

But when I was drinking, I just kept ignoring it. The Grandfathers would say, "Get your butt in gear. Do what you're supposed to do." I'd say, "I ain't going to do it. What are you going to do, kill me?"

Then, when my boy died—I don't know how to explain this—but the Grandfathers will only be patient for so long. When they finally say something to you, they don't kid around. They can be awfully tough on a person. They can get to you where you think they can't. They might have had to go through my kids to get to me, but they got to me. And it was a hard, hard lesson. But if a person is cut out to do something, he'd damn sure better do it. If he doesn't, he is going to get knocked. One way or another, he is going to get it.

That first sweat I ran by myself was special. But every one of them is special. Anytime you come before your Creator in a sacred way, in that way, it is special. And every one of them is different, even though they might look the same on the outside. When you go in the sweat, you strip yourself of everything and go before Him in a humble way. Just the way you are. You have no pretenses. You only have what you are. You go before Him and say: I'm here . . . and I'm asking you for this or I'm thanking you for this, and I'm doing it in a completely honest way.

Inside, I'm responsible for everybody. I have to pick up on if somebody is having a little trouble, or if they are sick. Now, this is hard to explain, but I pick it up not necessarily by sight. I feel it. Yet, while I am there, all I do is pour the water [on the rocks] and run the sweat. I'm no different than anybody else. We're all the same. I just make sure the water gets poured on the rocks, and it don't get too hot for the little kids or something.

The sweat humbles you. It cleans you out. Your outer body. All the poisons go out of your system. So it doctors you, too. The only thing is, the experience of the sweat—you can't explain that. I've had hard-nosed white people, nonbelievers, come out of a sweat. They come out crying. They say they've never experienced anything like that in their lives. But anytime you come before your Creator, it's a pretty startling thing. And even though it is a little, humble place, when you come before Him in that way, you can really feel it in your heart. When you leave, you know you've been in His presence.

We have wild meat that we grind up. It's like a sacrament. We take a little bit of it at the end of the sweat. And we thank God, for that meat represents all the animals that fed our grandfathers, fed us. By this simple thing, we say, "We thank you for this and ask you to bless the spirits of all these animals that give their life for us." Then we have berries. We do the same way with that. We say, "Thank you, my God, for all these things, everything that grows upon this earth." This is a humble way [to worship], a simple way. But we think of Him that way.

Now, I've been running sweats for many years . . . , but I'm having trouble now. There is a lot of turmoil here [on this reservation]. People are drifting off. Usually, our people start really coming [to the sweats] when they are right on the bottom. That's when they remember God. When they got everything they need, they forget about God. Like everybody else, they don't realize He is the reason they have it. It's when they are hurting, when they ain't got nothing, that they think maybe I'll pray a little bit.

But we knew this was coming. We were told this was coming. We were told this tribe would be right down to its knees, financially, because they think that's where their strength is, in that money. But it isn't. Money doesn't make them a tribe. The money has broken them up. Just shattered them. The Grandfathers told us—not only me but a couple of other medicine men—that this was coming. They told us this same thing, almost word for word. And you can see it going down now. And they are not done yet.

The hell of it is, we *all* got to pay for it, because we all let it happen. For me, the one thing I *know* is I'm going to keep my sweats going. I can't let this [trouble] stop it. Because the only thing I can do is be around to pick the pieces up. I know there will be people who will come and need help, and that is the only way I can be here to help them. I'll trap, I guess. Get a job where I can. But the sweats are more important. That is what the people are going to need when it comes to it. And I've got to be here. The only thing I can do is to be here to pick my brother up and say, "Maybe I can help you get back on the right trail."

The other night a man come up. He was going to kill himself. His wife ran off. She had been drinking. He was about half drunk. I talked to him for about two hours. I told him he's got a lot on the ball. He said he couldn't see it. He said there was no use him doing anything. He just came up to thank me for making his boy's powwow outfit, and he said he was going out to finish himself off.

Now, damn it, I talked to him and talked to him and talked to him! I told him his people were in trouble. Why is he only thinking of himself! Well, he

ELISE COHO PAWWINNEE, 85, UNCOMPAHGRE ELDER

I started attending boarding school at Randlett when I was eight years old. I stayed in school till I was quite old. They tried to make us talk English at the school instead of Indian, but we never quit talking Indian. My mother didn't come [to see] me most of that time because they were way out in the mountains. Most of the Indians lived in the mountains at that time. They would stay out there in the summer and come back [to the agency before winter] to receive the rations the government had put aside for them. They got sugar, flour, coffee, beans, and meat.

When I got to be around sixteen, my parents stopped going to the mountains. They started living right here along this road, where there were a lot of cabins. My family had a lot of sheep then. My husband's grandmother used to herd them. She was lame, but she went out with the sheep every morning. When she was too old to go out, she left them to my family. She was quite old when she died. . . .

Now, when a family member died in those days, the old people used to mourn for a year. They cut their hair and shed everything. They threw away all their belongings and wore their oldest clothes. If you went to [the Ouray] cemetery forty years ago, you would have seen blue and white enameled pitchers sitting on graves. Sometimes people put these water jugs on the grave because they thought the person might need a drink [on the way to the other world].

We never had coffins in those days. We dug graves, then put sticks across the [tops of the] graves, shelf-like. People put the dead person's things at the corners, and the dead were wrapped in blankets and laid there. The whole thing was covered. Most of those up on the hill are buried like that. They would just lay there until it all caved in.

went out feeling pretty good. He figured he had somewhere to go, some goal to go to. . . .

One night I had a young boy come to the house. He had been drinking. And I didn't want to get up and talk to him. He was just like a son to me. I told him, "Oh, go on in the house, lie down on the couch, and go to sleep. I'll talk to you in the morning." I didn't take the time to talk to him. And I'll be darned if he didn't go out and kill himself. So I don't give a damn now what time of night it is or anything. I'll *never* do that again! I'll talk to anyone that comes and wants to talk. That was the stupidest thing for me to do, but I didn't realize he was actually going to do it. He really needed somebody to talk to, somebody to care. No one cares down here anymore. They don't care about their own people. I've seen them walk right past people lying in the gutter, drunk. Walk right past and laugh, instead of reaching out to them and picking them up, saying, "Come on. I'll clean you up, help you." That's the stage we're at. And it can't be that way. It has got to be different. We have got to be different.

Clifford Duncan. *Kent Miles*

CLIFFORD DUNCAN, 57, TRIBAL MUSEUM DIRECTOR, SPIRITUAL LEADER, NATIVE AMERICAN CHURCH

Clifford Duncan was born in Fort Duchesne, Utah, on April 10, 1933. One of thirteen children, he grew up near the town of White Rocks and attended the Uintah Boarding School and Union High School. In 1951, he was drafted into the United States Army and served for two years. Upon returning to the reservation, he was sent to Denver under the auspices of the BIA's Relocation Program and then to Salt Lake City, where he apprenticed, under the GI Bill, as an electrical technician. In 1960, encouraged by his father, he traveled to the Comanche Reservation in Oklahoma to become a Damo-ene (one that is responsible or gives instructions during a Peyote ceremony). His teacher was Baldwin Parker, the son of Quanah Parker, a pioneer organizer of the Native American church in North America.

My mother's people were medicine men, and they handed down their spiritual and medicinal knowledge. My father's people were involved with the Peyote ceremony. Five generations that I know of, beginning with John Duncan, my great-grandfather, have been part of this Native American church. And the older I get, the more my life is wrapped in our religious ways.

I have no [conscious] sense of when my instruction in our traditional ceremonial ways began. The awareness of it is part of my body. Like the sagebrush tea that was given to me for colds when I was a baby—I have no beginning of that, because I already knew its bitter taste when I began to make sense of it. When something is this way, you have no way of cutting it off. If I were to walk away from it, it would call me back.

Each nationality has its religious ways. The Indians have had a lot of medicines, a lot of sacred objects that they used. As time went on, though, they began to lose their power. An Indian story says peyote will be the last one—the one we have to hold on to and the one that will carry us through the rest of our Indian life. So we must take care of it. It is our sacrament. Peyote is grown in the southern part of Texas, in the Rio Grande Valley. To us, this is sacred ground and the area where our religion began. This is where the Apaches, the Comanches, and the Kiowa learned about the Peyote religion and taught it to others—like the Sioux medicine man who taught it to my people and to my family.

Now, Peyote is an Indian religion. The Peyote ceremony lasts all night. If you take part in it, you have to be there for the whole of it. During a tepee ceremony around here, the rituals and languages may be of the Shoshone, the Ute, or the Navajo, but we all recognize one central spirit—the person we call Peyote. He is a man. He is a spirit that lives forever. Born a long time ago when God made him, there is no death in his life. His spirit lives today just like the day lives.

My father used to explain the Peyote ceremony to me this way: "White man's cathedrals and churches stand high to God. Their altars stand high and in front of them. Someday, a big fire will come to destroy the world, and all things standing up in front of that fire will be destroyed. But you will notice that our fireplace, our altar with the Peyote on top of it, is on the ground. It doesn't stand up. It is part of the earth. And when the fire goes over the world, it will not touch that altar. Only the tepee standing up above it will be destroyed."

My father said that while some of our traditions will die off, the Peyote ceremony will be the one to carry us through the rest of our Indian life. He said, "Each time you come to the ceremony, you must talk to that Peyote spirit. You must talk about your entire life, and you will see your life back to the time you were born. You will see the road that's marked from the beginning to the end of your life, and you will see where you are on that road."

Before we are taught about the medicinal ways [of peyote], we are shown how to participate in a Peyote ceremony, how to move around in the tepee. You do not walk into a tepee blind. You always walk to the left, you always circle to the left, and you must never turn completely around.

To join in an Indian ceremony, you must believe in it first, because it is like life itself. It is not something you have to "try" to accomplish, but something you believe in and will accomplish because of that belief.

Some of our ways are different from yours. As a spiritual man, I describe it like this. An Indian's day starts at noon and not at midnight. My day started at noon today. The night will be the middle part of the day, and when it comes to another day tomorrow, I will go into another day when the sun is straight up. That's why at the end of an Indian's day, there is no darkness.

Our month begins with each new moon, and each lunar month has a special name to it. There is only one star that doesn't move, and that is the center of the world. All the other things that go around are storytellers. Each star, and each group of stars, has a story to tell, like the stories of the animals and the creation of the world. You must learn to [listen]. [The stories] sound like folklore, but the person who believes in the Peyote ceremony will find what the animals say is real. And what they say will be a guidepost for him to live by.

I myself believe in the Peyote religion. I use it as a tool to pray to the Supreme Being. When I say pray, I mean talking. God listens to you when you're sincere. You will cry. You will laugh. God likes to laugh, too. And He knows I love certain things, so I tell Him that. To Him, my life is an open book. He knows me. And it was through this religion that I learned this. It was through a dream that I experienced this.

I dreamed that I died and was walking through darkness. It was a long walk, and I came to a light, a light on the ground. A man was sitting there. He was dark. He had a blanket, and I could only see his silhouette. He was big, about the size of those Buddhas you see in China.

I was supposed to tell this man my whole story. The story of my life. He was the one that was going to help me to move on to the next world. I talked and talked, telling him pretty near all my life. Then he said, "You didn't tell

FRANCIS McKINLEY, 66, UNCOMPAHGRE ELDER

I used to talk to the old people about my grandfather. They would say he was very strong willed, very authoritarian. He wanted his people to do what he said, because that was the only security they had. If they violated that, then they were gone.

My grandfather's name was Charlie Shavanaux, and it's my understanding that he succeeded Chief Ouray somewhere in the early 1880s. Chief Ouray decided that he wanted to remain in Colorado after he signed the peace treaty of 1880 in which the bands that I belong to gave up their lands. And he appointed my grandfather as chief of the band with the agreement of everybody else. [Shavanaux] was the one that led them from Colorado to Utah in about 1882.

My grandfather was a leader of the band which was located around the vicinity of Montrose, Colorado. Our tribe wasn't known as a tribe then. We were bands, and as bands we were identified by the area we lived in. For example, Uncompahgre refers to a lake in west-central Colorado. And part of the Uncompahgre group were called Biha. They came from the area close to Grand Junction. And the White Rivers were known by different subgroups, like Yampa and Yiparca.

I imagine it wasn't a happy occasion when they were being sent to a strange place like Utah. Many of them didn't want to come to a place that consisted mostly of a pile of rocks and desert, unlike the green valleys, the pines, and the forests they were vacating. Many were depressed, anxious, frustrated, maybe even asking for violent action. My grandfather must have had strong control over them, strong influence, in order to make them listen. It must have taken a very authoritarian, almost military[like] control to guide people who were broken down spiritually, emotionally, and in every other way.

---

me about certain things. What happened to that?" I had to go back and search out my life and tell him about it again. I told him everything [this time] that I had separated from myself before. And I found that this man knew everything about me from the time I was born to the time I was right there in front of him.

Suddenly the light went up, and I said, "No wonder you know everything about me. You are the other me." He said, "Yeah, you can never lie to me, because I *am* you. How can you lie to yourself and live in this world?" Then he told me to go back—and I woke up.

I try to explain these experiences to my children—and to my brother's children. That you have to answer to yourself and accept the blame for your mistakes. This is what they passed on to me, and now I am passing that on to my children.

One of our teachings says before the world "accepts" you, you're really just a spirit. Before a tree grows in this world, it is a spirit. The spirit that the tree has and the spirit that you have has no separation. You can't tell the difference, because they're the spirit of the same thing. It's after they "appear" that one is a tree and one is you.

You were meant to [appear this way] when you live in this world, and so was the tree. So this tree spirit and this spirit that is you are brothers. When a tree dies and when you die, you will go to this other place and meet again as the same spirit. All things are that way, and that's how we believe. So the tree that stands in one place all its life will know what's on the other side of the hill, because it possesses the power to do so.

Now, you can describe the colors of the world, the things you see with the naked eye—the people, their clothing, their skin. You can describe them, identify them, saying this one has light skin or this one had dark skin. This one is brown. But in the true spiritual world, it's not that way.

If you really want to see the true color of this world, take a good look at it through the other world. Then you will know the true color [of everything]. Maybe then you'll discover that the white man is really not a white man. Maybe you'll find out that an Indian is not an Indian. This is my people's way of thinking.

LARRY McCOOK, 41, INMATE, UTAH STATE PENITENTIARY

This interview was conducted in a closet-sized conference room in the Minimum Security Section of the Utah State Prison on May 6, 1986. Two months earlier, McCook and other inmates filed a class-action lawsuit against Utah correction officials for prohibiting Native-American inmates from growing their hair long, in the traditional style, and erecting a sweat lodge. McCook's group stated that since nineteen other states and the federal government permitted sweat lodges in their prisons, Utah's refusal to give permission (claiming sweat lodges posed an unwarranted security threat) was a violation of their civil rights.

A muscular, ruggedly handsome man, Larry McCook was the spokesperson and apparent leader of the effort by Indian inmates to retain their traditional way of life at the Utah State Prison.

I was born in a little house, right there in Randlett, on August 15, 1945. My parents are deceased. Okay? My uncle, Franklin McCook, is my parent now. He's my brother, my friend, my father.

My parents weren't married at the time I was born, so my grandma raised me until I had to go to boarding school in White Rocks. I couldn't grasp the English language then. Then my mom took me. By that time, she had married [someone else], and they were building a house at La Point—an all-white community—where my stepdad was going to farm. There were only five

Larry McCook. *George Janecek*

Indian kids out there, so that's where I learned to speak English. I went to school there until the fourth grade, then we moved back to Randlett to take care of my grandma.

After she died, I started Union High School [in Roosevelt]. I didn't like it, though. We didn't learn anything. The teachers just didn't pay attention to us. They thought we were ignorant and didn't try to teach us. So we played the role of being ignorant, gullible. We played the role, and that's the way it was. We were even discounted in sports. So what happened? It led to juvenile delinquency. When I was in the ninth grade, I robbed a trading post store with three other guys.

After that, I didn't go back to Union but went to an Indian school in Albuquerque, New Mexico. My athletic potential came out, and I played football. But I broke an ankle and had to come back home. By the time I came back, drinking was nothing on the reservation. Everybody was doing it. My parents were drinking. It was just an everyday thing. We could get drunk anytime we wanted. I tried to go to school again at Union High School, but then I took off for Phoenix instead. My mom had me picked up—put me on a bus and drug back. I went to another Indian school, didn't like it, and ran away again. Home life was becoming violent, though. People were drunk and there was fighting all around. I was in it, too. I was fighting.

But the seeds that my grandma and stepdad implanted in me—the Indian ways—survived that. My stepdad, Tommy Thompson, was a Sun Dancer for twenty years. He taught me things I'll never forget. One summer, he took me down to a Sun Dance in Southern Ute country—Ignacio, Colorado. After the dance, I stayed there with his people—the old, traditional people. I lived with them for a year, before he and my mom came and brought me back. I learned then that they work, those Indian ways and the blessings. And I remember those years real well . . . when I learned to love and respect my tradition and culture.

One time, when we were kids, my cousin, Ed Lonebear, and I got in some trouble at home, so they sent us down to a Mormon foster home in East Los Angeles. That's where I learned more about prejudice. We were the only Indian kids there to play first-string basketball and football in an integrated school. We liked the sports. We liked the school, and I learned a lot down there. I found out about the Mormon experience, and it was disgusting. My foster father would tell us, "Shut up. Quit talking Ute." He'd punish us and treat us real bad. But I didn't do nothing about it, because I liked the sports and the school. Then they'd coerce us into going to church, and I'd get stuck. We'd both get stuck. We'd get into the Book of Mormon, and they'd say, "Hey, you're Lamanites, God's chosen people." They'd say, "One day you're going to turn white. You're going to become delightsome, like us." They'd literally say to us, *"You are going to turn white; you are going to be like us."* And I'd go, "Yeah, yeah, I guess that's the truth."[12]

And this was just like yesteryear when [the] white man came into Indian country, took away children, and sent them to faraway boarding schools and taught them to be embarrassed of their Indianness. When the children went home in the summer, they looked at their people and said: "Our people are unworthy, so we're unworthy." They felt small. And this is important, man! This is where our suicide and drinking come from, and this is still being per-petrated. Kids go away to foster homes, Mormon homes, and then come back and get into this identity crisis, wondering what kind of Indianness is real. People go around asking, "How come Indians drink so much? Is it heredi-tary?" It's simply what I told you: the brainwashing and the prejudice. If you really looked into it—you'd see it!

I was a gifted child, I guess. I was a cute kid, you know, and I was always loved. Then, gradually, I had this desire in me to go. I'd tasted travel as a kid and I wanted more.

After high school I went into the marines. Breezed right through boot camp. It was beautiful. Then they stuck me down at Alameda Naval Air Base. Two months, three months went by. I was pulling KP and said: "Oh, heck with this man's trip." So I started going AWOL. They caught me, put me in the brig for sixty days, then kicked me out of the service.

After that, I just moved around, goofed around, drinking, carrying on, going to powwows, going all over the country. I lived on Indian people, on my wit, and on my ability to manipulate. I lived in the Mescalero Apache Indian Reservation and then in Zuni, New Mexico, shacking up, cohabitating, you know, the Indian way. Then I went north and lived at the Crow Agency, then in the San Carlos Indian Reservation.

I went all around and finally got married. I met this little gal. A Pueblo. We didn't get married right away. She got pregnant, and after I came back from Albuquerque, New Mexico, I married her. I've got three kids down there; they're grown now. But one day, I said to her, "Bye." She said, "I'll always be here for you." You know, just like that. No, I'm not lying, I'm not trying to play stud. I said, "Okay—bye." You see, the same restlessness was still in me. I had to move. So I split.

Finally, in Arizona, I was traveling with a bunch of Indians. We were moving, and I picked up hot credit cards and signed them along the way. A few months later, the police got me and gave me three to five years in Florence, Arizona.

Florence is a tough joint down by the old Mexican border. Its walls got to me, and that's where I snapped. I wrote my old lady, "I'm in jail, and I'm looking for consolation." She says, "Nope. You hurt me too much." Then she gives me divorce papers, and that kicked my ass. Then I started getting calloused; I was getting calloused. They had a TA—transactional analysis—group down there and I joined it, okay? I didn't know at the time that I was only polishing up my act. I really can manipulate, you know, and there I was, within three months, polishing it up instead of using it constructively. Polishing up my crazy act.

I've been in jails all over, okay? The first was the brig. Then Frisco. That's where they [sentenced] me, gave me a year for fighting. [Then Florence.] The last time was after New Year's Eve, when I was out partying with my sister. We went barhopping. When the bars closed, I went home, got into a fight. Got picked up for assault. And with my record, they gave me zero to five [years], and here I am, here I am.

Now, there aren't many Indians here [Utah State Prison]. Most of them go to federal joints. But when I moved over here, there was a Miguel Q. working here. He was the ethnic resource specialist, but he didn't do anything for the spiritual aspects of the Native-American inmates. When they asked for the right to have long hair, he wouldn't do anything about it. When they wanted their powwows, he'd set them up but discredit them, too. After watching him, I finally said to the Indian people, "Our white brothers, the non-Indians— they got their own churches and it all comes in under 'Church.' But we don't

HENRY WOPSOCK, 75, WHITE RIVER ELDER

My grandfather's name was Wopsock. That was the name attached to him at the time the reservation opened up. A lot of the people wanted money [as payment for tribal lands]. But instead of money, my grandfather wanted the cedars as his stake. And Wopsock means "the cedars is my stake." That was his wish, because he wanted firewood in the future.

I think this should be known, too: During the time I was young, after the reservation opened up, my grandfather used to talk about a certain place. He never did mention this place by name or say that there were white people there. Yet there was a man, he must have been an outlaw, and this man came to our place at night. His garments were black. He had black guns, two black horses, and a black saddle. About the first or the middle of August, that's when he'd come. And the only person he associated with was my grandfather. He came to the table for his meals, and he'd stay about a month. But just before he left, he'd give my grandfather a lot of money. I found out later it was stolen.

Well, after the war, in 1946, a bunch of us got a special permit to go hunting in Brown's Park. When we checked in, I saw an old man and I knew it was him—that same outlaw. I expect he was in his twenties when I first met him. And many times now I wish I had spoken to him, because I knew him as soon as I walked in. He looked at me a long time, and I expect he kinda knew me, too. He could have told me a lot.

One day, my grandfather told me to come to his house in the evening and sit by him. I had just started school. He asked me, "What are you learning?" I told him, "Reading, writing." He said, "Don't drop it. Learn all the white man's ways, because the time's coming that the Indian language will be gone. So learn two languages, but don't forget about your Indian language. Speak it, so in the future you can live it." He said, "You take these Indian people in their long hair. In the future, it won't be long. Mostly the people will have it cut short. You're going to see a lot of change in your lifetime. Remember when we used to go on up the hill and see all that sagebrush and that dust down there? It's going to be a different kind of dust. There's going to be farming machines. It won't be horses, and all the best fields will be fenced up." He said, "The best way to meet these changes is through education. You'll never have any trouble that way. You'll be just as good as they are." Now the time is here. It's here just as he said.

---

have any of that. Let's associate with the Native American Brotherhood, so we can do some of our traditional things."[13] I asked Miguel to help, but he stalled. So we're working through our medicine man, Clifford Duncan. We're going straight to our people on the outside [and to the courts] to get our hair rights and our religion in here just like the non-Indians.[14]

In the past, most of the Indian ideas got shot down. The prisons don't want anything to come in here that works [for us]; [especially] anything new. They don't like anything that shakes the bushes. But I don't mind, you know, 'cause I'm a veteran of hard time. See, the reservations were designed to be outdoor prisons. Before the Utes got their land claim monies, we were poor and prejudice was rough. And I'm a product of that. I remember the prejudice in the nearby towns. I've seen the adversity that comes from them stealing our homelands. And it's still there. Maybe I still got a lot of love in me, but I'm calloused from doing time and seeing prejudice. Yet I'll confront it. So when I seen my Indian brothers down like this, I said, "Hey, man, we need to do something for us."

So we're on our way now. Before, we were unnoticed. Our self-esteem was down, and we were shit on. Now, we're starting to be noticed. There's a little more pride; there's a little more respect for us. During circle, we pray.[15] Our medicine people are starting to come in. It feels good.

Myself, I'm a model prisoner. I haven't had a write-up or anything. I know the ropes. I don't smoke pot. It's all over here, man. You can get it easy. Booze, too. I jog. I participate in all their stuff. I play basketball, read a lot, watch constructive things on TV. And I share a lot. I share a lot. People come to me, hurt or sick. Sometimes, I get into them—because I know TA and I can give them real constructive stuff. If they come to me sincerely, I'll share with them. But I do my own time. I don't try to carry everybody else's troubles around. And, hey, you know what? I'm happy in prison, because I know my destiny. I know where I'm headed.

I'm a Ute. And our religion, culture, and ways have been here a long, long time. We've survived the adversities, the stealing of our homeland, and the prejudice. I've been part of that. It's been frightening, but also an awakening. And now that I know how to cope with it, I want to be a role model for my people and take what I know back there to help the Indians that are stuck deep in the reservations. I want to use my prison experience as an asset, to help my people to quit buying into abstract [white man] theories that throw them into confusion. Because reviving our Indianness, that's where it's at. Our songs and prayers and ceremonies are the answer to these troubled times.

Postscript: On March 16, 1989, in the U.S. District Court for Utah, Central Division, in a room packed with Utes and Navajos, Judge J. Thomas Greene declared, "There is no valid, rational connection between the regulation banning sweat lodges altogether and any legitimate penological interest. . . . The court notes that other religions have access at the prison to facilities for their religious ceremonies. . . . On the other hand, the Native American religion is not being accommodated . . . and in that respect the regulation operates to disfavor and punish those inmates belonging to the Native American religion." Consequently, the court ordered the prison "to allow the building and use of a sweat lodge by the inmates" on prison grounds.

Carleen Kurip. *Kent Miles*

CARLEEN KURIP, 38, DIRECTOR OF PUBLIC RELATIONS FOR THE UTE TRIBE

In an old wooden barrack built by the BIA at the turn of the twentieth century, Carleen Kurip described the spiritual legacy bequeathed by her grandparents and the way this inheritance informed and instructed her daily life. "I base a lot of my daily feeling on what I'm taking into my body and what I see," she said. "I may be able to see a certain bird flying, or maybe it's just going to land. I feel that presence all the time. If I don't feel it, I can begin to see why: I'm getting too involved in the fast pace [of today's life]. So I just back up. I've been taught that everything has a life, has an existence. Whether you abuse or take care of it, that's how your life is going to be. So, before the sun comes up, like I've been taught, I drink my water and I say a few words [of prayer] and hope it's going to be a good day. I don't think too much about what's going to happen. I just take each minute as it comes."

There was an abundance of elderly people when I was growing up. I felt secure because there were so many of them. My own grandparents, survivors who had been moved out of Colorado to Utah [by the U.S. government], were strong people. They were a very important part of my younger life. Because of their teachings, I've held on to my culture, tradition, and language.

John Ignacio Pawwinnee, my grandfather [on my paternal side], was on the original Tribal Council. He was a politician and a leader—that's what he was. He'd say, "First, help the tribe as a whole. Second, think of yourself last."

My grandmother [on my maternal side], Maggie Eutt Mountainsheep, also taught me a special lesson—that I was an individual. My grandmother raised me for my first-quarter years. She shared whatever she had with me. A good horsewoman, she could even beat men. And because of that ability, she was allowed to wear the warbonnet, the headdress. When I think about it, I don't visualize women in Ute society doing what my grandmother did. I grew up imitating her. I thought if she could do those things back then, well, I can do some things now.

In other words, I haven't limited myself as a woman. When I was growing up, neither of my grandmothers worked, and my mother never worked while I was in school. But some women of my age-group have had careers, some have even served on the Tribal Council. But I believe if I hadn't [become aware of] the opportunity from my grandparents, or seen or heard of their experiences, I probably wouldn't be doing the things I'm doing today. Even so, when I was young, I didn't always understand their experiences and just kept them inside me. Later, though, in my own life, I've had their experiences and words to fall back on. And now I've tried to carry these things on with my own daughter. . . .

While I was growing up, Ouray was a family community. Most of the people living there were in livestock. They had cattle or sheep. In the summer, everyone would desert Ouray, taking their livestock and horse herds out to the Hill Creek Extension of the mountains. Ouray was the Uncompahgre Agency. There were many homes, a general store, a livery stable, and a blacksmith shop. At Easter, we had a big rodeo; in the spring, the Bear Dance would take place. Yet that's not the way it is now. After the older generation died, I guess the younger ones didn't want to be involved with that type of livelihood, so people left the area.

Nowadays, I have fond memories of that life. I appreciated seeing the tail end of the older Indian generation, and I wish my daughter could experience some of it. These people were so close to nature. They knew life was hard. They had to haul water and kill the deer for food. And it made them survivors. Family life was closer because they all lived together. My grandparents even had a few older people living with us, so I had the experience of having uncles, aunts, and grandparents. And life was slow. Back then, the Indians had more respect and pride in themselves. You don't see that anymore.

I feel close to them. I feel their presence in me. . . . I believe there's a biological something—that one of my ancestors might have been a certain way that is part of me. I might not know who, but sometimes I feel like I've lived a life before, that this isn't my first life. And that's the way they used to feel. They taught me that life doesn't just end here and it didn't begin here. They'd tell stories like, "Don't be this way and don't be that way, because in your next life, you might come back as something you won't like." But the kids nowadays, they don't think life is worth living. They don't want to get past thirty. But me, I want to be old like my grandparents. I want to enjoy old age. That's when you have wisdom and knowledge and you are due respect.

My grandparents wouldn't let me go to school until I was seven years old. When I went to the first grade, I didn't speak a word of English. To this day, I still try to think how in the world did I make the change from a Ute speaker to English in a year's time; how did I learn to read. I think what drove me was that it was something I had to do. My grandfather told me I had to learn the white man's ways so I could help him. See, he didn't speak any English.

I never paid any attention to prejudice until I got into junior high. Then one girl said she wouldn't sit by me because I was an Indian and I was black. I knew I was an Indian. I knew I was different. But I didn't think people felt that way. So that was my first experience, and I've always been aware of this. But even so, I got a good education. Maybe it was because I wanted it and I would ask for it. All the [other] Indian students would naturally sit in the back of the classroom. I knew they were pushed back and didn't really learn that much. But the teachers didn't try to bring them up and involve them. They just allowed them to sit there. . . .

About a week ago, I was doing some statistical data for our Personnel Department. It was on all the people I grew up with and went to school with. More than half of them are now deceased. Maybe only about three men are employed today, and I'm the only female working. This is out of forty or fifty of us, so it kind of makes me wonder—what happened? I also found only a few people are over age sixty, so I can imagine what is going to happen when I become elderly. I guess it's pretty scary to me. The people that we lose every year—these older people. Every year, as we lose one of them, we lose something of importance to us. Soon, there's just going to be a few of them left.

I started work for the Ute Tribe when I was eleven years old. I worked for them clear up until 1980. During that time, we were selected by the Tribal Council to get involved in education. I did, and I began to like it. I wanted to do something in the public schools for a better education. I felt our young people were not getting the quality education that they deserved, so I went to work for the Uintah School District as a counselor at the junior high.

I helped the ones that were labeled troublemakers, handicapped. I encouraged them to come to school, to get involved in their lessons. The school district said they had behavior problems. They didn't. They just didn't have confidence in themselves. Or they didn't care. Education didn't mean anything to them.

At first, I was intimidated. But then I told myself that I was there for a purpose. And I got to where I could work with the staff. Towards the end, they pretty much came to me for advice on Indian students. They also stopped intimidating the children like they did before. They didn't punish them like they did before. And I felt like I accomplished something. I think we have a tendency to back down and quit. But I learned from my grandparents that you just don't do that. No one is better than you. You are equal to the next person. My grandfather used to say that if you're in a situation where a number of Ute people are involved and they don't speak up for themselves, you do it for them. I did that.

After my grandmother passed away, I quit working for the school. I needed time away from work. But I was used to working and after four months became bored. I applied for a job as head of the Public Relations Department and got it. My main jobs are to get the *Ute Bulletin*, our newspaper, out to the tribal membership and to educate people about political issues and cultural awareness. I like the job. I guess the position was established in the early '70s so that our relations with the local chamber of commerce and the governor would not be so strained. As director, you're spokesperson for the tribe. So sometimes I've had to do things for the Tribal Council that I might not have agreed with. But they want me to do it—so I did it.

Pretty much, though, I've always been informed about the tribe—the organization and the political aspects. I listened a lot to my grandfather and to my father. Sometimes, I'd ask my father for assurance. "Am I becoming too white because of material things?" His answer was always no. He'd say, "It's how you feel inside that makes you different. If you begin to not care about your people or your land or why you're here, and these material things consume you, then you are white."

But today's Tribal Council is different from the early ones. It's not just me that says this. Some of the people are saying they wish we still had some of our old people alive. We don't have a leadership anymore. The ability to lead people isn't here anymore. Common sense isn't used anymore.

I remember at the general council meetings, old men would stand up and talk the issues out. Some people would get emotional. But a decision wasn't made unless everyone else was involved in it. There was time to think on it, sleep on it, and ask God for guidance. Sometimes it took three or four days or maybe even longer before a decision was made. Now, it's over—just like that! People can't sit down and talk things over and decide what's best for the tribe. There's self-interest, immediate self-interest, rather than tribal interest. If our Tribal Council worked in unison, really representing the people, we could have a lot of impact. If we had a council that wasn't afraid of making waves, we could become a self-sustaining government and tribe. We could upgrade our land and people and quit having to depend on others to help us. . . . But a lot of people prefer not to get involved in politics. There's a lot of anger and hostility against our Tribal Council. People feel they've been used. I do, too. Particularly on how the council handled the [recent] enrollment issue, an issue that dates back to the split between full-bloods and mixed-bloods.[16]

I was always told that the family you married builds the blood stronger. I was told you don't marry someone with a disease, because you will pick it up and it will get into your blood. See, I'm from a mixed-blood family. And [my family] said that "other" blood makes you crazy. You don't think black *and* Indian. You don't think of the land and the earth and the values that are Ute. You get involved in other things that will hurt your family, your bloodline.

There are others, though, who feel our blood is not strong enough. Many of these are council members that feel we need new members to build a better tribe. Apparently, all of them have children of different blood that didn't meet the five-eighths [quantum Ute blood] requirement, and they want these children enrolled. They feel just the opposite of what I feel [and] what others feel. So there's a controversial issue here. There are two factions. And not being able to sit down and talk about it, not being able to go to the communities and really get the people's feelings, created a lot of problems.

We had a tribal referendum on different options about the degrees of blood. I was appointed chairperson. For three months, I actually went out and talked to people, had weekly meetings, answered questions, sent out letters, called people on the phone, and worked very closely with the old people. We wrote their viewpoints in the *Ute Bulletin*. The old people felt that whatever was worthy—the values they were raised with, the value of Ute blood—is today nothing. Essentially, they felt like they were nothing. So it's hard for them to understand what these younger people [those opposing the five-eighths option] are doing. They couldn't see why they were doing this.

Well, the five-eighths option won, which was the standing requirement anyway. But a month later, the Tribal Council reversed the referendum and came out with a policy of open enrollment. People felt deceived. They felt they had been lied to. I felt used and lied to.[17]

Will I accept what happened? I never will. I have to live with it, but it doesn't mean I have to accept it. I bet you twenty or thirty years from now the Indians won't have a voice. The person that has traditional values won't have any place here. Times are changing so fast. People accept the change. They forget their language, their culture, and their religion. That reminds me of what the old people used to say about the future. They said there was going to be nothing left of the Utes, just very few. They used the word *chawah* to describe this. *Chawah* means boiling coffee over and over and over—the grounds—until there's no taste left. Then you just have to throw it away. You can't get anything out of it anymore. That's what was told to me when I was young. I couldn't visualize this then because the tribe was so strong. But now I know this is what they meant. Remnants.

Shirley Reed and daughter. *Kent Miles*

JULIUS MURRAY, SR., 79,
UINTAH ELDER AND MEDICINE MAN

If you [as a white person] tried to live the life of the Indian, [other white people] wouldn't let you. I found that out. You can only do so much with Indians. Don't go beyond that. If you do, your people will be right on you. I've seen that happen. I'm talking about the white people here that try to help Indians. They get on them for trying to help. They'll do the same to you. They'll come down on you; they'll call you "Indian lover." They'll get you hemmed in no time.

So why are you so determined to know these things? You can't change the overall complex; you can't change the overall belief of the non-Indian people. They'll say, "Here's another [white] guy writing about Indians."

I would say the time is not yet right for all these things to become known. There is too much dissension. There is too much turmoil. There is too much distrust among people [so] that anything that you tried to bring out you wouldn't get to first base. Of course, there are a lot of good people in every group, but there's the majority that isn't. And within white society, the thing that's uppermost is that the majority rules, right or wrong. So it's hard to make a dent in something that's contrary to what you're bringing out. Because the fact is that people get to the point where they don't want to know the truth. They want to hear everything but the truth.

Even if [our story] were brought out, would these things be accepted as something real, or would they just say "that is something the [Indian] people have drummed up"? Can they get beyond [their preconceptions] to see how the transition from one way of life into another that is completely alien has affected us? These things have gone on for so long that it's become hard for people to realize what has actually happened. It will be hard for them to accept. They'll say, "Oh, these Indians are getting all this and that [from the government]," and they won't realize all the hardships we go through to live within this other way.

Do you see now what I'm trying to point out? Do you see what I'm getting at? How many of the people that read this will say, "Oh, that's bosh. They're human beings. Why can't they adjust?" But it is just like taking a crow and throwing him in with a bunch of peacocks. [They're] all beautiful things. Why can't he become a peacock then? Why can't he live like a peacock? Why can't he? Well, he just can't. Regardless of whatever you do with him, whatever you do for him, he'll be that crow.

SHIRLEY MURDOCK REED, 50, SOCIAL WORKER

Born on the Ute Reservation on January 21, 1935, Shirley Reed was one of the 490 mixed-blood Utes who were terminated from the tribal rolls by Public Law 671 in 1961. The termination program was an attempt by the U.S. Congress to mainstream Native-Americans by severing their treaty-based relationship with the federal government. While many people were emotionally and financially devastated by this short-lived and short-sighted effort, Reed was motivated by it.

"Termination," she said, "is the real reason I decided to go back to school. I wanted to do something to better myself and my children. I also felt education was going to be magical. I had the idea that if I could gain knowledge, that would give me the credibility to say, 'This termination, this division of the people is wrong.' And the tribe would listen and understand, because it is wrong! You can't split families strictly based upon who has how much Indian blood. It doesn't make any sense."

Shirley Reed received her B.A. degree from Brigham Young University and completed her master's degree in social work at the University of Utah. At the time of this interview, she was both a lecturer at the University of Utah and a consultant to Indian graduate students preparing for careers in social work.

I've lived off the reservation for eighteen years now. I sometimes say, jokingly, that I live in limbo. But what I mean is that I have to really function well in both places. While I'm here [in Salt Lake City], I'm doing something here. I work. But when I go home, it's like going into a whole different country, a different world. The other night, as a matter of fact—let's see, it was about three weeks ago—I was driving home. It was very late. I was traveling through Strawberry, and there was a moon, a bright moon. And everything was sort of lit up around me, covered with white. At the same time, there was a mist, a fog. I could see the bright stars. But every once in a while a wispy, little fog would sort of drift across the road and make things shadowy.

In front of me, the highway stretched . . . way out. And on that highway there was a fine, dry snow, and it was sparkling white, as if I was traveling on a highway of diamonds. And I imagined that it was diamonds, thousands and thousands of diamonds. It was like I was on some other planet. And it was so apropos, because I was going home. I was traveling back. And the whole area reflected the sense of where I was going. My lights only reached to a certain point, then it was black. It was like I was hurtling through space. I was moving through space. It was peaceful in some way, but it was not comfortable. And I noticed that everything seemed to fit—the fog seemed to fit, the little diamonds on the highway seemed to fit. It was a crazy experience, a crazy feeling. It stuck in my mind.

It made me realize that it doesn't matter how long I've been away from the reservation. It doesn't matter how well educated I am. There's still something within me that belongs there, that always remains there. Indians have a spirituality that is different, you see. There's a reverence for everything. Everything has a spirit. There's a spiritual quality about trees, about the land, about the sun and the moon. They all have a spiritual essence. I'm not sure that non-Indian people see trees as spiritual things because wherever they live, they cut down trees and they make their own space. They plant things, they make it different. Certainly, they've caused the most destruction to the air and the water. It's a matter of course.

I wake up in the morning and I hear on the radio, "If you have heart trouble or if you're old, don't go outside because you might have trouble breathing the air." Can you imagine—don't go outside, don't breathe the air? I don't think that's spiritual. How can you say it is if you allow chemicals to poison the very air that we breathe. Yet we accept this as a matter of course. We are not shocked by that. It's amazing to me sometimes.

Now, I have to add, I'm not sure the younger people within the reservation understand this difference anymore. Somewhere, maybe within my generation or the one preceding that, there was a break. There was an idea that maybe the Indian way of looking at things was not the best way. Or maybe our ideas were not coming down as clearly defined as they once were. Maybe the older people were not willing to share their way of thinking as they once did. I say this because I see things occur that really concern me: the breakdown of the extended family, the troubled kids, the suicides. That's saying to me that there is really some trouble in trying to find out who we are. . . .

We are approaching a very significant, an extremely crucial, time. Whatever happens right now, I believe, will determine if the tribe will exist or not. If the people decide that, yes, Indianness is a good thing, [that] they must not lose that perspective of the universe, then they're going to have to do something *now* to preserve that. But we have to decide. Someone *has* to decide. Somebody has to say, "We have to wake up. We have to do this together as a tribe, as a community." It has to be done. Only three percent of the children speak the language now. If the language is lost, something is going to be lost forever. It will be another step toward complete loss of tribal identity. So if Indianness is important—and I think it *is* significant—then the people within the community are going to have to say, "This is the way we are going to behave. This is the way we are going to raise our children. This is how our community is going to work."

Let me tell you one of the really wonderful things about the Indian way of life. An Indian dealing with another Indian person may feel anger, but there's also the idea that one shouldn't make another person uncomfortable. So if I feel angry or frustrated, it's better for me to be miserable than for me to say something to make you uncomfortable. I see this over and over and over, particularly with the older people. My father-in-law is a fine example. Let me give you an instance—just a humorous little episode—but therein lies something really important.

My family went to a Thanksgiving dinner. And my father-in-law, a very old, traditional man, really likes lemon pie. He's loved lemon pies since he was a young person. One of my husband's brothers' wives really cares a great deal for her father-in-law, so she baked him a lemon pie. He was the first one through with dinner, and she . . . cut him a piece of pie. And he ate it. They asked him, "How was the pie?" He said, "Fine." He had this pleased look on his face. Someone else finished dinner, and it was time for him to take a piece of pie. There were several kinds to choose from. He chose the lemon. He took one bite, then locked his jaws. He said, "Oh, my gosh, that's terrible." She'd forgotten to put sugar in. But my father-in-law had not said one word about that. He ate that sour, sour lemon pie with the look of someone who really enjoyed it.

His idea of social life is that you don't create any problems for anyone else. If they've done something that infringes upon your rights, you don't even deal with it. To become involved with their behavior says something about you, too. So, if someone does something you don't like, you distance yourself from that. You don't get involved in that at all. What that kind of behavior assumes, though, is that other people have the same values and they will not push or create problems for you, either. Of course, that's not the case. But the people of my father-in-law's generation had that notion. And they were kind, caring, sensitive people.

One day, I remember, my father-in-law was standing by the corral outside our house. He's built these corrals wherever he has gone to hold the animals that he's breaking. He was standing there, looking off toward the mountains, and he had tears in his eyes. I walked up to him and I said, "Chalmers, what's the matter?" "Oh, I was just thinking of all the old people [who are gone]," he said. And I cried for him. I cried. That really touched me. Because something *is* gone. Something he knew is gone. And I feel the loss even though I never knew it. I feel that loss, too. And I worry that that loss will become greater when people of his generation die. Because we don't know whatever it is that he knew, and he hasn't shared with us whatever it is that is not here anymore.

Whenever I try to explain to my white friends how my people view things, how they view themselves, how they view their God, what comes to mind is that my father-in-law, a very spiritual man, used to be up before the sun and rarely went out after dark. You see, every morning, when the sun rises, it brings the blessings of the day with it, the strength of the day. So he needed to be there. He needed to be there when the sun rose. Many Indian people believe this. The Navajos have a saying [about it] that goes something like this: "If you're not up when the sun comes up, then you're dead for the whole day." You might as well sleep all day, because for all practical purposes you're really dead for the day. There's some element of [universal] truth in that. Now, I'm not sure that every person is up before the sun these days, but the sun was significant in the lives of most Indian people at one time. What bothers me is that it isn't so anymore.

Things have changed so much. We've sort of given up the idea that Indianness is important. We've said, "Okay, it's not that important." We've let other ideas come in. We've let others define who we are. I've tried to think about when it began. When did we begin to let go? But I don't know the answer. I do know I am a good human being. Being born and raised on the reservation has given me a clear idea of my place in the universe. So I know I am a good person, and so are the things around me. Trees are good, birds are good, animals are good. And we shouldn't be trying to destroy them—we shouldn't allow them to be destroyed.

NOTES

1. A graduate of Westminster College in Salt Lake City, Utah, Forrest Cuch was thirty-one years old and in his ninth year as director at the time of the conference.

2. At the time of the presentation, oil royalties were being distributed to tribal members through monthly per capita payments. At the height of these payments, each enrolled member received four hundred dollars a month.

3. Ruby Crumble was one of the 490 mixed-blood Utes who were terminated from the tribal rolls through Public Law 671 in 1961.

4. The Native American church is the incorporated name of the organization sanctioning the sacramental usage of peyote. A Pan-Indian religion that grew out of pre-Columbian practice in northern Mexico and southern Texas, the "Peyote religion" spread among the southern Plains Indians in the nineteenth century and was introduced to the Utes in about 1914. Although the church has no general creed, members believe in peyote's sacred power to create visions and induce profound feelings "of fellowship and solidarity." Nightlong meetings, accompanied by drumming, singing, praying, and consumption of "the small spineless peyote cactus, emphasize sobriety, brotherly love, family responsibilities, and an intertribal outlook. On the Ute reservation, over fifty percent of the population are believed to be members." Ake Hultkrantz, *Native Religions of North America* (San Francisco, Calif.: Harper and Row, 1987), 82–83.

5. Menstruating women traditionally occupied a special shelter or a secluded corner of their home for several days.

6. Sun Dances originated with the Plains Indians in the eighteenth century, and the Utes began "sponsoring" their own Sun Dances in about 1890. As white settlers occupied greater portions of Ute territory, forcing the people to compromise or abandon their traditional lifeways, the Utes turned to the Sun Dance to reassert the tribe's personal and collective integrity.

Sun Dances are held annually today, usually in July and August. Each dance is based on dream instruction received by the Sun Dance chief and is a vehicle to open personal and collective communication with the Creator. Dances are held inside a corral, which looks like a great wheel. A large cottonwood is cut and placed upright in the center. Twelve smaller trees are placed upright on the circumference and connected to the center pole. Entry into the corral is from a doorway opening to the east.

To the accompaniment of drummers and singers, participants dance toward and away from the center pole for three days and nights while abstaining from food and water and praying for guidance. The rigors of the dance and the fast induce the visions that renew the lives of the dancers and the community. At the conclusion of the ceremony, Ute dancers traditionally drink water brought down from Big Springs. Fred Conetah, *A History of the Northern Ute People* (Salt Lake City, Utah: Uintah-Ouray Ute Tribe, 1982), 3–5.

7. In 1950, the U.S. Indian Claims Commission awarded the Confederated Ute bands thirty-two million dollars as compensation for their lost Colorado lands. Of this amount, seventeen million dollars went to the three bands on the Uintah-Ouray Reservation, and the rest went to the Southern Utes in Colorado. Due to widespread poverty and unemployment on the Utah reservation, the government permitted one thousand dollars to be distributed to each tribal member in 1951 as emergency relief. The rest of the funds had to be used in long-term economic and social development programs.

8. In 1953, the U.S. Congress, in a dramatic reversal of the New Deal Indian programs, issued a joint resolution declaring that it intended to free Indians "from Federal supervision and control" by terminating its trustee role and curtailing all federal

services to tribes. A concomitant of this policy was the relocation of Indians from reservations to urban centers, where employment opportunities were greater. Relocation centers were established in Los Angeles, Chicago, and Detroit to aid Indians in their transition from reservation to city life. Francis Paul Prucha, *The Indians in American Society* (Berkeley and Los Angeles: University of California Press, 1985).

9. Chapoose's first term as tribal chairman (1974–1977) marked a particularly creative time period for the tribe. According to Public Relations Director Carleen Kurip, the establishment of Ute Fabricating, Ute Hide and Tannery, Ute [Bowling] Lanes, and the Bottle Hollow Motel and Convention Center represented the tribe's first major economic development effort. "The aim of it," Kurip explained, "was to help the tribe become self-sustaining by creating craft-oriented work for men and women. Ute Fabricating made cabinets for local hotels, motels, and the Ute Housing Authority. Ute Hide and Tannery processed sheepskins imported from Australia and converted them into jackets and vests. And Bottle Hollow was our pride. It expressed our uniqueness [as a people] and our belief in our destiny. It was built to attract tourism and to increase employment for tribal members."

10. Chapoose was defeated in his 1977 reelection bid by Ruby Black, a traditionalist who represented a contingent of people who believed that the tribal business ventures brought an unhealthy intrusion of white values into Ute society. The group also believed that distributing oil royalty funds to the people through direct, monthly, per capita payments was more in accord with Ute customs than sustaining a system of highly paid white managers overseeing Ute employees.

11. Because he is not listed on full-blood or mixed-blood rolls, Gardner's genealogy is a bone of contention for some people on the reservation. They claim he has no business running sweats since he is not "legally" an Indian.

12. Starting in 1947, the Mormon church created a "placement service" to give deserving "Indian children . . . the privilege of living in LDS homes where they could not only be taught in [public] school[s], but . . . could be taught the principles of the gospel." Although it was begun modestly, by the 1980s the program had expanded to the point that a total of seventy thousand young Indians had participated. Although the church guaranteed that no proselytizing of young people would take place, proselytizing was, as McCook's interview indicates, impossible to prohibit and often had disastrous effects. This situation, of course, resulted from the Book of Mormon belief that Laman and Lemuel, the purported ancestors of today's Native-Americans, were cursed with "a skin of blackness" and became "an idle people, full of mischief and subtlety" for going against their father's prophecies. According to Mormon belief, after reembracing the LDS gospel, Native-Americans will again become "white . . . and delightsome" people. Robert Gottlieb and Peter Wiley, *America's Saints: The Rise of Mormon Power* (New York: G. P. Putnam's Sons, 1984), 159–165.

13. The Native American Brotherhood (NAB) was created by Native-American inmates as a means of organizing and protecting themselves while they were serving prison terms. The organization is national in scope and consists of "local" chapters.

14. In addition to wanting to wear their hair in the traditional style, the Native-American inmates wanted permission to build a sweat lodge on the prison grounds.

15. Group ceremonies take place in a circle, which is the symbol of life's unity and coherence.

16. The rivalry between the mixed-bloods and full-bloods on the reservation became a serious problem after the tribe adopted Indian Reorganization Act legislation in 1937 that created a corporate charter and a tribal constitution and made provisions for the election of tribal leaders. Traditional leaders, leery of this "white" form of government, refused to run for office. The vacuum in leadership was generally filled by the mixed-bloods. They controlled the newly created Tribal Council positions until 1961, when the U.S. Congress, through Public Law 671, terminated 490 mixed-blood Utes (people with fifty percent or less Ute blood) from the tribal rolls.

17. In 1980, several tribal members sued the tribe in tribal court for prohibiting their children—who had one-half Ute blood—from becoming tribal members. The Ute Tribe, in its defense, claimed that when Public Law 671 went into effect, resulting in the termination of 490 mixed-blood Utes, it established a quantity of five-eighths Ute blood as the amount needed for tribal membership. The aggrieved, however, held that the Ute constitution—ratified by referendum in 1937 and stating that a child could be enrolled if one of its parents was enrolled and was residing on the reservation at the time of birth—predated the later ruling and was, in fact, the official standard. According to these people, the five-eighths blood quantum stipulation was therefore "unconstitutional" until the constitution was amended by referendum. In 1985, Chief Tribal Judge Norma Jean Gray ruled that the plaintiffs were correct and ordered the Tribal Council to enroll several hundred "mixed-blood" children. The council, eager to circumvent the ruling and to deflect any negative political fallout, quickly held a tribal referendum, which sustained the five-eighths Ute blood quantum as the amount necessary for tribal membership. Chief Judge Gray, however, stated that the new constitution was not retroactive. The children still had to be enrolled. Organizers of the referendum (including Curip) and other "traditional" people felt confused and betrayed. They believed the council misled them when it allowed the referendum to be reversed. They also believed that enrolling these mixed-blood children would weaken the tribe's ability to maintain its traditional lifestyle.

BOOK TWO
AFRICAN-AMERICAN COMMUNITY

PREFACE

Ronald G. Coleman

The voices of the twelve interviewees in this chapter individually and collectively provide an understanding of the experiences of African-Americans in Utah for most of the twentieth century. Their stories build upon a history of African-Americans in Utah that began with such men as James P. Beckwourth and Jacob Dodson, who were members of fur trapping and exploration expeditions in the valleys and mountains of the region in the 1820s.

Permanent settlement of African-Americans in Utah began with the arrival of three African-Americans who were members of Brigham Young's advance party in July 1847. They were slaves of southern Mormons and were sent to help prepare for the arrival of the rest of the Mormon parties en route to Utah. By 1850 approximately sixty African-Americans were living in the Utah Territory. The majority were slaves, but a few were free persons of color. Although slavery was not legally sanctioned in Utah until 1852, it existed there from 1847, with the arrival of the Mormon advance party, until at least 1862, when the U.S. Congress abolished slavery in the territories. Whether the few slaveholders in Utah complied with this 1862 congressional act is unknown. Free African-Americans who migrated to Utah during this pioneer period did so primarily for religious reasons. As members of the Mormon church, they went to Utah to escape influences hostile to the Church of Jesus Christ of Latter-day Saints and to join their fellow Saints in building the newest Zion.

In the latter part of the nineteenth century the expansion of the national transportation network, the growth of the mining industry, and the military presence in Utah increased employment opportunities for African-Americans in the state and directly influenced the growth of its African-American population. Various companies of the U.S. Ninth Cavalry helped build and were stationed at Fort Duchesne in Uintah County from 1886 until 1901. The Twenty-fourth Infantry regiment occupied Salt Lake City's Fort Douglas from 1896 to 1899. The presence of these black soldiers influenced the social and cultural life of Salt Lake City's African-American population. By the 1890s the small African-American community had grown to numbers sufficient for the community members to establish their own churches, newspapers and political, social, and fraternal organizations. As elsewhere, the churches served the secular as well as the spiritual interests of the community. Black Utahns maintained communication links with other African-American communities throughout the country by regularly sending information about local activities to African-American newspapers in San Francisco, Portland, Pittsburgh, Seattle, Saint Paul–Minneapolis, Denver, and Chicago. Similarly, the African-American press provided black Utahns with information on issues of concern to African-Americans nationwide. Prominent African-Americans, such as Booker T. Washington, were warmly received by Utah's black residents when they visited the state.

However, with the increase in the African-American population, racially based discriminatory practices expanded in Utah. State law prohibited the issuance of a marriage license to interracial couples if one person was white and the other person black or Asian. The first African-American selected to serve on a jury was removed after complaints from white jurors. African-Americans were routinely denied access to public accommodations. Black Utahns were in a position similar to that of other African-Americans throughout the United States: They were residing in a nation in which the majority white population believed in white superiority and black inferiority. In Utah, blacks had to contend with being less than one percent of the total population in a state that was approximately ninety percent white and numerically dominated by a religion that until 1978 adhered to theological restrictions against black males. LDS religious proscriptions against blacks reinforced the discriminatory secular attitudes and practices of a significant segment of the religion's adherents. Many non-Mormon whites with similar beliefs of white superiority have historically felt very comfortable in Utah.

The oral histories in this chapter represent a broad spectrum of the historical experience of African-Americans in Utah. Five of the twelve interviewees are native-born Utahns. Three accompanied their parents to Utah when they were between the ages of six and ten, and four relocated to Utah in their early adult years. One left Utah as a young adult. Two are members of the Church of Jesus Christ of Latter-day Saints, and one left the Mormon church at the age of thirteen. Eight are men and four are women. The interviewees ranged in age from thirty-six to eighty-two.

The first four stories focus on the early decades of the twentieth century. Two of them were told by descendants of black pioneers who arrived in Utah between 1847 and 1871. These pioneers, like a number of other black Mormon families and their descendants, resided on land in the vicinity of Twenty-third East between Thirty-third South and Thirty-ninth South in Salt Lake County. They engaged in farming and were relatively self-sufficient. Three of these four interviewees spoke of "a nice family life," but none of them were financially well off. One of the four, born of parents in a mixed marriage that ended in divorce, was traumatized when her white mother remarried a white man and gave her away to a mixed couple. The agony of this rejection by her mother and the resultant sense of inferiority she felt for many years led her to a lifelong, deep devotion and commitment to ensuring a viable extended family structure.

World War II and the ensuing years had a dramatic impact on African-American life throughout the West. The development and growth of railroad centers, defense contract industries, and military installations in the region influenced a number of African-Americans to relocate to the western part of the country in search of better opportunities. Utah's small black population grew significantly, particularly in Weber County. One of the interviewees provides a unique glimpse into African-American life in the burgeoning western urban communities during the war years.

Throughout the country the World War II period and its aftermath was a watershed for African-Americans and their continued quest for freedom, justice, and equality. Black Utahns, like blacks elsewhere, became increasingly more vocal about local injustices. They responded to injustices in ways similar to African-Americans in other areas, although they did not respond as readily as many others. Still, there was a resurgence in support for the Salt Lake branch of the NAACP, and a branch of the association was established in Ogden. Four interviewees discussed the effect of the modern civil rights era on their lives, providing insights into how their levels of consciousness were raised, both on the local and the national level. They described how some local civil rights activists expressed impatience with some of their colleagues within the struggle, whereas others expressed concern about the militancy of these relative newcomers to the movement. Conflict over what were the best strategies for achieving justice and equality could be seen in many of the state's African-American communities during this period.

Racial prejudice and discrimination in Utah form the most dominant theme of the interviews. The majority of the interviewees recognized how the priesthood issue in the LDS church impacted the status of African-Americans in Utah.[1] Blacks were viewed as "unworthy" by many Mormons, and the Mormon religious beliefs and practices reinforced the rigid color line that had emerged during the last decades of the nineteenth century. Racism was evident in the public school system and was supported by the actions of some teachers and administrators. Several of the interviewees commented on how "mean and nasty" some of their white schoolmates were in their interactions with them. Indeed, race relations became increasingly difficult for many African-American students as their school years went by. The Rotary Boys Club was one of the few places in which African-American and Hispanic youth could gather without feeling the pains of exclusion. In the hope of achieving some semblance of equality of opportunity, a number of young black Utahns, like one of the interviewees, relocated elsewhere.

Individual and collective challenges to the racial slurs and discrimination form a second theme of the interviews. Interviewees described how members of the African-American community turned out in protest when an attempt was made to restrict blacks to a certain residential part of Salt Lake City in 1939. They also described how African-Americans, recognizing the influence of the Mormon leadership in local affairs, protested nonviolently in support of the state civil rights legislation at the LDS church office building, which was then located on South Temple Street.

Some of the interviewees noted that independent institutions, such as religious and fraternal organizations, within Utah's African-American community served black Utahns in ways similar to such institutions in African-American communities throughout the United States. Even today, they remain important to the leadership and the social, cultural, and spiritual vitality of the community, both individually and collectively.

The final interview suggests how far African-Americans in Utah have journeyed and how difficult this struggle has been. In 1978 the leadership of the Mormon church announced that "all worthy males" would be given the priesthood, a revelation that formed a landmark in the gradual changing of the racial landscape for Utah's African-Americans. In 1986, the Utah legislature's adoption of Martin Luther King, Jr.'s birthday as a state holiday formed another landmark. This legislation was introduced by the second African-American to serve in the Utah House of Representatives. The adoption of Martin Luther King Day illustrates a racial tolerance in the legislature that is important to all of the state's constituencies. Through the voices heard in the following interviews, one learns about the African-American experience in Utah from its rural roots to urbanization and the continuous struggle to overcome the barriers of exclusion and racism. With hope, "We shall overcome."

NOTES

1. Until 1978 black males were not admitted to the priesthood in the Mormon church.

Frances Fleming. *George Janecek*

PROLOGUE

FRANCES LEGGROAN FLEMING, 77, ELEVATOR OPERATOR, MAID

When we arrived at Ms. Fleming's home, we found an iron gate guarding the front door. After scrutinizing us through the peephole, Ms. Fleming opened the inner door, unlocked the gate, and then ceremoniously stood aside to let us in. The house was small and neat; the furniture, Victorian. A tiny, energetic woman, Ms. Fleming wore an ankle-length dark dress and a dark blue, button-down sweater. Her hair was tied into a bun on her head.

Francis Leggroan Fleming was born in Salt Lake City on September 25, 1906, to Nettie James and Louis Leggroan. A member of the Church of Jesus Christ of Latter-day Saints, she grew up on farmland in the southeastern quadrant of the city. In 1930, she married Monroe Fleming, the son of a Baptist minister, and the couple had two children. Ms. Fleming worked as an elevator operator at the Newhouse Hotel, as a maid at Auerbach's Department Store, and as a lunchroom cook for Prudential Life Insurance. Her husband was employed as a waiter and a coatroom attendant at the Hotel Utah. At the age of fifty-seven, at the behest of his wife, Monroe Fleming joined the Mormon church.

Throughout the 1940s and 1950s, the couple arranged to bring nationally acclaimed "Negro artists," such as Marian Anderson, Roland Hayes, Paul Robeson, Clarence Cameron White, and Hazel Scott, to perform in Salt Lake City. The aim of these programs, Ms. Fleming explained, was to introduce Utah's predominantly white population to the nation's celebrated black artists. Monroe Fleming passed away in their home in 1982.

I grew up right here. Not in this house, but in this area. Our place was six acres. It was a frame house, three rooms, a coal stove, no lights, no running water. We'd go to the ditch that was separating the property on the back and carry water [to the house]. Once in a while, Dad would hitch up the horses, put barrels and tubs on the wagon, and fill them up in the mountains. We grew everything we needed to eat. On about half the land, we grew hay and wheat; [on] the other half we had potatoes, peas, and beans. We had everything we wanted. We had chickens, rabbits, and pigs. We didn't even have to go to town for our meat, because Dad and his half-brother would slaughter a pig, then divide it.

Ned Leggroan was my grandfather. Amanda Leggroan Chambers, who married Samuel Chambers, was his sister. I don't know where they were from. I really don't. I just loved them. They lived on what is now Evergreen [Street]. We all lived in this area.[1] My grandpa Ned, who later moved to Idaho, was a small man, slender. At eighty-three, he could jump up and click his heels three times before he hit the floor.

Both my grandfather and grandmother were slaves. She was a mulatto. They told us some awful stories about slavery. Grandfather said he was picking cotton but he was leaning with his elbows on his knees, and his master beat him. Grandfather said if he could have found his master's body after he had died, he would have stomped it. I said, "I don't blame you, because anybody that mean needs to be stomped."

Grandmother didn't say much. She was kind of quiet. But you can imagine how horrible it was, because white people could be nasty, nasty mean then. They lorded it over anybody that was in their way, especially black people.

When I was going to school, the white kids were mean and nasty. Oooh! I went through that all the way through high school. It's a wonder I know anything. I carried an umbrella every day whether it rained or not, just to beat the boys that were so nasty from Holladay. If we met, they'd tease me all the way to school. They'd say the nastiest things they could put their tongues to. But white people don't want to believe that. [I remember] they'd come in on the streetcar, and either I had to get [to school] ahead of them or wait till they got to school [and] then run like mad to beat the bell.

There was one fellow who wouldn't leave me alone for nothing. He'd call me names. He'd pull my hair. And the teacher would just sit there. I said to her one day, "You make him mind his business or you're both going to be sorry, because I'm telling you I'm not taking this anymore." She laughed and said, "Oh, he won't hurt you." Well, one day he went into the boys' lavatory. He had a cap on his head. When he came out, I was waiting for him. He stooped over, and just as he stooped over, I threw a rock. It cut his head [right] through that cap and made it bleed. The teacher said, "You'll lose your noon recesses for two weeks!" I said, "Fine. That won't heal his head." I said, "I hope he learned a lesson, because I'm not taking any more of your punishment."

The prejudice wasn't as outstanding when we first started school. But the higher the grade, the more the prejudices were prevalent. My parents used to say, "Actions speak louder than words." As we grew, we found out exactly what that meant. They had another saying: "Still water runs deep, and the devil lies beneath." Well, you just watch. People who try to be so mighty much, all of a sudden will show their true thoughts, their true actions. Nobody has to explain it to you. You know what it means. When I used to go to Primary and religious class [at the local ward house], they'd say, "You can come in, but you can't take part." So it was hard. It was hard growing up here. They talk about the South, but Salt Lake was no better. No better.

But white people don't want to think it. One woman told me I was lying. "Was you there?" I asked. "Were you in my shoes? How do you know I'm lying? You didn't have any of the problems I had." She said, "Oh, I don't believe that took place." I said, "I don't care what you believe. I don't even care what you think. It didn't hurt you, but I've got the scars. They're not on the outside. They're in on the inside."

Things didn't change for us until the revelation [in 1978].[2] Then some of them whites were a little different. Some of them will never be different.

Neither will I in a lot of ways. After you've been in it for over sixty years, and been told you're not the right color, you are not going to be openhearted overnight. You are the same individual as you were. It's just like using . . . have you ever used an indelible pencil and made a mistake and tried to erase it? Well, [it's] the same. Once you are marked [by prejudice], you don't erase, and you don't forget.

We have a notion in our community that unless you know where you come from and where you are going, you'll never get anywhere. That's an old adage, but you need to know where you come from. You need that bridge to cross over. If you don't know where it is, you're going to be in trouble.

—Pastor France A. Davis, Calvary Baptist Church

MRS. LUCILLE BANKHEAD, 71, FARMER

Mary Lucille Bankhead was an acknowledged pioneer of Utah's African-American community. Proud, reclusive, and fiercely self-reliant, she was born in Salt Lake City on August 9, 1902, and grew up within the Church of Jesus Christ of Latter-day Saints. Legend has it that Green Flake, her great-grandfather and a former slave of James M. Flake, was Brigham Young's wagonmaster when the Mormon pioneers made their historic journey from Nauvoo, Illinois, to the Salt Lake Valley in July 1847.

Little reliable documentation is available on her other relatives, but Mrs. Bankhead is unfazed by that. "You know," she quipped, "it's always good to know where your roots are if you can find them. Sometimes I look at people saying who they are. They don't know who they are, but they think they do. I've got too many nationalities in me to say I'm this or that. So I just tell them I'm American."

I was born in 1912, August 9th, right here on this property, when all this land from clear up to the road on Twentieth East and back down there and back over there was ours. It was homestead land given to a Mrs. Jones by President Ulysses S. Grant. She later sold it to my father. It's been in our family for over one hundred years. I farmed it until I couldn't keep up with it anymore and my boys pulled all the weeds they were going to pull. So most of the property has been sold except the part I'm still living on.

When we were growing up, this was a busy place. We had chickens, rabbits, pigs, and other animals. We raised wheat and hay and corn. My father bred horses, and we always had a garden, an orchard, and all kinds of fruit. But black currants and peaches were our main fruits. And I'll tell you, picking those currants was an important part of my life that I'd never wish to repeat.

We made a good living off of selling those currants. Mother would ship

Lucille Bankhead. *George Janecek*

them to customers in Wyoming. But picking them was a chore and took all day. Mother would bring our lunch to us, and we'd stay there till almost dark, picking currants. They're tiny—little tiny things—and we'd have to rub them in our hands and blow the trash out of them and then put them in quart cups and pack them in cases, twelve to a case, for shipping.

Before my father bought this land, he was a cowboy in Vail [Colorado]. He was part Indian and part black. He didn't talk very much about it, though. He'd tell us where he was born, how he worked up in Bountiful, and he would tell us about horses. He always had a good grade of horses. I preferred the horse and buggy myself, but sometimes, when the snow was bad, I'd have to sit behind my father on horseback just to get out to the main road. Sometimes the snow got so deep on Twentieth East, Dad would have to take a shovel in at night so we could shovel out in the morning. And, why, when that east wind blew, you had better stay in the house. I've seen snowdrifts up to the roof of our house.

Now, my father didn't do much talking. Mother done the talking. She was younger than Dad. She did the talking, and you did not talk back. It seemed like if you did, she'd cry, and once she cried so loud it just got next to me. So I said that I'd never do anything to make her cry, and I didn't.

My family—and others in the area—always had their home health remedies. Some were terrible, like that asafetida which my mother would cut up in pieces and make us wear in little bags around our necks to ward off measles. It looked like some kind of hard gum, and it was the stinkiest stuff that ever was. It smelled like garlic. But we weren't the only kids who wore them. The white kids did, too. We all had to wear it to school, but I couldn't stand it, so I used to take mine off and put it under the culvert down here by Mrs. Peterson's house and pick it up when I was ready to come home.

There weren't many people around in this area—a lot of space between farms—but it was a close community and everybody was friends and helped each other out. When anyone needed wood for the winter, my father would take his six horses and a wagon and go up into the canyons with the other farmers to get firewood. At harvest time, they'd help whoever was doing the thrashing.

The only time they'd get together for socializing, though, was through the [Mormon] church on Sundays or when they'd have a dance or a party. We used to peek at them dancing, and we just had to laugh at a lot of the way they danced. During the summertime, we'd all picnic up the canyon. Sometimes, we'd have friends sleep over at our house, or we'd go to theirs. It didn't matter if you were black or white. We all got along.

I grew up with three brothers. All are dead now but George, who works at the airport. We had a busy house. My brothers had friends. One of them, Roy, used to visit a lot. I didn't know at the time that he was interested in me or that we were going to marry four years later. He would visit a lot during the wintertime when it was snowing. The east wind used to blow so hard, oftentimes he wouldn't be able to get home, and the boys would let him sleep over in their room.

Every once in a while, he'd wink at me, and, oh, I'd get indignant, and mother would find a way for me to go someplace else. But I didn't have an inkling that he was really coming to see me. At first, I'd just pay no attention. Then, I noticed that he was looking at me. After a while, we'd sit on the stoop, on the front step, and talk. Since my mother's bed was in the front room, looking out onto the porch, every night when he visited she'd say, "Lucille, it's nine o'clock. Time for Roy to go home." She didn't want me to marry Roy. But that's what happened.

My in-laws did everything possible to keep Roy from marrying me, too. They had the idea that I was too black and my hair too nubbly. But I had a good marriage, an awfully good marriage with a good husband. He worked hard, and when his check came in, he'd lay it on the table for me. He knew I knew what to do with the money and how to pay bills. All he wanted was about four dollars to go fishing. He'd want me to go with him and I would, because he did the same thing for me. He never said no. So I wouldn't say no to him, even though I didn't like fishing.

Roy and I had eight children. We lost one child to pneumonia. We were rushing to get him to the county hospital when he died in my arms on Fifth

East and Twenty-first South. I daren't say a word to Roy, because he was driving so fast I thought he'd be too emotional to hear that. I was afraid he'd run off the road.

We were a close family, and I had a lot of pleasure raising my children. When I was growing up, my mother never told me about life, and I had a lot of questions in mind. So I determined that at the dinner table, my children were allowed to ask any questions they wanted to ask—no matter if Roy had to get up from the table, coughing, and have to go outdoors until I finished answering.

Those days were eventful. When Ralph was two, he almost drowned in the canal before two boys plucked him out of the water near Thirty-third East. Once, I had to jump up on a chair with a butcher knife to whack off a noose around Donald's neck. He was only six years old and playing cops and robbers with his friend, and they were about to hang him. Boy, he came down and just all the wind came out of my baby.

Then I'll never forget the time when I went out on the porch and saw a coffee can walking across the floor. Ralph and Dick were giggling. They had put a water snake in the can, and it was moving all over. I had a hard time getting that snake off the porch.

Now, my mother went to [the LDS] church all the time, and she insisted that all of us children go, too. I don't remember my dad going. But I've always been a very staunch member of my church. My husband went to all the entertainments, and he volunteered on some church projects, like gathering eggs for the church's welfare program, but he didn't go to church meetings. If I had to go to meetings and it was cold or stormy, he'd sit out in the truck and wait for me, but he wouldn't go in. I never asked him why. I figured he was grown, and if he wanted to go he would have went. I don't push nobody to go to church.

Now, I've never wanted to leave my religion. A verse in the Bible says the Lord is no respecter of persons. I've always believed that, even though there have been times that I've been torn about it. I know that Mr. Abner Howell, my father-in-law, who lived in Holladay, had to hear the services while sitting in the vestibule in the Mormon church [because he was black]. He couldn't go into the congregation. But he did that—sat in the vestibule. That didn't happen at our church. If I couldn't have gone in the meeting room, I wouldn't have gone.

All my boys fell away from the church. They had always gone with me and their friends, but when it was time for the boys to become deacons and my boys had to sit it out because they were black, they stopped going. I feel sorry about that, too. I feel bad that Mr. Howell didn't get to live to see blacks recognized in the priesthood. But I feel like this: That was people doing that. God doesn't do this. So, as long as I believe that, you can't change my mind. Besides, I never believe a lot in what people say, and I don't go to church to socialize. I believe in God, and I go to church to hear the message. It don't make no difference whether you say howdy-doo to me or not.

I think highly of Martin Luther King. Yes, I do. I know that [racial] violence was a way of life in some parts of this country. I heard terrible stories and some that will always be on my mind. But the truth is, we didn't know about violence here—against blacks. We didn't have that kind of trouble here.

If I had problems and didn't like what someone was doing to me, and I thought I was right, I'd just open my mouth and talk about it. And somebody was going to hear. If they don't like it, why, that's just too bad. I'm like everybody else. I'm a woman. It don't make no difference what color my skin is. My blood is red like yours is, and I'm going to say what I want to say.

I did have an incident when I went to the Daughters of the Utah Pioneers meeting once. I had been their secretary for four years and was going to make a speech. The doorman opened the door for my friends, but before I could get in, the door closed on me. He expected me to go around to the kitchen entrance. I wasn't about to go to no kitchen door. So that main door opened for me, and I went in and gave my speech.

Sometimes, I've had to correct people who say things that aren't right. There was a [white] woman, Sister B., and every time she'd go to Relief Society, somebody would ask her how she was doing. She'd say, "Oh, I'm so tired, I've been working like a nigger." I was determined to break her out of that saying. The next time I was at Relief Society and someone asked me how I was doing, I said, "I'm so tired, I've been working like a nigger." You could have heard a pin drop in the ward house. I just whipped her with her own stick. And I haven't heard that expression since.

I remember best the time, in 1939, when the legislature was in session and a Utah senator was suggesting that all blacks from where we were and from Seventh South form a black district elsewhere in the city. He even had a black man, dead now, helping him. Probably gave him a lot of money to do it. Well, at that time, I belonged to the Camilla Art [and] Craft Club, and when several other women and I discussed this, we thought it was a ridiculous idea. So I hitched up the horse and wagon and we rode up to the capitol. We sat up there in the legislature all day. And, of course, we told them what we wanted and that we was not going to move—that what they really wanted was our land and we had no intentions of selling. That was the first time we ever been up to the legislature, but we just sat there waiting to be heard. Most of the ladies were dressed pretty good, but there was Mrs. Leggroan with her big, white apron on and wearing a white dust cap. And I was nursing my baby and had a basket for him to sleep in. We brought our lunch and ate it up there. The newspaper got on it and wrote quite a bit about it. And we stayed till we knew the legislature realized what they had to do. Then we went home. I guess the people at the legislature was glad to see us go. I have to laugh about it now.

Postscript: Lucille Bankhead passed away in Salt Lake City on June 16, 1994.

DOROTHY STEWARD FRY, 78, MAID, FARMER

"If you can persevere, you come out somehow. You don't come out the wealthiest in the world, but you survive." Dorothy Steward Fry spoke these words to us with the poise and precision of a person who had faced her demons and survived.

One of twelve children, Mrs. Fry was born in Pueblo, Colorado, on July 14, 1906, and came to Salt Lake City with her family in the summer of 1913. Her father worked as a temporary laborer in the construction of the State Capitol before becoming one of the city's underground public toilet attendants.[3] Mrs. Fry graduated from high school with the intention of becoming a registered nurse. She married and continued to live in Salt Lake City. But when she realized her skin color would prevent her from entering a nursing program there, she and her husband moved to Seattle, Washington.

In March 1984, she returned briefly to Salt Lake City to help Edward Steward, her younger brother, recuperate from an illness. This interview was conducted in the living room of his central city home.

We moved to Salt Lake in 1913. I had my sixth birthday here in the summer. That fall I started school at the old Fremont School on Fourth West, and that's where I had my first real taste of prejudice toward black people. The children were prejudiced. They didn't take kindly to black people. (We were called Negroes then.) This was a Mormon city and a Mormon state, and the Mormons did not believe blacks were quite human. We're not supposed to have [had] souls. We were never supposed to go to heaven. If [blacks] were Mormons, they could belong to the Mormon church, but they could never hold the priesthood because they were cursed by their blackness. That was taught to their children and they used that against us.

One of the things that has remained in my mind to this day was an incident in school on Valentine's Day. On Valentine's Day, we had Valentine boxes in school. Everyone could bring valentines and put them in the boxes for their friends. I had no friends, because the white children didn't play with us. But I made valentines also. And I can remember, very clearly, we had red paper to cut out our red hearts, and we could write something on them. The teacher said, "If you want to send the valentine to a friend, you may put their name on it. On Valentine's Day we will draw them out of the box, and you'll receive your valentines and you can take them home." All the children's names were called that day but mine. I got my valentine [back]. Then the box was empty. The teacher then stood in front of the classroom, and she had a valentine for every child in the room except for me. She called everybody's name. Everyone went up and got a valentine from the teacher except me. She could see the hurt in my face, so she just turned her back to the class and started writing on the blackboard. There were many incidents like that.

At home, though, we didn't discuss discrimination. But I remember one time my father said, "Don't be antagonistic unless it's absolutely necessary for you to defend yourself. Don't go and start fights. But if the fight is brought to you, try to defend yourself." He did not tell us to just take all these abuses. But he always taught us not to start fights. And we didn't. But we had a lot of fights. I mean *real* fights, not just this name-calling. And we *had* to defend ourselves, because as long as someone thought they could beat up on you and you'd be cowed down, they would do it. It would happen four or five times a year at school. Each year [when] we'd go to a different class, we'd have to start all over again letting them know we could protect ourselves. This is the way it was, and all this sort of thing, going on year after year in school, [while] being kept from doing things other children were allowed to do, created a lot of hate in my heart.

We had a nice family life, though. We were very poor, but we were always well fed, clothed, and we always had a roof over our head. Coming from a large family, we always had our own entertainment. My mother wasn't an accomplished pianist, but she could play and we'd dance. We also had a little old-fashioned gramophone. It was one that played the little cylinder records that slipped in over a handle and had a big horn on it. We played those and danced with our brothers and each other. There were eight girls and four boys, so we had a lot of company.

Mother was a very domestic person. She made our dresses. She baked loaves of bread by the dozens and always prepared biscuits and corn bread and pies. And she taught me how to cook. She taught all of us [girls] how to keep house and cook. She also joined the [black] Masons with my father and became a member in the Order of the Eastern Star. She liked that, and she liked her church work. So she was, I would say, a very docile, domestic sort of person. And she was kind. She was kind to her children. She was kind to the people in the neighborhood. She was even kind to their animals. In fact, any stray cat or dog that came along, she would feed it because, she said, "It wouldn't be straying around if it wasn't hungry." [*Laughs*]

I have known my mother to sit up all night long trying to get our dresses made in time to wear to church on Christmas Eve or Easter Sunday. She'd sew for weeks to get them ready. Then she would comb our hair. For everyday, she would part my hair in the middle and braid it on each side and tie a ribbon on each braid. For Sunday, she'd make my hair into ringlets and put a big bow on top. She did this for most of the girls, except for my older sisters who were self-sufficient by then. So life had its sweet side. But things were sure hard for blacks.

My sister Thelma, in fact, was one of the instigators for organizing the NAACP here. Along with my father and other people in the community, she got it started. I don't remember too much about why. I was quite small. But I remember my father and Thelma sitting at the kitchen table one evening, talking. She said this banquet was going to be held and a public meeting. He said, "How are you going to finance it? Are you going to sell tickets?" "Well," she said, "there'll be no charge for people to come in, but they'll have to pay to get out." So apparently they were going to take up donations, and it all worked out very successfully. They were able to get their charter in 1919.

I also remember that a Mr. White, the organizer for the NAACP all over the country, came here at the time. He traveled around and organized groups wherever he could get enough people together. He came and held this mass meeting [to see] if there were enough Negroes interested. I don't know how long he stayed, but he got a lot of people involved. And they all put their funds and their efforts together and got it organized. A man by the name of MacSwane, a bailbondsman in Salt Lake many years ago, and an old soldier, Sergeant Jackson, were prominently involved. Then there was a Mr. Burgis, an old-timer—he was interested. I don't remember other names. But I do remember that it was well organized and well attended, and they held it together. Somehow or other, they've always managed to keep that organization together here.

Sometime later, another thing happened here. It wasn't just the NAACP that was fighting for us, you see. In April 1929, I married my husband. He was a pullman porter. Tomorrow, in fact, would have been our fifty-fifth wedding anniversary if he had lived. When we married, the pullman porters and the dining-car waiters had no union. If they talked about forming a union, they were fired. But there was a man by the name of A. Philip Randolph who went all over this country organizing black people, especially pullman porters, into a union. He came here and held several meetings, and I met him.

I was grown by that time. And Mr. Randolph really impressed me. He was quite an organizer.[4] Before the union started, the porters had to stay up on their feet and work for hours and hours with no rest. They just worked until they got back home. After they got the union going, they had some protection. Yet, for a time, as soon as anyone found out that a porter was organizing or even interested in organizing, he was fired. My husband's father lost his job because of this. He was a very dynamic man, and the Pullman Company offered to buy him off if he'd just forget the union. But he told them, "You know, you sold my mother and father, but I'm not for sale."

I attended one of the meetings where Mr. Randolph spoke. He was a very sincere, very dynamic speaker. And after listening to him, I was convinced that what I needed was some additional education for the work I wanted to do. Yet if I stayed here, I'd never be able to attend a nursing program or go into business, because they just wouldn't hire black people in those jobs. You could get a maid's job, but there was no way in the world you'd ever be hired to do any professional work. My sister Blanche was an expert typist, but she couldn't find a job here. She went to Seattle, and she couldn't find one there either. They just wouldn't hire black people to do those things [then]. That was just the way of life.

So my goal was just to get a good general education, and someday, perhaps, I'd be able to go farther and do better. I always dreamed I'd leave Salt Lake City. There just had to be a better place. I didn't know how I'd ever get there or what kind of place [it would be], but I always dreamed there'd be a reason for me to leave. I felt I *had* to leave. I would die if I stayed here.

When I say I would have died, what I mean is I would never have amounted to anything, because the whites here were so cruel to my race. They thought all black people were ignorant, lazy, shiftless, dirty, and unkempt, and that made me hateful. I hated them so much I couldn't speak civilly to them; I always had a sharp answer. It's really hard to describe all this. But this is something that was within me: I had that race hatred in me.

I don't suppose you'll ever understand this. It's a little hard to make you realize this could have happened. I don't know how my brother feels about his life here. But boys generally survived better than girls. All I could look forward to was growing up and getting married, if I could find someone who would take care of me. And the worse thing in all this, the thing I rebelled against most, was the discrimination. And it really didn't make any difference for you to protest, because whites didn't care anyway. Of course, we didn't protest like they did later in the '50s and '60s, when they marched and all that sort of thing. It wasn't like that. My rebellion was within me. I know many other young people felt the same way. But maybe it didn't affect their lives as deeply as it did mine, because I didn't get over my hatred until I was an older woman.

I finally had to fight within myself to get over my hate, because hate can destroy you. Finally, I just felt . . . well, it's all over. Life is better now. You can be over it, be rid of it, and work it out. I think I've just about overcome most of it. Some of my worst enemies now are friends. I guess you could put it that way. And maybe they were not as bad as I thought they were. Maybe they weren't the enemies I thought they were.

HOWARD BROWNE, SR., 82,
COAL MINER, FARMER, REDCAP

Tall, slender, cautious, and soft-spoken, Howard Warren Browne felt he had fought hard for everything he attained. He believed racism and discriminatory practices so pervaded Utah life that every step forward for a black man came against the grain.

One of two children, Howard Browne was born in Kansas City, Kansas. His father graduated from Howard University with a degree in law, but due to segregation he was unable to develop a practice in Kansas City. To appease the black community, the local auditor's office gave him a token patronage position, which he held until he was laid off, years later, during the Depression.

Mr. Browne's parents divorced shortly after World War I. Following the separation, he spent each school year in Kansas City with his father and paternal grandparents and each summer with his mother, who had remarried and moved to Rains, Utah. After completing high school, he enrolled as a premed student at the University of Kansas (following in his paternal grandfather's footsteps), but his education was cut short by the Depression and his mother's desperate financial situation.

He and his wife moved to Utah in 1929 and spent ten years in Carbon County, where he both farmed his mother's land and worked as a coal miner. In 1938, he found

Howard Browne. *George Janecek*

employment as a redcap with the Union Pacific Railroad and, the following year, resettled his family in Salt Lake City. He held a position with the Union Pacific until his retirement in 1979. Mrs. Marguerite Browne (who worked as a maid, janitor, laundry clerk, and program evaluator for Model Cities) passed away in 1988.[5]

My place of birth was Kansas City, Kansas—October 18, 1911. My mother was Mary Isabell Warren; that was her maiden name. My father was Howard Reginald Manlius Browne. He graduated from Howard University as a lawyer, but he never worked as one. After World War I, he was appointed to work in the local auditor's office. They put him in there because he had smarts and because he had graduated as an attorney, and this guy that was running for office placed a black in there to satisfy the black community. There were a lot of black people living in Kansas City at the time. So he worked there until the Depression came; then they laid him off.

My mother was an off-breed from a German family back in Maryland. My grandmother on my mother's side was working for this family, and the young boy got my grandmother pregnant and my mother was born. So that's where I come from on my mother's side. My parents met while my dad was going to school, taking up law. My dad's father was a doctor in Kansas City, so he brought her back to Kansas City, where I was born. My grandfather brought me into the world.

Then my mother got interested in land, and, at that time, why, you could homestead a certain amount of land out West. So she decided she wanted to homestead out in Colorado; so she and my dad homesteaded 640 acres of land down in southern Colorado. But while we were down there, why, World War I broke out, and my father joined the service. He wanted my mother to come back to Kansas City [while he was gone], and she just didn't want to go. Anyway, he joined the army and went on over to France as a first lieutenant. When he was discharged, he went back to Kansas City and wanted my mother and me to come back where he was. She didn't want to go back. So he said, "Well, I'm going to stay back here to take care of those from whose flesh and blood I come, in preference to those that are of my flesh and blood."

He sent for me to come back to Kansas City, and that's where I went to school. I came through grade school, junior high, high school, then went to the University of Kansas. I stayed for a while with my father [in my early school years], and then he married again. I tried staying with him and his wife, but since I was having such difficulty with her, why, I went over to my grandmother and stayed [with her] through junior high and high school. In the meantime, in the summertime, when school was out, I'd go out to Utah to visit my mother. She had remarried a coal miner from Kansas named Ausie Kimber, who had come out to Utah in the early '20s.

Now, I may not be phrasing this right, but during that time the mining industry all over the country was having [labor] problems, and they were bringing black people in to break strikes. And that's what they did in Utah. In 1922 or 1923—I don't know which year—they started bringing people from down South to come in here to break strikes. And that's the main reason why most of the blacks (including my stepfather) got in Carbon County, other than those that were brought in by Brigham Young as slaves. By 1922 or 1923, they were bringing blacks in regularly to Carbon County.

I came here about that same time. I was eleven or twelve years old when I arrived. The first time, my mother [and stepfather] was living in a coal camp out by Helper, called Rains. There were about twenty blacks living there, working in the mine. There were ten or fifteen black people living in Helper. There were several living in the coal camp below Rains called Latuda. There were several living over in Castle Gate, working in the coal mine there; several in a coal mine called Kenilworth; and another twenty or thirty living and working in the Utah mine on the way to Hiawatha.

All of the black people [in Rains] lived on the far end of the coal mining camp in bunkhouses. Most of the white people lived in homes down below. Bunkhouses were close to the mine. They had a post office there and a company store where the miners could trade; then on payday, they could pay the company store. They also had a small schoolhouse, a grade school for the kids. Miners made pretty good wages in those days. They made pretty good money. I remember, between the camps, [which were] situated a half mile apart, there were saloons—what they call[ed] coffeehouses. These were run mostly by Japanese people. I don't think there were any Japanese working in Rains. But the next camp down, Latuda, why, they had a big Japanese community. They had pretty near everything they wanted just in their own camp. They had their own blacksmith shop, where they sharpened their own tools because they weren't satisfied with the way Americans sharpened tools.

And as I remember, I enjoyed it. I had a lot of white boys that were friends of mine. They were from Polish, Austrian, and Italian families. And all of them were real friendly. At the time, my stepfather worked as a miner and my mother took in washing and ironing for the white people and some of the blacks in the camps. Most of the coal miners weren't married. They were bachelors. So she would wash their clothes and make and sell [them] beer. She learned how to make it from a Frenchman. All in all, she was a very thrifty woman, and she saved whatever she could spare. She started saving [she told me] while she worked in Colorado Springs at a hotel, and every nickel she got, why, she put it away, put it in the bank.

When I was nineteen, my mother had saved enough to buy a piece of property. She bought a forty-acre place down in Carbonville, which is between Price and Helper; and they started farming. Then my stepfather got sick. When he got sick, why, I was [living] back in Kansas. I had just gotten married, and my mother wrote me, told me her husband was ill and [asked] would I come out to Utah and help her out. So I jumped on a freight train and came out to Carbon County to help her out. And, well, I've been here ever since.

Now, when I got here, they were in Carbonville, but they were in bad shape. They didn't have a home or anything. So, when I came out, why, we made a dugout. We dug a great big hole in the ground. It was twice as long as this living room and about as wide. [Then] we went up in the canyon and got timber and stuff to put the top on. And we lived down there in that hole in the ground for several years because it was warm down there [in the winter] and cool in the summer. We lived in that hole—my mother, my stepfather, me, and my wife. We had shelves built along the dirt walls to put our personal things. We dug them out. [*Laughs*] Then my mama wanted a house built. So I knew something about carpentry, and I built her a house on the property. But before it was completed, why, she got cancer and we had to take her to the hospital, where she had four operations [before she was stabilized].

Anyway, we lived there and farmed this land. It was a good piece of property and raised real good alfalfa. We could get twenty-eight to thirty dollars a ton, and that was a good price in them days. The area around us, I remember, had a lot of houses. People owned property all around there. Down through the area, they were mostly foreigners—Greeks, Italians, and Austrians. And that's the main thing that kept us going, because the other [white] people [in Price], why, they were very antagonistic toward blacks. But the Italians, Poles, Austrians, and Greeks were friendly. They didn't want you talking to their women, but otherwise they were okay. [*Laughs*] So this side of Price, we could go anywhere we wanted to go. Helper was in the heart of coal mining country. But Price, well, that was off-limits to blacks.

Now, I was, you might say, quite an independent person. I say that because one motivation for coming out here [other than my mother's request] was because I'd fell out with my dad's people back in Kansas City. And I swore I never wanted to see any of them again. What brought this about was that I married. I felt like I was a man, yet still they tried treating me like a child. And I resented it. I couldn't do nothing on my own. So I said, well, I'm going to get as far away from them as I can. If I make it, okay; if I don't make it, okay. But they won't be able to say they did it for me."

So I came out, and I did make it. Of course, my mother helped me a lot, but she wasn't always throwing up to me what she was doing for me. So I made it: I raised four kids, built me a home here in Salt Lake. So I think I did pretty well. Also, I don't think I've got too bad a character, because I've always wanted to help other people. And I've helped a lot of people. I have several skills, and I've done a lot of things I've never charged for. I've tried to be a Christian. Yet I've probably done some people wrong. But I've regretted it and never intentionally did anything to [hurt] anyone. On the other hand, another part of my disposition is that I don't want anybody to do anything to hurt me. It takes quite a bit to make me angry, but once I get angry—well, that's been kind of the story of my life. I try to keep from getting angry, because once I get angry, I could go crazy.

There were several instances, I guess, where I had occasion to be angry. One was when we were first living in Carbonville. I was farming in the summer, and in the winter, why, I'd get a job in the coal mine. And I remember this one occasion. We were in the mine, and an Italian was working on the [drilling] machine. In the coal vein, every once in a while, they'd hit a real hard rock with the machine and it would dull the [drill] bits. The white guys called this a "niggerhead rock." So we were down to the main entrance, eating our lunch, and this guy was talking. He said, "By God, I hit that damn niggerhead up there and dulled my bits." Then he turned to me and said, "Oh, excuse me, Howard . . . I wasn't talking about you."

Well, that's the only thing that made it bad, see—picking me out that way. I said, "If you hadn't said a damn word to me, why, everything would have been all right. But I know you weren't talking about *me*, because if you had been talking about me, then you and me would have been tearing up this main entrance here." I didn't pursue the conversation. If he had pursued it, if he had said, "If that's the way you're going to take it, you so and so . . . ," why then, him and me, we would have been in it. But he didn't say anymore. So I just let it go. That was one occasion.

I remember another time, this was over in Price. Now Price was the same as being in a different place altogether. Like I said, there wasn't any blacks that lived there. It was more of a white element—Mormons and Catholics. And they were quite prejudiced. But I used to go over there. They had what they called pool halls. They were places you could go in and buy beer, buy liquor, and, if you wanted, gamble—play cards.

Well, one night I was sitting down playing cards at a table, and there was a tall Mexican fellow playing cards, too. There were several other people there. Well, this Mexican fellow, he treated everybody fine, but he was a bad guy. This one guy, he didn't know this Mexican was real bad. [*Chuckles*] And some dispute came up in the card game, and this Mexican said something to him. He [the other man] jumped up and said, "Do you know who you're talking to? You're talking to an American white man!" So this Mexican fellow said, real low, "I'm just as much of an American as you are." This guy said, "Black as you are, you can't be as American as me."

The [Mexican] guy never said no more, [but] I knew he was hot then. Well, this fellow done made me hot, too. I said, "Hell, you can't be as much American as him or me. Some of my people come from the Cherokee Tribe, and you people came over and took this country away from us. So how in hell are you going to be as American as him or me?" Well, he saw I was hot, so he never said no more, because I was ready to tie into him. And this Mexican always carried a pistol or a knife, and I knew he would have killed him right there if they had got into it. But incidences like that—just blind hatred and prejudice on the part of those white folk—was hard to take. You never did get used to it.

Now I'm going to tell you another story. Part of what I know [about it] is from hearsay and part is through what my mother showed me. The way I remember it is this: [In 1925] there were black people, bachelors, living up in Castle Gate. There were two guys batching together, and one of them was having trouble with the town marshal. The marshal told him, "You be ready,

86   African-American Community

because next time we meet, one of us is going to get killed." Sure enough, they met under the tipple. But this black guy killed the town marshal, then took off into the hills.

I used to know his name, but I've forgotten it. Anyway, he took off. In the meantime, they got a posse out for him, and they were hunting him all over. They couldn't find him. But he got hungry and tired and sleepy, and he thought he could come back to where he was batching with this other guy, get a little rest and something to eat, then he could go on again. As it happened, he laid down and he fell asleep immediately. While he was asleep, his partner went and got the posse. They came and got him while he was laying there, then took him over onto the outskirts of Price. That's where the lynching took place.

I know the guy's name that turned him in. In fact, he's got two kids here. They're grown men now in Salt Lake City. I'm not going to call their names. Anyway, that's what my mother told me. The rest of the story my wife got from the manager of the country club. (Our farm [ad]joined this golf course, and it had a country club. My wife worked at the club for a while.) The way he told her, he was a young fellow at the time. He was at the lynching and, he said, he was never so sorry of anything in his life, because they took this man, hanging there, and they cut his fingers and toes off and threw them to the kids as souvenirs. I don't know whether any more happened or not. That's what he told my wife, and what my mother told me. As far as arrests—there wasn't anything done about it that I know of. Nothing that I know of. I guess they thought that's what's supposed to be done to a black person who kills a white person.[6]

Postscript: Due to failing health, Howard Browne left Salt Lake City after his wife's death and moved to Sacramento, California, to live with his son. He passed away in Sacramento on December 5, 1996.

RUBIE LUGDOL NATHANIEL, 76, ELEVATOR OPERATOR, MAID

Rubie L. Nathaniel was born in Salt Lake City, Utah, on January 1, 1907, to a white mother and a black father. When she was four years old, her mother unexpectedly "gave" her to another mixed couple to be raised. "That was the biggest hurt in my life," she confided to us. "It took me a long time to recover from it."

Married twice, she raised three children, two daughters and a son. Her mildly retarded son was living with her at the time of the interview. Her eldest daughter left the state in the 1950s after being told her color would prevent her from obtaining employment as a department store buyer. A recent widow, Ms. Nathaniel spoke in a delicate, disarmingly girlish voice.

My name is Rubie Nathaniel. I guess my mother came over from Sweden when she was just ten years old and later became involved with my father, and she had a little boy. This was before they were married. Her family put her [my mother] in a home of some kind, and when the baby was born, they adopted it out. After that my parents went to Idaho to get married, because black and white couldn't marry in Utah. But they separated before I was born (my father died shortly after), and my mother married a white man.

[When I was young] we moved next door to her mother, who had a big family—seven boys and three girls. And there I was, the only little dark spot in the family. *[Chuckles softly]* So, when I was about four and a half, my mother gave me to another couple, a Negro man and a white lady. I was old enough to know that she had given me away, and I couldn't understand it. I thought there was something wrong with me, because mothers just didn't give away their children, you know. I didn't know what was wrong, but I knew there was something terribly wrong for her to have given me away. And this made me very afraid of people. I would just hide when anyone came to our house.

When it came time to go to junior high, I remember, they had just built a new junior high school on Sixth South, just about two blocks from where I lived. When it came time to go there, my [step]mother took me over, and they wouldn't let me go there. My mother didn't press it or anything. They said I wasn't in that district. But then I had to go clear to West Junior High, which was two miles away. And part of the time, I had to walk. My parents were very poor. Sometimes they didn't have carfare. And I had to walk these two miles even in the winter.

The two years in that school, as I remember, were the most lonely years I ever spent, because I was so shy. I guess that was partly it. I can't remember many other students in that school. I remember one teacher and two other Negro children, a brother and a sister. They were quite light. But neither of them spoke to me the whole two years I was there. And I don't remember anybody else having anything to do with me. I didn't know a lot of black people, and being so lonely and so out of it, I would sometimes wish I lived someplace where there weren't any white people at all. Oh, it was a terrible two years!

When I got into high school—I went to West High—I finally realized what was wrong with me and why I spent a lot of time by myself. In thinking about it, I realized I had this inferiority complex and that it was from my mother giving me away. But it just seemed I was too bashful to do anything about it. I was just still afraid of people. But I figured it *had* to be that, because I didn't know why else I was that way. And, finally, I sort of got over it. But it took me a long, long time. Even when my children were little and I would have to go to school for some reason, I would just be so afraid. It was a terrible chore for me to have to go to school to face their teachers.

Now, my stepparents never told me they were becoming my parents.[7] It was something I just understood: They were Mama and Papa. That's the way it was. And they meant more to me than my own mother and father, yet they were an unusual couple. My father was completely illiterate, while my mother had two years of college. She did teach him, finally, so that he could write his name. And I remember how happy he would be when he could read the headline in the paper; he was just so proud of himself. But they were very different. And as I grew older, I wondered what in the world was it that drew her to him, because he had a terrible temper. He never hit her or anything, but, boy, he could scare me. He had such a temper and a big voice, and he could use terrible language. She was very different. She was well brought up and everything.

And I remember—I couldn't have been more than seven—when my mother's sister came out from Ohio and tried to talk my mother into leaving him. They made me go outside and sit on the step when they started talking. I did, and I heard them in there, and her sister got all over her about marrying my father. Oh, they really went at it. They screamed at each other, and this woman tried to make my mother leave him and go back to Ohio with her. Well, that was a bad time for me, because she was the only person I had left to hang onto. And here this woman was trying to take her away from me, so I cried. But, of course, she wasn't thinking of going anywhere. I don't know why, but she really loved my father. She really did. He was tall and big and good-looking, and he could be very jolly.

I lived with them until the age of nineteen; then I married and went on my own. I was married twice. My first husband was the youngest of four boys and, as it turned out, pretty spoiled. After we got married, we went to live with his mother, who had a big house. His brother and sister were there, too.

Now, my husband had what was considered a good job—he was running an elevator in the Continental Bank. So I kept after him, because I wanted a place of my own. But he was just spoiled. He was making fifty dollars a month, which was good money, and we were only paying three and a half dollars a month for our room, so he didn't want to go. But with all those people around, I wasn't happy. So, when I was pregnant with my second child, I told him, "I am not going to live like this anymore. If you don't get me a place of my own, I'm going home." He halfheartedly looked for a house, but he really didn't want the responsibility. So we got a divorce.

Not long after that, I married Henry Nathaniel. We were married forty-six years before he passed away. I met Henry at Trinity AME [African Methodist Episcopal] Church. At the time, he was working in the garage of the Ford Motor Company. He was making twelve dollars and fifty cents a week. I was working, too. I've worked all my life—between babies. I worked on the freight elevator in the Newhouse Hotel. That was considered one of the best jobs in town for us [black women], because all we could get was maid's work.

Anyway, after we married, Henry figured he could do better with the railroad, so he started working as a pullman porter. But then the Depression hit, and things got really rough. They sent him all down the coast, into Texas, over into Florida. He'd be gone as much as six weeks at a time, and when he was gone, I thought he was never coming back. Then the hotel cut my salary from fifty dollars to thirty-five dollars a month, and I had to pay a lady two dollars and fifty cents a week to look after the kids while I worked—so it was rough.

I've often thought of those years, because the Depression frightened me. I was scared because Henry was gone so much and it was so hard to feed my kids. Oh, it was an awful time. I thank God my minister was there. He lived a couple of doors down from us, and people were always giving him food. So a lot of time, he'd give me part or all of what he got. And that helped. I never went on welfare, and I don't think my kids ever went hungry. But they sure didn't have much of what they wanted.

One time, I remember, we got so low we couldn't pay our rent. The landlord, in fact, didn't even come to collect it. Then the kitchen got to leaking. I had pots and pans sitting all around to catch the water. Then the ceiling fell in. It was just awful. I remember, after the rain quit, my husband and I got cardboard boxes and nailed them up to the ceiling. Then we got some paper and papered over that. He thought he'd patch the roof, too. So he got roofing material and got up there and thought he had it fixed. But the next time we got a big rain, we got up in the morning and here was the cardboard and stuff all hanging down in the kitchen. I told the kids, "I used to have to put on galoshes to cook." [*Laughs*] Oh, dear, it was a frightening time, but we came through it.

Now, Salt Lake City always had its segregation. We never had to ride in the rear of the bus or the streetcar (when we had streetcars), but you couldn't sit wherever you wanted. You couldn't go in dance halls, you couldn't go in restaurants, and you couldn't go to shows except in certain places. And, well, you just couldn't go anywhere. But I learned to take it and do my best. I wasn't as bitter toward whites as a lot of our people were. I don't know—maybe it was because I was raised with them and didn't know many black people [at first]. But so many of our people were so bitter, and I wasn't that way. But I had my bad times, too. My bad times came, I guess, when white people would hurt my kids' feelings. Then I would just get really upset, and I would get in there and be ready to fight and argue with anyone.

But that didn't happen too often, because when my kids got older they fought for themselves. My oldest girl, well, she would fight in a minute if anybody said anything to her out of the way. I would try to tell her that she shouldn't fight so much. But that's the way she thought it should be. They didn't like the way they were treated, and they were going to do something about it.

When kids at school made remarks or called her names, for instance, it would hurt me, but it would make her mad. I'm glad she was not afraid like I was. She graduated from the University of Utah, and she was very outgoing. She would call her professors, talk to them on the phone. The dean of women was very friendly with her. I told her one day, "Natalie, I wish I could be more like you. You just seem to meet everyone, and you're not afraid of anyone."

She said, "Ma, they're just people. They're just like you and me." I said, "I wish I could feel that way, but I'm still a little leery of [white] people."

Natalie worked at Auerbach's in the china department. They had a big [department] store on State Street and Third South, and she worked there all the time she was in college. She helped put herself through college. When she graduated, though, the buyer, the head of the department, told her, "Natalie, you know as much about this department as I do. You could take it over in a minute, but I can't give you a job [as a buyer] because you're black." So Natalie had to move to Chicago to find work.

And I have to tell you, I hated to see her leave. But she had no choice. She couldn't get a job here. So she went to Chicago and stayed with old friends of mine. And in two weeks she had a job as a buyer at Carson, Peery, and Scott in the china department. She's lived there since. She has just turned fifty and she has done well. She married an attorney, and they have four children. So, she did much better than she could have here. What could she have done here? [In those years] even when our kids graduated college, they still had to shine shoes or be janitors or waiters. So they just picked up and left. Many of them left the state.

Postscript: Rubie Nathaniel passed away in Salt Lake City on May 13, 1989.

WILLIAM PRICE, 56, PROFESSIONAL BOXER, EQUAL EMPLOYMENT OPPORTUNITY OFFICER, BUREAU OF LAND MANAGEMENT

A slender, frail-looking man with gentle, inquisitive eyes, William ("Wee Willie") Price did not look like a fighter. One of six children, he was born in Helper, Utah, on January 27, 1929. His parents had migrated to Carbon County following World War I, when large numbers of blacks were recruited to come in as strikebreakers. In 1935, his father died of black lung disease. Two years later, the family relocated to Salt Lake City.

Price started boxing at the age of ten, he said, in order to protect himself from white bullies. But he enjoyed boxing so much he turned professional at the age of seventeen. He estimated that he had 120 fights in his career—"amateur and pro"—and just missed the big time in Madison Square Garden because of a perforated eardrum.

After retiring from "the fight game" in his mid-twenties, he hauled "lead dust" for the Tooele Smelter, then became a supervisor of a supply unit at Hill Air Force Base. When the air force made diversity training mandatory for military and civilian personnel, he became "a specialist in race relations." He later transferred to the Bureau of Land Management, where he now manages its office of Equal Employment Opportunity.

I started boxing when I was ten years old, 'cause I was getting beat up by white kids so much. They'd taunt me after school and then they'd form a circle around me and get their toughest guy to take me on. So I was all the time running home to my mother, crying. She finally said, "I'm tired of you coming home like this, son. You need to start fighting back." So I started boxing for self-defense, and I liked it. I wanted to fight as an amateur, so I joined a boys club. That gave me an opportunity to do something for myself. Because out there in the ring, you're by yourself. There is no way an individual can beat you [simply] because of your color. So, during the time in the ring, I felt like I was king of the hill, and I needed that.

I started [boxing] at Jackson Junior High, then I transferred to the Rotary Boys Club, which is no longer in existence. It was on First South, between Fifth and Sixth West, right next to Neighborhood House. The club was kind of the gathering place for the boys and girls in the area, and it was self-sustaining, because each member paid dues. We even helped build the gym. Each kid bought one cinder block, and that's how we got it up. I don't know what it cost, but we each donated thirteen cents; the city and private contractors did the rest. As a result, we had one of the largest gyms in the state. And it was full every night. You could find three hundred kids in there every single night.

In addition to the gym, we had a shop, we had a band, we had a pool, we even had a little recreation area with a pool table. We [the kids in the club] also had our own court system set up. We elected our own judges, police officers, attorneys, the whole works. So, if you were caught acting up, you were issued a ticket, and you went before your peers and they judged you. The punishment was paddling for the most part. So they could either order a number of paddles, or they could tell you you could no longer come to the club for a week or a month, depending upon what you did. But it was a good system, I thought, because it was fair and it was peer judging peer. We didn't have adults running out, saying, "You're out, you're out, and you're out." You were just issued a citation, and you had a chance to get all your witnesses and go before the court and have a good chance to argue your case.

'Course, I went before the court a lot. [*Laughs*] My problem was that I liked to run from the main clubhouse to the gym. To reach the gym, you had to go underneath and pass the shower rooms, locker rooms, and I used to like to run up and down those stairs and holler like hell. When I got caught, I'd have to go before the court. My excuse—as I told the court—was that I was trying to improve my voice because I wanted to be a singer. They didn't buy that but one time. [*Laughs*] But the club gave me the opportunity to travel through the state as a part of a fight team. We went to all the small cities in Utah and Colorado. I remember going over to Denver, Colorado, in 1946 and representing our region in the Golden Gloves tournament.

Considering the time, [the club] was a unique place. There was no racial bias at the club. Our officers were of all races and all colors, and it was set up this way. The directors just didn't tolerate any discrimination. If you behaved yourself, paid your dues, you were entitled to one hundred percent use of the facilities. But what really made it special for me was the warmth. When you walked in, they treated you like they'd known you for a hundred years. It was a kind of haven [from the outside]. They always had pictures on the walls of kids that had done something that week, or that month, or that year. All these rewards were provided you. So the club was like a large family. I'd say thirty percent [of the kids] were Italians, ten percent were Hispanics, a few were Greeks, and the rest were a mixture of blacks and whites.

And we felt secure there—we felt protected. If you were part of the club, and the club had a function someplace, everybody hung together. So you didn't worry about the outside, because you knew you had four or five buddies with you. And when you traveled, you didn't have to worry about whether you were going to get support. You *knew* you were going to get support. If you did something wrong, you were still going to get support from your club members when you were out. You'd catch hell when you got back, but you got support at the time. And they could care less about the color of your skin or your religion. So it was a super place. And I think it saved—in fact, I'm sure it saved—thousands of young people from ending in the State Industrial School and going to prison!

Now, the Giacoma brothers, all five of them, were our first trainers. They were older than us, and you had to fight each of them. There wasn't this sparring with someone your size all the time. You put the gloves on with those bigger guys, and they didn't hold back very much. I weighed 112 pounds when I started; I finally got up to 126. But I was tall for my weight. Most of the guys I fought were shorter, so that was an advantage I had and used. And we were rewarded [for fighting well]. If you won so many fights, you got a nice jacket that said "Rotary Boys Club" and your name. Every kid was proud to get that jacket. Trophies had to be earned as well. Our coaches were all volunteers. And they spent six hours each night at the gym working with us.

At the time, quite a few clubs around the city supported boxing, so we always held tournaments.[8] First, you'd have a fight off in your club to see who was going to make the team and travel. Sometimes that was worse than fighting those other guys, because *everybody* wanted to make the team. So, once you had the box off and the winners were selected, they'd load you in a car and take you to the next club, where you'd fight for a hot dog and drink. Winners and losers got the same. To me, though, getting that hot dog was like getting a million bucks. And it wasn't just the food. It was the total experience. You'd walk out in the ring, you'd hear the crowds cheer, and, afterward, if you fought well, somebody would pat you on the back and say, "You're one hell of a tough fighter." And you felt great.

I loved it. So did my mother. She was a great supporter. I remember we used to fight right across the street from the Elks Club, and she was always there [at the fights]. One time they brought a guy in; he was the amateur champion from Pocatello, Idaho—a lightweight. We were having a contest to see who was going back to represent us in the Nationals. I was a featherweight, but interest in us had built so much that [the local promoters] wanted to see us fight. So I said, "Hey, I don't care if he does have me outweighed by ten to fifteen pounds, I'll fight him. It doesn't make any difference." I never laid a glove on him. In the second round, my mother climbed up in the ring to protect me. [*Laughs*] That was a little embarrassing. But she never missed a fight. She traveled with me wherever I went. If she could manage it, she was there at ringside, cheering me on. But when she climbed into the ring, I told her, "Mom, I can take care of myself." She thought I was getting hurt, and that day I was. I was getting the hell beat out of me. He was a good fighter. Afterward, I swore to her I wouldn't fight guys that were over my weight anymore.

At seventeen, I decided to turn professional. I wanted to be the Champion of the World and I wanted to make some money. We didn't make very much then, but it still seemed like a lot. My first fight, I remember, was in Idaho. I can't forget it, because I had to put my age up. You had to be eighteen to fight professionally in Idaho. The fight was a ten rounder for the Intermountain Featherweight Championship, and I blew it. I got the hell beat out of me! See, the first three rounds, I was all over him. But I didn't know how to pace myself yet, so I just ran out of gas. I learned, though. I learned I had to get me some four and six rounders and gradually build up to a ten-round fight. And that's what I did.

I had two managers as a pro. First Pete Giacoma, then Marv Jensen handled me. Jensen was the [former] Middle Weight Champion of the World and managed Rex Lang, a top Utah heavyweight contender. Under Jensen, I started traveling a lot. I went to Oregon, Idaho, Los Angeles, San Jose, and I fought one of the top contenders for the featherweight [title] in Reno, Nevada. I don't recall his name now. The only thing I remember about the fight was that Reno was so damned prejudiced, it was pitiful.

I remember Jensen sent me down on my own because they couldn't afford to send a manager with me. When I met the promoter of the fight, he said, "Well, we're going to have to take you out [of] this neighborhood," because it turned out that I couldn't even sleep at the local YMCA [Young Men's Christian Association]. So they got me in a car and carried me off to the black community, where there was a dinky, little hotel. That's where I stayed, and it was a frightening experience. Come fight time, I was more concerned about these conditions than I was the fight.

I mean, if you walk into a town and they say [to you], "You can't stay in town; we're going to cart you forty miles away," then you're not sure how people are going to react to you when you fight a white fighter. I mean, what do you do? Do you lose or do you win? If you win, what's going to happen to you? If they're so prejudiced that they won't even let you stay in the YMCA, that's hard to take. At least it was for me.

But even when we traveled to Denver to fight in the Golden Gloves, they had separated the fighters. The black fighters had to live in Five Points. The white fighters had to live in another part of the city. They would not let our team stay together. And that didn't change until [the Civil Rights Act of]

1964, when a lot of changes [in public accommodations] came about.

So those were the situations we faced. We accepted them because we were told to accept them. But we didn't like it. And it affected your fighting. See, before a fight, you needed to divorce yourself from everything and just zero in on that guy who was gonna try to punch the hell out of you. But you couldn't do it. In Reno, I couldn't get my fight plan together 'cause I was down there by myself and [because] they hired some local guy who didn't know me from Adam to be my second. He was telling me to pull a left hook, and, hell, he didn't even know if I could throw a left hook. So that disturbed me. Then I could hear the white people along the ringside shouting, "Kill that nigger!" That was just common talk. People nowadays think these things happened a hundred years ago. Well, it didn't happen to me a hundred years ago.

But, all in all, I think the fight game did me some good. First, it provided me an opportunity to take a good look at myself and say, "I'm as good as you are, and I'll prove it to you. Let's forget all this racial hanky-panky. Let's put on gloves and get in the ring and see who's going to come out the winner." Second, financially, I did pretty good. I bought my first two homes strictly off what I made in the fight game. Of course, I missed my big opportunity in Madison Square Garden. I got hurt in a fight. But that couldn't be helped.

I had the contract all signed, you see, but because I had taken that tune-up fight in Reno, I didn't make it. I won the Reno fight, but I perforated my eardrum and spent a couple of thousand dollars and the next three months trying to get the ear patched up. That caused me to miss the fight. Then my doctor told me, "You could fight again, but you're taking an awfully big chance. You could get killed in the ring." So I fought one more time, then I called it quits. By that time, I had three kids, and I was more concerned with being around to be a daddy as opposed to winning the world championship.

All told, I fought for fifteen years. I quit in my late twenties. Since I was the smallest, skinniest guy on the team, the coaches bought me a robe and put "Wee Willie" on the back. That was my ring name. But my close friends in the fight game called me Blinkie, because I had the habit of always blinking my eyes. So whenever anybody said "Blinkie," I knew who they were talking about. But in the ring, I was "Wee Willie." That's what I fought under for a long period of time.

NATHAN "WOODY" WRIGHT, 67, ASSEMBLY-LINE WORKER, SPERRY UNIVAC

Machinist, electrician, hotel manager, bartender, cook, hustler, and street philosopher, Nathan "Woody" Wright "had done most anything anybody else had done." "I've been on the good side of society," he said, "and I've been on the bad side of society, and I've been in between. So I know it all. Well, I don't mean 'all.' I mean, I've had enough experience to know right from wrong."

A sultrily handsome man, Wright was born on February 6, 1916, in Havana, Cuba, and spent the first eight years of his life in New York City, where he was struck by a bus, lost his legs, and acquired his distinctive sobriquet. At the start of the World War II, he joined the Civil Service and was sent as a machinist to Hill Field Army Air Base, where he spent four years repairing gun turrets and machine guns and finally working as an aircraft electrical inspector. In 1948, he left the base and began working at the Railroad Porters and Waiters Club on Ogden's Twenty-fifth Street. He was an employee of the club until it closed in 1970. From 1971 until his 1982 retirement, he was an assembly-line worker for Sperry Univac. Our interview with him was conducted in his apartment at the Salt Lake City Multiethnic Highrise.

I was born in Havana, Cuba, but the first thing I can recollect is living in a tenant house on 127th Street and Fifth Avenue in New York. I lived there till I had my accident; then we moved to the little town of Greenwich, Connecticut, which is about thirty miles north of New York.

Do I remember the accident? Hell, I remember it just like I'm sitting here! In New York City, you don't have too many places to play but the street, see. So me and some kids had built this car from an orange crate and skate wheels. Well, it wasn't really a car. Just an orange crate, a board, and some wheels. Anyway, we was on 127th Street, trying it out. The street ran off a hill down into Fifth Avenue. And me and this boy were on the wagon. It had brakes and everything. But when we got down to the bottom, we couldn't stop. The brakes went out right when this bus arrived. He [the other boy] got killed—instantaneously. I didn't. I was luck—lucky. The doctors didn't give me twenty-four hours to live, but, well, here I am. I was seven years old then; I'm sixty-seven now.

They took me to a hospital right away, and I was in the hospital for almost two years. For six months, I didn't know nothing; I didn't remember nobody. Young as I was, I had what you'd call a psychological problem. I felt that life was no more. Meantime, my parents had moved up to Greenwich. And by the time I got out, they had bought a home in this ethnic neighborhood. That's what they call it now. We just called it "neighborhood" then.

It was an area composed of Italians, Poles, Irish, and Germans. And the kids in the neighborhood took to me; and that helped me come out of myself. They'd take me out in my little wagon and pull me around the block. They'd take me to the fields where they played ball, like nothing had happened. And when I started back to school, walking on crutches, they helped me learn to use my artificial legs. See, at that time, we had to walk to school, because there was no such thing as a school bus. We lived about a good half mile from school, as I recall. So, in the morning, they'd come and get me, take me to school, and I walked. When we came out, we used to go to an Italian grocery store across from the school, buy a pop or an ice cream cone, then head for home.

Well, these guys would take my crutches and make me walk without them. First, they made me walk about eight or nine feet. Then they'd increase it.

Eventually, I just threw my crutches away. I didn't even walk with a cane until about maybe nine or ten years ago, when I got these new limbs. Anyway, I went to [elementary] school, then high school, and managed three years of college before I came out here. And those kids helped me realize I could do anything anybody else could do with two good legs.

Now, my parents worked as domestics in the town of Greenwich. They lived on the estate of the people they worked for and came home on weekends. My father's sister, my aunt, took care of me while they were gone. My parents had their own living quarters, and they were servants. That's putting it plainly, I guess. But they were very unusual people.

Though they weren't well educated as far as books were concerned, they would sit down and explain things to me. My dad talked to me about the ways of the world, how things operated, what the government was up to, what was happening. He'd take me fishing, take me to ball games. I was his only child; so anywhere my dad went, I went. My mother also sat down and explained things to me. Strange as this may sound, she told me all about sex. I knew more about what took place in a woman's body than any kid my age.

In the house, we had lots of books. My dad had oodles and goodles of books. You see, whatever the boss man, Mr. Mallory or Mrs. Mallory, bought for their kids, they would buy for me. I remember we had a medical encyclopedia about four inches thick. The pages were illustrated, and I'd look through it. I didn't always know what I was looking at, but I was fascinated. My folks never had to buy me clothes either, because Mr. Mallory had a son my age. When he'd buy his son a suit, he'd buy me one. So I was fortunate that way. I had things the average poor kid didn't have, and I never had serious problems with the opposite race.

Oh, every now and then, I'd get into a little fight, but that's part of life. You know, some kid would call me "nigger," or I'd call him "guinea" [Italian] or "Polack son of a bitch." But what the hell. We all went to school in the neighborhood. And it really didn't make no difference whether you was black, green, or purple.

In 1937, I started college at the Lincoln University in Pennsylvania. I wanted to be a lawyer and a musician. I became a musician, but I had to quit that. I played alto trumpet, French horn, bassoon, but I had to quit because my lungs wouldn't take it. The doctor ordered me to stop. So, thinking of becoming an attorney, I spent a year in Pennsylvania, then two at the Lincoln University [campus] in Missouri. But in my junior year, the war [World War II] started, and everybody was going off to fight. So, as a patriotic American, I thought I'd join the effort, work during the war, then go back and finish school. But that's not what happened. I came out here in 1942, got to fooling with electronics, and just never went back.

Now, when I joined the Civil Service, they had two openings: Birmingham, Alabama, and Ogden, Utah. At the time, [I thought] I'd rather come to Utah than go down to Birmingham. So I came here. I [had been trained] as a machinist, went right to Hill Field, but didn't get hired. The supervisor of the machine shop, a Mormon, told me he had "a lily-white shop" and he was going to keep it that way. So I asked this young white captain to find me something else to do. He sent me to OJT, on-the-job training, and I got into repairing machine guns, which was kind of fun. After repairing them, you took them out on the range and fired them. So that was fun, that was kicks.

When I was about to finish OJT, another instructor asked me how I would like to get into hydraulics. So I got into hydraulics, working on gun turrets. Then I got into the electric shop—I got in there because the machine shop got slow in work. And what they would do, see, is lend you out to various jobs. So I got into the electric shop, and I learned to wire airplanes and all this kind of ole stuff. It was really unique, because you had to be able to read blueprints and schematics. It was sharp.

They also had an opening in the battery shop, which was part of the electric shop. So I learned how to rebuild batteries. We'd go and service the planes and change batteries and all that kind of jive. I ended up in inspection. When I left Hill Field, I was an aircraft electrical inspector. And the only reason I quit—I could have retired out there—was because I got screwed out of another job.

See, they brought a young white boy in. He'd been on a mission for the Mormon church. I taught him everything I knew, but when a supervisor's job came open, they give him the goddamn job. They told me, "Well, there'll be another opening in about six months and we *might* be able to work you in then." I said, "The hell with this might shit. Give me my money." I had almost ten thousand dollars of retirement money. I thought, shit, I can draw this son of a bitch out, and I can live off of that. Ain't nobody [to take care of] but me. They tried to get me to stay, but I took the money, bought me some clothes, and partied in Wendover, Las Vegas, Reno. You name it. I had me a ball. Then I came back and started working at the Porters and Waiters Club. I worked there until I run out of gas. [*Laughs*]

When I started at the club, it wasn't my first time there. I had been going there all the time, 'cause that was one of the only places in town you could go to socialize outside of the [black] church. I mean, if you was the flip class, where you drank, wanted to meet women, things like that, that's where you went. It was sort of a gathering place. You'd go there to socialize, drink, play cards, shoot the breeze. You had [black] railroad men staying at the club from Nebraska, Chicago, Denver, Kansas City, Los Angeles, Frisco—a smattering from everywhere.

Billy Weekly started that club far back as World War I, I believe, because them black railroad people, stopping in Ogden during their layovers, didn't have no place to go.[9] See, before the war years, most of the blacks that were in Ogden—what few there were—were railroad people. It was only after the war came on that they had an influx of blacks. Then people just started being transferred in. Hill [Air Base] was one of the contributing factors. A lot of blacks came to work there. Those that didn't work at Hill worked at installations like Clearfield, which was a navy base; Second Street, which was an army depot; the Arsenal, which was an army depot; and Tooele.

The club was [off Twenty-fifth Street], half a block from the railroad station, and all the railroad guys that stayed there were under contract. Both Union Pacific and Southern Pacific had contracts [with the club] to house their people when they came to town. All they had to do was sign up. And every month—well, eventually, this became my job—I would send a report on how many cooks, how many waiters, how many chair-car porters we had, and where they was from. Boom, boom, boom. Then we would get our checks. And after I worked a while, when a guy came in, I knew where he was from. As a matter of fact, I knew what day he'd be in town; and when I saw him come through the door, [I'd] automatically sign him up and give him his keys.

Now, during this time, Twenty-fifth Street was rated as one of the worst streets in the nation by *Life* magazine. *Life* made a survey of cities and their red-light districts, and it rated Twenty-fifth Street as the fourth or fifth worst street in the nation. This was during the war years [and right after]. At that time, you could do anything on Twenty-fifth Street that you did in New York City. Anything. It was a pretty rough street. But then, it wasn't too rough: I lived on it, hell, and I ain't come up with no scars. And I was a pretty rough dude in them days. I mean, I did a little of everything: drinking, stealing, mugging people—all that kind of shit. So I've come a long way, baby.

Now, if you look down Twenty-fifth Street today, you can see people three blocks away. But I remember a time there'd be so many people out, you couldn't see the next block. I remember when at midnight there'd be so many people out, you'd think it was day.

On Saturday nights, the place was full of black servicemen. During the war, that's all you'd run across on Twenty-fifth Street. Jovies [civilians] like you and me didn't have a chance. The servicemen ran Twenty-fifth Street. When I first came out, they were the reason Twenty-fifth Street got desegregated. Really. 'Cause they were going in them places, and [the businesses] were refusing the black soldiers. And rather than adjust, [the black soldiers would] just literally tear up the place. If you told them, "Well, I can't serve you because you're black," they'd go right out and get a gang and come back and tear up the joint.

They had a couple of theaters where you couldn't sit downstairs, a couple of crow's nests. So this night, [they went in there and] they almost had a riot. They had to bring a general off the base to cool them cats down, 'cause they went back to the base, got guns, and they were getting ready to do it up real good. See, most of these guys didn't want to be in the service. So they were hostile to start with. Then they found out they were going overseas. And some of them figured, well, maybe I'll get back and maybe I won't. So what the hell!

It was a wild place, no question. And there's definitely a story in there. But it's hard to describe, 'cause it was a mumbo-jumbo world. It was all mixed up. There were prostitutes, gamblers, working people, all thrown in together. All jumbled up. There used to be some characters on Twenty-fifth Street you wouldn't believe. There was a prostitute named Rose who had a leopard for a pet. She was a tiny girl. And if you wanted to do business with her, you had to do it with the cat in the room. But this is the way it was. And it takes all kinds to make the world, babe.

Twenty-fifth Street went strong for a while. But in later years, the place began to change. It changed because you had a change in uptown officials. During the war and immediately afterward, they had a mayor over there that, you might as well say, owned Ogden. When Peery was mayor, he went for the wide open stuff. But when Peery died and they got new officials, they closed the town down. And when government changes, a town changes. Things that happened couldn't happen no more. Gambling, hustling, everything was wrong. You couldn't do nothing, man. You couldn't even spit straight.

As for me, well, I have no regrets. I've never been bitter about life. See, most of my life has been a gift to me. I guess I've been blessed. After the accident, the doctors told my parents I wouldn't live twenty-four hours. But I've lived this long. So I've had to be blessed. Someone had to be working for me. And I've never had to beg nobody for nothing. I've always been able to maintain myself. Of course, sometimes I slipped a little lower than I was supposed to. But I've always come out of it.

And I got an education. I didn't get no sheepskin. But what I got, nobody can take away. And I got sense enough to keep myself going. This is something you've got to learn yourself. You can't be taught. You don't get this in school. You get this in the school of hard knocks. I always say book learning isn't worth a damn if you don't have some experience behind it. You can have all the book learning you can get, but if you don't have outright experience, book learning ain't no good. I've seen people in my life that have nothing but book learning, and, man, when they get out in the world, they ain't worth a damn. They's like a snowball in hell.

Postscript: Nathan "Woody" Wright passed away in his apartment on June 7, 1995.

Albert Fritz. *George Janecek*

ALBERT FRITZ, PRESIDENT, SALT LAKE CITY BRANCH OF THE NAACP, JOURNEYMAN ELECTRICIAN

Albert Fritz ran away from home as a teenager and eventually lost contact with his mother and siblings. A discreet, dignified man, he reluctantly admitted during the interview that he was still deeply affected by his rashness in running away and its unforeseeable consequences. "I never discuss it, but every single day of my life I regret having made the mistake of leaving. Yet, because I didn't do what I should have done toward my own family, I've tried to make a contribution by helping other black people attain their goals in life. I think of this constantly."

Born in Lansing, Michigan, Albert Fritz "rode the rails" into Salt Lake City in 1928. After briefly working as a busboy, he made his way up the ladder from janitor to journeyman electrician at the American Smelting and Refining Company (later Kennecott). His association with the Salt Lake City branch of the NAACP began in 1939. Between 1955 and 1964, he served as branch president.

On June 14, 1989, Albert Fritz passed away in a Salt Lake City hospital. In honor of his lifetime contribution to the black community, the Salt Lake City NAACP created the Albert Fritz Award. The award is now presented annually to the "civil rights worker of the year" in "recognition of dedicated services to the community and humanity."

I can tell you right off: Nothing's come easy for blacks in Utah. Even after the steelworkers organized in 1937, whites in the union were still promoted over minorities, even when they had seniority. So I objected. The whites came at me with, "What do you want? Aren't you satisfied that you have a job?" I told them, "Look, all I want is the same opportunities you have." I wasn't too smart, but I knew that much. I wanted the same rights, and I wanted to be treated like a human being. And I was outgoing. If I thought something was wrong, I stood on my feet and complained about it. They criticized me, but it didn't change me. They tried to discourage me, and oftentimes I would have to tell them off in no uncertain terms. I used curse words when they would say, "What do you want? Do you want everything?" When they used derogatory words toward me, I decked a few of them. And the only reason the American Smelting and Refining Company didn't fire me is because the job I was on was so dirty whites didn't want it. Plus, I could outwork any two men on the job. I had a strong back, I guess, and a weak mind. [*Laughs*]

But, well, I don't know what made me fight back. People have asked me, "Why have you done this, Fritz? Why did you, through the years, go through this and that? What was it?" I said, "I can't tell you or anybody else, even now, why I did these things. I just know there's a certain drive within me to do these things because we're in America. This is my home. And in spite of what's happened through the years, I still love the country and feel that we are Christians, human beings, and should be treated as such. And as a black man, I feel I should be given the same opportunities as whites. And if I'm not able to aspire to the position I would have wanted to be in, then I feel young blacks should have this opportunity. Like all Americans, they should be given every opportunity to attain their goals in life."

I was born in Lansing, Michigan. But I won't give you my date of birth. I don't want it published. I stayed in Lansing until the age of fourteen, and my life was rough. We were poor and we didn't have much. My mother did maid work, janitorial work, and we children would help her mop [floors] and dust desks for banks and [other] business establishments. My father was a mechanic at the Oldsmobile factory, but I didn't ever know him. Then, like some boys who get the idea they're smart, I left my house early one morning and didn't ever return. I didn't hate it there, but when you read stories of other places, of western cowboys, that's what intrigued me. As far as this country, I knew nothing of the states I later traveled through because I wasn't prepared to go; I just left. I really don't know why. I just got the idea that I would leave, and I did.

I went by freight train through several states. I had a little bundle of clothing, no money. And I just hopped little passenger trains, when I could get on 'em, and [I'd] hide between the engine and the second car. Most times, I got kicked off. I survived by knocking on doors, asking for a job or for food, and sleeping in hobo jungles. But it was hard, because I was too young to get a job.

I remember one particular incident. I was in a city back East, and there were three more fellows on the train. And we were pulled off the train, and they took us into the station. They were asking where we were from, because they knew we were underage. I was, especially; perhaps the others were, too. I don't even remember their names. Anyway, we were forced to stay at the station. Then the officer who picked us up telephoned back to our homes. He said to my mother, "Well, we have this Albert Fritz, and we're going to send [him] home." She said, "Well, that's not my son, because he wouldn't be there." She didn't dream I was that far from home. So they took us to a hotel, through the back door, fed us, and took us back to wait in the station. They were going to send us home. But after a day and a half of waiting, we snuck off one night, got on a train, and left town.

I hoboed for about a year before I came to Utah. I came in from Denver and hopped out somewhere near 2100 South, where there were a lot of railroad cars. I got off the train, walked to town, and began knocking on doors for work; otherwise I'd have to go out and sleep in a boxcar. I got a job washing dishes at a café between State and Main [Street] on Second South. I ate the leftovers from the plates customers had. I also got a room for a dollar fifty a week. I finally found a room with a black family, because the whites, regardless of whether they owned dilapidated hotels, wouldn't rent to colored people. They just wouldn't rent to you. When you went to the door, they just told you, "No!" It was that blunt.

Later, I met a colored fellow on the street. He told me to go to the Hotel Utah to bus dishes. So I got a job in the Sky Room; it was later called the Roof Garden. One day, this white family came in. The fellow noticed I had no soles on my shoes and took me for a traveling man. He said, "You're not from Utah." I said, "No." He pointed to the stacks out there [on the west side of town]: "Before you leave, you want to go out there. That's where they make copper."

So, two days later, I went out with a friend of mine. We rode a freight train out to Garfield (to Kennecott). It was owned by the American Smelting and Refining Company then. And the man [in the office] said, "Do you boys want work?" We said, "Yes." He said, "Come back tomorrow." So we came back the next day, and I got a job working out there for three dollars a day. The work they gave me was cleanup in a big building.

Now, I hadn't been out there more than a week when the employment agent came along. Above where I worked, it was awful dusty and dirty. You couldn't see your hand before your face when you looked up there. He said, "I'm going to lay you off." I said, "Well, I really need this job." He said, "Either I lay you off, or you go and work up there." And up there, like I said, it was filthy dirty. It was so dusty you'd have to get a sponge, wet it, wrap it in gauze, and keep it over your nose and mouth so you wouldn't breathe in all the fumes and dust.

See, Kennecott had these ore trains that went from one building to another to dump the ore after it had been roasted. I'd been working under them, and that's where your fumes came from. They ran these cars from one building to another, and they were uncovered. And fumes and dust from the roasted ore would go up into the air and fall all over. The odor was so strong your nose would bleed, your eyes would burn, and you would cough. If I blew my nose, black dust would come out. When I'd spit on occasion, my saliva was black. It was a dirty job, and whites didn't work on it. They didn't have to. The Mexicans, the Greeks, the Japanese, and the colored people worked there. And the reason they kept me, like I told you, was because I could outwork two men on the job, *any* two men. I worked there for eight years before I got promoted.

Now, I didn't get involved in the black community right after I came into town because, well, you didn't see many blacks then. You'd go downtown, and if you ran into two or three in a week, why, that was setting some kind of record. The majority of them that were here worked at the Hotel Utah and the Newhouse Hotel, and they were railroad men. And blacks, if they congregated, had one or two places of their own they would mingle at. One was called Mineral Springs on Beck Street. Then there were one or two black cafés. [Blacks] weren't permitted no place else.

I'm thinking about a way to tell you what brought about the change in me, but it's hard to come up with it. I was only married a short time [to my first wife], but through the difficulties of the marriage I learned I was inexperienced in many ways of life. After we split up and I lived alone, I kind of grew up. I started seeing the ways of the world: how my country operated, how this state operated, how a state law allowed an establishment to refuse you service, and how blacks were being treated. And I resented it. I resented it when they told me to go upstairs in a theater. I resented walking into a café and being told, "We don't serve colored here." And I resented the way salesmen in the stores would take your money, with a smile on their faces, but wouldn't let you try on clothes before buying them.

Then, over on Seventh South and Second East, there was more blacks concentrated there than any other place in Salt Lake City, and whites were resentful. There was talk that a Mormon bishop named Sheldon Brewster and members of several wards and the city council were trying to get blacks moved out north, near the stockyards. I don't know how they planned on doing it, but that was the talk for a while. . . .

So I joined the NAACP in 1939, because it was a good organization and the only organization trying to bring about changes. I didn't get too deeply involved at first. I just paid my membership [dues] and attended meetings. We didn't have large meetings—maybe ten, twelve, fifteen people. But there was always discussion about the conditions we encountered in the city, the negative attitudes toward blacks, and the way children were treated at school. They just weren't accepted.

But back in the 1940s, we weren't making much progress. Abner Howell was president of the NAACP. He and his family had quite a lot of [farm] property up on the east bench. He was a fine man, the first black to graduate from West High School in Utah, but he was passive. And, being LDS, why, he didn't want to approach [church] officials about [making] changes. Looking back, I can see why. Conditions weren't favorable toward blacks at that time. And many blacks felt it was useless to approach [white] people in an attempt to make changes. They weren't going to accomplish anything. Of course, some feared they'd offend someone or lose their jobs if they spoke out. They didn't say so in so many words, but this is the condition they were laboring under.

In 1955, I became president of the NAACP. Now, this opportunity didn't exactly present itself. Being president was thrust upon me. The former president was leaving town, and neither the vice president nor others on the board accepted the position. So the president persuaded me to take it. He didn't talk me into it alone. The president of my local union, W. Madil, who shared many of my views [toward discrimination], also pushed me into it. He told me, "Look, A. B." (he called me A. B.), "I'll back you up. If you need help, I'll back you."

I'll admit, I was afraid. Not of people, but of handling the organization. The Salt Lake branch never had any money to speak of at that time. Yearly memberships were two dollars [per person]. One dollar went to the national office in New York to help them fight for civil rights in the South; the other dollar stayed here. We had no office. We had no telephone. Every once in a while we would send out correspondence, but most times it was word of mouth. When I became president, I used my home phone and traveled at my own expense. Plus, if I took a day off during the workweek for a speech, I'd work on Saturday or Sunday to make it up. [At first] I didn't know if I could manage that.

The more I got into it, though, the more at ease I felt. In the background, people talked to me, encouraged me. Blacks supported me. Then Dr. Landau, a wonderful man, had me come up to the University of Utah to speak. I was unused to public speaking, so I shook [during the presentation]. But I wanted to take this step and challenge the people by telling them that we blacks wanted the same opportunity others were getting . . . that's all. I eventually was invited to speak at the Kiwanis Club, the Rotary Club, the Exchange Club. I wound up lecturing all over the state.

I don't know whether "guts" is the proper term to use, but I was never afraid of white people. I always made it a point to tell people what I thought. Maybe I wasn't smart enough to have any fears, because I *was* threatened. I don't remember the first time, but I remember one incident clearly. I had spoken at the Christ Methodist Church, up on Twentieth East and Thirty-third

South, in the morning. I spoke about encouraging other denominations to work with us toward bringing about equality of opportunity. And, evidently, there were some newspaper reporters there, and somebody wrote it up.

The next morning, there was an article in the paper on what I said concerning the treatment of blacks and how they weren't given the same opportunity in jobs, housing, and public accommodation. Later that night, about three o'clock A.M., my phone rang. Some fellow said, "Is this that Albert Fritz, the head of that nigger organization, the NAACP?" I said, "I'm not a nigger." He said, "We're going to run every nigger out of the state of Utah, but you're going to be the first one." I said, "Now if you talk so big, you come on over. If you come alone, I'll kick the hell out of you. But if you're not alone, you'd better come prepared, because I'm going to shoot the hell out of all of you."

I slept with a rifle by my front door. But they didn't ever come. He called me back, always at two or three o'clock in the morning, cursed me, and told me they were going to tar and feather me and run me out of the state. They were going to run every nigger out of the state. But they didn't ever come. Several times, after meetings, cars followed [me]. I would drive around, then finally go home. Then there were letters. I got [many] threatening letters. But during the time I remained president, I kept pushing. It seems when my morale got low, there was always someone or something to bring me up again.

In the 1950s, Dr. Ralph Bunche came here to conduct a model United Nations Assembly at the University of Utah. They sent a car from the university, and I had breakfast with him the day of the session. Then I watched him conduct the session, which was followed by a question and answer period, and I felt really fortunate to have met him. He was a distinguished and intelligent man, and he inspired me. I knew I'd never get the education he had, but I knew within me that I could keep working to help blacks here that weren't being given equal opportunity. I knew I could do that.

When Dr. King came here later, the same thing happened. He gave a talk at the University of Utah, then had a question and answer period. This went on until he barely had time to get in his limousine and return to the airport. I rode back with him, and I can remember the very words he spoke to me. I said, "Dr. King, we're trying to get public accommodation [legislation passed] here, but we're not making much progress." He said, "Just keep trying. Don't give up. You'll get it. It will come." Those were the very words he told me.

JOHN OSCAR WILLIAMS, 42, POSTAL CLERK

Born on May 19, 1944, in Forest, Mississippi, John Oscar Williams was the fifth of eight children and the last, as he said, to be born in the "old country." "That's what we called Mississippi when we were growing up," he said. Then he explained, "Dad's often told us that he didn't want any of us growing up there, because there wouldn't have been any opportunity for us to advance. So he worked to earn passage for us to come out here."

Eddie Williams, John's father, arrived in Utah in 1946; his wife and children followed two years later. John Williams grew up in Salt Lake City and graduated from South High School in 1963. From 1960 to 1968, he was intensely involved in the NAACP and the civil rights movement in Utah. From 1964 to 1968, he and his wife, Judy Lawrence Williams, created and produced a weekly radio show, in which they presented the social and cultural history of African-Americans from a strictly "black perspective." John Williams received a B.A. in behavioral science from Westminster College in 1986. The same year, he was employed by the U.S. Postal Service in Provo, Utah.

The first thing I remember about growing up in Utah is *always* having to go to Calvary Baptist Church on Sunday. Our family was very active in the church. So, regardless of anything, we had to be at church in our little, short white pants, all dressed up and learning our memory verses and Bible names. That's my first memory. My second memory is starting school, and that was a horrible experience.

At that time, we were all centrally located. Half the blacks went to Grant School; the other half went to Jefferson [Elementary] School. I went to Jefferson. There was about six blacks that started there, and I remember J. T. She was Greek and black. I've often thought about her, because her perception of herself was that she wasn't black. She was very light, and her parents and her grandmother didn't want her to have any association with blacks. So that was J. T. Then there were the others.

I can remember, in kindergarten, how we sat around the teacher, who would read *Little Black Sambo* to us. [Then] we'd go out for recess, and the other kids would call us little black sambo. J. T. was obese; her nickname was Aunt Jemima. I can remember white kids running around the schoolyard calling her the biggest nigger they'd ever seen; and [I can remember] how J. T., myself, and others used to battle. We'd be out there battling them over the name-calling, and we were always brought in and told, in no uncertain terms, that we couldn't fight it forever. It was something we were just going to have to accept. I've always wondered why they never called in the other kids to tell them it was wrong.

So, the few of us [at Jefferson], we caught a lot of racial abuse. I guess it would be equal to any place during that time, 'cause the teachers weren't sympathetic. They were mostly white and LDS, and they all knew you were the curse of Cain, because this was what they had been taught. I remember one teacher from Ireland. She would get up in front of the class on St. Patrick's Day and tell us, with an Irish accent, how she just loved to hear "those old darkies sing."

So we were treated as inferiors. We were always placed in the non-thinking, nonfunctioning groups. We were never able to achieve, and it seems like we were never given the attention the others got. The teachers, who were supposed to be educated people, used the words "nigger" and "darkie" and thought nothing of it. They would think *absolutely* nothing of it! The kids at recess parroted them, and so we became exactly what the teachers called us.

My dad always said he never got an education. But I've told my sister, "Much as I kept him in school for the trouble I caused, he probably got a Ph.D." You see, our parents were always going to school because of what the teachers here in the city were doing to their kids. My parents had to go to West High once because my older brother, Percy, hit a teacher. He had stayed up all night and worked on some paper, and the teacher wouldn't pass him because he didn't think blacks were capable of doing that kind of work. He told him he cheated, and my brother fired him up.

But that's the kind of abuse we took all through elementary school, junior high, and high school. The education system here was just blatantly racist. And I was always striking out in anger, because I *knew* it wasn't right, and I was always getting suspended for fighting. My parents would go down and try and reason with those teachers, but there was no reasoning with them. So we fought and we kept on fighting.

It wasn't just in school, either. When we'd go to the Utah Theater, the Capitol Theater, all of the theaters, we had to sit in the balcony. That was the only place they would let us sit. On Saturday nights at ten thirty, we skated at the Normandy Skating Rink and paid double the price. Every black. The cops had standing orders not to enforce the curfew on Saturday nights against the blacks, because this was the only time they had to go roller-skating over at the rotten Normandy Skating Rink. I remember the manager's bald head, [his] shiny, bald head, as he took our money. There would be about a hundred blacks there, and we were all giving that guy our money. Just giving him our money! [We] never should have done it, never should have done it. [Yet it was] the only time we could go skating.

All through my youth, I never heard my parents *ever* use any derogatory terms to describe any other race or group. My dad always said, "If you call somebody out of their name, you'd better be ready to whoop them. And if you do and *you* get whooped, don't be bringing it home because you were *wrong*."

The first time on our street where I remember seeing real anger, real hatred, and real bitterness [toward whites] was in August 1955, when they lynched Emmett Till.[10] I was eleven, and Ted Steward [a neighbor] came up the street. We were sitting on the front porch. He came up the street and said, "They ought to just take a machine gun and shoot every goddamn one of *them*." Those were his exact words after they had lynched Emmett Till. I didn't understand, at first. I didn't understand what lynching was about or why they killed him.

The comment, I remember, was that he was "lynched for looking at some no-good, goddamn, fat, white bitch." That was the comment. We [kids] weren't supposed to hear that or the discussions that went on here, but there were a lot of discussions about that lynching. You'd go to the barbershop and they'd be talking about the lynching of Emmett Till. It had a profound effect on this black community.

The way I [finally] got into it—I got to look at *Jet* and *Ebony* at Butch's barbershop. I got to see pictures that were taken [of Till] and published. And there he was, his head beaten, out of shape, in a box, a kid from Chicago, and all he did was wolf whistle at a white girl in Mississippi. The hostility in this black community was so intense you could just feel it in the air. You could feel the rage everywhere after the so-called trial, when the perpetrators were let go. It was rage, real rage.

A lot of times, I think the lynching of Emmett Till was what gave birth to the civil rights movement. [Because] it was graphic, it was really graphic. I mean, that picture of Emmett Till, a kid, who had been beaten and killed and thrown into the river, and the picture of a gigantic white woman and those two white men and their statement that they were defending white womanhood. The papers all over the world showed that picture of him in a Chicago funeral home. What made it cut so deep, though, was TV. The national news, crude as it was, showed you what happened. There had been lynchings all the time down South, but for some reason *everybody* got to see this picture of Emmett Till.

Now, in school we never read any black history. I remember looking through the old South High [School] library for things about black people. They had two books. I can remember a music class that I was taking [where] they went through the *Porgy and Bess* [musical] and W. C. Handy. And I remember I had a book [put out] by *Ebony*. There was a picture of W. C. Handy [in it] with his trumpet in his hands. I took it to school to show the music teacher. But she wanted [to keep] the picture. My mother just got so pissed. I've never seen her that angry, but she didn't want to give up the picture. She felt the teacher should have had her stuff together enough to have pictures [of black musicians]. She was appalled by the ignorance of them teaching a class and they didn't have or were too lazy to get the materials.

Then . . . how can I say this? In high school, there developed an even heightened difference in the thinking of blacks and whites, because we weren't allowed to participate in high school activities to the best of our abilities. [We] never were.

Out of my class of sixty-three blacks, five graduated. That's a horrible percentage. But the thing was set up. When they brought out all those aptitude tests in our junior year, and these career [guidance] people were called, hell, we knew we wasn't going to graduate. They gave us all IQ tests. We'd all get together after these tests was done and compare notes, and, you know, [the results showed] *none* of us were fit to go to college. It came down that we should stick to a trade school or that we should be domestics. But we never believed it, 'cause we knew it was fixed. Shit, every one of those kids was fit to go to college or better.

But, you see, the criteria was set up in your junior year. If the teachers had the information that you weren't "college material," you were just sunk. You didn't get the college preparatory classes. For me, I thought the best thing I could achieve was to end up working on the railroad. I mean, that was the limit of my expectations: to get a job on the railroad. I never saw a [black] doctor or a lawyer. I didn't even see a black schoolteacher. *They didn't exist.* And with a healthy dose of "you're not college material," what would you look for?

In my senior year in high school, 1963, I was shining shoes at the [Salt Lake City] airport. I made good money, but I hated the job. Other black guys [my age] were shining shoes at Florsheim on Second South. The white kids, meantime, had their nice grocery store jobs. Very few of us had what you would call a legitimate part-time job. They were murder on blacks for employment. So that's what I done. After a while [though], I got tired of it; then something [in me] just snapped. I got too militant is what it was. I just got tired of taking that stuff.

From the time I entered high school, you see, to the time I graduated in 1963, the civil rights movement had really grown. So we started feeling this personally; we became aware of these things. We got to see the troops at Little Rock, Arkansas. That's a perception you never forget—the state National Guard standing with their bayonets, keeping those black kids out of school. You were glued to the TV for that little news spot. You also got to see it in the newspaper, so you were getting a constant barrage of, hey, this country isn't all it's cracked up to be. In other words, you became aware that you are black, and that you are mistreated.

I remember seeing those little black kids in their white dresses and those armed troops and that ranting and raving [mob] and the horrible foulness of all those screaming people. And you were praying for Eisenhower to do something. Eisenhower was debating over what he should do. Finally, he federalized the guard and let the kids in, and that made us feel good—it really did—to see them damn bigots have to escort those blacks kids into the school. I think we breathed a sigh of relief, but you never forgot the confrontation.

And that kind of thing was going on *all over* the South! I saw people breaking down segregation in all kinds of ways, and I started thinking about all these things that happened to us here. I thought about sitting in balconies, going roller-skating, not being able to find decent jobs. And I came away realizing it's no different here than down there. I had that idea, and I *know* the other black kids had that idea, because we used to talk about it. So we said, hey, it's time to change things.

The first thing we did was start having Junior NAACP meetings. We [also] had kind of a clandestine group at the start and we met on Saturday nights, because we knew the leader of the NAACP youth just wasn't doing the job he should. So what happened was people decide to get me to run for president, 'cause they figured I'd do a better job. So we bought all the two-dollar memberships we could. And on voting night, I had thirty-five of my followers there. He had nobody. So we voted him right out of office. I got to be president, and I had them vote in my ex-wife, Judy Lawrence, as vice president. And since we all shared the view that we were getting royally shafted, those Saturday nights became times for us to vent our anger.

But that group of young people—the class of '63 and '64—that was the cream of the crop of our black community. I mean, you had Annette Howell, who was the [state's] first black to win the Sterling Scholar Award. She was our Junior NAACP secretary. My wife was the valedictorian at West High School. I think our membership got as high as 125 or 130 active members. It was a very special bunch. There was a lot of skill there. We manipulated it so we could get a [sympathetic] white vice president. So we knew what we were going to do, and we did it. That was a brilliant group of people.

What we wanted, initially, was to do away with skating on Saturday nights—Norman Dee's racist policy. That was our first goal. Our second goal was to send money south to help Dr. Martin Luther King and the NAACP carry on their fight. Those were our original intentions.

But, more importantly, we had something that made a difference in the long run. It *really* made a difference. We had four seats on the executive board of the [Senior] NAACP—voting seats. So when Dr. Nabors got going, he was constantly assured of four votes.[11] That made a difference in the long run, because a lot of the things he wanted to do and push for were difficult to achieve because he wasn't president. Albert Fritz was president. So those four votes made a difference for progress. They *did*. And it was time. It was time. Everybody was fed up with the way things were going. *Everybody* was sick and tired of it. We just weren't going to take it anymore.

What did we want? We wanted our freedom. We wanted access into *everything* we were qualified to get into. We wanted to be able to go to schools. We wanted to be able to go to college. We wanted to be able to compete openly in the marketplace. And we wanted equal access to *everything* that the white power structure controlled without regard to race, creed, or color. On the other side, the white establishment wanted us to wait. We called that gradualism. We had three hundred years of that. We weren't going to wait anymore.

DR. CHARLES "CHUCK" NABORS, 51, ASSISTANT PROFESSOR, DEPARTMENT OF ANATOMY, AND ASSISTANT DEAN FOR MINORITY AFFAIRS, SCHOOL OF MEDICINE, UNIVERSITY OF UTAH

Intense, articulate, mercurial, Dr. Charles James Nabors brought verve and vitality into the fight for civil rights in Utah. Born in Cleveland, Ohio, on January 11, 1934, he attended Wabash College in Crawfordsville, Indiana. In 1956, he accepted an invitation to pursue graduate studies and conduct research in the anatomy department at the University of Utah. He earned his doctorate in anatomy in 1965; and from 1967 until his unexpected death in 1986, he was an assistant professor in the department and a nationally recognized researcher on cystic fibrosis.

Charles Nabors. *Kent Miles*

Dr. Nabors's accomplishments as a civil rights activist and community organizer, however, rivaled, if not overshadowed, his academic career. Between 1961 and 1965, he was on the executive board of the Salt Lake City branch of the NAACP and was regarded as the organization's most charismatic leader. In 1968, he founded the Utah Non-violent Action Committee (UNAC), a multiracial organization dedicated to aggressively exposing and rectifying black problems. The same year, he became Utah's first elected black delegate to the Democratic National Convention, and in 1972 he was appointed state chairman of the McGovern Presidential Campaign.

When I agreed to come to Utah in 1956, my parents went nuts! They did *not* want me to come here. They had heard of the image of this state. Utah had and still has, although somewhat diminished, the image of a place that is extremely hostile to black people. The Mormons were thought of as outright racists. So I probably wouldn't have gotten to Utah if I didn't have my own plane fare. But I flew to Salt Lake City one day and went straight to work, literally with suitcases unpacked, because we were starting a [research] project. This was still during a time when the [national] civil rights movement was cranking up slowly. At the time, I was kind of an eager, young guy who was extremely interested in research. I think I've always been the kind of person that kept up with current events, but research was the whole ball game for me at that time—the entire ball game.

Now, the university, and particularly the medical school, had a very strong liberal tradition at this time. The medical school was, if you will, a colony. The department chairmen and most faculty were non-Mormons. It was a colony even within the university itself, let alone within the rest of the community. But, initially, I didn't pay much attention to it. I just hacked away at graduate school. I was publishing papers and working for a professor from Mexico City, and we worked like crazy all the time, doing research and consulting. So it was a very busy time.

When I could get time off, I'd go home. On one trip, I allowed my sister to fix me up with a blind date. Her name was Joan Washington. She was from Dayton and was very lovely, very beautiful. We started dating. She grew up in Tuskegee Institute, Alabama, and her father, who had retired, had been the executive director of the Urban League for twenty-five years.[12] He was a unique man and very successful at what he did. And, I remember, every time I'd drive to Dayton to take Joan out, I'd always end up sitting down and talking with her father. She'd have to finally butt into the conversation and say, "We're going out now," 'cause her father and I'd be sitting there talking civil rights and Urban League business.

Joan and I eventually got married in Dayton, and I brought her West. We drove out, and Joanie started off in the profession of child development. She has done a lot in that field. I guess her career began the second year we were married. That must have been 1961, and by then the freedom riders had gone into the South.[13] And I [definitely] could feel what was starting to happen [in this country]. I remember having long debates with my father, who wanted nothing to do with it. He just wanted to be a respectable Negro. "You are going to be a Ph.D.," he told me. "Do your job and stay off the streets." But I wasn't about to stay off the streets. I had seen enough crap in Salt Lake City by then that I was not about to do that. There was gross housing discrimination here. Blacks were crowded into about half of Central City and near the West Side. Those were the only areas in town, with very few exceptions, where black people lived, and I was not about to put up with that.

So, that same year, we attended our first NAACP meeting in the city. It was held on the patio of a black family's home on Eighth South. During the meeting, Joan and I looked at each other in disbelief. These people were talking about world affairs and drinking tea. It was as if they didn't know what was going on out there. I got up toward the end of the meeting and said, "Folks, we got problems in Utah. We got problems all over the United States. What is this talking about world affairs?" I got a cold shoulder, a very cold shoulder.

We started going to NAACP meetings regularly. Pretty soon, along came a number of local blacks, all of them young, and others who recognized this nationwide issue [discrimination against blacks]. So, pressure for action suddenly started coming from all directions. At that time, in Salt Lake City, they had given up segregation in most movie theaters and restaurants. But other types of public accommodations and facilities, like bowling alleys, had not, and housing discrimination, as I said, was rampant. Utah also had an antimiscegenation statute on the books [prohibiting cohabitation or marriage between a white and black or white and Asian person]. So the first thing we did was to lobby Governor Dewey Clyde for a repeal of the act.

Now, one of my friends, a Republican, urged me to make an appearance before the Platform Committee of the Republican party. I went in, made an appeal for civil rights, and presented arguments against the antimiscegenation statute. What a riot that was! At that time, Ernest L. Wilkinson was still alive and doing his vindictive, nasty little things.[14] When I finished talking, he stood up, holding his suspenders—he always wore suspenders and was easily the most obnoxious man on earth—and gave me a lecture about [how] "this isn't the right thing to do at this time." And you could hear the heels clicking in the room like it was a meeting of the gestapo. They all stopped listening, and our time was wasted. But we hung in and managed, with help, to lobby it through the Utah State Legislature in 1963. . . .

About this same time, I remember, my home phone started ringing! Once you get active, you know, and people know you're active, your home phone starts ringing. People [called me] complaining that they couldn't get apartments. People complained about a lot of things, because I was the "enfant terrible" of the NAACP! I was out there while the others were still discussing world affairs and still hanging onto that old-line attitude [of] "We are Negroes." And this conflict goes all the way back, I guess, to the fight between W. E. B. Du Bois and Booker T. Washington and their philosophies.

Booker T. Washington, you see, stood up in Washington, D.C. [in 1895]—he was president of Tuskegee Institute at the time—and he said to a white audience [justifying segregation], "In all things purely social, we can be as separate as the five fingers, and yet one as the hand in all things essential to mutual progress."[15] W. E. B. Du Bois, on the other hand, was very progressive and a very militant opponent of segregation. And, I suppose, my relationship with the local branch was like the relationship between Du Bois and Washington, because they were very conservative here. A lot of them were black clergymen. So this squabble was continuous. Albert Fritz and I argued all the time. He wanted to take more moderate actions [against discrimination], and I was building up for that first [public] demonstration.

At the time, we were going around and using a technique called "a sandwich" [where we approached a problem from two sides] to collect evidence on housing discrimination. We'd send in a black couple to rent an apartment, and if they were turned down, we'd send in a white couple to see if they were offered the place. Now, our activities were being absolutely, totally ignored by the local press. Nobody, and I mean *nobody*, would cover our stuff. "That [kind of segregation] doesn't exist here," they said. "We don't have those problems in Utah." I'll show you, I thought.

I'd heard that blacks couldn't bowl at Rancho Bowling Lanes, over on

North Temple. So we ran a sandwich on it with witnesses, and, no dice: Blacks couldn't bowl. I can't remember what day it was—it was summer. We put a picket line in front. And since I realized the local press wasn't going to cover us, I called AP [Associated Press], UPI [United Press International], and several local radio stations. I also called the Salt Lake Police Department to let them know what we were doing. And I led the picket. I led every single one of them! We picketed in orderly fashion. It was really squeaky-clean non-violence. Then the [local] press came up [and asked], "Who's leading this thing?" Their next question was, "When did you get in from New York?" They couldn't believe anybody who lived here would be so "uppity" as to picket a local business. So that first picket line really shook the place, and we finally got some coverage.

Back at the NAACP, do you know what they were saying? "If Nabors wants to bowl, why doesn't he build his own alley?" The old guard felt I was an outsider. I was not of the Utah black culture. Not all of them, but these were the lines that were drawn. Their attitude was sort of like the prisoner-of-war syndrome, in that if you're suppressed long enough, you begin to think that's your rightful role. It's a reaction to expectation. I mean, if all your schoolteachers, most of whom are Mormon, expect you to be inferior, you begin to live your life to those expectations. So, what the NAACP was telling me was: First of all, you are not one of the boys and girls. You're just a smart college boy who came here. Second, we don't expect things to get better. We have no expectation of that.

So there was a real counterpoint between the civil rights atmosphere in Utah in 1962, 1963, and what was happening across the country. Black communities across the country were enormously hopeful and motivated. But Utah was gazing at either the Wasatch or the Oquirrh mountains. So there was a definite and serious lag here. And the Salt Lake City public, when they saw what we were doing, said, "You're radicals. You're out of line." They did everything but call us Communists, which they couldn't do, because I wrapped everything we did so tightly in the flag you would become nauseated to see it.

Now, our most dramatic public action occurred with the passage of the first civil rights bill in Utah, the Public Accommodations Act. [This came] after the historical 1964 Civil Rights Act was passed by [the U.S.] Congress. Our debating point was, "It's the national law. Why not make it the state law?" But [it] came down to the last four days of the Utah State Legislature—Thursday, Friday, Saturday, and Monday. And one of my friends in the press corps came to me and said, "Chuck, it's not going to pass. We've counted the votes. It will not pass the state legislature." I said, "You want to bet?"

That Thursday afternoon, three or four of us went in to ask the leadership of the LDS church if they'd help us get the legislation passed. They told us, "We only get into politics on moral issues." It took me a minute to regain my voice. I said, "Isn't the way one human being treats another a moral issue?" Well, we didn't get what we wanted, so on Friday morning I put a civil rights picket line in front of the offices of the LDS church down on South Temple! I called United Press International and Associated Press, and they covered it. They put it on the "A wire," which means it went to all their subscribers nationwide. Three days later, on a Monday morning [in 1965], the Civil Rights Act was passed by the Utah State Legislature's House of Representatives sixty-nine to nothing. Do I need to say more!?

After that victory, picketing became a constant tool [for us]. When we wanted a fair employment law, we put the picket line back in front of the church offices. When we wanted a fair housing law, we put the picket line back in front of the church offices. There remained a lot of hostility towards what we were doing; there were nasty letters, phone calls. I called the Justice Department in Washington three times because threats were made to me and other people involved in the movement. But, fortunately, we had superb coverage from the local police department. They hauled people away a couple of times and disarmed a guy when we were picketing the school board.

The potential of black violence, of course, had to be checked, too. In 1968, I remember, during the Stokely Carmichael–H. Rap Brown era, there was a group of young blacks in Central City who definitely didn't think we were radical enough.[16] I spent more than one night till four o'clock in the morning talking to them, negotiating, reinforcing the idea in their heads that if they got violent, there was a vast majority who would get violent back. We managed to prevent violence. It would have been absolutely disastrous in this community, because the reaction would have been an absolute, outright rejection of anything we were attempting to do.

So, gradually (you know, nothing succeeds like success), the black community came wholeheartedly on our side, even those folks who didn't jump on the bandwagon from the beginning. We always had a large number of whites picketing with us who were as committed as any black on the picket line. We initially had more whites than blacks. But, gradually, that ratio changed, not by the attrition [of whites], but [by] the addition of more black people.

So, we changed a lot of minds in the '60s. A lot of Utahns said, "No more of this." There's not a neighborhood now where you can't find blacks living. In most offices and banks, you'll find black employees. You still won't find blacks moving into the executive echelons. That's still missing, but in other ways there are enormous changes.

The event of recent years, though, that is going to make the *most* difference is the revelation by the LDS church. This will have a profound effect on this community, because faithful members of the church do what the church tells them to do. So I've been telling my black friends, "If you want to make a move in this community, go for it. Now is the time. The level of acceptance has made a quantum leap, because, all of a sudden, the Lord has told everybody to play fair. And, by God, they'll play fair." They *will* play fair. For a while, they may even play more than fair. [*Chuckles*]

JAKE R. GREEN, JR., 51, OFFICER,
SALT LAKE CITY POLICE DEPARTMENT

A trim, muscular man with chiseled features, Jacob ("Jake") R. Green, Jr., was born in Salt Lake City on May 5, 1936, and raised in a religiously "mixed" household. His father belonged to the African Methodist Episcopal Church (AME), and his mother was a Mormon. At the age of thirteen, Jake Green severed his connection with the Mormon church and has not been formally affiliated with any religious body since.

Mr. Green was employed as a redcap for the Union Pacific Railroad and as a medical assistant at the Utah State Prison before becoming Salt Lake City's "second black patrolman" in 1968. The city's first black patrolman, he noted, was his great-grandfather, Paul Cephas Howell, who moved to Utah from Mansfield, Louisiana, in 1888. Jake Green retired from the force on July 1, 1976. At the time of this interview, he was working as a customer services representative with Delta Airlines.

The first home I tried to buy was out on 6400 South and Third East. They painted a skull and crossbones on the door and put up a sign saying "No Niggers Wanted." I was twenty. It was a piece of property that had an acre [of land], and I always loved horses and wanted an acre of property to raise them. There was a tiny house and a lot of potential with the ground. I was going to live there, raise horses, and build a [larger] house later. I didn't have big dreams. I worked hard—I always worked two jobs—and I wanted a home, and I wanted to raise kids. I didn't go to college because there was a lack of opportunity [for employment] around here. But I was raised by as shrewd of an old man as you'll ever want to see.

My dad was super shrewd. I remember during the Second World War . . . I was sixteen or seventeen, and southern black soldiers were being stationed at Camp Williams and Camp Kearns here before going to Fort Lewis, Washington, and then overseas. Gas was on rationing, and tires you didn't get. My dad would get off [work] at midnight at the [Union Pacific] Railroad Depot, and these guys would all be down at the Porters and Waiters [Club].[17] My uncle owned that club. At closing time, the soldiers always needed a ride back to the base, and [my dad] would tell them he didn't have enough gas because it was rationed. "It's all right, Pops," they'd say. "Just go to the gas station." They would go with him, get out, and pump gas into his car, damn the ration stamps. After he'd drive them to the base, he'd syphon the gas and sell it for bootleg prices. If somebody needed tires, he'd do the same thing. He did all them shrewd things.

But these black guys [the soldiers], let me tell you, they were a cut above. They didn't play games, and you didn't mess with them. See, you've got to realize, at the time, most Utah blacks were uneducated. We were doing whatever whites would give us to do. And jobs weren't plentiful. Most of my friends who graduated college had to leave the state to find employment. There were few opportunities here. We didn't know how to use the press. We rode on the back seat of the bus. And if a black woman nine months pregnant had to jump up and give a white man [her] seat, what did you have? What was there to fight for?

These guys knew they were going overseas, so they didn't take no shit off anyone. They'd as soon kill you as look at you, and they didn't care. They were going overseas to kill for freedom, and they were going to have some freedom here before they went. The [white] people [here] were very intimidated and threatened by [the black soldiers]. You would be, too. The country needed them, and [white people] had to start paying their price. They had to start paying, but they didn't like paying in full.

Now, growing up here in Salt Lake City, we never knew any lynchings. But you were never entitled to your free cut of anything. My dad worked as a redcap for the railroad; he was with them for fifty years. He also did all the bootleg plumbing for blacks in Salt Lake City, because there were no apprenticeship programs here for blacks. They weren't allowed plumbing licenses. Ed Steward, the first black plumber, had to go to Kansas City to obtain his license. So Dad bootlegged. If people wanted a hot-water jacket hooked up in their old coal stove, he did it. If they wanted a faucet fixed, or any type of household plumbing, he did it. He could have been one hell of a plumber in his day. He was a sharp man. All he had to do was see it done once, and he could do it. But his day is over now.

My father, I used to say, baled cotton. I never saw cotton. I [once] told him, "You baled cotton, not me." I said that because I wanted to show him that he *had* to take these jobs. He had to be kicked in the behind. He [once] worked in a hothouse. He could take a rose off a bush, stick it in the ground, and it would grow. He crossed the old lady [his boss], though, down in Texas, and she fired him. This was the way it was. Blacks knew their place [then], and they stayed in their place.

In Salt Lake, they didn't go to the Terrace Ballroom. They had their own little clubs—the Dixieland and the Porters and Waiters. And if you wanted any black social life, you had to go to one of these clubs or to the black church. I remember [when] they used to have big dances, everybody would go there. You could be a pimp off the street or you could be singing in the church choir, you'd all be in there. There were no black societies. The pimp could go wherever the Christian went.

In 1956/1957, I started reading all kinds of black history. I was in my early twenties, and it was the day of Dr. Martin Luther King, Jr. [He] was one of the best things that ever happened for blacks in this country. When he pulled off what he did in Montgomery, Alabama, with the bus boycott, you no longer felt growing up in Utah had to be this way. You no longer felt you had to jump when "the man" said "jump." Laws started changing. Civil rights laws started coming about. There was representation. And the [Salt Lake City branch of the] NAACP was probably at its strongest. You [also] had Stokely Carmichael starting up.[18]

I remember traveling to Detroit. That was the first time I went into a black ghetto, into a mass of blacks living below human standards. And the song back there was [that] either there was going to be change or they were going to burn the place down. At the time, I remember, white storekeepers were taking the milk, the bread, and stuff off the shelves on the East Side and selling it on the West Side, where the ghetto was, for higher prices. And blacks demanded it be stopped. They also wanted to do something with the tenement housing. I went down one morning, at six o'clock in the morning, into the ghetto. I was digging in the gutter, and I kicked over a 1948 newspaper. It was 1962. The gutter hadn't been [properly] cleaned down there since 1948.

I remember I asked myself which direction I wanted to go. Did I want to fight [whites]? Did I want to burn things down? What did I want to do to release my frustrations? I was very belligerent, very bitter, very hostile. At the time, I voiced my opinion to a lot of white people. [I said,] "Either I'll have freedom or I'll fight you." In Detroit, they said every black had to kill nine whites in order to survive. [I said,] "If I have to kill my nine, I'll take my nine with me."

There was a lot of hostility during that time. It was very frustrating not to be able to go where you wanted, even if you had the money. I had worked [as a busboy] in the Empire Room at the Hotel Utah. I could spit in your food and serve you, but I couldn't go in there and eat with you. That's how basic the discrimination was. If you came to Salt Lake, tired as hell after driving across the highways, as a black person you couldn't get a motel here and had to drive through. And Vegas was even worse. So if you left Salt Lake, you had to drive all the way to the coast or sleep in your car. You weren't going to get a room anywhere.

I remember going into Vegas in 1953 for the [Union Pacific] Railroad. A guy fed us breakfast in the closed part of the café. When we came back for lunch, he couldn't feed us because he had it opened to whites. I jumped up and called him a bunch of sons of bitches, told him he had fed us breakfast, what the hell was the problem now? We were denied there. We were denied a place to sleep.

I remember cutting up a railroad car, totally destroying it. There were twenty of us there from Salt Lake City. The railroad had us down there to pick up Boy Scout troops. They had brought us in twelve hours earlier. We couldn't get a motel room. It was 119 degrees outside. So we went and demanded the railroad do something for us. "We're employees," we said. "We were required to work all night. We need a place to rest." They said they'd put two pullman cars on refrigeration. We could break the berths down, but there would be no linen. We agreed to that. We allowed them three hours. We waited in the cars. The cars were about 140 degrees inside. [When they didn't come] we took knives and opened up every piece of upholstery, tore fountains off, busted the handles.

Let me tell you, it doesn't take much to want to burn a place down. I feel extremely lucky that we didn't have more civil violence than what we had. We were very lucky as far as I'm concerned. What really saved this country was [President] Kennedy supporting Martin Luther King, Jr. Dr. King was outspoken, and [he] made a lot of difference. He gave you hope where there was no hope. He showed us what we could do en masse. Stokely Carmichael and some other black leaders told us we could burn it down. But Kennedy and King offered us a little light— something to keep you going and not abort the wagon. It would have been very easy to jump off the wagon. But they gave us some light where there was no light. So we were very lucky that a social movement, as large as that one, was able to go on without more bloodshed than what we had. You can say what you want about Martin Luther King, Jr., but if he hadn't taught love, if he had taught hate, if the black leadership at that time had been Stokely Carmichael and Malcolm X, we would have had a bloodbath.

EPILOGUE

TERRY LEE WILLIAMS, 36, SENATOR, UTAH STATE LEGISLATURE

One of eight children, Terry Williams was born in Artesia, New Mexico, on March 22, 1950, and moved to Utah with his family in 1960. He received a B.A. from Weber State College and an M.A. in economics from the University of Utah. On November 2, 1980, he became the second black person ever elected to the Utah State House of Representatives; and on October 27, 1982, when he was appointed to serve out a resigning senator's unexpired term, he became Utah's first black state senator.

When I arrived [in the legislature] in 1980, most of the people [in it] were here through the auspices of the LDS church. And that's why I received some ridicule. I mean, they thought I had no place [being] here, because I didn't come through channels. So, I was not only a fluke [in their eyes], but after I got here I was not afforded the same respect and access [to the system] as others. I mean, it was like I had no business here.

There was a movie—I'm sure you're aware of it—called [The] *Birth of a Nation*. It appeared in the '30s, and it showed, graphically, what happens if you let blacks into government. It showed an all-black [state] congress. And these black gentlemen in their three-piece suits had whole watermelons in their arms [and were] digging their heads into them and passing outrageous laws. It's a tremendously horrendous movie.[19] But it was saying, "This is what you can expect if black people are ever in positions of decision-making power."

And I bring it up only to say there was a concept in this country, especially in the more conservative communities, that black people aren't capable of making decisions on behalf of the society or themselves, so whites are chosen

Terry Williams with Coretta King. *Kent Miles*

by God to make decisions for their welfare. That's the biblical foundation for apartheid. And that existed here.

So when I arrived, I met legislators who didn't believe a black person could walk and talk intelligently at the same time. I mean, I was speaking the same language they spoke, I was coming up with the same kinds of ideas, and they were amazed, just amazed, I could do that. They expected a character out of *The Birth of a Nation,* I guess, only from a youthful, militant point of view. They thought, in other words, that I was just going to pound racism at them.

My very first day here in 1980, I remember, we voted for a resolution. Ronald Reagan had just been elected, and a representative sponsored a resolution that said we congratulate him and embrace his policies. Well, I was very green. So, since I didn't believe in [the resolution], I voted no. One of my colleagues kind of sidled up to me, nudged me, and said, "Look up on the board [where the votes are tallied]." I looked up, and there were seventy-four "yes" votes and one "no" vote. He said, "This is a resolution. It doesn't mean anything. Go ahead, change your vote." But I was so green I didn't realize a resolution had no force of law. So I said, "I can't vote yes to something I don't believe in." I said, "I'll just take my vote off." But once you push the yes or no button, you can't electronically take it off the board.

Now, unbeknownst to me, in the hall outside the chamber, one representative asked another, "Whose is that 'no' vote up there?" This guy said, "Oh, that's that black boy across the way." Well, to make a long story short, the press in the hall overheard the comment and reported it. And over the next few days the NAACP and other organizations contacted the Speaker of the House and said, "This man [the one who called me "that black boy"] ought to be censured. He ought to be kicked out." So, on the tenth day, this legislator stood up in the chamber and made a public apology to me. Feeling obligated to respond, I said, "I accept your apology. I know there's no hostility in your heart, and let's be about the business of working for the people of this state."

Now, I'm telling you all this because I *didn't* stand up, pound my desk, and call this guy a racist. So it's not what I did, it's what I *didn't* do, that gained me some initial credibility.

Now, I first sponsored the Martin Luther King, Jr., Holiday Bill in the 1985 legislature. It never saw the light of day. The powers that be up here never let it out of committee. In 1986, all I did was resubmit the bill, the same bill, but in the interim a lot of things happened. Forty other states passed the bill. President Reagan said some kind words on its behalf, and there was a renaissance [of interest] in Dr. King and the civil rights movement throughout America.

So, in my mind, we had a whole year of activities and efforts that lent themselves to the popularity of the concept and the passage of the bill. As a result, when I reentered it, [I] naively thought it would pass. It has national precedent, and it's the right thing to do. I had absolutely no idea that the bill would create a clash of philosophies [here] or that it would receive the negative reception it did. But that's exactly what happened.

And halfway through the legislative session, for all intents and purposes, the bill was dead [in committee]. It was dead in the water. We introduced it, and they killed it. Only they didn't kill it, they tabled it—which is essentially a kill, if you don't enact measures to resurrect it. That's when I went about to get it out of the committee table. [I] finally did that. We got people to vote it out [of the committee and onto the Senate floor]. They didn't want to, but . . . one senator [seemed to speak for others when he] said, "I'll vote it out. But when it gets to the floor, I'm going to vote against it. But I'll vote it out so [Senator] Williams can state his case; then we'll kill it there."

They nearly did. Senators made comments like, "I'm not prejudiced. It's just that it [the new state holiday] will cost [the state] a million and a half dollars." Or, "I'm not prejudiced against Dr. King; it's just that his [civil rights] movement in America is still a secret record with the FBI. And since the records won't be revealed [in full] for fifty years, we ought to wait." Or, "Did you know Dr. King was associated with Communists?" These were ridiculous arguments. But senators came up with every possible argument to defeat the bill rather than speak their true inner feelings.

What they really felt was that they didn't like Martin Luther King, Jr. They didn't believe the civil rights movement did anything for Utah. I heard that many times [off the Senate floor]. They believed this black minister, beginning out of Montgomery, did something good for blacks in the South. They really believed that. But that's it. They didn't know Dr. King spoke up in their behalf as well as everybody else's and that the passage of the [national] Civil Rights Act of 1964, opening public accommodations in hotels, motels, and tourism, was to their benefit, too.

We had the fortunate opportunity [at that time] to bring Mrs. Coretta Scott King in [to address both the Senate and the House], because there [was] a lot of concern about Dr. King's association with the Communist party, his preaching treason, wanting to overthrow the government of this country or to change the constitution.[20] With her help, we began to refute all of those arguments, so there was no question about constitutionality or his associations.

I told my colleagues that in the early '60s anybody who spoke on behalf of civil rights was painted red. Dr. King just fell into that category, and [J. Edgar] Hoover [director of the FBI] didn't like him. And Hoover charged everybody with being a Communist, including [Attorney General] Bobby Kennedy.

But I [soon] realized this wasn't what really concerned people. When it came right down to it, they didn't want to create Martin Luther King Day by displacing Columbus Day or the emancipator's [Abraham Lincoln's] holiday.[21] That was blasphemy to them. They didn't believe this black man did anything [of that stature] for this country, much less the state of Utah. And this [maneuver] simply wasn't in keeping with their personal philosophies. They would state this to me individually in rooms like this or in the hallway or in the bathroom.[22] But they couldn't bring themselves to say that at the microphone, before the press and the people who elected them. So we were in a tough spot.

[Finally,] after weeks of debate, we got thrown into what's called a conference committee, because the House wouldn't agree with what the Senate did and the Senate wouldn't agree with what the House did. We got four members from each body, and we met in this very room, on this very couch and these chairs. There were ten of us gathered here, including staff members, to talk about what conclusion we could come to.

Well, I knew this was the time and [this was] the place. A decision had to be made one way or the other. Either we were going to get the bill or we weren't. And I said, "Every Thursday we send these beautiful young men out of this state." This was my quintessential argument. I said, "We send these fine gentlemen out on United Airlines every Thursday morning to all parts of the world to be missionaries [and] to proselytize for the LDS church. What do you think is going to happen to them when they go to other states in the Union?" I said, "They are going to get off their planes, and people are going to say, 'You're from that state that didn't pass the Martin Luther King Holiday, aren't you?'"

I just said that, being desperate. . . . And you could have heard a pin drop in this room. I could see the pondering thoughts on their faces, and one of the senators spoke up: "You know, I never thought about that. Senator Williams, you are absolutely right." What brought them to the brink and over was the recognition that what we do here, regardless of whether we [fully] believe in it, would affect the status of this state and how it stands in the nation. [If we didn't pass the bill] when forty-nine other states had chosen to do what the president had embraced as a national holiday, we would be singular in our denial.

So, I touched a nerve in the Mormon mentality, because I learned a long time ago that the Mormon church is proud and places itself in the public eye in the best light possible, all of the time. And this decision would have detracted from that. It would have reflected badly upon their religion. And that's when I knew I had it, I had the bill. Within four days, we came to a consensus about technical matters.[23] Then the bill was sent to Governor Bangerter. He signed it right away.

NOTES

1. She is describing the Holladay area of Salt Lake City, which was home for a sizable number of black Mormon families at the turn of the twentieth century. The Leggroans, the Bankheads, the Chambers, and the Howells (descendants of the first blacks to enter Utah Territory as slaves) all farmed there.

2. On June 8, 1978, the president of the Mormon church, Spencer W. Kimball, announced that he had received a "revelation" from God to rescind the 130-year ban preventing blacks, the seed of Cain, from holding priesthood in the church. "He has heard our prayers," said Kimball, "and by revelation has confirmed that the long-promised day has come when every faithful, worthy man in the church may receive the holy priesthood. . . . Accordingly, all worthy male members of the Church may be ordained to the priesthood without regard for race or color." Lester Bush, Jr., and Armand L. Mauss, eds., *Neither White Nor Black: Mormon Scholars Confront the Race Issue in a Universal Church* (Midvale, Utah: Signature Books, 1984), 225.

3. In an interview conducted by the Oral History Institute on June 13, 1983, Edward Steward, Mrs. Fry's younger brother, described the underground rest rooms: "On the corner of 3rd South and State Street, there used to be two restrooms: one for men and the other for ladies. They're torn down now, but they were by the Centre Theatre, below the walk level. There was urinals along one wall, toilets on the other. The floors were all white tile, and the roof was made of a heavy glass. The toilet at the end was for my dad's private use, but he used to rent it out for a nickel. He also had a locker room, where you could check parcels for a dime; shoe shines were ten cents; soap and towel were five cents."

4. The Brotherhood of Sleeping Car Porters (the pullman porter's union) was begun on August 25, 1925, in New York City. A. Philip Randolph, publisher of the pro-labor magazine *The Messenger*, became the union's central organizer. Jervis Anderson, Randolph's biographer, explained Randolph's efforts on behalf of the union in *A. Philip Randolph: A Biographical Portrait* (Berkeley: University of California Press, 1986): "[Randolph] looked upon the Brotherhood as . . . a symbol of the strug-

gle by black Americans to build and sustain movements for their own political and economic salvation" (p. 193). The Pullman Company wasn't sympathetic, though. It refused to meet with Randolph and threatened, fired, or suspended porters suspected of joining the brotherhood or helping organize on its behalf. The first signed agreement between the company and the union came in 1937, twelve years after the formation of the brotherhood.

5. Part of the legislation enacted under President Lyndon Johnson's Great Society initiative, the Model Cities program sought to give low-income people and elected local officials greater control over federal resources earmarked for urban planning.

6. Historian Ronald Coleman's account of the hanging differs slightly from Browne's. According to Coleman, Robert Marshall was taken from his Price jail and hung in stages. "The rope was pulled until he lost consciousness; he was then revived by burning his soles with matches. The pulling and burning continued until Marshall died to the cheers of men, women, and children who smiled for a photographer." Ronald G. Coleman, "Blacks in Utah History: An Unknown Legacy," in Helen Z. Papanikolas, ed., *The Peoples of Utah* (Salt Lake City: Utah State Historical Society, 1976), 115–140.

7. Their names were Gertrude and Edward Browne.

8. The Kiwanis and Elks clubs in Salt Lake City, the Gemmel Club in Magna, and the West Jordan and Fairmont clubs all supported boxing programs after World War II.

9. The Railroad Porters and Waiters Club was started by Billy Weekly in 1912 to house black railroad employees during their layovers. The club accommodated approximately fifty men when it opened. In 1920, twenty-three additional rooms were built, and by the beginning of World War II, the club was able to house over one hundred men at a time. In 1959, due to the decrease in national railway traffic, the hotel portion was closed, and the Porters and Waiters Club was transformed into a night club/restaurant. In 1970, Mrs. Anna Belle Weekly closed it up and had the building torn down.

10. Emmett Till, a fourteen-year-old Chicago boy, was visiting relatives near Money, Mississippi, on August 28, 1955. According to news stories, Till, his cousin, and other youngsters were headed to a local store to buy gum when he whistled at the wife of the local, white storekeeper. Later that day, Till was kidnapped and murdered by the storekeeper and his half brother. Four days later, "the youngster's body was found weighted with metal, floating in the Tallahatchie River. Young Emmett had been shot through the head and, with seventy pounds of weights tied to his head, thrown into the river." *Salt Lake Tribune* (February 11, 1989).

11. Dr. Charles Nabors was on the executive committee of the Salt Lake City NAACP. Dr. Nabors' interview follows. In those early years, Dr. Nabors was regarded as one of the more radical members of the board of the NAACP.

12. The National Urban League was founded in 1910. According to the CBS News reference book on civil rights, by 1970 it was considered "one of the most . . . effective of all civil rights groups." It had 101 affiliates in thirty-four states and the District of Columbia. Dependent on contributions from individuals, the federal government, and industry, the league emphasized furthering the economic power of blacks through training and apprenticeship programs. Joan Martin Burke, *A CBS News Reference Book—Civil Rights: A Current Guide to the People, Organizations, and Events* (New York: R. R. Bowker Company, 1974), 115–116.

13. To compel the U.S. Justice Department to enforce a federal statute prohibiting segregation "in vehicles engaged in interstate travel . . . [and] at all terminal accommodations," James Farmer, the director of the Congress of Racial Equality (CORE), issued a nationwide call in March 1961 "for volunteers to conduct freedom rides through the South." Seven blacks and six whites (including Farmer) responded; and

on May 4, 1961, "split into two interracial groups," they left Washington, D.C., on a Greyhound and a Trailways bus and began their journey into the deep South. The aim of CORE was to create a major racial confrontation—something the freedom riders were sure to do simply by having blacks and whites ride together—that would force the federal government to intervene. Following brutal attacks on these freedom riders by mobs in Birmingham and Montgomery, Alabama, and their arrest in Jackson, Mississippi, the government did intervene. On September 22, 1961, the Interstate Commerce Commission "announced that interstate carriers and terminals *must* display signs stating that seating '*is without regard to race, color, creed, or national origin*'" [emphasis added]. A year later, CORE proclaimed that "the battle of interstate travel had been finally won." Harvard Sitkoff, *The Struggle for Black Equality 1954–1980* (New York: Hill and Wang, 1981), 96–110.

14. Ernest L. Wilkinson, an attorney and a state legislator, later became the president of Brigham Young University.

15. The speech Dr. Nabors is referring to, "The Atlanta Address," was given by Booker T. Washington, the founder of Tuskegee Institute in Alabama, on September 18, 1895. Called upon to address the southern cotton states and the International Exposition in Atlanta, Washington emphasized that Negroes must concentrate on winning the respect of whites by acquiring manual skills. His focus was on the Negro's need to pull himself up "by his own bootstraps," rather than on civil rights. In effect, Washington condoned racial separation, encouraging, instead, economic cooperation between the races.

16. H. Rap Brown, whose real name was Hubert Gerold Brown, succeeded Stokely Carmichael as the chairman of the Student Nonviolent Coordinating Committee (SNCC) in 1967. He received national attention when, on July 22, 1967, at a Washington, D.C., rally, he said: "This country was born of violence. Violence is as American as cherry pie. Black people have always been violent, but our violence has always been directed toward each other. If nonviolence is to be practiced . . . it should be practiced in our community and end there." Burke, *A CBS News Reference Book,* 19.

17. The Porters and Waiters Club in Salt Lake City was a separate entity from its Ogden namesake. In addition, it had no sleeping facilities; it was a private black nightclub.

18. Stokely Carmichael was one of the founders of the Student Nonviolent Coordinating Committee in 1960. Six years later, he became one of the leading proponents of the Black Power movement. The movement advocated self-defense, when necessary, for blacks and repudiated Martin Luther King, Jr.'s, strategy of nonviolence. In the book *Black Power: The Politics of Liberation in America* (New York: Vintage Books, 1967), which Carmichael coauthored with Charles V. Hamilton, the authors explained: "The advocates of Black Power reject the old slogans and meaningless rhetoric of previous years in the civil rights struggle. The language of yesterday is . . . irrelevant: progress, non-violence, integration. . . . Such language . . . misled some into believing that a black minority could bow its head and get whipped into a meaningful position of power. The very notion is absurd. . . . From our viewpoint, rampaging white mobs and white night-riders must be made to understand that their days of free head-whipping are over. . . . Those of us who advocate Black Power are quite clear in our minds that a 'non-violent' approach to civil rights is an approach black people cannot afford and a luxury white people do not deserve" (pp. 50–53).

19. D. W. Griffith's *The Birth of a Nation* appeared as a silent film in 1915. It was later reissued in 1930, when Griffith added a sound track. The movie chronicled the South's loss of the Civil War and the alleged "horrors" of Reconstruction. Griffith solemnly celebrated blacks loyal to the South's rigid caste system but presented blacks seeking political and social equality with whites as buffoons or as venal, treacherous,

vindictive monsters. A nearly all-black South Carolina State Legislature was shown on a normal workday. One legislator sat with his bare feet on his desk, another surreptitiously slipped a bottle of whiskey out of his jacket pocket and took a hearty swig, still another was engaged in heated debate, gesticulating wildly, while holding a huge drumstick. The Ku Klux Klan were the film's heroes. Through the force of arms, they restored the social order. Blacks were put "back in their places," and the reins of government were returned to whites.

20. Addressing the combined Utah Senate and House, Mrs. Martin Luther King, Jr., said, "Martin lived his philosophy of nonviolence. It was a way of life for him. . . . He always said that it was easy to do right in public but it is much more difficult when no one is watching. If one is consistent in one's philosophy and behavior, people will begin to respect you and follow you. . . . He was believable because he was an example of what he taught. . . . He did so much for America at a [critical] time. . . .

"When we celebrated the holiday [for the first time] last January 20th, . . . we tried to bring people together in this nation in a day of nonviolence [and] solidarity. We wanted it to be an all-American holiday, and I think it was in character the kind of holiday that we would like to see it continue to be. . . . We thought that it was important that it not be just a holiday for black people or just any one group but for all people. This is the message that I continue to carry around the country. Martin Luther King, Jr., Day must be a day that is all-inclusive. If we seek to make it anything else, then it is not true to his spirit." *Journal of the Utah State House of Representatives* (February 6, 1986, Day 25), 427.

21. After Senator Williams introduced his bill, amended Senate and House versions of the bill appeared calling for the Dr. Martin Luther King, Jr., holiday to replace, respectively, Columbus Day and Abraham Lincoln's Birthday. Both bills were ostensibly aimed at keeping the state from spending additional funds on the new holiday.

22. The interview was conducted in one of the Senate's conference rooms.

23. To mollify social and fiscal conservatives, the committee renamed Washington's Birthday, celebrated on the third Monday in February, "Abraham Lincoln/George Washington/Presidents' Day." The final compromise thus added a new holiday, maintained previous holidays, and kept the state from incurring additional costs.

BOOK THREE
JEWISH COMMUNITY

PREFACE

Jack Goodman with Michael Walton

The United States is a nation peopled almost wholly by immigrants from other lands and their descendants. Aside from Native-Americans occupying sorry remnants of their once pristine lands, the nation's people are, in the words of Franklin D. Roosevelt, "Americans all, immigrants all." FDR himself descended from early Dutch and English settlers of the Hudson River Valley. Even those thoughtless Daughters of the American Revolution who refused to let Marion Anderson raise her glorious voice in their Washington, D.C., hall had as forebears English, Scots, Irish, Welsh, Danes, French, Spaniards, or Portuguese who emigrated to the new land prior to 1776.

The nation has been considered the Goldeneh Medinah, the golden land, by many peoples. To be sure, some settlers arrived in the new nation earlier than others. Some religious outcasts escaped the Old World on board the *Mayflower*. Many others came as slaves, unwilling cargo penned in fetid holds. By the middle of the nineteenth century, English, Irish, and Scandinavians crowded aboard speedy clipper ships. Later still, immigrants, many Jews among them, paid for steerage passage on crowded Nordeutscher Lloyd or Hamburg-American vessels. Most of those Jews bade none-too-happy farewells to the lands of kings, czars, or the Austro-Hungarian emperor, sailing mainly from Bremen or Hamburg.

Whatever the port of departure, most would never again venture on the high seas. Instead, offering fervent prayers of thanks for their safe passage, they spilled out across a continent broader than most could imagine. A majority settled in coastal cities, traveling as far west as St. Louis, St. Joseph, Chicago, or Cincinnati. Of the few who ventured beyond the Missouri River, fewer still crossed the Rocky Mountains prior to the completion of the transcontinental railroad. But a handful of adventurous men and women of Jewish faith

With Michael Walton's permission, the editors incorporated a small portion of his unpublished essay, "The Jews of Utah," into this preface.

did reach the Great Basin almost simultaneously with the 1847 arrival of the Mormon pioneers' first wagons.

Although no Jewish names appear as 1847 "First Company" participants on the Brigham Young monument on Salt Lake City's Main Street, some Jews certainly rode aboard the slow-moving Mormon wagons en route to the West Coast. In his carefully kept journal, Mormon leader Lorenzo Brown wrote, on March 1, 1851, "Called to see some Hungarian Jews living in the ward . . . emigrants bound for the [California] mines . . . forced to leave their native land because of the revolution." He was referring to the revolts of 1848 that rocked sizable sections of Central Europe, the old Holy Roman Empire. When the revolution failed, thousands were forced to flee to the shores of a new land.

One of the most adventurous Jewish newcomers was Solomon Nunes Carvalho, who reached Utah in 1853 but did not linger there long. A South Carolina native of Portuguese and Sephardic Jewish descent, this thirty-nine year old artist, cartographer, daguerreotypist, and writer was a member of John C. Fremont's military mapmaking expedition that was crisscrossing the trackless Rocky Mountains and Great Basin in 1853 and 1854. Carvalho's name appears prominently in accounts dealing with this military venture into the unknown West.

Carvalho's *Incidents of Travel and Adventure in the Far West* remains a little-known classic. In it, he wrote of concocting a Rosh Hashanah meal featuring "horse soup and horse steaks fried in buffalo tallow" with expedition members, all of whom nearly perished of cold and starvation near today's Parowan, Utah. After finally reaching the Mormon settlement and thawing out, the intrepid Carvalho backtracked to Salt Lake City, where, before leaving, he produced portraits of Brigham Young, Daniel Wells, the Indian chief Wakara, and other Native-Americans. His portraits give anthropologists a rare, authentic record of the headdresses and clothing of Great Basin tribes.

The first Jews known to have made their homes in Utah and prosper in merchandising were Julius Gerson Brooks and his wife, Isabell, who was rather inexplicably nicknamed Fanny. A Silesian, Julius spent some years in New England, working as a peddler, before returning to Silesia to marry his child-bride (she was just sixteen years old) and journey to Salt Lake City. In cities and towns throughout the nation, Jewish immigrants similarly found new lives in the new land.

One story concerning the Brookses may or may not be apocryphal but is worth repeating. Heading west by way of Illinois, they encountered an ex-army officer who told fascinating tales of opportunities in distant places—tales that spurred Julius and Fanny on their journey west. The former army officer turned farmer was Ulysses S. Grant, who was himself never too successful in any occupation until he returned to army service when the Civil War began.

Traveling with a train of fifteen wagons, Julius and Fanny Brooks reached the valley of the Great Salt Lake in July 1854 and decided to make Salt Lake City their home. In a few months, the Mormon *Millennial Star* listed, among the new city's twenty-two business establishments, "Mrs. Brooks' Millinery and Bakery." Mrs. Brooks apparently settled down immediately, but restless Julius went on to Boise and San Francisco, trying his hand at storekeeping, before returning to Salt Lake City. The Brookses were soon to join forces with Samuel S. Auerbach, who drove into town in 1859 with a wagonload of "store goods" from California, where he had been in business with his brothers, Frederick and Theodore. The Prussian-born trio ran tent stores at such gold rush towns as Bodie and Rabbit Creek, California.

While Samuel, the youngest brother, began a new life in Salt Lake City, his brother Fred traded at Camp Floyd, a Utah post set up in 1857 by troops under Colonel Albert Sidney Johnston, before going on to Salt Lake City. The bluecoats of "Johnston's Army" had come to Utah when President James Buchanan sought to quiet the near warfare between Mormons and the far-from-evenhanded federal judges and territorial governors assigned to the belligerent region.

Later, after a reported conference with Brigham Young, Fred Auerbach, with Samuel as his partner, established "the People's Store" on Salt Lake City's Main Street. Meanwhile, Theodore moved to New York.

F. Auerbach and Bros. flourished, moving into larger and larger quarters and finally settling in a department store at State and Broadway that was for many years the city's best-known non-Mormon institution. When a Brooks son married Fanny Auerbach, the families joined to build the Brooks Arcade which is still standing at State and Broadway.

By the time the Auerbachs set up their store, the rails of the Union Pacific and Central Pacific had been joined with a golden spike at Promontory, and numerous other German Jewish merchants had arrived in "Zion." Among them were the three Siegal brothers, Ichel and Abraham Watters, Charles Popper, Simon Bamberger, Nathan and James Ellis, and Nicholas Siegfried Ransahoff. The latter became a good friend of Mormon leader Brigham Young and lent him ten thousand dollars to purchase Camp Floyd's entire stock of pork when the post's troops went off to the Civil War. Ransahoff, who apparently held Orthodox dietary principles, must have been unwilling to buy the pork for his own profit, due to his distaste for *treyfa* (unclean) meat.

During this time, the Auerbachs and the other Jews of Salt Lake City, all labeled "Gentiles" by the Latter-day Saints, became enmeshed in an economic war resulting from Mormon charges that non-Saints were outrageously overcharging LDS members. The conflict centered around the church's newly formed Zions Cooperative Mercantile Institution (ZCMI). Although church leaders looked with more favor upon the Auerbachs, Ransahoffs, and other Jewish merchants than other non-Mormon tradespeople, the former were not spared the ire of the Mormon leadership.

Fearing Brigham Young's wrath, most "Gentile" merchants fled the city, establishing a new community at Corinne, near the shores of the Great Salt Lake, where the railroads, wagon trains from the Montana mines, and even a lake steamboat exchanged goods. ZCMI, meanwhile, its signboards reading "Holiness to the Lord," flourished and opened cooperative branches in many

Utah towns. But Brigham Young soon halted the economic warfare, and by the 1880s most merchants—Jewish and genuine Gentiles—moved back to Salt Lake City to resume business and to build a community. At the end of the decade, ninety-one Jewish businesses operated in the city, and approximately two hundred Jews lived in the state.

By 1910, the nation experienced the second, and by far the largest, in-migration of European Jews. Previously, uprisings against the Habsburgs had impelled hundreds of thousands of Jews to migrate to the new world. But refugees fleeing Czarist Russia's pogroms, anti-Jewish ordinances, and military conscription now arrived by the millions. A portion of these immigrants, their families, and their children—whose vivid recollections form this chapter—became Salt Lake City's first sizable generation of peddlers, storekeepers, merchants, and miners. The years between the world wars became the heyday of Jewish merchants, who set up shops on State Street, Main Street, and the cross-streets between South Temple and Fourth Street. Some shops sold workingmen's clothing; others, stylish millinery. Jewish peddlers sold produce from fruit and vegetable wagons or bought and sold scrap metal, sacks, barrels, and sheepskins. On State Street, Ben Ramo's Golden Rule store sold workingmen's clothes to railroad laborers and construction workers. Gallenson's Jewelry was a door or two down, and Max's clothing store, the Hub, Tannenbaum's Army and Navy, Wolfe's sporting goods store, and Axelrad's furniture store were nearby. The Tannenbaums became semiofficial purveyors to park rangers, servicemen, mail carriers, and policemen. Soon every Utah man made a seasonal pilgrimage to Wolfe's or rival Zinik's on Main Street to purchase reels and creels, wading or hiking boots, skis, snowshoes, or hunting equipment.

The names of other newly arrived merchants easily come to mind, such as the "Mad Hatters," Adolf and Ed Berkowitz; Harold Findling of the Boston Store; Harold and Ben Roe, who owned an emporium; Joshua Shapiro, who owned a luggage store; and Aaron Hirsch, who sold menswear. Nearly all of their shops employed Jewish alteration tailors and salespeople. Showing preference in this way was not unusual; after all most Mormon establishments employed chiefly Latter-day Saints.

In the beginning of their lives in Mormon Zion, most Jewish immigrant peddlers and neophyte shopkeepers lived with their families in downtown alley streets, such as Kuster Court off Fifth South or behind small State Street shops. However, Salt Lake City had no enduring ghetto, no festering slum. Although life was hard in the local equivalents of "cold-water flats" or tenements, there were quiet backyards, often with trees, behind many shops. There were schools at which Jewish newcomers were admitted and educated. And there were shuls (houses of worship) or at least a *melamed* (a teacher) who ran a cheder where thirteen-year old boys could prepare for bar mitzvah.

Prior to 1875, the majority of Salt Lake City's Jews were from parts of newly unified Germany. But in subsequent decades, the more massive immigration of Russian Jews occurred. The initial immigrants spoke German; the newer arrivals spoke Russian and Yiddish. In Utah, as elsewhere, a schism among Jews developed along religious, social, and language lines. The earlier arrivals developed the city's Reform congregation, comprised mainly of German-speakers. In 1883, they built the heavy-domed, gray-painted Temple B'nai Israel, a building still standing on Fourth East that is now the home of the Office Pavilion design company. In 1904, in the midst of the heavy influx of Russian and Polish Jews, the more orthodox Congregation Montefiore opened on Third East, housed in a structure graced by twin towers, each topped by a Moorish-style dome.

The structures housing the congregations are themselves of considerable interest. A young German architect, Philip Meyer, brought to Utah by the Auerbach family, modeled B'nai Israel after a Berlin synagogue that was later bombed and burned in Allied air raids. Meyer, who returned to Berlin after B'nai Israel's completion, perished along with millions of fellow Jews in Hitler's death camps. The style of Congregation Montefiore's synagogue can be partially traced to the influence of the Moors, who brought their culture to Spain before Columbus discovered the New World.

As in larger centers of faith in New York, Cincinnati, Los Angeles, and even Montreal, bitter battles often occurred between members of the Reform congregation with services in English and those of the more orthodox synagogue with traditional services in Hebrew and Yiddish. At the prime of the life of both synagogues as ideological centers (ca. 1900–1940), the perception of the congregations was that the rabbis of B'nai Israel often acted as community ambassadors to the Mormons, whereas the rabbis of Montefiore were primarily concerned with maintaining faithfulness to rabbinic, or traditional, Judaism. Although the members of the congregations interacted regularly through secular Jewish organizations such as B'nai Brith, these contacts did not overcome cultural and ideological differences. The marriage of a member of one congregation to a member of the other was laughingly considered a "mixed" one.

During the ensuing years, tempers cooled, and as a result of post-wartime cooperation, Americanization, and economic integration, traditional and Reform Jews moved toward each other socially and religiously. In 1969, the two Sunday Schools united to reduce the expense of maintaining separate Hebrew school faculties. In 1970, a consolidation committee was established; and in 1972, the two congregations officially merged to form Synagogue Kol Ami, a name that means "All my people." After seventy-five years of wrangling, Salt Lake City Jews, as historian Bob Goldberg observed, "had removed the organizational wedges that divided them."[1]

Today, Congregation Kol Ami serves about 550 family members; and Utah estimates its statewide Jewish population at five thousand people, five times the total at the turn of the twentieth century. Today, there are at least as many Jewish professionals in Salt Lake City as there once were Jewish merchants. The major "brain influx" began shortly after World War II, when the University of Utah's new four-year medical college attracted men like Dr. Maxwell Wintrobe, a world expert on hematology, and Dr. Louis Goodman, whose books on pharmacology were deemed "bibles" in the profession. In the meantime, Dr. Louis Zucker gained a considerable reputation in the English department of the university, and almost simultaneously, Maurice Abravanel abandoned Broadway musicals and the Metropolitan Opera to become the long-term conductor of the Utah Symphony.

In other fields, radio entrepreneur Sid Fox established KDYL-TV, channel 4; Sid Cohen fostered a mysterious something called "cable"; and news correspondents such as Allan Moll, Allen Frank, and Dan Rainger became active in both radio and television. Throughout the 1960s and 1970s, professional ranks of the Jewish community were swelled with the arrival of university-affiliated professors, researchers, and physicians and university-trained social workers, therapists, teachers, and attorneys. When American Express and other corporations moved their operating centers to Salt Lake City, they also brought key personnel, some of whom were Jewish and became active in the city's developing Jewish community.

Yet, even with this steady in-migration, there are still few neighborhoods in Salt Lake City in which Jews are more than a tiny minority. Like small Jewish communities elsewhere in America, Utah Jewry faces the need to preserve its identity in a nonnurturing environment. It is not that Jews face open hostility from members of the Mormon church. On the contrary, nowhere in America is there less anti-Semitism, greater interest in Judaism, or a warmer expression of camaraderie from an organized dominant religious group. Indeed, Mormons are largely confused about the status of their Jewish "cousins." They believe the Jews are descended from the Israelite tribe of Judah, and they trace their own descent from Joseph, through Ephraim. With their similar backgrounds, are Jews to be classified as a special population? And how can the Jews be grouped with "Gentiles"?

Nevertheless, Jews suspect that this brotherly love is sparked by self-serving motivations. Invitations to Jewish youngsters to participate in Primary and Mutual and Mormon youths' involvement with Jewish youth in meaningful social relations are presumed to be efforts to attract them into the church.[2] Certainly, the LDS church does not discourage such conversions. So, no matter the extent of social ties among Jews and Mormons, this source of tension usually lies beneath the surface.

Jews, like many other minorities in Utah and elsewhere, suffer most from the absence of any "recognition" of their presence. A common complaint is that community decisions made by Utah's political and legal authorities (especially Mormon religious authorities) usually do not take into account the needs of the state's non-Mormons. The Mormons, the argument goes, act as if society were homogeneous, whereas the minorities seek pluralism. Consequently, the culture that has evolved among Salt Lake City Jews is one of a special adaptation to the circumstances of another's culture. Physically isolated in the Intermountain West, Utah's Jews struggle to maintain a strong sense of Jewish identity and community. They strive to embrace and integrate the increasing numbers of Jewish newcomers who settle in the state and make it their home.

As the following interviews indicate, they have accomplished and are still accomplishing this task with ingenuity, determination, and élan.

NOTES

1. Robert Goldberg, "The Jewish Community in Utah," in Helen Z. Papanikolas, ed., *Separate Journeys* (Salt Lake City, Utah: Repertory Dance Theatre, 1991), 21.
2. Primary is a class for boys and girls between the ages of three and twelve. The children meet at the neighborhood ward house each Sunday for an hour of religious instructions. Mutual is the organization for young men and women between the ages of twelve and eighteen. They meet twice a week (one of those days being Sunday) for religious instruction and related social activities.

Ed Eisen. *Kent Miles*

Doris Guss. *George Janecek*

PROLOGUE

HARRY ISADORE SMITH, 71, CHICKEN FARMER

With his face weathered and lined, Harry Smith looked well-scuffed by the years. Born on July 12, 1912, in Ogden, Utah, he was raised on a chicken farm where hard work for little financial gain was the way of life. After graduating at the top of his accounting class at the University of Utah in 1928, he sincerely believed he would lead a better life away from farming. But tight money during the Depression caused him to leave the Stanford Graduate School of Business and compelled him to return to chicken farming. He purchased his own farm on the southeast side of Salt Lake City in 1940 and, following a period of feverish wartime activity selling eggs for the war effort, settled into a routine in which survival became the norm. Smith sold his farm in 1972 and, at the age of seventy, began a second career by opening a Men's Army and Navy Store.

What my dad did coming out West was to become a peddler. He went from house to house or farm to farm to gather up what was considered practically worthless merchandise, or if it had some value, he'd give a very small amount of money to take it away. He would then sell it to his brother-in-law, the junk dealer, Joseph Kraines. That was in Ogden.

Originally, both of my parents were from what was Poland at that time. My mother came from Tow Pruzanski Breza Kartuzka. I remember that because, as a young boy going to junior high school, I was the one who was instrumental in bundling up bags of clothing for our relatives and writing their address on at least ten different labels so that each package had the right permission to be delivered to the right person in Poland. Of course, we didn't know whether those packages ever got to them, but that didn't deter us from trying.

After my family settled in Utah, my father and an uncle went up to Preston, Idaho, for the sole purpose of survival—to find work. These trips were very hard on my mother because he'd be gone from home for weeks at a time, looking for low-cost merchandise to resell. When he did get a job in Salt Lake as a mattress maker, the location of the company was a two-hour drive by horses. So, aside from the minimum ten- or twelve-hour day (there was no such thing as an eight-hour day), he spent an additional four hours traveling. He would come home just to sleep, and early the next day he'd be on the road again. That went on for years. Finally, the whole thing got to be too much for him and my mother, and he got out of that line of work and started a poultry business in Ogden.

Now, raising poultry was a risky business. Medicine was about as backward for humans at that time as it was for chickens. Anybody who regarded himself as an authority on chickens was a fake! And no matter how many chickens you had, if you had chickens, you had trouble! There were epidemics, I remember, that no medicine would help, and a disease like "laryngo tracheitis" could take thirty percent of your chickens. Vaccinating chickens against chicken pox also wasn't practical, because they'd still come down with the disease. Fifty percent of your chickens could get wiped out easily.

So there were never any easy years because of "this" disease or "that" disease. Still, my dad did everything that he could. His hours were long. I would say long and bitter. In his determination to stay home, though, he was willing to work seven days a week, week after week.

Dad was written up as one of the early pioneers in the poultry business. In the 1920s, people like him didn't know about protein, carbohydrates, starch, or fats. For instance, he didn't know how to control diseases or what to feed chickens or even how to feed them. He didn't know that cod-liver oil incorporated in chicken feed could prevent lameness that struck five to ten percent of chickens during the winters, or that your chickens were bound to get worms if you didn't put cement floors in your chicken coop. I'll tell you, raising chickens was an unproven existence, and he learned many things by "intuition" alone.

I remember that he fed his chickens horse meat for protein even though he didn't know about protein. He even made a trip to California to buy a bone grinder, because he believed bonemeal was nutritional. After a hard day's work, and long after we'd gone to bed, he'd stay up late at night, grinding bones for feed. After using the carcass for chicken feed, he learned how to salt the hides for sale. He made use of everything. Later on, we'd go with him to Utah Lake and buy truckloads of carp, another great source of protein, to feed the chickens. There was so much to learn, I think Dad paid a big price for being a pioneer in the industry.

A lot of our early business was with the railroad that bought all the eggs we could produce so they could provide their travelers with fresh eggs for breakfast. An egg is comprised of eighty percent water, and it is important to minimize the evaporation of water in the egg by supplying a barrier of moist air onto the egg. Since these were the days before air-conditioning, we provided the moisture by laying wet gunnysacks over the eggs. By 1940, though, air-conditioning came into effect, and we put in refrigeration.

I did a little of everything on the farm. At times, we had eight thousand chickens, which was a lot in those days, and depending on what year I was in school, I would feed the chickens, gather the eggs, and candle them, checking for blood spots. In the warmer weather, I'd say I worked six hours a day after school, putting in an average of forty hours a week, without even questioning whether I should or not.

The Great Depression hit us hard. Eggs were nine cents a dozen, and the cost of feed was eight cents. Still, we felt lucky we had a place to work and a way to make a living, no matter how small. And we got by. After high school, I attended the University of Utah. I had a car by then. It may have been an affluent thing for a boy to have during those times, but I did enough work to warrant it. I worked on the farm in Ogden from Friday afternoon until Sunday and then drove to Salt Lake Monday morning in time for classes. It was an hour's drive if I broke the law long enough, which I did.

Going to the University in Salt Lake was wonderful. It seemed like there would be opportunities to do worthwhile things in such a big city. I graduated in accounting and worked in an accounting office as an apprentice for two years. But the Depression was very tough. The firm couldn't keep me on after my apprenticeship. It had nothing to do with me personally. They just didn't have the work.

I began graduate school at Stanford School of Business on a two-year scholarship, but there was no money for books, food, transportation, or housing. And there was no promise—no chance—of employment. I went back to the poultry business. After all that schooling, it was quite a letdown for me to have to remain in the poultry business, working with my father for a long period of time. I had few friends, and socially, those were very, very quiet times; but having a place to work was a godsend.

I stayed in Ogden until 1940. Then I got married, and following in my father's footsteps, I bought a chicken ranch out at Seventieth South and Twenty-third East. On that day, my dad said, "Harry, you've just made ten thousand dollars." Little did he know that it was going to be very, very profitable for only four to five years.

See, World War II had started, and people were going away into the army. Every person who grew three thousand or more chickens, however, was automatically classified as essential to the war effort and could stay at home on the ranch to produce food. Well, I had twelve thousand chickens, and my ranch became more profitable. I worked very hard, but I didn't mind it because of two reasons, which were the strongest reasons in the world. Hitler was my mortal enemy, and I was blessed that I could stay home and raise enough eggs to take care of the troops.

Right after the war, I was a little ambitious and, following another man's idea, built a twenty-thousand-square-foot building that was round in nature. Unfortunately, while a round building can keep an operator happy, it's death on chickens. I'm used to sickness, so at first, when the chickens started dying, it wasn't startling. But when we started losing one hundred a day, I couldn't understand why. I looked at myself as being an experienced farmer who had gone through all the chicken diseases in the world, but I'd never seen anything like this. Within two days, a chicken's comb would turn black and she'd be dead.

Looking for solutions, I barked up all the wrong trees. All the authorities could do was find secondary invaders and tell me to spend one hundred dollars a day for sulfur drugs. I knew that wouldn't work. Finally, my heart told me what to do. I told my men, "Don't ask me why, but let's move out half of the chickens, whether they're well, sick, or dead, into the vacant coops. And in [the round house], we'll put in fans to pull the air out."

Would you believe it? Within three weeks, it was an entirely different picture. The chickens were fine. The problem was in the design. There was no easy flow of oxygen in the round structure. See, in our old coops [that were] twenty feet wide, all you had to do was open the window and you'd get easy circulation of air. But in the round building, with its 150-foot diameter, there was so little air, the chickens were dying from breathing in their own carbon dioxide.

Well, I operated here until 1968. Actually, in 1962, I reached the conclusion that I couldn't continue any longer under the same basis, because I became obsolete. It's interesting my obsolescence came through another invention. We used to put five hundred chickens to a coop, with each coop close by and the younger chickens a distance away for safety purposes. Well, a guy from Minnesota had a brainstorm that if he were to put thirty thousand chickens in one room, they would give off enough BTUs [British thermal units] per hour to heat a building in the frigid Minnesota winters. There was no way I was going to be able to—or wanted to—borrow two hundred thousand dollars and put in sixty thousand layers [hens]. I wasn't going to do that.

Of course, you don't just give it up like that. You've got chickens; you've got coops; you're still in business. You say to yourself, it might be unprofitable this year, but maybe next year it will be better. That's what the family always says: "Next year will be better." But after another three years, I could see it wasn't getting any better. So I had another brainstorm—to become a breeder of pedigreed eggs without having to change the ranch itself. For a couple of years, I did pretty fair as a breeder. Then a California company broke our contract. And even though we had a legal battle and I won some money, it was just a stopgap. I now realize the whole damn thing was a stopgap. See, even your ego can be false. You can think you know what it's all about. . . .

DORIS N. GUSS, 75, HOUSEWIFE

"I'm from the old school," Doris Guss confided near the end of our interview with her, which was conducted three months after her husband's death. "For the first thirty days [after Sam died], I didn't go anywhere; I didn't do anything. That's the way I was raised. My son is saying Kaddish for the whole year.[1] That's the way we are. And it isn't just mourning when you say the Kaddish. The Kaddish means that you pray you can be a blessing to his memory—all that he was and all that he is. That none of us do anything to desecrate his name. That's what a memorial is."

Born in Chicago, Illinois, on December 16, 1909, Doris Guss and her family moved to Daisy Creek, Idaho, in 1916 to homestead 160 acres of farmland. The wide-open land was exhilarating for a city girl, Doris recalled, but "too isolated for my mother, who was a very religious person." So the following year, they relocated to Ogden, Utah, where her father found work with the Union Pacific Railroad. At the age of seventeen, Doris met her husband, Sam Guss, an immigrant from Wlodova, Poland. They were

NORMAN NATHAN, 86, MUSICIAN, BUSINESSMAN

My father emigrated from Russia in 1889; he came to Salt Lake in 1890; and he became a citizen in 1895. Since he was the first in his family, uncles and cousins followed. He helped them come, and they settled near us in the blocks around Ninth South and West Temple.

I'll never forget Joe Doctorman [my cousin] chasing a cow down West Temple with a tree branch, chasing it to the slaughterhouse, I presume, where they would slaughter it and pay him. He'd buy one cow; pretty soon he'd buy two. In later years, he went out and brought a truckload.

My father decided there were so many small settlements in surrounding counties that he could take out a load of merchandise, sell it, and make a living that way. He ordered men's and ladies' clothing and household goods from M. E. Smith in St. Louis. Then he got himself a covered wagon with two strong horses, and he'd load that wagon and go out for two or three weeks. He'd come back with hides or furs that he'd purchased along the road and sell them, also.

He worked hard, and as he went further and further into the territory, why, he learned to really appreciate—this was all he looked forward to—coming home on a holiday or just being with his family for a week or two before going out again. My mother would make him pudding and gefilte fish. But he used to like to work on a soup bone. He liked to eat the gristle off that soup bone. [*Laughs*] So mother would usually have a big bone waiting for him.

As he got older, he tried staying off the road. He tried a grocery store, then a junk house, but he was never successful. He finally went into the hide and fur business; he bought furs and hides for a Los Angeles outfit, and he did all right there. He'd go on the road and buy carloads of sheep, deer, or beef hides. Sometimes the sheep were the fatalities of a snowstorm. Shepherds would skin them and take them to a hide buyer, who would sell them to my father. Sometimes slaughterhouses sold him hides. He paid ten cents to twenty-five cents a pound. The peak, I remember, was twenty-five cents a pound.

The hides had to be salted. When I worked with him, I'd take a sack of salt and spread it on a hide. I'd take another and do the same, until we'd have great stacks. After they're salted, they dry, and that brine draws out the impurities in the hide. Then it's "cured." Afterward, they're sold to a tanner, who makes them into leather. I don't know if you're familiar with the tanning process. It requires soaking hides in chemical solutions. The chemicals solidify them and make them impervious to wear and tear. On most hides, the hair is removed. And since leather varies in grades, different leathers are used for different articles, such as shoe leather, leather coats, leather jackets. It's quite a process. But that's what we did.

married in the Montefiore Synagogue and settled on the southeast side of Salt Lake City, where they raised four children and established the family business, Jordan Meat and Livestock.

We moved to Ogden, Utah, in March 1917. There, my father got a job painting railroad boxcars in the roundhouse. We arrived just as the War [World War I] was coming to an end and couldn't get housing, so we had to move in with a [Jewish] family. I don't recall the name of the family, but the man was a *melamed,* a teacher. And he felt sorry [for me] that I couldn't understand a word of Yiddish, and my mother refused to speak English to me.

See, I never wanted to speak Yiddish in front of [my American] friends—I was embarrassed. I remember, in Chicago, when we'd take the streetcar and my mother would take out the *Jewish Forward* to read, I'd say, "Mama, please, put it down!"[2] She would constantly tell me, "Doris, never be ashamed of who you are. Don't do that to yourself, because you'll never be a happy person."

So, after we settled in Ogden, this man [the *melamed*] recognized that my mother wanted me to learn Yiddish, and he taught me how to speak and how to write. And I was really happy, because I became a part of [my] family. After that, my mother spoke English to me, so I could really understand she wasn't doing it to hurt me, but rather to make me realize how important it was to be proud of who you are and what your language is and never be ashamed. To this day, I'm grateful for that lesson.

When I was not quite thirteen, my father passed away. He had what they called dropsy, where the fluid drowns the heart. He was just a young man, forty years old. At that time, my mother had my sister Annie, another sister who was four, and the baby, who was three months old—four girls. So it was quite a struggle for her. I was in the eleventh grade then; I went through school quite rapidly. And because I had done so well, and because of the situation at home, I had the privilege of being asked by the Jewish community if I wanted to learn a profession so I could help my mother. So the Ogden community helped me go to a business college, where I learned shorthand and typing and got myself a job. I worked for several years. Then, when I was seventeen, I met my beloved. He bought and sold cattle.

I met him at a mutual friend's house in Salt Lake City, and it was love at first sight. He gave me my ring on my birthday, and we were married the following June. [Through him] I had the blessings of another family; his mother and father were like another set of parents. I spent most of my days with his mother after I got my little house cleaned up. I was a young bride and I had new furniture, and it was like playing house. I'd put the dessert plates out first, because they looked prettiest. I'd set it all up, then I'd go down and visit her. She spoke little English but she was the sweetest woman. Then I'd come home and fix dinner. Saturday was "our day." We'd go out and oftentimes buy a record, and in the evening, after dinner, we'd turn it on and dance, just the two of us.

Then I remember noticing Sam's strong attachment to his parents.

Oftentimes, he'd stop at their house, and when he'd come home he wouldn't be hungry. I would say, "Well, what did you do?" He'd say, "Oh, Mother had this and that, and I tasted a little bit of it." Being a young bride, tearfully, I'd say, "Why didn't you come home first and then we'd both go and visit." "Oh, I'm sorry," he'd say, "I just wanted to see how they were."

But [my mother]—to this day, she is a blessed memory to me—had a philosophy. She said, "Doris, reverse the situation. If I were living in Salt Lake and Sam's parents were in Ogden, don't you think he might have to call and say, 'Doris, when are you coming home?' Don't begrudge him visits with his parents. Don't ever do that, because they're not here forever. Let him have them as long as he wants. If you feel badly about it, go down and visit with him."

I did . . . and it drew us together. Sam and I grew very, very close. That's the way our life was. [At home] we didn't say very much to one another, our thoughts were so much alike.

Then, when my mother [suddenly] passed away, leaving my two sisters behind—one I had lost right after I married from a heart condition—we took them into our home and raised them. They were eleven and sixteen; and it wasn't easy, because we had three of our own by then. And millionaires we never were.

Yet, if I ever got disturbed because my sisters weren't helping me and I'd say [to Sam], "Why don't you say something to them?"—he'd say, "Don't ask me to do that. They're your sisters. If I say something, they'll [only] feel I've hurt their feelings. But if you say something, they'll be angry, but they'll forget it." Even his own children he would rarely reprimand in a loud voice. When our son was seventeen, I remember, we were sitting at the table here, and for the first time in years we were discussing something and our voices got loud. I guess we got much louder than usual, because my son got up from the table and said, "Now, don't be upset, Mom and Dad. I'm just going out for a little ride, and I know you'll settle down once I come back." Well, that cleared the air right there. We didn't realize we had raised our voices.

All through our life, when it was good, it was good; when it was bad, we comforted one another. Oh, we had words like all human beings. But never did an evening pass that it wasn't all smoothed out. We never went to bed angry at one another. Never, throughout our almost fifty-seven years together. So I can say we had a beautiful life of love from the very beginning. He was always by my side, because there was never a night we went to bed—as God is my witness—that I didn't say to him, "May God give you to me all the rest of my life." He would say, "I thank God for you."

Unfortunately, a year ago, we found out Sam had a tumor on his pancreas. At the time, we were not told how long it would take for the tumor to show. There was always a question of how long it would take for it to activate. Then, just all of a sudden, he started building more blood than he needed. They took two quarts of blood from him. Then, in February, we took him into the hospital, and they gave him four transfusions. The doctor didn't know why he was suddenly losing blood.

We took him again in March, and they said cancer was causing the blood loss. We still didn't know it was a matter of how long. . . . But when he was in the hospital, he started not feeling good—he started failing. Then the rabbi came to see him, talked with him, and asked him if he wanted him to pray for him. He said, "Yes, I would like that." Then the rabbi said, "Sam, everybody is praying for your well-being." He said, "Rabbi, I want you to know, I'm not afraid. God owes me nothing."

A week later, before they moved him into the hospice unit, we tried to talk. But he could hardly make himself audible. So Joe [my son-in-law] helped. I put my body actually on [Sam], and Joe helped Sam put his arms around me. They were like dead weights. Sam looked at me with his blue eyes and didn't say anything. But the question was there. I said, "Sam, don't worry about me. I'll be alright." He said to me, "Are you sure?" I said, "Yes, I'll be alright."

Those were his last words, because he started swelling up [and he lost consciousness]. Then the cardiologist was called in, and he asked me, "What would you like me to do?" My kids were all around me. I said, "My children may think I'm cruel, but I don't want you to let him suffer." He said, "I'm glad you feel that way, because there's absolutely no hope." On the chart, I remember, he wrote: "For God's sake, let this man die!" That night, my children looked at me, and I thought maybe I hurt them. But they put their arms around me and said, "Mother, we're glad you did what you did, because we feel the same way."

You see, I couldn't stand to see him on life support. He was a man so full of love, so full of life, that it would have been heartbreaking. It still bothers me sometimes, but I prayed to God, almost every moment of the day, to please take him. It was selfish of me, but I couldn't stand it. He was such a part of my life that I couldn't stand to see what was so beautiful be so tortured when there was no hope. They would take a little water and put it in his mouth because it was so parched, and the minute they put it in, it would flush right out. So what was there? [Cries softly] Nothing. Sam died the day after our eldest daughter's birthday, the twenty-third of March [1984].

JOSEPH ROSENBLATT, 79, RETIRED PRESIDENT, EASTERN IRON METAL COMPANY

The Rosenblatt family saga has acquired the quality of legend in Utah. Nathan Rosenblatt, Joseph's father, arrived in Salt Lake City as a penniless teenager in the summer of 1880, and by 1895 he had become the proprietor of the intermountain region's largest scrap-metal yard, Utah Junk. In subsequent years, he and his sons built the state's first foundry, erected its first steel mill, and, in the 1930s, through Joseph's initiative, transformed the family's already thriving, multifaceted enterprise into the inter-

ED EISEN, 64, OWNER, UTAH BARREL COMPANY

When I was growing up, we had all of the institutions that are established in most every Jewish community. We had early religious-school training, we had a Jewish bakery, and we had a kosher butcher shop.[3] Mr. Kaplan was well known by all the old Jewish inhabitants of the city. His West Side store sold kosher and nonkosher meat. In addition, he was also instrumental in the third synagogue that was established here, Sharey Tzedick. He helped found the "nyer shul."[4] The cornerstone was laid in 1918, and the ceremony was officiated by the only Jewish governor we had in this state: Simon Bamberger.

Now, I don't remember 1918—I was born in 1916—but I remember going to that synagogue. We lived just a few blocks away, within an area of the city that most of the [newer] Jewish people settled. It was the area between Main Street and First West and [between] Third and Tenth South. It was a ghetto-type life, because we had few very wealthy Jews. Those that were, were [German Jews who were] either commercial merchants downtown in the retail stores or in the mining trade. Hotel Newhouse, which is just about to be razed, was built by Samuel Newhouse, who was a very wealthy Jewish mining man. He also built the Boston Building. But most of us just lived on Eighth or Ninth South, right by the railroad tracks.

We lived on that side because my father was, and I say it without fearing any derogatory implication, a junk peddler from Hungary. He was born in Miskolc and originally followed his father here. Now, do you know what a junk peddler does? He rents a horse and wagon for a dollar a day and goes house to house buying discarded items you might see in garage or salvage sales: old clothes, old bottles, anything. And that's why the Jewish people were in the discarded business, because nobody else wanted that.

But the Jews made an industry out of this. For instance, scrap iron was melted into iron ore. Nonferrous metals such as brass, copper, aluminum, and zinc were melted down and sold to the smelters to be reused, just as aluminum cans are reused today. So my father picked up junk. He'd get it during the day and work deep into the night, sorting and cleaning, separating brass from iron, and so forth. When he got enough for a sale, he would sell it to one of the regularly established junk dealers, who were also Jewish. The Peppers were one, and the Rosenblatts were another. And they sold to smelters, to reusers. Most of the peddlers went to one of them.

nationally known mining machinery manufacturer, the Eastern Iron Metal Company (EIMCO).

Throughout the 1940s, EIMCO's revolutionary "rock loaders" were transported to most of the major subsurface mining operations in the world. In 1956, when manufacturing included complex filtration machines, EIMCO employed two thousand people locally and had established manufacturing plants in England, France, India, Italy, and South Africa. At the time of its 1964 sale, the company was considered "the world's

Joseph Rosenblatt. *Kent Miles*

largest builder of machinery for removing solids from liquids."

Proud and reclusive, Joseph Rosenblatt was reminiscent during his interview of the nineteenth-century industrialists who equated commerce and civilization; he believed industry was synonymous with human progress and produced leaders exemplifying the highest attributes of civilization.

My parents were both born in Brest-Litovsk and came over as very young people. My father came in the spring of 1880. He was about fourteen years old. He often told the story that one afternoon, when word had reached his family that the Russian Army was taking boys twelve years and over, his father came [home] with a ticket to Hamburg, Germany, and enough money to buy passage to America, and said, "Pack. You're getting out tonight." That was it. And without any more preparation, he was on his way to Denver, Colorado, and his parents' friends. But when he reached his destination, he found people so desperate they barely had enough food to care for their own family. So he stayed only a short time in Denver and that summer got himself to Salt Lake City.

Mother emigrated several years later. [My father] barely remembered her [when she arrived]; she didn't remember him. But the families had been good friends in Brest-Litovsk and a match had been made years earlier. So they met in Denver and were married. They stayed a few years; but hope for a better life was not there, so they returned to Salt Lake.

They got here in 1889, I believe, and my father started off as a peddler. He had a [push]cart and went door to door, industry to industry, trying to find out what people would be interested in buying and then finding sources of supply to fill their need. He dealt with almost anything, but primarily retail things at first: clothing, linens, simple household goods, dry goods that were given to him by the Auerbach brothers to sell on consignment. That pretty much became his start.

One of the classic [peddling] experiences that became part of family history was his driving a team of horses from Salt Lake to Spokane, Washington—almost a thousand miles away. By that time, he had switched from selling dry goods to supplying parts for mining machines, and he left early in the spring with a wagon full of parts for the mining camps. The story he told is that he got into Spokane anywhere from four to six months later but became stranded because of the Panic of 1907, when currency had no value. To survive, stores, banks, everyone issued script. That was the only way people continued to exist.

But he was in real difficulty. The exchange value of script was only useful in the neighborhood in which it was given, where barter was possible. And since there was no way he could get out of town without some currency that was of uniform exchange value, he was stuck. He wasn't able to come back until the following spring. He often told us about that experience. And no matter how sympathetic I felt as a youngster, it was [always] hard to understand how such struggle, such deprivation, could have been possible.

Now . . . my father was a man who didn't hate. He disliked things, but he rarely used the word "hate." Yet [the word] was reserved for anything Russian. [He had] great bitter feelings for Russia—for all it stood for and all it represented, [for] the unbelievable adversities the ghetto life created, and the limitations on people's opportunities—bitter limitations. In his mind, Russia represented the lack of the kind of freedom we had learned to depend upon and to love in the United States. This freedom was solely absent from his youth, and so he didn't like to talk about the past.

He confined himself to talking about the present. He had a great emotional feeling for freedom as he knew it in this community. Occasionally, he was critical of the Mormon church. In fact, one time, he even encouraged my older brother to actively oppose the church in its efforts to teach Mormonism in the public schools, because he felt the dread of religious persecution in Russia must never be permitted in this country. He felt this was really a land of the free, so he was vigilant. . . .

But his vigilance was not a violent slamming-on-the-table kind of effort. It was a gentle, persuasive effort. The authorities in the Mormon church were an aristocracy for him. He believed they were people concerned about right and wrong, people who recognized America was *not* a country in which you could impose religious beliefs. Because the unique accomplishment of our American way of life *was* the separation of church and state. It was completely unknown anywhere else in the world, so it was a principle which had to be protected. And he did his best to do that. [*Chuckles*] He was really a flag-waving, United States of America citizen! He was very thankful to be here.

Of course, my father was ambitious, and his business ventures prospered—but not without risks and setbacks. When I was five or six, my father expanded the [junk] business—he and my oldest brother built a foundry. And, let me tell you, for them to have had the guts to do that was really something, because it was a massive undertaking. In addition, they themselves were not really schooled in things mechanical, and there was an absence of people with industrial skills [in the area]. So they were dependent upon employing [out-of-state] people who had that training. And, in an effort like that, you make lots of mistakes. The learning curve gets to be a very long one, and the price of ignorance is quite high. But he did it! He put up with all of the hardships and the failures until he succeeded.

A few years later, he and my brothers built a steel mill. Now, my father ventured into these activities because in those years there was always the need to find markets for the tons of scrap the junkyard accumulated. The Murray smelter used some scrap; my father [regularly] shipped to them. But he was always looking for a market that would leave him independent of just one buyer. He eventually realized that if he was going to successfully market scrap metal, he'd have to find a way to become his own best customer.

Now, it's often said that it was easier [to succeed] in those days, because it was possible to do things with a small amount of capital. You know the classic stories about the low cost of labor, people working for ten cents an hour. But [what you have to realize is] everything was in proper relation to everything else. A dollar was a hard dollar. And earning that which represented entrepreneurial possibility was *very* tough. Entrepreneurial possibility is my phrase, of course. My father didn't know it. *Chutzpah!*[5] That's what he knew.

So, when the Midvale smelter came up for sale in 1913, he bought it to build a steel mill. And that was unheard of for this area! Inside the buildings, I recall, there were tall steel structures with overhead traveling cranes. He decided that was the ideal way to market his scrap—turn it into steel. So he built the mill. He bundled the scrap, rolled out the angle iron and reinforcing bars and mine rail, and then, lo and behold, the war [World War I] started. And, immediately, there came a demand for steel products that couldn't be filled.

Unfortunately, that was his undoing. Because [to meet the demand], they expanded the operation they originally started with into a sizable steel mill. By 1916/1917, they were employing three thousand people out there. [*Chuckles*] It was a great enterprise! But they were up to here in debt. And when the war ended, there was trouble. [Government orders ceased] and the steel mill went into receivership, which was a heartbreaking experience.

I was fourteen then, and the part I remember was the night the family gathered around the table, after the steel mill and Utah Junk had been lost. My father didn't know what he was going to do. The after-war years were as destructive a depression as we ever had. He didn't know where he was going to get the money [to start repaying debts]. Then Mother said, "I've saved what's almost twenty-five thousand dollars; that will get us started." [*Chuckles*] And it did. Somehow, through all those years, out of household money and this and that, she saved it. And it was of massive help, because my father—in the push to expand the mill (which, by the way, won him the best-business-man-in-the-state award)—had signed his personal guarantee with several loan companies.

And although our attorneys told him he was free of the commitment to repay, he made arrangements to pay it off. It was his feeling that if he was to measure up to what is expected of a man in the USA, particularly a Jew, it meant meeting a standard of conduct that could not be criticized as being improper and certainly not, heaven help him, illegal. So he paid it back. It took ten years, but I remember his joy at being able to say, "It's all paid off."

One of the activities we were engaged in [in 1926], after I graduated from the University of Utah with a Juris Doctorate, was the purchase of mining plants where the mines had played out and the processing mills were sold for their value as used machinery. In other words, rather than purchasing for scrap, because the prices paid were much beyond the value of scrap, we bought and restored equipment for its value as usable machinery.

In 1928, we made a huge investment in a processing plant in Arizona that had belonged to Kennecott Copper. I was fresh out of school, and my assignment was to go down, hire a crew, and take charge of the operation—dismantle it, sell it, and [if necessary] send it back to Salt Lake for repair. It was the first time I had been away from home for any length of time. Living in a remote mining camp without any shoulders to lean or cry on very quickly changes a person from being young and dependent into somebody who's slightly tough and independent. And as I look at it now, with the benefit of fifty years or more, it was a wonderful experience in making a responsible businessman out of a kid who had things pretty easy.

The first thing I did, I remember, as I walked through this plant, where rattlesnakes were the only living creatures around, was decide there was some value in the residue that had been left in the processing machines, particularly the filters. So I went back to visit with the head of Kennecott in that area and made some inquiries. He said to me, "Kid, from the way you're talking, I have a notion that you think there's some cleanup left in that plant. To save you some disappointment, I just want to tell you we swept that place clean. There is *nothing* there!"

Well, I felt there was something there worth going for. So, the first crew I hired was a clean-up crew, and, sure enough, there was a lot of stuff. [*Chuckles*] We gathered two loads of copper concentrate, a couple of months' work. There were two smelters [nearby]: one which belonged to Kennecott and another, fifty miles away, which belonged to Magna Mines. I shipped it to Magna Mines, thinking it might be less controversial. It went through. Copper was selling at eighteen cents a pound, and I got a little less than twenty thousand dollars [back], which was fantastic! That was quite an experience.

The entire venture made a tremendous impact, though. I realized [when it was over] that we had enough know-how to move independently. In short, we could stop buying secondhand machinery and reselling it, and start designing and making machinery on our own.

You see, all through those early years—when we were strongly involved in the mining industry—a lot of engineers and metallurgists came to us looking for improved ways of handling the ore and getting the [mineral] values out of it. They wanted to increase the percentage of recovery of values so more zinc or lead or gold or silver would be extracted.

These people came to us because we were [also] a custom plant—the only substantial machine shop around. We didn't initiate anything, but people continually came to us with their designs, and we'd build them. Over the years, we built flotation devices, filters, special pumps . . . so we accumulated all this experience. And I said [to my father], "We've got to take advantage of this." So, on that basis, we went ahead and designed a rock-loading machine. We began in 1932 and started marketing it in 1934. Once we decided to go ahead, it happened quickly. We didn't have a great deal of competition.

But we did have one large hurdle before we could manufacture successfully—money! It was hard to come by locally, because Utah banks had no experience in dealing with a manufacturing plant like ours. So, at the close of 1937, I decided there was no way I could get [additional] financing here. I would have to go to New York to find a banking connection.

That winter I went to New York to see a friend. I can still see myself sitting in his office. He said to me, "Hell, the best thing for us is start at the top!" So he got on the phone and he called [J. P.] Morgan and got me an appointment. I was frightened beyond all understanding. [*Chuckles*] Here was the House of Morgan, on the corner of Twenty-third and Wall Street. It was historically important, and there I was, in the middle of the day, walking up the bank steps.

When I got inside, into the vestibule, there were three men standing guard, obviously armed, interviewing everybody who came into the bank. I finally got inside and talked to one of the people and described why I was there and what I wanted. I hadn't come to seek a loan but to seek a connection that could become familiar with us and what we did and how we did it. "Our growth [potential] imposed upon us the need for outside help," I said. He listened and said, "We've never handled anything like this before. But we're interested; we'll let you know."

I came home and didn't hear a word from them for four months. Then this came in the mail: "Dear Mr. Rosenblatt, We have finished our investigation and we've decided we'd like to have you as an account." [*Chuckles*] Well, with that, we were off and running!

I never did borrow any money from Morgan, but the prestige of the connection was exactly what I had hoped for. It was a great help to say to a large corporation we wanted to sell equipment to that they could check on us at Morgans. Salt Lake City, you see, was a remote place. For anyone undertaking manufacturing of heavy machinery in a specialized industry, Salt Lake City was unheard of! What kind of cockamamy deal was that? So the Morgan sponsorship opened doors, and we really started growing.

JOEL SHAPIRO, 60, MERCHANT

Intense, probing, articulate, Joel Shapiro is the unofficial chronicler of Jewish life in Utah, with quotable remarks found in local newspapers, articulated in speeches, and archived in numerous historical accounts. Born in Salt Lake City on March 22, 1922, he graduated from the University of California, Berkeley, in 1943 and then served two years in the U.S. Army. From March 1944 to the end of World War II, he was assigned to G2, XV Corp, a French-based counterintelligence unit specializing in the analysis of aerial photographs and prisoner interrogation. On April 18, 1945, as a member of G2, he accompanied the forces that liberated Dachau.

After the war, Shapiro decided against graduate school and settled in Salt Lake City to expand his father's modest luggage store. Originally consisting of one downtown shop, Shapiro's Travel Goods and Gifts now has stores in five different Utah locations. "If you're looking for the punch line," Joel Shapiro told us, "the fascinating thing is that my three sons are now involved in the business with me. It's rather astonishing, because I never thought it would happen, and I never planned for it. But there it is. And there aren't many small, specialized, family businesses left in America today."

My father was born in Russia, near Minsk or Pinsk. He was born in 1879 and entered this country with his father and another brother in 1890 or 1891. He came in the great Russian-Polish exodus to America, and whether they came because the two sons were threatened with conscription, I don't know. It's the usual story: The grandfather came first, then the mama [grandmother]. The eldest son contracted consumption, as they called it in those days, and he was sent to Denver [Colorado] to cure it. Accompanying the eldest son was my father, who was at that time seventeen. Not long after they settled in Denver—within a year—the brother died. So that is how my father, at the age of seventeen, came West.

He used to tell me he immediately tried to meet Jewish people [with whom he could discuss the Bible], because he was a very well-educated man for having his education stopped at a young age. He had only had a Jewish education. He hadn't gone to public schools in Russia. But he had been a yeshiva *bocher*.[7] So, from the minute he was able to stand, he was trained. Those who knew

Joel Shapiro. *Kent Miles*

him, both within the synagogue and without, always commented on his range of knowledge of anything to do with the Bible. His basic life philosophy and responses were out of that background, not out of a public school background. So his closeness to Jewish peoplehood—he wouldn't have called it that—but certainly [his] emotional closeness, caused him to become immediately engaged with the Denver Jewish community.

His first job, he would often tell me, was selling soap. Somebody in those days gave young boys soap to sell door to door. The idea was to ring a door-bell, and when the lady of the house answered, instead of launching into his products, he would give her a little bar of the soap as a present to get the door open. He told this story many times. He no sooner started out on his first job than he was arrested for selling without a license. They took him to the precinct headquarters, and he was horrified. What a terrible thing, he felt, to be arrested and all he was trying to do was sell soap. Two bars for a nickel.

He was taken out of jail by a Jewish man he had met in Denver, whom he had called. This man came down and got this poor youngster out of jail, and so his soap-selling career was quite short. Then he got jobs which are the antecedents of my work. He got jobs working for traveling salesmen. He was a packer and unpacker. People in those days would come to Denver, which was already a pretty large community, selling soft goods, hard goods. And they would come with trunks. They'd stay in hotel rooms, and they had to have someone unpack and spread their wares out. So he became a packer and unpacker.

He worked hard, and as he liked to tell me, he was recommended from one [salesman] to another. Eventually, one man took him on and asked him if he'd like to go on a trip with him, and that man happened to be in the trunk business. So he went to work for this salesman and started selling trunks.

Now, that sounds like an odd thing, but if you move back to 1910, before World War I, trips were undertaken by people only with a great [deal of] preparation and the expectation of being away a long time. So trunks of different sizes were the basic travel container for personal goods. He eventually got a line of trunks himself and worked for a company out of St. Louis known as Herbert and Meisel. They existed until the 1930s, and he carried their products throughout Idaho, Wyoming, Colorado, and Nevada.

He often reminisced about his travels through those areas. He would talk about being a traveling salesman in the West when men still wore guns on their belts. Guys were pretty tough. He was about the same size as me, five feet eight inches, and not muscular. He had never built up his body by being a miner or a cowboy or a rancher. He was a city boy; he was a city boy when he was born and he was a city boy when he came West and got into the soft goods trade. He was not a hard-fisted man. I rarely heard a curse word from my father. It was just not in his language. He spoke excellent, structured English, but laced with kind of an Old World perception.

So while going into the little towns of the West—a young, skinny, sallow-faced, Jewish salesman—he . . . was [often] made the butt of jokes. These tough cowboy types would seize on him, as a little, skinny Jew boy, and play

HELEN FRANK SANDACK, 65, HOUSEWIFE

My father was born in Grodno, Russia, in 1873. His name [was] Arthur Frank. The family name was originally Fratovnick, I think. It was changed, as many were, when people came here. My father arrived in America in 1903. He was already married to my mother, and they had three very young children who were all under the ages of five or six. My grandparents never came over. I never knew them. Of course, it seems astounding to us "now" that families could leave families, knowing that they'll never see them again. But I didn't think much about that when I was little.

My mother's brother, Berrin, came to Utah first. He lived in Salt Lake or in the little town of Brigham City. My parents thought they would settle in New York. But I remember my mother saying, after she had been in New York for several weeks, [that] she couldn't stand it. "There were so many people, it was like another ghetto. I didn't come to America to live in a ghetto," she said. So they came to Utah.

Now, Father became a successful retailer in this city; he was well known. But Mother was remarkable in her own right. She had the most wonderful sense of humor in the world. She could cry, but then she could laugh. It seemed that whenever we'd get together as a family, somebody would say something that would strike her funny, and when she laughed, she had such a contagious laugh we would all laugh with her until we cried. Half the time, we didn't even know what we were laughing about.

She was a short, little lady and quite plump for a long time. Then she lost weight and became very vain about the way she looked. Meticulous and well groomed, in her later years she wore three-inch high heels. Sometimes, going downtown, she'd practically fall off the sidewalk. She had a little trouble with

jokes on him. As he told the story, he was in a saloon one afternoon, and they set him up to take out a saddle horse with somebody. He said he'd go. It would be a nice ride in the countryside. He was a fair rider, not a great rider. And unbeknownst to him, this was a horse which had been trained to go out to the edge of the city, then turn around and race in. This was an exceptionally fast quarterhorse, I suppose.

And, to repeat, the custom was to take these horses out and then race inward and finish in front of the saloon. But as soon as that horse would reach the "turn point," it would take off like a bullet. So my father and this set-up companion got on their horses and ambled out, and [at the turn point] the man said, "What's this in back of us?" And the horse took off like a streak with my father hanging around his neck. "When I got back to town," as he told it, "everybody was out there in front of the saloon, laughing, and [there was] great hilarity." But this is the kind of thing they did. They made a fool of him. And he learned to get along with that because he'd come to the little town to sell his wares.

her heart by then, a little hardening of the arteries. It might've got into her brain, because it would make her dizzy. I'd say, "Mom, why don't you take a cane?" "A cane?" she'd say. "Do you want me to look like an old lady?" She was about eighty then. [*Chuckles*]

Of course, as hard as Mother could laugh, she could carry on just as hard the other way. I had a sister, for instance, who got a divorce, and that was just unheard of at the time. I'll never forget the day. I was in my teens. She was married to a wonderful Jewish man, marvelous society background, lots of money. They lived in Portland, Oregon. It was everything parents would want for their oldest daughter, supposedly. So when she came home and said she was getting a divorce, I thought our world would collapse. I remember I was sent upstairs; then doors were closed. And the crying and the screaming! My mother, well, she almost died, because "nobody" got divorced then. So it was terrible. It was a tragedy! I'm telling you, if somebody said my sister committed murder, she wouldn't have been as disturbed.

Mother was extremely devoted to our family. During holidays like Passover and Rosh Hashanah, the whole family would gather and she'd be preparing food in the kitchen for days.[6] Her favorite expression was, "This is really good, if I say so myself." After Daddy died, I thought it would be impossible for her, because after the years of early struggle, he had treated her just like a baby. I mean, she never drove a car, never wrote a check. He paid all the bills. He made all the decisions. If they went on a trip, he was the one who planned it. And he loved planning trips. And it didn't matter if it was Europe or Nephi, it was all a big thing with him. He'd think about it for weeks; he'd get out road maps and plan the itinerary. And whatever he wanted to do, she went along with it. So when he died, we thought, "How will she ever get over it?" But she had that same inner strength he did. She was terribly lonely, but she managed quite well.

And, no doubt, these penetrating kinds of incidences molded his response to the larger community when he [finally] settled down and became a merchant. In that period of the '20s, my father was the kind of Jew who made no bones about being a Jew but who, in his public life, never wanted to "rock the boat." He had a tremendous sense of what is correct, but publicly he was apolitical. I remember, when I returned from the army [after World War II] and participated in local political activities, it bothered him. He was the kind of guy that blessed both parties. Whoever came in was all right. I hate to use the word "submissive," because he wasn't submissive. But in the public part of him, he learned not to "mess in the white man's affairs."

Mother was different. She was Colorado born—a little town in Colorado—and was a very well-educated woman. She had obtained a master's degree from the University of Denver in about 1915 or 1916. She had a degree in English education when most girls weren't even going to school. So the marriage of my mother and father, when I look back, was a strange mixture: he being a European with a yeshiva *bocher* education and she being—from one side of her family—German, very modern, and well-educated. I've often said she was born sixty years too soon. Had my mother lived in this era, she would have been, no doubt, a crusading feminist.

In a way, she was a crusador then, too. She worked for Neighborhood House and other public agencies; she liked to work with newly arrived Americans; and she got into the social services, the various relief societies, both in the Jewish and non-Jewish communities. So, there was my mother, out as a public person working in the community, while my father represented the point of view that if you want to survive in business, don't get messed up in politics.

On the Jewish level, my father belonged to both [local] congregations, but he was more at home at Montefiore.[8] I remember going to visit my father in Montefiore when the rabbi was still giving the sermon in Yiddish. Now, things being what they were, that was not pleasing to my mother, who believed the American synagogue ought to be an [exclusively] English synagogue. So, if I was a child in conflict, in *Jewish* conflict, it was between those extremes.

My mother tended to dominate my Jewish education, because we were essentially Reform synagogue goers. And in the Reform temple, in the '30s, I certainly didn't speak any Yiddish. I can't imagine anybody saying much of anything in Yiddish in that congregation. Even the amount of Hebrew used in the service was minimal. There weren't many theological concepts [discussed] in the Reform synagogue. We were trying to fit into what was deemed acceptable by the larger community.

Now, I don't mean to denigrate what happened in the Reform synagogue, because it filled a function. It integrated us. The people of the Reform synagogue, in the 1930s, were those Jews in the city who, by and large, were making it in America, being reasonably successful in whatever economic enterprise they were doing. We had a substantial merchant class at that time. We don't anymore.

But, anyway, the separation between the synagogues throughout the '30s, until after World War II, was a *real* separation. "These people" didn't go with "those people" for a card game or a movie or what have you. Kids, not knowing these differences, sometimes played together. But there was that subtle "down-home" expression that would tell you that "you ought to play with your own kind." So there was a real separation. There were two groups. And, as I saw it, those in Temple B'nai Israel were busy establishing themselves economically and integrating in the [larger] community, whereas the Montefiore folks [kept] more of their European ways and their religious formalities, which were really objectionable to B'nai Israel people.

Now, our numbers are such that even at present it's possible for a grade-school child to be the "only Jew" in his class. So the time we're speaking of, when I was growing up, it was even more likely. And I remember occasionally—it wouldn't happen a lot—being harassed as a Jew on the campus grounds: "You killed Christ" kind of thing and kids chasing me around. This happened several times. I don't think it ever occurred to the family to protest. In other words, in the '20s and '30s, those families I represent as the Reform families knew there was anti-Semitism just under the surface, but they just had the basic "get along with the system" attitude, [the] "Let's conform to whatever's required of us" [attitude]. Placed against today's standard, that seems way out of joint. Yet we were a group of people who just wanted to get along.

In 1938, I remember, an odd incident [occurred], because my mother, almost infuriated, was about to run to the school system. I had a very fine teacher in high school. She taught a class we called "civics," which dealt with contemporary [national] and international affairs intended to make a young person aware of the world. And this woman was very good, lively, and she made us read. The incident [I'm referring to] grew out of the fact that she visited Germany and now was giving us two or three days of her impressions, stressing how wonderful Germany was and Hitler's autobahn and the trains that ran on time.

We kids were amazed, because we knew local trains didn't travel on time and they were musty and dirty and full of bugs. And these German trains were glistening, beautiful things which ran on time. When you describe these things to youngsters, who are very automobile conscious—six-lane highways, 150 miles long—it's very impressive stuff. Very impressive to a young man's mind. Those were the [world's] first freeways, she said, and *Hitler* built them!

So I came home and told my folks about these wonderful things Hitler had done for Germany, and they were outraged. "What else did she say? Did she say anything else? Did you hear anything else?" I remember that incident quite clearly, because they just about flipped out. What's additional, they started to pump me with information which I was directed to go back to class and pour in on the German story. [I tried] but I don't think I did well. I wasn't much able to bring the emotional factors to merit, because I just didn't dig them at the time.

But I wonder if any seventeen-year-old is ever very wise and knowing about anything much farther than the end of his nose? That's not said with any meanness. I just think growing up in America is a strain enough on a young body and mind, just sticking to what's required of you. If you're a middle-class person, that means the social and academic life. So, generally speaking, the American Jewish young people of my age, who ended up the ones going to war, did not really have an in-depth understanding [of what was happening in Europe]. And I don't believe you really can understand [massive anti-Semitism] until you confront it yourself or through the experience of someone close to you.

By the time I got in the service, I certainly had a better understanding of what was happening in Europe, and I was no longer terribly innocent. That was in 1943. So I was a latecomer. I went through the ROTC [Reserve Officers' Training Corps] system [in college]; then I was inducted into the army. The actual physical induction, from which there was no going home again, occurred here in Salt Lake City. Then I went to Fort Benning, Georgia, and from there to Louisiana; then I volunteered to go overseas. I volunteered because I got sick and tired of digging foxholes in the Louisiana mud, and, very frankly, I wasn't happy. I was trained to be an officer in the infantry, and four days before graduation, I got thrown out for overstaying a pass. That's a minor story. Anyway, I ended up going to northern Ireland, where we were told "we were there to fill dead men's shoes." This was in May 1943. I was in charge of a training group.

Well, one morning, a young officer called me into his office and looked at me and said, "Looks to me like you could do something better for the army than be a [line] corporal." I said, "I agree with that general premise." He said, "You have one of the highest IQs in the ETO [European theater of operations]." (I remember this statement although it's self-serving. . . .) "We ought to be able to do something with you. Can you take a typing test?" I said, "I can take it, but I can't pass it." He turned his head while I typed and scratched me out to meet the minimum standard. Then he said, "I'm sending you to higher headquarters."

So, in the middle of the night, they picked me up in a truck and we drove, drove, drove, drove. I ended up in a headquarters somewhere, and I sat around there for five days 'cause nobody knew I was there. Then they drove me to another place, where I sat for another five days because nobody knew I was there. [*Laughs*] But even though this unit didn't know it, I had been assigned to fill a shortage in their intelligence section. When this was finally discovered, I was assigned to a G2 unit for the rest of my time.

Fortunately, I was placed with a fine group of people, and our job was the acquisition of battle information: finding out what's happening on the other side. I was a "general outfielder," as they say. I ended up doing a little typing and interrogating—in short, everything. There were two German-Jewish boys there, and they were superb interrogators. I never saw them threaten a German prisoner, nor did I ever see one that declined to answer. This included officers.

The unforgettable fact from my military career, though, was the experience of going into Dachau. I was in on the liberation of the camp, and that's a memory (I mean, a Jewish memory) that won't go away. A small detachment from our headquarters was sent in. I asked to go with them. I had no "official" reason for being within the confines of the camp. But I wanted to see it.

[I remember] the countryside around Dachau was beautiful: grass, peach trees, neat streets, no dust or dirt. White houses, neatly painted, well-kept flower beds. A pretty, typical, German countryside town, as differentiated from a French countryside town, which tended to be cluttered with chickens, cows, and pigs. There was a railroad spur leaving the town; then there was this tremendous encampment. When people speak of camps these days, they often misunderstand. They think a [concentration] camp is the size of a large play-ground. These things covered acres. Tens of thousands of people lived there.

There was a trench around the encampment to prevent escape. It was perhaps eighteen feet wide and cut deep into the earth. Inside of that were high fences, a double row of fences. Instantly, after the American troops arrived, they placed guards all around the camp to prevent mass exodus. Although several thousand people got out, it was imperative the rest be kept there, at least momentarily, because they would rampage the countryside. So the first irony that struck me was that one guard had been replaced with another. However, the atmosphere of those being kept in was completely different. There was joy. Nevertheless, the guards didn't let anybody out.

We found some SS ["Schutzshasfel"—Blackshirts] guards lying dead along the periphery of the camp with their fingers cut off. The prisoners did what had been done to them: took the gold from their hands.

The railroad spur coming into camp had little cars. They were full of human corpses, and one could see that the side doors had been opened and a machine gun had sprayed down the sides. You could see the line of bullets that riddled the interior of the car. Each car had a pile of bodies. In the crematoria, there were two rooms with a pyramid of naked bodies—skeletons, inmates—who had not been burned. You asked what I saw? *THIS IS WHAT I SAW!* Each was waiting to be burned and cremation was continuing under American guard, because there was nothing else to do [with the decaying bodies].

I walked around the encampment. I walked into the so-called hospital, which was a dreadful, dreadful sight, and talked to people there. I eventually ended up speaking to a young Polish boy, who had gone to school in England. His English was flawless, and he became my escort. We went through the hospital. People were in all stages of dying. They saw me, they screamed, it was crazy. They just wanted to touch. Many dead had not been removed. Many had great, gaping, ulcerated sores, because the inmate doctors had no more medication or bandages. Doctors did what they could. But they had no supplies.

The boy said, "I want you to meet one man. He kept our barracks sane. He's a great man!" These were huge, typical, army barracks, which held maybe 250 people, and down in one corner, you had a sergeant's room. It had a door on it. In this one was the barracks' leader. He had a little cot, because he was head man, and he was [sitting] on it. The boy introduced me, and as I began to interview him out came a story you've heard before. The barracks' leader was the man who chose who would live and who would die. But this boy was very confident of this man.

Then, this Polish prisoner, the barracks' leader, a former captain, turned the interview on me. He had one overriding concern, which he kept hammering at: What is going to happen now that Roosevelt is dead? The liberation of Dachau [occurred] five or six days after the death of Franklin Roosevelt, and he hounded me about what I knew of Truman. Who was this man? How [would he govern]? There was this unbelievable sense of elevation that the figure of Franklin Roosevelt held, not only for American people but for the Europeans. He was *the hope*! And this man was virtually despondent over his death. This Polish prisoner in Dachau. In the absence of Roosevelt, he couldn't believe the United States would not become a tool of the Russians. How would the United States know the right thing to do?

There I was, a young fellow, and, of course, I knew who Harry Truman was. I knew he was a midwesterner, a down-to-earth guy. I knew he had been the head of several committees. But most of all, I knew more about the constitutional process in the United States than this officer. I kept telling him about it. But he kept asking me about Harry Truman's ideals, his courage. What would he do after the war? These things I couldn't answer. I explained that America had a constitutional process and that men somehow grew to their jobs. He would not be another Roosevelt, but he would be a good man. I wanted to give this Polish prisoner, who really did not have the strength to get off his cot, some confidence, some hope, that everything would be all right. So there I was, selling America to those forlorn, skeletal, decrepit people, many of whom were political prisoners.

Now, to the youthful mind, the three-day visit to Dachau might have wound up as [just] part of the total war experience. It *was* part of a total experience. But as one matures, you single out the experiences which are the most important; you separate the most important from the most ironic. So as a Jew in America, [I know] the Dachau experience is a historical experience. Its impact on me lasts to this day. When I see political forces which would deny there was such a thing as the extermination of ethnic groups in Germany, my witness, obviously, has value. Whenever I show the pictures [I took] or tell my story to people, I try to make clear that it *did* happen. It's not fabrication, it wasn't imagination, it happened.

More principally, I point out man's inhumanity to man—the old story which people, it appears, need to be reminded of again and again and again. What the modern young person has some difficulty grasping is the massive extent of it. Having lived well in this country, with full bellies and strong muscles, to see European Jews reduced to skeletal forms seems almost unbelievable. They see it and can't comprehend how an organizational structure inflicted that sort of life on others. And that's the reason for telling the story. We need to be educated and educated, again and again and again, if, indeed, the Jewish aim of the perfection of the human being is to be realized.

ROSE ARNOWITZ, 75, HOUSEWIFE

Rose Leibowitz Arnowitz was born in Cleveland, Ohio, on November 21, 1908, and was raised in an Orthodox household. She met her husband, Michael Arnowitz, when she attended his brother's wedding in Cleveland in 1930. Three years later, "on February 12, 1933, Lincoln's birthday," they married and, after a brief New York

Rose Arnowitz. *Kent Miles*

honeymoon, settled in Salt Lake City, where Michael owned a men's clothing store on State Street.

"When I first came [here]," Arnowitz remembered, "the Jewish community was very cliquish. But my husband had three brothers living here who had social contacts in both congregations, so I was automatically part of things. In the following years, I'd often hear of Jewish couples who moved here, were not accepted, and left. I think the [unspoken] feeling in the Jewish community [at that time] was, 'There's enough of us here. We're fine like we are.' "

I was born in Cleveland, Ohio, on November 21, 1908. My parents were Anna and Abraham Leibowitz. They were from Romania and married there. I have a copy of their wedding invitation. I have the ribbon that was on the candles on the wedding table. I have the coat my father wore to his wedding. It looks brand new. They came here because he didn't want to serve in the army and because of the pogroms.[10] During a pogrom, soldiers would steal everything from you and beat you if you were Jewish. My father's sister was beaten during a pogrom. They killed her husband and left her for dead. Well, she wasn't; she came to America, too. But she was left with a tic from that

SADE L. TANNENBAUM, 85, SECRETARY

When I got older, I became involved in preparing the dead [for burial]: washing and dressing them. There were a group of women who did it for the women and a group of men who performed that for the men. Each woman did it for many years. As one passed on, her place was taken by someone else. I deemed it an honor when they asked me to join.[9]

The preparation is quite simple, really. You sponge the person a little at a time. Nail polish is taken off, if there's any. The hair is washed and left plain. We don't comb the hair. We say a special prayer, then put the shroud on and put the person in the coffin. The shrouds are prettier now than they used to be. They have a little lace on them. There's also a little cap, with a veil over the face. Of course, the casket is closed, unless the family wants to see [the deceased] before the service. Ordinarily there is no viewing.

I can remember we used to have men and women that sat with the body until it was buried. No one does that now. And when my mother died—well, this was a rather gruesome thing. She died at home in her bed, and I remember they brought her down, put something on the living room floor, and washed her right there. That was very, very hard, to have it in the house. They didn't use funeral parlors at the time. Then they brought a very crude box. It was just plain wood. They placed her in that, and her shroud was just a sheet. That's what they had then.

The service was in the house, too, and there was a crier, a neighbor who came and was beating her head against the wall. I remember I told her, "Look, that's uncalled for. You're not going to bring her back or anything." They used to have a bag with Israeli soil. She couldn't be buried until we had that in the coffin. Also, this I had to do: they had to see that she had covers for her eyes so they wouldn't open. It will always be with me, it was so crucial. Now they take them to the funeral parlors. You don't see any of that.

---

beating. She could never stop her head from shaking. She used to tease, "You know, I always say no."

My grandmother lived in a little town, what they called a *dorf,* a country town. She had a restaurant, but it wasn't like a restaurant as we know it here. You could call it a little inn. People knew what a fine cook she was and made reservations to eat. This is where my mother learned to cook as well. Of course, they brought this knowledge to America and [used it] at every gathering at our home, where taste and presentation of food is very important.

My mother, father, and grandmother, and my mother's single sister and my brother, left Romania in 1906. They got as far as Holland when my father was detained because of an eye ailment. My grandmother and my aunt traveled on, but my father and mother and their son had to stay until he was declared cured. Then they came on to America. They came by boat, of course. And they went to Cleveland, because my mother's two brothers were living there.

My family was not destitute, even though no one was allowed to take anything out of the country and my family left much behind. My grandmother used to tell us how she made a slit in the lining of her coat and fitted gold pieces inside.

Soon after they arrived in America, my father opened his own grocery store, which my mother managed while he worked for a big creamery, candling eggs. That was his business, too. I can still remember, as a child, watching him looking at eggs under a light, [which] was really a little tin can with a bulb in the middle and a hole in the front. He would hold each egg up to that light. Sometimes, he would hold a dozen eggs at a time and wiggle them in front of the light, grading them, checking for blood spots. "Leakers" and eggs that didn't pass his inspection would be tossed into large tin cans and sold to the bakeries. It took years before any of us ever ate anything that the bakers baked, because we knew what kind of eggs were in the baked goods.

But that used to be my ambition when watching him—to be able to hold at least three eggs in my hand at one time. He was very apt at that. He was a young, vigorous man and worked quickly. He was paid by the case, you see. When he finally accumulated enough money to buy his own truck, which was a horse and wagon, he went into his own business as a distributor. Then he fixed a stool for me to stand on so I could reach the counter, and he let me check the eggs and fill the cartons. The eggs arrived stacked in wooden cases. We'd check them and then pack them into egg cartons that were made of paper and came flat. I would open them up and fit in the little sections that separated the individual eggs. Oh, I was in my glory! I finally learned how to pick up three at a time, and then six, and pack them.

My mother told me they opened their store in a non-Jewish neighborhood. She said they never planned to be open on Saturday during the day and were told that they would lose business [because of that]. Well, that was the only location they could get, with living quarters in the back of the store. Surprisingly, the non-Jewish people flocked to the store after dark on Saturday nights. That's when many of them came in to do their shopping. So there was always business.

My mother said she ran the store all by herself; even when she was pregnant with me. Later, she said, I had real black curly hair and white skin and that I was so tiny and walked at such an early age, people used to think I was a windup artificial doll.

Still later, my parents sold the store and moved to a different neighborhood, a Jewish neighborhood, and into a triplex. My grandmother and aunt lived on one side upstairs. We lived on the other side. And my uncle, who had five sons at the time, had the downstairs. My father had a barn and a horse and wagon that he used to deliver eggs.

The bakeries that sold cakes—and used the tinned eggs—were in the Gentile neighborhoods in those days. The Jewish bakeries only carried bread, rolls, and challah.[11] As far as it went for pastry, they made kichelach [little puffed-up cookies] out of unsweetened dough and eggs. Sometimes they were baked plain, and sometimes they were sprinkled with sugar. They use them at kiddush, or for a bar mitzvah or a brit or for Passover—most of the Jewish celebrations.[12] They serve them with whiskey on the Sabbath because they don't require you to wash your hands like you must if you use a challah or a raised bread.

I remember the challah my grandmother made. She always took a piece of it, sprinkled some yeast on it, and let it burn as an offering. I don't know why, though. [She burned] a piece about as big as a walnut. I remember my mother or my grandmother lighting the candles, passing her hands three times over the flame, and saying a prayer as she covered her eyes with her hands. Her head was always covered. I still have my grandmother's head covering. It is 150 years old now and made of pure silk. I think of her every Friday night and holiday that I use it. My grandmother came to my shoulder [in height]. I can still see her beautiful little face. I can see her lighting seven candles on Friday night—seven candles on her brass candlestick holder. It had three branches to hold the candles, and it is now at least two hundred years old. She got it for a wedding gift. In those days, you see, people gave you something they had. They didn't buy you something new. I don't know why my grandmother lit seven candles or, for that matter, why my mother lit five. I have it now, here on my table, and I use it just as they did. It brings back a lot of memories.

My father was a cantor.[13] He had a beautiful voice. He went to shul on Friday nights and every Saturday. When I was a child, I sat right next to him. But as I grew older, he couldn't bring me in with him. I had to go upstairs and sit in the balcony with my grandmother and all the other women and children.

My parents were Orthodox Jews. It was a way of life for us. But they left us alone. What I mean is, they never pushed us to be the way they were. Still, we didn't dance on Friday nights, and on Saturday mornings we walked to shul. After services, since my mother's mother was living at our home, all the relatives would march into my mother's home for kiddush and for a very big meal. My grandmother and mother were just marvelous pastry cooks, among everything else.

My grandmother, I remember, always knitted special heavy white socks that my uncles and my father wore to shul only on Yom Kippur. They were made of very fine white yarn—yarn that you don't see nowadays. The men wore them without shoes. Do you know that custom?

My mother didn't go to shul regularly because people were always coming over to our house afterwards. I think that was the way with a lot of mothers: fixing up the house, preparing the meal, waiting for us to come back. Later in the day, we kids would walk over to a cousin's house or go out on the porch and listen to my dad tell a story. It never occurred to us to go to a movie. We'd listen to my dad, fascinated as if he were just making up stories. We never realized until we were older that he was telling us Bible stories. He'd replace names with ones familiar to our neighborhood; he'd include some neighbor-hood tidbit [and there would be] a moral to the story.

That's the way it was for years; we were a religious family. When my brother became an attorney, they knew in the courts that they didn't ever schedule a trial on Shabbes [the Sabbath], because he would not be there. He had a beautiful voice, like my father. He prayed daily at home and wore his tallith and tefillin.[14] He always walked to shul. In fact, he died in the syna-gogue, when he was just fifty years old, a very young man. He walked into shul, sat down, and he was gone.

I married my husband, Michael, in 1933, and we moved to Salt Lake City. I've always said that the women of the Talmud Torah, B'nai Brith, and the Sisterhood met me at the train station and joined me up right then and there.[15] I quickly became part of a social group that was from the Temple B'nai Israel as well as Congregation Montefiore because my husband's three other broth-ers belonged to one or the other. But I have to say, because of my upbring-ing, I was most comfortable at Montefiore.

At that time, we lived on Thirteenth East and South Temple, in the Knickerbocker Apartments. It was a lovely place but a far walk to shul. During Rosh Hashanah [each year], we moved down to the Belvedere Hotel on State Street near South Temple, so that we could be within walking distance of Montefiore. It might sound easy, but it was quite a chore. Of course, the suite came furnished with dishes and pots and pans, but I would never use them. We've always kept kosher—even in Utah. So we took our own dishes and silverware, table cloths and napkins, candlesticks and candles. And we brought in all the food I cooked and prepared one or two days before the holiday.

I would tell the maids, when we went to service, not to move anything. Usually the maids were Mormon and interested in what we were dong. They felt related to us—to the Israelites, as these young girls would say. So I'd explain to them why we brought everything in ourselves. Then they would light the stove—I wouldn't light it. When I left for services, I'd leave them a note that said "Please do not turn this off."

We did this for almost twenty years—taking everything from our house to the Belvedere Apartments. This was, of course, before our sons married. And always, somebody would call asking "Could you take a student?" or "Could you take a soldier?" We always did, which meant dragging more dishes, more dish towels, and more food. Sometimes [during World War II], I'd have ten or twelve soldiers sitting at the table.

Those were special times. Our entire Jewish community—especially our women—volunteered many, many hours. There was a time we must have had six hundred to seven hundred Jewish soldiers stationed out here—eastern Jewish boys from New York. While some would just bum around for the hol-idays, many were used to Jewish services and wanted a place to go. It wasn't unusual to see them coming in and out of the old Covenant House, where the LDS Business College is today. The Jewish Welfare Service, to which most of us donated, supported many of [the programs offered to soldiers]. Many of our women spent hours there, helping these young men and women in the armed services. From Hadassah, National Council of Jewish Women, B'nai Brith, and Sisterhood, we were always called upon to help.[16] On Friday nights, someone would conduct services at the different camps. On Sundays, women volunteers made brunches for them. Once a month on Saturdays, we held a dance in the big ballroom. B'nai Brith raised enough money to rent a room at the Elks Club so these servicemen would have a place to hang around, talk, and write letters. I remember, too, making five gallons of horseradish for a seder when there were so many Jewish soldiers here; the only place big enough to have it was in the South High School cafeteria.[17]

We also sold war bonds. We distributed the rations for meat, sugar, and gasoline. For a certain number of hours a week, I worked down at the City and County Building, checking credentials and issuing stamps. See, only so much could be given away. In fact, when these soldiers came to dinner in our homes, they'd bring their stamps so we could buy enough food to feed them. I remember those years. Our volunteer war effort was cited in the papers. We received letters from President Truman, Secretary of the Treasury Henry Morganthall, Jr., and others commending us on our work. I have these letters right here.

I remember when Rabbi Cardin came to Salt Lake. That was the same year my father died. The rabbi had a mellow, deep voice that somehow just embraced you when he talked. And he was that way in his sermons. Even when he was giving someone "hell," it was done in a nice voice.

I remember one thing in particular. There was a group of women—like Rosie Pepper, Claire Bernstein, and old Mrs. Mednick—who prepared women's corpses for burial. They had asked me to do that, too. The rabbi asked from the pulpit. He didn't see why anyone should be afraid. Well, when my parents were alive, I always discussed everything with them. And when I told my mother, she said, "Oh, you serve the community in many other ways. Don't do that." And I was so glad to have her tell me that.

Some people said Rabbi Cardin was a strict man. I don't know what is meant by "strict." He was observant, he kept a kosher home, he would not eat meat out. He lived near the synagogue and wouldn't ride on the Sabbath or on holidays. But there were some who disagreed with him because he wouldn't marry a Jew to a non-Jew; and he wouldn't allow anyone on the pulpit who was married to a non-Jew. That was in those days.

We used to have kosher dinners at Montefiore—Purim dinners, Hanukkah dinners. Two or three hundred people would eat. One year, I baked the cakes for it here in my kitchen. I was the only one [for whom] Rabbi Cardin allowed to have anything out of the kitchen come into the synagogue. My kitchen was the only one. I baked upside-down cakes—many of them. My son was home from school and helped me wash the pans and the bowls, so as soon as I was finished with one, I could make another. When we had enough of them, he'd load up the car and take them down to Montefiore, where the other women were cooking the meats and preparing the salads. After he took the first batch down, I remember in particular asking, "Well, what did they say when you brought those cakes in?" He said, "Oh, they said they looked like a picture." I smiled—and he said, "Now, if they only looked like a cake, we'd have something!"

I never did prepare bodies for burial. Eventually, though, I was on the board of all the Jewish women's organizations, and I spent a good deal of time with the Jewish Relief Society, which helped the people in this community as well as the indigents and the travelers.

There were about twenty women on the board—all active and involved. I remember them. Mrs. Abe Bernstein, Mrs. Abe Klein, Mrs. Seymour Freidman, Mrs. Lawrence Goldsmith, Mrs. Sam Hentleff, Mrs. Saul Karsch, Mrs. Joseph Levin, Mrs. Richard McGillis, Mrs. Ben Pepper, Mrs. Ben Roe, Mrs. Max Siegeal, Mrs. Pisar Sobel, Mrs. Tannenbaum, Mrs. James L. White, Mrs. Max Golnick, and Mrs. David Zinik. We met once a month. Somehow or other, someone knew of someone in need. It wasn't a formal process. A name would come up, and we would see what we could do. Primarily, we helped with food and clothing. But there were times we paid bills, found housing for refugees, and even provided funds for medical services.

In those days, Holy Cross Hospital wouldn't admit anyone unless they paid. The county hospital was awful, but that's where the indigents had to go. It was a horrible place. The stench was terrible. I visited in the men's ward once, where there were maybe fifteen of them in there—one sicker than the other, and no one fully clothed in hospital wear. They were so afraid their meager belongings would be stolen, they kept them right under their bed. Instead of crutches, I remember they gave out two-by-fours, slabs of wood, to use.

Within our community, we provided food. Some people had lost their jobs; others had gotten sick. Some women were raising children alone and on practically nothing. Some people would take [the food] only after we put it down by their door and left. Others were so hurt they needed help, they turned us away. But we went wherever we felt we could do some good, and it was always done on a very, very confidential basis.

We took care of transients coming through town. That was one of our biggest problems. These transients would make it a practice to go door to door, merchant to merchant, asking for money. They needed it. They were stranded. They had a sick baby or a broken-down car. For some transients, downtown Salt Lake City became a stopover for money as they migrated east to west and then back east again.

After a while, the merchants really began to complain. They didn't know who to give to or how much to give, or whether they should give to everybody that came in. So that's where Mrs. Zucker came in. Soon word got around there were funds for the worthy and that Ethel Zucker would be distributing those funds. She used to live on Second South, near downtown, and she took care of them. And, I'll tell you, that helped eliminate a lot of the *schnorrers*, the phonies. She knew exactly who had just seen her or who hadn't left town when he should have. And they knew this. So the minute a merchant would mention her name, these phonies wouldn't go near her at all. She was fair, but she was not easy.

From the beginning, funding for the Jewish Relief Society came from the community—one dollar from each family. Once a year, we had a "meeting" which was really an affair: the Jewish Relief Society Tea. It took place at the Covenant House, from two to four in the afternoon, and was really quite formal. The tables were set with beautiful lace cloths and napkins. A silver tea service at each end of the table held coffee or tea. A silver bowl held lumps of sugar; a silver plate showed off the lemons. There were beautiful cakes, cookies, and flowers. We never had speakers, but each event would honor certain women, who would sit and pour the tea or coffee. Amy Schiller, the oldest member in my day, was always given an honor. For years, her chore was to fix the lemons. She'd slice them and then decorate them beautifully with cloves.

Almost all the women—possibly seventy-five percent—in the Jewish community would come to this tea. They would all be beautifully dressed. In those days, women just wouldn't go anywhere without a hat and gloves. No one wore dungarees. They would come to donate their dollar, talk with their friends, and just see what everybody was wearing.

We were an effective board. I think we filled the [definition of volunteerism] and were well rewarded by our efforts. But as time went by, volunteering changed. When I was president, the name itself had been changed to Jewish Family Services and [the organization] became a "professional entity." It changed the atmosphere, and, in a way, the volunteer spirit. Instead of word of mouth, instincts, and personal volunteering efforts, social workers, counselors from the state, county commissioners, and other public administration services drew up policies, gave out copies of personnel and practice codes. They required that we attend volunteer institute training programs [and] that we be supervised, especially when we were dealing with family and children's issues. We also had to attend regular mental-health meetings. We had to produce progress reports and follow a continuum of high-level professional practices. It was a change for the good, I believe. Part-time help was hired; health networks were organized. But at the same time, it became an obstacle course for us. And, I think, it affected the spirit of volunteerism. Instead of working from the heart, we went to work from the rules. And it never quite felt the same.

SAM BERNSTEIN, 72, ATTORNEY

Dad came here from Austria in the 1890s and did what any healthy Jewish person would do: anything where he could make a dollar. He couldn't speak or write English, but he had a strong back, so he peddled. He'd go out, buy metals or a few cattle, and sell them.

Dad used to tell me he wasn't the only Jewish person in Salt Lake City in that predicament. For instance, there was a Jewish fellow here by the name of Eisenberg, and he said the other Jewish peddlers used to rib him. Like Eisenberg bought himself a white horse. So Dad told me they picked up a large egg—I don't recall what kind of egg—and put it in the manger where this horse was at night and tried to convince Mr. Eisenberg this horse laid an egg. He also told stories of how they were in competition with each other, buying junk, and he'd tell me they would get Mr. Eisenberg to buy items that weren't even salable, just as a joke.

I remember, too, that Mr. Eisenberg was a very religious man. He'd get up early in the morning and start his chores, buying junk, and he'd [still] be saying his morning prayers and wearing his tefillin on his arm and on his head. And Dad said he would come to some place asking if they had any junk and would be told that a man with boxes on his head had already beaten him to it. [*Laughs*] You know, it [just] amazes me, when you look back at those days, how these men survived.

SIDNEY MATZ, 64
CRANE OPERATOR, KENNECOTT MINING COMPANY

Wearing a short-brimmed brown cap rakishly tilted over his fully bearded face, Sid Matz looked like a storybook sea captain or everyone's favorite renegade uncle. Born in Garland, Utah, on November 28, 1919, and raised in a predominantly Greek and Italian community, Matz said he was more comfortable living among all nationalities than among only his "landsman."[18] "I'll always be Jewish," he asserted, "but I know I don't feel part of the Jewish community—even today. My sister Bernice married a Jewish boy. My sister Ruth married a McCrimmon. My dad wouldn't speak to me for a year because I married a shiksa—an Italian who knows more about Judaism than I do. But my kids, all of them, believe they're Jewish. They go to synagogue when they want. And when my granddaughter comes up to me and tells me she wants to be Jewish, I put my hand on her head and tell her she is."

A second-generation Jewish-American, Matz retired from the Kennecott Mining Company, where he worked as a crane operator for thirty-four years.

My grandfather was a rabbi in Russia.[19] He was also my dad's only teacher; he learned him how to read down in the basement of the shul. Who knew how my dad learned more, since that was the only schooling he ever had. But

Sidney Matz. *George Janecek*

he was a genius at numbers. He added faster than a machine. In fact, when we were growing up in Garfield, Utah, a bunch of guys would get together in a pool hall and they'd fix numbers, and then they'd bet how fast it'd take the old man to get the answer. And he had some way that he could add stuff up. These guys would use an adding machine and he'd do it in his head, and he'd beat them every time. Sam Matz, my dad.

My dad literally walked out of Russia and into South Africa when he was thirteen years old. He used to tell me about pogroms in his village. Cossacks came in on horses and just slaughtered the Jews in the town. When they started killing the young Jewish boys, my grandfather gave [my father] a two-and-a-half-dollar gold piece and sent him to an older brother in South Africa. He had to do this on his own. He made his way through walking, working on a boat, then joining a caravan going across the desert. To this day, we have that gold piece.

After a few years in South Africa, he worked his way to Canada. He got a team of horses and a wagon and put some pots and pans and dry goods and yard goods and everything else in it and traveled around the country as a trader—a peddler. Soon he made his way down into Idaho, where he heard about this Russian Jewish family that had a farm. He went out there and met my mother, Annie Fogel. She came from a Russian village near his, but they had never met before. Somehow, she was put on this farm and worked like a slave. That's what they did: brought kids over and worked them on the farm as cheap labor. My mother was illiterate—never learned to read or write. But she had a natural instinct about people and money, and she could never be fooled. A customer would come into the store, buy something, and write the price down, and she would just "know" if it was right.

Anyway, they married and moved to Afton, Wyoming, where my dad opened up a store and my oldest sister, Bernice, was born. After a while, the family went to Garfield, Utah, where Kennecott Copper owned the town, and my dad opened up a business called The Fair Store. Like always, he rented the property.

It's interesting that he never owned a building. I guess in Russia they couldn't own nothing and whatever they had was always taken from them. So Dad never bought nothing, and he ended up paying fifty times what he could have [paid for] the whole building and the hotel up above it and the two buildings beside it—if he had bought it. But he never did. Every month, he paid rent.

But he knew how to run a business . . . his way. If he ever saw a kid walking up the street with raggedy shoes or barefoot, he'd bring him inside, sit him down, and fit him up with a pair of shoes. If they said, "How can I repay you?" He'd say, "When you grow up and work at Kennecott, you'll know where to come and buy your shoes." He built his whole reputation that way. In fact, he run that store where people would come in and buy something, take it up to the counter, write what they got on the books, and leave. And all the while, he'd be sitting over there with a bunch of other people, telling stories and this and that. And he never lost a dime. To him, everybody was honest.

My dad wasn't interested in making money. He should have been a philosopher. He knew the Bible forwards and backwards. He had—what do they call it?—a photographic memory. If you asked him about a passage in the Bible, he'd tell you the page and line. And he read other bibles and knew a lot about other religions. I remember there was this one bishop, Evans was his name. He came in once and said, "Sam, would you let us give you seven lessons about Mormonism?" He said, "Yes, if you let me give you five lessons on Judaism." So they came in, and he quoted from both bibles until finally they said, "Sam, we can't come down anymore because you're going to make Jews out of us before we make a Mormon out of you."

He could have been a rabbi. In fact, he officiated at some funerals where they couldn't get a rabbi. Yet, this [same] man was also an agnostic or an atheist. He didn't believe in the way they got God pictured, you know, as a person or whatever. He knew his religion, and he knew science. He took a scientific view of it all. When I'd ask him about Moses, he'd say, "Moses was a terrorist, you know. He brought pestilence; he killed the Egyptians." My dad would call him a terrorist. [*Laughs*]

When I was growing up, we lived in Magna. The population was small, and Kennecott owned a lot of the land. Dad's store was on Main Street, and we lived in the back in a two-room place with a kitchen and a little bathroom. There weren't many Jewish people there, and I guess you could say we were raised with Greeks, Italians, and Mormons. That's how we lived.

I went to Hebrew school for a while. But I never lived like my dad and my mother wanted me to—like being bar mitzvahed. When I was twelve, my dad was a member of the shul. I used to come in here, to the rabbi, to learn lessons. But I fought with every kid in that place. I guess they rubbed me wrong and I rubbed them wrong. The rabbi finally told my dad, "You've got to get him out of here. He's always fighting." So I left. It wasn't any more my fault than theirs. That's how it went. I just didn't feel comfortable with the Jewish community. I didn't grow up around them.

But I knew I was Jewish. I'd never deny it. I remember in grade school in Magna, we'd go there and we'd sit down and everybody would have to bow their heads and say the Lord's Prayer—"in the name of the Lord, Jesus Christ." Well, he's not my Lord. So I'd always say "Moses" or something like that.

Another time, this teacher told the class the story of Jesus and how the Jews took him out and crucified him. Well, all the way home from school, kids threw rocks at us—me and my two sisters—and hit us with sticks, calling us Christ killers. We ran into a store. My older sister, Bernice, said, "Why did we do that?" "Do what?" "Kill Christ." "We didn't do it!" I said. In fact, the Jews didn't do it; the Romans did.

But there was quite a bit of anti-Semitism in those days. I remember, in 1923/1924, they burned crosses on the hill by Kennecott here. There'd be all these guys in robes. We saw them on their horses, coming through town, and heading up there. Well, I had this friend, Pete Karakas, a Greek kid. He was the toughest kid in town. He helped me fight some of my battles. Anybody who touched me or anything, Pete was one of the guys that would step in.

I remember, this one big guy, four or five years older than me, got me down one time at the park. He just threw me down and really started in on me, saying, "You Jew so-and-so." Well, Pete happened by, and that's the last time that guy did it. Pete just about killed him.

Pete and I were inseparable when we were kids. We built bikes together. We built this shack. As we got older, he'd fix anything that went wrong with my car. We hung around in school, went to California together, and even joined the army together. The people in Magna always said that the Karakases had twin boys and that they took Sid Matz, who was Pete's twin, and left him on Sam Matz's doorstep. Karakas got the good twin; Matz got stuck with the bad one. [*Laughs*]

But this one time, like I said, the KKK [Ku Klux Klan] were burning their crosses up there, and me and Pete snuck up in this canal to look. It was hot, and [after a while] they took their hoods off. And when they did, we saw a couple of people we knew. I can't mention any names because I don't want to start any big deal. But one of them was a Mormon bishop and the other was a businessman in Magna.

What broke up the Klan was that they kidnapped a kid name Jim. He was a young Greek kid, awfully big. According to the story, they took him up the mountain—not to kill him but to scare him. Well, this was the biggest mistake they ever made. When people got wind of this, the Greeks and Italians all got together and went up there with guns and trucks, and I imagine they really went berserk. And that ended the Klan here.

Magna and Garfield were small towns. Most of the people in them worked at Kennecott. In fact, everybody worked for Kennecott. Mothers, fathers, kids—they all worked there. It was like a big family, and the town was a good place to bring up kids. There were schools nearby, and the company houses in Garfield were cheap. Fifteen dollars a month got you a four-room house with two bedrooms and a nice yard. Gas cost next to nothing; lights was for nothing; and Kennecott furnished the power. Not much to look at on the outside, [the houses] were nice inside. It was an ideal place to live. Close to work. I'd walk three blocks and be at my job.

During the Depression, the towns stayed alive because Kennecott kept everyone working. Maybe they'd work only three days a week, but the paychecks kept coming, and that's a hell of a lot better than going on welfare.

Since water was the most important thing during these hard times, Kennecott would send a crew down to Garfield with a drill. They'd go up and down the streets drilling wells—just so people could pipe water in to raise their gardens and get them through the hard times.

After World War II, Kennecott had a policy to rehire everybody who worked for them before going into the service. They even gave credit for time spent in the army. But I guess I messed up too often. I had quit Kennecott nine times before, and they weren't anxious to hire me back. By this time, though, I was married, had two adopted children, and was ready to settle down. With some help—and 'cause I was Sam Matz's boy—I got rehired. I went out there, I remember, determined to stick with it. So when everybody else would go on a break, I'd keep on working. I worked and worked. That's what I did. I started with Kennecott when I was sixteen years old, a school kid, went through World War II, a bunch of different jobs, and ended up working back there for thirty-four years until I retired.

BERNARD L. ROSE, 72, ATTORNEY

Bernard "Bernie" Rose (1911–1988) was born in New York City to Louis and Rebbecca Rose. He went to high school in Bayonne, New Jersey, and attended New York University and the University of Colorado before finishing his final year at the University of Utah Law School. After passing the Utah State Bar, he lived in Salt Lake City and practiced law there for most of the next fifty-four years. A combat veteran during World War II, he served in the army for three years as a field artillery unit commander in the Asiatic-Pacific Theater of Operations.

Two years before his death, Rose was presented the Community Service Award at the Salt Lake Jewish Community Center "for serving the Jewish community in his profession and as a volunteer." Among his many contributions, he was recognized for giving to the needy "according to the true definition of Maimonides" as an "anonymous philanthropist"; for "his anti-Defamation work," wherein he "single-handedly contacted every school superintendent in the area to ask that religion be omitted from public school curricula"; and for his support of, and guidance in, the Salt Lake Jewish Welfare Fund Drive, the proceeds of which are annually divided between Israel and Utah's Jewish community.

I was born in New York City, and I don't know if it's important to know that I was born in a charity ward there in the hospital on March 11, 1911. I suppose the charity ward enters in to some degree, because after World War II, I needed my birth certificate for a passport to go overseas, and I couldn't get it. All my records—from school, the board of health records, and even the military—had me as Bernard L. Rose. But when you're born in a charity hospital, and you're Jewish and a boy, your name was Isadore, all of you. And if you were a girl, your name was Sarah. With the Irish, it was Patrick and Mary. So this is how I got my name on the birth certificate, assuming that it's my birth certificate.

I grew up in the Lower East Side of New York. My father left my mother and was some place out in the West. I was raised in the home of any one of my mother's five sisters. I'd stay with one aunt until she had so many kids there

DAVID ALDER, 81, INSURANCE AGENT

My mother and I came from Libau, Latvia, in 1909 to meet my dad, who'd already been here four years. Our first night we stayed at the Rosenblatt house, because my father was working for them as a bookkeeper. Then we rented a house on Ninth South between State and Second East—869 Foster Avenue. Now, among Jews, where we lived was called "the ghetto," because the Jews from Russia and Poland and Galicia all congregated in that location. As I recall, across the street lived Bilsky, a hazan, a cantor. He had two daughters. Next door were the Cohens—Henry, Izzy, and Morris. Then there were the Zlotnicks and the Bernsteins. We all lived on Foster.

A few years later, after we settled in, I remember I took a summer job with Heinz 57 Varieties, the nationwide concern that sells pickles. While [I worked] there, a man came to me and wanted me to become secretary of an association called the Workingman's Progressive Association. This was a credit union. The people who belonged to it were peddlers, or small storekeepers. They each paid in a specific sum to become a member of the association. Then, if one of the members needed to borrow money, he'd arrange for another member to sign with him. So if Guss needed fifty dollars, he'd go over to Hayden, and Hayden would sign his name, and Guss would get fifty dollars. The interest would be very minimal, and this man wanted to know if I would be the secretary.

I told him, "Yes, I would," and that's when I really met a lot of the people in the Jewish community. I met the Mednicks, the Eisens, the Haydens, the Roes. I met all the Jews who peddled or had little stores along Regent Street. And I learned from them that there was a distinct cleavage between the [newly arrived] Russian and Polish Jews and the German Jews. The German Jews had been the first to come to Utah, and they were established in business. They were in dry goods, wholesale, retail, liquor, mining. But these Russian and Polish Jews, they became junk peddlers, hide dealers; they ran secondhand stores. So they were [considered] a lower class of people entirely.

But the thing I want to say is that when I think about what the children of these peddlers [accomplished], it's marvelous! I have a friend whose folks came here and eventually became dealers in [secondhand] gunnysacks—that's a burlap sack. Well, their son, Izzy Wagner, is a multimillionaire today—not entirely from burlap sacks—but he is in with the elite of this city as no [Jew] has ever been. I was recently in his office when he was preparing for "a date" with the mayor—and the phone rang. I answered it, because he was busy on the other line. It was the governor calling.

was no room for me, and then I'd go to the next aunt. I stayed with my grandmother for a while, until she died—one month after my bar mitzvah. Then I moved in with another relative. There was no strangeness about all this moving around because we were a very close family, even to today. The area I had the biggest difficulty was when I went to one house where they were ultra-

Orthodox. I lived with these people until I finished high school. I was raised along with the children, and just like her sons, I had to go to cheder.[20] I had to go to shul, and I had to daven every morning.[21]

I remember davening and looking out a window, daydreaming because you don't have to daven out loud. It gave me time to think. There were times, though, that I lived with relatives who weren't religious—although by association and their involvement, they all felt Jewish.

I can remember being hungry in our earlier days, back when I was three, four, and five years old. I can remember taking a knife and a loaf of bread up to my mother and my mother cutting me a piece of bread. I would be inclined to say there wasn't always even bread in the house. I think that's the big reason my mother turned me over to my aunts, you know, one at a time. She'd never have turned me over except for care and security, and she paid what she could. I saw my father a couple of times when I was growing up. He was working with a furrier in Montana. Then he, too, went into the fur business. Once, during the last summer before I graduated high school, he sent me a ticket to visit him in Casper, Wyoming, and I spent a month there.

Now, growing up, I always seemed to get in trouble—not with the law, but at school. Once, I went to school with dirty fingernails, and I probably had a dirty neck, and certainly dirty ears. Well, we had an arithmetic teacher who would examine us. When she saw my dirty fingernails, she took the edge of a ruler and whacked me across that hand, and—oh, Lord—I turned in my seat, put a left hook in her belly, and dropped her on the floor. That's the kind of thing I'd get in trouble for.

There wasn't any Jew-baiting in my neighborhood, because it was a Jewish neighborhood. But if we wanted to go to a movie, say a half a block outside our neighborhood, we didn't go unless we went six or seven kids at a time. That was the way it was for everybody of all nationalities then. You knew where your boundaries were, and you stayed close to home. I can't ever remember seeing a Jew being ganged up on in an Irish neighborhood or an Irish kid being ganged up on in a Jewish neighborhood. I don't remember any shootings or anything like that. Most of the time, it was all fists, and then we'd be looking for boards. Maybe once in a while somebody would get laid out, but it wasn't anything. . . . I mean, everybody would get laid out at one time or another.

Of course, later, when I was going to school and looking for work, I'd see ads in the paper, and I'm not excluding the *New York Times*, that had "NJNA" in them. It didn't even have to be spelled out. I mean, every Jew knew it meant "No Jews need apply." When I got a job working as a delivery boy at a lace house, I denied I was Jewish to get the job, but [I] didn't deny it the day after I got the job. It was up to them to fire me. If I ran into any [overt] discrimination, though, it was usually an isolated case where someone would say, "Hey, Jew!" and a fight would start over it.

It wasn't a big thing—fighting. In New York, you'd walk along the street in West Colfax and you'd see a guy wearing a pair of boxing gloves and another pair lying on the pavement. You'd go over, pick up the gloves, put them on, and fight the guy until he got tired or you got tired. That's the way it was. (When I was in Denver, later, it was more sophisticated. They had rings.) I've always said I learned to fight in the streets of New York, but actually I learned from a cousin of mine who was small for his size, but, oh, could he fight. I mean, he was a born boxer. Nobody had to teach him anything. And he used to take me around and pick fights for me. Invariably I'd get whipped. But, ultimately, I developed some kind of skill as a boxer.

During my era, it wasn't unusual for a Jew to be a boxer. In fact, certainly in the lighter weights, all the Jews were champions. You had Bennie Leonard, Luke Tendry, Barney Ross—all Jews. Max Bair. Well, I don't know that he was ever Jewish. Maybe his grandfather was. But when you hung a Jewish star on [a boxer], boy, it made him important at the gate. In this part of the country, you had Harry Miller, who used to fight as Bobby Miller. He was good, but he didn't fight very long, because that professional life was a hard life compared to the amateurs.

Anyway, I left New York after I attended New York University, boxing on a sports grant. I was in a match, got hit, and hemorrhaged. After a very quick diagnosis of tuberculosis at some hospital—I can't even remember the name—the next thing I knew I was in Denver at the Jewish Consumptive Relief Society Hospital for five and one-half months. By the time they released me, their diagnosis was that I didn't have tuberculosis at all but a lung abscess that had burst. When I left the hospital, my father sent me a ticket to join him in the southwest corner of Wyoming. So I did, and I knew then that I'd never go back East.

See, on the Lower East Side streets of New York, you're always going sideways so you don't get pushed around inadvertently. If you wanted to see a piece of sky, you'd have to go to the park. Everything—the spaces—seemed too confining. The streets were not free to drive in. They were not free to walk in. They were just not free, period. Here, I have a tremendous appreciation for space. I'm always telling my wife, Mary, to open up the curtains so we can see the whole world from our living room.

Anyway, after I left the hospital, I transferred to Colorado University. I got maybe two or three letters a month from my mother, and there wasn't one letter that didn't contain a dollar bill in it or maybe even five dollars. But she never wrote that things were either good or bad, and I didn't know until years later that things were bad for her.

While I was in school, I worked all the time and fought on the school team. I was in quite a number of amateur fights. We weren't permitted to fight in tournaments or we'd lose our school eligibility, so we would go out into different clubs and fight amateur. We'd go to informal bouts, and sometimes we'd fight at "smokers" all through the school year. A smoker is when guys from different departments, say engineers, would get together to smoke, drink, play poker, and watch the fights. They'd make a night or a weekend of it. I was pretty good then—a little bit better than pretty good. And sometimes we'd get as high as ten dollars for fighting. It was better than what I got from my only professional fight, when I got the hell knocked out of me! I've got to tell you, all through that fight, it never occurred to me to lay down. I won it for one round, and then I ran out of gas. See, I had the capability to beat him, but I didn't have the strength, speed, or the endurance to beat him, and, boy, did he give me a trouncing by the time it was over!

See, I have a personal philosophy, and that is, I don't care who the hell you are, you can only take so many punches—for some it's a hundred, for others it's a thousand—before you get punched out. For me, even on the amateur level, I was good, but I was already meeting fellows whose gloves were on the tip of my nose a split second faster than my glove could find its way to theirs. After I got into law school, I fought for one more year and then I stopped.

I first came to Utah in 1932 because times were bad and [because] my father, who by then had moved to Salt Lake City, told me I could get work in a refinery they were building here and go to the University of Utah Law School. His letters said, in effect, "Well, I can't promise you meals, but I can surely promise you a bed." So I came here to find a bed. That summer I met a girl. I married her in 1933 and entered my last year in law school.

By 1934, I passed the bar. That's when poverty came in. There was no way to practice and no way to open an office. Maybe it would have helped if I had known people or stayed active in the Jewish community. But, at that time, I didn't do either. Anyway, to make any money, I used to pose in the nude for an art class up at the Art Barn on Thirteenth East and South Temple—for sixty cents an hour, with nothing on but a jockstrap. At first I was embarrassed all to hell. But we needed the money. Then, when Ketchums [construction company] started tearing down an old theater, I'd clean bricks after my so-called office hours, which involved [modeling and] walking the streets, trying to pick up cases. How do you pick up cases on the street? You don't. During the Depression there was the feeling that there was no work, and there probably wasn't. Some people had reserves, but we had nothing except the positive feeling that one day this would be over. Those were hard days.

In 1936, my wife and I were divorced. She was a very fine person, but she was a Mormon and I was a Jew. And even though I was divorced socially, if not religiously, from the Jews and she was divorced from her community, I guess we ultimately recognized the fact that she couldn't live the way I wanted to live and I couldn't live the way she wanted to live. My second marriage might have gone all the way, but the war intervened, and by the time I came home she had found somebody else. By the time I married my third wife, I was already bonded to her kids. I still am—in fact, there would be no conceivable tomorrows for them without me—but it didn't work out with her either. I was married four times, and interestingly enough, none of them to Jewish women.

Do I think I've had a fair percentage of successes? Yes, even in the area of my most miserable failures. Fortunately, as far as my work is concerned, soon after my first divorce, I was walking down the street and ran into a Jewish lawyer, Harry Goldberg, who had an office in the Felt Building. He offered me his office to practice law from, and that's how I got my start in the mid-'30s.

In the late '30s, I remember, all we did was read about Hitler. He was a constant subject of conversation among Jews. Some people thought [his tyranny] would pass: Everything passes, and this will, too. Others, like me, felt a nagging sense of frustration that it wouldn't. But, for a while, you had every shade of opinion—from those who turned their back on it, to those who bowed to it, to others who sat there and bit their fingernails because what else could you do except bite your fingernails? To our discredit, there were also some people who said, "It couldn't happen to nicer Jews than the German Jews." I can tell you [that] a number of people in Salt Lake City said that without any concept of what was going on there. Of course, we're talking about the early days, when they were just getting pushed around. When it really got serious—I don't mean they were going into death camps, but when they were being isolated for what was considered war camps—then we started losing the sense of it happening to "German Jews." By that time, they were "Jews" getting pushed around. Am I making myself clear? Then they became real, living Jews to us.

Now, I've got to jump ahead to tell you I built up in me such a hatred for Hitler that I just couldn't wait for the United States to enter the war. And when it did, I ran down to the recruiting station to enlist. As far as I know, Izzy Wagner was the first [Utah] Jew to enlist in the marines. For me, for one crazy reason or another, it took me a while to get accepted. But by March of 1942, the army took me in.

I got appointed to OCS (Officer Candidate School) and was there for ninety days. I came out as second lieutenant and went overseas to Hawaii. After two months of doing very little, I volunteered for Guadalcanal, the Twenty-fifth Division. Even though they were taking a whipping from the Japanese, they accepted me, and I got involved in every amphibious training exercise there was. I commanded up to eighteen men and spent three months sopping wet, climbing up and down ship nets and into little LCBPs—one-unit [landing craft] deals. We'd go around and around in circles, waiting until everybody else was off the ship, and then the lead boat would head to shore. You'd get nauseous all the time, going around in those little circles. You'd always be on the verge of vomiting. It was terrible.

Well, the next thing I knew, we were on boats and two days from landing on Luzon in the Philippines when I was given a change of assignments—the command of a survey team and an ammunition train. Let me tell you, an ammunition train team is usually comprised of every guy that ever had a stockade record, all of them guilty of acceptable crimes. An unstable group, none was able to stand the boredom of waiting to move out, so they were always in some kind of trouble. And yet, after six months in action, when we came out, there wasn't a man in our outfit that didn't respect another man in the outfit.

We had 180 days in one campaign, but—honest to God—I can't tell you that I was in the war for any more than three to five days. We had one day that we got shelled, shelled badly. As a matter of fact, it was two days after Roosevelt died, and it seemed like the shells were never going to stop flying. Time just stretched out like it was going to go on forever. The reason I know it was two days after Roosevelt died is because, when it was over, there was a quiet silence that was totally thick, and cutting through it came this voice out of a foxhole, "We want Roosevelt back. This never happened when he was in office!" I laugh about it even now, the sense of humor that comes up in any circumstance. That's also when I got a face full of gravel and thought I lost my eye. But I didn't. I didn't.

I joined Montefiore Synagogue in Salt Lake City before World War II, but I didn't go too often until after the war, when my mother would come to visit and say, "You make me ashamed. How can I walk the streets when my son doesn't go to shul?" So that's when I started walking on a familiar path with some degree of frequency. After my dad died, in 1954, I said Kaddish for eleven months and [gained] a stronger commitment. Saying Kaddish was a warm satisfaction for my mother, because she knew I would say it for her, too. From that time on, you could consider me a regular. I started going to shul out of habit, but it became for me a matter of curiosity, too. I got interested in where the Jews fit in the whole scheme of things. I started reading everything I could get my hands on, and the more I got into it, the more it became a part of my religious education and [a part of my life].

I can't tell you what Judaism is. It's certainly a religion, but it's more than that. It's a tradition, and it's more than that. It's a culture, and it's more than that. It's a history, and it's more than that. It has a cement or a glue in and of itself that's more than being Jewish. It's a composite of all of these things, and it's even a nationality; it's part of a race. And it's more than any one of all those things. It's you who goes to shul; it's you who doesn't go to shul; and it's you who only remembers you're a Jew when you're given a lox and bagel. It's all these, and it's more than that.

EPILOGUE

DR. VICTOR KASSEL, 68, GERIATRICIAN

Brash, assertive, controversial, Dr. Victor Kassel represents the group of East Coast professionals who began arriving in Utah in increasingly large numbers during the 1950s and 1960s. Shaped by culturally diverse Jewish communities, they altered the makeup

Victor Kassel. *George Janecek*

and social outlook of Utah's Jewish community. They brought it a certain ethnic cockiness and were generally less tolerant of the provincialism of Mormons, whose ideas of Jewish life were extrapolated from Bible study classes.

Born in Brooklyn, New York, and raised accompanying his father on house calls in Bedford-Stuyvesant, Kassel grew up knowing he would become a physician. At family gatherings, he was called "Doctor Victor" to distinguish him from the other boys with his name. After graduating from the Kohut Jewish School, a boarding school in upstate New York, he attended the University of Maryland and the Long Island College of Medicine, which, like most medical schools of the era, permitted a maximum ten percent Jewish enrollment in its freshman class.

During World War II, Kassel was stationed at the Kearns Army Air Base and served as a flight physician in the U.S. Army. Following the war, he returned to Salt Lake City and married Frieda Pepper, whom he met while stationed at Kearns. Since no residency openings were available in Salt Lake City, he completed his residency at *the Harvor General Hospital in Los Angeles and, in 1951, settled in Salt Lake City to start a private practice in geriatrics.*

Called by colleagues the "first geriatrician in private practice in America," Kassel waged a one-man crusade for years in behalf of Utah's and the nation's elderly. He developed a one-hundred-bed geriatric unit at the Salt Lake Veterans Administration Hospital (which many felt was the finest geriatric care unit in the VA system) and lectured extensively on the problems and special needs of the aged. His moral fervor, biting wit, and unwavering personal commitment awoke many to the needs of a neglected segment of the population. In 1994, Dr. Kassel retired from his practice.

What got me interested in geriatrics was a talk Oscar Kaplan, professor of psychology, gave at the University of San Diego during the war [World War II]. I believe it was written up in *Time* magazine, and he prophesied about the growing problem of the aged that would occur after the war. Now, I was always interested in chronic disease and long-term care of people. Recognizing this, when I was head physician at Harvor General Hospital in California, I could see that my house staff, interns, and residents were not interested in the chronically ill. When we began admitting chronic lung patients from a hospital in Long Beach, which was closing, I tried getting interns and residents to assume responsibility for these patients, and they didn't want to. They considered these elderly patients "crocks"—terrible word. But that's what these patients were called. So I assumed responsibility for them outside of my ordinary duties, and I began to realize this was a growing problem.

When you deal with elderly, you see, they require a lot of attention and a lot of knowledge. It isn't a contracted, stilted practice. Geriatrics is the branch of medicine concerned with people who have a variety of medical, surgical, psychiatric, and social problems. On the other hand, internal medicine only takes care of a person's disease; general practitioners in those days only treated symptoms. Nobody was interested in taking care of a person's needs completely. But this was a challenge in geriatrics. This was the fascinating part—medically.

When I started my practice, though, people thought I was very foolish. When I came for my interview to get a Utah license, the physician in charge thought I was just absolutely out of my head. Who would ever want to take care of elderly people? Let me pursue that further. When I met with the American Medical Association's Committee on Aging in Denver in the '50s to discuss the problems of aging, one of the committee members looked at me and said, "You don't really specialize in the care of the aged, do you?" "Oh, yeah." He said, "It's insane to do that. Why do you want to waste your time taking care of elderly people?" I remind you this was a man who was selected by the [American] Medical Association to be on the committee concerned with the problems of aging. This was the sort of attitude he had, and this was the attitude I encountered out here.

So it was a difficult undertaking. But I've always felt that people who are discriminated against should be helped, and as I found out, no group was suffering more discrimination in this country than the aged. It still exists today. But I'll also point out to you that Dr. Nascher Ignatz, the physician who developed the word "geriatrics" in 1906 and who was interested in developing a specialty that would prevent the decrepitude of old age, was Jewish. Stricklets, another pioneer, was Jewish. The developers of [the field of] geriatrics in this country were Jewish. The first Department of Geriatrics in a medical school was at Mount Sinai. The first head of a department dealing with long-term care was Jewish. In fact, the leaders in care of the aged in America *all* came out of the Jewish community; so I saw this as a part of my heritage.

I also recognized . . . in California that in order to introduce the idea [of geriatrics] to people, I would have to become a public speaker. So, during my residency, I spent good money and took the Dale Carnegie course, and I became a very competent public speaker. And when Frieda and I came back to Utah, I looked for a way to introduce people to geriatrics.

Now, I wasn't interested in dealing with colleague physicians. To me, they represented the most prejudiced and anti-aged group in America. So I evolved a talk entitled "What a Jew Believes" and had my first invitation before an LDS group. [*Chuckles*] I went to the ward house because I knew members of the Mormon church were "interested" in learning more about Jews. What they were interested in, of course, was converting us. But I recognized this and took advantage of it. Typically, what I did was explain basics: why the name Jehovah was an artificial construction, why the Jews do not accept Jesus, what is a Jew, et cetera. Then, toward the end of the talk, I'd mention geriatrics and the [Jewish] concern with aging. Before I knew it, I was invited back for another talk dealing with aging. So this is how I distributed information throughout the community.

Further, when I came back to Salt Lake City in 1951 and started to practice, the new Veterans Administration (VA) Hospital at Fort Douglas activated a program for elderly patients [suffering from] tuberculosis and psychiatric and neurological problems. The old VA hospital had dealt with surgery and medical programs. The new VA hospital at Fort Douglas created a geriatric unit.

Well, I got a telephone call one day from Hardin Branch, a professor [at the University of Utah] and the head of the Department of Psychiatry, asking me if I would be interested to work part-time and build this geriatric unit. I accepted the job, and it became a godsend. It took me ten years before I brought money home so I could eat out of my private practice, so I lived on income from the VA. Also, it was a marvelous opportunity. Where else would they pay me to do my specialty and develop a program—a very fine program, by the way. . . .

I developed what was considered to be the outstanding geriatric unit in the VA system in the country. You see, the prevailing prejudice toward the elderly then was that chronological age, in and of itself, produced decrepitude. And this was just not so. People are not impaired by chronological age. They are impaired by disease. The trick is to work out *all* the diseases that negatively influence them and then try to improve the situation. So, if you're dealing with an elderly individual who has fifteen different disease entities and you improve each one of them a little bit, you end up with the marvelous result of improved health. That [I learned] is the whole trick in geriatrics.

The concept was new, of course. I invented it as I went along. For instance, it occurred to me that when I saw an elderly patient who limped, I didn't say his limp was due to old age. I took an X ray, and I found he had a bad hip. Next to him was a seventy-two-year-old who walked perfectly well, yet when he exerted himself he got short of breath. Well, the shortness of breath was not due to seventy-two years of age. If it were, everybody aged seventy-two would have the same problem. His shortness of breath was due to heart disease. Another individual, aged seventy-two, found he couldn't remember anything. It's ridiculous to say his age produced memory loss due to some inevitable brain derangement.

So, as I spent time with these patients and began to look for solutions [to their problems], I saw the need for doing comprehensive histories, physical examinations, and whatever laboratory work was necessary before making a diagnosis. I called it a Geriatric Diagnosis Profile or, for a while, to annoy my right-wing friends, the Troika Diagnostic Profile. [*Laughs*] Troika in Russian means three. And it consisted of medical and surgical problems in the first category; psychiatric and psychological problems in the second category; and social problems in the third. These were the three major diagnostic groups. What I would do is work out what the difficulties were in each. Then I knew with what I was dealing.

It was all original thinking. I began recognizing the uniqueness of it when I was appointed by President Nixon in 1971 to the Advisory Council to the Administration on Aging and I got to know my colleagues. They thought it was amazing. But I didn't think of it as a major breakthrough. I just found it fascinating to do something constructive, and I always had the idea that [for] some reason or other this was my calling—mind you, not a religious calling, but a secular calling.

In a secular calling, one has an obligation to one's fellow man. [In other words,] on the basis of his need, man has certain requirements. As a fellow human, I saw this as my obligation to help ease the pain, the problems, and whatever requirements that come along. I didn't see that God expected me to do this and [that] if I didn't, God would punish me. I did this because the individual is important in and of himself. Someday, in fact, I'm going to speak to God and have him answer for why he created Alzheimer's. He or she, however you like it, has to answer to me for the creation of this sort of agony and horror. In the meantime, I don't have any reason to answer to God for my behavior. I do what I think is proper on the basis of the other person's needs. I don't do it for profit, though I do have to have an income. I do it because I think people who need care are entitled to it. I think it's a horror that in America the aged do not get the care they need. There is so much discrimination against the aged now in hospitals. Patients are allowed or even compelled to leave before they are well enough, and the attitude of the Republican party is a shame. I think much of the attitude in this state is horrible. Elderly people are still the most discriminated-against group in America. . . .

Now, I'll admit, I occasionally regretted coming to Utah, not because of the prejudice against the elderly but because of Utah's terrible materialism and provincialism. The Jewish community, unfortunately, was no exception. In my [Jewish] upbringing, ignorance was frowned upon. In the tradition I knew, we were the people of the book. What carried us through the ghettos was that we deified learning. The important person in the ghetto, in the shtetl, was the student, not the moneymaker. This is the way I saw things. I alienated people in this community because I was critical of the fact that their value system wasn't Jewish enough. I had not seen this where I grew up. I had no contact with the notion that the important thing was to make a great deal of money. [What I'd learned was] that the important thing was to become knowledgeable.

The provincialism [of the Mormons] was also terrible. In the early '60s I was president of the Community Services Council, the big council in Salt Lake dealing with the development of services for all social service agencies. We had our annual meetings at the Hotel Utah dining room, and the place was always packed with representatives of various state and private agencies. This one year, Eva Hancock, my executive secretary, set up the agenda for the luncheon meeting. As president, I chaired the meeting, and I saw that there was going to be an opening prayer. I don't know who gave it. It may have been a member of the LDS church. He went up, made the traditional sort of prayer, and ended with, "In the name of our Father, Jesus Christ," and sat down.

I said, "Just a minute. As a result of this prayer, you have excluded a certain group of people. There are Jews here, there are Unitarians, there are others who would not be included in this prayer. I think it only obligatory that we continue the prayer to include those people." I said, "I will give you the prayer that Jesus himself would have given." I always carry a yarmulke [skull-cap] with me. I took it out, said the *bracha* [traditional Jewish prayer, here said over bread], broke the bread, and said, "Now, you may eat, because we are all included in the prayer." I did it deliberately. I sort of felt an obligation to rub their noses in it. And since then, I understand, they do not restrict prayer at the annual meeting. But this is what I'm talking about. I found the [Mormon] people here very provincial. They just didn't understand [the needs of] other cultures. A year or two ago, the Utah State Medical Association held their annual meeting on Yom Kippur [a major Jewish holiday]! You'd think *they* would have more brains than that, but they don't. It never occurs to them. I fought it for a number of years, then got tired of it and just went on my merry way . . . because it recurs and recurs.

When I left the VA in 1963, I became a full-time practitioner and gradually built up the practice. I did more speaking, joined more organizations, developed more programs. So now I earn a living—not a particularly good living, but I don't starve. Geriatrics is a respected discipline now, except people still don't want to do it. They want to spend time at the university teaching courses on it. They want to do research on geriatrics, but they don't want to *do* geriatrics. They don't want to get out in the community. Geriatrics is very demanding. People are always calling you on the telephone. You're dealing with chronically ill individuals who are elderly and very vulnerable. And when you take care of these people, you end up with all sorts of problems, disturbances, impositions, and people simply do not want to be imposed on that much.

The average physician wants to work twenty hours a week and make a hundred thousand dollars a year. He doesn't want any headaches. And it's a sad commentary on the medical community, because they put profit before people. The practice of medicine should be service oriented. But it's profit oriented, maximization of profit. The primary motive is to make an income. But what can we expect? We live in a capitalistic society, and what we see is a reflection of capitalism.

But you feel for these [elderly] people. Their problems are enormous. Today, I started off my day at 9:15 A.M. A husband and wife were brought here from Idaho by their son. The wife is beginning to show evidence of Alzheimer's disease. She has arthritis and rheumatism; she has aches and pains; she bloats; and she has a million and one complaints. Yet when you try to explain what these problems are, because of her impaired memory, she doesn't remember what you said. So she starts the complaints all over again. And there is no resolution. On the other hand, the husband had open-heart surgery fifteen years ago, and he can't really take care of her. They live in Idaho in a small home, and they're both going to fail.

Just before you came into the office, I did a complete examination of a seventy-two-year-old man who has epileptic seizures and is beginning to lose his recent memory. He knows there's something wrong and wants a solution. I'm convinced he's beginning Alzheimer's disease, and there isn't a thing I can do to treat or improve it. I did another physical examination on a man who is going to be seventy next week. He's very competent. His wife has Parkinson's disease. She's becoming more and more frail, more and more helpless. I have no solution for him either, other than to try to ease his burden as much as possible. And this is the way it goes all day long. The only satisfaction you get is that you're rendering a service. You try to help people deal with inevitable tragedies—people who all day long come in and tell you, "Doctor, old age is hell. Will you give me a pill so I can end it all?"

So that's what I do. I won't abandon them. Most of the physicians in town don't want to take care of them. I can't abandon them to that. I saw the problem in the '40s, became involved in trying to effect an easing of the burden, so I can't abandon them. I have a responsibility. Oh, I'm sure other doctors could assume responsibility for their care. I don't think they'll do it as well. You can't get them to make house calls. You can't get them to respond on the telephone. But I don't feel as angry anymore. I don't detest those doctors. I don't hate them. They chose to be ophthalmologists, cardiologists, chest men. Everybody has their own taste. I selected this. I just think I have a talent for this particular service, and I do the best I can. It rolls down on top of me, of course. But in answering God's question to Cain—"Where is Abel?"—I feel I am my brother's keeper. I believe, "Do *not* do unto others as you would not have others do unto you." I mean, what right do you have to three homes when other people have no home? Why should a sick person be denied care if he or she can't afford it? If people need food, they should be able to have it. But what is prioritized—what priorities come along—are that I have to see a profit before I do this. I think that's shameful.

NOTES

1. After a spouse's death, the widow or widower traditionally mourns intensely at home for seven days. This period is followed by thirty days of less intense mourning by the spouse and eleven months during which the son, or sons, of the deceased daily intones the Kaddish prayer, a public affirmation of God's greatness and holiness. According to legend, a child is able to rescue a parent from suffering after death by saying Kaddish during daily services for eleven months. Alan Unterman, *Dictionary of Jewish Lore and Legend* (London: Thames and Hudson Ltd., 1991), 110-111, 142.

2. Established by a group of Socialists in 1897, the *Jewish Daily Forward* became "a journalistic institution" in the immigrant community. With Abraham Cahan as its editor, the *Forward* became the major Yiddish newspaper of its day. According to Stanley Feldstein, author of *The Land That I Show You,* "The Jewish working class flocked to its bosom for protection, [and] sought its counsel on how to deal with employers, and . . . how to handle their everyday problems." The *Forward* was also a useful vehicle of acculturation because of its "in-depth" and "explanatory" coverage of the nature of the U.S. political system. Stanley Feldstein, *The Land That I Show You* (New York: Doubleday), 179–180.

3. A kosher animal is one that has cloven hooves and chews cud. As described by Alan Unterman, kosher killing is performed "by drawing a sharp knife," with a perfectly smooth blade, "quickly across the front of the throat." The slaughtering is done by a trained adult male who has been accredited by a rabbinic authority. "After the slaughtering has taken place . . . , the internal organs are examined to see that there are no . . . signs of disease or lesions on the lungs," which would make the animal *treyfa,* or nonkosher. Unterman, *Dictionary of Jewish Lore,* 180.

4. Sharey Tzedick, Utah's "nyer shul"—new synagogue—was founded in 1916 by a splinter group distressed by the dilution of orthodox practices in the Montefiore Synagogue. According to the *Salt Lake Tribune,* the shul was dedicated at afternoon services attended by Governor Simon Bamberger on

March 28, 1920. Initially well supported, by decade's end the congregation had run out of steam and money. Most of its congregants, according to other informants we interviewed, returned to Montefiore by 1930.

5. "Chutzpah," a popular Yiddish term, means nerve, cheek, impudence. As defined by Alan Unterman, it refers "to that quality of lovable audacity thought to be characteristic of Jews. . . . The concept is sometimes [humorously] defined in the story of the man who murdered both his parents and then asked for mercy from the court because he was an orphan." Unterman, *Dictionary of Jewish Lore,* 54.

6. Passover is the spring festival that commemorates the Exodus of the Jews from Egypt and the religious and social unification of the Jewish people. During the seven-day holiday, no leaven is eaten or used. Matzo, a flat cracker, is consumed instead of bread to remind people of the Jews' precarious condition while fleeing oppression and to rekindle in them wonder for their ancestors' journey. On the first night of Passover, a family meal is held that symbolically reenacts the passage from slavery to freedom.

Rosh Hashanah (Hebrew for "head of the year") begins on the first day of the Hebrew month of Tishri, which usually falls in late September. On this date, God is believed to have created Adam. Rosh Hashanah also marks the start of the ten-day period, ending with Yom Kippur, during which "God the heavenly King sits on His throne and determines the destiny of each individual in the year ahead." The prayer and repentance characteristic of these ten days "are meant to ensure that one's name" will be included with those who "will survive the year and not be punished [by death] for their sins." Unterman, *Dictionary of Jewish Lore,* 168.

7. A yeshiva *bocher* was a student in a rabbinical academy or "a Talmudic college for unmarried male students." Beginning usually in his teenage years and sometimes continuing into his early twenties, a young man studied portions of the Bible and sections of the Talmud dealing with Jewish law. Learning was "undertaken for its own sake as a religious duty," so most students left without formal rabbinical qualifications. Unterman, *Dictionary of Jewish Lore,* 206.

8. The dominant congregations in Salt Lake City at the time Joel Shapiro was growing up were B'nai Israel and Montefiore. The former was established by German Jews in 1891 and was identified with the Reform movement, under which many traditional ritual practices were curtailed or drastically modified; the liturgy itself was predominantly in English. The latter, established by Russian and Polish Jews in 1904, used the Conservative service, which, in part, came into being as a reaction against the "liberal excesses" of the Reform movement. Though the Conservatives also identified themselves with the rational, scientific, humanist spirit of the age, they believed it was essential to keep the core rituals and tradition of Judaism intact.

9. As described by Alan Unterman, members of the burial society, or Chevra Kadisha, "wash the body, anoint it and dress it in a shroud" before burial. Men may be prepared by women or men, but women must be pre-

pared by members of their own sex. Burial should take place as soon after the death as possible, preferably on the same day. Mystics believe a delay in burial will keep the soul from resting. Unterman, *Dictionary of Jewish Lore*, 42–43. See also Mark Zborowski and Elizabeth Herzog, *Life Is With People: The Culture of the Shtetl* (New York: Shocken, 1962), 378.

10. "Pogrom" (Russian for "destruction") is a term often used to describe the Russian attacks on Jewish communities in the Pale of Settlement at the turn of the twentieth century. As described by Alan Unterman, "The Czarist government encouraged pogroms to . . . provide a scapegoat" for the Russian masses reeling under the burdens of poverty and powerlessness. "The series of pogroms which led to the mass exodus of Russian Jews to the West began in 1881 in Kiev, after the assassination of Czar Alexander II, and reached their peak in the Kishinev massacres in 1903." Unterman, *Dictionary of Jewish Lore*, 159.

11. "Challah" originally meant the "tithe taken from dough before baking and given to a priest." Today, it refers to braided loaves of bread that are prepared for the Sabbath and festivals; the tithe is symbolically represented by a pinch of dough that is burnt in the oven while the bread is cooking. Traditionally, two loaves are prepared as reminders of "the double portion of manna" God gave on Fridays and on the eve of festivals during the years the Jews were wandering in the desert. Unterman, *Dictionary of Jewish Lore*, 46.

12. Kiddush is a blessing made over a cup of wine to consecrate the Sabbath, a holiday, or a celebration.

"Bar mitzvah (Hebrew for the "son of the commandments") is the ceremony recognizing a Jewish boy who has reached the age of thirteen and has formally assumed "the religious duty and responsibility" of a man in the community. The event is solemnized by "calling the boy up" to the Torah on the Saturday following his thirteenth birthday to read the weekly portion of the Law or the "prophetic lesson" before the congregation. Dagobert D. Runes, ed., *Dictionary of Judaism: The Tenets, Rites, Customs and Concepts of Judaism* (New York: Citadel Press, 1991), 31.

Brith Milah (the "covenant of circumcision"), commonly called "brith" or "bris," was first performed by Abraham. In modern times, the foreskin of a baby boy is removed by a professional circumciser, or Mohel, on the eighth day after birth. At the end of the ceremony, the child is given his Hebrew name.

13. The cantor, or hazan, is "the synagogue official who leads the prayers, particularly on Shabbat [the Sabbath] and festivals, and who may also read from the sefer torah [the scroll containing the Five Books of Moses] and teach the children of the congregation. He is also known as the *sheliach tzibbur*, or 'messenger of the community,' since he recites the prayers which can only be said . . . on behalf of the worshippers. In modern times the chazzan [hazan] is appointed primarily for his singing ability, and a whole category of cantorial music has grown up for the virtuoso chazzan." Unterman, *Dictionary of Jewish Lore*, 48–49.

14. "Tallith" ("tallis" or "tallit") is the prayer shawl worn by male Jews around their shoulders during prayers in synagogue. "It is said that a Jew wrapped in a tallit is like an angel of the Lord of Hosts, and many . . . Jews of the old school wear their tallit over their heads as an expression of awe in the presence of God." Unterman, *Dictionary of Jewish Lore,* 194.

"Tefillin" (Hebrew for "prayer objects") are the two leather boxes containing quotations from the Pentateuch that a Jewish man wears on his forehead and left arm during morning prayer. They are thought to "inculcate humility, and the reward for wearing them is long life. . . . Though there are stories in Jewish literature about the protective powers of tefillin, they are not regarded primarily as magical charms. In the meditation [said] before putting them on, the tefillin of the hand are understood as a reminder of God's outstretched arm when he took the Israelites out of Egypt." Unterman, *Dictionary of Jewish Lore,* 196.

15. "Talmud Torah" was the name traditionally used for educational institutions for orphans and poor children supported by the Jewish community. In the present context, it probably refers to an elementary school attached to the synagogue.

The fraternal order of B'nai Brith (Hebrew for the "sons of the covenant") was founded by twelve German Jews in 1843. The members initially met to discuss the lack of unity among Jews outside the synagogue and the growth of anti-Semitism in America. The broad purpose of the organization, which has made it the "largest and most influential Jewish faternity in the United States," was stated in the preamble to its constitution: "B'nai Brith has taken upon itself the mission of uniting [American] Israelites; . . . of developing the mental and moral character of the people of our faith; . . . of supporting science and art; [and of] alleviating victims of persecution." Feldstein, *The Land That I Show You,* 77.

The Sisterhood was the women's organization most closely affiliated with the synagogue. The mission of the present Kol Ami Sisterhood, as stated in its bylaws, is "to promote in every way possible the welfare of the Congregation in preserving and fostering the precepts and traditions of Judaism." Kol Ami Sisterhood Bylaws, 1989 edition, Salt Lake City, Utah.

16. Hadassah, the American Zionist Women's Organization, was founded by Henrietta Szold in 1912 to focus the awareness of the Jewish community on the dire health needs of the first Jewish settlers in Palestine. Through her extensive campaigns, Szold organized Jewish women throughout the United States to help bring "medical units of doctors and nurses . . . to improve the health, medical care, and education of the people of Palestine." More than any other Jewish organization, Hadassah has been responsible for bringing "Israel's hygienic, medical, and health standards" to the level "of most advanced Western nations." Max I. Dimont, *The Jews in America: The Roots, History, and Destiny of American Jews* (New York: Simon and Schuster, 1978), 211.

Because of the large numbers of Jewish immigrants being unnecessarily detained at Ellis Island and deported from the country at the turn of the twentieth century, the Hebrew Immigrant Aid Society (HIAS) and the National Council of Jewish Women (NCJW) were formed. The former was created to help Jewish men and families pass through the immigration labyrinth, and the latter, founded in 1903, was created specifically "to deal with the problems of unaccompanied female immigrants." In the ensuing decades, NCJW grew into one of the most socially active Jewish women's organizations in the country. With chapters in nearly every Jewish community, it organizes community resources to deal with the needs of the indigent, the elderly, families, and Jewish women in general. Ronald Sanders, *Shores of Refuge: A Hundred Years of Jewish Emigration*, (New York: Henry Holt and Co., 1988), 217.

17. The seder is the formal Passover dinner.

18. "Landsman" refers to a person who lived in the same European village before emigrating to America.

19. A rabbi (Hebrew for "my master" or "my teacher") is an "ordained scholar . . . licensed to decide on questions" of Jewish law and ritual. In the past, Rabbis were not paid for their services, so they held other jobs in order to earn a livelihood. Today, they are "salaried synagogue officials, with wide preaching and pastoral duties." In general, rabbis are not viewed as intercessors between the congregation and God. They represent, instead, "the chain of tradition through all the generations of Israel." Unterman, *Dictionary of Jewish Lore,* 162–163, and Runes, *Dictionary of Judaism,* 189.

20. "Cheder" (or "heder") is a Hebrew word meaning "room." "Religion classes were often held in a room attached to a synagogue" or in the home of a teacher, a *melamed.* "It was traditional for boys to start cheder at three or five years old, learning to read Hebrew from a primer" and translating portions of the Pentateuch into Yiddish. Unterman, *Dictionary of Jewish Lore,* 49.

21. "Daven," a Yiddish word, means "to pray."

BOOK FOUR
CHINESE COMMUNITY

PREFACE

Anand A. Yang

The following narratives by members of the Chinese community in Utah arrest and move us because they are both familiar and unusual American tales. They are immigrant stories shared by many people; yet each has a special sensibility. They are also compelling stories, because for all the similarities characterizing the remembered pasts of Raymond Hong or Thon Gin or Ed Kim or Helen Ong Louie or William W. Louie or Bob W. Louie or William Tang or Helen Gim Kurumada or Gordon Su, the recounting of individual experiences can touch us all.

At the heart of these stories are issues regarding identity: They tell of experiences that made first- and second-generation Americans of Chinese descent adhere to, and be distinguished by, their Chineseness even as they were striving to become part of a larger whole. These accounts do not evoke the celebrated metaphor and myth of the melting pot but instead evoke the traumatic image of the scalding wok, for Americanization for minorities is never just a matter of becoming Americans (by birth or through naturalization) in due time; it is about struggling to acquire the legal and public entitlements of citizenship, to gain fundamental rights and liberties in a land ostensibly of opportunity and of the free. Indeed, theirs is not the narrative of any immigrant group but of people whose experiences were and are linked indissolubly to questions of race and ethnicity, as if the hyphen that ties such Americans to their national or ethnic origins is a tightrope and not the bridge that it has been for Anglo- or Euro-Americans[1]

Conspicuous, therefore, in these stories are the tensions and drama entailed in negotiating the transition from being immigrants or sojourners to being citizens. Those tensions are what make for the richness of these stories, a richness of color and detail that highlights the foreignness of the United States as perceived through first- and second-generation immigrant eyes. And as these Utah vignettes clearly reveal, foreignness was not just in the eye of the newly arrived beholder; the dominant community, legally through racist legislation and informally through everyday patterns of behavior and values, kept the newcomers apart, a separation that reminded them that they were undesirable and unequal aliens. To use the telling phrase applied by Ronald Takaki to describe the Asian-American experience, they were treated as "strangers from a different shore." What transformed Asians into 'strangers' in America," Takaki wrote, "was not simply their migration to a foreign land and their lack of indigenous and organic ties to American society, but also their point of origin and their specific reception."[2]

Thus, lodged at the core of the remembered pasts of the Chinese community are memories of incidents and occasions that pertain to the exclusion and alienation the Asian-Americans felt from the life and times of the larger community. The stories cast far less light on Chinese shores. China, in these testimonies, appears largely as an imagined place of ideas and customs that formed part of their Asian-Americans' sentimental education and part of the education and cultural baggage that they felt they had to pass on to their progenies.

Although these stories claim a bit of Utah history for Asian-Americans, they focus only on its twentieth-century chapter. The earliest date situating the families of the storytellers in Utah is mentioned by William Louie, whose father came to Utah via California in 1909; all the other stories are, at the earliest, located in the 1920s and 1930s. Neither here nor elsewhere in published materials is much told about the many Chinese who lived and toiled in the region in the nineteenth century. But their ghosts inhabit the silences and gaps of these stories, reminders that many who came earlier were uprooted by the inhospitality of the local society and culture and left the region, leaving few traces behind. Neither descendants nor other tangible reminders speak of that history.[3]

The experience of nineteenth-century Chinese-Americans was epitomized by the term "Chinaman's chance," meaning no chance at all. Indeed, the place in history of several hundred thousand Chinese immigrants who made up the pioneering generations that reached the shores of America—mythologized as the Gold Mountain—in the wake of the gold rush of 1849 has only recently begun to be documented.[4] As many as eight to fifteen thousand Chinese immigrants made their way into Utah around the middle of the nineteenth century, engaged in the construction of the Central Pacific Railroad from Sacramento, California, to Promontory Summit. Their deeds have been justly celebrated; their monumental achievements, which required them to pour sweat and blood into bringing the railroad across the High Sierras and the Nevada plain and desert into Utah, have endured long after their names have been all but forgotten. Yet, at the 1969 centennial of the 1869 joining of East and West, marking the meeting of the Union Pacific and the Central Pacific railroads in Utah, speakers paid glowing tribute to everyone involved in the enterprise except the Chinese, the people who built the Central Pacific line. At the Promontory site, only one sign commemorates their contribution, a sign that describes a remarkable feat of construction: ten miles and fifty-six feet of line built in one day, April 28, 1869.[5]

The early Chinese immigrants felt the alienness of the United States as soon as they set foot on its shores. For Raymond Hong, the immigration center at which he and his uncle were processed was "like [a] jail." But even reaching the United States was a major undertaking, especially after the U.S. Congress passed the exclusion laws, beginning in 1882, that prohibited the immigration of Chinese laborers except for returning laborers and the wives, children, and parents of those already here. Although the exclusion laws were not repealed until 1943, Chinese newcomers did manage to evade them by coming in as "paper sons and daughters," as fictitious relatives who were legally eligible to enter. Helen Louie, for instance, whose real family name is Ong, arrived in the late 1930s as a paper daughter under the assumed name of "Yee." An event in the life of many pre–World War II Chinese immigrants, the memory of the era of false papers shows up in Ed Kim's testimony as well.

Once the Chinese immigrants arrived in Utah, home for many was Salt Lake City's Chinatown, Plum Alley—51 East Second South, located parallel to and between Main and Regent streets. At its height in the late nineteenth and early twentieth centuries, as many as one thousand people may have resided in this area of less than a city block. Chinese immigrants also lived in other parts of the state, in such places as Park City, Corinne, Ogden, Terrace, Mercur, Pleasant Valley, Fort Duchesne, and Silver Reef. As William Louie recalled, his father moved from San Francisco to Park City at the turn of the twentieth century, when it supported a "good-sized Chinese community."

When Helen Kurumada's family arrived in Plum Alley shortly after the Depression, it was, she said, "less than a half a block long." Its decline had clearly set in by the 1930s, when its inhabitants numbered only about fifty. Although still intact in 1945 when Thon Gin returned from the service, Plum Alley had by then largely become the meeting place of the "old Chinese." As Gin recalled, they went to Plum Alley "mostly to gamble. There were few residences. It was essentially a neglected alley with old storefronts. Nothing in it that didn't smell of a slum. . . . Just old dilapidated buildings and storefronts, with interiors that weren't much better." In 1952, Plum Alley was abandoned.

Even in its heyday, however, its denizens never made up much of a complete community. Like so many other Chinatowns, Plum Alley was predominately a male place. Because of the demographic configuration of Chinese immigrants to this country, many more men than women immigrated and therefore many men were "bachelors" and remained so until their deaths.[6] Not surprising, therefore, is the paucity of references in the impressions recorded here of links and ties to other families. As Raymond Hong stated, young people and children were scarce in Plum Alley.

Similarly, there were few linkages to the wider, dominant community. Ed Kim accurately sized up this lack of connection when he stated, "Our relationship with the larger community was nonexistent. My relationships were with Chinese and mostly through the family. . . . Our world was a very small world, which revolved around our family, our community."

This exclusion from the larger community left Ed Kim, in his own words, with an "inferiority complex." Perhaps it also heightened his sense of "being Chinese," an identity that his father, he told us, had also emphasized. Indeed, one refrain echoing through many of these stories is the sense of being construed as the "Other," a construction that often reinforced and enhanced an individual's sense of ethnic and cultural identification. Some, however, opted to downplay their "ethnic background." Bob Louie represented this school of assimilation when he said, "I'm not saying I've renounced Chinese people. But hey, I feel we're [living] in a country were everybody is the same. So I don't feel like I should segregate my social life or my feelings."

To be a Chinese-American or just plain American, however, was not a choice prior to the late twentieth century, when the world of Chinatown and of the Chinese was circumscribed by the fact that the United States was, to use one expression, a "white man's country." As Helen Louie observed, "When I came over [in the 1930s], the United States discriminated against Oriental people. They looked down at you. They really looked down." Such treatment was expressed in verbal abuse—"Chink, Chink, Chinaman" was one epithet in common usage. Discrimination also assumed the form of apartheid and segregation. As Helen Kurumada recalled, "Discrimination was absolutely public in Salt Lake. We couldn't go to city swimming pools. . . . When we went to a movie at one of the better theaters, we couldn't sit downstairs. We had to go . . . to the balconies."

Nor were jobs available to Chinese immigrants in the 1920s and 1930s. As Bob Louie testified, job choices were limited to managing or working in "a restaurant, a laundry, maybe a small grocery. That's about all. They didn't have any other opportunities. They couldn't go out and walk into an office and get a job." To Raymond Hong, this reality meant going "maybe five years—to American school. I don't know anything else. I same as born in a restaurant." Likewise, Ed Kim did not give "a lot of thought of going out to be a physicist, or an aviator, or a doctor. Those avenues were not available to us. . . . The [white] people in that town thought we'd always be in the restaurant business, that we would never venture out of that field. So we weren't motivated. We weren't pumped full of golden dreams by our teachers. We were just like clouds in the sky, passing by, just there for the moment."

But not all Chinese-Americans of that generation met the same fate. Some were helped by parents or grandparents who worked unendingly to create a better future for their sons and daughters. Two Chinese-Americans in Salt Lake City whose career trajectories followed avenues outside the restaurant field were Thon Gin, whose family was in the laundry business and who went to school on the GI Bill, completed a Ph.D., and secured a managerial position with U.S. Steel, and William Louie, a fourth-generation Chinese-American who became a prominent Salt Lake City architect.

Much has changed since 1965, when immigration laws were instituted that opened the shores of the United States to many more Chinese (and Asian) immigrants. No longer are Chinese-Americans overwhelmingly from Guangdong (that is, Cantonese) as they were in earlier generations and as most of the sample represented here were. The new wave of Chinese immigrants has come from Hong Kong, from Taiwan, and, more recently, from the People's Republic of China; in the late 1970s and 1980s, some also came as part of the refugee exodus from Southeast Asia.[7]

The contemporary experiences of Chinese-Americans and of Asian-Americans in general have been hailed as success stories, in the popular media especially. These groups have been called the "model minority," a misleading myth that ignores many realities and pits minorities against one another.[8] Indeed, as post-1965 immigrant Gordon Su indicated, much about the present has a familiar ring to it. For, notwithstanding the differences between the experiences of the current generation and those of the earlier pioneering generations, questions of identity persist. "We're not *completely* absorbed," Gordon Su said. "We still maintain our independence. . . . We do our own thing." And, as a recent publication commemorating Chinese-Americans aptly concluded:

> The Chinese American society of today is going through rapid changes. It is certain, however, that the major Chinatowns will continue to flourish into the foreseeable future as long as immigration continues from Asia. On the other hand, the process of Americanization also will continue as Chinese Americans participate more and more in the mainstream of American society. But whether they are recent immigrants or Americanized Chinese, they are all Chinese Americans, one of the many groups that make up a pluralistic American society.[9]

NOTES

1. In *Asian Americans: An Interpretive History* (Boston: Twayne Publishers, 1991), Sucheng Chan used the term "Euro-Americans" to "create a conceptual parallel between Americans of European and Asian ancestry" (p. xvi).

2. Ronald Takaki, *Strangers from a Different Shore: A History of Asian Americans* (New York: Penguin Books, 1990), 12. Other synthetic histories of Asian-Americans include Chan, *Asian Americans*, and Roger Daniels, *Asian America: Chinese and Japanese in the United States Since 1840* (Seattle: University of Washington Press, 1988). The works of Chan and Takaki particularly frame Asian-American history within the context of the histories of minorities in the United States and thus, show Asian-American history as being fundamentally different from the history of European immigrants.

3. Even for the twentieth century, the published literature is quite limited concerning Chinese-Americans in Utah. Sources include Don C. Conley, "The Pioneer Chinese of Utah," in Helen Z. Papanikolas, ed., *The Peoples of Utah* (Salt Lake City: Utah State Historical Society, 1976), 255–277, and Dean L. May, *Utah: A People's History* (Salt Lake City: University of Utah Press, 1987), 141–43.

4. See, for example, Sucheng Chan, *This Bitter-Sweet Soil: The Chinese in California Agriculture, 1860–1910* (Berkeley: University of California Press, 1986, for one brilliant reconstruction of the nineteenth-century story.

5. See George Kraus, "Chinese Laborers and the Construction of the Central Pacific," *Utah Historical Quarterly* 37 (1969): 41–57.

6. In 1900 the ratio of Chinese immigrant men to women in the United States was 1,887 to 100. Although this ratio changed slowly, it remained heavily skewed in favor of males. In 1910 the ratio of Chinese men to women was 93.5 to 6.5; in 1920, 87.4 to 12.6; in 1930, 79.8 to 20.2, and in 1940, 74.1 to 25.9. Shih-Shan Henry Tsai, *The Chinese Experience in America* (Bloomington: Indiana University Press, 1986), 40, 98.

7. The fastest growing minority in the United States, Asian-Americans—including Pacific Islanders—in the 1990 census constituted 2.9 percent of the country's population, or almost 7.3 million people, a sizable increase from the 1965 estimate of barely one million. Chinese-Americans made up the largest group in this category: 0.7 percent, or 1,645,472 people, of whom 5,322 were counted in Utah. "Economic and Statistics Administration, Bureau of the Census," *United States Department of Commerce News* (June 12, 1991); *New York Times* (June 12, 1991).

8. An article that attempts to set the record straight is Ronald Takaki, "The Harmful Myth of Asian Superiority," *New York Times* (June 16, 1990).

9. Him Mark Lai, Joe Huang, and Don Wong, *The Chinese of America 1785–1980: An Illustrated History and Catalog of the Exhibition* (San Francisco: Chinese Culture Foundation, 1980), 94.

Ed Kim. *George Janecek*

PROLOGUE:
PLUM ALLEY, SALT LAKE CITY

RAYMOND HONG, 74, RESTAURATEUR,
POST OFFICE CLERK

Raymond Hong was born in Kwantung Province, Toishan District, on February 13, 1925. He emigrated to the United States in 1937 with his uncle and came to Salt Lake City immediately after being released by immigration officials in Seattle, Washington, to join his father. During World War II, he served with the Twenty-seventh Infantry in Okinawa. He returned to Salt Lake City after the war, and for twenty-three years he owned and operated the Ding Ho café, which was located on the corner of Broadway and State Street.

I come to the United States with my uncle [in 1937]. And when you are young, it's not sad to leave [your home country]. It's kind of exciting. We come to Seattle. We have to go to some kind of [immigration] center there, like [a] jail, you know. You couldn't go anyplace until they interview you. I forget how long it takes—maybe a couple of weeks. Some stayed several months. In those days, you can't bring wife. Just men come. Those people ask you a lot of questions. They want to know who lives next door to you, what relative. All kind of things. And when they ask my father [who met me at the immigration center], both [sets of answers] have to be correct.

After that, I come to stay with my father. In those older days, there's no place for Chinese to rent in Salt Lake. My dad, like other Chinese men, lives in a little hotel in Plum Alley, which [was] between First and Second South, between State and Main Street. That's Chinatown. In our hotel room, there was no heat. You burned coal to keep warm. There was only one toilet for ten rooms. Downstairs, they got some kind of store. People sit. The Tong men [members of the fraternal organization known as Bing Kung Tong] gamble.[1]

When I first come, there are only two young guys like me that come from China. They both live in Plum Alley. Then there is a boy named Gim. He is born here and lives just a few stores up. That's the only children I remember.

I went to school till I was seventeen. But my dad don't want me to stay [in school]. He want me to open a café near my uncle in Pocatello [Idaho]. So I did. But I stay only six months, because I lost money. Then I come back, and work here as a waiter. I have no choice. I have to do restaurant work. I only go—maybe five years—to American school. I don't know anything else. I same as born in a restaurant.

THON GIN, 61, EXPLORATION MANAGER, U.S. STEEL

One of twelve children, Thon Gin was born in Washington, D.C., on July 13, 1925. His parents settled in Park City, Utah, in 1927 and for the next fourteen years operated the Hoopoo Laundry in Park City's Chinatown. Thon Gin served in the Army Air Corps during World War II and, using the GI Bill, completed his education after the war, earning a Ph.D. in geology from the University of Utah in 1953.

When I returned from the service in 1945, Plum Alley was still intact, but I didn't go there much. The only people that really visited there were the old Chinese. And [they went] mostly to gamble. There were few residences. It was essentially a neglected alley with old storefronts. Nothing in it that didn't smell of a slum—if that's a term that can be used. Just old dilapidated buildings and storefronts, with interiors that weren't much better.

The old guys, a cross section of those who worked in restaurants, usually ended up in Plum Alley after work. They played ping, which is a Chinese domino game, and fan-tan. Now, this fan-tan was played with a big pile of buttons. They'd put a [large] cup over it, then they'd pull [those buttons] out and you'd bet on the residual sum, after dividing by four. The dealer would count off the buttons by fours, then the fraction that was left over was the winning number—anything from zero to three. They also played a Chinese version of keno, only they had eighty numbers. I mean eighty characters. Keno is an adaptation of this.

My father went on occasion, but he wasn't an avid gambler. I didn't gamble at all. First of all, I didn't understand the games. Second, the people who gambled weren't particularly the young people [born in the United States]. They were more the people from China. The people who worked in the restaurants. I remember I asked one of them once [why he gambled]. I said, "Gee, you come from China. You work like a dog here in a restaurant. You make fifty dollars a month. Yet, as soon as you're paid, you run over to Plum Alley and lose it. I can't understand your reasoning." His answer was, "When my dad was over in the United States and sending us money, we were considered wealthy. I didn't have a thing to do. I lived a rich man's life. So my dad finally brings me over. I work like a dog here [but I don't earn enough to go back]. And I see no way out of it. If I go gamble, I might be lucky and make a fortune and get out of this trap." That's the best explanation I could get, but it was only one man's opinion.

If my father told me once, he told me five hundred times. "This is a white man's country."

—From *Longtime Californ':*
A Documentary Study of an American Chinatown
by Victor G. Nee and Brett De Barry Nee

ED KIM, 56, RESTAURATEUR

That we are shaped by our history is a truism most people acknowledge but few actually own. For Ed Kim, a student of Chinese-American history, however, the past and present are inextricable. A burly, heavyset, intense man, he realized that the experiences of his father (and others like his father), who emigrated to the United States near the turn of the twentieth century, were his legacy—that to come to terms with his own life, he would have to come to terms with theirs.

The eldest of five children, he was born in Lewiston, Idaho, on September 30, 1929, and raised in a "conservative" Chinese household. In 1964, he settled in Salt Lake City with his wife and daughter, and after working in private clubs for fifteen years, he opened the China Doll restaurant on the city's West Side. He was, at the time of this interview, the president of the local chapter of Bing Kung Tong and an acknowledged leader in the city's Chinese "restaurant community."

I'll start at the beginning. The United States was a highly coveted place by the Chinese during the 1890s, 1900s era, when my father was growing up. During that time, conditions in China were terrible. They were going through semirevolutions, semireforms, which were not welcome by the imperial government. The reformers or revolutionaries would regularly disappear. These conditions continued right through the overthrow of the imperial government in 1911. Then, for the next twenty years, the republican government of China was not a broad-based government. There was a series of civil wars that left the peasants in China, their livelihood, in shambles. As my father related it to me, they used to harvest two crops of rice a year in the Toishan District, and the taxes and the land rent were so prohibitive that unless you had somebody in this country sending you money, you could not make it.[2] So what the Toishanese did is ship their most valuable product—their young men—to this country. And this country became a surrogate country for most Chinese. It was never meant to be a permanent home. They were told to come here, make their fortunes, and return.

But it was very difficult for these Chinese to immigrate to this country at the turn of the century. My father came here in the 1920s through nefarious means. And, if it was not for a brother-in-law who helped make the arrangements for him to come, I would probably not be sitting here today for this interview.

Immigration difficulties for the Chinese began right after the completion of the [continental] railroad. All of a sudden, the coolies, or the laborers, found themselves unwelcome. There was even some conservative thought of sending all of them back to China. Instead, an immigration law was passed that compelled every Chinese to register with Immigration, regardless of how they had entered this country. The law permitted them to come and go, provided they documented their going and approximate return. But families were not allowed to unite from the old country. Chinese women were prohibited from joining their husbands here. And the law allowed no immigration of relatives. Sons and daughters [could come] only prior to their sixteenth birthday. So it was a very, very restrictive law.[3]

[To enter the country,] Chinese immigrants developed ways of beating the system. In a span of anywhere from three to six years, they made several trips [back to China]. Each time they returned to the states and passed through Immigration, they declared a larger and larger family—mostly sons, of course. A man may have had only two sons, but by the time he came through for the third time, he declared four, with two being fictitious. These fictitious sons, called "paper sons," he could then sell off to various other candidates, who would assume his family name in order to get into this country.[4]

A returning Chinese was [usually] approached by people who wanted to come or had relatives that wanted to come. And after they agreed on a price, the seller then gave the buyer his biographical and geographical background. And this person would memorize back as far, in some cases, as the great-grand-father on the mother's side and the father's side. He would memorize the lay-out of the village, how many bridges it took to get to a crossroad, which way the buildings faced, which streets ran east to west or north to south, whether he lived in the middle of the village or at the end. They were quite thorough in detail.[5] Then [upon arriving in this country], he would use his inability to speak English to hide many things that were not obvious. Many, many Chinese of my father's generation came here with these false papers. Although Immigration in the 1950s allowed people to come forth and confess and be given immunity, only some did. Many did not, because who wanted to take a chance on being deported from the country of the golden nautilus? [Laughs]

So, as far as Social Security, as far as their driver's license, people maintained their assumed identity, while their real name also was known in the community. Many times, as a young man, I was confused by this. I'd ask my father, "How come he's known as Mr. Lee when everybody calls him Wong?" My father would say, "You have to understand, Mr. Lee was his paper name. Wong is his real name." Then he would caution me, "If anybody other than a Chinese asks you, you don't know why." [Laughs]

My father came here in 1922. He came by the cheapest method, steerage, which occupied the bottom two layers of the boat. In fact, they were not allowed on the deck with the higher-class passengers. So, the travel conditions were, at best, terrible. The ship was very cramped, the food was terrible, and the journey was long. It took something like forty-five days on the sea, with several stops in the Far East, before they arrived in Seattle, where the immigration authorities got hold of them. My father went through an inquiry that lasted from four to seven days. As he told us, the interrogation was arduous and very searching. They were looking for things all the time. They tried their utmost to trip him up into making statements that would not be beneficial to him.[6]

After that, he came into Lewiston, Idaho, to an area that Chinese had settled in. Once there, he went right to work to repay the financial indebtedness for his piece of paper, which, as I understand, with passage and everything was several thousand dollars. He worked seven days a week, fifteen hours a day, for fifteen cents an hour washing dishes in a restaurant.

As a young man, I remember our local meetinghouse. It was a boarding room, grocery store, and social club, all rolled in one. In the winter, it held approximately two hundred middle-aged to elderly Chinese men. My mother, my great-aunt, and the lady who was married to a cousin were the only Chinese women in town.[7] Most of these men worked in lumber and mining camps scattered throughout northern Idaho, on the North Fork and Clearwater, where the mining and lumber industries were big. They worked as camp cooks and stayed there in the spring, summer, and fall. When winter came, they'd go into town.

Now, the ultimate goal of most Chinese was to be in business for themselves. They were obsessed with creating businesses of their own. At the time, though, most of them worked for others. Eventually, however, many [opened] privately owned businesses. Sometimes they bought out the owners they worked for. Sometimes they saved their money and got along on essentials until they could buy something. My father—after paying off his indenture and working an additional three or four years—built up a nest egg of a roaring five hundred dollars and bought a complete restaurant. This restaurant seated approximately fifty people and had all the essentials restaurants should have. But by today's standards, it was very primitive. Dishes were washed by hand. All the vegetables were prepared by hand. And there was no natural gas—we used coal burners. I remember one of my first jobs after I got out of the third grade was to carry six buckets of coal to fill up the coal bin.

Now, my father was very proud of being Chinese. So he imparted much of his knowledge of the language and the courtesy, the respect for elders, to us. In my adolescence, if I walked into a room where older Chinese were present and I didn't address them by the proper age-group respect, I didn't wait to go home to catch hell. I got it right there. Sometimes the reprimand was verbal, sometimes it was a crack across the head with his knuckles. It didn't take many lessons to get the point.

And at the time—and really from my first memories on—our family led a very sheltered life. Our relationship with the larger community was nonexistent. My relationships were with Chinese and mostly through the family. The old Confucian teachings in China held that the most important structure was the family, regardless of who was running the government. The ultimate authority in a Chinese family was the eldest. That was my father. His authority was absolute. There was no challenging him without dire consequences.

My mother was completely obedient to whatever he thought was right. There was no quibbling, no arguing, no debating. He did what he thought was right for us.

My father stressed hard work in school and responsibilities to the family. His thoughts were not on weekend movies or school dances. They were not important. Athletics were not an important facet in the life of a conservative Chinese family, either. In fact, my father and I came to odds over my trying out for football. He thought it was frivolous. I thought it was important. I remember it almost came to the point that he threatened to commit me to reform school if I didn't listen to him. But through a good Caucasian friend, we convinced my father that if I were able to carry out my responsibilities as far as school and family were concerned, I could try out—and I did.

But it was truly against his wishes. He was against anything that deviated from the traditional Chinese family lifestyle. He was so conservative, in fact, that he expected if he returned to China, nothing would have changed. In elementary school, it was my father's wish that I would return to China as a preteen and finish my education there. I looked forward to that. I really looked forward to living with my grandparents, uncles, and cousins and acquiring a Chinese education. But the logistics of World War II and the continuing Chinese civil war precluded all those plans. So I feel robbed of the chance to do that. I would dearly love to be literate in Chinese, to be able to delve into some literary things that are now available to me.

I'm an anomaly, though. Today's Chinese aren't concerned about their ethnic background. And I feel they are evading themselves by not delving into these things. I think anyone who has such a rich heritage shouldn't ignore it, shouldn't forget it. But many of the succeeding generations are not even conversational in the language, let alone literate. They have accepted the ways of this country; they have become Americanized. The only thing that reminds them they are Chinese is the pigmentation of their skin. And that's a crime. That's really a crime.

Most Chinese have documented roots that take them back fifteen to twenty generations within the very locale from which they came. In my father's case, we have documentation for thirty-eight generations. And it's really staggering when you think about giving that up.

My father never could. Even in his mid-eighties his thoughts were still with his family and the different branches of his clan. While growing up, so were mine. My early ventures were all family oriented. This held until high school. Then I began having dreams of other careers and other roles. As far as careers, however, there wasn't a lot of thought of going out to be a physicist, or an aviator, or a doctor. Those avenues were not available to us. Our world was a very small world, which revolved around our family, our community—but not really around school that much. There, we were only tolerated. The [white] people in that town thought we'd always be in the restaurant business, that we would never venture out of that field. So we weren't motivated. We weren't pumped full of golden dreams by our teachers. We were just like clouds in the sky, passing by, just there for the moment.

You have to understand, we were amongst the *first* generation of Chinese children in that town. Everyone else was anywhere from ten to fifteen years older than we were. And the younger ones from the immigrant generation [the next older generation] that went into the public school system were only there to acquire enough English to do business in the restaurants. That's all. We were the first Oriental children that went from first grade to junior high to high school and to college graduation in that small town. But although we progressed, our perspectives were narrow. I thought I'd stay in that "one-horse" town for the rest of my life, working in the family business. I really did not think I would ever work for a large company.

Circumstances [fortunately] dictated differently. When I found out that boys are different than girls and began going with a Caucasian girl, I changed fast. Of course, that scared the hell out of my father. But it was an awakening for me. This [Caucasian] girl made a tremendous impact on me. You see, I was introverted. I didn't have the ability to really express myself. And I had an inferiority complex. I was paranoid about being Chinese. But she made me extremely proud to be Chinese. She made me feel that I was the equal of anyone around. She made me climb out into the sunlight. She probably didn't realize what kind of a monster she turned me into. [*Laughs*] But she gave me confidence in myself. She gave me the tools to work with.

We went together for four years, and I know she suffered some indignities because of her association with me. I'm sure she suffered tremendous pressures, not only from her parents, but from mine. My father wasn't even courteous to her. He would just not hear of his oldest son marrying a Caucasian girl. His question to me every day was: "When are you going to get rid of her?" At least my mother was nice. But that situation created some real paradoxes for me. And she, realizing that I lived in constant fear of alienating my family, finally decided to break it off and seek something else. Having gone through such an emotional sandstorm, of course, I ended up marrying a Chinese girl. I married her when I was thirty. It made my family very happy. Some people have alluded to this marriage as a self-sacrifice. But I don't view it as that. Now that I'm older, I see there's a definite reason we birds, we robins, fly together. I see a definite reason for it. So I don't advocate mixed marriages. Even a marriage between a Chinese and a Japanese, at best, is difficult.

I stayed in Idaho after getting married. . . . But I left the restaurant and went to work for a large retail clothing outfit for nine years. I became their merchandising vice president, in fact. And I must admit, for a while there, it blew my ego to think of me, this Chinese kid, right in the heart of the white man's world—right in the fashion business, the rag business. But when I finally realized my title would always be bigger than my paycheck, I left. I took off my key ring one day in 1962 and said, "My office will be clear in twenty minutes." They tried to get me back, but my mind was made up. And two short years after that, I jumped in my '64 Ford with my wife and ten-year-old daughter and came down to Salt Lake to take over the food operation in a private club. . . .

Now I've lived here for twenty years. Five years ago, I finally opened up my own restaurant. At fifty-some odd years, when most people are looking towards an easier road, trying to find a cushion to soften the blows, I'm off here looking for an empire. [*Chuckles*] I realize this is a step I should have taken in my mid-thirties. But I wasn't mature enough then. So this is probably my last chance to make a mark in the world with a grease pencil. That's my analogy for the kind of mark it'll be. The first good rainstorm comes by, it will be erased. But it doesn't matter. What matters is that I have a strong character, that I know right from wrong, and that I take charge of myself.

For me, being Chinese definitely gave me the inner toughness I need to survive in this country. It gave me the drive to want to make it. In dealing with others in business, I've always felt I can manipulate them. They could not manipulate me. And if you take someone of my background versus someone who was born and raised in this country, how many of them will tell you they have an edge? Maybe it's just a dream. Maybe I'm working on my dreams. I don't know. I know that I care about everything. But [like my father] I care about my family numero uno. Above god, above country. Above any god and country! I would sell out God, I would sell out country, before I'd sell my family out. My drive is to provide for them. In the Chinese scheme of things, they give us the family. Nothing else counts if you can't provide for your own.

Now, I know I'm never going to become financially independent. That's not my goal. My goal is to get my children to college. See them along on their way. And to have a little [for myself]. Not a lot. I don't need a lot. I've had my fun. I've had a rich life despite some cobblestones. I don't fit everybody's mold. I know that. I'm an American-born Chinese, and that is not all that palatable to the foreign-born [Chinese]. But I can't change that. My character is Chinese. I think Chinese. And with my family I convey and insist upon that. I insist that my girls will not marry Caucasians. They'll marry Chinese. I teach them that—not from the time when they find out boys are different [from] girls, but from when they're about nine or ten. I convey to them that if this is not carried out, the results would be catastrophic from my standpoint.

HELEN ONG LOUIE, 60, RESTAURATEUR

The King Joy restaurant is located off the corner of Broadway and Main Street, in the heart of Salt Lake City's old financial district. Opened after World War II, it has been in the Louie family for nearly forty years. Helen Louie, a small, energetic woman, told us she's "the mother" of the restaurant. "That's what all the waitresses call me," she said, " 'cause I never find anything wrong with anybody. I can't even tell a drunk to get out."

Born near Canton, China, on January 6, 1926, she emigrated to the United States four years before the repeal of the Chinese Exclusion Act. "There was no way for my dad to bring me over legally [at the time]," she confided, "so he just pretended I was

Helen and Harry Louie. *George Janecek*

somebody else. I came in with an assumed name, as a child of another family. 'Yee' is my passport name. My real name is Helen Ong. But back then, lots of people came over as children of other families. 'Course, you have to pay that family to use their name. [Immigration] checked on me a couple of times. They'd say, 'How come your name is different from your brother's and father's?' I'd tell them I took my mother's [maiden] name. Then they'd let me go."

When I came over, the United States discriminated against Oriental people. They looked down at you. They really looked down. If you did something wrong, you were afraid that they might deport you. My dad taught me there were a lot of things you keep to yourself. "The government's got ears," he'd say. "Don't tell anybody what's going on. Whatever they ask, don't let the outside know." 'Course, my father knew all about this because he'd been through it. Since 1965, it's been different. No problem.[8]

My grandfather came to the United States on a businessman's adventure. They used to call the United States "The Golden Mountain." You could come over and not do anything except bend down and pick up all the gold you wanted. That was the impression in those days. They believed anybody who came from the United States was just loaded down with money. So these guys would leave their families in the old country and come here to make a living. My grandfather had three sons and one daughter. The oldest son, he decided to stay home and take care of the family. So my father, the third son, came to the states when he was fourteen years old. That was a few years before World War I. But when the war started, Grandpa got scared he'd be drafted, so he took him back to China and got him married. After the war, my father left his wife in China and returned to the U.S. As soon as he saved a little money, though, he would go home and visit his family. I was born during one of those visits. My brother was born during another.

When my dad first came to Utah, he and his father lived in Salt Lake. They even spent time in Plum Alley, which was full of gambling joints. Of course, my grandfather smoked opium. And they slept in the same room, so the smell of the opium went right into my dad's clothes. When he'd go to school, the teacher would question him about it. My dad was in high school then, at West High. That's when he found out about discrimination. He found out he couldn't go to certain theaters or swim at Wasatch Springs. And when he'd go to school, they'd call him "Chink, Chink, Chinaman," which is a disgrace, you know. Nowadays, anybody call you that, you just go sock them in the face. But that's when he said he learned to keep to himself. He was afraid of being deported.

When Grandpa was about fifty-five years old, he retired from business and went back to China. But my dad stayed here. Around 1935, he met an elderly Chinese couple from Phoenix who owned a grocery store but were also looking to return to China, so he took over their shop. It was a regular grocery store in a black and Mexican neighborhood, and Dad sold meats, vegetables, and canned goods. It was a struggle, though. For example, a loaf of bread at that time cost ten cents, and pies were a nickel. Dad always said he'd just love to eat one of those pies. But if he did, he would have to sell four more pies just to make up the difference. So he wouldn't eat it. But that's how he worked [his way] up. And he struggled—struggled until he earned like, maybe, fifteen hundred dollars to make a trip back to the old country to see Mother. Then people in China would see him and say, "Boy, here comes a millionaire from the United States, from the Golden Mountain."

When my brother was four years old, my father brought him and my mother to the U.S. They left me back in the old country, where I went from relative to relative. Of course, wherever I'd go, my father always sent money, so each relative fought for me to stay with them just to get the money. Then, when war broke out [with Japan] in 1937, Dad decided he better bring me over to the United States before the war got too big.

But, you know, I was really disappointed with this "Golden Mountain." In China, before I left, I was living with my mother's sister and her husband, who was an architect. My uncle made good money. He had a chauffeur, a cook, servants, and two maids to do the washing and cleaning. I never had to wash my own clothes. If they were dirty, I'd just throw them in the corner. The next thing you know, they'd be washed, ironed, and put back in the drawer. I think if you were upper-class and didn't have to work, you would be very well off in China.

But most people [in China] were poor [farmers]. My dad made life easier for our family because he worked in the United States. And at that time, one dollar maybe equalled thirty dollars or forty dollars in China. A hundred dollars might be three thousand dollars in China—enough to live on for a whole year. But in the United States, a dollar is a dollar. I found out that everybody has to work, and up till now, we're still working! Of course, the Chinese are known as very hardworking people. Very few go broke. They have a saying: "If I can't make it in eight hours, I can put in sixteen hours and make it." Of course, most Chinese love to gamble, too. And my dad was a bit of a gambler. If he won in Chinatown, he'd come back [home] and he'd have money—see, spending money, maybe thirty dollars. I remember one day my brother and I saw a nice car parked in front of our house. Walking in, we asked whose car it was, and Dad says, "I bought it. I won it last night." He won sixteen hundred dollars and went out and bought the car—the first car we owned.

When I came here in 1939, I was already a teenager—thirteen years old. They put me in the second grade. But the kids were nice. And soon they pushed me up, and I skipped over grades. My mother died shortly after I came here, but I was never any trouble for my father. He made arrangements with the school principal for me to have two hours at noontime so I could make him lunch. Then, every day after school, my brother and I worked in [his] grocery store. If we needed money, we'd get it from his safe. He never locked his safe. He knew we wouldn't spend money foolishly. Then, when Dad went back to China to get his new bride, he turned the store over to us. My brother and I ran it for him till he came back. It's the way of the Chinese people. You don't have to put your foot down or be strict. Just mind your folks. Whatever they say is okay.

When my dad brought his new wife back to the United States, life became a little different, and I wanted to get out of the way. It happened that my father's friend had a son, Harry, and the two men thought they would try to match us. See, they figure [that] after you reach a certain age, you should get married.

I remember, I just come home from work and Dad decided that it was time for me to marry. He said, "Look him over first. If you like him, it's okay. If he likes you, all right. [But] you don't have to marry him if you don't want to." So he [Harry] came for us to meet. The reason I really wanted to get married was to get out of the house, and that's what I did. Did I love him? Well, Americans talk about love at first sight. But I don't think there's such a thing. See, maybe you like a guy a little bit, but you really don't love him. Love is come after. You have to learn to love a person. It might be you like that person at first. Then you live with him and he's opposite, but you learn to love him. It's different.

With some old-timers, there wasn't even an introduction. Usually a girl is almost twenty when a matchmaker asks her to get married. The bride comes to the [groom's] house, whom she's never even seen before. Never. And after she's married, she might sit up for three nights or for a week before she can go to bed with him, because she doesn't know him. That's the old way. The old time. They don't do that no more, though.

I married Harry in 1950 and moved to Salt Lake City.[9] We got married in March, and my father passed away in June. He had high blood pressure, and in those days, there was no cure. There's an old Chinese tradition to have everybody live in the same house. So I've lived in this house for thirty-six years [along] with Harry's family. As our children came along—we had eight in thirteen years—the biggest problem was space. It was tight quarters. But eating was all right. We'd go to the restaurant.

I worked with Harry at the restaurant. His sisters worked there, too. In the '50s, there was lots of business. Before TV, this street was loaded with people on Friday and Saturday nights. I'd come down and relieve my sisters-in-law. It was very busy. There was no time for anything. We worked 364 days a year. Only Christmas we got off. We didn't know what a vacation was. Chinese people just stayed at their work. If you close a week, you think you're going to lose all your customers. That's how it was.

But right now, this place is dead. People don't come downtown anymore. So I'm thinking about closing this joint and just going home. After working for so many years, you know, kids all grown up, you think, "That's enough." But I don't think Harry's ready [to quit]. He's like the old family. His work is his life. For his part, if this place closes, there's nothing for him to do. He has no hobbies. Me? I got a lot of things to do. I love to work in the yard and see things grow. I love to sew, crochet, knit, fix things up around the house. So I tell him, "This place is becoming an expensive 'hobby.' You know, we get the joint open and by the time we pay our overhead, there is nothing left. And we have to keep digging out the reserve." So I tell him, "Why not forget it?"

But he just ignores me. He doesn't want to leave. Maybe he wants to pass it on. I don't know. But I don't want the kids to run the restaurant. Why run a little restaurant? I wouldn't encourage a kid to come work in this place sixteen hours a day. When they were growing up, I'd always tell them, "Go get a profession. If you can't make it, there's always stove work for you. Cooking, you don't need an education." I say, "The only thing I can give you is your education. And nobody can take it away from you. If I give you money, you spend it. It's gone. But an education, you can keep [forever]."

Postscript: Harry and Helen Louie closed the King Joy restaurant in the spring of 1991. Harry Louie passed away in Salt Lake City on March 9, 1996.

WILLIAM W. LOUIE, 62, PRINCIPAL IN THE ARCHITECTURAL FIRM OF SCOTT, LOUIE, AND BROWNING

Silver-haired, impeccably dressed, a strikingly distinguished-looking man, William W. Louie spoke in a soft voice, at times a whisper. Although unaccustomed to disclosing details of his personal life, he spoke to us, he said, to inform his children and grandchildren "that all of history here isn't Mormon history. Other minorities have a part, a share, in making Utah."

A fourth-generation Chinese-American, he was born in Ogden, Utah, on January 18, 1923, and raised in the city's Chinese enclave.[10] Upon completing high school, he joined the Army Air Corps and served in the ground crew of the celebrated 354th fighter squadron, which, he said, "shot down more airplanes in Europe than any other group in the air force." In 1945, he returned to Utah and, with the aid of the GI Bill, attended the University of Utah's newly formed School of Architecture. He graduated in 1951, a member of the university's first architectural class.

My father left Toishan, a farming district close to Canton, in 1909 and like his father and grandfather before him came to the United States, to San Francisco, to find work. As with most Chinese men of the time, he left his wife behind in China.

Between 1909 and 1917, my father worked at the Senate Café in Park City, Utah. Why he moved to Park City he never said, but it seems like such a strange place to come after San Francisco. He probably knew someone who offered him the job, and at that time Park City had a good-sized Chinese community. While [he was] in Park City, my father's first wife died, and it wasn't until 1919, when he was thirty-four years old, that he went back to China to marry [my mother]. In October 1921, he brought her to Ogden. My brother Harry was born the following month. I was born two years later. . . .

Now, my father was an uncommon member of Utah's Chinese community, because he had a family here. In Ogden in the '30s, there were only three Chinese families among two hundred men. Most of these bachelors talked about going back to China, whereas my dad—especially after he started to raise a family in the U.S.—never did. I remember him as a slender man, smaller than I am now, about five feet six inches tall. I look a lot like him. He was a hardworking person, always struggling to make ends meet. He dressed Western style, never wearing anything like you see in photographs of the older Chinese in Chinatown. He spoke the Toishan dialect, which is different from Cantonese. Perhaps it is more crude—a peasant-type language for those out in the sticks. We all spoke this dialect as we grew up. My father never became fluent in English. And it didn't matter; because in the restaurant, he was usually in the kitchen, and even as a waiter he would hardly have to use it. My mother never spoke much English either. A sort of frail woman, slightly taller than my father, she wore simple cotton dresses instead of traditional Chinese clothing.

William Louie. *George Janecek*

My parents were really reserved with us, but that is part of the Chinese character—to not be too demonstrative. Among their friends, I don't remember seeing them go beyond a handshake. But I do remember once when my sister was sick and cried in pain, so did my dad.

We rented our house in Ogden for twenty-five dollars a month. It was west of the main shopping area, between Twenty-fourth and Twenty-fifth streets, where all the Chinese lived. At that time, the residential district was right behind the business district, and one of our neighbors still had a barn and sheds. In fact, when the farmers came to town, some of them kept their horses in his barn. Looking back, I can see what a poor house we had. A frame structure, everything inside was minimal. We had a front porch with wooden steps and a wooden sidewalk, all worn out from wear. In the backyard, we had a garden and a coal shed. We burned coal for heating, and us kids had to go out in the cold mornings to get it.

The house had a living room, two bedrooms, a kitchen, and kind of a dining room. Seven kids (there were nine in our family) slept in one bedroom, while my mother and father slept in the other. In the living room, the sofa opened into a bed for my older brother and me. My mother did our cooking on a gas burner, like a hot plate, that sat on top of a table that had rollers on its legs. For meals, she would roll the table into the kitchen, prepare food on the tabletop, then roll it back into the dining room. Everybody sat around it and ate. We had rice at every meal and a simple Chinese dish that today could be considered a delicacy. Oh, yes, that room contained the coal stove. In the winter, when the heat was on, that was the warmest part of the house.

Religiously, my parents were Buddhists. I don't think they went to any kind of organized church in China, and at that time there wasn't a Buddhist temple in Salt Lake or Ogden. Instead, they followed a set of rituals—for example, when to light the incense and make sacrificial dishes for the kitchen gods or ancestors they revered. Growing up, we didn't have any formal religious training. We just followed the Chinese customs and traditions. As a community, we really kept to ourselves. We didn't have any big social interaction with our [white] neighbors.

The immigration problem may have been the cause of our isolation. Though we never had any specific action taken toward our family, when you grew up in the Chinese community, there was always this fear among everybody, because the majority of the people came here illegally. Consequently, they were always afraid some federal employee would catch up with them and investigate their family background. To protect us, I guess, my father never told us how he got here. But we were always aware our Chinese name was different than our American name. And when we got old enough, this became a shadow or question mark we always carried with us. . . .

Until I was ten or eleven, the central spot for the community, and in our lives as well, was the "Chinese store." There were two or three in Ogden. For the Chinese bachelors, who represented ninety-five percent of Ogden's Chinese population, the stores were more of a community center than anything else. Generally, each store represented a different clan. The front end of a store had token shelves containing medicine, tea, dishes, and other merchandise. And maybe they did sell some of that stuff. But, actually, the store was a front for illegal gambling. Three or four different types of gambling went on in the back—keno, dominoes, fan-tan, and at times they had slot machines.

My father worked in one of the stores. Since most of the bachelors lived in hotel rooms, each store [also] had a cook for its employees and bachelor "guests." As kids, we too got to eat dinner with them almost every night. We were probably the only Chinese kids these men ever saw, and going there became a way of life for us.

I did not speak English until the first grade. But then I learned quickly. My dad always wanted us to get a good education. Both of my parents pushed us to better ourselves. For themselves, though, they never had any big goals. Every day, they were just trying to subsist. My father never had a car. We always rented a house. We didn't have many luxuries.

From the age of ten through high school, my main passion was aviation. I didn't dream of flying airplanes; but I liked making them, just like other kids enjoyed making model cars. In junior high school, in fact, I joined a model club and got involved in quite a few competitive meets. When I left high school, I applied to Hill Air Force Base to be on a government civilian program working on planes. After I completed a training program in Sacramento, I worked in the instrument repair shop [at Hill] and on gyroscoping flight instruments. Six months later, September 1942, I joined the regular Army Air Corps and eventually became part of the 354th fighter group.

Now, prior to my military experience, I experienced some name-calling. After Pearl Harbor, Ogden kids who thought I was Japanese called me "Jap" and worse. That happened to many Chinese people at the time; in desperation, I remember, we came out with a badge that stated "I am Chinese-American." I wore one, too. Once I got into the military, though, that kind of intimidation didn't happen often.

After completing basic training, I was sent overseas and stationed about forty miles from London, in Colchester. I was part of the ground crew for the 354th. I remember writing long letters home to my parents, especially about the blitz. But I was never really homesick. I was fascinated by airplanes, and, as it turned [out], I was in the glory part of the business. See, our fighter group was selected to use the new P51 Mustang. And by the war's end, we had shot down more enemy airplanes than any other fighter group in the air force. We wound up with over a thousand planes destroyed. So we were glamorized. We were constantly in the English papers and magazines.

Later in the war, our assignment was to follow and support General Patton's Third Army. So, after the June 6, 1944, invasion of the mainland, we flew over to France. We followed on the beachhead within a month. Then, since the advancing ground troops needed air support, we'd set up temporary hangars and lay down runways in hacked-down country fields. We followed Patton this way across France and into Germany.

My military specialization slated me as an instrument technician, but I had a talent for artwork and so spent much of my time painting and repairing damaged planes and doing my specialty—nose art. Have you seen those names, cartoons, and even figures of beautiful women painted on the bombers, on their noses in particular? Well, that's the kind of work I did.

For example, our squadron commander, James Howard, who had come in from the Flying Tigers in China, asked me to paint "Ding Ho"—which in Chinese means number one, the best—on his plane. I did that. Then I painted [symbols for] all the planes he had shot down in the Pacific—there were six, I think. Later I added a swastika for each plane he shot down in Europe. Other pilots in the squadron came to me, too, when they wanted to personalize their planes. And I was happy to do it. I felt I was really helping them, helping their morale. In the heat of battle, these markings also helped our antiaircraft people identify the planes. My "Ding Ho" design later became famous. When I returned to the U.S., I found a facsimile of Howard's plane among the most famous World War II model airplanes. It was a complete replica, right down to the lettering I had done on the nose.

After the war, I got on the GI Bill and went to college in Utah. For a while, I boarded with a mixed-marriage couple, the Yungs. It was sort of an unusual family, because Mrs. Yung was Caucasian and her husband was an old-time Chinese fellow, somewhere in his fifties then. At that time, antimiscegenation statutes were still on the law books making it illegal for Orientals to marry whites. That type of marriage in Utah was rare, anyway. But I wondered about them a lot, because I had been brought up with a strict taboo against marrying outside the Chinese race. Yet there was something typical about them—and familiar. He worked in the Chinese stores [like my father], was out most nights, and dominated her just like other Chinese men did their wives.

When I began dating in college, there were few Chinese girls to go out with. Most of the [Oriental] girls I knew were Japanese who had come here with their families because of the relocation policy and, after the war, had remained. The difficulty and stigma in dating them came from my parents and other Chinese. They actually thought it was worse to go out with a Japanese woman than a Caucasian, because Japan and China had been at war with each other. My mother objected more strongly than my father, particularly when I became serious about Mary [who eventually became my wife].

To me, though, it was easier dating Japanese than Caucasians, because they were at least Asian. But Mary and I had to sneak around. Since my mother died in 1949, before we were married, she never had to become totally disappointed with me. My father, I think, finally accepted Mary before he died; at least he softened after we married in 1951.

After I was demobilized, I began college in the engineering department, then switched over to the Fine Arts School for a commercial art degree. When they started the Architectural School in 1949, I switched again. It was an ideal combination, a blend of engineering and art, and I did well. After graduating in 1951, I worked for architects Scott and Beecher. Scott was my present partner's dad. After Mr. Scott died, Walt Scott, Bill Browning, and I formed a new firm.

Now, I don't think being Chinese affected the work we've pursued or gotten. I'm sure some people looked negatively on them for having a Chinese partner, but no one's said they weren't going to choose us because I'm not white. What affected us more is that none of us is LDS, and that's a rarity for architectural firms here.

Personally, as an architect, I feel like I'm an example to Chinese kids coming up. For a long time, the average white person here in Utah associated Chinese with restaurants, laundries, or railroads. Now our children are realizing that it's possible to be successful in other businesses, without being white. But I never forget I'm Chinese. When people ask, I describe myself as Chinese-American, and physically, I'm always aware I'm different from most people around here. When I go into a store or into a strange gathering, and I'm the only Chinese among a hundred people, I can't help but feel like I am spotlighted. But I don't want you to get the idea that I feel close to the traditional Chinese community. I don't. What I feel close to is my ancestry. I come from six generations of Chinese, and I am proud of my culture and heritage.

BOB W. LOUIE, 59, INSURANCE SALESMAN, NEW YORK LIFE

Born on November 27, 1927, Bob Louie (William Louie's younger brother) believes he helped recast "the mold" for Utah's Chinese population. In his mid-thirties, he left the restaurant milieu in which he was raised and became, he said, New York Life's "first" Chinese insurance agent. The interview with him was conducted in his office in downtown Salt Lake City. Louie sat beside his desk. On the wall behind him there was an enormous, fully opened Oriental fan.

I've been so doggone busy earning a living these last twenty years that I haven't really reflected much on my life. But when I came into this business, most of the people who hired me never thought I'd survive in this jungle. Yet here I am—twenty-two years later. I fooled everybody. Really! There are those here that still remember when I started. There are a few. We still think about that, kind of joke about it. But it wasn't a joke back then. There was a lot of trepidation on whether or not I could make it in this business. A lot of them said, "Give him three months, [then] he'll be out doing something else." They never thought I would do it.

So, [looking back,] I'm glad I made the move [into insurance] at an age when most people are too afraid to start a new career. Because I think—even though I was born here in the United States—in a way, I pulled myself out. I pulled myself away from a mold here in Utah that most Chinese people were in.

You see, in my era, when I was a youth, things were tough for everybody. The Depression for one thing, [and] coming from a large family for another— it was difficult. It was really difficult for people to achieve. Everybody was out trying to earn a living to help the family out. That's everybody, not only Chinese. But I think for me and many [other Chinese-Americans] like me, some things were particularly tough. You had to work, and you had to help out with the family. So all your free time was taken up. There was no way to meet anyone outside your community.

While my [white] schoolmates were out playing, I was already working in the restaurant business. And life continued like that. And in the restaurant business, we worked fourteen hours a day, six days a week, with no vacations. So up until the time I came into the insurance business, it was really difficult to meet anybody socially. We were kind of stuck with our own. Some people rose above this and achieved greatness.[11] Others remained in that rut. So . . .

Bob Louie. *Kent Miles*

as I reflect back, I *know* why I took to the insurance business. Because for the *first* time in my life, [after I got into it] I could say, "My God, I've got a white man's job!" [*Chuckles*]

You see, coming into the insurance business was just like going from one world to the next. The hours were long, of course. But they were of my own choosing. And all of a sudden, I was meeting entirely new people. So it's been good [for me], and it's been a lot of fun, too. I've gone to [new] places, I've made a good living at it, and I've had a lot of time to enjoy my family. I probably would not have been able to do that if I had stayed in the restaurant business.

Unfortunately, though, over the years and because of new business commitments, I've pulled away from the Chinese community a bit. Although some of my clients are still Chinese people, and I keep in contact with them and would help them if they need help, I just haven't stayed active in the community.[12]

But, you see, most of us who were born here in the United States see things differently than our parents. What we feel is this: When Chinese people came and settled in this country, if they wanted to make their life in this country, they did what they had to do. But being born in this country, we're mingling with other people who were born here. And whatever the fashions are, we adopt to a great degree. So, although many Chinese talk about the old cultural things they brought over with them, I think it's just the minority of them that still cling to that way. Most of us want to be able to say, "Hey, we are of Chinese descent, but we are Americans and we want to be recognized as such!"

I was recently talking to a person I've known a long time. He's a friend, and he's a client of mine. We were talking about celebrating the Chinese New Year. Now, this friend of mine has always worked for Chinese people. Although he's Caucasian, he's been very friendly with many Chinese. And he was showing me some invitations he had to Chinese New Year parties. I said, "That's sure great, Steve. You're getting invitations and I'm not even getting them." He said, "Bob, they probably think you're just a white man now." [*Laughs*]

So maybe that's it. Maybe that explains [some of] what I'm saying. My children have all kinds of friends today. I, myself, I think that's good. Although, like I said, I've dealt with a lot of Oriental clients. I respect them. If they need help, if they want me to help them, I will. So I'm not saying I've renounced Chinese people. But, hey, I feel we're [living] in a country where everybody is the same. So I don't feel like I should segregate my social life or my feelings.

I've always felt that [segregation] was the [real] problem for most Chinese people in this country. Unlike other races who came here, the Chinese came because they didn't have any other way to make it in China. So most of the early [Chinese] immigrants who came into this country were workers. Their whole thinking was just to come over here, save enough money, then go back to China. Japanese people came over to this country because they wanted to settle here. So they got into the mainstream of America more rapidly.

[Historical] circumstances, however, made that [adjustment] especially difficult for the Chinese people. In the first place, many of them didn't earn enough money to go back to China. Second, until 1965, they couldn't bring their families over, either. So there were few Chinese families here. Third, many of them—even if they *couldn't* accomplish it—went [through their lives] feeling, I'm just going to save enough money, then go back to China and die. Few thought of settling in Utah permanently.

And what did most of these people do in the '20s and '30s? They ran a restaurant, a laundry, maybe a small grocery. That's about all. They didn't have any other opportunities. They couldn't go out and walk into an office and get a job. For one thing, the language barrier kept them out; for another, no one would hire them. I don't care how qualified they were, the language and racial barriers kept them out. Those were difficult times.

Today, I think it's wide open for Chinese people. If they qualify [for a job], they can do whatever they want. Of course, to a certain extent, racial discrimination is still here. It's not as widespread or as vocal as it was back then, but it's here. Yet [despite discrimination], there are opportunities available for you to find your niche and feel comfortable. Other doors are available—doors that I couldn't get into twenty years ago. For instance, I have a lot of

Caucasian clients now that I might not have had then, and I get along fine with them. They trust me. So, looking back, I think today's business climate has opened up tremendously.

As far as the children are concerned, I think it's going to be even easier for them. When I was a young kid going to school, life was segregated. The white kids did their thing, and we [Chinese] did our thing. Today, the kids are growing up with each other. They're going through school together, they're socializing, they're becoming one, so to speak. So, on a business-type basis, because of this, the trust will be there. They won't have to hear, "I don't know your kind, so I won't even let you through the door." They're already *in* the door.

WILLIAM TANG, 64, RETIRED MERCHANT

William Tang's office is in the southeast corner of his now vacant supermarket. All morning, on the day of our interview with him, he had taken potential lessees on tours of the store, and now he led us to the office. We climbed the back stairs, passed through an attic-like space cluttered with crates and old cash registers, and entered a midsized room whose walls were covered with calendar photographs advertising "ideal" vacation spots around the world. The images were bright, colorful, and unreal.

Tang's appearance was casual (corduroy shirt, jeans, denim jacket); his speaking style was agitated and self-probing. Although he was at first reluctant to speak of his "personal life," as the interview progressed, he relaxed; his eyes softened and brightened, and he spoke comfortably, albeit within self-imposed limits.

Born in Canton, China, on December 22, 1922, William Tang came to the United States at the age of sixteen. After paying off the indenture to his uncle for bringing him over as his "paper son," he started his steady climb toward financial independence. He settled in Salt Lake City in 1942, and following a brief trip back to China after the war (during which time he married), he bought and operated, in succession, a Chinese restaurant, a grocery store, and finally a supermarket at 428 East 900 South. An ambitious man with a dream of "making it big," he learned to balance his gambler's instinct with sharp-edged, almost bitter, pragmatism.

I came to the United States with my uncle in 1938, after the Japanese invaded Shanghai. My uncle had been back to China a number of times. Like most Chinese, if they were good people, they went back and forth every few years. You might ask why they did that. It had to do with the stupid immigration laws. They didn't permit Chinese citizens to bring their wives over. So the only way [to live] was to go back, stay with your family a while, then come back here to work. People got by. [It was] not the way they'd like to [live], but they got by.

I guess you've heard from the other Chinese that the only way to get in the country was by coming as someone's son or daughter. Have you heard that? Well, my uncle reported that I was his son, and I paid him so much for the

William Tang. *Kent Miles*

piece of paper that recognized him as my father. This was illegal. But the only way you could come over was as the son [or daughter] of an American citizen.

Now, I didn't know much about the United States. I knew my uncle wanted to take me over, and my family liked it. And I knew the stories about [life] here from other people—all those fantastic stories about opportunity. We saw people returning to China, and it seemed they were always rich. It seemed there was always more money here than in the old country. Whether they were actually rich or not, I didn't know. That was the impression.

Actually, when you're a youngster, how much "knowledge" do you have? You don't know enough [about the world] to judge. Sometimes what you hear is the truth, sometimes it's a lie. You don't know how to tell the difference. You make decisions [based] on what you hear. Besides, when you're a young kid [in China], you don't have much to say; the family does most of the saying, see? We talk about individualism here as if choices are always ours. But how in heck do you expect a teenager to make that kind of choice? It's foolish. He can't do it. He doesn't have enough knowledge. More or less, it's a family decision; they okay it.

I came with a suitcase and a duffel bag. We sailed on the *Princess Russia* from Hong Kong to Seattle, Washington, in nineteen days. It was a big steamer, the kind you see in movies. The boat was divided into sections: first class, second class, third class, and so on. In the third class [where we were], they combined a group of people, and each [person] had a bed to sleep in. I don't think they let you go into first or second class. But I don't know. I was such a greenhorn, I just stayed close by my uncle. [*Laughs*] Sometimes I stepped out a little bit [on my own], but not that much.

After I got in the states, I went to Pennsylvania; that's where my uncle had a laundry shop. I stayed a few weeks, then I went over to my number-two uncle, who opened a place in Johnstown, Pennsylvania, maybe sixty miles south of Uniontown. And I learned to wash and iron clothes. They had [washing] machines, but you had to check colors and put clothes together by hand. Each material had to be washed a little differently. You had to learn how to treat a certain color, and you had to make sure colors didn't fade.

When I think back, I guess I felt good the whole time I was there. You see, I was just a kid. I didn't have to depend on anyone. I was kind of free. I didn't make much money. But the system was that you worked in the shop; they paid your room and board. You slept with so many people in a room, but you had your own bed. You all ate together at a big table, and you didn't worry about anything. So it was pretty good. I missed my family. But that's what happens when you grow up: You come out into the world. Either you stay in your community or you go someplace [to find work]. Some of my school friends went to [find work in] the Philippines and South America. . . . I came here.

I worked in the laundry for three years. But I consider myself pretty lucky, 'cause I heard of people who came over and had to work for a particular person for years and years. I was not that way. Before coming over, I knew how much he was going to charge. Then I just accumulated money to pay him. It was a good deal. My uncle charged me one thousand dollars. Of course, at the time, one thousand dollars was still quite a bit of money. But I heard other people say it took them years to pay back many thousands of dollars. So my uncle was pretty considerate; it was a good price. Under the immigration law, of course, that [transaction] was illegal. So I was glad when a number of years later they changed the law, making all those illegal citizens [like myself] legal. Because a person could have been a good person, yet he was still an illegal [alien]. Of course, we still have a lot of stupid laws. And sometimes you just have to wait for the right situation before a particular law can surface and you can do something about it.

In 1942, three months after the war [World War II] started, I moved to Salt Lake and started school here. I had a relative here; he found me a little place in Plum Alley. Plum Alley had four Chinese stores at the time. People did a little business in the store[fronts], but in the back, they gambled among themselves. They had to do it that way—keep it quiet—because it was against the law. But since they didn't make trouble, the law could pretend it didn't exist. They closed one eye, which, I think, is right. Because gambling is part of our nature. You can't draw a straight line [and expect it to fit everyone's lifestyle]. You have to make the line a little crooked, because human nature is still human nature.

I attended Horace Mann Junior High mainly to learn the language, and after school, I worked in the New China Café. I remember [that] Jimmy Leo, a friend of mine at the time, took me over [to the school]; it was [located] kitty-corner from West High. During the war, Jimmy had a café on Main Street called the Rice Bowl. Anyway, I went to school and I worked. I never worried about jobs. During the war, the jobs came looking for you. There were so many soldiers in Salt Lake, the cafés were always full, especially on Friday or Saturday nights. [I remember,] as soon as we filled up, we closed the doors. When a table was open, we cleaned up, let the people out, before we let the next party in. We couldn't let people wait inside, because we couldn't work then. . . .

During the war years, there was a lot of discrimination here. Blacks were still called Negroes, and Negro and white soldiers had separate camps. Even in the movie theaters they were separated. There was a lot of prejudice. Chinese people couldn't purchase property in certain areas. A friend of mine tried to buy a home on Thirteenth East. They wouldn't sell it to him. So I would say at the time there was a racial line [separating people].

In 1945, I was drafted into the army. I served for a year, then I decided to go back to China for a visit. At that time, my entire family was still there: my father, my mother, my grandparents. And when you're from an old country, somehow, over time, everything you had there becomes beautiful to you. *Everything.* Somehow that was in my head, so I went back. And in some ways, the place was beautiful; in other ways, it was not. After the war, a lot of things were broken down. The Japanese soldiers had been through there and caused a lot of damage. People lost a lot of money. Not many businesses were operating. But, in other ways, the place was just the same.

I found a wife in the old, customary way, through friends or relatives. I know arranging marriages sounds like a crazy idea to Americans. But the notion of love at first sight sounds crazy to the Chinese. Maybe [in America] we have more open[ness] between a man and a woman. You can go to a party, see a girl, get introduced to her, then get to know each other. Maybe you're in a big hurry, you call it love at first sight, and you get married. [*Laughs*] But what does it prove? People still end up in divorce court. So it makes you wonder. Is it actually better? [White] people laugh at Chinese backwardness; they compare arranging marriages to mating cows or pigs. But I think it all depends on your point of view. It all depends on who is writing the story.

My wife was from a village eight miles from my village. The villages were all separated by rice fields. The fields were always covered with water, deep water; that's how they farmed the rice. Anyway, my wife's aunt met me in the marketplace. She knew I had come back from America, so she asked me if I was married. I said, "No, not yet." She said she had a niece [and] I could see if I liked her. So she introduced us, and I said okay. That was it. A lot of times, you just have to take a chance. In everything we do we have to take a chance, because nobody, absolutely nobody, knows the outcome before making a move. You might call it a calculated risk, but it's still a risk.

When we came back [to Utah], the owner of the New China Café asked me to come and run his business. I ran it until the Korean War started in 1950; then we went into business together. We leased a place on the corner of State Street and Second South and called it the Little Dragon. We worked together for five years, then I started looking for a business by myself. See, a partnership usually fails because of differences of opinion. You might feel the place is too dirty; you should get someone to clean it up. He says it's clean enough; don't waste manpower on cleaning. You'll say, this is a good cook; he'll say the cook's lousy. Things like that. None of them a big deal. But they reflect other things. So you just separate.

Afterward, I opened a little grocery store on Second West and Sixth South: the United Market. It was just a small grocery. We sold produce, groceries, dairy products, and beer. But I'll tell you, when I think back, it was hard. I remember I didn't have a garbage man. Once or twice a week, I had to empty my bins and take the garbage to the dump. It was hard to get steady meat from the butcher supply house. I needed a dairy case to shelve milk, and I couldn't afford new refrigeration. So I bought an old-fashioned unit with three doors for one hundred dollars. I also had to ask the bread companies to give me racks for shelves. But I didn't know if they would do that. If you sold their bread, would they give you a bread rack? [*Chuckles*] I laugh about it now, but when I think back at those times, I wasn't laughing [then]. I was even afraid to ask them for bread racks. [*Chuckles*]

Now, my customers were mostly working people who lived off Second West, an industrial area of the city. At the time, the freeway [I-15] had not come in there. But Highways 40, 89, and 91 all passed by the store. And during the summer, Mexican workers came up to pick cherries. When they came through town, they always pulled off the highway and stopped in at the store. Boy, they bought a lot of lunch meat. I had a meat slicer, and I cut them baloney, pressed ham, salami, cheese—whatever they wanted. I remember, they also bought a lot of sandwiches. I sold them for twenty-five cents a piece, and I made very good money.

When the freeway came in, we lost a lot of the neighborhood. They tore down a lot of houses and built the Holiday Inn, the Travel Lodge, the Roadway Inn, and that's when I knew I'd have to move. I think that was in 1966. I bought the Super-Saver here on Ninth South, and I came over with my little American dream. I had noticed what Dee Smith did. He started with a small store in Roy, Utah, and built a supermarket empire. 'Course, I don't know if the chain belonged to Dee or to somebody behind the scenes. But, at one time, I hoped to have a few more stores, and the dream never materialized 'cause I had a hard time going from a small grocery to a supermarket.

You see, I went from twenty-five hundred square feet to about nine thousand square feet, and I made a mistake. I miscalculated. According to my figures, I should have come out ahead. But it didn't work out that way. There were a lot of things I didn't see. First, I took over the name Foodtown. When you do that, they advertise weekly for you and you pay Associated Foods for your portion of the ad [regardless of your advertising budget]. Then, they had Gold Strike stamps [trading stamps purchased by grocers for customer use]. That's expensive stuff. I felt the pinch of that every day. It seemed I couldn't make any money.

I started staying up in the office here in the evening after everybody had gone. I sat here, opened the books, and tried to see why I wasn't able to make money. You know what? When I looked at those figures, a chill went through me; I felt a cold chill inside, and I broke into a sweat. I said, "It can't be." This wasn't just once or twice; many times when I looked at my books I felt the same chill and sweat. Then I said to myself, you have to cut the overhead. This is your business. You have to cut the overhead. I finally went home and told my wife, "This is the situation. We have to make a move. Otherwise, I'm going to be dead soon."

Well, I knew I couldn't move. The only thing I could do was knock the ghost out of the way. So I tore my Foodtown sign out—I had a beautiful electric sign outside. I tore it down so I wouldn't have to pay as much electricity. Then I changed the name of the store to Super-Saver Discount, laid off some people, and, somehow, it worked. I could feel the release. Before, I took money out of my pocket each month. Once I made the change, I stopped losing money. Then I knew I could make it. I felt a lot safer.

Lots of times, you see, you don't know exactly what you're supposed to do until you are *in* a situation and [the reality] hits you. At that time, you have to face it. And you better find an answer; and you better find the *right* answer to solve your problem. Fortunately, I did. My dream never came out. I dreamt I would get big, and it didn't work out. I will never dream that again. So I said [to myself], well, just hold on to what you've got. Do it in a smaller way. Don't try to fight it. You can beat your brains out. Maybe you'll get a little further ahead. Maybe you won't.

Of course, I still had my headaches. Safeway, Albertson's, Food King, and Smith's were all in the area. They all gave me headaches. Even 7-Eleven; they like to sit themselves right next to a big store. But, somehow, each store, over time, develops its own customers. You might say each store has its own personality to please a certain group of customers, and they become a unit. People will drive a couple of blocks to come in and give you their business. Sometimes your next-door neighbors won't shop with you; they'll go elsewhere. But you'll get customers from quite a few blocks away coming just to shop with you. That's pretty common. I had good meat, good produce, low prices, and, eventually, customers I began to call friends. So it all worked out, because I learned to let things go a little, not to press so hard. This way, I might live a little longer, enjoy life a little bit more.

HELEN GIM KURUMADA, 69, DIRECTOR OF THE OFFICE OF ASIAN AFFAIRS, REAL ESTATE AGENT

Helen Gim Kurumada learned about the fragility and uncertainty of life sooner than most young people. One of four children, she was born on May 17, 1919, in Mackey, Idaho, and settled with her parents in Plum Alley after the stock market crash of 1929 wiped out her father's restaurant business. When she was thirteen, her father passed away from heart failure, and two years later her mother suffered a fatal nervous breakdown. Helen became the sole supporter of her siblings at the age of sixteen. Remarkably, she did not turn bitter. Adversity became a spur for personal growth and, later, for community activity and political advocacy. During World War II, she worked with the Utah Japanese American Citizens League (JACL) to resettle Japanese-Americans forced to evacuate the West Coast; in the late 1960s, she participated in the Utah State Board of Education's initial effort to incorporate ethnic history into public school curricula; and in 1980, she became Utah's first director of Asian affairs.

I've always thought the Chinese community is years behind other minorities in organizing themselves for their own benefit. Here in Salt Lake, where the roots of the community go back to the old immigrants and the old attitudes of working sixteen hours a day for pennies in a restaurant, little has changed. The same conditions exist in the Chinese restaurants now that existed when I was young. In fact, my nephew was so mired in it that it really upset me. I told him, "You've got to get out of this. You'll never get anywhere." So he's gotten out. But you can waste your life working in those

Helen Kuramada with her
husband, Jun Kuramada.
Kent Miles

restaurants. You work sixteen hours a day—and at the end of the day, what
do you do? You go to a furnished room or a gambling house. You have no
social life. Your relationships with the opposite sex are with prostitutes. And—
good grief—*all* this was going on when I was a girl!

But Chinese won't discuss this. Yet, there are people coming over as they
were a century ago and still getting stuck here when they are sixty and seventy
without a family. No one knows anything about them. They've worked in
Chinese restaurants all their lives. And all of a sudden, they're seventy, they're
sick, they're living alone, and there's no one to help them. Because there are
no Chinese churches here. There are no temples. There's, in fact, no organized Chinese community.

Recently, I've been thinking of writing about what it was like to grow up
Chinese in the Intermountain West . . . because what I've read—though it's
well written—doesn't contain much nitty-gritty stuff. People say "nice"
things. Now, I'm not necessarily wanting to drag up the seamy side, but it
wasn't like that. And for our children's sake somebody ought to say, look, we
went through terrible times. People called you "Chink." They pulled their

eyes up at the corner. They beat you up. In fact, as [school]children, we hid in bushes until everybody went home so we wouldn't get beaten up. And we weren't just beaten up once in a while. We were beaten up every single day.

I don't know much about my mother's family, but I do know about my father's. My grandfather came over in the very early days of immigration. He came on what was called a business visa. And somehow he got his wife here, too, 'cause the records show she came over and had three children. The oldest child was a son, my father was the second, then they had a daughter. In the 1870s, my grandfather [apparently] realized a wave of anti-Chinese hysteria was coming, so he took his family back to China. They had three more children there, twin boys and another girl.

When my father was twelve, his father sent him and his sixteen-year-old brother to San Francisco to work and send money back to the family. Now, the older brother, who had the promise of a job, was supposed to look after my father. But growing up, I always heard how terrible this brother was. He gambled and visited houses of prostitution. And when my father told him, "You're not supposed to do this; I'm going to write home to mother," his brother beat him up. After several beatings, my father said he ran away to a mining camp somewhere else in California and, gradually, worked his way up to Oregon. He was smart enough to realize, though, that as long as he was in mining camps [with other Chinese] his brother could find him and—in the exaggerated mind of a twelve-year-old, he thought—kill him.

So, in Oregon, Dad made friends with a young Caucasian who was working for the Union Pacific Railroad. One day this fellow told him that he was being transferred as a brakeman to the run between Mackey and Blackfoot, Idaho—where there were no Chinese. [He said] that if he came along, the brother would never find him. So, hidden under sacks of mail, father rode to Idaho.

And his friend was right. He *was* the only Asian in Mackey. For a while, he worked in mining camps. Then, when he was fifteen, he borrowed $115.00 and bought the consignment for a lunch counter at the [railroad] depot. It had six or eight chairs, and I believe it took him two years to pay the money back. Apparently, he did well, because years later, when he was about thirty-eight and married, he had made enough money to open a restaurant and buy a ranch of several hundred acres. He had the first Sizzler idea, I think. He wanted to raise beef to use in his restaurant. . . .

But then the big [stock market] crash came, and beef prices plummeted. Then in the spring of 1929, Idaho farmers discovered that Idaho Power and Light, which controlled their irrigation water, decided to make a land grab. So, following the crash, the company raised their irrigation rates. They charged something like twenty-seven dollars per acre of water, which ruined everyone—forced many to leave their homes.

[When we were] coming down from Idaho to Salt Lake, I recall that our train was like a funeral train. We were riding with people like the Longhursts, who owned six or seven thousand acres of land and had simply left it behind. In a way, that train ride was like the [later] Japanese evacuation from the West Coast, because these people weren't able to take any possessions. Where could they put them? Everyone was crying.

My mother continued to cry after we arrived in Salt Lake. Unlike my father, she always looked on the dark side of things. But considering her background, I can see why. You see, her aunt had gone back to China and told my grandmother she [the aunt] could take Mother to the United States. She'd make a better marriage here. She'd have a place to live with my aunt, and she could go to school and get some knowledge of English. But that wasn't the way it happened. What my aunt got was a free maid, who cooked, washed, and cleaned in exchange for room and board. And mother never got over it. She felt life had really handed her a bum deal. So, after we arrived, I remember her saying, "I don't know. We may even starve to death." My father said, "We'll find something. We're not going to starve."

Now, we didn't have any kin in Utah. But we knew there was a clan of Yees here, so my father felt we wouldn't be alone.[13] He felt there would always be something to do to feed the family. And that's why we came. [Chinese] clan obligations are similar to extended family obligations, except they are even less elective. It is your duty—no matter how you do it—to make sure these people don't starve. . . .

I remember arriving in Chinatown—Plum Alley—which was less than a half a block long. Supposedly, there was a place for us there. It turned out to be a tenement house. This was a tremendous comedown. In Idaho we had a house. But this place had rats and cockroaches. It was old and dirty. My mother grew even more depressed. But my father had some money, and he and another fellow bought a restaurant on First South called the Bon Ton Café.

Unfortunately, though, my father's health started to fail. He probably had high blood pressure, which was not diagnosed. So he began having heart trouble and got pleurisy. And when I was thirteen, he died. I remember—he came home and asked me to put on some hot water for tea. As I did, he leaned back in his rocking chair and said, "I'm so tired. . . ." Then he was gone. I was scared out of my wits. He must have had a massive heart attack. But there was no autopsy. The authorities didn't care. It was just one more Chinese dead. His clan made the arrangements for the funeral. And they buried him in the city cemetery—in the Chinese section.

The next day, I remember, I had the distinct feeling I was going to have to be responsible [for all of us]. So at Christmastime I got a job at Kress's [Department Store]. We lived in Plum Alley for another year and a half. I think it was my nature to accept my father's philosophy. Yet things were hard, and I can understand how my mother felt. She had four kids, there was no welfare, no way she could get help, and she didn't know how she was going to cope. I kept telling her, "We're not going to die. We're going to be all right." But she felt like, you don't understand anything!

Then [two years after my father died], my mother was sitting in the apartment one day, and all of a sudden she started saying things that didn't make sense. She took out her purse and said, "Look—we've got lots of money!" But there was less than four dollars in her purse. We called a doctor. He came . . . and told us, "Your mother's had a total breakdown. She has to be committed to the Utah State Hospital. There isn't any other place for her to go." So she was, and she eventually died there. The doctors told us, "She didn't want to live."

[After they took Mother away], the Children's Service Society came down for us. And since we didn't have any adults who were responsible for us, they arranged for us to live with a Caucasian family until I finished high school. My cousin, whom my father helped go through the university, found out about our bind and began sending us fifty dollars a month. The Children's Service Society contributed something like twenty dollars a month. And our clan made arrangements for a moving company to take our possessions. We didn't have much. And we went to live with a blue-collar Mormon family.

Now, this family did the best they could with us under the circumstances. The mother wanted us, but her three boys felt it was a disgrace to have "Chinks" living with them. I remember there was instantaneous gossip throughout the ward about this family taking in Chinks. Then there was a daily parade of [curious] neighbors who came through to look at us. Yet this wasn't a first for me. The first time I faced racial slurs was in Mackey, when I was about six. Above J. C. Penney's was a social hall that people always rented for parties. All the [Caucasian] kids were talking about this upcoming party. I remember I was talking to my mother about the dress I would wear when my father said, "We're not going to the party." I asked, "Why not?" He said, "We were not invited." "Why aren't we invited?" He said, "Because we are Chinese." Now, all the kids used to call me Chink, but it never entered my mind until then that I wouldn't be invited to a party because of that.

Anyway, slurs weren't new. What surprised me, though, was school here. That was a culture shock. I remember I walked into the high school cafeteria on my first day with my lunch. I was going to sit down close to some Caucasian kids, and this Japanese girl suddenly appeared out of nowhere, took my hand, and said, "I wouldn't do that." "You mean sit over here and eat lunch?" I said. She said, "Don't do it. You'll make trouble for yourself. Come and sit with us." She was referring to the Japanese kids. I said, "Okay." I didn't know the rule, see, that all minority kids sat in their own groups: The Jewish kids sat together, the Asian kids sat together, and the Mexican kids. But thanks to previous experience, I knew "trouble" meant you were going to get beaten up.

Still, I remember thinking, what's the big deal? They're eating their lunches, I'm eating mine. Why can't I sit where I want? But after the Japanese girl's warning, a Jewish girl, Rachel, said, "Listen, don't try anything. You'll get in trouble. Your parents will find out; then they'll give it to you, too." Now, I hadn't considered that. So I decided it's not worth it.

But discrimination was absolutely public in Salt Lake. We couldn't go to city swimming pools. Our parents paid taxes, but we couldn't swim in the Liberty Park pool. When we went to a movie at one of the better theaters, we couldn't sit downstairs. We had to go upstairs—to the balconies.

I remember our sixth-grade class went to Wasatch Springs one day to learn something about the hot springs. I was the only Asian in the class. And I can remember the look of absolute disgust and despair on our teacher's face when the manager came out and said, "This girl can't go in here." The teacher said, "Why not? She's part of my class." He said, "What is she—a Chink or a Jap?" I remember him saying that! The teacher said, "What does it matter?" "We have our rules," he said. "Won't you please make an exception this time?" the teacher pleaded. "I'm responsible for these children. I can't be in there watching them and out here watching her, too." So he made an exception, and I remember, distinctly, he said, "Don't you ever try this again."

In high school, I began attending the Japanese Church of Christ and making friends in the Japanese community. I was attracted to the Japanese, because as a community they were better organized. They had a higher standard of living, and they were ambitious.

Plum Alley, well, it was like a collection of seedy bars you'd see in New York. It was the equivalent of that. All these single, mostly old men were there, gambling. And they had terrible personal habits. Their clothes were dirty, and they were generally unkempt. I knew there was dope dealing. Nobody talked about it, but it was there. I also knew better than to let on that I knew. Because that was one thing we were all taught early on—you don't repeat *anything* you hear *to anyone*. . . .

So I wanted to move as far away from Chinatown and that strata of Chinese life as possible. Plum Alley just wasn't a place you wanted to live. None of these men living there had much of a future. They weren't going to make enough money to go back to China. They talked about it. But unless one had a stroke of good fortune while gambling, they were never going to make it. And who was going to go back to China broke? It wasn't the way it was done. What would you do after you got there? So this wasn't pleasant stuff to be around. These men led miserable lives. They died one by one and were usually buried by some relative or clan member in the city cemetery. The only way they made it back to China was if their family organization sent money to exhume their bodies and take their remains home.

After I graduated high school, we moved out of the foster home and went on our own. Through the WPA, I got a temporary job at the State Engineer's Office. From there, I found full-time secretarial work with the Utah Forestry Service.

I was definitely lucky to find work! But the thing I marvel at, in hindsight, is that Judge Reuben Clark allowed me to take care of my brothers and sisters. I was sixteen—definitely under age, you see. Judge Clark was in his second year on the bench. I remember the four of us went into his office, and we told him we don't want to be separated. We don't want to be adopted out. The kids were crying. He said, "You don't need to worry. We'll work something out." Then he asked me, "Do you think you can take care of these children?" I said yes. He said, "All right, I'm putting you on trial. It won't last forever. We'll have a policewoman come down and check on you once a month. You won't know when she's coming, because she's not going to let you know. And we'll see how well you take care of these children."

Well, I had just rented this little house by West High School. And, gosh, I remember I felt tremendous tension. I washed all the kid's clothes weekly. I gave them heck if they got *anything* out of place. 'Cause I never knew if this policewoman was coming. Now, honest to Pete, she was *only* coming once a month. It seems like a joke when I think about it today. Yet we were petrified! We wanted to have everything just so. So, Betty [my younger sister] was always spotless. I washed her clothes every chance I got. I thought if I took her down to Neighborhood House and she seemed unkempt, they'd say, "This girl looks terrible. Her sister brings her down, but heaven knows how they live."[14] I remember there'd be times I was so tired from housework, I'd just see champagne bubbles. When you're really fatigued, prior to passing out, I guess, you see little bubbles.

Now, I was well ensconced in the Japanese community by the time I started working—at least among the young people. I was an officer in the Christian endeavor. I remember, after church we had these get-togethers. We'd make punch; somebody would bring cake. Then, once a year, we also had [high school] graduation parties. And that's where I met my husband.

I met Jun Kurumada while he was in dental school. I shouldn't say this, but we had this tremendous physical attraction. Yet we were very, very different. I was sort of a volatile person. I would really tell him off. He was, and still is, more circumspect. And our interests weren't the same. As he's gotten older, he's gotten more liberal. But at the time, he had an overexaggerated notion of [the importance of] place in society and what was proper.

He got this from his parents. 'Cause as soon as they found out about me, they were adamantly opposed to us going together. His family lived out in Murray at the time, and Jun lived in a hotel room in Salt Lake when he started his practice. But anytime he visited his family, they'd give him this rough time. Then, when we would have a date, he'd be [sullen], quiet. He would want to go for long walks. And I interpreted this as he didn't want us to be seen together.

I remember I was having lunch at the office one day, because there was a lot of work to do, and Jun called. We were supposed to see *Gone with the Wind* that evening, and he [evidently] didn't want to pick me up. So he asked me, "Would you mind meeting me in the lobby of the theater?" Well, I was so fed up with our situation that I told him, "No, I'm not going to meet you in the lobby, or down an alley, or under some rock. And while I'm telling you this, you might as well know that your family may be leaders in the Japanese community. They may, in fact, have a better grade of manure on their shoes, but they are still farmers!" And I hung up.

We would've thrown in the towel if a coworker at the WPA office hadn't intervened. She came over to me one day and said, "I'm so tired of seeing you come back from lunch in tears that my husband and I are just going to take you two up to Heber and get you married." So one summer afternoon, we drove up to Heber with this Caucasian couple and were married by a justice of the peace.

Thinking about it now, I realize Jun didn't marry your "normal," single girl. I was more like a divorcee with children. After we got married, my six-year-old sister lived with us, and though my brothers were in college, they stayed with us on weekends. So Jun didn't just marry one gal—he married a whole dang family.

We hadn't been married long when the attack on Pearl Harbor came, and World War II broke out. I remember it was Sunday. We were in our apartment. And we felt horrified. To complicate matters, Jun had recently been drafted to be the president of the local JACL—because the other fellow's term had expired—so, after the Japanese attack, I remember, [local] reporters swarmed all over him.[15] They wanted a statement. "How do you feel that Japan bombed the U.S.?" Well, Jun and I realized right away that they were connecting all the Japanese citizens here with Japan, because we're physically different from Caucasians. So as soon as the war broke out, we sat down to draft a statement to give out to reporters.

Now, my brother Ben (who was studying to become an attorney) and I helped Jun write the statement, because it wasn't his forte. I remember I told Ben, "We have to say something that cannot be misunderstood or turned around." I don't know where I got the wisdom, but I just really felt that this could not have any ambiguous terms that could later be used against us. It had to be a clear, ringing condemnation. Which it was. We said that "Japanese-Americans are Americans first, and we condemn the bombing of Pearl Harbor. We are shocked and outraged." We said this because we both sensed that there would be this nebulous thing about where our real loyalties were. We sensed this because we both realized—don't ask me how—that when it comes down to these emotional kinds of things, people are not rational. When it comes down to really crunchy, rock-bottom things, our civilization is less than a sixteenth of an inch thick!

A short time later—after President Roosevelt issued the executive order to evacuate the Japanese from the West Coast—I found myself really active in the local JACL.[16] Giving a deadline of March 15, 1942, the government said if the Japanese did not [voluntarily] vacate their homes by then and move east, they'd be placed in camps.[17] So, many started to leave [the West Coast]. Some headed [to the] East. And some chose to locate in the West to be close to relatives who had gone to the camps. Jun and I opened an office in the city. When people came into town they'd stop and ask for information, and we'd tell them what we knew. If they wanted to stay, we'd also try to find them lodging and employment. . . .

I got to hear some really heart-wringing stories then! I mean, just suppose your father had farmed land near the Salt Lake airport for forty years. Then, all of a sudden, the government declared you "a menace," and you *had* to leave in forty-eight hours. Now, where would you go? What would you take with you? What would you sell? What would you leave behind? And who would you ask to take care of your things while you were gone?

The Japanese evacuation reminded me of when our "evacuation order" came through in 1929 and we had to leave Idaho. Just like these people, we *knew* we were innocent. But now that the die was cast, we had to go. Friends and neighbors came over, they brought food, people cried. It was the same during the war. People just had to get out. They had to take their possessions, without knowing where they were going or how they were going to fare. The evacuation took *everything* away from people that had been dear to them.

During the war, the *Pacific Citizen* (*PC*) [a Japanese newspaper from California] moved out here. They also moved the JACL national headquarters here. The *PC* was housed in the Beason Building on Second South between the Walker Bank and the Mint Café. Larry Gihari and his wife ran it. They were professional journalists. And Larry helped us keep things in perspective. Because when you're in this kind of cauldron of feeling, you want, on the one hand, to disprove all those people who think you're going to spy or disrupt things. On the other hand, you're so indignant, so angry, that you tend to lose the perspective that nothing goes on forever.

The Giharis knew this. They helped us understand it. They also helped us realize that the things we say are going to have consequences. For example, we became very conscious, if there were incidences of violence, of how that would look. You have to remember, these war relocation camps were under the army's command. So we felt we were all on trial and that anything we did or said could affect a lot of people. Personally, I just tried to give people support. You can't think, "I'm glad that's not me." Maybe there is a part of you that feels that way. But you can't afford to separate yourself. So, when people told me their stories, I tried to comfort them. At the same time, I helped to keep control of the situation. We knew if there was a collective surge of this anger and pain, we might not be able to control it.

So, in everything we did, we tried to show, I'm just like you. We had to dispel some of the hostility and suspicion that was built up because of our physical differences. So we did not emphasize our ethnic origin. That was a period where we all wanted to become totally assimilated with the majority. We didn't want to show that we had different feelings or different thoughts. And we tried not to be conspicuous by congregating in big groups. We had JACL meetings. But when we met, we put the American flag and the state flag up. There was that feeling that the more distance you could put between yourself and your heritage, the better off you were. One girl, I remember, told me she forgot how to use chopsticks. I can laugh about it now. But at that time I thought she must be terribly threatened to say that. So those of us who lived here became real bananas—which our kids say is being yellow on the outside and white on the inside.

Those were very painful times. It's difficult, you know, even after all these years, to talk about them. It's kind of like opening an old wound. . . . Yet the war really opened up all our eyes. Personally, it made me think about things more deeply. I am aware now that what people do has consequences. So, today, it really pushes one of my buttons when people talk glibly about the "American way of life"—as though it's already "achieved." "We don't discriminate," people say. "Everyone is free to come over here and make their own way." They like to talk about that in one breath and in the next say, "If we could just get those lousy Vietnamese out of our shrimp beds; if we could just keep these Mexicans from streaming over our borders."

So as far as I am concerned, the American way of life has not been achieved. It's not achieved when we have incidences in Detroit where a Chinese kid, an engineer, is beaten to death with a baseball bat by displaced autoworkers. This was just two years ago. We all cherish the American dream, where everyone is going to be treated equally, where everyone has a place at the starting line. But we have to realize we have not achieved it.

I learned during the war that all minorities are in the same boat. You may be in the steering part and not getting water splashed on you. And somebody else may be in the back getting half drowned. But don't think you're not in the same boat. You are! Sometime or other, you're going to be back there, and that other guy's going to be up front. So people have to know they can't exploit each other just because they're in a more favorable position. They've got to know this, or we're not going to survive. To survive . . . *together*, we need to be constantly aware of the fact that we cannot exploit each other. And when there's injustice done and people feel rage, then you have to really see it in perspective and think of ways to arrive at a better solution.

As Americans, it's our blessing and our curse that we're restless. We want instant solutions to problems, and we want it done yesterday. But I think we have to realize that other cultures have ways of doing things also, and if you can just strike a commonality with them and not order them around, and call them names, good things can be accomplished. So I think it behooves us to realize that whether we're members of minorities in this society or members of the majority, we're all going to be minorities someplace. And we must not forget the past. We must not give in to the mentality that says, "Having lived through it once, let's not go raking through all the coals again." Because if we don't talk about the past, we'll forget it. And I won't permit *anyone* to forget the evacuations or Plum Alley or the blatant segregation we suffered. By golly, these people—the fourth and fifth generations of Chinese and Japanese—must hear about these things. They have to know what really happened to us.

EPILOGUE

GORDON SU, 46, COMPUTER PROGRAM ANALYST, HERCULES CORPORATION

Gordon Su was born in Taipei, Taiwan, and came to the United States in 1968 as a graduate student in business administration. A graduate of Southern Illinois University's School of Business, he sees himself and the other Taiwanese who came to the United States after 1965 as the "second wave" of Chinese immigrants to enter the country.[18]

When I was young, America seemed almost a paradise. People never had problems there. On the material side, they were always sufficient. It seemed just like a utopia—America, the land of possibilities, the land of wealth, the land of opportunities. But not everyone could go [to America] at the time. The only way to go was to study there. But you had to be an excellent student to be admitted by a university. It seemed out of reach. By the time I was in college, many of my classmates were going, and suddenly it seemed possible. We realized it would still be tough. We had friends who went and wrote us of their experiences. We knew it would be tough. But when we considered that after graduating we could have good jobs and all the material things we dreamed of, it seemed worth the effort. What we didn't take into account, though, was the enormous cultural shock. Everything would be different.

I came over in 1968. I [often] tell people, I came to the states twice. The first time I came, I saw all the differences. How differently [Chinese and] Americans live. The second time I came, I saw how similar Chinese and Americans are.

I had one suitcase [when I arrived]. I was one of the few students who brought lots of jeans and casual clothes. Most Taiwanese students brought very formal dress. But that's the only aspect of American life I was prepared for. Everything else was shockingly new and disturbing.

When I first arrived, American people seemed astonishingly beautiful to me. The Caucasians represented the standard [for beauty]. Even today, you know, Chinese beauty tends to be modeled on Western beauty. [Everybody wants a] high nose, high brow, fair skin. Plus, American movies—Hollywood—promoted beauty in their standard, and the style was Western. That was the only way to go. And, in most cases, American people *were* beautiful. They were wholesome, healthy, and energetic. They had good nutrition. The women were tall. They had good bodies. The Caucasians seemed very impressive.

In our time, nutrition was a serious problem. After the war [World War II], Taiwan was extremely backward. We lacked in every material thing. There wasn't enough food, enough meat, enough clothing. So we had many stunted or deformed people because of poor nutrition.

Also, Americans in a small town are very friendly. They say hello, they smile at you, and they are always courteous, even though you are a stranger. In Taiwan, in the cities, people are rude. It's impersonal. If you go to a shop, you hardly get any service. On the other hand, the Chinese always seem to have a way of getting what they want. If a shop closes at five and you arrive ten minutes late, you can usually talk your way in, and the proprietors give way. There is also a thing called "a personal touch." You can use your personal relationships to accomplish things. In America, I would say, people went more by the rule. And the guy who seemed so friendly the first time you met might forget you completely the next day. Taiwanese people didn't make friends easily. But when they did, it meant a lifelong friendship. You could almost ask for anything if you were having [serious] difficulties.

That first time I came, I also found it hard to adjust to the American way of study. The system I attended in my early years in Taiwan was harsh. Our elementary and secondary schools didn't try to develop your "individual talent." There was one system. They taught it, and you learned it. And you didn't talk back. If you got in trouble, you were punished. They flogged you with a ruler or a stick. There were some very, very strict teachers who really punished you. This wasn't "symbolic" punishment. They really beat you, because at that time the teachers were under the influence of the [old] Japanese system, and the Japanese system is very severe. They take corporal punishment for granted. And our parents, of course, approved. They said, "Oh, this teacher is so good. He is severe and he punishes the students so hard."

Our schools were pretty much modeled on army discipline. We boys had our heads shaved, and the girls had their hair cut short. We wore khaki and had an insignia on our shirt, with a number on top of our pocket. And each morning we stood at attention, sang the national anthem, and raised the flag. Then we'd drill, exactly the way they do in boot camp. We'd do aerobic exercises and listen to speeches about expected behavior. So it was a harsh system. School was not a place you went to enjoy yourself. You had to be careful in school. You had to be cautious. And it created a strong sense of insecurity in a lot of Chinese people. That's my personal feeling. But because of those harsh early days, you were always looking over your shoulder. You always felt that you were being watched, and so you [had] better behave. I think I have overcome that feeling, but I know a lot of people who haven't.

Regimentation continued on the college level. There was no corporal punishment, of course. There was no need for it. We were well indoctrinated by then. And in college, the work was hard. We always had a lot to do. But the curriculum was fixed. All you really had to do was study the text and pass the tests. And the tests were uniform. Everybody took the same exam. You didn't have to do much creative thinking, for instance, to understand cost accounting or auditing. You had to solve problems based on the textbook. But here in America, you had to do a lot of creative problem solving. You had to come up with your own ideas, you had to do your own research, and you *had* to make presentations and be witty when you did it. All this was especially hard for foreign students who hadn't mastered the language.

I remember I envied my friends who were in engineering programs. They didn't have to make so many presentations. Going for an M.B.A. I made a lot, and I didn't do well. Sometimes I felt the whole thing was a fiasco. [*Laughs*]

But after completing my M.B.A. program at Southern Illinois University, I was prepared to settle in, because it seemed easy to find a job. After one year of work in New York, however, my concept changed. This was in 1970, right during the Vietnam War, you see, when American society was in chaos. Even the campuses were in chaos. We didn't have a commencement because of student riots. So I began to get disillusioned about American society. There was no order. There was nothing left. In addition, the corporations that were once considered very glamorous institutions had bad images, and there I was, an M.B.A. major stuck in an ugly, crowded, violent city. I worked in the Chrysler Building, in Times Square, and I hardly ever saw sunshine. I was always scared [by the chaos in the city], and I didn't have a lot of friends. So I thought, if I'm going to live [like] this, I might as well go back to Taiwan. I won't have as much opportunity, but life will be less painful. So I called it "quits" after a year and went home.

My family and friends were very surprised to see me. I was one of a very few who were returning to Taiwan at that time. But Taiwan was really starting to develop as an economic power then. They had ambitious plans to industrialize the nation, and they gave lots of advantages to foreign companies who wanted to invest. I got a job with a European company, where my American education was a tremendous advantage, because everyone in the company spoke English. On the job, I interfaced with Dutch, British, and German people, and I did well. And all of a sudden, I realized that not all white people are the same. They come from different backgrounds, they have different experiences. So I was happy, I felt confident. I had my own department, and I quickly earned everyone's respect.

A short time later, I got married. And one day, my wife announced that she wanted to come to the states. Most of her family had already immigrated, and [she told me] she wanted to join them. So I said, "Okay, let's give it a try." It was as simple as that. My wife was excited. But the second time around, I had no illusions. I knew what life would be like here.

In 1976, we flew to California. Later, we visited my wife's brother in Salt Lake. Now, at the time, the Utah job market was really active. And when Hercules offered me a job as an [in-house] accountant, it looked like a good opportunity for us. And it was. After nine years, we are quite comfortable here. We like the environment; we like Utah's outdoor life. So we're staying.

But most Chinese people won't come to Utah, though. They want to settle in California—especially those from Taiwan—because they cannot handle the cold. I know some families who [wanted] to move out of Utah after their first winter here. And if they could have gotten to California or Arizona, they would've moved, just like that. But, more importantly, California has a large Chinese population. Everything is handy. And since most Chinese prefer their own lifestyle, their own diet, their own food, Chinese movies and entertainment, California is their mecca. People go there to get what they believe is necessary for life. They believe they *must* go to Chinatown [in California] to buy groceries. But, frankly, I kicked the habit. I don't need to buy Chinese groceries. I know many families who stick with the traditional way of preparing food and other things. That's the way they were raised. But I don't need it. I'm able to do without it.

Chinese culture, of course, is another matter. We have a strong culture, a strong legacy, and we should maintain our heritage. No doubt about it. I personally believe, though, that the strength of Chinese culture is that it will prevail by itself, without any political actions. A lot of Japanese-Americans say, "You Chinese are strong people, because you're the only Orientals who have maintained your culture in this country." They say, "Look at the Chinatowns in the major cities. They're thriving, while the Japanese, German, and Italian neighborhoods are all gone—all assimilated. Yet Chinatown is *still* Chinatown. It's unique and it's isolated from Western society."

This is what they believe. But it's not quite what I see. Chinatown *is* Chinatown. But the forces behind it, the reason people's lifestyle and language are different from the mainstream culture, are due to something else. My theory is that the old-time Chinese people [from Toishan] came here as laborers. They were not intellectuals. They had very poor educations, so they couldn't adapt to the local society. They had to isolate themselves to survive. But this second wave, my group, we're intellectuals, we're professionals. We are the students and the scholars. And we can accept a new way of living, because we have the skill and the knowledge to hold jobs in the mainstream society. The Toishanese didn't have that. So they had to bunch together to create their own society, whereas a high percentage of the Chinese from Taiwan seem to be absorbed into American society.

Well, let me qualify that. We're not *completely* absorbed. We still maintain our independence, but we don't have the same group structure. We do our own thing. Utah, in particular, is very different from California, because there isn't even the temptation here to isolate yourself. A good proportion of the Chinese here have jobs with American companies. Some, of course, do own restaurants as in the first wave. And we do have our Taiwanese group to maintain our heritage. But we are more on our own. We have been more accepted by the system, and we have more American friends. The early Chinese *had* to have their Chinatown to survive. But, you can see, Chinatown and what it represents is over the hill. It doesn't represent Chinese culture as it is now. We're the new center, and we're coming up.

I recently helped start a Chinese language school here. I'm in charge of it. We started out with a few parents who wanted to teach their children the writing and reading of Mandarin, our official language. Our group originally started out as a social group. Then we adopted this agenda, because this was something we all supported. We hired teachers, and now we have regular classes on Saturdays. And these Saturdays have become a regular meeting time for the parents and a very important community activity. And we hope that our children will be able to read and write Chinese, because our language is such a different system from English and such an important part of our culture. Almost all Chinese culture is based on our language.

I used to try to explain to knowledgeable whites that China has been China for so long because of our language. A lot of them would say, but Mandarin is unscientific; it's hard to learn, hard to speak, hard to write; you cannot put it in a computer; there are all these drawbacks. But these people forget that the Chinese language is a written language. It is a symbolic, or pictorial, language. You [Americans] see a picture of a heart, and you say that's a sign or symbol of love. Well, that's exactly how the Chinese language functions. Now, the character itself won't give you a hint or clue as to how it's pronounced. It's not a phonetic system. You won't know how to pronounce a Chinese character unless you've been taught it. What's so good about this? Well, the thing is that the written language cannot be corrupted by pronunciation. It doesn't depend on it. So whether you are Toishanese, Cantonese, Taiwanese, or a Mainlander, each with a distinctive pronunciation unknown by the others, the writing system is the same. I might not be able to speak with the Toishanese here, because of our different pronunciations, but I can always communicate in writing. The writing system is the same, although we each pronounce the symbol for love differently.

So every Chinese character is a symbol of communication. And this is something we must never forget. I want my son to understand this. When I am dead, and my boy signs his name and spells it "S-U," I want him to know what this represents. [I want him to know that in China] we have many names spelled S-U, but each of those names could consist of different characters with each character having its own [historical] origin. And if he doesn't know Mandarin, how will he know where his name comes from? How will he know his identity—that his Chinese name represents a certain family and dates back many thousands of years? I would hate to see my child only know his name as two English letters and not know what is behind the name we have given him. That's what I want my boy to remember. That [knowledge] will keep the Chinese one nation. If my boy can maintain the writing system of his ancestors, eventually he'll be able to identify himself as a Chinese.

NOTES

1. Patterned after secret, fraternal, patriotic societies in seventeenth-century China, the Tongs spread to Hong Kong and Southeast Asia over the next two centuries. Author Peter Kwong noted that they were "introduced to North America" during the latter part of the nineteenth century "by individual members of small and weak clans who did not want to be pushed around by the powerful and prestigious Lees and Tams, or . . . the Toishanese [Cantonese]."

In the first three decades of the twentieth century, Tong wars were fought in major Chinatowns in the United States for control of economic opportunities; these opportunities included the sale of opium, gambling, prostitution, and other illegal activities. After World War II, the Tongs attempted to clean up their image by starting and operating legitimate businesses.

According to our informants, Salt Lake City's Bing Kung Tong, a branch of the national Bing Kung Tong whose headquarters is in San Francisco, was only peripherally and briefly engaged in illicit activity. The organization functioned, instead, as a social center, rooming house, and hiring hall for single men who did not have family associations to turn to for help and fellowship. Peter Kwong, *The New Chinatown* (New York: Noonday Press, 1987), 97–100, 107–110.

2. Most Chinese emigrants to America during the late nineteenth and early twentieth centuries came from the Sze Yup districts (Sunwui, Toishan, Hoiping, and Yanwing) in the densely populated Pearl River Delta in Kwantung Province, with the majority of these people coming from Toishan. Victor G. Nee and Brett De Barry Nee, *Longtime Californ': A Documentary Study of an American Chinatown* (New York: Pantheon Books, 1973).

3. Nearly twelve thousand Chinese "coolies," or laborers, constituting approximately ninety percent of the Central Pacific's workforce, were employed by the railroad between 1866 and 1869. They laid more than eighteen hundred miles of track through some of this country's most impassable terrain. However, in the decade following the May 10, 1869, ceremony at Promontory, Utah, marking the creation of America's first continental railroad, the West Coast and the intermountain states exploded with anti-Chinese sentiment. Politicians, members of fledgling labor unions, and armies of unemployed whites, reeling from the 1870s recession, which had gripped the nation, directed their ire at the Chinese, who they believed were flooding the West with hordes of "cheap labor." Reacting to this volatile situation, Congress passed the Chinese Exclusion Act of 1882, which suspended the immigration of Chinese laborers for ten years. The law proved unsatisfactory to anti-Chinese forces, though, and the more restrictive Scott Act was passed in 1888, followed by the Geary Act four years later. These acts not only provided for the exclusion of nearly all incoming Chinese (only merchants, students, children of citizens, and diplomats were exempted), but, by denying immigration to the wives of Chinese laborers already in the United States and by prohibiting Chinese from becoming citizens, were also aimed at the "slow termination of the Chinese population [then] living in the United States." Nee and Nee, *Longtime Californ'*, 55.

4. From 1900 to 1943 (when the exclusion act was repealed), many Chinese entered the United States as "paper sons." "Under U.S. law," explained historian Peter Kwong, "all persons born in this country are automatically citizens, as are the children of citizens even if they are born abroad. Few Chinese at the turn of the century were born here. However, the San Francisco earthquake destroyed most immigration and birth records. Thus, it became impossible to disprove a Chinese claim to citizenship; a Chinese man could [as a result] return to China and claim to have fathered a son, who could also claim citizenship. The 'slot system' soon evolved into a lucrative racket in which individuals paid fees to become 'paper sons' of Chinese Americans." Although the exact number of fraudulent entries during this period was never determined, the practice was widespread. Peter Kwong, *The New Chinatown* (New York: Noonday Press, 1987), 14; and David R. Chan, "The Tragedy and Trauma of the Chinese Exclusion Laws," in *The Life, Influence and Role of the Chinese in the United States, 1776–1960* (San Francisco: Chinese Historical Society of America, 1976), 199.

5. Great care was taken to acquire information about the background of the person whose identity was being assumed because "it was the policy of immigration officials to presume all Chinese entrants 'guilty' of illegal immigration until proved otherwise." Nee and Nee, *Longtime Californ'*, 56.

6. It was not unusual for incoming Chinese to be detained for questioning at the port of entry for weeks or even months.

7. Families were a rarity in pre–World War II Chinese communities. The National Exclusion Act, coupled with local antimiscegenation laws that prohibited Chinese men from marrying white women (Utah's law was not repealed until 1963), created veritable bachelor societies.

8. World War II brought the first change in the immigration status of Chinese-Americans. In 1943 (after the United States and China signed a treaty of alliance against the Japanese), the U.S. Congress repealed the Exclusion Act, permitting 105 foreign-born Chinese to enter the country each year. Although the change was significant, its impact, given the minuscule immigration quota, was negligible. The major change in the immigration status of the Chinese came with the passage of the Immigration Act of 1965, which established a flat quota of twenty thousand immigrants per year for *each* country outside the Western Hemisphere and brought the era of legislative discrimination against the Chinese to an end. Kwong, *The New Chinatown*, 20-21.

9. Harry Louie was the eldest son of the nine children in the Louie family. Interviews with two of his younger brothers follow.

10. "My great-grandfather and grandfather were both citizens of the United States," William Louie explained. "My great-grandfather left Toishan in 1850 and came to California because of the gold rush. He worked in the mines for five years, then returned to China to get married. He came back again in 1857 and in 1860 sent for his wife. She arrived the following year, and their son, Louie Ah Yim, was born in the United States in 1861. When Louie Ah Yim was nineteen, he also returned to Toishan and married. Five years later [in 1885], my father was born. Now, my grandmother stayed in China, while my grandfather returned to the states again, but I don't know much about his story from there on."

11. For Bob Louie, "achieving greatness" meant acquiring an education and leaving the restaurant business.

12. When Bob Louie became an insurance agent, his early clients were predominantly Chinese.

13. "My father's name was Yee Hing Gim," she explained. "Gim was not his surname. But when he gave his name to Immigration at the point of entry, they wrote it down so that Gim [his first name] became his surname. But there is no Gim clan in China. There is a Yee clan. Strange as it may sound, of all the millions of Chinese, there are only about 150 surnames."

14. Neighborhood House was a day-care program that catered to low-income people. For a minimal fee, a working parent could leave a child there during the workday. It is still in existence today.

15. The Japanese American Citizens League was created by second-generation Japanese-Americans (Nisei) in the 1930s to combat racism against Japanese in the United States and to create a forum through which they could address and articulate issues vital to the survival and development of the community on a national level. The organization consisted of numerous local chapters, published its own newspaper, and sent representatives to Washington, D.C., to lobby the U.S. Congress. At the time of the evacuations of the Japanese from the West Coast, the JACL was the only national Japanese-American organization, and many Japanese/Americans looked to it for leadership.

16. As author Harry H. Kitano wrote, "On February 19, 1942, President Roosevelt signed Executive Order 9066, which (1) designated military areas under military commanders could exclude persons, and (2) authorized the building of 'relocation' camps to house those excluded. This set the stage for the evacuation of more than 100,000

Japanese, both citizens and aliens, from the West Coast." Harry H. Kitano, *Japanese Americans: The Evolution of a Subculture* (Englewood Cliffs, N.J.: Prentice Hall, 1969), 32.

17. Voluntary evacuation was actually allowed until April 27, 1942. After that, all evacuation procedures were controlled by the U.S. Army. Kitano, *Japanese Americans*, 33.

18. Historian Peter Kwong called the second wave from Taiwan "the Uptown Chinese." "Between the mid-1960s and the mid-1980s," he wrote, "close to 150,000 Taiwanese students came to the United States for graduate education. Today they are the largest single group of foreign students . . . in America. Some 97 percent have remained here after graduating. . . . These . . . immigrants represent a large proportion of the Uptown Chinese, and they have had the most significant impact on the [new] reputation of the Chinese community in this country." Kwong, *The New Chinatown*, 60–61.

BOOK FIVE
ITALIAN COMMUNITY

Preface

Philip F. Notarianni, Jr.

Italy, politically unified in the 1870s, loomed in its early years as a nation of emigration. Economic and natural disasters set in motion a migration of peoples that spanned from the European continent to North and South America and to Australia. In the context of this mass exodus, the state of Utah hinged as an important destination for Italian immigrants entering the American West. They were attracted by Utah's growing industrialization, primarily in the railroad and mining industries. Italian laborers in search of economic opportunities thus provided Utah with yet another group of European-born citizens.

Small villages situated in the majestic mountains of the Tyrolean region, the fertile valleys of Piedmont, the farmlands of Rome, the Abruzzi, the picturesque hill towns of Calabria, and the coastal regions of Sicily were thrust into the realm of Utah history. The names of various Utah cities and towns, such as Salt Lake City, Helper, and Sunnyside, echoed in these villages and surfaced as sacred places where relatives, friends, and neighbors had gone for better opportunities. The word "America" embodied many expectations and often was used to indicate the area from Canada to South America as well as Australia.

The first significant waves of Italians into Utah consisted of single, young, male laborers. Just after the turn of the twentieth century, Carbon, Salt Lake, Tooele, and Weber counties housed most of these immigrants.[1] Some trekked specifically to Utah, whereas others settled in the East, working in the coal mines of Pennsylvania and Virginia, and then wound their way West, perhaps stopping first in upper Michigan, Minnesota, or Montana or traveling further west to Wyoming or Colorado and then continuing into Utah. They journeyed to find work on the railroads or in the gold, silver, and coal mines of the West. Once in Utah, many immigrants set in motion a chain migration, writing home to entice fathers, sons, brothers, uncles, and cousins to follow in their footsteps.

In Utah, particularly in Carbon County, Italians quickly became attracted to organized labor. They surfaced as the main group of laborers in the 1903–1904 coal miners' strike in Carbon County, mainly in the camps of Castle Gate and Sunnyside. The United Mine Workers of America (UMWA) eagerly sent Italian organizer Charles Demolli to Colorado and Utah as an ambassador of labor. Demolli campaigned against the abuses coal operators inflicted on the miners. The *Salt Lake Tribune* called the leader from Lombardia (the Lombard-Milan area) a "silver-tongued orator," whereas the *Deseret News* labeled him as "no better than the average Italian fruit peddler." The poor conditions in the coal and metal mines, and in mills and smelters, led many Italians to look to organization as a way of improving their lot.

Virtually all of these industrial immigrants intended to earn enough money to aid their families in Italy and then return to their homeland; but in ten to twelve years, most of them, weighing the relatively secure life in Utah against the poverty in Italy, decided to remain and call Utah home. Women began to arrive: wives called from the "old country" and the brides of men who had returned to Italy explicitly to find wives. Italian families settled in many of Utah's rural mining and railroad towns as well as in the urban areas of Salt Lake City and Ogden.

Photographs that can be found in family albums attest to the importance of "image" for these laborers in correspondence they sent back to the homeland. In the 1920s, coal miner Frank Mangone of Castle Gate, for instance, had a photo taken of him proudly handing over the money he received on his first payday to his wife, Teresa. Seeing the photo, Teresa's family in Italy would be assured that she was being well taken care of in Utah. In addition, family photographs placed on gravestones or adorning living room walls provided a necessary link of people to places. The family served as a basic social unit in Italian life.

Some laborers who had apprenticed in the trades in Italy had the economic skills that enabled them to leave mining and embark on business careers. Others, primarily second-generation sons, found opportunities in the professions. Still others returned to the centuries-old skills of agricultural farming, goat and sheep herding, or dairy farming. By the 1920s, Utah had become a place of destination and settlement for Italians.

In many of the mining towns and in cities such as Salt Lake City and Ogden, "Little Italys" formed, usually on the West Side near the depots of the Union Pacific or Denver and Rio Grande Western railroads. In those areas, sights and sounds abounded that reflected Italian life. Italian-owned saloons, grocery stores, tailor shops, shoe shops, restaurants, and barber shops lined streets like Second South in Salt Lake City and Twenty-fifth Street in Ogden. In other towns, such as Price, hotels like the Pensione Italiana catered to Italians traveling from town to town in search of work. In Bingham Canyon, Italian-owned enterprises also dotted the street of String Town (Main Street).

Although the Italian immigrants attempted to adapt to the realities of the Utah environment, second-generation children typically found themselves caught between two cultures. Family life centered around Italian ways, varying in accordance with the regionalism that existed in Italy. Language, too, varied, for in Italy dialects often differed in villages only a few kilometers apart. Food traditions also varied, from the polenta (corn meal) eaten by Tirolese (Tyroleans) and Piemontese (people from Piedmont) to the spicy tagliatelle (pasta) enjoyed by Calabrese (Calabrians) and Siciliani (Sicilians). Yet, children, whose immigrant parents stressed education, attended English-speaking schools, where "American" customs and traditions became the norm. For the immigrant families, change and accommodation occurred gradually.

Restrictive immigration legislation enacted in America in the 1920s effectively curtailed Italians from entering the country. And during the Depression, Italians, like others, left Utah in search of work in nearby states, such as California. These Depression-era years proved stressful for many of Utah's immigrants, testing the survival skills they had mastered during the immigration process. For many, an emphasis on family gardens and the importance of family-produced and stored food carried them through these lean years.

The 1940s and World War II produced some paradoxes for Italian-Americans in Utah and elsewhere. Whereas some felt sympathy toward an Italian government bent on expansion, others proudly purchased U.S. Savings Bonds and sent their sons to fight in U.S. military uniforms, possibly against their own relatives and friends in Italy. During the Allied occupation of Italy, Italian-American soldiers from Utah visited relatives, bringing Utah and Italy even closer together.

The postwar years witnessed many Italian-Americans sending for additional family members to join them from Italy. Throughout the 1950s and 1960s, many financially secure Italian-Americans sponsored these arrivals. Even into the 1970s, Italians found their way to Utah. Some remained, but others returned after a time to Italy, which was no longer choked economically by the problems it had encountered during the mass migration period. In the 1980s and 1990s, members of the Church of Jesus Christ of Latter-day Saints have been successful in bringing Italian converts to Utah in a new era of immigration.

The oral histories presented in this chapter highlight a wide range of experiences of the Italian immigrants who settled in Utah, including their trials, tribulations, and triumphs. From the immigrant generation, born in Italy and raised in Utah, to the second and third generation, born in Utah or elsewhere in the United States, these respondents provide us with the voices and stories of experience. Although Utah did not attract the large numbers of Italians that can be found in New York, Chicago, and San Francisco, "Italianness" continues to live in Utah. The interviews that follow convey the "sense of feeling," the deep love of family, the dignity and pride in hard work, the satisfaction with America's promise, and the beautifully expressed optimism of the Italian immigrants to Utah, whether money was plentiful or scarce. The stories illustrate that *Italianità,* the best in the Italian character and traditions, has been transmitted from generation to generation.

Mary Juliano and Vito Bonacci lived the immigration experience, as did John Crus (who came to Utah as a child). Mary Juliano was born in San Giovanni, in Fiore, a beautiful hill town in the Sila (mountain) region of Calabria. The buildings of the town currently sprawl over the hillside, with much of the new building construction made possible by immigrants sending money back home. Mary's interview, like many others, conveyed a deep love of family. She told us of the agony she felt over being separated from her grandmother when she emigrated to the United States: "I was raised in her arms," she said. "I slept in her arms. . . . It almost killed me to leave her." Mary has filled the void of separation with memories and poetry, composed in Italian and English.

Both Mary Juliano and Vito Bonacci told of their families traveling across the United States from the East to reach Utah. In a previous interview, Vito told of eating a banana for the first time in an eastern railroad depot and not knowing the peel had to be removed. Both shared experiences of fathers who worked in the East, then moved West. Hard work and the success it ultimately brought emanate as major themes in both interviews. Mary noted, "We didn't live fancy, but we lived good."

Vito Bonacci, also born in a Calabrian town, recounted his experiences as a coal miner and union man. For many immigrants, the realities of tense, sometimes violent struggles between management and labor raised questions about whether freedom and justice existed in Utah. Italians, Greeks, and South Slavs fought for the recognition of labor unions in Utah. One of Vito's relatives, Frank Bonacci, helped to champion the cause of the United Mine Workers of America. Suffering from blacklisting and evictions from company-owned property as a result of his union work, Frank's family became tangled in a life of uncertainty.[2]

The name "Bonacci," with its ties to the labor movement, proved to be a source of difficulty for Vito in his mostly unsuccessful trek from camp to camp in search of work. When he found work, he was laid off in the summer. When he protested once, the superintendent told him he was laid off because he didn't "spend enough in the company store." He related how the Mormons were against the labor movement and how, when he argued with a Mormon bishop who worked in the shop with him, he was told, "You're in the minority. We are [the] real Americans." Only the New Deal, under Franklin D. Roosevelt, brought union recognition to Utah's coalfields and, subsequently, the untold loyalty of numerous Carbon County residents to the Democratic party. Vito's son Joe, talking of his father's active role in the local St. Anthony's Catholic Parish in Helper, remarked that if Jesus Christ ran for political office as a Republican, "Dad would vote against him!"[3]

John Crus, also born in Italy, was raised in Salt Lake City. Like most other informants, he spoke of his deep love for his mother and his pride in her achievements—making salt pork, bacon, salami, and sausage, as well as knitting. "She washed by hand and knitted," he said. "Even when she sat down at night [she] was knitting . . . always something." From the railroad to farming to boardinghouse ownership, his family set about finding a niche. As with all the other informants, survival became the key. John Crus, at age eighteen, did better than many, embarking on a highly successful career as an oil distributor.

Second-generation Italians Filomena Bonacci, Dominic Besso, Mary Ravarino, and Eugene Barber all shared a vital sense of family and closeness to the Italian culture. Filomena Bonacci, born in Sunnyside, Utah, told of her father, who went back and forth between Italy and Utah: "He was a quiet man; yet when he talked, you'd think he was arguing with the world." Her mother, she said, was the center of family life. "My mother . . . was a jewel. . . . She's been gone about twenty-five years, and I still miss her." Filomena shared an anxiety and fear of coal companies with her husband, Vito Bonacci. Their fear was rooted in the potential to be evicted from their home because of Vito and Frank Bonacci's union work. Home for many Italians represented their place in time and space—an anchor.

Home often provided a link between the Italian-Americans' places of origin and destination. An example is the home of Camillo Manina, who lived near Vito and Filomena Bonacci in Spring Glen.[4] Manina constructed his home much in the old-country style found in his native *paese* (town) of Novalesa, near Torino. Animals were penned on the ground floor; the family living quarters were above it.

Dominic Besso, whose roots were in Torino, Italy, was born in Rock Springs, Wyoming, and raised in Price, Utah. His father learned the craft of shoemaking in Italy but, after immigrating to the United States, tried farming before returning to his trade. The trade was passed on to his son, Dominic, who maintains the family-owned shop. Like other informants, Dominic recounted his family's struggle to survive, describing how survival meant the need to be adaptable. This adaptability is a hallmark of immigrants. After all, they began the process of adapting by emigrating in the first place.

Dominic Besso told us of the Italian communities of Price and Carbon County. Distinctions between north and south Italians and between Tyrolean-Italians and others remain fresh in his memories. His perceptions of the years of Prohibition and of those community members who prospered as bootleggers reflect the survival instinct of the immigrants, but also something more. To Italians, wine represented more than an alcoholic beverage. It symbolized cultural tradition and sociability. Italians appreciated wine. Besso recounted how his father made the best wine for company and a second wine for table wine.

For Italian-Americans, wine—and food in general—must convey a sense of quality, because they reflect upon the family.[5] Although the form of food changes with time and place, the value of quality remains constant. Italians understand this concept, as illustrated in the incident Besso recalled of the "Mormon" who thought he was pulling a fast one by drinking the family wine when in essence it proved to be vinegar. This classic tale of being "duped" exists in most folktale repertoires.

Mary Ravarino described the special closeness she feels to her family and cultural roots in the Trentino region of northern Italy. When she asked her mother why she left the beautiful Tyrolean region of Italy, her mother replied, "When you're hungry, you move to where you find food."

Mary's father, an immigrant to America, journeyed back to Italy to marry and then returned to make America home. "I don't think my father ever wanted to return [to Italy] after he and my mother made America their home," Mary recalled. Her father, like many other Italian-Americans, moved from the uncertainties and danger of mining to farming. The family eventually settled in the Ogden area, among other "Tyrolean Italians." Mary recounted how her family clung to their traditions, centered on hospitality and song. She described how her mother, in typical fashion, made their home "a cocoon of love and security."

Outside the home, the immigrants often sought the security of belonging to Italian fraternal and social organizations. Mary Ravarino's father, in this spirit, began the Friendly Club in Ogden—a group serving the needs of Ogden's Italians of Tyrolean descent.[6] This group and others founded by Italians in Utah since 1897 became vehicles for maintaining traditional ways and, at the same time, providing immigrants with the means for making transitions to their new environment.

Eugene Barber's reminiscences centered on family. His parents adhered to rigid rules of honesty. His father, he said, was "a good, moral man." During the Depression, when Eugene and other "kids" stole a sack of potatoes, his father, Eugene told us, "made us bring it back. Times weren't good for us. . . . It got so bad for us at one time that my mother had to keep us out of school. . . . We just didn't have enough clothes [to wear]." His mother "set the atmosphere in the home," and his father implanted in the minds of his children the concept of hard work. For Eugene, "the way [his parents] acted, the way they lived their lives, rubbed off on our entire family."

As a third-generation Italian-American, Tom Barberi provided a look at the legacy of one Italian immigrant family—the success made of opportunities found in the new land and the interaction of traditional values with that new land. Tom knows his roots and proclaimed them proudly. Like the second-generation informants, Tom stressed how his parents taught him the "work ethic," which served as a "rudder" for him through his voyage in life. Tom readily admitted, "I grew up in an old-fashioned Italian family," something that became a point of pride and strength for him.

Parents in the Italian–American community have stressed the importance·of education and have provided their children with anchors in a world of change and diversity. In a world that champions individual rights, Tom Barberi stated, "the rights you had as a child were given to you by your parents." Authority was not questioned. For Tom, the vicissitudes of time seem to have tempered some elements of his culture that youngsters often viewed with contempt. Now, for him and others, those elements are seen as strengths, just as his parents had said.

The informants in this chapter speak of a process set in motion by immigration. Their experience was part of an international movement. Italians in Utah have accommodated to the land and environment. The Italian community has become a part of Utah life in ways perhaps unforeseen years ago. Italian sections of towns and cities no longer exist, but their presence continues to be felt. Italian fraternal and social organizations contribute to general community causes and projects; and many Italian men and women have entered the professions, business, and educational, social, and political positions of authority. The dreams of grandparents and parents have been realized.

A second-generation Italian who, on a trip back to the region of his parents' birth, was asked to speak at a university there, speculated during his talk on how it was possible for him, with a doctorate from a Utah university, to be lecturing at an Italian university in the very locale of his parents' birth. Would his parents ever have imagined this possible? he wondered. "Of course," he said. For they were dreamers, doers, and survivors.

NOTES

1. An overview of Italian immigration into Utah can be found in Philip F. Notarianni, "Italianità in Utah: The Immigrant Experience," in Helen Z. Papanikolas, ed., *The Peoples of Utah* (Salt Lake City: Utah State Historical Society, 1976), 303–331.

2. For additional information on Frank Bonacci, see Philip F. Notarianni, "Rise to Legitimacy: Frank Bonacci as Union Organizer in Carbon County, Utah," *Rendezvous* (Idaho State University Journal of Arts and Letters) 19 (1983): 57–74.

3. From interview with Joe Bonacci conducted by Philip F. Notarianni in Spring Glen, Utah, September 1, 1990.

4. For a discussion of the Manina house as well as additional information on Vito and Filomena Bonacci, Mary Juliano, and Dominic Besso, see articles by Philip F. Notarianni, Steve Siporin, and Thomas Carter in David A. Taylor and John Alexander Williams, eds., *Old Ties, New Attachments: Italian-American Folklife in the West* (Washington, D.C.: Library of Congress, 1992): 68–111.

5. More information on the role of food among Italian-Americans in Utah can be found in Richard Raspa, "Exotic Foods Among Italian-Americans in Mormon Utah: Food as Nostalgic Enactment of Identity," in Linda Keller Brown and Kay Mussell, eds., *Ethnic and Regional Foodways in the United States* (Knoxville: University of Tennessee Press, 1984), 185–194. See also Steve Siporin, "Our Way of Life Was Very Clear," *Northwest Folklore* 8 (1990): 3–18.

6. On the Tyrolean-Italian heritage and the Friendly Club in Utah, see Amanda De Lucia, "Tyrolean-Italian Heritage in West Weber, Utah," M.A. thesis, University of Utah, 1991.

Tom Barberi. *Kent Miles*

Eugene Barber (standing far left) with his family.
Kent Miles

EUGENE ROBERT BARBER, 70, RAILROAD WORKER, TRUCK DRIVER

Tall, robust, and gregarious, Eugene Barber has swung passionately in his life between the poles of family and work. "In the environment I grew up in, I never thought much about an American dream. We were raised under the influence of hard work. My parents were hardworking people, both of them. They planned that one day it was going to be our responsibility to make a living, take care of the house, provide for the family. Those were the things they implanted in our minds. I don't know if that's a dream or not. That's just something we knew was going to happen in our lives."

One of fourteen children of Jenny Madeleine and Dominick Barber, Eugene was born in Salt Lake City on June 1, 1924. After graduating from West High School, he worked for a year as a loader "on the docks for the Rio Grande Railroad" and then, in June 1943, was drafted into the U.S. Army. Assigned to headquarters in the First Cavalry Division, he was responsible, he said, for setting up "[Pacific] command posts and providing security for the commanding officers."

Following his discharge in December 1945, he returned to Utah and his job at the Rio Grande Depot. Five years later, when the railroad moved its headquarters to Grand Junction, Colorado, he decided against relocating his young family. With the help of his older brother, a salesman for Bullough's Insulation, he was hired as a truck driver with the same firm. At the time of this interview, he was beginning his thirty-fourth year of employment with the company.

I'll tell you what I know about my father. He came from a little town in the province of Calabria, right in the toe of the boot. He had two brothers, one older and one younger. The older brother came to America first. When he got a job in a mine in Pittsburgh, he sent for the other two. My father was about thirteen years old when he got here, and he was kind of a little rebel. They used to work different shifts [in the mine] so they could all live in a one-room place. They worked these shifts so the apartment wouldn't be too crowded. But the older brother kept the money and doled it out as he thought they needed it.

Well, my father decided he didn't want to live that way. So, he just took off and hitchhiked back to the West. He came West and wound up in Salina, Colorado, and got a job on the Rio Grande Railroad. He worked there for quite a number of years. That's where he met my mother. Then the railroad transferred him to Salt Lake City. He worked for the railroad up until 1922. He was an instigator in getting a railroad union in Salt Lake City. As a matter of fact, [together] with a man by the name of Cunningham, the master mechanic at the railroad at the time, they struck and they got a union started. But the ones who were [labeled] "instigators" were not called back. So my father got a job as a bartender, and he bartended the rest of his life.

In them days, it was just beer joints and ten-cent beers, you know. My dad worked in a number of places, jumped around a little bit on Second South. I don't know if you've been told this, but Second South, between about Sixth and Third West, was called Greek Town. That [area] was spotted with [establishments that were] Greek coffeehouses and [Italian] beer joints—what they called taverns. On one side they had booths for the ladies; on the other side, men would drink beer at the bar. Ladies were not allowed on the bar side— that was not ladylike—but they were nice places.

In the front of the coffeehouses, they had little stumps of trees with little round [wooden] boards placed on them. The men would sit out there and drink coffee. Then, at certain spots along the street, they used to have jails. They were just perforated metal boxes, about the size of phone booths only closed in. The policemen walked the beat, friendly to everyone they knew, and if they found a drunk, they would throw him in the box and hold him until a paddy wagon came. The wagons were the old-fashioned closed-in types. They would pick him up, cool him off in a jail cell, and let him go again.

My father was a short, stocky guy. He looked like a wrestler. No neck. We [jokingly] called him an ape, because he had long arms that stretched way out and he was bald on top. We don't have many pictures of him. The few we have showed he used to have a big handlebar moustache—a great big, huge one. I think it was the sign of the he-man. But he was a lovable guy—not churchgoing. Yet I'd consider him a good, moral man, and very honest. We could never think of doing anything dishonest in our lives.

I'll tell you a story. About Twenty-first South, in that area, it was all farm- land in the days when we were growing up. And there were a lot of garden- type farmers. It wasn't trees and orchards. It was vegetable-type farming. Well, we [kids] went down there one night and stole a sack of potatoes out of some guy's garden, and my father made us bring it back. Times weren't good for us. We lived in the Depression era. In fact, I'll tell you, it got so bad for us at one time that my mother had to keep us out of school. This was in 1932, just before Roosevelt [got into office]. I was going to Franklin Elementary School, and I remember staying home because we just didn't have enough clothes [to wear]. But that's how honest he was. He was a good, honest, strong man.

I'll tell you another little story. One of the beer parlors he worked in used to sell liquor under the bar. They were not allowed to do that because liquor was not sold in Utah at the time of the Prohibition. But if one of their good customers came in and wanted a little glass, I think most of the bars would sell them a glass of whiskey. Well, [Dad] happened to be on duty at the time an undercover cop came in, and he sold him a glass. So he got thirty days in jail for that. But in the city jail, he entered this wrestling tournament. He became the champion wrestler at the jail after thirty days. So, like I say, he was a good, strong, tough man.

Dad worked at Tony's Place for a while. Tony Picanelli owned that bar and another one up the street. The Shamrock was also up the street. Pete Malachi owned that; [Dad] worked for him for a while, too. When I was twelve or thirteen years old and in junior high, he'd start [work] about six o'clock in the morning, cleaning up the bar from the night before, and I used to help him.

He had enough sons, so each day one of us could go in to mop the floors, clean out the toilets, and wash those old, big brass spittoons. We used to do all that stuff when we were kids. My brothers and I took turns helping him get ready. Then he would open about seven thirty in the morning. I don't know why anybody wanted to drink beer that early, but those railroad people did.

See, the place was right down by the Rio Grande and Union Pacific depots. Trains were going in and out of there all the time. There was a lot of activity, and my father really liked it. He liked his work, and he liked the neighborhood. We were a poor family, material-wise, but we got along well with most of our neighbors. If you want me to spell it out, with most of our Mormon neighbors. While we were growing up, Mormons weren't too pushy about their missionary program. After the war [World War II], they started to become more [aggressive]. That's when I started to notice it. But early on, we'd go down to the Fifteenth Ward [the neighborhood Mormon chapel]. It was the only place that had a gymnasium. The caretaker lived next door, and we'd ask him if we could play ball. He'd say, "Sure, as long as you don't wreck the joint."

So, we used to play basketball all the time. Everybody played. Gee, we had blacks, Greeks, Italians, Mormons. We all grew up together, and we didn't realize [differences]. So I can't tell you why in my lifetime becoming adults made such a difference. As children it didn't make a difference. But as soon as we became adults, all of sudden your culture, your color, my culture, my color, made a difference in our lives. I don't understand it. Never did. Growing up, I didn't have that problem. I don't have that problem now. As far as I'm concerned, I don't care if a black or a Jew or a Greek lives next door to me. I don't care. He's got as much right to that house as I have. But to a lot of people that seems to be a big problem. [They worry] the Vietnamese are moving in; the Tongans are moving in. I don't know why. I can't answer that.

During the war [World War II], we were all drafted. All six of us [boys]. And my father had six stars in the window. When you had a boy or girl in the service, you got a star to place in your window. My father had six of them placed across [the glass]. But since he was not a citizen, he couldn't get out of the house [after] nine o'clock at night. He was kept on a curfew because we were at war with the Italians. Japanese were the same way—probably more so. Germans were the same. We were at war with Germany. But nobody ever stopped to think, "Why would my father send six sons without raising Cain if he was not going to be a good citizen?" That upset me. That upset me quite a bit. He's got six sons overseas. He's worried sick about them, and somebody's telling him he can't go outside his house after nine o'clock at night. That didn't set right with me. But we lived through it, and everybody got back alive.

And my parents—God bless them!—they were as charitable as people could be. I mean, we were a large family—fourteen children. We didn't have anything, but we were raised in an environment of love and caring and sharing.

My father was a strict disciplinarian. He liked to show the rough side of him, as far as "You do this, or else." But my mother controlled it. She set the atmosphere in the home. For instance, my older sisters got married young. They got married when they were sixteen, because that was the Italian style, or maybe the old-country style. Anyway, we had a houseful of people. My brother-in-law ran a produce house. He had a driver running back and forth to California, hauling fruit. His name was Johnny Baldini, and he stayed at our house when he came into Salt Lake. I had a cousin, Freddy Scallione. He lived with us. I had another cousin, Robert Gray, who lived in California. When he came into town, he stayed with us. My mother took them all in. She didn't care.

We lived in a fourteen-room duplex owned by an Italian called Amandi. The second floor was exactly like the first floor, only we made every room [on the second floor] a bedroom. There was a screened porch upstairs, just like downstairs. We boarded it and made it a room. There was a kitchen upstairs, same as downstairs. We made the kitchen another bedroom. And we had people jammed in them little rooms, three in a bed. My mother—I can remember—used an old washing machine with the old hand-crank wringer. She used to wash all our clothes. She would go from morning till night baking bread, cooking, darning socks, sewing, yet she was happy. It was not a drudgery [for her], as I look back on it.

There was work. There was a lot of *hard* work. I didn't realize how much when I was seven or eight years old. But she was always laughing. She liked to sit and talk to people. Everybody would gather around the kitchen and sit there for hours, talking and having coffee. My father drank coffee out of a bowl. There was no cup for him. He made it in a saucepan and drank it out of a bowl. He'd sit there for hours, talking. She'd darn, she'd sew, she was doing all kinds of things, and my sisters would do the same. In them days, you grew up to be a housewife, so you had to learn all those things. So they learned. They cussed about a bit, as we [boys] did when we had to bring in the wood and the coal. But we did it, and it was fun.

Once each month, my brothers and sisters . . . we get together with our wives and husbands for dinner. We've been doing this for as long as I can remember. We're very close, and we get together and [often] reminisce about our mother. How she used to calm my father down, telling him, "Calm down, Dom, calm down. It's not that bad." What the heck, we were roughhouse boys. We liked to roughhouse it in the house, and my father, in his broken English, would say, "Knock it off, or I'll give you the back of my hand." My [older] brother can talk just like him. He tells these stories, and I bust out laughing. Tears come to my eyes, 'cause he talks just like my father talked. But my mother would calm him right down. And my father *adored* my mother. He adored her.

They wouldn't go to shows. Their pastime was visiting friends, and they had a lot of friends. I mean, we lived in Little Italy. Our neighbors were Italian people. But my parents mostly went out with Mr. and Mrs. Nicastro. Tony

Nicastro owned a lounge by the New Grande Hotel, just down the street on Fourth South. My parents would visit their house, and they'd come to ours. They'd sit on the porch in the summertime, or they'd take walks. That was their pastime. The parks used to have band concerts. In fact, Pioneer Park was a thriving place at the time, not the bum hangout it has become. Families also used to go to Liberty Park and spend Sundays listening to a military band from Fort Douglas.

So, we like to reminisce about the [hardships] my mother and father must have gone through. But how should I put it? If at any time my mother was a tired, haggard woman, she never showed it. I often think about this. I think it was her attitude. My mother was so in love with my father and so in love with the children that her attitude was, "This is not work. I love to do this." There was no unhappiness in our family as far as that was concerned. Maybe that's bragging. But I think it's the truth. I think that's a fact. My mother did what she had to do. She worked hard, but she did it out of love for her husband and her children.

I teach a confirmation class at the Guadalupe Church for high school seniors. About three weeks ago, two sisters in my class got into a violent argument outside of the classroom. I happened to overhear them, and I walked over and asked what the problem was. One said, "I can't stand her." The other said, "That's because you're always saying things that hurt me." I tried to help them, but I didn't settle their argument. I think they continued arguing.

Afterwards, I got to thinking about it. We had a family dinner just last week, and I brought this up. I can't remember when we had violent, hateful arguments. Oh, we argued. You get fourteen kids together, and everything's not going to run smoothly. I don't mean to say it did. But there was no hate. That's what I'm trying to say. There was no hate. There was a lot of love, and there was a lot of sharing. When we were going to junior high, my brother Bob was trying to make up a little bazooka band—you know, bazookas and harmonicas. He used to get ten cents for lunch each day, and I didn't have a bazooka. Do you know what he did? He saved a nickel each day out of his lunch money, so he could buy me a twenty-five-cent bazooka. It's a small thing, you know, but I remember that.

I'll tell you a final story about my sister and her husband in Helper. He's a retired coal miner in his eighties, and he wanted to paint his house. Now, my brother Bob, who I was just talking about, is an insulation salesman. On his circuit, he sometimes has to go through Helper. When he stopped in last summer, he saw our sister, and she said she needed the house painted. They've got a great big two-story frame house. But because of Dominick's age, she didn't want him climbing a ladder. When Bob came home and told us about it, all six of us brothers and our sons—thirteen in all—got three pickup trucks, and one Saturday, we borrowed the scaffold from where I work and drove down to Helper.

We left at six o'clock in the morning, set the scaffold up, painted the house, tore the scaffold down, and were back here by five o'clock that night—in Salt

Lake City. He can't get over that yet. Helper didn't know what hit them. It's a mining town, you see. The streets are narrow, and people's houses are very close to each other. They didn't know what was happening to Dominick's house. But we had a system. We put four guys to a side. We got on all four sides, and—bingo!—we painted the house in nothing flat. We did that, and it was fun. We enjoyed it. That's the way we operate.

And I attribute all of that to the teachings of my mother and father. The way they acted, the way they lived their lives, rubbed off on our entire family. Really. If you do something begrudgingly, you'll probably get an ulcer. But if you do it because you want to, if you do it out of love for another person, it's not work. That's a true statement. It's people's attitudes, what they do and how they do it, that makes the difference. We just have a different attitude. The way to go about a lot of work is to have fun at it. So, if someone's house needs painting, we *all* paint it. If somebody's house needs roofing, we *all* roof it. That's why I say we were poor materially. We were not poor spiritually. We were very, very rich.

MARY JULIANO, 83, HOUSEWIFE

Afternoon sunlight streamed into the living room of Mary Juliano's brick home in Price, Utah, on the day of the interview. The walls were covered with crucifixes and family photos. "You know why I have so many crucifixes?" she asked us. "Because we need reminders of Christ. We need to see him on the cross to understand what he gave us."

Barely five feet tall, Mary Juliano wore black pants, black cotton slippers, a stark white blouse buttoned to the neck, and a black jacket. When she spoke, her body came alive. Her fingers carved air; her torso craned forward; and, feigning embarrassment over her boldness, she playfully buried her head in her lap.

One of ten children of John and Maria Teresa Cortese Nick, she was born on September 2, 1904, in San Giovanni, in Fiore, Italy, and "was brought" to the United States at the age of five. Three years after graduating from Carbon High School (where she dreamt "of becoming a linguist"), she married John Juliano, an Italian immigrant, and began to raise a family. In her mid-forties she suffered what she characterized as "a nervous breakdown"—crying fits, anxiety, and depression. Local physicians recommended electroshock therapy, but Mary refused the treatment and brought herself out of the dark through prayer, poetry, and what she pointedly described as adoration of "the Creator."

A coal miner and jack-of-all-trades, John Juliano died on August 5, 1984. Mary Juliano, a mother of five and grandmother of six, passed away on December 9, 1993, and was interred in the Price City Cemetery.

Well, I'm arrogant, dear Mother of God. Ask my son—he'll say I'm as arrogant as ever. But then, like that priest from Helper said, "You can trust arro-

Mary Juliano. *George Janecek*

gant people. You know where they stand. It's them *sweet-eyed ones* you've got to worry about. You don't know what they're thinking."

I was born in Calabria, Italy, and raised in my grandmother's house. I was raised in her arms. I slept in her arms. She was the love of my life, more so than my mother. That's why it almost killed me when I had to leave her. My father had left earlier to come to the United States, the country of providence and work. He worked in the mines back East and then moved to Sunnyside, Utah. After five years, he saved enough money to send for my mother and me. I was five years old when we came to this country. We came by ship. I can remember going on deck to the edge of the ship and watching the fish jump up and splash me in my face. And I remember going right to Price, Utah, and then Moreland. But leaving my grandmother behind was the biggest trauma in my life. That's why I'm so much like, "Hey, everything is hunky-dory!" on the outside, but on the inside I'm a very sad person.

My sister Angie was born in Moreland. When we moved to Hiawatha, three or four more were born. Two were born in Spring Glen, and the last one was born in Price. There would have been thirteen or fourteen altogether, but my mama lost two or three. We were a big family—sometimes, four or five in a bed. But we enjoyed it even though it was a lot of work.

When I was about ten or eleven, my father bought a farm just past the city limits going towards Wellington. It wasn't much of a house—too small. But Papa laid out plans for another house, and the three of us built it. Mama and I nailed so many boards—narrow laths, not the panels you have today—we got stiff necks for a week. I chiseled the doors to put in the locks, and Papa and I put up the doors. It had four rooms, and we added a little kitchen in the back. We did the best we could, and the house still stands.

We worked hard on the farm. Besides keeping up with the vegetable garden and weeding the wheat, Mama and I kept the ditch banks clean of weeds. Papa made special wines. We made four or five kinds of cheese, and we cured meat. We sold everything. It wasn't easy, but we made a living from it. I went to school, but I had my chores to do, and so I used to run home and beat the school bus. By the time it passed us, I would be in the garden working. Kids would shout, "Hello, Mary!" And Papa, who was from the old school, would yell, "Whatsa' matta? Whatsa' matta? 'Ello, Mary! Who is this?" "The kids I go to school with, Papa." He was very strict. Once, when two boys stopped by to ask about a school assignment, Papa said, "You better go. Mary can't talk." He went into the house and came out with a shotgun. They sure left in a hurry. [*Laughs*] I think my papa was afraid one of these days I would leave him, and then who would he have to rely on?

Papa worked at the Sunnyside [coke ovens] off and on to make a little extra money. In the summers, we'd load his wagon with forty or fifty dozen ears of corn and peddle them throughout the mining camps. Papa and I. In fact, I still have this wart from the time I used to tie the vegetables. We sold all kinds of vegetables. Sometimes, we'd sell ham and cheese, like provolone. At first, we traveled by horse and buggy, and then Dad bought a Dodge truck. We'd go up the canyon to Standard, Rains, Castle Gate, and all along the road to Carbonville and Kenilworth. People would know who was passing. They knew the peddlers. If they needed something, they'd stand by the road and wait for us. They were nice—never rough or violent.

I worked hard all those years. By the time I was in high school, I'd get up early in the morning to milk the cow and get my brothers and sisters ready for school. I sewed their shirts, cobbled their shoes, cut their hair, and took care of the gardening. I cut Papa's hair, too. We didn't live fancy, but we lived good. We had good food, fresh vegetables, fresh milk, and we made a living.

Since I was the oldest child in the family, my mother and dad gave me all the trust. God love them, Mama wouldn't even handle money. Papa worked, and if he brought money home, he'd give it to me to take care of. Now, don't get me wrong. My mother wanted it that way. She was smart, but she couldn't speak English well. Anyway, we got along pretty good, and I took over. Eventually, I had the will, the farm documents, and everything else pertaining to the property. If something had to be bought or something had to be done, Papa would come to me. Maybe that's why I'm so tired today and don't care anymore.

People don't understand that [although] I was educated in the modern way, I still clung a bit to the old-fashioned ways. You know, I wasn't about to let the world ruin me and hurt my mother and dad. Don't you see what I mean? I didn't want to go away from home to work. I wanted to stay close. So I obeyed my parents. I never defied them. I have that to remember. It didn't matter what the world was coming to, you know? I'd ask my papa, "May I go visit so-and-so?" If he said no, I didn't go.

I did want to bring my grandmother here. I even crocheted a quilt that I was going to raffle off to pay for her passage. She had granulated eyes. (That's when you can't always open your eyes.) I had it, too, because we slept in the same bed. So she couldn't pass the [health] inspection. But I wanted to go to Washington, D.C., to get a special visa for her. Papa wouldn't let me go. "Oh, no. Oh, no," [he said]. He was afraid. You know what I mean? He was afraid I'd leave home. So she died over there, and I never saw her again. Of course, a few years later, I did leave home when I married John. Then I pulled out of the property and turned it over to my brother in California and to my sisters. By then, I said, I had enough.

I didn't think I wanted to marry. I wanted to be a linguist and travel. I wanted to speak every language, so I would be comfortable wherever I went. That's what I wanted to do. I took language classes in school. I liked to imitate people. I had a pretty good accent. One time, when Papa and I peddled, there was a Greek man that used to come and bother him. "You wanna buy some-ting—string bean, patata?" Papa would ask. "Na, na! I wanna buy Marie!" "You wanta buy whot?" "I wanna buy your Mary!" He was joking. He was a good man. My daddy said, "My Mary not fa' sale. So you bettah ski-dooo and go-go-go!" [Laughs]

That's what I meant to do—be a linguist. I already had several proposals for marriage before John came by. Tony had a beautiful accordion. He told my father he would build me a house. "I know she's modern," he said. "I'll give her anything." But then here comes John. He worked in the mines with Mr. Olivetto. So you know how it goes. "You wanna get married?" Mr. Olivetto asked him. "There's a nice woman, a daughter of a dear friend of ours. . . ." That's how it goes.

[John] came in the afternoon. I saw him come up the road, walking like a captain or a colonel. So there he was, and there is Tony. I didn't know what to do. But I knew who I was going to choose. John walked so straight, and I could see the pride in his face, that I guess I wanted to see what made him tick. So I told Tony I wasn't ready to get married. [Laughs] Then I married John. He was some man. Tough. A good worker and a good miner. An A1 miner. He didn't have enough education in English, but he was one of the best [workers] in the mines. He was tough. He had to be, because he was on the rescue team. And he was a good husband. He must have been for me to live with him for fifty-seven years. Of course, like I say, sometimes he wanted to be right and I wanted to be right. But as a rule, he was a good husband. A good provider. Strong in body and strong in mind. He wasn't afraid of anything. Try as I can, I can't forget that special man.

When we lived in Sweets, we lived in a shack, but it was as good as anybody could have because it was a new camp and kind of small. It was like living with a big family. I remember I made a mystery cake with three layers of chocolate, vanilla, and strawberry. Nobody locked doors then, and I'll be a dirty chicken if sometime during the day that cake wasn't gone. I thought, well, what's the big deal and walked down to the superintendent's office. There he was, Thomalson, with the clerk, eating it all. "Don't you think I would have given you a piece of cake? You had to take the whole shebang!" [Laughs]

We lived further down from the mouth of the mine, but I could see what was going on there. Whenever when there was an accident, all the women would climb the hill, running like crazy. That always upset Thomalson. He'd say, "Those darn women!" Because when somebody gets hurt, it's like John said, you have to give them all the room you can. You can't crowd around, because they have to work with that person or maybe he needs more air. One time, Thomalson started to cuss. "Those damn women—they're always here to make it worse." He said they ought to put up a big fence to keep them out. I said, "Sure, you'd be the first one to watch me jump the fence!" See, I've always been outspoken—very outspoken.

We stayed in Sweet Mine for five or six months, then my mother had a mis[carriage] in September. She almost died. That was her last baby. I was so afraid of what happened to her, I told John we had to get out of there because there wasn't a doctor close by and I was in a family way. So John said okay and got a job in Standardville.

We had our babies at home. The only one of my five I had in the hospital was Vince, my last one. The doctors were good—all of them. Dr. Frank

Gorishier and I became friends. [When I was in labor] he would come to the house. I'd ask if he wanted coffee or something to drink, and he'd sit on the edge of the bed and stay with me until the baby was born. When my Frankie was born, John, well, he was in the poolroom. I sent for him, and he didn't come right away. But Dr. Frank stayed with me. Then John came home and lay on the other side of the bed and fell asleep. Dr. Frank said, "Some husband you have." And I said, "Well . . ."

John liked to go to the poolroom and play a game of cards once in a while. I could have gone with him. But I didn't like cards, so I never did. Even when he'd play solitaire at home, I'd tell him I didn't want to give my time to those stupid cards. But as a rule, in other ways, John and I did things together. We'd take walks, go places, talk. Like I say, John could be ornery if he wanted to. When I got older, I started to get ornery, too. Then we'd start that phrase, "All the time, the yakity-yak." Once, I aggravated him so much, he got up on his chair. I was over there, on the other side [of the table]. I said, "You want to conk me one?" See, I'm that kind of person. I speak my mind! "Come on, get up! Get up! I'll wait for you!" I said.

Once, we were arguing about something, and I said, "Why in the name of hell did you marry me if you didn't like me?" He said, "What the hell?" Just like that! "What the hell? You think I marry you if I no like you?" He wasn't a very tender man. You understand what I mean? He couldn't show me affection because he was the old-country way—had to be the big cheese! But man is just another human being with feelings and habits like a stupid woman. Some men are afraid to show they're a little bit tender. They're going to lose their manhood! Ah! I could tell by the way he talked about his mother and his dad that he was a little bit tender. And in the way he treated his children— aiyeeee—that daughter was the apple of his eye. Oh, mama mia. "Oh, my Jeannie," [he'd say] . . . So there you have it. He was a decent man. And now I wish I had played cards with him.

I don't think anyone knew the real me. I had high goals. I don't know what it was, but I wanted to do or be something special. And it didn't happen. I had heartaches, and I was disillusioned. In 1945, I was so low, I was afraid I could have done something [to hurt myself]. I don't know exactly what happened. It's like I said—I was okay on the outside, but inside I was unhappy. Maybe, too, it was from having children born close. Or the humdrum of life. Maybe it was the change in life. I cried too much. John used to get uptight with me because I cried so much. And I couldn't make up my mind about anything. Should I do this, or should I do that? You see, indecision is one of the worst things for the nerves. I was disillusioned about something. I don't know— whatever it was, it was a crucial part in my life, and I guess everything just piled up. Don't you see what I mean? I was unhappy about something. I wanted to do something special. My ideals were too high. John used to laugh at me. I don't know, but I thought . . . oh, gee, a horrible thought came in my mind. End it all. And I thought, "Oh my God, what a sin."

Then I had a nervous breakdown. My nerves broke. For nine days and nine nights I didn't sleep. My doctor suggested shock treatments. "Mary, get shock treatments or you'll lose your mind," he said. I said, "You don't put the juice in my head." See, I was arguing with doctors. Yakity-yak. I said, "I'm not going to lose my mind because the Master that give it to me will help."

When I was young, Mama and I talked about Jesus. We sang songs about him. I even went to the Mormon Sunday School just to sing with them, because [the songs] were about Jesus. "Rock of Ages." "Jesus Loves Me." Don't you see what I mean? I've been through all the churches. I go to Greek church for funerals. I go to the Mormon church, the Methodist church. Jesus is one, don't you see? And wherever they mention his name, I will go. I'm Catholic, yes. But if there's no Catholic church, I'll go where they talk about Jesus. Is that bad? Jesus is Jesus. He's the Master. I don't know where He's going to send me, but I know it's up to Him.

That's why you see Him around my house. We need to see Him there on the cross to understand what he gave us. He must have created us because we were important enough to create. And how could He give us all the beauty of the world if He didn't have it in himself? And He doesn't want us to destroy it. See what I mean? So we have no more right to destroy ourselves than to kill somebody else. If you get something bad, you have to fight it off because you're not the boss of yourself. Your Creator is.

So when I got sick, I prayed all the time. I thought about Jesus, and I acquired a feeling of importance, a selfishness for me, which is something you have to have if you're going to fight for yourself. I learned how to let go. When I went to bed, I learned how to relax myself and rest my mind so I could sleep. I wrote poetry as a way to get courage for myself. I looked at the sky above and saw His creation of beauty and love. And little by little, I worked it off. The doctor tried to give me pills. But I told him to take them himself. I'm not much for pills and medicine. He almost give up on me. But I told him, "Nuts to you, Doc!"

VITO BONACCI, 86, COAL MINER, UNION ORGANIZER

Vito Bonacci was in a serious car accident approximately a year before our interview with him. His oldest son confided to us that he had worried that his father "would go downhill" after the accident. But, as he had done all his life, Vito Bonacci faced adversity with courage and spunky determination. A month after the accident, he was back on his feet, vigorous and feisty as ever.

Born on November 5, 1901, in Decollatura, Italy, a village in the province of Catanzaro in the region of Calabria, Vito Bonacci came to the United States in 1919 to work alongside his father, Dominick Bonacci, in a coal camp. After sifting coke ash for a year near Venango, Pennsylvania, they moved to Sunnyside, Utah, and became part-time workers at the coke ovens, filling in for absentees on the midnight shift.

Vito Bonacci. *George Janecek*

"We done that for seven months before we got a steady job," Vito Bonacci recalled. "But then that didn't last too long, because we went on strike in 1922." The strike for union recognition convinced Bonacci of the necessity of collective bargaining. When his father returned to Italy several years later, Bonacci remained in Utah and continued to advocate in behalf of the United Mine Workers of America. Together with his wife's uncle, Frank Bonacci, he became instrumental in the effort to organize Carbon County's coal miners.

When I first came to Sunnyside, Utah, in 1921, I had to keep my mouth shut, because this state didn't believe in unions. If they knew you're a union man, they won't give you a job. Well, I was a union man from Pennsylvania, because over there any job you were doing in the coal camps you had to belong to the union. It was a hundred percent union in Pennsylvania. So we come over and we tried to organize. We talked to the miners and told them it'll be better if we joined the union because we'd get better wages and be treated more like white people. A lot of people won't like what I'm saying, but them days, the coal miners were treated like slaves. We need[ed] a union to be treated like white people. So I helped out, went all over [in that 1922 strike].

Two days after we went out [on strike], I remember, the company kicked us out of the company houses. Then, just below Sunnyside, what in them days they call Draggerton, east of Carbon, the United Mine Workers gave us a big tent, and we lived there. Now, we was in pretty good shape at the beginning. But later we had too many [Mormon] scabs come in. The majority come from Emery and Sanpete counties. [Most] had never been in a mine before. They all worked on farms. But during the strike, the company let them have all the work they want. So they made big money.

I remember, when we lived in that [big] tent, which was pretty close to the highway at Sunnyside, we had three or four union miners in a [small] tent behind the Rio Grande Depot in Price. There ain't no depot there no more. And every time a train would go by, they'd inspect it, and they used to tell us if there's any scabs coming to work. Scabs came in cars and on the trains. The majority used to come on the trains.

Well, one day a bunch of us were sitting around, over by the track, talking, having a good time. There was an old store up there. I think it's closed down now. They had a telephone, and these guys used to call and let us know if any scabs was coming. This time they said there was two loads of scabs coming up; one [car] was run by the Sunnyside superintendent.

Well, we figured, we'll stop them. One young guy, a little older than me, kind of husky, said, "The best thing to do is pull a couple of ties from under the railroad track. When a car comes across and hits that, it'll stop." That's what we done. The guy in the store had an old pick. We went over, dug ties from under the rails. But when the car hit them things, it went over [the space]. It didn't stop. So this guy—I don't even remember his name now— you know, it was a long time ago—he had hid a gun in the bushes. He couldn't keep it in the tent because they were searching all the time [for weapons]. So he took a shot at this one car. The car never stopped. Went clear over the ties and clear up to the mine. We didn't get nowhere.

Two days later, we got the [state] militia. They brought the militia from Salt Lake because of that shooting.[1] He didn't hit anybody, but they thought there's going to be big trouble. So them guys come down, and they took *everything* we had. There was an old lady over there. She had one of those old-fashioned ovens to make bread—big, round, Italian-style bread. The only way to eat it was to cut it with a knife. But the militia even took our knives. So we had to break it with our hands.

After that—I'll tell you what happened—I couldn't get no other jobs around here. Every time I asked the superintendent, the boss, or whatever, for a job, I had to give them my name. Frank Bonacci, my [wife's] uncle, was one of the main organizers [for the union]. So every time I told them my [last] name is Bonacci, [they said] "No job."

They told me there's one place in Spring Canyon. They said, if you go over there, this superintendent named Jack Jones will give you a job. Everybody talked about how mean he was. But I went up there, I went into the office, and he talked nice to me. He made me sit down and said, "What can I do for you?" I said, "I'm looking for a job." He said, "Yes, no trouble." So I felt good about it. He asked a few more questions. Then I was supposed to go from Spring Canyon up to Standard, 'cause that's where the [company] doctor was. [I had] to pass the examination before I got the job.

I told him, "Fine, I'll go see the doctor." [The superintendent] said, "Listen here, [that'll be] twenty-five dollars." In other words, he wanted me to pay him twenty-five dollars before he okayed me to go to work. The only thing I said [was], "If I had twenty-five dollars, I wouldn't be looking for a job." I had walked up there from Helper because I didn't have any money, see. I was broke—*real* broke. But that's how it was.

So I wrote to a guy in California. We come together from the old country. He was a boss, a foreman, on the Union Pacific. He sent for me, and I went over there. It was a pretty nice job. I worked on what they called the traveling gang [and went wherever they needed us to work]. They used to take railroad cars and fill them up with gravel. They was building a new yard in Los Angeles, and they had to have gravel to put under the ties. The only place they could find any gravel was over in Anaheim, California. It wasn't [good] gravel; it was kind of sandlike. But it was the best they could find.

So we went over, and they used steam shovels to load the gravel. In fact, there was an orange farm there, and when they picked up the sand with the shovels, there would be trees and everything thrown in these cars. We took everything to Los Angeles, and we made sure the cars were in good shape. Then we moved to Las Vegas. They had some work over there. We worked two months there. From there we moved by the [Utah] State Prison, [at] the Point-of-the-Mountain. They got a gravel pit there that belonged to the Union Pacific.

Two or three days after we got there, I told this foreman, "I'm close to Helper now. What about giving me a week off? I'll go see my uncle and my friends." He said, "Sure, go ahead." Well, two days after I got in Helper, he call[ed] me on the telephone and said, "Don't come back, because you ain't got no job." He gave my job to another guy who had a beer joint in Salt Lake by the Rio Grande Depot. See, in them days, you couldn't sell whiskey. They caught this guy selling it and closed him up. So he got my job and I got left over here [in Helper] again.

This time, I got mixed up with my wife's family. My wife's older sister's husband was driving a team of horses at Kenilworth and delivering coal to the company houses. He had a house here on the other side of Spring Glen, and he told me, "You come up with me one of these mornings and talk to the super[intendent] and see if he's got anything." So I went up with him.

The superintendent was a French-Canadian just out of the army. Everybody said he was rough and tough. I went and looked at him, and I figured he must be rough and tough. He was a real big man. But he was educated. He said, "Please sit down and we'll talk [things] over." He'd just built two new houses at the camp, he said—one for him and one for the mine foreman, his wife's cousin. He wanted those houses fixed up nice. He said, "How about clearing the yards, firing the boilers for heat, and doing this stuff?" So I went, and I built roads, planted trees, grass. In other words, I was his gardener.

Then, I don't know what happened, but a lot of those Emery County guys decided to go home. So the superintendent told the tipple foreman to give me a job. Well, he gave me the worst job they had. I had to clean inside the tipple, the place where the coal cars got dumped.

Now, this was an old-time wood tipple, two floors high. I was down on the bottom, cleaning up, keeping the tracks clean. And it was dirty. They dumped the coal about fifteen, twenty feet over my head. And all the dust and little chunks of coal used to hit me on the head. Them days, you never wore hard hats, just regular caps. So it was a mess. You were sweating. That dust came down, and it stuck to you. You couldn't even move. I got home at night and I had more dirt, more coal dust, inside me than outside. But every time I asked that foreman for something better, he never had nothing.

One time he told me, "Listen here, buddy. You're drinking the sauce." See, the guys from Emery County were [always] bringing him a chicken or half a calf. Well, he liked wine, and he expected me to give him some to pay him off. In other words, he expected me to buy the job like everyone else. But I didn't believe in it. The union believed you should work and get paid for it. So he didn't care much for me.

The company also had a policy that if you didn't buy everything from the company store, they'd let you go. They had everything there: clothes, food, tools. One time, after they changed superintendents, the new guy laid me off during the summer. I asked him, "How come I can't stay in the summer?" He said, "You don't spend enough in the company store." I said, "How can I spend it if I don't make it?" But he didn't care. So for fifteen straight years, I worked in the winter and got laid off in the summer. That's how it was. If the superintendent felt like giving you a job, he'd give you a job. If he didn't like you, he'd give you a pink slip and away you'd go. [*Laughs*]

One time, in fact, the super[intendent] in Kenilworth found out Frank Bonacci's younger brother, Joe Bonacci, had been organizing. So [Joe] was told to leave Kenilworth. He decided to move back East with his family. [By then] I was living in Spring Glen with my wife's family. But when I heard he was going to Connecticut, I walked up there to tell him good-bye. They used to have a track that went straight up from Spring Glen. I walked the track, and when I got to about sixty feet from the first house in town, here come an old man on a horse. They called him Frank. He was [a company] cop, and he was mean. He'd shoot you like a dog if you tried to argue with him.

Well, Frank got his rifle [pointed at me] and said, "Go back." So that's all I could do. Turn around. No talking. I couldn't get up there. So, like I said [earlier], we were slaves. You couldn't go into the camp to see somebody. You couldn't talk about the union because they had spies listening. In fact, Kenilworth put a cop inside our camp. He was a friend of mine; yet he listened, and if you said anything about a union, he'd tell it to the office and away you'd go. They'd kick you out.

So right today, I say the only two guys that freed the laborer in the United States was John L. Lewis and [Franklin D.] Roosevelt. We had no right to organize before Roosevelt got to be president. Once he legalized it, we [at least] had a chance.

I remember another time we went to a place called Consumers to set up a picket line. It was way up in the hills, and they had a tough superintendent. He claimed more than half his men didn't want to join the union. When we got up there, we sat down on the right side of a big wash and got to talking. We figured that at night, when the miners were coming out of the mine, we'd talk [to them] and see if we could get some interested in hearing more about unions.

There was an old [Italian] lady in that village. She lived up there, and she sat down with us. She must have been about my age now—mid-eighties. She was with us when here comes that superintendent. He had one leg shorter than the other. A tough guy, I tell you. He told us to move out. We asked, "Why? We aren't doing nothing. We aren't hurting nothing. We're just having a hell of talk amongst ourselves." He said, "I want you guys out of here. I don't want you guys here."

This lady said, "Listen, I live here. I pay rent to the company. I got a right to sit where I want." "No, you don't," he told her, real cocky-like. So the old lady [went up and] shoved him, and with that short, crooked leg, he rolled way down the wash, about twenty-five feet. An hour after that, by golly, we saw a bunch of guys with horses and rifles [coming up] from Price. A fellow by the name of J. Bracken Lee, an insurance man in them days, was leading them. He come up on a white horse. He got to be governor [of Utah] later. The other guys were on different horses.

One by one, they got around us with rifles [and told us], "Keep walking." Bracken Lee got behind me. We had to walk from up on top of that hill, way up there, clear down to the road that goes to Price. Every time I slowed down a little, he'd hit me with that gun [muzzle]. So I just kept walking. What else could I do? I didn't figure he'd shoot me. I didn't figure he had the guts to do that. But it's hard to tell what somebody will do in that situation. You don't know what to think.

Years later, after we got the union, I was working in the [machine] shop at Kenilworth, and I was grinding some tools, and J. Bracken Lee was running for Congress. It was the first time he was in politics, and my boss, who was his campaign manager, brought him up to the shop and straight over to me. They wanted me to shake hands with him. Now, my boss never did call me by name. He was shorter than me, but he always called me "Shorty." Anyway, while I was sharpening tools, he said, "Shorty, [come] meet Mr. Bracken Lee." I said, "That son of a bitch! Not me." He went to about thirty guys in the shop. He gave each of them a button. He didn't give me no button 'cause I told him I wouldn't vote for that son of a bitch.

So that's how it was: Utah was a rough state to organize in because the Mormons was against it. And in this state, if you ain't got them behind you, you ain't going to get nowhere. But we finally did it. We made them [miners] believe. We told them the difference between belonging to the union and not belonging. A lot of them didn't know nothing. They didn't know the union could do anything for them. When I first joined back East, I didn't know I could [eventually] get my pension and hospitalization out of it. I joined because I figured if the company did something I didn't like, I had somebody to defend me. So we did all right. I'm well satisfied.

Lots of times, though, I think back East we wouldn't have had all this trouble with strikes and the [Mormon] church against us. I [still] don't know why they didn't believe in it. But I work[ed] with a lot of strong Mormons. And they were always trying to tell me they were better than we were. One guy, a bishop, worked with me in the shop. He was a good friend; we worked together. But every time we argued about something, he said, "You're in the minority. We are [the] real Americans." That's just what he said.

I'll tell you, right today, I don't think we're treated like we should be [by the Mormons]. They still think we're foreigners. I talk to a lot of those guys. We're friends now. I say, "As far as the church is concerned, that's your business. You believe in that religion, and more welcome to it. I belong to my church. But I don't like you mixing church and state. I don't like the laws you're making." I don't know if you noticed [that] the last time [the state legislators met] they had to ask those big guys in the Mormon church if it was all right to make a certain bill. I don't think they should have anything to do with the [making of] laws. I ain't got anything against them [as a religion]. But I don't think they should pass laws to satisfy themselves. The laws should be passed to satisfy everybody.

FILOMENA FAZZIO BONACCI, 77, HOUSEWIFE, SEAMSTRESS, LAUNDRY WORKER

An even-tempered woman with an innate sense of modesty and proportion, Filomena Fazzio Bonacci was born on December 20, 1910, in Sunnyside, Utah, and raised in Spring Glen, a nearby farming community. She married Vito Bonacci at the age of sixteen, and the couple lived for a decade in the Kenilworth coal camp, where their first son, Dominic, was raised. Their second son, Joseph, was born and raised in their present home in Spring Glen.

After enrolling her children in school, Ms. Bonacci supplemented her family's income by working at the Kilfoyle Tamping Company in Price, where she made tamping dummies for the coal mines.² She also worked for a time as a presser for the Price Steam Laundry. Following her husband's retirement, she worked as custodian and caretaker at the Carbon County Country Club.

An active member of St. Anthony's Catholic Parish in Helper, Ms. Bonacci was for many years responsible for the annual fund-raising banquet for the Notre Dame Catholic School in Price. In 1985, the parish acknowledged her years of devoted community service by naming her "Woman of the Year."

My full name is Filomena Fazzio Bonacci. My father's name was Rosario Fazzio. My mother's name was Filomena Bonacci Fazzio, the opposite of mine. They were married in Decollatura, Italy, and then my dad used to migrate. He migrated four or five times. He'd come here and go to work, then he'd go back, stay a year, come back, and go back again. My mother finally told him, "If you're going back [to America] again, don't come back anymore. I can't live like this." She didn't like him coming home, getting her pregnant, then leaving again. Even Grandpa told him, "If you're not going to take her or you're not going to stay, don't come back here again."

But he loved Mama too much to leave her, so he brought his family over in 1908, and they moved to Sunnyside. Mama had three children and was pregnant with my second brother when they came, so he was born here in the United States. A year later I was born. I was the first one that was originated all the way through here. The first child. Then she had four more. I had three more sisters and a brother after that. There were nine of us [in the family].

My father was a coal miner. While he was going back and forth, he worked at the coke ovens in Sunnyside. Then, when he brought the family over, he didn't want to bring us up in a coal camp, so he bought this farm and got a job in the Kenilworth mine. He was picking and loading coal there until he quit. He was a quiet man; yet when he talked, you'd think he was arguing with the world.

My mother—I couldn't describe my mother. She was a jewel—she was just out of this world. She was friendly to everybody. She rarely got mad. When there was trouble, she was always there to make peace. *Always.* If anybody was arguing, she'd say, "Now, come on, come on. Can't we talk this out without

Filomena Bonacci. *George Janecek*

getting our tempers up?" Oh, she was a wonderful mother. She's been gone about twenty-five years, and I still miss her. Oh, I just miss my mother.

When I was a young girl, she would take me out in the fields. Starting at about the age of seven, she'd say, "You come with me." So, to this day, I like working outside in the garden better than I like being in the house, because I was "the outside girl." My sisters worked in the house, and I'd be outside with mother, planting our garden, hoeing and cultivating. We cut our wheat with hand scythes. I [could] cut about four acres of wheat [with her], and she'd make a knot with the wheat itself, then tie it to make bundles of grain. She couldn't read or write—neither could my dad—but she was very good in everything she did.

Oh, my mama, she'd always make some little party for us. You know, we didn't have the neighbors we have [around us] now. We had only one way down there, one up here, so we couldn't play with our neighbors' children. But when she had time, she'd sew our doll clothes, show us how to play with our dolls and how to take care of them. Then, when my sister got married, she [and her husband] moved [beside us]. And once she started having babies, we started taking care of them. It was a lot of fun. We grew up not like nieces or cousins but like one big family.

Later on, people started moving in and started building. Then we had a few more friends. But our closest friends came when we went to school. That's where the friends were. I remember they converted a two-room house [for school use]. From there we went to Carbon High School. I didn't go clear through Carbon High, though. I got the love bug and got married. [*Laughs*] I was sixteen at the time. I still remember he was going with another girl, and he came over to see my sister. I went out on the porch—he had this girl on his arm—and he said something to me. I told my mother, "Oh, I could just knock that man down. He thinks he's a smart aleck. I despise him."

We got married in 1926. Then Vito got a job in Kenilworth, and we moved up there. I think we lived in Kenilworth for seven years. Dominic, my first child, was born there. Then Mother said, "Oh, you better come down here. We'll give you a lot, and you can put a house on it." So we moved down, and Mother was a great help to me, just like she was to everyone.

She wasn't exactly a midwife, but she used to go around the neighborhood [and help the women give birth]. They'd come and get her, and she'd say, "I'll come and assist you, but I want you to get a doctor." But lots of times she delivered before the doctor came. I think she delivered babies to every one of the families around here. She also was with me when I had my kids. I don't think I could have gone through it without her by my side. I don't think I could have.

She was so tender with my babies, and when my first boy was born, I had a very hard time. After the delivery, the doctor said [to us], "He's dead; he's born dead." He laid him on the bed, and as he was working with me, my mother grabbed the baby, went into the kitchen, and she worked with him. Pretty soon, the doctor jumped up. He said, "What did you do, Mama? What did you do?" "I brought him back to life," she said. I don't know what she did. But when there wasn't any response, she grabbed him and went in the kitchen and the doctor heard the baby scream and he ran in there. She'd always tell me, "You take care of that little boy. I brought him here, so you take good care of that little boy."

She was there when I had Joseph, too. And if anything went wrong with them, I'd run to her, and she'd say, "Oh, it's all right. Don't worry about it." Then she'd work with them a little bit. She'd do something with them, and they'd be all right. She never had no education, but she just had something in her that told her what to do, I guess. I don't know what it was. One time a lady told me, "Maybe she does witchcraft." But she didn't do witchcraft. When we got sick, her medicine was hot lemonade. Once in a while, if you were older, she'd put a little drop of whiskey in it. When the boys got older— seventeen, eighteen—and they'd get a cold, she'd always put a little drop of whiskey in with the lemon juice. But she was heavy on that lemon juice. Or when one of the kids had a cold, and I'd tell her "I don't know what I'm going to do," she'd say, "Get some hot milk and put some sugar in it until it's so sweet they can't stand it. Give them a couple of spoonfuls of that, and that'll cure their cold." And it would. I'm not subject to colds very much, but once in a while if I get a sore throat, then that darn hacking cough, that's what I do, and it takes my cough right away.

After I got married, the thing I worried about was Vito getting hurt on the job. I'd always say a prayer when he left [in the morning], then a thank-you prayer when he came home at night because the mines weren't like they are today. They would explode. Miners didn't have the know-how they got now, either. They know how to keep the dust down. Back then they picked by hand. And that coal bounced around quite a bit, so I'd always worry. And I was always thankful. I'd kiss him good-bye and ask the Lord to take care of him during the day. Then, when he came home, I'd always thank the Lord for bringing him back.

Oh, those mines were a constant worry. I remember when I was younger— twelve years old—they had that '22 strike. My mother's brother, Frank Bonacci, was the one who organized it, and his brother used to go around with him. And during the strike, they moved down to live at my dad's place. The union give them a tent, but they moved down here. And I remember at night, the search lights just kept a'going, and [I thought] they could see every-thing that was going around our place.

The light was on this hill [above us], and all night it'd just keep flashing. And, oh, I'd go to bed every night with fear and worry. I'd wonder if they're going to come and get us because my mother's brothers were both here. I thought they were going to come and cause us trouble. They never did, but that searchlight put fear in us. [We thought] they knew everything that was going on down here. They could tell who was here and who wasn't here.

After the strike, my uncles moved away. They didn't bother Dad anymore. The only thing is, the mines wouldn't give Dad any more work. So we kids had to peddle the vegetables my mother grew. We had a little buggy. We'd fill it up, and we'd peddle in Helper and Kenilworth. We'd sell every bit of it, too, because all the miners bought from us. But it was hard. Without Mama's garden, we'd never have made it.

By the time the Depression came, Mama and the boys had got a little dairy going. I remember she'd give us meat and milk. Dad still couldn't get steady work. But after the dairy got off the ground, my brothers found work, and Dad took over the dairy. My sisters helped, but mostly my mom and dad worked it. And over the years, they built it up. When they quit about ten years ago, they had around a hundred cows. They were doing big business.

For me, my hardest time was in 1942, when Dom was in the service and Joe was about six. I had a terrible scare. Vito got strep throat. I told him, "Don't go to work," but he went anyway. Well, one night the kids wanted to go to the movies, and he said, "Why don't you drive them to the show?" I did, and when I came home I found him in a great deal of pain. He said, "I can't move my legs, I can't move my hands!" I called a doctor in. He said it was "inflammable arthritis." He was all swollen and laying flat on his back. The doctor told me, "I can't give him any medicine. There's nothing I can do. He's going to be a cripple." I says, "Not if I can help it, he's not. . . ."

So I took his legs and pushed them off the bed, and I said, "Now, you grab your arms around my neck and pull yourself up," and I drug him around. I did that every day, every day, until little by little, little by little, he started to move his legs. After three months, he was good enough to get up. A couple of months later, the guys came down from the company and said, "You can come down if you can sit; you don't have to do anything."

But I remember that Christmas was terrible. I was working at the Price Steam Laundry so we could eat. Dom was still in the service, and I told Joe, "Santa won't come this year." He said, "Mama, I don't want no Santa Claus. I don't want no Santa Claus." My sister-in-law said to me, "Oh, you're mean; you could go and charge something for him." I said, "I'm not going into the hole just to buy him something." He was seven years old, and he had to give up his Christmas gift. So that's the worst Christmas I've ever spent in my life.

The worst thing about it all was that, in the meantime, Mama developed sugar diabetes, and every morning I had to leave Vito in bed, run over, and give Mama her shot. She couldn't give it to herself. So that's one year I will never forget. I never even want to remember it. It was terrible the way his bones tightened up and they thought he wouldn't be able to walk anymore. But I drug him. It was hard on me. But I drug him all over. I'd drag him from there over to here [from one side of the room to the other], and from here to over there, until he couldn't stand it. He was so tired and in so much pain. But then God helped him. After six months, he got up and went to work, and he's been working ever since.

What was bad, too, was that after he started working, the FBI spied on him to see where he'd go, what he'd do. He didn't know it, but one of his [co]workers told on him [that he was a possible saboteur or spy]. So they followed him, and that was terrible. I didn't think we deserved it. I told one guy, "He's got his mother, father, brothers, and sister in Italy. He's working here and buying United States government bonds so the army can go and kill his parents and you're following him around? It makes no sense."

But you know what? We survived it. And right now, I'm in heaven. I really am. I'm in heaven. Everything is going our way. I take my time, I can do what I want, and I don't have any debts. I don't have much money. But I don't have debts, either, and that's [being] rich. Lots of times, I'll have an extra dollar, and I'll give it to my grandchildren. It makes me happy when I can help them. Joe says, "Mama, with your small pension, you can still save ten, fifteen dollars to give to the children?" I say, "When I was twelve years old, I started school barefooted, because Dad was on strike and he didn't have money to buy me shoes. So I'm glad to give it to my grandchildren—even if they have the best shoes in town." Vito sometimes gets mad and tells the grandkids, "When I was young, I didn't have this, I didn't have that." I says, "Thank God they haven't got what you had! Let them have what they want."

DOMINIC BESSO, 70, SHOEMAKER

One of four children of Martina Ferraro and James Besso, Dominic Besso was born on December 15, 1915, in Rock Springs, Wyoming, and raised in Price, Utah. He described the Price of his youth as "wide open," with rampant prostitution and bootlegging. It wasn't only "the Greeks, Italians, or Bohunks" who engaged in these activities, he told us. "Plenty of 'fall-away' Mormons bought moonshine or whatever else they could lay their hands on."

Besso learned the art of repairing shoes from his father, who had apprenticed as a shoemaker in Turin, Italy. By the fourth grade, he was actively involved in the business. After school, he delivered shoes and swept the store, and on Saturdays, when the shop remained open until nine P.M. to cater to the coal camp trade, he sat and stitched designs into the handmade boots his father sold for fifteen dollars. "Those boots would sell for a hundred today," he remarked.

In 1939, when his father suffered a stroke, Besso took over the business and worked hard to maintain the quality that was his father's trademark. Over the decades, by dint of its remarkable longevity, the Besso shoe repair shop became a Carbon County landmark. On August 19, 1989, family and friends gathered at the Price Elks lodge to honor the sixtieth anniversary of the little shop located at 41 East Main Street.

My father worked in Rock Springs, Wyoming, until he got it in his head that he was going to be a farmer. He didn't know a thing about farming. That was about the same time my brother, at the ripe old age of ten, was hopping freights and going to places like Rawlings, Wyoming, 110 miles away. I think that took a lot of guts to go that far. But the railroaders would tell my dad he'd

Dominic Besso. *Kent Miles*

better watch that damn kid, or one of these days he was going to get cut in two. Well, I think my dad was a little bit disgusted with that. So when his good friends, the Buonomos, said they were looking for a better place to make a living and moved to Price, my family followed. There, in 1917, they homesteaded a farm, and my dad lost his shirt.

In the early '20s, there were about three nationalities in Price and in Helper: mostly Italians, Greeks, then Bohunks. The reason they went there in the '20s was because they were always following work. See, when they came to this country, they'd go to West Virginia and southern Illinois first; then west to Colorado, New Mexico, and Utah—wherever they heard of work. If one mine didn't work out as well, they'd get word from somewhere else where they were hiring, so they'd drift from mine to mine in search of better working conditions.

Being foreign and coming from the old country, most of these immigrants couldn't read or write. They had no skills other than common labor. Those that stopped in Carbon County worked in the coal mines, because that's all there was for them. Others came up to Bingham and worked on the section gangs fixing the railroads, doing what amounted to slave labor. A few of the ones that were educated, the shrewder ones, got into business. I guess some were honest, and some I wonder about their [business] practices.

It was the ones that bootlegged that made a lot of money, because it didn't cost them much to make the stuff and they would sell it. I don't know how many bootlegging joints there was in Helper. I recalled being told the bigger majority of them were owned by southern Italians. They also had hotels with floozies in them. I was just a kid then, but I saw a few of them on Main Street. They were dressed to kill and that. Of course, they [plied their trade], and we were all ears and our mouths wide open, you know, looking at the other side of the world. In the Central Hotel there was a madam. Now her husband, I think, was Italian. I don't know about her. She was a huge woman. She wore short dresses and was always really well groomed. I remember she had a Packard convertible that was always parked in front of that hotel.

Helper was noted for having more bootleggers than Price. But Price had its share. The wealthier people down there, all of them came by their money by bootlegging, because no one made money by going to work in the mine at the menial wages they got. People bootlegged until they had buildings and stores and houses. That's the way it was in the '20s and early '30s.

Now, my dad learned shoemaking in the old country. So, of course, he made shoes after the farming experience took everything he had. In the middle '20s he had a shop downtown. He left there and had a little shack at home. Then he went back downtown in 1926. We were on Carbon Avenue. He didn't own the building, but he had some friends, coal miners, and I think he borrowed all the money from them. They took him back to one of the old coal camp houses and dug behind the wine barrels, where they stored their money in those old Sego lard buckets. And this one guy took out the money—gold pieces they had—and gave it to Dad. That's what they did in those days. They buried the money in those Sego lard buckets. That's how Dad got enough money to buy a building. Then in 1929 we started at the present location that I'm still in—the one that became the morning gathering place.

See, this was the only Italian establishment where people could stop by anywhere from three or four o'clock till ten o'clock every morning and find out what the news was. Most of them didn't know how to read or write or anything like that. The bootlegging joints didn't open in the morning. So all the men from the old country would come into my dad's shop and have him read their letters or write some for them. In his small village in Italy, my dad's father was the schoolteacher. He had four boys and was going to make priests out of every one of them. He sent them into the seminary, and the oldest boy did become a priest and later was in charge of all the schools in that area. But my dad went into the seminary, stayed quite a while, and didn't like it, so he left.

He didn't tell his dad. He just left, and in those days, in order to learn a trade, you moved in with the people who taught you. So my dad went into a place that made shoes. Not fixed them. He didn't fix shoes until he came here. But my dad got enough of an education to read and write Italian, and English, too, although he never mastered the right pronunciation. He also spoke fluent French, because as kids they would cross the border. So there he was in this shop [in Price] with his countrymen, and then—since it turned out there was any number of Frenchmen that had sheep outfits in Price—a lot of Frenchmen came in with their shoes and letters from the old country.

When these people prepared themselves for citizenship, they would take my dad to Salt Lake with them. While he was away, I would have to stay out of school to take care of the shop. If I recall right, the rail fare was two fifty a round-trip and they bought him his dinner. My dad was a good-hearted person known by all these people. They came to him for his opinions about this and that. And he'd give it, but he never took a dime from anybody.

Like I said, the ones that made money made it by hook or crook. They didn't take it out of the mines. This one guy, one of these Tyroleans who didn't claim to be Italian, bootlegged into the '30s. He was an old man, this one—married, but they didn't have any children. All they had was a pure white spitz dog with a curly tail and turned up nose. Well, this man had a fermenter right in his house. It was about six feet by ten feet wide and five or six feet high and made out of cement with a spigot in the bottom. He got his grapes from Colorado and California. He would put three or four "tons" of grapes in a big vat, stomp on them, and dump them into this machine, where they fermented and were made into wine. They called it a *tina*.

He had money and everything. He made wine in the basement of his house, and nobody ever bothered with him. Hell, you didn't have to have an education to do this. During Prohibition, this other guy was running moonshine from Utah to Wyoming. His car had so many holes in it—from agents shooting at it—but he'd keep going. He couldn't read nothing. And in order to do anything that he would do, he would put an X on the line. He knew the value of the dollar, though. And he knew if he put a nickel in [his business], it would hatch a whole bunch of little ones.

My dad would buy twenty-two to thirty-five boxes of grapes and maybe ten boxes of muscatel. And we always had wine at home. But he never sold it, and nobody ever bothered us about it. Dad made a first wine and a second wine. The first wine they would put in barrels or bottle it. That was for the best, for company. The other wine they would take and use as table wine. My mother occasionally drank a little glass, and my dad had one during a meal. That was the extent of it. Then they would take whatever was left over from the grapes—the sour mash—and make it into vinegar—really good, strong, wine vinegar that would knock your head off! I remember in the summers my family had a table down by the canal, near a bunch of trees, where it was shady and cool. They ate dinners there because it was so hot in the house. One time, the water master, a Mormon, passed by and saw a gallon jug, one of those crocks, on the table. I guess he thought it was wine and was going to get over on these "Wops," so he took the jug, hoisted it up over his shoulder and drank and drank and drank and drank, and my mother said he should have just choked to death on that damned vinegar. But, God, he got through and said, "Ahhh." And all of her life, she just never got over that fact that the guy drank that homemade vinegar thinking it was wine.

In those days, those guys would drink just about anything. After the Castle Gate explosion in 1924, I was told that a lot of women buried their husbands and were left with a whole house full of young kids. Must have been 175 people who were killed.[3] And it seemed like darned near half of those people were the older sons—fourteen and seventeen years old—who helped out their families by getting paid for the coal cars they loaded. Until they came out with a better deal, most of these widows got paid only enough money to bury their men. Nothing else. There's one woman I'm thinking of who had eight or nine kids to take care of, so she made beer in her kitchen and sold it. One guy told me they were in the front room, the living room, drinking beer, and they drank a little too much, so they had to go to the outhouse out in the back. They went through the kitchen, and there was a great big crock boiling by the stove—fermenting, you know. And on the top of it was a whole layer of flies, just like waves, floating around. I guess, the things they drank—it's a wonder some of them are alive!

There was instances where they would make moonshine in carbide cans, and I remember two guys drank some of that and were killed. Poisoned. Some even drank wood alcohol. They drained it from their Model T Fords. Of course, they died from that, too. They would try just about anything. Why? I don't know. They wanted to get drunk, I suppose, and just never come to.

We drank, too, as kids. We never told our parents. Nobody did. They might have suspected, and my mother, I remember, would cover for us when we sneaked in late at night. She would always threaten to tell on us, but she never did. A lot of people drank in Price and in Helper. That's why they had the name of being so rough. Of course, Salt Lake had its problems. There used to be a hotel up there by the name of the Black Stone. It was supposed to have had a flock of hussies and a lot of drinking. It was just on a higher scale.

But there were plenty of people—plenty—that did their fair share. When I had the Seventies Books store in my building, six different LDS ladies volunteered every day. I knew them all, and when they started to get on about their families, why, I had to come to a sudden stop and go around the corner, because I knew what their grandparents and great-grandparents were. And in most cases they were all the town drunks, alcoholics, deadbeats, you name it. That's what was there in those early days. Even today, with seventy-three percent Mormon and twenty-seven percent of us Gentiles, the liquor stores run well over eighty million dollars a year in business. And I know damned well we don't have that many tourists!

But hell, today if I say I drink a fifth of booze a year, I'd be stretching it. And I don't smoke. My other brother does—and coughs and coughs and about chokes to death. But he's seventy-seven years old, and I figure if he hasn't got better sense by now, I can't tell him different!

My mother and father were never, ever drunk. They had a little glass of wine with their meals. That was it—like in the old country. Like most people from the old country, we didn't speak English at home. And most of the time, the men were downtown on business, and you didn't even know who their wives were, because they were at home. My mother hardly ever left the house. Once in a while, she'd visit a few of her friends, and once in a while, they'd visit with her. But when I was a kid, I used to do all the grocery shopping. Anything we ate, I had to go buy. I even bought her clothes. I would go down to Penney's, which was about the only good thing here at the time, and my father's friend, who was the manager, would have the saleswomen get five or six dresses for me to take home to my mother. The part that used to really gripe me was when my mother wore those old black bloomers and the salespeople would throw some of those in, and I'd go home loaded like a damned horse. She'd pick out what she wanted, my dad would pay the bill, and I'd return the rest. I must have been about thirteen or fourteen years old at the time. My dad wouldn't do it. And she wouldn't go downtown.

It wasn't until years later, after I was married, that she changed. My father had a stroke. He wasn't an invalid, he just couldn't do a lot of things. So my mother made a list of things she needed and gave them to my wife. Finally, my wife told her, "Grandma, you're as healthy and as strong as I am. And you know what you want. You're going to the store with me and buy what you want. You can do it just as well as not." So she went. After a while, with my wife speaking English and my kids speaking English, my mother started speaking pretty good English.

But life for many from the old country was like that for years. The women did for their husbands just like they were "Indians"—slaves. It was bred into them—to cater to their husbands, totally. And in some families, discipline was harsh. Too harsh. I think the men amongst some of the foreign people were most generally quite brutal disciplinarians. That resulted in a lot of the girls, when they were sixteen or seventeen, running away from home. Or marrying young. It was a custom, amongst the Greek people and the Italians from the south, to marry their daughters off to men twice their age just because they had jobs in the mines. Sometimes these girls would go off with some of these old guys because of the rotten life they were getting at home. Sometimes their lives got better, and sometimes it got worse.

I never dated an Italian girl. Why? Because there was just no way. There was a girl from Helper I quite liked. I ran into her at a dance hall called the Rainbow Gardens. She got to the dance, all right, but sitting on the sidelines was [her] grandma. You know, they'd bring the girl, then the girl could go out and dance, but there was the whole cockeyed tribe—grandma, mother, aunts, and what the hell—. . . down there watching her and you. There could be ten of them there; their eyes were just like radar. They knew damned well that the girl wasn't going outside or anything like that. I could have taken her out to a show—my mother was her mother's friend. But after two or three dates, they would have started wedding preparations. That was the custom. But I wasn't ready for that. I couldn't afford to keep myself going, for one thing. And I was not in any frame of mind to get married. So it just went right over my head, and that was the end of that. No, I would never take out an Italian girl. I met Marge when I was twenty-three or twenty-four. She was different. Independent, like her mother. A German. I married her in December 1941.

The following year, the day before Christmas, I got my "1A classification," had the radio on, and heard about the Hawaii deal. People were volunteering left and right, and they were taking two quotas out of Carbon County every month. I thought for sure I was going to have to close my doors. When you had a 1A classification, you can just as well kiss everybody good-bye. But on the first of April they declared a shoe rationing, and within a week I had a deferred classification. I was in an essential industry. Shoes were on ration stamps. And they got only so many stamps for leather shoes, so they wanted us to fix as many as possible.

Then—out of fear they weren't going to have any shoes to wear—people started bringing them in. Oh God, they brought everything they had in their closets and in their basements. Moldy, smelly stuff. It's a good thing I couldn't fix all of them, because I would have been stuck with three quarters of them [because people didn't pick them up]. I had an awful lot of shoes left when the war was over. And you know how I got rid of them? After the liberation of Greece, I guess since shipments couldn't be guaranteed to get to the people, families here decided to buy leftover shoes to send. I sold them for a dollar fifty or two dollars a pair. I got the cost of my material out of them. And they'd spend five or ten dollars and send a whole bunch of shoes—just in case their relatives didn't get them, they wouldn't be out a heck of a lot.

There was an Italian POW [prisoner of war] camp in Utah, up in Logan. The big thing was there was no television and you didn't [read about the camp] in the newspapers. . . . And your gasoline was rationed, and so no one came up to see any of them, unless they were related. So nobody knew much. And where we were, nobody worried about the thousand or so Italians and Greeks who were working [in Utah]. When the war was finally over, we had a big celebration at the Silver Moon. My dad was one of the leaders, and we decorated for at least two thousand people.

My dad was, I would say, as good as an American as anyone who was born here. There was always an American flag hanging out on the porch whenever there was the Fourth of July or any American holiday. He never thought about going back to Italy. There was a few old men who talked about the old country, but not one of them went back. Oh, maybe a few, but not very damned many, because they didn't have a damned thing to go back to.

JOHN CRUS, 75, PRESIDENT, CRUS DISTRIBUTING COMPANY

The quintessential self-made man, John Crus had a gambler's demeanor and the speaking style of an auctioneer. His sentences crackled with street slang and moved with the speed of automatic rifle fire.

One of nine children, Crus was born on February 2, 1910, in Rocca, Italy, and was raised on Salt Lake City's West Side. Because of his father's early death, he worked as a full-time gas station attendant while still in high school and helped his mother raise his siblings. An ambitious youth with a flair for entrepreneurial schemes, he progressed rapidly into self-employment. He leased his first gas station at the age of nineteen; several years later, he started his own gasoline distributorship.

In the decades following World War II, Crus financed and constructed his own gas stations (fourteen in all), expanded his distributorship, then made the fortuitous and savvy decision to become a wholesale supplier of "lubricants" (motor oils) as the industry was expanding. After a rocky start, Crus Distributing developed steadily. By the mid-1980s, in Crus's estimation, the company had surpassed all other Utah distributors in volume of sales and had become the state's major supplier of lubricants.

There were nine children in my father's family—seven boys and two girls. The boys were all, more or less, railroad carpenters. This is how come they wandered around Italy. When the railroad decided to run a line, they would move there. If the railroad was running a line from Salt Lake to Ogden, just as an example, they would come to Salt Lake. When that was completed, they would migrate to the next stop. They all came to America, all the boys. In those days, this was the land of gold and silver. So they all came, and they all, more or less, got into the carpentry end of the deal. Not house building—industrial stuff.

My mother and her brother came to America when she was fourteen and he was sixteen. Their folks had died when she was probably ten years old, and

John Crus. *George Janecek*

they lived with aunts [in Italy]. Four years later, they hopped a freighter and worked their way over as a dishwasher and a deckhand. That's how they came over.

They stopped in Valpraiso, Indiana, for, oh, I don't know how long—maybe a year and a half. They had relatives there, and she went to work, and he went to work as a carpenter. Strange . . . even my five brothers, with the exception of me, took up the building business. It must have been in their blood. Anyway, while my mother was in Valpraiso, she met my father. Then they moved to Glencoe, Wyoming, where they were married.

My father's brothers kind of went this way and that. Two of them died right after they got here. A couple stayed in Indiana, then two followed on to Wyoming. My parents stayed in Wyoming for a year. When the railroad went to Washington, they went to Washington, where my sister Anna was born and my brother Tony. They thought Anna died of a heart condition at the age of three months, but she could have died of anything. In those days, what did they know of how she died? But that's the story I got.

Then the railroad sent Dad back to Glencoe to work on the line, and this was where they stayed for a time. My parents opened a boardinghouse, and my sister Jennie was born. Now, Jennie was sick [from birth]. She wasn't an invalid, but she also had a real bad heart deal. So, when she was a year old, the folks decided they should go back to Italy, where the elevation was lower, to see if it would help. Unbeknownst to my mother, I was already conceived. So I was born in Italy, right in Pratiglioni, which was, like, across the street from Rocca [my father's birthplace].

We stayed in Italy until I was about four months old, and we came back to Wyoming—same place. They didn't sell the boardinghouse, just went down to see if it would help Jennie's health, which it didn't. At any rate, in 1912, when mining in Glencoe started petering out, they sold the boardinghouse, came to Salt Lake, and bought a little hotel called the Columbus.

It was located on 252 West South Temple, and we ran that damn place for several years. It had about twelve rooms upstairs that were occupied mostly by miners from Bingham. I can remember that. Downstairs we had a dining room. In my mind, as a kid, that room looked as large as a warehouse, but it wasn't that big. Yet we used to have about ten boarders. In the morning, my mother made them breakfast, and she would pack their lunches. They'd grab their buckets and be gone [to] wherever they went to work.

Now, the Columbus had a big dirt basement. And for some reason a story was going around that the Mormons had hidden gold in the basement. [Laughs] This is really funny, because my dad believed it. One day he was down there picking into the basement. Actually, he was making wine. All the Italians made wine. Anyway, he would bottle this wine, then he would dig a big hole in the basement to put the damn stuff in there, because during those years anybody caught making wine, God, they'd break the barrel and that was it. So he's digging, and he hits a coffee can. He opens it up, and there are about twelve gold watches in the damn thing. Of course, gold in those days wasn't worth a hell of a lot. But all of a sudden, all of us kids were picking down there. We never did find anything else. [*Laughs*] So maybe somebody just planted the damn thing there.

Anyway, my father ran the hotel, but my mother was the chief cook and bottle washer. And, gosh, she would make pies, bake bread, and, Lord almighty, she was so busy. She always had a kid on her back. Hell, she was either carrying one inside or carrying one outside. Everyone in our family was born about eighteen months apart.

But she was a fine-looking woman. Really, my mother was a fine-looking woman. Quite tall and a really good Christian. None of us kids ever went to church, yet she was probably the finest woman in the world as far as religion was concerned. Oh, my gosh, even during the Depression—God, I don't know how she did it. I mean, here this gal was with eight kids, and anybody on the street that she saw that was needing a meal or something—in those days there were so many that looked like they hadn't eaten for a week—God, she'd drag them in and give them a bite to eat. She was so good about everything that you can't believe it.

Of course, I was only six when my dad died, so I didn't know him as well. What happened was one of my father's brothers had been farming in Price. And he kept coming up about every six months and saying to Dad, "Gosh, you've got all these kids. Why don't you buy a farm and put the kids to work?" Finally, my mother and dad bought a farm down on Sixty-fourth South and Ninth East in Murray. Boy, I don't think my father had ever used a shovel in his life. He knew no more about farming than flying kites. But his brother was a good farmer, and he was going to come down, live with us, and teach my father and all of us kids how to do it.

Anyway, my father went down to old man Fisher to buy a team of horses—this was the Fisher of Fisher Feed and Grains. I remember him down on Second West just as if he were right in front of us. Then [Dad] went over to Conwagon Machine Company and bought a brand-new wagon with the big, high seat. The damn thing was to haul stuff in. Okay, so they hooked the horse and wagon, and they started off for the farm. They went down State Street, and at Forty-fifth South the horses got excited and bolted right down State Street. My dad was flipped up out of the wagon. It lit on his back and broke his neck. He died instantly. That's what happened.

Well, my mother said we're still going to the farm. So we went to the damn farm. We lasted three months and she said, "This is no place for us. Let's go back to the hotel." See, my uncle was a good farmer. But, God, he didn't believe in modern implements. It was all the old stuff from Italy. Damn hoes and this kind of crap. I shouldn't say that. [*Laughs*] But it didn't work. It didn't work a bit. So we came back, and [we] sold the hotel. We kept the farm—leased it out to some people from Glencoe—and we all started working. The minute any kid was big enough, he was out delivering prescriptions or *Liberty* magazines—just anything to make some kind of money. It was a real struggle.

But my mother—you can't believe it. I never saw her angry. Never—really!

She was my mother, but, God, she was considerate with everybody. Jesus Christ, I remember old Mrs. Tarro. She was one of those old gals who didn't have anything. Her husband was kind of a screwball. I think he was drunk half the time. And Mother would go down to the farm, get bushels of stuff, and just give it to her. As a matter of fact, [Mother] even helped the people who leased the farm. They come down from Glencoe with nothing, only their belongings, and she helped them for a couple of months.

Oh, man, she was something. I'd get such a kick out of her. She never learned English. She only spoke Italian to us till she died. And we used to have an old aunt who would come from California each year and spend a month with us. She was a really religious old gal. Anyway, you know what kids will do. One day, I said to her, "Jesus Christ." And she come over, she grabbed me by my ear and said, "You little bastard, don't you ever take the Lord's name in vain again!" [Laughs] The next day, my mother [who didn't know the meaning of the phrase] started telling a couple of us, "You little bastards, come here." So my aunt says to her, "Do you know what you're calling them?" Man, when she found out, it was the last time she ever called us that. [Laughs]

[Mother] was a great lady. She would buy a whole pig at a time, and my two older brothers—they were better [at it] than I was—would cut it up, and she'd make ham. She'd take all the skin off and make salt pork and bacon. She did all that stuff. She would buy potatoes and onions by the one-hundred-pound sacks. And we had a lot of Italian food, all different kinds of pastas and meat. She would make salami and sausage with a little hand grinder. Then, we always had a few chickens in the backyard. She would cut their heads off, skin the damn things, and cook them. She did all this. Plus, she washed by hand and knitted. Gosh, even when she sat down at night, she had a damn spool and was knitting, darning socks, sweaters, always something. She kept that up, I'll tell you, until she died. She died young, too, darn it. She never smoked in her life, yet she died of lung cancer at sixty. Fortunately, she didn't take long to die. It wasn't one of those deals that take months and months.

As for me, I don't know what kind of [career] idea I had in mind. Growing up, I just wanted to be a salesman. In those days, they weren't full of malarkey—you know, full of baloney. You sold a product, and that was it. Of course, today, we have a lot of people—even our own salesmen—boy, they stretch that truth to where it breaks, which is not right. So we have to pull them back a little bit. But back then we would look at a salesman and think, God, I wish one day I could be a salesman. They were kind of upper echelon as far as the job market was concerned.

In high school, I took a doggone course in accounting, I took shorthand, typewriting, math, all this sort of stuff. I wasn't big enough or heavy enough for sports of any kind. I always went out, but I never made a first team in my life. [Laughs] I was always too small, or too light, or too this, or too that. Besides, damn it, I didn't have the time to do it. Once we moved across the street from West High, I started working in a gas station about two blocks away. I'd get out of school at three thirty, come home, grab a quick sandwich, go out to the station, and work until eleven. On Saturdays, I'd work from eight A.M. until eleven P.M.; on Sundays, eight until noon. So I had half a day off, once a week. My other brothers did the same. All of them worked hard.

I remember thinking, "When I leave this doggone place, I'll lease a gas station instead of just being a helper." In 1929, as soon as I got out of high school, that's exactly what I did. God, I was just a punk kid. But the Shell Oil Company was interested in the fact that I had worked in a service station for a couple of years as a flunky. So I leased a place from them. I lied about my age—told them I was nineteen—and I lied about every damn thing else, too. [*Laughs*] Anyway, that's the way the damn thing started.

They leased me this station on Sixth South and Main. Then my two brothers leased service stations. And we bought our gasoline from Shell at wholesale and resold it. That was the deal. We also changed tires, washed and greased cars, changed oil. It wasn't a big thing. But during the Depression—say between '29 and '31—we was about the only ones making any money. Everybody was out of jobs. Even bank presidents would come in and buy two gallons of gas. Hell, I can remember one of the vice presidents of the Walker Bank jumped off the ninth story of the building. He just couldn't stand this mode of living.

Oh, the Depression was terrible. Really, it was horrible. Nobody had jobs. I had young girls driving into the station from Nevada or some damn place offering to go to bed with me for five gallons of gas so they could move on. Those were tough times. So the gas business was like a godsend. I mean, every day these poor guys would come and use our rest rooms. We had rest rooms off to the side of the building. These poor guys, toward night, would go in and want to sleep in the rest room. We had to kick some of them out of there. It was a rough go back in those days. Really!

But we all sold gasoline, all three of us brothers. None of us were married yet. Then Shell Oil went on the NRA [National Recovery Administration] deal. They took our stations from us—from lessees—[and] put us on salary. The salary was $60.00 a month, where before I had been making $150.00 a month, which was more than bank tellers were making. So I quit. I went over to the Producers and Refiners Corporation, which had about seven service stations, and I leased one of theirs. I leased the station right on the corner of North Temple and Second West—right where the Triad Building is—the exact corner.

I stayed with them about eight months. Then Sinclair Refining Company came into the picture and bought out Producers and Refiners. So I went down to see them. I said, "How about getting me a wholesale job as a salesman?" They said, "We don't need any salesman. But if you want to set up a little commission deal, you can buy yourself a gas truck and we'll sell you gasoline. Then you can go out and peddle to whoever will buy from you." So I did that, because I wanted something a little better. I mean, God, I'd been running stations for so long, I thought why not take a chance.

I went out and bought a used truck. It cost me a hundred dollars and ten bucks a month. And it went along like that. Then, God, the past manager of Shell moved to this company, and he insisted I lease a bunch of stations and release them. He was a highfalutin guy, you know what I mean? And, gosh, I was a screwball! So I leased these stations. And, my God, these guys would put up a little money to lease from me. I'd deliver gasoline to them. They'd sell it and then abscond with the money. Well, to make a long story short, after six months I went bust. I went completely bust. It took me four years to pay my damn bills off! God, that was a rough go! By then, I was married, so it was a good thing my wife was working, making her fifty-five dollars a month as a bank teller.

Anyway, I went back to Producers and Refiners to see if I could lease another station. I thought, well, damn it, I learned my lesson. Let's start all over. So I leased a station from them, and about a year later, I got the same commissioned deal. I became a commissioned agent [selling gasoline]. I bought another truck. As a matter of fact, I bought back the same truck. [*Laughs*] And that's how I got started. After a year of that, I gave up the service station and went into the commission agent deal. This is how it all come about. And I've just been there ever since.

Of course, for the two years I was in the army, my wife ran it. She ran it and still worked at Walker Bank. My brother Don somehow or other started drinking too damn much, and he almost depleted the business. But my wife kept [it] alive till I came back, then I just went right back to work. This time I also built service stations and leased them to Sinclair. I'd buy the ground and put up the building. Say, for example, the ground cost twenty thousand dollars and a building cost thirty thousand dollars; that's fifty thousand dollars. Now, Sinclair would give me a noncancelable ten- or fifteen-year lease. Okay, I could take that to the bank and borrow the money to buy the ground and lease the station. All I did was supply the gasoline and make a commission there. This is the way it ran. At the end of ten or fifteen years, it was my gas station. I built fourteen of them.

Now, the bad part came when the leases expired. Some of the buildings were old, and Sinclair wasn't interested in releasing them. So I would sell them as quick as the leases expired. Some, I would make a nice profit; some, I would be behind. It all depended on where the station was located. In fifteen years, one section of town would die down, another would develop.

Then, ah, about fifteen years ago, I got clear out of the gasoline business. Clear out of it. I stayed right here, this same place, but I severed all connection with gasoline. Why? Because gasoline was getting hard to get, really hard to get, and because I'd lost a couple of gasoline drivers. Their trucks tipped over . . . and, God, it got so bad that every time there'd be a siren blowing across the freeway here—you can hear it very easily from here—I'd think, oh, God, one of my goddamn trucks has exploded on the freeway. It just got to the point where it started to get to me.

Years before, one of our drivers lost control of the truck coming out of the canyon, and it just tipped over. The fellow tried to jump out. As he jumped, the truck just plopped right on top of him, killed him instantly. The other one happened just about the same way. There were two in a few years, and in those days, damn, we didn't have too much insurance on these poor guys. So it was a bad deal. That still stays with me.

So I got out—clear out. Then I had a lucky break. A guy has got to have a few lucky breaks to get by in this doggone world. When Sinclair moved out of here, I bought this place, [which stretches] clear up the street. They practically gave it to me. I think it was for $175,000 or $200,000 for the whole city block. Of course, since then, I've sold the front for a hell of a lot more than I paid for the back end that we still got. Anyway, we stayed here, and we switched into the oil end, which was just getting profitable.

Now, [at the] start, when we just worked the oil end, we had a hell of a time—you've got to believe me—because nobody was interested in us. Christ, we were small potatoes, and we didn't have any volume. But we started going after accounts—we hustled. Nobody comes to you, you know what I mean? So, God, we went to Kennecott; we'd go to little industrial accounts [and] put them in an oil pump dispenser to get their business. The turning point came when Texaco made us their oil distributor. When we got that, we were able to get into the commercial business pretty good. Then, from there, we got Quaker State, and from that point on, they came to us. See what I mean? We used to have to fight for them, and then they would come to us to see if we would take their line out.

Now, we sell—oh, Lord—we sell every kind of motor oil that is distributed in the United States. We're distributors for about the biggest part of them, and we [even] sell to the distributors. God, Dunn Oil Company is one of our best customers. Rainbo Oil is one of our best customers. Cargo Oil, Christianson Oil. Fortunately, we have the oil franchise, so they've got to buy from us. And a lot of the stuff we never touch—a lot of the stuff. See, we ship a carload of Quaker State to Dunn Oil, for example. We order right from Oil City in West Virginia, and the stuff gets dumped off at Dunn Oil.

We also pull certain oils out of Wilmington, California. Our castor oils we pull out of St. Louis. And we sell—you just can't believe it—carloads and carloads of oil to all the supermarkets. Safeway, Skaggs, Gibsons, Price Savers, Fred Meyers—they all buy the stuff by the carload from us. You'd be amazed at the amount of oil that is sold through supermarkets and stores today.

Gosh, you can't believe the amount of oil that goes through us. On top of that, we sell aviation oil; we sell all types of industrial oil. We sell to Utah Power, to Mountain Fuel, and to a lot of the mines down in Price. As far as just being in the oil end, the lubricants, we surpass them, all of them. Nobody can touch us. We supply a good portion of the state. So, hell, that's about the story of my life. As for heirs, my wife and I had no children, so my two nephews, my brother's boy[s], are taking over. And they're doing a nice job. The organization is going full blast. So I'm just going to slow down—completely. Well, not completely, but a lot. Hell, I'll be seventy-six years old in February. I come down daily. But what the hell do I think? I'm not going to live forever, for God's sake.

MARY RAVARINO, 70, HOUSEWIFE, TEACHER

An amateur historian, Mary Anselmi-Ravarino has amassed an impressive collection of documents describing the lives of her immigrant parents. Before the start of our interview, she showed us the receipt of the "first check" her father sent to his mother in Italy; her father's original hardbound journal, which he kept during his first decade in America; and numerous books she had acquired portraying the customs of the Tyrol region of northern Italy.

One of two children, Mary was born on September 8, 1924, in Reliance, Wyoming, where her father worked as a coal miner. In 1930, following a mining accident in which her father lost his closest friend, the family left Wyoming to purchase farmland. After traveling through Idaho and California, they bought a farm in Ogden, Utah, "near many Tyrolean paisani,*" and settled down.*

Ms. Ravarino grew up in "Utah's Tyrolean-Italian community." Upon graduating from Weber High School, she attended the University of Utah, where she received a bachelor of arts degree and acquired an elementary education certificate. For a few years, before marrying Frank Ravarino, she taught in the Salt Lake City School District. After marrying Frank, however, and while raising their three children, she functioned primarily as a substitute teacher. Once their children were grown, she became a full-time teacher of "gifted and talented students" in the Salt Lake City School District. Mary also served as president of the Salt Lake Council of Catholic Women for twelve years and participated in many other civic and community activities.

My parents left Trentino, the beautiful Alps of Italy, for the desolate, tree-less, sandy hills of Wyoming. I asked my mother once, "How could you stand being in that kind of environment?" "When you're hungry," she said, "you move to where you find food."

My father was from the little village of Brezarsio. His family lived in a large castle that had been converted into many small apartments. Their home over-looked the Valle d'Non, which is a picturesque little spot, really. But they had only a small piece of farmland to glean a living from, and they had many mouths to feed: six boys and two girls. So they were very poor, and it was a hard life for them. My mother was born in a neighboring village called Castilfondo, which means "castle." Her family had a little farm in the bottom area of the castle grounds, but they were very poor, too. She told me [that] once her brother was so hungry, he wanted to eat the last of the potatoes, but his mother said he couldn't. "If we eat all the potatoes, we won't have any to plant for the next year," she said. He went into the garden and ate three radishes for his lunch—radishes. It was a hard life. So hard, I don't think my father ever wanted to return after he and my mother made America their home.

My father worked in America for ten years before returning to Italy to visit his mother and meet my mother. Before this time, he didn't know her. But he had been living in a boardinghouse owned by one of her aunts in Rock Springs, Wyoming. When this woman found out he was going back, she gave him a locket to give to her niece. After he met her, he stayed for a year, court-ing her. They were married in January 1922 and left for America in February. They sailed on the [SS] *Belvedere* and arrived at Ellis Island in the beginning of April. It was a long voyage but a nice one, because they traveled second class. When my father first came over, he had little money and had to go third class, which is more like steerage. It takes courage for people to leave their land of birth and go into the unknown and start a new life—it takes people with strength of character. That's how I think about my parents.

Because my father spoke English, he was able to help other Trentini or Tyrolean immigrants get through Customs quickly. He told us that's where a lot of people changed their last names. Either the officers in charge couldn't understand the pronunciation and therefore shortened the names of people, or the immigrants themselves were so worried about discrimination they pur-posely changed their names. Bianco might then have become, simply, White; or Cardones [might have been] anglicized to Cardon. My father never changed his name, though. He was proud of it.

After getting through Customs in New York, they traveled by train to Reliance, Wyoming—where I was born—and moved into a four-room house with two bedrooms, a kitchen, and a small living room. The community was very diverse, with a lot of nationalities. I remember there was a number of our own nationality of people. Two uncles boarded with my parents. When more family members came to work in the mines, they took meals with our family, and my mother did all their laundry. She was very, very busy. She was also lonely. She said when my dad took her to Rock Springs to visit her aunt, she was overjoyed. It was like seeing the Lord just to get to see this aunt. When my brother was born, she got even busier, which I think helped. Whomever my folks met, though, strong friendships were developed. On days that the men didn't work, they would visit, drink wine, and talk about the old country.

I remember an experience about being inoculated. I can see this old kitchen table and the doctor pulling tape to hang down from the table before using it on us. He gave us the vaccination and covered it with a celluloid cup, then used this tape to cover over the inoculation. It's so vivid. I must have felt something, you know, because though I was very young then, I still have it—the trauma of that experience—with me.

Reliance was a desolate place. Since there were no trees, I remember we would make picnic lunches and eat inside sand caves—in little holes in sand hills. I will say this: As soon as people moved in, they made the soil work for them and planted vegetable gardens, flowers, and trees so they could have food for the body as well as for the soul. They transformed the area. My parents lived there for eight or nine years. I was six when my dad decided he had had enough.

At first my father worked in the mines, going in with coal cars and dyna-miting to get to the coal. Then he took on different responsibilities and became a weigh master, weighing cars, which carried its own dangers. There had always been a lot of mine accidents and numerous cave-ins, but when he witnessed an accident in which his best friend was killed and he was injured, he decided he could no longer do any kind of mining work. Apparently, my father was weighing coal cars, and nearby, a train car full of coal got out of control and was running down the track. His friend tried to stop the runaway car by planting a spike bar into the tracks. My dad ran over to help, but it was too late. The car was going faster than his friend thought. It pushed that spike bar into him and just ripped through him. It was a terrible experience, and my father wanted nothing to do with the mines after that.

Since he had been a farmer, he looked for a little farm to buy in California, Idaho, or Utah. When he heard of a group of Tyroleans living in Weber County, Utah, he bought a piece of farmland there, and we—along with my uncle—moved to Ogden, where ninety-five percent of our neighbors were Tyroleans. We had a stone house with three bedrooms, a living room, a huge dining room, kitchen, and bathroom. Yes, we had our own bathroom. And two coal stoves, one in the living room, the other in the kitchen. Later, they would put in a furnace, and when television came along, my parents were one of the first in the neighborhood to get one—and a telephone. Just like in Reliance, my parents were warm and open with their friends. My mother always had coffee on the stove, and if anyone entered, they would immediately sit down and be given a glass of wine or coffee. We had a nice yard with trees, flowers, and a garden, too. When the men, especially, congregated, they would sing some of their old songs, peasant songs.

By now we were living through the Depression, but we never suffered because there was always food on the farm. My parents had thirty-five acres and raised cattle, goats, and chickens. They also grew potatoes, sugar beets, alfalfa for their cattle, wheat, tomatoes, and corn. They milked their own cows and sold it to a dairy seven miles west of Ogden. I still have the milk cans in my garage. I remember they built a concrete fountain, where water ran constantly. They'd put these cans full of milk into the fountain to keep them cool until the milkman came to take them away.

My father was a very intelligent person. He had a fifth-grade education, wrote and spoke well, and learned English quickly. He always read books and instilled in us that learning and books were important. Soon, he became a community leader. Many Italian Tyroleans in the community would come and seek his advice. He belonged to the Farm Bureau, and during the war, he sold war bonds and worked with the Red Cross.

My mother was a very wonderful, kind, and gentle person. She was good to us and made our home a cocoon of love and security. She was also good to everybody else in need. She was widowed in 1951, and she carried on with the farm. She was a good farmer. She put concrete in all the irrigation ditches, just like all the other farmers were doing, and she took care of leveling her land. In fact, one neighbor asked her, "Maria, how do you know how to do all these things?" She said, "If you look, the land tells you what to do." She loved animals, and they loved her. I remember the minute my mother would walk down to the barn, the cattle would come and nuzzle her. She'd bring warm milk to the little calves, and they'd just adore her.

We made almost everything at home. My mother taught me how to sew and cook. I remember, and still use, some of her herbal remedies—chamomile tea for stomach aches; *Malva* plant poultice for [simple] infections. All this came from our garden. Two or three times a week, we ate polenta with our meals. Polenta is made from cornmeal. Similar to a cornmeal mush, it is very thick. The only way to make it is in a copper pot. And every [northern] Italian woman had her copper pot and big wooden stirring stick. It's very simple to make: Four cups of boiling water, and one teaspoon of salt to one cup of corn-meal. After stirring it for a good half hour, you add a dab of butter and put it out on a plate to eat with chicken and gravy or beef and gravy. Because my family raised their own vegetables, they would make sauerkraut for the win-ter. They would slaughter their pigs and make sausages, too. Sausage and sauerkraut are complements to the polenta.

They also made their own cheese. I can see my mother and uncle putting a great-big copper tub on the coal stove and then having to stir [the milk] with rennet in [it] to curdle the milk into cheese. My father made little frames with screens to put the cheese rounds in to cure it. They would be big and round, like you see today. It took two weeks to make cheese. Daily, my mother would go with a little pan of salt and a little bit of vinegar and rub the top of the cheese, turning it each day to make sure it would cure. The only thing my parents had to buy was the flour and sugar. Nothing was wasted in our home. My mother would render pig fat and make our own soap. And always, they made their own wine.

My parents were industrious people, frugal and honest. When my father and some of the neighbors were trying to figure out ways to save farming costs, they decided to join together and buy the machinery needed for the farm and take turns helping each other out. I remember my father took care of the books. Using one piece of equipment for four or five farms made quite a sav-ings.

When it was time to harvest the wheat, everyone would pitch in to use the [communal] thrashing machine. While the men worked in the fields, the women were in the kitchen preparing fried chicken, corn on the cob, fresh green beans and beets—all from the farm—and pies and cakes. When the work was done, or the men stopped for lunch, we all had a big feast. We kids thought it was a party.

When it was time to dig potatoes, the group worked as a unit again. Adults would dig the potatoes and sack them. Younger children would pick the pota-toes in buckets and put them in the burlap bags. I can see my father . . . hold-ing his big needle, sewing up the top of the hundred-pound bags. When we'd get to the end of the rows, we always had punch and cookies. I guess that's why we always thought it was a party.

Someone from Salt Lake usually came to buy the potatoes. But I remember one year during the Great Depression, they offered my father fifty cents for a hundred-pound bag. He was indignant. "All this work," he told me, "and I'm not even getting paid for the seed that I paid to get started with?" He told them, "I'll let them rot in the field before I'll sell them to you for fifty cents a hundred-pound bag!" They had their pride.

My parents worked hard from early morning to late at night. Depending upon the watering rights, they took turns irrigating the fields with the water that came from the canals. Sometimes, in the middle of the night, I can remember my dad putting on big boots and going out into the fields, in the dark, to change the water from one field to another. Generally speaking, they were up by five thirty or six o'clock in the morning. But always late at night, he'd end up sitting with a glass of wine and the newspaper. My mother would read her newspaper and he would read his—the *Ogden Standard Examiner* and *Trentino nel Mondo*, the Trentino people of the world.

They wanted to keep up with the news of their people. They also kept the traditions of their past. At home, we spoke the dialect of the Nonnes, the dialect of their valley. In 1937, six years after we came to Ogden, my father and his friends formed a group called the Friendly Club to continue our traditions. [Meeting] at their homes at first, they would socialize inside and then play boccie games on the lawns. Later, they bought an old canning factory and converted it into a club for dancing and receptions. I had my wedding reception there. I got married at St. Joseph's Church in Ogden, had a lovely brunch for a hundred guests at the Hotel Ben Lomond, then a big party with dancing, singing, and drinking wine at the reception hall.

I am very proud of my family. They maintained their heritage and taught respect for others. Honesty, integrity, and treating people right were paramount. I can still hear in my mind my mother's little proverbs. She'd say, "*Disliata, Mary, fai Pagota.*" That meant, Get going. Do something. Be busy and work. The work ethic was really instilled in all of us from a very early age. And when I got old enough to date, she'd say in Italian, "*Treni piedi en le scarpe.*" Always keep your feet in your shoes. [*Laughs*]

Our family life was very good. Our parents were concerned with our happiness and taught us with firm kindness. We didn't have great distress in the family. Outside, at school, we felt some prejudice, but we had such a strong unity of family and friends we were able to cope very well. I was going to West Weber Elementary School, and I don't know if the LDS people felt a little threatened by the influx of Tyroleans—Catholics—coming into Ogden, Taylor, West Weber, and Plain City, but there was discrimination and prejudice against us. Some kids called us names like "Wop" and "Dago." There was one incident that was very harrowing. It didn't happen to anyone in my family, but an eighth-grade [Italian] boy used some foul language, someone said, and a group of LDS boys took him and put him in a little cave and set it on fire. Luckily, the boy got out and didn't get burned. But I remember this vividly. What a terrible thing to do to someone.

I have to say [that] later these boys did a complete turnaround, so maybe they learned something. But one reason I wanted to become a teacher was to go back to that community. I thought, I am going to teach them to act as Christians and treat people as you like to be treated.

For the most part, though, we had good neighbors, and my parents were quite happy. Their lives were good. They had food and clothes. Their bills were paid. And their kids were becoming educated, which was very important to them. I had an aunt and uncle from California who wanted to move back to Italy, and they did. My mother said, "Oh, you're making a big mistake." She felt there was no place like America.

And they were deeply religious people. We weren't able to get out to church every Sunday because we lived seven miles out of the way. But, the church, St. Joseph's, sent priests out to our community. In the early days, we held mass in our neighbor's home, in an upstairs room, and we had religious instructions, the catechism. Then we had it in the Friendly Club hall. When a priest wasn't here, four or five older Italian women would teach us.

Although my father served as an altar boy when he was young, my mother was the one who felt we needed to attend church. Even when we went to church, my father didn't go as regularly as my mother. This is interesting to me. I've been back to Italy a number of times—probably twelve times. And I noticed in the little village where my mother received her first Holy Communion and confirmation, and was married, the men usually stood outside while the women were inside. In America, the men came in with us. But I guess they believe religion is more important than the rituals.

My father was fifty-nine years old when he died of cancer of the lung. His lungs had been full of coal dust, thanks to the mines of Wyoming. The irony of it is that after he died, a bill was passed to reimburse these people who had black lung. My mother never received anything, though. He died too soon. After his death, my mother assumed everything on the farm that he had done. She carried on, bought cows, went to the auction—did everything. And she always paid her bills on time. Both of my parents were very conscientious. If a bill came one week, it was paid the next. They never wanted any bills hanging around. They never wanted to be in a position to have someone else take care of them. I remember taking my mother to the cemetery so she could put flowers on his grave and then going with her to pay her bills. She never got behind.

My uncle continued living with us, but Mother became the head of the house and directed everything. My uncle liked to sit back, smoke his pipe, and relax. I used to call him my little alms uncle, like Heidi. He would sit and talk, whereas my mother . . . My uncle would say, "Your mother never walks, she runs!" As long as she was alive, she was always doing something—for the family, for the farm, for others. I see her at my sink peeling potatoes and helping to the very last day.

Even when she had cancer and was sitting in my family room, she'd say, "Mary, bring me some stockings to mend." She had to do something. I remember when she was dying in the hospital—even then—she gave to others. I was walking with her one day in the hallway, and she met a gentlemen who, we found out, was all alone and had very little. She said to me, "Mary, go see if he doesn't need something." She was seventy-two years old when she died. And up until that day, she was always thinking of someone else.

Now, just before the end, I knew she was suffering hard, and it bothered me that she suffered. Her doctor said she could live for three or four more months of absolute hell. I said to him, "Give her anything she needs so that she doesn't suffer." But I also prayed that my mother would die, even though I didn't want her to die. I said, "Lord, don't let her suffer. If you need to, please take her." And those prayers were answered. She went into the hospital for the last time very, very sick and had a stroke and died. So I think there is a Lord up above that doesn't let certain things happen. I certainly didn't want her to die, because she and I were . . . no one could have been closer than we were [*Cries softly*], but I couldn't stand to have her suffer. And you know what? Within six months, my little uncle died, too.

EPILOGUE

TOM D. BARBERI, 51, TALK SHOW HOST, KALL RADIO

One of two children, Thomas D. Barberi was born in Gilroy, California, on March 21, 1943, and was raised in a "traditional Italian household." Intent on becoming a professional football player, he attended San Jose City College on a football scholarship but had to give up his dream when an injury ended his career. He went into radio broadcasting purely by accident, he said.

Barberi apprenticed with several radio stations in San Jose, before moving to Salt Lake City in 1971 and becoming KALL Radio's notorious "morning man." At the time of this interview, he had been on the state's airwaves for more than two decades. He described his program as "the longest running radio personality program in this market." He is (it must be said) a genuine rarity in Utah—an inventive muckraker, a trenchant and unorthodox liberal commentator. The state's cultural life would not be the same without his daily dosage of pique and sarcasm, ridicule and affection.

Since 1986, Barberi has also written a weekly column of social commentary for the Salt Lake Tribune. Aspen West published a collection of these writings in 1991 in a volume entitled Barberi Attempts to Legalize Adulthood in Utah.

My name is Thomas D. Barberi. I hate to tell you what the "D" stands for— Dale. [*Laughs*] How I got the name is a long story. I was almost a "Junior," and my mother said, "No! We're not going to name anybody Salvino Salvatore Barberi the second. One of those is enough." That's my father's name.

I was born on March 21, 1943, in the Wheeler Hospital in Gilroy, California, the garlic capital of the world, which is the area my [paternal] grandparents migrated to when they came over from Italy through Ellis Island and across the country. I'm one hundred percent pure Italian. I'm half

Genovese and half Calabrese. My ancestors come from Genoa and Calabria. My father's father's name was Giuseppe Barbiero. When he came over, Italians were looked down upon as a minority, as were a lot of ethnic groups, so he thought he would anglicize his name a little bit and drop the "o." So it became Barberi, and we've all been Barberi since.

My mother's father's name was Casimiro Madrigali. It's a beautiful name. He was a musician and operated a saloon back in the 1890s and 1900s. His wife's name was Asunta D'Ricco. My mother was born above a saloon in South San Francisco. Anyway, those are the two families that came over from Italy. My parents met and married in California, where they were all farmers and vintners—wine makers. When the Prohibition came along, they stopped making wine and continued farming. So I come from a farm family; the whole family was farming in Gilroy.

Back when I was in the third, fourth, fifth grade, Gilroy had a population of about seven thousand people. It was strictly a farming community, and you were either Italian or Portuguese. Of course, at the time, we [also] had migrant workers. In fact, my father was an agent of the government for a while and would go to Calexico [California] and Mexico and recruit migrant workers to come up and work for the season. We would contract with a family, too— provide housing for them, and they would work our ranch during that harvest season. That's pretty much how that worked back then.

Then the government got involved and screwed agriculture royally. My dad finally decided to get out of farming when they wanted to put a meter on our well and tax us for our own water. He said, "I think it's time for this old farmer to look at better things." He could see the demise of the small farmer coming. Soon bigger groups started buying out small ranchers and creating big collectives. That's how farming is today. I still have a cousin who is a big grower in Gilroy. But that's the only way you can survive now. A forty-, fifty-acre ranch, eking out a living, is pretty tough. My uncles are wealthy [only] because they sold their ranches to [land] developers. That's how the old farmers made their money. They sold out to car dealerships and shopping centers. It's kind of sad.

But I grew up a farm kid in the "all-outdoors." We grew prunes, apricots, peaches, pears, and some cucumbers and tomatoes. But prunes were our primary crop and provided us with a very good living. It was hard, [though,] because you had to depend on the weather. I'll never forget one year [when] it rained after the prunes dropped. Prunes are picked off the ground, you know, not picked off the trees. And it rained after they fell. And if they stayed on the wet ground for too long, they would rot. So, being the incredibly hard-working guy he was, my dad bought a couple dozen bamboo rakes, and we raked forty acres of prunes—kept them turned—so they wouldn't rot. Then the pickers came along after us, picked them. So we saved sixty percent of the crop because of hard work—the work ethic. That's why I think growing up on a farm was terrific.

I feel sorry for today's inner-city kids. When I was a kid, my fantasy was to live on a street that had a sidewalk, 'cause you could roller-skate and ride a bicycle. I didn't know how good we had it because everything was ranches and dirt. I learned to drive a truck when I was eight years old. I mean, that was one of my toys. I also learned to drive a tractor. But I always thought city kids had it so good. When we moved into the city, I found out they didn't know what they're missing. You learn the work ethic from your parents, and kids don't have it today. I think a lot of our social ills today come from kids who have not learned the work ethic, so they don't have a rudder. No direction. And that's too bad.

I grew up in an old-fashioned Italian family. The word "respect" was one of our most important words. You respected your parents, aunts, uncles, and you revered your grandparents. They were the patriarchs of the family. Holidays were always great, because all the aunts cooked us food, tons of food. And all the aunts treated the kids the same. So Mom wasn't the only one who disciplined. If you did something wrong and this aunt caught you, you would get a whack like anybody else. There's an old saying that it takes a whole village to raise a child. I think it's a wonderful saying, because everybody was always involved in everybody else's household. It wasn't like visiting relatives only on holidays. We were together *all* the time. That's just the way it was.

And there was no questioning authority. What Dad said went, because it was necessary. I mean, being farm people, you had to live by your wits and hard work, and [it was understood that] he did things for the good of the family. So if you did something wrong, the discipline was sure and swift. It was usually a good whack. My mother was great at it. When she caught you, you wouldn't see it coming. She'd hit you on the back of the head. Boy, it would sting! [But] it was not [the physical pain] that hurt. It was the fact that you did something that made her angry. We felt like: "Oh, Mom doesn't like me." That was the biggest fear.

So they'd beat you to death, then they would love you [back to life]. That was the Italian way. Very demonstrative people. As I grew older and started dating, the first experience at a family dinner was really something, because my girlfriend thought everybody was fighting. I would have to explain, "No, Italians don't talk, they argue. That's the way they communicate. If you want to get into the conversation, you just have to yell louder than the other person." Because, you know, hands were flying, and everybody [was involved]. But it's wonderful. It's a great way to communicate. Emotion is always there.

I never understood quiet people, because I never trusted them. Italians were going to let you know what's on their mind. The beauty of it was that they were mad at you one second, then it was all over. There was none of this festering guilt and anger. If you did something wrong, you got a whack, or they yelled at you, then you were on to other things. None of this, "Wait till your father gets home." The punishment was instantaneous and well deserved. [*Laughs*] It was a great way to live.

Now if you look at your child cross-eyed, someone's going to yell "child abuse." It's too bad, because we've lost our culture, and we've lost respect for elders. When I would go out with my parents and they were doing business, I would be quiet and listen. That was how you were brought up. The rights you had as a child were given to you by your parents. You asked for permission for things. It's not like you were entitled to anything. Today we've lost that respect for other people's rights and feelings and property. That's not how we were brought up. You didn't take things that didn't belong to you. I mean, you didn't have to think about it. If it didn't belong to you, you didn't touch it. If you used something, you put it back. So the question of being raised in a moral atmosphere was a given. It wasn't "We're going to sit after dinner and talk about morals." You didn't do that, because you lived by example.

My father has more integrity than any man I've ever known. He couldn't lie. If you put a gun to his head, he couldn't lie. It's just not in his character. And if he said he was going to do something, he did it. A handshake was good enough. That's how most of them did business. You made a deal that you would sell prunes for four cents a pound, shook hands, and it was a done deal. I grew up in that atmosphere, watching my father deal with the seed companies, the food processors, and the other ranchers. So I thought that's how adults acted. They were honest. When they said something, you could believe it. Unfortunately, in today's day and age, you have to teach kids to be cynical, and that's too bad. I don't know how you get back to that [earlier way].

My parents' dream for me and my brother was not ranch work. As great a life as I think it was, they thought there was something better in America for their kids than working fourteen hours a day on a ranch. They hoped we'd go to college. Get better jobs, get an education. It was important to them. My brother didn't go on. He went into the service. I was the first one to go to college. And I got into radio by accident, purely by accident.

See, my dad was a pretty entertaining guy. He had a great sense of humor. So I got that from him. And I was always kind of the class clown. To me, teachers had all the straight lines and I had all the punch lines. So I was always a pain in the neck to my teachers. I was a funny kid, and I was always shooting my mouth off and getting in trouble with my mouth.

At twenty-one, though, I was lost—directionless. I went to college to play sports. I had no real career ambition, but I did want to play football, which I did. And I'm grateful to athletics, because it gave me a college experience. But I really didn't have any other goals other than to play sports. So I took classes just to stay eligible. That's what I was doing in college. Then I got injured, my football career came to an end, and I dropped out of school and started doing a whole bunch of jobs. I drove a truck, loaded boxcars, worked in a warehouse, sold cars, pumped gas. I did everything. But I looked at all these jobs as things I found out I *didn't* want to do for a living. [*Chuckles*] That was my research. After every job, I'd say, "No, I don't want to do this for a living!"

I had some high school friends whose dads owned radio stations. And one of my buddies said, "You really should think about going into radio, because you do funny stuff." I never thought about it for a living—but he introduced me to it and got me a weekend job. And it was the first time I ever got paid for sitting in an air-conditioned room. I always equated earning money with hard physical labor—working for the gas company, digging ditches, all that stuff. I said, "Hey, I can dig this. I get paid for sitting in an air-conditioned room, and the heaviest thing I've got to pick up is a record? Career? This I like." That was thirty some odd years ago. I feel like I've been retired ever since. Actually, I feel very fortunate that I've found something I can do and that I dearly love.

Relocating to Salt Lake was another accident. I was working at a radio station in San Jose, California, and I had some contact with radio stations in San Francisco. My goal was to work there. But I got a call from the people at KALL here. They invited me to come up, see the station, and talk about a possible job. I was doing rock and roll format at the time, and I wanted to get into an adult contemporary format. That's what I wanted to do. Anyway, they offered me a job, and I thought I would come here, hone my skills in this format, and go back to San Francisco. Well, that was twenty[-three] years ago. I've had so much fun here that before I knew it two decades have flown by. Oh, I miss some of the things in California—obviously, family. But I've grown to really love Utah. Working in a capital city with such an interesting culture and strange politics is like hunting in a game preserve for a person who does what I do. I mean, every morning I open the paper and there's goofy stuff going on, and it just makes for great radio.

So I've enjoyed it here, I've had a lot of fun, and I've gotten along. People ask me, "Don't you feel repressed? Utah is a repressed society." But there isn't anything I'm hindered from doing on the radio here that I would be doing if my show were in another market. There is nothing I feel repressed about, because my own built-in set of values guides me. I still do my shows thinking, "Would Mom be offended if I did this joke or that joke?" That's still in the back of my mind. It's not conscious, but that carries over.

So I feel total freedom in what I'm doing, because [I trust] my own sense of values as to what is appropriate for public consumption that has my name on it. My dad always told me, and he didn't originate the statement, "I have nothing else to give you, my son, but my name." But that is the greatest legacy you can get from your parents—your name. When he had it—and he does have it—it served him in good stead. It meant a lot. He wanted me to carry it on. The name you have means a lot. I respect that, and I try to make it respectable. So when I do a show, I do it the best way I possibly can, because its not called the Apollo Broadcast show. It's not the KALL radio show. It's the Barberi Show. So I want it to be the best it possibly can be, because name, handshake, respect, mean everything. If a man is not respected, what is he?

So for me, it all stems from where we came from. I came from Anita and

Sal, and, I got to tell you, to this day they don't change. I'm still "Tommy"; I'm still their kid. I will be till the day I die. We [recently] went with some friends to Pebble Beach for the weekend to play golf. After we finished, we were going by my folks' house to have dinner. I told my mother we'd be there around one P.M. Well, one thing led to another, we got a late start, and we showed up about three P.M. My mother was livid. She started hitting me. "Where have you been? Where have you been?" These friends of ours were stunned: What is this crazy woman doing? I was laughing and saying, "Mom, Mom, I'm sorry, I'm sorry we're late." "Well, the food is cold and you said you'd be here." She was just reading me up one side and down the other.

She even called my daughter here in Salt Lake. She didn't know what to do, so she called Gina. "Where's your father?" Gina said, "Well, Ma, he's in California." "Well, he's supposed to be here at one o'clock for dinner, and I want to know where he is?" Gina says, "If he's here, he's not going to make it to your house at one o'clock." But she didn't know what else to do. So I said, "Ma, we're just a little late." "Ah," she said, "the food is getting cold, the table is set." I said, "Okay, Ma, calm down, we'll eat." Then she got it out of her system, and we had a great visit.

But my friends, who had never witnessed this before, said, "My God, you're mother is really mad." I said, "No, that's just Mom. I was late. I said I'd be here at one p.m., and, by God, I should have been here." So, like I say, their [basic] attitudes never change. I sat down and she said, "Why don't you lose some weight?" Then—"Here, are you hungry?" [First] she's telling me I'm fat, then she's feeding me, and every ten minutes [she's asking], "Do you want a sandwich?" [Laughs] It's like I wrote in my Mother's Day column: "One thing is certain, no matter where I go or how old I get, there is one person I can count on to be the anchor of my world. I know this because I can go back [home] anytime and know that I will find Mom in the kitchen and spaghetti sauce and salami in the fridge, and I will feel like a little boy again—special.⁴"

NOTES

1. During the six-month-long 1922 walkout of Carbon County coal miners, three instances of violent conflict occurred between strikers and company guards ferrying strikebreakers into the mines. The first event took place on April 27 after strikers in Winter Quarters were evicted from their homes and boardinghouses. Shots were exchanged, resulting in the injury of three men—a mine guard and two strikers. The second outbreak occurred on May 22. John Tenas, a young Greek miner, was shot and killed by Deputy Lorenzo H. Young. And, finally, on June 14, shots were fired between strikers and the train crew and passengers of a railroad carrying strikebreakers. Arthur Webb, a company guard, was killed in the encounter, and two other company men and a miner were wounded. The following day, Governor Charles R. Mabey dispatched the National Guard to Carbon County. The guard imposed mar-

tial law and confiscated the strikers' weapons. Allan Kent Powell, *The Next Time We Strike: Labor in Utah's Coal Fields, 1900–1933* (Logan: Utah State University Press, 1985), 121–134.

2. Sock-sized containers of dirt, preferably clay, tamping dummies were stuffed into drilling holes, alongside sticks of dynamite, to concentrate and contain explosions in the coal mines.

3. Actually, 171 people were killed in the Castle Gate mine explosion.

4. The column was first published in the *Salt Lake Tribue*, May 8, 1988.

BOOK SIX
JAPANESE COMMUNITY

PREFACE

Nancy J. Taniguchi

I n the 1850s, Japan, Utah, and the administration of U.S. president Millard Fillmore all spun threads into a Gordian knot that took more than a century to unravel. How would such diverse people as the Japanese and Utahns interact? How would they adjust to one another? Would they ever become one? Personal tales of these transitions are told in the following interviews.

To a large extent, the presence of the Japanese in the United States, and in Utah, was due to Commodore Matthew Perry, who in 1853 sailed his "black ship" into what is now Tokyo Bay. Perry carried with him a letter for the emperor of Japan signed by President Fillmore that demanded the right of open trade between the two nations. Under Perry's guns, the emperor accepted the offer. The first American-Japanese treaty, signed in 1854, initiated a continuing relationship between Japan and the United States. Interestingly, President Fillmore had, just a few years earlier, set in motion a process in what is now Utah that would foster a relationship between that area and Japan, as well. In 1851 he had granted the domain of the Church of Jesus Christ of Latter-day Saints official territorial status. That action would eventually lead to Utah's statehood and its full participation in a nation increasingly involved with Japan.

The American-Japanese treaty of 1854 ended approximately two hundred years of Japanese isolation, allowing freedom of movement between Japan and the United States. Most travel by Japanese was highly regulated, however, and was initially confined to diplomatic missions. Official ambassadors from Japan first visited the United States in 1860, on the eve of the Civil War. *Harper's Weekly* reported on their visit, noting the mutual benefits of trade between the two nations and then further editorializing as follows:

> Our people will go to Japan and will endeavor to show the Japanese the best side of the American character. On the other hand, the Japanese—if good rela-

tions be established between the two countries—will send out some of their people to plant Japanese colonies in our territory. Of this interchange the benefit will be obvious and mutual. Civilized as we boast of being, we can learn much of the Japanese—if nothing more, we can learn the duty of obeying the laws.[1]

This statement, probably aimed at the increasingly recalcitrant South, nonetheless underscored a cardinal Japanese virtue. The Japanese did, indeed, obey the law. Japanese colonies, though originally welcomed (at least in theory) in the United States, later elicited fear and envy. Yet even when people of Japanese descent in America were threatened with the loss of their land and were imprisoned solely because of their ancestry, they acquiesced rather than break the law.

The mutual benefits touted by *Harper's* had to await the outcome of two civil wars, one in the United States and one in Japan. It was not until after the U.S. Civil War that the American-Japanese treaty was signed permitting Japanese to emigrate to America. As far as Japan was concerned, when the Tokugawa Shogunate was overthrown by the Meiji faction in 1868, the Meiji imperial government sponsored a few young Japanese men to go to America as students. Eventually, it even permitted "five young Japanese women of rank" to go to America in the care of the wife of the Japanese minister to Tokyo.[2] These young students added to the handful of Japanese, mostly castaway fishermen and sailors, who had already reached America's shores.[3]

Furthermore, in 1868, before the installation of the new Meiji government, Japanese labor agents had smuggled between 50 and 150 Japanese out of the country to work on Hawaiian plantations and about 40 more Japanese to work at an experimental silk-growing colony in Gold Hill, California. The silk colony failed, however, leaving few traces of the Japanese presence other than the grave of the first Japanese woman to die in America.[4] After this inauspicious beginning, Japanese colonization in America seemed unlikely to succeed.

Yet, from this tentative venture onto the mainland, Japanese immigration gradually increased. The first Japanese to visit Utah arrived in 1872: an official party headed by Ambassador Extraordinary Iwakura. Utah's first Japanese settlers came a decade later.[5] They formed only a tiny part of the overall Japanese emigration to the United States, which was also rather modest. The U.S. census reported about 24,000 Japanese in the United States in 1900, with the number increasing to approximately 72,000 in 1910. In 1920, the census counted 111,000 Japanese in America; in 1930, the number was almost 139,000. Corresponding census figures for Utah showed 417 Japanese in 1900; 2,110 in 1910; 2,936 in 1920; and 3,269 in 1930.[6]

This influx of Japanese into Utah, however small, had the following important results. First, the Japanese immigrants formed a variety of associations, some with traditional roots and other prompted by immediate necessity. Second, the growing numbers of "different-looking" people elicited nativist fears among Utahns, and other Americans, of "Yellow Peril"—fears that were previously directed against the Chinese. Both of these outcomes had local and national manifestations.

On the positive side, during the early twentieth century, the organizations formed by Utah's Japanese strengthened their traditional cultural values and enhanced community ties. Primary among these organizations was the Buddhist church, which had its start in Utah with a simple ceremony. In 1912, a Buddhist priest arrived in Ogden to conduct a memorial service for deceased Japanese pioneers. From this event grew two churches: one in Ogden and shortly thereafter a branch in Salt Lake City.[7] Other branches were later established in outlying communities in northern Utah and southern Idaho, including Honeyville, Corinne, Syracuse, Rexburg, Blackfoot, Pocatello, and Idaho Falls. The Honeyville branch, which also served the farming communities of Garland and Tremonton, remained as an independent temple with its own minister until the mid-1980s when, due to a diminishing population, it lost its independent status. It now shares a minister with Ogden but continues to serve the same area.

Other organizations met a variety of additional needs. For example, in 1913, Japanese business and professional men formed the Japanese Association of Utah, which served the function of a chamber of commerce.[8] Carbon County's Kyo Ai Kai (which is still in existence) provided pensions for the disabled and a proper funeral in case of death, two necessary functions in a coal community. In Salt Lake City, the Hiroshima-Ku enabled Japanese originating from Hiroshima to reunite periodically to pass along information about people from home. Similar organizations served people in the Sego, Eureka, and Bingham mining districts and in the farming communities of Elberta and Payson, as well as other areas.

The maturing of these Japanese communities did not always bring approval, however. The probability that these "outsiders" would multiply led to a growing American backlash. In fact, their "outsider" status had been enshrined in American law. The Japanese could not become American citizens through naturalization, a prohibition dating back to the Naturalization Act of 1870 and its later judicial interpretations. Thus, through circular reasoning, the Japanese were "unassimilable" partly because they were prevented by law from assimilating.

As anti-Japanese prejudice increased nationally in the early twentieth century, pressure mounted on President Theodore Roosevelt to "do something" to limit Japanese access to American land. In 1907 he responded by negotiating a "Gentleman's Agreement" with the Japanese government, which took effect the following year. In it, Japan agreed not to issue passports for laborers, skilled or unskilled, for passage to the United States, excepting only Japanese who were former U.S. residents and the parents, wives, and children of U.S. residents. As a result, females began to predominate among the immigrant population, transforming the earlier ratio of approximately ten males to one female to near parity.[9] Many of the wives who arrived in the early twentieth century came as "picture brides," as the interviews in this chapter attest. From the Japanese perspective, there was no subterfuge involved. Arranged marriages were common among the Japanese; this marital custom had endured for centuries. An ocean between the contracting parties did little to diminish its practice. In American eyes, however, the Japanese were trying to circumvent the naturalization law.

In an attempt to stem the flow of Japanese into America, the U.S. Congress passed two specifically anti-Japanese acts. In 1922, the Cable Act was passed depriving any American-born woman of Japanese ancestry of her citizenship if she married a man born in Japan. This statute remained in force until 1931. Then, in 1924, the possibility that any Japanese man or woman could emigrate to the United States was abruptly cut off with the Japanese Exclusion Act, which denied entry to all Japanese under a newly established immigration quota system.

This national backlash against the Japanese had its counterpart in Utah, although some differences existed. During the relatively peaceful decades of the early 1900s, the first Japanese settled in Utah. They were mainly converts to the Mormon church, who began arriving shortly after the opening of the Mormon mission to Japan in 1901. They were quickly followed by others who immigrated for economic, rather than religious, reasons. For example, the establishment of the sugar beet industry in 1903 prompted the hiring of one thousand Japanese to work the beet fields.[10] Others came as contract labor to mine copper at Bingham, to work on the expanding Denver and Rio Grande Western Railroad, to staff sugar refineries, and to dig coal in Carbon County. Most were men who wished to store up a nest egg and return to Japan, but others came as families, more likely to remain. The families formed the backbone of a number of businesses and professional offices in Salt Lake City and other urban centers providing many needed services for members of the Japanese community as well as others.

Many of the immigrants went into farming. Among the Japanese, farmers were traditionally held in high esteem because they "fed the nation."[11] Even those men recruited to work in the beet fields began to diversify, growing other crops on their own land. For example, the Japanese planted almost four thousand acres of sugar beets in Utah in 1910 and almost four thousand five hundred acres in 1914. But for roughly the same years, the amount of land they planted that was not devoted to beets increased from two thousand one hundred acres to an estimated nine thousand acres by 1915. On this expanding acreage, 402 Japanese were employed as farmers in 1924, and they, in turn, employed 213 Japanese farmhands and supported 1,138 dependents (who also worked very hard, as the interviews in this chapter show).[12] Utah's Japanese had particular success with truck gardening, especially with celery. Locally grown Sweetheart Celery and Jumbo Celery came to win national acclaim. Furthermore, the patent on Ever-Bearing strawberries made one Japanese a millionaire.[13]

This success did not bring universal approval, although according to historian Leonard Arrington, Utah's initial reaction was favorable. Utah's Mormons first admired the Japanese, noting similarities with their value systems, especially with their vision, organization, strong family ties, and industriousness.[14] In fact, the Church of Jesus Christ of Latter-day Saints inaugurated a renewed emphasis on worldwide preaching with its opening of a mission in Japan in 1901.[15] Yet, in the following decades, as more and more Japanese settled in Utah, many Utahns expressed the same fears as those felt nationally. Utah's Japanese remained a "different" population and experienced a corresponding amount of racial prejudice. Japanese were frequently, and derisively, referred to in print as "Japs," as in a telling 1913 Utah newspaper editorial that read, in part, "The 'Japs' are all right in their place, but that place is not beside Anglo-Saxon women, and the sooner the latter find it out the better for them."[16]

Fortunately, from the standpoint of that editorial, during the first half of the twentieth century, most people of Japanese descent in the United States did not intermarry. Unfortunately, again from the standpoint of that article, the absence of out-marriage resulted in larger numbers of Japanese-looking people, although they were increasingly American citizens by birth. The Nisei, or second generation, born to immigrant parents in America, resisted the marital arrangements of their parents' generation but also typically married within their race. As a result, the population of Japanese descent remained a distinct, and growing, unit within America. They were lumped together with the Issei as "Japanese," with no distinctions based on citizenship.

Despite the increasing anti-Japanese prejudice, a few Utahns remained firmly pro-Japanese. Outstanding in this respect was Utah's Senator Elbert Thomas, who had served a Mormon mission in Japan. From that experience, he acquired positive views about the Japanese—an outlook he kept throughout his life. In 1938 he wrote:

> Japan and America are neighbors. We have an ocean which is called the Pacific between us. If that ocean is to remain the ocean of peace it will depend on the ability of America and Japan to continue to be friends. . . . We have had differences, rather great ones, but all have been solved in a common-sense way and today there are fewer problems between us than there have ever been in my memory and I believe, too, a better will and a better desire to settle those problems in a peaceful way than we have ever known before.[17]

Thomas's hopes, however laudable, were dashed when Japan attacked Pearl Harbor. In America, the racist notion of "Japanese" as an all-inclusive category promptly predominated. Physical appearance became the deciding factor, not citizenship, allegiance, or personal loyalty. In a reversal of the American standard of "innocent until proven guilty," people of Japanese descent were considered to be universally guilty of the attack and were denied any chance to prove their innocence. The tragedy of this large-scale scapegoating is clearly evident in the interviews in this chapter. The Nisei, especially, expected to be protected by the U.S. Constitution, which was supposed to be their birthright. Understandably, they felt disappointment, frustration, and anger following the decision to evacuate all of California's citizens of Japanese descent, as well as most Japanese-Americans living in Oregon, Washington, and Arizona. But the Japanese responded to the decision with stoic acceptance and were incarcerated in concentration camps for most of the war. One of the camps, Topaz, was located near Delta, Utah, where the creation of a museum commemorating those who were interned there is now in progress.[18]

The ostensible reason for the wholesale incarceration of an entire population was to prevent sabotage, but not a single act of sabotage ever occurred. The forced evacuation of approximately 120,000 men, women, and children—two thirds of them U.S. citizens—had no motive other than those spawned by prejudice, jealousy, and hate. Yet, despite the overwhelming injustice of the internment, Japanese-Americans uniformly obeyed the law. They went to prison peaceably, silently bearing horrendous personal losses, both material and psychological. The resulting wounds have taken a long time to heal, as some of the interviews that follow reveal. Furthermore, West Coast racism left a local legacy. Several of Utah's current Japanese residents were Topaz inmates. Having lost everything, and facing what was sure to be long-lived hatred in their former homes, many Topaz inmates elected to remain in Utah. Typically, they gravitated to the prewar Japanese enclaves, such as those in Salt Lake City and Ogden. There they joined others who, like them, still dreamed the American dream.

This dream comes through in the following pages. The interviews mirror a strong wish for progress, most often gained through the hard work of men, women, and children. Recreation—except for the celebration of holidays and festivals—was not a frequent feature in the lives of Utah's Japanese. Clearly, those who came to Utah believed that America promised a better life, although it did not always immediately deliver. Yet the successes were many, and they were as varied as the people who clung to the dream of peace, opportunity, and hard-earned prosperity.

NOTES

1. Editorial in *Harper's Weekly*, May 26, 1860, quoted in Prince Tokugawa, "Friendship Between America and Japan," *American and Japan in Amity and Trade* (Tokyo: Osaka Mainichi and Tokyo Mainichi, 1938), 28.

2. Yamato Ichihashi, *Japanese in the United States* (1932, reprint, New York: Arno Press, 1969), 4.

3. Ichihashi, *Japanese in the United States*, 48–49.

4. Ichihashi, *Japanese in the United States*, 51; Mary Tsukamoto and Elizabeth Pinkerton, *We the People: A Story of Internment In America* (Elk Grove, Calif.: Laguna Publishers, 1988), 247, 256.

5. Helen Z. Papanikolas and Alice Kasai, "Japanese Life in Utah," in Helen Z. Papanikolas, ed., *The Peoples of Utah* (Salt Lake City: Utah State Historical Society, 1976), 336.

6. Ichihashi, *Japanese in the United States,* 60–64, 170.

7. "Buddhist Church of Ogden: 75th Anniversary, 1912–1987," privately printed, 4. Copy in possession of the author of this preface.

8. Leonard J. Arrington, "Utah's Ambiguous Reception: The Relocated Japanese Americans," in Roger Daniels et al., *Japanese Americans: From Relocation to Redress* (Salt Lake City: University of Utah Press, 1989), 92.

9. Roger Daniels, *Asian America: Chinese and Japanese in the United States Since 1850* (Seattle: University of Washington Press, 1988), 125–126.

10. Ichihashi, *Japanese in the United States,* 170–171.

11. Papanikolas and Kasai, "Japanese Life in Utah," 338.

12. Ichihashi, *Japanese in the United States,* 171.

13. Papanikolas and Kasai, "Japanese Life in Utah," 339.

14. Arrington, "Utah's Ambiguous Reception," 92.

15. *Deseret News 1991–1992 Church Almanac* (Salt Lake City, Utah: Deseret news, 1990), 290.

16. Editorial in *Carbon County News* November 6, 1913.

17. Senator Elbert D. Thomas, "Good Neighbor Policy," in Tokugawa, *America and Japan in Amity and Tragedy,* 85.

18. For information regarding the museum, contact Topaz Museum, Box 550, Delta, Utah 84624, telephone (801) 864-5013.

Kuniko Terasawa. *Kent Miles*

Chiyo Matsumiya. *George Janecek*

PROLOGUE: ISSEI

CHIYO MATSUMIYA, 85, HOUSEWIFE, SEAMSTRESS

Conscientious, determined, resourceful, Chiyo Ongino Matsumiya was one of the Japanese picture brides who arrived in the United States in the first two decades of the twentieth century and endured bitter labor, bigotry, and long periods of social isolation while raising her family.

Married to Jinzaburo Matsumiya (1890–1964) in Japan in 1918, she settled with her husband in Tintic, Utah, where he was a section foreman for the Union Pacific. One of the few women in the area, she cooked and washed for several Japanese "bachelors" who worked with her husband and ran a commissary to supplement the family income.

After the bombing of Pearl Harbor, her husband was abruptly laid off. The family relocated to Salt Lake City, where he took odd jobs until a head injury he received in a 1947 car accident forced him to retire. An expert seamstress, Ms. Matsumiya became the family's sole provider. She altered suits, slacks, and sports jackets for Hibbs, a men's clothing store in Salt Lake City, until her retirement in 1972.

My [maiden] name is Ogino Chiyo.[1] I was born in Fukui Ken, Onyu Gun, on April 10, 1899.[2] When I look back at my village, I realize it is a lot like Salt Lake. Near the Japan Sea, the mountains are always covered with snow and pine trees. By my village, a big stream borders on the back side. My home was a small place quite a distance from our [regional] school. I remember as a child walking to school and wearing long snow boots. I also remember, after a big snowstorm, making steps up to the temple roof in the snow and sliding down on a straw mat—just like skiing.

My father's name was Ogino Kimezo; my mother's was Ogina Masa. I had two sisters and one half brother. I am the only one left. We were Buddhists. My father was a very good man, a respected person considered the head man in our village. He farmed rice and loved to help people. The older people in the village who did not know how to read or write would ask him to read this or write that. And he would. When the farming season was over, he would bring threading material [obtained from a plant base] from far away and divide it among the older villagers so they could make thread for fishing nets. When the nets were made, he took them to sell in Osaka and other places. We used to hunt for mushrooms with him. During Obon Odori [dance festival], my father, who loved to sing, would beat a drum and sing in the middle of the [dancing] circle. Whenever he stopped singing, the circle would get smaller.

My father loved to play Go.[3] When the harvest was over, the village temple priest always invited him to play in the temple, and Father wouldn't come home until the following morning. One time, my mother suggested he take me along, so he would return earlier. But being a child, I fell asleep, and my father played until morning. Things like that I can't forget.

In the spring, we planted rice by hand, one by one. When it was growing, we'd go to the mountains to pick weeds to rot and use as fertilizer. Then we used our feet to stamp the decayed weeds between the rows. At the harvest, everybody helped—families and neighbors. There were no clocks in those days; [instead] a temple bell used to ring [before daybreak]. When it did, we'd say, "There's the bell. Let's get up." We'd work from daybreak until dusk. When one field was done, we'd go on to another neighbor's field until everybody's field was planted.

I stayed with my family until I graduated from grammar school and went to Kyoto. Since my school records were good, my father wanted me to become a schoolteacher. But in those days, the custom was to go to Kyoto and work as a maid to learn manners and etiquette—and then to marry. Besides, my mother said, "Oh, this child is just like a boy, and if she becomes a teacher, she will be so conceited, we won't be able to do anything with her."

So I went to Kyoto. I didn't work long as a maid, because I learned I was going to go to America [as a bride]. My parents had arranged the marriage. But I didn't see or know my future husband, although we were from the same village. At the time, he was working in the United States, and I went to the Kyoto Jogakko [a girls' school] for about three years to learn English. I studied really hard and my eyes were bad, so I had to go back and forth to see the eye doctor.

When Matsumiya returned to Japan, and I saw him for the first time, I remember thinking he was rather tall for a Japanese. I was, too, for that matter. We got married in Japan and came together to America in 1918. My father died before my marriage arrangements were made, so he never knew I went to America.

We sailed *tokuson*, special third class, which was between second and third class. There were lots of picture brides coming over from Hiroshima, Kusha, and Wakayama, but no others from my village. I didn't bring anything with me. No kimono . . . nothing. According to Matsumiya, I was to make dresses when I got here.

Most Issei had ideas of making money and going back to Japan early.[4] Matsumiya said [that] after we had two children, we would go back to Japan to educate them. But I wasn't even thinking of going back to Japan. I wanted to live in a wider place, like America. So I thought only of raising the children here. Matsumiya said if I didn't go back, the children would return to Japan and be taken care of by the grandmother. That is how most Issei thought, probably because they weren't eligible for citizenship.[5]

As the ship entered San Francisco harbor, I remember looking curiously around at the crowds of people on the pier. I watched picture brides look all over for their future husbands. We were taken by a small boat to the immigration office, where I had to stay one night with the other women. My husband stayed at a Japanese hotel, then came back for me. Later, we went up and down Market Street, window-shopping. I was surprised to see how tall the *hakujins* [Caucasians] were and how they wore long dresses and high hats.

At the hotel, Japanese merchants came to sell American-style clothing. A dressmaker measured me and said I must have this or that. Matsumiya took care of the money matters, and I just stood there in a daze. I don't know what happened other than I must have bought everything, [even] high-buttoned shoes. We stayed in San Francisco for three days, until my dresses were ready, then we took a train to Salt Lake.

Matsumiya worked for the railroad, so the train fare was free. We arrived at the Union Pacific station and went for provisions at a store owned by Dr. E. I. Hashimoto's father. He was a "big shot" in Utah. He sold groceries and supplied all the needs of the Japanese people. He took orders for clothes from the Japanese people living in rural districts, and he looked after the picture brides and other people who came from Japan. In his store, rice was stacked high, and tins of *oshoyu* [soy sauce] were piled one on top of another. These staples were sent to railroad sections in and around Utah. Whenever Japanese foods were needed, a letter was written, and Hashimoto would deliver. That's how he made his money.[6]

I think we stayed for about a week in Salt Lake and then moved to a place called Jericho, twenty miles from Eureka, which used to be a big mining town. We lived in one section of a house, and Yamamoto-san and his family lived in the other. We got our groceries from Hashimoto and had our orders delivered [from Salt Lake City] by freight. We had all kinds of Japanese items: *oshoyu,* miso [bean paste], *kanpyo* [dry gourd], *shiitake* [mushrooms]. Once a year, we made *osushi* [sushi] for New Year's.

Soon after we arrived, the influenza epidemic of 1919 caused many people to die. Even my husband had to be hospitalized. When Mrs. Yamamoto delivered her third child in Salt Lake and returned home, she brought the flu bug with her. You couldn't believe that one could get the flu in such a desolate place, but she brought it and everyone got it. I was the last one to get the flu, so I took care of the sick ones.

After we got well, we heard from my husband's friend Mr. Mori that sugar beets were selling at a good price of twelve dollars a ton. He also said farming was better than railroad work and why didn't we go into that? So, on the spur of the moment, we decided to move to Sandy, near Midvale, and farm for a while. We worked under Mr. Mori, who had about ten acres of farmland. It was very, very hard work. At that time, there were no machines to do the work. So we thinned the beets by hand and had such backaches, we couldn't stand or sit.

In 1921, we decided to farm on our own and moved to Benjamin, Utah. Within two years, my children were born. Those were difficult years. We were poor. My husband did all the hard work, borrowing all the farm machinery, and I did the housework, washing, cooking, taking care of the children. During that time, we raised sugar beets. The first year was good, but in the second year, a big hailstorm came and destroyed our crop.

Thank goodness, country people are good, kind people. They all help each other. We had good neighbors like Hirase-san and a German family named

Balzly. Mrs. Balzly looked after both Mrs. Hirase and me just like our parents would. When our children were born, she took care of us. She taught me how to cook, how to smoke ham and bacon, and how to prepare headcheese. She was just like Buddha. It never mattered who came to her door—she'd ask, "Are you hungry?" When all our children went fishing, I would prepare a Japanese lunch, because her boys loved Japanese food. And after fishing, she would give them pies or something to bring home. My children always looked forward to that treat.

Still, financially, it was bad, and my husband didn't care for farming. He didn't like the idea of borrowing equipment, because he had to borrow it after the [others had finished using it] and by then he was always late with his own farming. We realized then that no matter what we did, we would still be broke. So I said, let's quit. It would be better to return to our former job. In the fall of that year, we returned to Eureka and to Kimberly Junction, back to the railroad. Soon after, we moved to a small place called Tintic Junction, which had a roundhouse, a maintenance house, and maybe five or six homes. The public school was in nearby Eureka, and the children got there on the bus. By then, I had five children.

The name of Tintic was taken from the Tintic silver mines. It was at five thousand feet elevation. Being that high, there were hardly any cloudy days, always sunny ones. And the air was clean. Every train coming through from Los Angeles to Salt Lake had to come through the summit, through Tintic, and take on coal and water before going over the mountain. Trains coming from Salt Lake were pulled by two engines. There were numerous tracks.

Although the railroad company built regular homes, we lived in a freight car that was made by joining two boxcars together [width-wise] by the floor, making about six rooms, which was useful for our large family. It was really nice—warm in the winter, cool in the summer. Our house, coal, and water were all provided by the railroad. Until we had electricity, we used kerosene lamps. For years, I used to carry the lamp into each room; otherwise, the children wouldn't play. The house was already built when we moved in, and we planted trees in the front to make it look nice. From the outside, it looked like a regular house. Even there, Mrs. Balzly visited. Her boys drove the car, and she usually stayed with us for about three weeks or so. She was just like my mother.

My husband was a section foreman and supervised five or six Mexicans. They straightened the railroad tracks and raised or lowered the grades. He rode a motor cart here and there. In those days, that was the only work the Issei could do. At the beginning there were few Japanese around. During the Depression, others came to work under my husband. They were lonely men, some with wives in Japan. I felt sorry for them and so invited three or four of them to eat with us. I did this for about ten years.

But it was a hard life with no time for pleasures. I spent my time washing, ironing, and cooking. I rarely had a chance to talk to anybody. I think I got up about five thirty in the morning and made lunches for the three men—

three sandwiches for each man and one each for the children to take to school. I washed everything by hand, scrubbing those long pairs of underwear with bar soap. When the evening came, I was able to do some knitting and ironing. In those days, I still didn't know too much about cooking, so I prepared the same dinners every day, like cabbages in a big pot with a pork bone for flavor. Everybody enjoyed that. In the winter, we bought a hindquarter of beef and a whole pig and hung them in the garage. I would slice the beef to make sukiyaki. I used to watch Mrs. Balzly cook, so I learned how to roast, too. I also learned how to smoke bacon and ham and did it by myself. I charged the men twenty dollars a month [for the food]. But when I once added up the whole month's grocery expenses and divided it among us, we didn't come out well. I didn't charge for washing or haircutting, although when some of them got their paychecks, they bought cakes for the children. That was nice.

When the war broke out, we were completely surprised. America is a big country, and Japan is such a tiny nation. What are they talking about [—that the tiny nation of Japan could be at war with the United States—] was our attitude. We were living in a place where there weren't many Japanese. Maybe once or twice a month, when we met in town, we would greet each other. Seldom did we discuss anything. Still, we heard rumors that adults would be sent to one camp and the kids would be sent to another. It was worthless talk, but everyone was frightened.

In Salt Lake and in Garfield, there was some trouble. Someone diverted warm wastewater so it would run onto the railroad tracks—maybe to blame it on the Japanese. Even though the Japanese workers didn't cause the trouble, the railroad decided to lay off all Japanese workers to avoid further problems. My husband was given a leave of absence until the end of the war. But we were asked to move from our home within three days. They told us we couldn't go west, but if we wanted to travel any place east, we could go for free on the train. Some people went east. But we didn't want to go to anyplace we didn't know, so we went to Payson. We were told we could rent a house until the war ended, but the owner came back early and told us to move. I drove all over the place every day looking for a place to rent. Even a corner of a barn would do, but I was told it wasn't for rent to a "Jap." During that time, my husband did day work, picking tomatoes, beans, and peaches, while I drove around. Finally, we came to Salt Lake, to 2100 South and West Temple. It was still country then, and because we had chickens and pigs, we pooled our money and bought a house. Paid in full at the time of purchase.

Two of the children were with me. The boy was away at the University of Utah. Jeanne and my second daughter, Fumiko, were in Salt Lake. Jeanne's husband was in the army, assigned to Fort Douglas. There were many Nisei at Fort Douglas then.

Most of the railroad workers who went to Salt Lake could only find work at a restaurant or hotel. My husband worked as a dishwasher. That's how it was. But no matter what we felt about the war, we didn't talk about it. We had two children still going to school, and we had to live and eat as usual. And I didn't have bad feelings towards Caucasians. Most were good to us. This was something done by the higher authorities, so what can you do?

I remember there were groups of Japanese railroad workers and others who gathered at the Colonial Hotel and discussed the war, but we never joined them. We didn't talk about the war, not even with our kids. We just kept our mouths shut.

Postscript: Chiyo Matsumiya passed away on March 12, 1990.

HISAYE TSUTSUI, 86, HOMEMAKER, FARMER

A tiny, animated woman, Hisaye Tsutsui is blessed with extraordinary recall. Her interview was full of vivid details of daily life in turn-of-the-century Japan and in the interwar decades in the United States.

A mother of five children, she was born in 1898 in Kochi Ken, a mountainous region of Japan known for its wheat, barley, tea leaves, and corn. Farmers in her village were self-sufficient, and what they didn't raise, like fish, they acquired through barter. "The man selling fish always carried his stock in a basket hung on a bamboo pole," she noted. Her husband's family lived in the same village, on the north side; she lived on the south side, on higher ground. She never met her husband prior to their proxy marriage; he had emigrated to Hawaii when she was four years old.

Hisaye Tsutsui arrived in San Francisco on March 18, 1920. She believed she was "amongst the last of the picture brides, on the last ship." "After that," she said, "picture brides were not permitted to enter America."[7]

In my village, we raised silkworms and made paper from *yanagi* and *hajikusa* and other similar [willow] plants. We steamed them in a kettle, removed the skin [cover], put them in water to soak, then dried them neatly on a rack. We used some of the paper ourselves and sold the rest. That was our method of living, and with the money made from selling, we bought clothing and things we lacked.

We never purchased rice. When we ate it, we cooked only just a few grains, so you could hardly tell it was in the pot. Only during religious celebrations or holidays were the villagers able to eat all rice. On regular days, we ate corn, wheat, or barley. We'd pound the corn and cook it with a tenth of rice mixed in. We made powdered corn into *mochi* [rice cakes] and ate it that way. In the winter, we ate *kibi no gohan* [cooked rice made with broomcorn]. In the summer, we cooked *komugi* [wheat] and *oomugi* [barley] mixed with a tenth of rice. In Japan, people say if you eat barley, it prevents sickness such as *kakke* [beriberi], where your legs swell.

In Japan, people don't use much sugar, since everything is flavored with *oshoyu* and salt. Our sugar was not white nor brown but dark black and used only for confectionary or for *anko shiru* [sweet bean broth]. We grew *rakkyo* [shallots] for pickled scallions made with dark brown sugar, vinegar, and salt. They were delicious. Besides making *oshoyu*, we made miso [bean paste].

We lived in a mountainous region terraced for wheat first, [then] corn, then barley. We cut grass from the mountains and used it as compost. We raised rice in the wet, marshy land and used fertilizer made from the cut mountain grass and cow dung. We had good rice crops using a natural fertilizer. We also made our own *waraji* [straw sandals] from rice stalks, which were pounded, made soft, then woven. During the wet season, we grew sweet potatoes. We never had lots of chickens, and we were not allowed to eat eggs except when we were sick. There were no deer around and not many rabbits. Sometimes we'd trap small brown birds in a grove with a trap called *kobute*, which is like a mousetrap. But it was for amusement, not a meal.

We had no ceremony for planting rice. Neighbors would come to help us plant, and then we would go to help them. During *Tan Matsuri* [a festival], we went to worship at *omiya* [a shrine], which was spacious enough to accommodate large numbers of people. There, everyone brought all kinds of dishes and entertained. During *Honen Matsuri* [a harvest festival], when the crop was harvested, there would be dancing and sumo [wrestling]. There was drumbeating and singing. It was quite a happy event for everyone to gather from neighboring villages.

There were *muras*—small villages and hamlets—scattered here and there. The mura where I lived must have had about fifteen houses. The school was located further away, in Shimura, and was attended by children from five muras. After school, we had to take turns, *toban* [a duty], cleaning the classrooms. Sometimes we'd come home an hour and a half later because of the cleaning and the long walk. There was no such thing as a carriage. We all had to walk, in the rain, in the snow, in sunshine, and equip ourselves for each change in the weather.

The only hospital was located ten miles away in Kochi Machi. There was a doctor in Ikegawa Machi who made house calls and traveled by horse. But he was so busy away on calls, he could not always be reached.

My father died at fifty-three years of age due to kidney failure. We continued farming, but it was so hard without his help. My older brother went for an apprenticeship [*koko*], and my second brother went to war. We could not do it alone, so we hired a man who worked for us at a minimal wage.

I was married at my parents' home in 1919. On March 18, 1920, I arrived in San Francisco.

When my husband first left Japan for Hawaii, Okamoto-san and my brother went with him. I think they were the first from our village to go to the United States. I don't remember all the details, because I was only four years old. I do remember being carried on the back of my mother as we went to see them off and told to be a good girl and they would bring me lots of candies and presents.

After my husband heard how good life was in America, he left Hawaii and went to the States, where he worked as a railroad laborer in Montana and a farmer in Texas, then Utah. He was thirty-five years old when we got married. I don't know whether his parents asked him if he wanted to get married or not. I don't remember. Don't you think it was that way for most of the picture brides? Some of them didn't care what kind of a person the man was. As long as he wanted a wife, she was willing to marry him and come to America. Then she could be free to do anything she wanted. At least, that's what I heard. That's the kind of feelings some picture brides had.

In my case, I can't say I "knew" him, because I was so young when he left our village. Maybe I was chosen because it was his parents' wish to send a bride to him who was a close family member. I didn't know anything about my husband's business or what kind of person he was or about his feelings. All I saw was a picture of him, which was kind of vague. The main reason why I wanted to come here was because *ani san* [my brother] was working at an *udon* [noodle] business in Salt Lake City. And I would be able to see him if I came. I married by proxy with a legal ceremony in Japan, with *shimoda* and *montsuki* [formal wedding attire]. Then my brother's friends came and we had a party.

When I left my home for America, I walked through a tunnel and took a riverboat to a place called Io. My sister traveled with me for a while. From Io, I took an electric train, a tram, to Kochi City, a boat to Kobe, then a steamliner to America. As to baggage, I was given one blanket to be used on the boat. My clothing was stored in a *hori* [woven basket, trunk]. We slept in cramped rooms made even more narrow with bunk beds arranged in *kaiko-dame* [cocoon shelves]. I slept on the top bed. Some people got seasick, and I had a cold, but I wasn't scared or lonesome. My thought was to go to America, so I must have some courage. Also, everyone else on the boat was traveling a long distance with the same idea in mind, so it was good that way, and I knew I wasn't the only one.

When we arrived in San Francisco at the immigration office, we were fed dry, separated rice [Chinese rice] and some boiled fish. I remember the rice was hard and I couldn't eat it. I met my husband there. We had each other's picture, so I began to search for him as soon as we landed. There were lots of men waiting for their brides, and he was there early. I remember he had been farming and was dark with a sunburned face.

My brother's wife sent a hat for me to wear, and my husband brought it with him. It was a Western type of hat, and since the day was windy, I had to hold my hat down. Even when I put a pin through it, it wobbled. I also got high-top boots. I was used to wearing *zori* [sandals] in Japan, and these new boots didn't fit me in the same way. I was in pain whenever I walked. When I came to [the farm], I didn't need them anymore. But when I first arrived, I must have looked strange and amusing to others with my Japanese kimono and *haori* [cloak or garment worn over a kimono] and obi [sash], Western hat and boots.

Before going to my husband's farm in Payson, I spent a month with my brother and his wife in their apartment behind the Noodle Shop. When I arrived at the farm, six horses came out to greet me, and I remember seeing a barn, hay piled up high, and a sugar factory nearby.

The house was very plain, built out of wood, and not very comfortable. It had a kitchen, bedroom, and a front room, that's all. The bath was outside in a separate shack. It had a square wooden tub, and the fire was built underneath. My husband must have built it himself. I didn't have any particular impression. I thought this must be how it is. I just knew I had to learn how to cook rice [in an American house].

You see, in Japan, our house was different. There, we had a room with an *irori* [hearth, or fireplace] in the middle of it. From the roof over the fireplace, an adjusted hook holds a kettle over the fire. That is where we cook the rice, boil water for tea, and cook our meals. Next to that room is another one similar to our [American] kitchen, and below that there's usually a little garden with steps. That's called a *chanoma* and is a sitting room where we have our meals. In another room [*kamisuki ba*], we have an oven where we do our work cooking grass for papermaking.

Some practices, too, were different in America. Nowadays, when you get pregnant, you go to a doctor, have regular checkups. We didn't bother with that. I think most of the Japanese [Issei] women regarded birth as a very simple, natural process—especially when country doctors are miles away. In 1922, our first child, Tom, was born in small hospital in Payson. I remember when I was pregnant with him, I went out to dig some vegetables. My husband and I rode on a horse. I never rode on a horse before, and when I took the reins, the horse began trotting away and wouldn't listen to me. I got thrown off. Fortunately, it was by the fence where the weeds were growing thick, so I wasn't injured. But I was really scared. Our second son, Harry, was born in 1923, at home. He was a breeched birth. Mrs. Kato, a friend and neighbor whose husband worked with mine, must have been surprised seeing him come out feet first.

We had to order Japanese food through my brother in Salt Lake. I remember I wanted to eat *satoimo* [taro], but it was out of season then. This craving came during my first pregnancy, and I wanted to eat anything—even a cookie—made out of *satoimo,* but we couldn't get it. Oh, I had such cravings then for Japanese food.

Payson was a small town and far away from the cities. One time, when I needed to buy a baby buggy, we had to go to Provo. It took us a whole day by horse and wagon to get there. That was the only time I went to Provo. During the winter, we had few pleasures or amusements. I had a sewing machine, the old-fashioned peddle kind, so I took my old clothes apart and made them into children's wear. As [the children] grew, I'd sew coveralls and other clothes and outfits. We couldn't afford any luxuries and had to do with what we had, especially when the children were young. For a while, we made a good living on sugar beets. The price at twelve dollars a ton was considered good; fifteen dollars a ton [which we sometimes got] was even better. But one time, sugar beets fell to five dollars a ton, so it wasn't even worth working. Then, when blight struck the roots, the plants did not grow and the harvest was so small we couldn't make a living. It was a failure. That was when we moved.

We moved around a lot. I had five children in all, bearing one child here and one child there. Tom, Harry, Kate, Mabel, and Mary. I guess I sort of made the rounds! For a while, my husband went into partnership with Mr. Kato and worked in Draper, farming north of the state prison. But the land there was not suitable for sugar beets. It had too much salt, and so that business, too, failed. We planted different kinds of vegetables near the house. But we still did not make enough money, and when Mr. Kato decided to move to Sunnyside, we couldn't pay the rent and so we worked for wages, just barely enough to eat.

When we went to Arthur, Utah, we worked on a salary basis and lived in a company camp. They gave us a house, rent free, but with three children by now, it was too small. Since the house was built against a rocky mountainside, we dynamited the rock and dug out dirt to make the room larger, and that's how we managed to live. After three years, my husband went back to farming in Sunnyside.

We didn't have anyone to baby-sit the younger children, so the older ones helped. As they started school, one by one, I was able to work out in the field. When Kate was eleven or twelve years old, I taught her how to cook rice. As soon as Mabel and Mary came home from school, they'd change their clothes, grab a sandwich, and immediately come out to the field to bunch carrots and beets. Tom and Harry helped, too. That's how we were able to farm.

We endured a lot of hardships. But after hearing other people's stories about moving here and there, we know it was a way of life for most of us. I thought this must be the way it is [in America].

When we moved to Salt Lake City in 1930, Okamoto-san asked if we could start a partnership. So we started farming ten acres of land nearby from where we are. Near the railroad, we farmed another ten acres. We specialized in raising green celery. Between wide rows, we used our horse and wagon to spread horse manure. After the manure was spread, we took a fork and broke it up and cultivated it, mixing it with dirt. Then we made a small ditch and placed the celery plants. In the furrows, we also raised beets, carrots, and radishes.

Our farmhouse was at the end of this street. It was crude and built for two families. Okamoto-san lived on one side. On our side, we added a lean-to shed and were able to make another bedroom by laying beds side by side for the whole family.

During that time, we had no tractor. We put a harness on the horse and strapped the plow-cultivator around its body. Our horses would plow and cultivate everything. But constant use of the plow and cultivator made our arms so stiff, we couldn't bend them. I often wondered how we ever did it. Okamoto-san farmed with us for seven years, then pulled up stakes and went back to Japan. After he left, my husband had a difficult time getting the vegetables to market. After the war started, though, we sold our vegetables to the wholesale market. A man would come for the vegetables, and the entire family would help get them ready. That's how we got by.

In Salt Lake, we worked and worked. By eight o'clock in the morning, after getting the children ready for school, we were out in the field. We had horses to take care of, but no chickens or cows. We also kept rabbits, about ten. As to meat, it's not like eating steaks, as young people do today. If we bought one pound of meat, we cut it into small pieces for a side dish and never ate one pound all at once. In those days, we only had a small icebox, which didn't hold much. We had simple meals: rice, a side dish of a little meat, and vegetables. All our grown children still like cooked vegetables.

When our land was sold, we left and rented another ten acres to farm. We raised all kinds of vegetables but had to be on a specific water schedule set up by the county. We would water once every five days during daylight hours; but once a month, one of those times would fall during the night. After working all day, I would make my husband and me a breakfast, and we would go out to the field. I would sleep near a vacant chicken coop until two in the morning. Then we would water until eleven o'clock that day. It was dark when we started to water. I had to carry a bent pipe and lay it on the ditch so the water would flow through it. Once, after carrying the pipe across the street, I sat down and fell asleep. Fortunately, no cars came by. I suddenly awoke and realized I had fallen asleep. You know, you get tired, carrying the pipe and setting it down in the dark. That's one thing I'll never forget.

But, through all that, I never regretted coming to America. My husband is a rather gentle person. He farmed until he was seventy-nine years old. When things went wrong, he may have thought he should have stayed in Japan, but he was a gentle person and so there were no troubles. We became American citizens [in 1952], and we never went back to Japan.

NISEI

EDYTHE KANEKO, 68, HOMEMAKER

Despite her mother's insistence that she marry in the traditional baishaku, *or arranged marriage, method, Edythe Hariko Tanaka married the man of her choice, Noble Kaneko, in 1939. The couple lived in Gunnison, Utah, for a year and a half, then moved to Spanish Fork when World War II broke out. "There were people ready to come out and bomb us," she recalled, "but there weren't many. We had a lot of friends." Still, it was, she remembered, "a terrible feeling to have this country fighting our mother country and people wondering which side we were going for."*

After farming in Spanish Fork for twelve years, the Kanekos moved to American

Edythe Kaneko. *Kent Miles*

Fork, where Noble Kaneko became the supervisor of "the LDS church farm." Before moving, though, they joined the LDS church. "What brought it on," she explained, "is that all through the war, the church people were so good to us. They didn't care about the war. They invited us to all their functions and treated us as one of them. And, I think, that just drew us in. Made us feel so good." Her parents were startled at first. But like many Issei, her father believed it ultimately does not matter what church you belong to. "Just be a good member," he advised.

I'm Edythe Hariko Kaneko. I have seven sisters and one brother . . . two brothers, actually. The first one passed away in ten days. I was born on January 2, 1916, in Elwood, Utah—the home to which my mother first came [from Japan]. I remember living there for a short time, then [moving] to Salt Creek. I was talking to my mother about it the other day—that I remember our neighbor was close by, about a quarter mile away, [and she] tended me while my mother worked. And one day she came to get me. My mother was standing by the gate and I was reluctant to go. She had a hold of my hand, was dragging me down the dirt road, and I was just yelling and screaming. I guess I didn't want to go that day.

We didn't live long in Elwood before my father [and his friends] loaded up our furniture and moved us out to the Salt Creek Farm, where we stayed. We didn't have a car. We had wagons and teams of horses. And I remember the old white surrey with the fringe on top and an old black buggy with a little top. It was drawn by one horse. When we went visiting, we [kids] sat on the floor while Mother and Dad sat on the seat.

In those days, Salt Creek was quite a big [waterway]; it looked like a canal. Dad would run down there [in the summer] and go swimming, and we'd sit on the bank. There were three of us girls then. We'd watch him, and he'd scare us by going under the water. We'd scream and cry. We thought he was gone. When he'd come [up], everything was fine. But, I remember, he really scared us. We weren't old enough to realize he was okay. We thought, Dad's gone!

I remember Dad working those acres of sugar beets, and Mother out there helping him irrigate and weed. They were hard workers and worked long hours each day. Whatever had to be done in those days, everything was horse-drawn. It isn't like today. My father just had a one-blade plow, and it'd take quite a while to plow up that much ground. They worked hard, and we helped. When we were young, he'd give us each a hoe, and we'd go out and weed. When I was six years old, he said, "If you can learn to thin beets"—that is, to thin them out about ten to twelve inches apart—"why, I'll pay you."

So, just below the house, a patch of beets took up about one hundred feet, and I thinned about six to ten rows, quite a width, and learned how to thin. He came out, checked it, and said, "That looks very good," and gave me a dime. Then he hitched up his horse and said, "We'll go and get some ice cream and celebrate." Now, when I got that dime, I thought I was at the top of the world! I was just so tickled. That was the first money I earned. So he hitched up the horse and the buggy, and we went to town.

The winters, I recall, were quite hard. The ice on the creeks and ponds would get about two feet thick. Men would go down with ice saws, cut blocks, and bring them up to store in the big shed at the top of the hill. See, the ice man had built a house with cement foundations thick enough to hold in the cold. Rows and rows of blocks would be stacked in there, covered with sawdust, and the ice would last all through summer. So, when it was warm, we'd go and get ten or twenty cents worth of ice to make a freezer of ice cream. My mother mixed the cream, and we'd churn it in one of those wooden buckets. That's how we made it.

Our house was a big, [sprawling,] two-story place. Upstairs, we had five bedrooms; downstairs, a bedroom, living room, dining room, and kitchen. But we had no indoor plumbing, no running water. Before [we came], a cistern was built, and we used a pump at the end of the lawn [to bring up water]. I remember Dad saying we purified the water by running it "through" the underground gravel. It was stored in a tank, and we'd pump it out. Then we'd turn a crank, and when the water came out of a spout, we'd fill up a bucket and haul it into the house.

Eventually, most of us had a room to ourselves. But the house wasn't heated. We just had a cooking stove in the kitchen, a potbelly stove in the dining room, and one in the living room. That's how we heated the place. The upstairs didn't have any heat. When it was cold, we used blankets, and quilts about a foot thick. If it was *very* cold, we'd heat bricks on the stove, wrap them in a blanket, and put them under our covers to warm up our beds before we went to sleep. But I know when we crawled into bed, we were shivering for quite a while before the bed warmed up. In the morning, we didn't dare get up. We could see the windows were all frosted, and the ice was hanging on the eaves of the house. Outside, it went below zero every day.

We grew up in that house. And since my parents couldn't speak any English, when I started grade school, I couldn't speak a word either. I had a first-grade teacher who really worked with me, though. Her name was Amelia Christianson, and I guess she adopted me. She lived with the Hunsakers in town, and she just took over everything. In my first school program, I was a little sunbeam and wore a little orange costume with ruffles. Mother didn't know how to make it, so Mrs. Christianson bought the material and made it for me.

One night, after she made this costume, she took me over to her place after school and fitted it to me. Since there was no way we could reach Dad to get me, she and I walked the three miles out to our home. It was getting dark, but she was good enough to walk with me. About a quarter mile from the house, I said, "I can walk the rest of the way." So she left me and started walking back. And all of a sudden, there came an open car, coming down that road. It was Mr. Hunsaker. He must've got worried about her and come after her. And I remember feeling quite glad, because that was a long walk back in the dark.

Now, in grade school, the prejudice against us was quite strong. You'd often get a kid who'd try to be smart and call you names. We didn't like the word "Jap." The white kids knew that, and so they called us Japs. In about the fourth grade, this one boy, a real smart aleck, always called me that. Every time I turned around, every time I'd do something different, he'd say, "What do you think you're doing, you Jap?" And that hit me hard—that made me feel like crawling in a hole.

We didn't socialize much with white kids as we grew older. For instance, when it came to [school] dances, they wouldn't ask us for dates. Besides, our parents didn't think it was right to date people of other races. So we socialized with our own. I remember we had a [community] picnic every spring. In the early years, it was held by the little adobe building the Japanese Association rented in Garland. We celebrated New Year's and other holidays there, too.[8]

We met there until the Japanese Association bought a big, two-story building in Honeyville that the sugar company owned. Then we started having picnics and other socials there. The picnics were a big event. Held in the first of May or late April, they had races and children's games, and prizes for every event. We all ran in the races. The first three would get the big prizes; the rest would get little prizes. But everybody got something. They also had races for men and women, and they eventually worked into [sumo] wrestling. Oh, the women used to bring lunches, and that was a big deal. Every family fixed their own lunch, then they'd bring blankets so they could sit on the ground and eat. I would say that was one of the big social events of the year for us.

As we grew older, the [Nisei] boys started [all Japanese] baseball teams in different towns. Every weekend, I remember, we'd go to a baseball game. That was our summer recreation. Sometimes, we'd follow our team to other towns, just follow them wherever they went. As we got into our late teens, we formed a social organization. I can't remember what we called it. We'd hold a convention every fall and have a dance at every high school graduation. The dances were held in Ogden or Salt Lake. Each city would take turns being the host. The older folks didn't think it was wise for the boys and girls to mingle, so my mother and dad always went with us as chaperons. They went with us to every dance and stayed with us till midnight [when the dance ended and we'd all go home].

At the fall conventions, we always had a main speaker; then we'd hold meetings and discuss the things we could do to better ourselves. This wasn't the JACL yet. But it merged into that. I remember we always tried to get a prominent Caucasian, like a city official or a school principal, who thought a lot of us to address us. We did this because we wanted to prove we were not what [the whites] thought we were. A few people thought we were [permanently] separate from everybody else. So we organized these conventions to prove we were Americans. I mean, we were going to be if they would let us.[9]

After my high school graduation, I told my mother I wanted to train as a nurse, but she said that was too hard. I wanted to go to business college, too, but Dad didn't think it was right for girls to leave home [alone]. In 1937, they gave in and said, "You can go to the Kister Tailoring School on 500 East South Temple, for three months." Located behind Backer's Bakery, the school was run by a little old lady, who taught us how to draft patterns and make clothes. My friend and I rented a room in a Japanese hotel on First South, right in the middle of the city's Japanese community. Every day, we walked four blocks to and from the school. On Saturday afternoon, we went shopping downtown. For me, to actually live like that, to be able to experience some city life, when all I knew was farming and country life—that was glorious!

I would have liked to have stayed, but in March [1938], I had to go home and start farming again. Then, as I was getting to the age of nineteen, twenty, my folks thought they'd better find me somebody, get me married, or I'd become an old maid. If you weren't married by twenty, you see, you were considered an old maid.

Now, my parents had go-betweens [baishaku] representing their families [before they married]. They brought that custom over and thought it was going to work for me. I remember they'd come and tell me [that] a certain Issei wants a wife. Then the go-between would bring him to meet me. I was supposed to be in the kitchen fixing a meal, putting on a good front. He was supposed to be in the dining room, visiting with my parents, and just eyeing me up and down to see if I was okay. Of course, they all said I was okay. But I didn't approve. Most of the men were in their late twenties and thirties—I counted a dozen—and they were too old for me and too steeped in the old Japanese customs. "I'll never get along with one like that," I said. My mother said, "You'll never find a Nisei your age, because you're one of the oldest ones. You'll be too old for them."

As I passed twenty-one, twenty-two, things got worse. Then—am I supposed to tell this? [Giggles]—there was a couple [who were] good friends of my and my [future] husband's folks. They came up and told me, "There's a nice looking man living down in Gunnison." Then they went and told him about a nice-looking girl up in Tremonton. Before they could [formally] get us together, though, he just jumped the gun and came up to visit. From then on, we dated, and things really started popping. I was twenty-three when we got married, and he was twenty-six, and everything worked out. In fact, it's forty-six years since we met.

Now, I must tell you, I've really tried to keep my parents' ways. But over the years even customs like New Year's Day have become Americanized. And there isn't anything you can do. We are still a close family, though. My parents taught us to be close, and we have really done that. We're more lenient with our kids than our parents were with us; and our kids stick to their own American ideas. Yet it still works. My mother once told me, "I don't want any intermarriages." They both insisted on that, as did most Nisei. So a big share [of our generation] are married to their own people.

When you get to this third generation, though, it's completely different. My mother has forty-one grandchildren and between sixty to seventy great-grandchildren, and, I think, the biggest part of them are intermarried. In our own family, only the oldest boy is married to a Japanese girl. The others all married into the white race.

But we don't mind. We knew it was going that way, and, I say, as long as they can find themselves a good mate that they can live and work with the rest of their life, that's fine. I've got two [white] daughters-in-law and a son-in-law, and I tell people we couldn't have done better if we had picked them ourselves. They treat us like their own parents. They are really good to us. So, now, it doesn't matter to us at all. Every one of them fits into our family just like that's where they belong.

YUKIYOSHI "YUKUS" INOUYE, 71, FARMER, UTAH COUNTY COMMISSIONER

Yukiyoshi "Yukus" Inouye was dressed casually for our interview, wearing work pants and a flannel shirt. His manner was warm, cordial, unhurried. He offered us a large scrapbook to peruse. It contained yellowed newspaper photographs of prize hogs he had raised; copies of letters written to the local JACL nominating him for the "Man-of-the-Year Award"; articles about him as county commissioner.[10] Everywhere he was depicted as conscientious, compassionate, concerned.

Born on a small farm in Taylorsville, Utah, Inouye grew up in a typical rural Utah community, where parents worked hard for modest rewards, neighbors helped one another, and children hunted, fished, and played football. World War II shattered this relatively stable world. Remarkably, it did not shatter Inouye's hopes. "I promised myself I wasn't going to get discouraged by the bigotry," he said. "I believed in the principles of this country, and I made a commitment to get involved and be the best citizen I could be."

Over the years, he did just that. He served his community as scoutmaster, member of the Soil Conservation Service, and Farm Bureau president. In 1958, after farming for twenty years, he sold his "operation" and went into real estate development, initiating "the building of the Alpine Country Club," the first club in the state to accept Nisei members. In 1973, the Utah Democratic party appointed him to fill the final two years of an unexpired Utah County Commission term. Two years later, he ran for a full term and became the first Nisei elected into office in Utah.

My father, Chokichi Inouye, came from a small village in Shimane-ken. In America, he said, he worked for the Utah Idaho Sugar Company and, at the time, . . . didn't know a sugar beet from a sunflower. In fact, he was chewed out for leaving the sunflowers in when he was thinning beets. [*Laughs*] He learned, though, and three years later, when he moved to Taylorsville, Utah, and leased some ground, he started farming on his own. At that time, most of the Japanese farmers were growing beets. I can remember, when I was four or five years old, working with my dad cultivating beets. It was all country back then. All country.

When I was in the second grade, we moved to Union. By Union, I mean up Creek Road. It was there that I planted apricot and silver poplars that are

Yukiyoshi Inouye. *Kent Miles*

still growing. And it was there I started trapping and selling skunks, getting five dollars for three skins at the American Fur, which was right next to Eddie Hashimoto's store. Mel Proctor, the caretaker at Murray Power House, taught me and my buddy Tom Erickson how to trap. We would walk the three miles up to the power house just to learn how to do it the right way. The first skunk we trapped, we drowned in the creek and, boy, did we hear about it from the people down below us who drank out of the creek!

I'll tell you, though, Tom gave up pretty fast, because the skunks' spray got to him. It was as strong as beet pulp. But it didn't bother me. So I bought his interest out, bought his traps, and that winter went trapping alone. I had a little pony, and early in the morning, I'd ride out to check my traps. That was during hard times—1928—but I was an independent kid and caught twenty-odd skunks that first winter and made close to fifty dollars. My wife jokes that I had to give up trapping or lose my friends. [*Laughs*] So I got into the rabbit business for about four or five years, then started raising broilers for Kentucky Fried Chicken when I was in high school. My project was sponsored by the FFA [Future Farmers of America] because I experimented with raising [the chickens] on straight skim milk and high protein mash made from ground corn, wheat, bran, and bonemeal. The chickens done real well, and they tasted good.

My father was forty-two when I was born. I was the youngest child and the only boy, so they depended a lot on me and I had a lot of responsibility. My mother was uneducated; she couldn't read or write, but she had lots of wisdom. She used to say, "Words in your mouth are like saliva. As long as they stay in your mouth, they can be swallowed. So be careful what you say." She also used to tell us, "Never burn bridges, because you don't know when you or your son or your grandkids will have to cross that bridge again." She was a gentle woman. She never woke me by hollering. Instead, she would caress me and say, "Yuki, *okinaka*," meaning, "Yuki, it's time to wake."

By the time I was a teenager, we were into truck farming. Actually, there wasn't much money in sugar beets, so most Japanese farmers started truck gardening—raising berries, lettuce, potatoes, celery, and those types of crops. Everybody worked hard. And, since few Issei spoke English, they all relied on each other. In Murray, the Matsumoris, Ushios, Nambas, Moris, Tadeharas, and Fujikawas all knew each other well. All the farmers were close-knit.

I learned a lot about truck gardening from the Fujikawas. They made money during the Depression and went back to Japan. They were good farmers. Mr. Fujikawa used to tell me, "If you're going to plant a crop, take care of it. If you're not going to take care of it, don't plant it." Kay Fujikawa was known for "Kay's lettuce and celery." He always used the same grade of produce, so if you looked at the top, you'd always see the bottom with his packing. Some people didn't do that. In fact, onions and potatoes were often chimney packed, which means they would be filled with number two grade onions in the center and number one on the outside. People like Fujikawa frowned on that. They believed in and practiced integrity. They taught us, "You can't buy it, you've got to build it, because that which you buy won't last."

My family raised strawberries, and before I'd go to school, I'd get up at four o'clock in the morning to haul the produce to the Growers Market in Salt Lake. The original Growers Market stood right where the Hilton hotel stands today. There were wooden platforms and rows of barns. Most of the people drove horses and wagons and came in from Bountiful and neighboring areas of Salt Lake. I drove my dad's Model A pickup, although I can't remember if there was an age limit [for driving]. I know I didn't have a license.

Now, I was always an independent and inquisitive kid. I received a Union Pacific Agricultural Scholarship to attend Utah State University, but during the Depression having a college degree didn't make it any easier to find a job. So, in 1933, after graduating from high school, I looked to branch out on my own. I knew about the Japanese camps in Ely and Ruth, Nevada. I got use of my dad's Model A and loaded it up with vegetables. I remember I took eggplants, cucumbers, onions, lettuce, and radishes and headed off for a smelter camp in McGill, where I met Dr. Toyota, the Japanese boss who took me under his wing and helped me sell the produce.

I made some money from that trip. When I came back, I bought a thirty-three and a half ton truck for $975.00 and started trucking into Reno regularly. I also opened a little fruit stand in Ely. There used to be a popular song called "Hot Cha Cha," so I called my shop the Hotcha Market. My brother-in-law helped me that year. Then, because I was a workaholic, I thought I might as well farm in the summer and haul in the winter. So, starting in 1935, that's what I did.

I'd work sixteen to eighteen hour days then and not know what tired was. I had energy and drive and the desire to be somebody. If a person told me I couldn't do something, I'd do it just to show him it could be done. Besides, I wanted to make a little money, which I did. During the Depression years, from 1933 through 1936, I made one hundred dollars a week trucking.

Boy, I could give you a lot of trucking stories! I remember I cashed my checks in Reno, then worried about getting [all that] money [safely] home to pay off the farmers. I didn't want to carry the money on my body, so I'd hammer a nail through it into the back of my truck. Sometimes, too, we'd have accidents. Once, we slipped off the icy road and tipped over in Beaver, then again at Wendover Flats. I'd always bring spare parts to fix bearings that might go out and brakes that might lock—which they did, generally at night. Once, after breaking down in Farley, we got out of the truck, started a fire, and, oh, you couldn't see anything in the darkness, but you could hear the coyotes howl. Those experiences were harrowing, but they helped me grow.

I got married in 1938. That was the same year my wife said, "You're not trucking anymore!" and I bought my first tractor. My wife was from Tremonton. She's a farmer's daughter and right from the start was a big help on the farm. We met at the annual picnic. I was sumo wrestling, and her father, who was a sumo enthusiast, said, "Hey, why don't you come up and visit us?" [*Laughs*] That's how we got started.

We worked very hard. She drove the tractor while Tom Matsumori and I hooked the horse cultivators on the end, and, man, we'd really go to town! Then I rigged up a horse-drawn plow so I could put it behind the tractor. We farmed from 1938 until 1941. My parents were living with us and I was getting pretty well acquainted with the business world of Salt Lake when, suddenly, the war broke out.

It was about this time we started running into discrimination, too, and during the war, things got worse. Boy, I remember hearing the news on the radio. We were on our way to the celery field when we heard that war had broken out, and we both had a "now what is going to happen" kind of feeling.

Now, Sheriff Beckstead knew me and my family because I played high school football, but from that day on, we were watched closely and kept to a nine P.M. curfew. I can tell you how closely they watched us. I used to have a single-shot .22 rifle for killing skunks. Since I couldn't have it around, I gave it to my neighbor Orrin. About ten days later, when we were having lunch, the sheriff pulled into the yard and said, "Yuk, we're sure mad at you." I said,

"What have I done?" He said, "You gave that gun to Orrin Van when you were supposed to deposit it with the sheriff's office."[11] To this day, I don't know how they found out. But somebody was watching me that close. Well, I took it right down to the sheriff's office. I had a little camera and took it, too, and burned a lot of the papers and pictures my folks had from Japan. A lot of families did that, because they were fearful of the connection with Japan. Looking back, I wish I hadn't done that.

Other people who knew us changed towards us. I used to stop at Red's Café in Sandy, but he wouldn't feed me. He said, "Yuk, I feel bad, but if I had you sitting here, I don't know what would happen." I went to my barber to cut my hair and he said the same thing and wouldn't cut my hair.

In 1943, I bought an eighty-acre farm in Utah County from W. D. Chapman, and he was really lambasted by the people in the community. "How come you sold that farm to a Jap?" they wanted to know. But being a real Christian, after we moved in, he took me down and introduced me to everybody in the area: grocery-store owners, bank officers, other farmers. He was really impressive.

Still, things were tough. I was cleaning the ditch in front of my house with a fellow by the name of Fred Bugle, a kid who stayed on from Chapman. I waved to these three kids who were going by one day, going hunting. Fred waved, too. They said to me, "Don't you wave at us, you yellow bastard! We'll shoot you!"

In 1943, there were only forty homes in this whole community. So, right then and there, I made up my mind to get involved socially. See, I have a philosophy that strangers are only friends you haven't met. Many of my Japanese friends went into a shell at that time. I'm grateful I didn't, because I would have taken my whole family with me. So I told my wife what I planned to do, and she was real supportive, worked right there along with me. You've got to have the support of your wife to make it work.

When Bill Hyde, a neighbor, asked me to work with the Scouts, I jumped at the idea. But can you imagine [a Japanese] walking into a bunch of Boy Scouts in 1944? These kids took one look at me and said, "What's a Jap doing here?" I also joined the Farm Bureau, became president of the Utah County Farm Bureau, and was involved with the County Crop Growers Association Board and soil conservation work. And this is what I would like to tell you: If you're willing to work with integrity, be dependable, and have a good attitude, people will recognize you for who you are.

Of course, it took a lot of my time and energy. I remember once, when I was harvesting our Utah Sweetheart Celery, I slept only fifteen hours that entire week.[12] By the end of harvesting, I went [in]to our outside toilet, and my wife had to come out and wake me up. I had fallen asleep in the outhouse! Another time, I fell asleep on a truck full of peas. But I never turned anything down, no matter how much extra work it involved.

In 1975, I did a lot of soul-searching and threw my hat in the ring for the County Commission race. I wasn't a scholar, but I knew I could talk to people and I had the practical experience of working with people. I also wondered if I—a Democrat in a strongly Republican county—could be the first Japanese-American to throw his hat in the political ring and stay in. Well, I did it and I won.

I got [to work on] all the human resource programs, including mental health, human problems, and government youth programs. The other commissioners didn't want them; dealing with low-income people, alcoholics, and minorities were headaches for them. I was glad to get them. I wanted to work with these people. I felt we ought to let their stories be heard, and I knew if we didn't listen, we wouldn't understand them. I worked hard. I knew everybody was watching me. I knew everybody throughout the state was watching. When someone referred to the Japanese as those "yellow bastards," I didn't let it bother me. I couldn't. All I could tell them is, "People are people; we're all part of each other."

As a commissioner, I stood firm. I wasn't wishy-washy. They always knew where I was coming from, and I stuck with my principles. And I'm grateful that when I got into the commission, I got to see things without blinders—because unless you get involved and take your blinders off, you'll never see the wider picture. And you won't be able to grow, to change. This can be a great country if we all learn that we need each other and must accept each other.

I often tell a story to young people. There's a fifteen-year-old boy, a smart aleck in the community, a know-it-all. You know that age. There is an eighty-five-year-old blind man [who is considered] a wise man living in the community as well. This young fellow thought he'd put something over on him. So he got a little bird and went to the old man and asked him, "Wise old man, you're the wisest man in the community. I've got a bird in my hand. Is it dead or alive?" The young fellow thought whatever the old man says will be wrong, because if he says the bird is alive, he will kill it; and if he says the bird is dead, he'll let it live. The wise old man said, "Son, the decision is in your hands."

EDWARD HASHIMOTO, 73, PHYSICIAN, PROFESSOR OF GROSS ANATOMY

Outspoken, playful, irreverent, Dr. Edward Ichiro Hashimoto had the reputation of living life on his own terms (or nearly so). Born in Salt Lake City on February 24, 1911, to Edward Daigoro Hashimoto and Lois H. Niiya Hashimoto, he was raised in his father's sizable shadow (Hashimoto senior was known as Daigoro Sama, or "Great Man," in the community).

Edward Ichiro, however, wasn't impaired by his father's stature. To the contrary, inspired by his father's achievements, he excelled: He was a student prodigy, graduating high school at the age of fifteen, college at eighteen, and Harvard Medical School at twenty-four. He joined the faculty at the University of Utah Medical School in 1937 and was professor of gross anatomy for more than forty years, receiving numerous "Distinguished Professor" awards.

Edward Hashimoto. *Kent Miles*

Dr. Hashimoto credited his legendary teaching acumen "to telling dirty stories." "I found out," he quipped, "that during slide lectures, ninety percent of the kids went to sleep when the lights were off. So [to keep them awake], I'd tell them a dirty story. The freshmen would be so shocked they'd go down and tell the dean, 'Dr. Hashimoto's telling dirty stories.' The dean would say, 'Don't worry, I had to take his class, too.' [Laughs] The key, of course, was that the stories helped them recall the anatomical points I was illustrating." [Chuckles]

My father's store was located at 163 West South Temple. The store to the east was the *Utah Nippo* [building], the local Japanese newspaper run by Mr. Terasawa. Just east of that was a secondhand store run by Spitzer. One hundred yards further, on the corner of West Temple and South Temple, the Bamberger Depot had lines going to Ogden. Its tracks ran behind our store.

Further west was a grocery store. In fact, two grocery stores were on that block. Going east, [there] was a small Japanese restaurant owned by Mr. and Mrs. Kanigae. Next to that, an alley led into an open courtyard surrounded by a rooming house—a two-story adobe building—where quite a few Japanese bachelors stayed. I don't remember the name of it now, but we used to practice judo and kendo in the hall.

All of this was actually one block south of Japanese Town, which was on First South. There they had more Japanese stores: a fish market, restaurants, the Rocky Mountain newspaper, several rooming houses, and another dry goods store, which rivaled my dad's.[13] For half a block, there was also a row of open-stall vegetable markets run primarily by Italians and Japanese. They even had a public bath on First South between Second and Third West, an area that was mostly fields and gullies. The public bath was oblong shaped, about ten feet by twenty [feet]—a pretty large place. We'd go [there] after a baseball or judo practice. You know how the Japanese take baths to relax. They take a little pan, soap, and a cloth, and they throw the water over themselves. Get everything as clean as possible. Then wash the soap off. Then they get into the bath. Naturally, they don't wash off, because they're already clean. It's the temperature that makes you look hot, like a red-legged lobster. It's really hot. There was a dividing partition for men on one side, women on the other. You'd carry your little towel with you if you wanted to cover yourself strategically, but we didn't bother as kids. We'd spend maybe ten minutes to scrub the dirt off, then sit around for a while. Later, we'd get a snack at the Pagoda restaurant, which was about half a block away. . . .

My father's full name was Edward Daigoro Hashimoto. He was born in Wakayama prefecture, the southernmost province on the Pacific side of Japan. As it was the Japanese custom for the eldest son to go out and earn a living, my father was invited by his uncle to come to America. He arrived in 1896 at the age of sixteen. He had no formal training and very little education except a Japanese high-school one. With his uncle, he started his American life in Seattle, where the Great Northern Western Railroad terminated, then moved to Los Angeles, Montana, and eventually Ogden and Salt Lake when the Denver and Rio Grande was being built as an eastern terminus for the Western Pacific.

His life was much more interesting than mine. He was sent out on the Great Northern railway as a cook. He didn't know anything about cooking. Once, they gave him a hundred-pound sack of flour and a ham to cook for the railroad workers in his little section gang. He made flour balls and cooked them in salt water, which doesn't sound very palatable. Since the ham was covered with mold (as all hams were in those days), he thought it had gone bad and gave it away to a tramp. Those poor workers had to subsist on a hundred pounds of flour for a month.

As far as telling us stories about his early years, Father rarely spoke of his adventures and was known as the Great Silent Hashimoto. He very rarely said anything [at all] except to grunt in the affirmative or the negative. [*Laughs*] At that time, though, . . . the railroad gangs were mostly Oriental—Chinese or Japanese—or Irish. And the cowboys in Montana didn't like these foreigners invading their country and putting the "iron monster" through their open plains. One time, some drunken cowboys came into railroad camp and shot it up, killing some of the laborers. Father escaped and hid out in the mountains. After a month of walking alone during the night and hiding out in the daytime, he walked about five hundred miles en route to Salt Lake City.

He studied a lot by himself. As a result, he became a better-educated man than most college graduates and an influential individual around here. He established the E. D. Hashimoto Company, a country store. I remember there was a big basement which had a warehouse. Essentially, all sorts of canned stuff were down there that would be sent out to the gangs on the railroad. He stocked rice, soy sauce, and other Japanese food. Upstairs, he had clothing—suits, overalls, shoes, socks, and underwear. I remember working during my high school days, loading hundred-pound sacks of rice and taking them down to the depot and shipping them out to various section gangs. I can't lift twenty-five pounds today.

But that was in the 1920s. Twenty years earlier, my father had been very instrumental in furnishing labor for the building of the Western Pacific Railroad. He contracted thousands of workers from Japan, arranged their transportation here, and set them out in gangs, consisting of maybe ten people, along the railroad so they could maintain the rails. He furnished them with food and clothing. The railroads paid him, and he, in turn, paid his laborers, who, for the privilege of coming to America, paid him a dollar a month. He had a lifetime pass on the Western Pacific Railway because of his job as a labor agent. He was a contractor and paymaster—the whole works. During the time the gangs worked, he had a steady income of one or two thousand dollars a month—all this in 1900!

Dad died at an early age, sixty, with diabetes. I remember he got the first insulin that came west of the Rockies. It wasn't too purified, and he had to be injected with it. And, as those days were hectic sometimes, if you got a little too much, why you'd wind up in the hospital in insulin shock. If you didn't have enough, you'd be in a coma. So I grew up at Holy Cross Hospital, since he was there half the time.

But he never let it slow him down. After the railroads were completed and up until his death, he was always busy doing something. He furnished the labor for Bingham Copper and the coal mines in Sunnyside, Price, and Helper. He was called a *mikado* [emperor] because everyone came to him for work and help. He was one of the starters of Tracy Loan Bank in Salt Lake and had his fingers in practically everything—getting a contract to furnish beets for Utah, Idaho, and Clearfield canneries; starting a colony of Japanese in Delta, Utah, to grow sugar beets; investing in silver and gold mines down in Chihuahua, Mexico; starting oil wells in the Casper oil fields in Wyoming; and investing in Gilsonite mines; and extracting oil from the enormous oil deposits in Vernal. During 1914, about the time of World War I, when the Japanese and Chinese labor ran out, he imported Mexicans and became the honorary consul general of Mexico in Utah and southern California.

He was fifty years ahead of his time, but always underfinanced. He'd get this idea, gallop off, and before he could get the thing rolling, why, the stupid thing would collapse because of lack of money. He was also called Boom or Bust Hashimoto. He'd be dead broke one year and rolling around in dough the next. [*Laughs*] I remember back in the '20s, before Redman started Western Airlines, my father got involved in growing fruits in Mexico and importing them into America. He put them on railroad cars. But when they had a strike, he lost all his money because the fruit spoiled. Everybody trusted him, though. He had maybe a thousand boys [young men who were laborers and sometimes students] that he knew he would always be welcomed by, and all the bosses were indebted to him. So he managed to scrape by.

Of course, he always had to battle against the fact that he was a foreigner, and, obviously, you can't change the color of your hair or the color of your skin. He had a chance to make a killing with a silver mine in Salmon, Idaho, but the natives burned it down one night.

When I was born, we had the second house on the block at 315 South Twelfth East. Our house was like most others. It wasn't Japanese style. In fact, my mother became very interested in Mormon antiques and decorated the house with them. We also had a radio with speakers; Baldwin invented a superior headset for radios, and Father received the rights to sell it overseas.

We grew up as a Christian family, but my father wasn't religious at all. My mother was brought up Episcopalian. She was rather religious and went to missionary school at Colby College. Mother helped build the Japanese Church of Christ downtown by going around to all of Dad's business associates and friends and collecting enough money to build that little church.

I was closer to my mother; my father was down at the office most of the time. He had friends, although I don't know how good they were. You know, when a person becomes influential, politicians gather around. The governor was a good friend; President Taft visited. Mother used to entertain a number of politicians in the front parlor—have big parties.

Between 1920 and 1927, since the Japanese were heavily involved in railroads, mines, and farming, the community was larger than it is now. In the state, there must have been about ten thousand Japanese workers and their families.

In Salt Lake, they also had Japanese schools, where they taught Japanese and where I probably became the best marble player in town who learned very little Japanese. The classes started right after school and ended at five o'clock, after which I went back to the store and came home to eat about six o'clock. There were usually one or two Japanese schoolboys from the university who taught at the school or worked around the store—doing handiwork, helping out, and looking after me, since I was usually hiding or in trouble.

Growing up, I had my Japanese friends through Japanese school, but none of my close friends lived in my vicinity. Since I lived in an all-white area, my neighborhood friends were all white. These were the ones I would pal around with, be in Boy Scouts with, or go to the shows with. But segregation and blatant separation were quite evident throughout the 1920s. And discrimination, when it occurred, was painful to bear. Once, when our Boy Scout troop went to swim at Wasatch Springs, a public swimming pool, the manager wouldn't let me swim. Well, the Boy Scout troop pulled out, and we went across the street to Crystal Springs. Another time, we went to the movies, and some of my white friends sat up with me in "nigger heaven," because I wasn't allowed to sit in the main lobby. I don't believe I went to any movies for a long time after that.

These things were painful, but they also made me very angry. You see, I didn't recognize I was Japanese until I looked into a mirror. My mentality and way of life were just as American as anybody else's. But I'm not exactly stupid, and I recognized a certain amount of difference between myself and the rest of the people. And I already knew I couldn't fight particular differences on a fair, equitable basis. "So," I thought, "well, damn them—if that's the way they feel about it, I'll beat them at their own game!"

As my few Japanese friends were going to college, I, too, naturally planned for college. And anybody knows a man who studies six hours a day will be better than a man who does one hour. So that's what I did. In the face of prejudice, I worked harder. Even in high school, every morning, I would say, "Come on, Hashimoto, you've got to put out a little bit more." And I did. I graduated from high school when I was fifteen and from the University of Utah in 1930, when I was still eighteen. In order to do that, to graduate in three years, I had to see President Thomas at the university who said, "What are you trying to do, Hashimoto, show up the white boys?" I said, "Yes, sir, and I'll do it."

At first, I thought about going into law but realized that even though my position might be respected, I am Japanese; and when it came down to the nitty-gritty of guilty or not guilty, my clients would lose out. Even my father lost several law suits simply because he was Japanese. I decided on medicine.

When the war broke out, I felt embarrassed, to say the least. I didn't have any ties with Japan other than my black hair and yellow skin. Still, I had to teach that day, and I was concerned about how the students would react. When I went before the class, they watched me nervously. I gave my usual lecture and then asked, "Why [are] you looking at me? I was born in Dublin." Right away, that cleared the air; and ever since, I've been known as the Irishman. I've always said, "Never lose your sense of humor. If you do, you'll end up in a deep depression."

During the war, my parents stayed with me. With the influx of Japanese from the West Coast, I was one of the busiest surgeons around. On the whole, I was under the wing of the university, and none of my colleagues at Holy Cross Hospital ostracized me. Educated people knew I had nothing to do with the war. My days passed fairly normally. I walked into the grocery stores and bought my groceries, and nobody bothered me. Nobody threw ashes on my front lawn or broke windows or smashed my car.

Of course, I wasn't on the West Coast, where there was a certain amount of hatred against the Japanese. Or in Hawaii, where it must have been worse. That's where the "Go for Broke" Japanese-American 442nd Battalion started and made a name for itself. The most decorated unit in the United States Army, they had the most fatalities and the most casualties, too.[14]

I remember one day, though, I was parked down near the water pumping station around Sixth South and Eleventh East. Some guy came up and knocked on the side of my car window. When I looked up, the damn fool was pointing a big .45 right at my head. It scared me to death. "You're in a forbidden zone, you blinkity-blink Jap! Are you trying to blow the place up?" This man was guarding the place, *on his own.* Also, some kids vandalized the [Japanese] cemetery. They shot at the tombstones with rifles and pushed some, like my uncle's, over.

On the West Coast, some Japanese tried to act like they were Chinamen, but they were invariably picked up by informers and thrown in the concentration camps. That's what they were, of course—concentration camps with barbed wire, guard towers, and searchlights. You couldn't call them anything else.

I was so angry, I said I would volunteer for the medical corps, but President Thomas said no way. I tried to resign from my teaching, but he said no way to that, too, and that my life would be on the line if I got captured. I was finally exempted from military service and spent my war years here, teaching and having a full medical life.

I never had a patient with any war hysteria or induced psychosis. The Japanese philosophy is one that acknowledges what will happen will happen, and there's not much you can do to change it, so we go on from here. They don't let themselves be eaten up by anger. They figure it is just the way the world turns. They lose everything and they begin again. My wife has no bad memories of the concentration camp or the internment. Of course, Japanese families like hers put their entire household [belongings] into government storage warehouses, their safety guaranteed by the government, only to return to find nothing there—nothing at all. But she doesn't feel vindictive about it. She has the philosophy of *Shikata Ga Nai*—it can't be helped.

Postscript: Dr. Hashimoto passed away at his home in Salt Lake City on August 23, 1987. He had lived in the house built by his father since birth.

JIM YOSHIO TAZOI, 65, FARMER

We spoke to Jim Tazoi in the kitchen of his childhood home, where he still lives. A modest, unassuming man, and a veteran of K-company, Third Battalion, 442nd Regimental Combat Team, Tazoi said he was shipped to Europe in 1944 just in time to fight in the "Rome-Arno" campaign. He also participated in three other major campaigns, which culminated in the now well-known Battle for the Lost Battalion.

On October 27, 1944, in northern France, in a battle that became emblematic of the 442nd's fighting spirit, the team, as described by author Chester Tanaka, "received orders to break the German ring surrounding the 'Lost Battalion' of the 141st Regiment, 36th [Texas] division." During the next five days, the unit "engaged in some of the

Jim Yoshio Tazoi.
George Janecek

war's bloodiest and fiercest fighting." The fighting was "hand-to-hand, head-to-head, tree-to-tree, an inferno of grenade and small arms fire."[15]

The 442nd incurred more casualties during this engagement than in any other European campaign. I and K companies were hardest hit. They suffered, respectively, ninety-five percent and ninety percent casualties. Tazoi was injured and awarded the Distinguished Service Cross (DSC), the second highest honor bestowed on a soldier by the army. "Eight of us got the DSC," he said. "But only me and another guy in K-company didn't get killed."

I was born right here in Garland, Utah, on August 28, 1919. My parents were from Kumamoto-ken. That's down in the southern end of Japan. My father came over as a young man [in] 1910, about the time a lot of young Japanese fellows were coming over. He came to Hawaii first, then San Francisco, then inland to Wyoming, and then to Utah. We used to have a sugar beet factory here, and they recruited stoop labor. That's the reason he came. He probably worked in the fields a while, then started renting ground and sharing rent, and eventually he bought our little farm here [in Garland].

I can remember—oh, over fifty years ago—we were living in a little place called Fielding before we [came back] to Garland. I started school there while we were farming on sugar factory ground. The factory owned a lot of ground, and they'd rent it out. The farmers had about thirty acres. It isn't much [by today's standards]. But in those days it was considered quite a bit of ground.

We farmed with horses then. We had no tractors, and most labor was hand labor. I remember my father cut irrigation ditches by hand. We didn't have beet toppers, we never had herbicides to control the weeds, and we had no way of leveling the ground. So, everything was hard. Our lifestyles were different, too. In those days, we stayed around home, and it seemed like all we did is either work or sleep. There wasn't much recreation.

But I have a lot of fond memories of Fielding. I started school there, and I don't think I spoke much English. In fact, since my folks only talked Japanese, I don't think I spoke any. But I made a lot of good friends, and eventually I got so I could talk a little. [*Laughs*]

After the seventh grade, we moved back to Garland. My parents had a chance to buy this little farm, and, of course, we continued raising beets. Everyone did. When we finished harvesting, we'd go over to the factory and process the beets in the winter. The sugar factory was a big thing in this valley. Sugar beets probably paid off more mortgages than any other single crop.

After high school, I went to the Utah State Agricultural College for two years. Then war clouds started hanging over [us], and the army wanted to draft people. They said [that] after serving one year, why, we could come home. So a lot of us decided to join the National Guard. I went in with the fellows in this area. There were over a hundred who went with the Guard.

We left here in March 1941 and were sent to Camp San Louis Obispo [in California]. Seven months later, the 7th of December, the war started. Most of the [Caucasian] guys ended up staying in the service for four or five years.

In our case, when they started evacuating Japanese off the coast [in 1942], they evacuated [Japanese-American] servicemen, too.

Since I was one of five Japanese fellows from Garland, they sent me to Texas, where I asked for a discharge. I wanted the discharge because I was the oldest boy. My elder sister [had] recently died, and my father was quite a bit older than my mother, and his health wasn't good. So I wanted to help him on the farm. The army let me out, but they didn't discharge me. They transferred me into the reserve. And that's where I was until they formed the all-Japanese unit—the 442nd—and I was recalled and sent for basic training in Camp Shelby [Mississippi].[16]

I remember a lot of the [Japanese] boys in Shelby were upset. Their families were evacuated and sent to concentration camps and held behind barbed-wire fences as if they were prisoners and enemies of the United States, and here they were volunteering for service. That wasn't easy.

I still remember, just before I got recalled, [the army] sent out a [loyalty] questionnaire. I'm not sure you're familiar with what I'm talking about. It's the same kind of questionnaire [used in the camps]—that "no-no, yes-yes" deal.[17] Well, when I got the letter, I couldn't communicate with my folks good enough to ask them about it. So, I remember, I sat back under a tree, and I think that was one of the hardest decisions I ever made. It wasn't that I wanted to be disloyal. I wanted to do *everything* I could for this country. Yet the wording of those questions made it real hard to answer. So I agonized over that for a long time. Finally, I wrote "yes-yes."

But a lot of those fellows [in camp] answered "no-no." [It was] not because they were disloyal. They were just mad at the government for giving them a few days' notice, then taking them out of their homes, putting them in concentration camps, and, *on top of that*, giving them that kind of questionnaire. Nobody felt good about that. Nobody could feel good about something like that.

Now, basic training wasn't too difficult. But I was lucky. I'm a country boy, and I was in good shape. A lot of town kids had it rough. We were in the infantry, and we went on twenty-five-mile marches with full field pack. And, gosh, I was five foot eight, and I was one of the bigger guys. Our average height—I read it somewhere—was about five feet four inches. Some men, quite a few, were even under that. The army must've relaxed their regulations, because they said nobody under five feet would be accepted.

We trained from October 1943 until March 1944; then, in April, we got the call to go overseas. We landed in Italy and went into combat right after the fall of Rome. I don't remember the names of all the campaigns now. But we fought on the Arno River, and after going through a part of Italy, we were sent to France. And all the way [up the peninsula], it was just old-fashioned, front-line fighting. The infantry are the front-line troops, so it was just a matter of slugging it out.

When I got wounded in France, the enemy was six feet away [in places].

We were in the mountains in northern France, trying to advance on them. They had a lot of advantages. They were sitting back, waiting for us. So we were just like sitting ducks. This particular battle was [called] "The Rescue of the Lost Battalion." There was about two hundred Texans trapped in that. And we suffered eight hundred casualties getting those guys out.

Now, the Lost Battalion wasn't really "lost"; we knew where they were. But the Germans had let these Texans in, then closed in behind them, cut them off. So they were trapped. I guess their situation was getting desperate, 'cause for two days the Second and Third battalions of the 141st Regiment made several attempts to reach them, but each time they were beaten back. Finally, we were given the orders to get them.

In most of our campaigns, we got support from the artillery. But, in this particular case, [where we were] advancing through a dense forest, the shells flew over the top of us or landed in our midst. Artillery support was almost useless. Those were two or three days of the fiercest fighting our outfit encountered in the entire war. A lot of time, we were shooting from the hip. These Germans were good soldiers. Many of them stayed put [as we advanced]. We couldn't hardly see them. They wore camouflaged uniforms, and we could come right up to them, within eight or ten feet, before they'd finally get up and run. Then we were shooting them from the back.

I remember, on the afternoon I got hit, I killed one particular German kid. As we were going up [the hill], it was real hard to see anybody. As we advanced, they didn't stand up and say, "Here I am." So, ten or fifteen minutes before I got hit, I come up on this little draw, where the rain had washed through this ditch. It was maybe a foot and a half deep. I just happened to come up to that place, stop, and kneel down to see if I could see anybody. I looked down, and right there beside me, in that creek, was a German soldier. He was hoping the first wave would go over. I'm sure he wanted to give up. But in the heat of the battle, you're not thinking of taking a prisoner. I mean, he was lying [beside me] right quiet. So I raised up my rifle, and when I did that, he let out a real scream. I still emptied four or five rounds into him.

If I had to do it over, I might think, "Gosh, he wants to give up." But then, that's the guy who seconds before was shooting at us. Besides, we couldn't afford anybody taking prisoners back to our lines. Because even one extra man up there [with you] gave you a lot of help.

Now, near the creek, there was a big fallen tree. Our artillery knocked it down. As we were approaching it, I thought there were German soldiers on the other side of it. And because there was so much shooting, I thought, well, one place is as good as another [to fight], so I started crawling over to the tree. But before I got over, why, I got shot through the chest with a machine gun. After they knocked me down, I guess I was lying there, groaning. So they started lobbing hand grenades just over the tree. I remember two or three grenades exploded around me. Finally, one exploded on top of me. But these were "potato mashers"—concussion grenades. If I was inside a house or a building, they might have killed me. But out in the open, it wasn't too bad. It just tore me up a little.

Now, I'm going tell you about an experience I had up there. I laid there for a while before the medics come up. I suppose I laid there a half hour, and all that time I could hear real pretty music. [I remember] I was just laying there listening to that, [thinking,] Gosh, that's funny, being up here in the mountains, listening to music. Then, I might have been dozing off. So, I thought, I better try to stay conscious all the time. Later, a doctor told me the bullet went through my chest within a fraction of an inch from my heart. In fact, he said the concussion of the bullet moved my heart over.

But that music was a kind of music I can't describe. I never heard it before. And being up at the top of the hill, I began wondering—when I come to— Gosh, what's wrong. Gosh, I better try to stay awake. I think I was pretty near gone.

The day I was injured we made contact with the Lost Battalion. But we really got roughed up in the process. The Third Battalion took the brunt of the attack. We had three battalions. They usually sent two battalions up and kept one in reserve. It so happened, I guess, that it was our turn to be up there. Our company had the normal strength of around two hundred men. We ended up with seventeen riflemen. All the officers were gone.

I spent eight months in the hospital, recuperating. The bullets also shattered my ribs, so they took some ribs out. When they cut you, it takes a long time for nerves to grow back. I still have a tingling sensation from it. I remember the doc telling me, "Well, it might grow back in your lifetime; it might not." So that's what happened. The 442nd suffered more casualties than any other battalion during the war. I'm not sure why. Maybe it was our pride. Some of our guys used to say, "We have more guts than brains." But that's not necessarily the case. Maybe when you're fighting, you don't like to be pushed back. Maybe that was it.[18]

After I recovered, they gave me my discharge, and I came home to Garland. But I kind of felt real bad. There was still quite a bit of prejudice. People would make remarks to you. I remember somebody telling me to "get off the street and go home," even when I had my uniform on. Just lately, even, I was someplace and people started talking about the war and somebody asked me if I was in the service. I said, "Yes, I was in the service." They wanted to know which side I fought on.

SACHIKO WADA SEKO, 57, WRITER

Sachiko "Sachi" Wada Seko did not conceal her role as community gadfly when she spoke with us. "I am very conscious of the unconventional pieces I've written, whether about family life or the camps," she said. "Other people didn't write about those things because they were uncomfortable topics. But I thought it was time to shatter the image of us being such a nice, bland, [polite] people."

The eldest of four children, Ms. Seko was born in Los Angeles, California, on August 2, 1927. Her family (including maternal grandparents) lived in Boyle Heights, the city's Japanese section, until 1939, then moved to Santa Maria, where they lived "until the evacuation." Like a number of Japanese-American families, hers was physically separated as a result of the WRA's loyalty questionnaire. Her grandparents, who voted "no-no" and requested repatriation, were moved from Gila, Arizona, to Tule Lake in 1944, then returned to Japan.

In 1945, the Wada family resettled in Salt Lake City, Utah, and bought the California Market, a small grocery store situated in the city's Japanese community. Ms. Seko reluctantly gave up her personal writing goals and helped sustain the family business for two decades. After her mother's death in 1970, however, she returned to journalism, and for the following twelve years she wrote a column for the Pacific Citizen *(the JACL national news organization) satirically titled "From Happy Valley."*

My father was a second son and, like most second sons, wasn't going to get anywhere by staying in Japan, so he came over to the United States to seek his fortune. I think he was sixteen years old at the time. My mother came with her mother, because her father was already here. Actually, my mother came to attend a women's college for Japanese immigrants in San Francisco. She must have been sixteen as well. My grandmother came to find out why her husband hadn't returned to Japan as promised. [She discovered] he had accrued a twenty thousand dollar gambling debt and there was no way he could return, so my grandmother decided to stay with him and help him pay it back.

I was born in Los Angeles—Boyle Heights—which, I later learned, was one of the centers of the city's Japanese community. We lived there from 1927 until 1939. We then moved to Santa Maria, California, until the evacuation. My mother was a pampered woman. Exceptionally beautiful and very bright. One of the brightest women I've ever known. When I was an infant, my mother would nurse me and read Shakespeare out loud. I liked to nurse, but now I loathe Shakespeare because that's what she breastfed me on. [*Laughs*] My first words were "*Chi chi boko nana*"; *chi chi* means breastfeed, *boko* is book. My grandmother said I talked by the age of one, and I know it was all Shakespeare, because that's all I heard—I mean, bits of Shakespeare being quoted all the time—up until my mother died. In Japanese, yet! [*Laughs*]

My grandparents lived with us from the moment I was born. My grandmother only cooked Japanese food and did all the cooking. She was a great cook. My mother mostly read and wrote—she was a prolific writer—or would go chasing off with her friends. In the concentration camp, she was named "Poet Laureate" because of her haiku. After the war, she volunteered as the community letter writer for other people [in Salt Lake] and got to know many people in Japan without ever meeting them face-to-face. She never accepted money for doing this. But people would repay her with vegetables, and that she would accept. She also arranged funerals for people, and on Thanksgiving we always ate late, because she was so busy fixing trays of food for people who didn't have families or were poor or sick. The war took everything away from us. But I think it was a great equalizer. It taught some people like my mother [to have] great compassion.

I was never really close to my father and never really knew him, even though we all lived in the same house. He was a timid, servile man. At the produce market where he worked, if he carried something out for a white man, he would "Sir" him all the time. If the man told him *not* to "Sir" him, he was appalled rather than complimented. And he was afraid of everything: poor health, depression, sugar shortages, muggings, the FBI, you name it. There's a term for it: *Ki gachi sai*, meaning small hearted. He was like that. When we moved to Santa Maria, he chose to stay in Los Angeles and come home for holidays and weekends. We didn't mind. He was sort of like a black cloud [over our lives]. We didn't have the same admiration or respect for him [as] we had for our grandfather.

My grandfather was the patriarch of the family. He was my hero. In my eyes, he was an unusual man and as large as God, probably. He was a treasure to us. When he wasn't working, he'd take us to the parks. He'd make us wagons and kites and cages for our guinea pigs and rabbits. He epitomized masculinity to me. We felt almost invincible because we had a grandfather like him. When we were young, we'd bring our friends into the house and say, "Do you want to see our grandfather?" Isn't that silly? But we did. "There's our grandfather, over there," we'd say.

My father had a loud laugh and was garrulous. But that doesn't denote a sense of humor. Grandfather was gracious, more of a listener than a talker. You don't have to talk a lot to be gracious. He was also meticulous. Everyone who knew him concurred there was never another man quite like him. During the Depression, relatives say he would come to Utah unannounced and show up at their homes carrying sacks of rice. Without his help, some of these families could not have survived.

My grandfather ran the household. My parents were both bilingual—having attended schools here—but out of respect for my grandparents, we always used Japanese in the house. A very formal Japanese. We [children] didn't go flying out of the house, like my son later did, and say, "Bye, Mom! See you!" It was always "*Iti maeri masu*," we'll be leaving. When we came home, it was always "*Tadaima*," I've returned. In the morning, we always said, "*Ohayo gozaimasu*" [good morning] to our grandparents, and we always bowed. Then we got dressed and ready for breakfast. At breakfast, my brother would be served first, because he was the male child. I would be served next, because I was the oldest female child, and so on down the line.

You know, many Japanese men came here to escape the draft, not just to seek their fortune. My grandfather could not tolerate this type of immigrant. At affairs such as weddings, or after funerals, when people gathered and sang nationalistic songs, praising the emperor, my grandfather would sit with the most contemptuous expression on his face, because he knew damn well why they were here; whereas, he had served his time. My grandfather was truly the emperor's man. The army had contoured him so that even after forty years he was still an army man. That discipline, that walk, the household rituals [were unmistakable], which is why on the day of Pearl Harbor, he said, "I'm going to ask for repatriation"—and he did.

This is not to say that my grandfather was an ultranationalist—far from it!

He never expressed negative sentiment about American life. Referring to Anglos, he never used the derogatory term "*Keto*," the hairy ones. It's almost as bad as saying Nigger or Jap. Although I heard most immigrants, including my father, use it, my grandfather never did. He always bore in mind that we—his grandchildren—were Americans. This was our future. We would have to survive in this society, entirely separate from him. So there was considerable restraint and understanding in addition to his dignity and resolve.

I recall the night he told us he wanted to be repatriated. It was the evening of December 7th. We were sitting around the dining room table, talking and eating oranges, as we always did after dinner. He said he was returning to Japan as a matter of personal honor and loyalty—not out of military zeal or to help in the war effort. He actually believed Japan would lose the war. At the time, many people, claiming loyalty to Japan in their hearts, planned to go back if Japan was victorious. He simply believed you went where you belonged. He said, "No matter how your country fares, you still return to your country in time of war." Then he said a curious thing [to me]: "Twice it will happen in your lifetime. You will be caught in between cultures. Now and once again, at some later time, and you will have to endure it." He was right.

Now, most Americans talk as if Pearl Harbor happened on December 7th, and they were all shocked out of their wits. That wasn't true. People saw the war coming for months. What was stunning, though, was the actual attack. I mean, I don't think anyone thought we would become involved in a war right here on American soil.

I remember my mother and I were in a Greyhound station, on our way back to Santa Maria, when the attack was announced. We caught our bus around noon, and that was the most eerie bus trip I ever made. People didn't attack us or make any derogatory remarks. They just looked at us in silence. Everyone was stunned. We reached the Santa Maria Depot and nothing happened. And then Monday, when we went to school, things started to change.

The other thing that stunned us, of course, was the evacuation. I didn't believe it would occur. I thought the churches would rescue us. I really did. We *all* did. In our hearts, even with the luggage packed, we thought there would be a reprieve. [The idea of evacuation] was a nightmare, you see, that you thought was not going to pass. We all evacuated together and went to the camps by train, which is why I can't stand the sound of trains even today. Every time I hear the click-click-click-click of the wheels, I think about that exodus and the feeling of being estranged from mainstream America.

Actually, at first, we went to Tulare [Assembly Center], which at least meant we were still in California.[19] But when we got on the train again, going far, far away from home, a feeling of separation, of desolation came over us. The MPs [military police] on the trains were armed. All the [window] shades were drawn, and all you could do was peek out into unknown. It was hot, miserable. Everyone ate lunch and collected money to tip the black porters, who were very kind to us. That would be the last fancy meal we would have for three and a half years. The trip itself must have taken at least twenty-four hours, because I remember waking up and seeing the brightness outside. It was late afternoon when we reached Gila, got off the train, were placed in army trucks, and hauled to the camp.

At the time, I don't think you stopped to think, why is this happening to me. I don't think those kinds of deeper questions impacted you until after you were inside an internment camp and you realized you were not going to leave this place for a long, long time. And you didn't know what the consequences of being there were going to be. I remember, when we walked into the concentration camp, my grandfather told us to walk straight, walk proudly, keep our dignity, and not let the people gawking at us know how we feel.

In Gila, we were assigned to one room in a barrack. At least that was better than the horse stable in Tulare. Someone dropped our baggage off. Then people said we had to form lines to eat at the mess halls. They showed us where the latrines were. I don't remember anyone breaking down, so it surprises me when I see these [documentary] photographs of Issei women dabbing at their eyes. Maybe our group was more stoic, more resigned. I don't think there was any show of anger, either. Just resignation.

After a few days, everyone started building. My grandfather was good with his hands. He discovered piles of scrap lumber at the end of our block. He dragged pieces back and made partitions, so we would have privacy between the cots. He made frames, too. We had cloth, and so we covered the frames. Then he made a table and a sofa. Grandmother made the cushions.

It's a funny thing, but when the War Relocation Authority brought in distinguished guests to investigate or examine the camps, they would ask us if we would be willing to show our particular barrack section as a model.[20] Our place did look quite livable. My grandfather dug out ironwood from the desert dirt and polished it. My mother made paper flowers and put them in floral arrangements. But our barrack was nice because of my grandfather's handiwork. It was not a typical room. The [visitors] should have been taken to the more ordinary barracks. Then they would have noticed how sad things really were.

You see, everyone's life was really deranged by being in these camps. I mean, stuck away like that, I don't care what people say, you develop a reservation mentality, like the Indians. Things lose their luster. Things are not acute. I mean, there were crises when everything was sharp and the images were bright. But, in general, you sat there in the camp and you went through [only] the motions of living, because the future was not within your grasp. You couldn't visualize it clearly. You had no real time. Your roots were gone. So you acquired this mentality where the days and the months blended together. Time just went. You were not occupied with the projects of the future.

Structurally, the top portions of the barracks [between the partitions and the ceiling] were open. There was never any privacy. You heard neighbors talking or quarreling. You heard children yelling or crying. At any time of the day, sounds penetrated the entire dwelling. Some people never got to see the out-side beyond the fence. You made do with clothes or you acquired them through a catalog. You didn't see shops, cars, traffic signals, people of different colors—all these things were no longer part of your life.

People tried keeping busy. The women made their paper flowers; but how long can you make flowers? It's not a longtime deal. You ate your meals in the barracks, so you didn't even plan ahead to the next festivity. You didn't have such an option. Your options were gone. It was awful.

Yet, let me emphasize, harrowing as this sounds, if someone asked me today what happened in the camps that to this day remains a source of mental anguish for the Japanese-Americans, I wouldn't refer to any of this. I'd have to say the most divisive and decisive issue in the camp was the loyalty issue. The issue did not come to a formal head until the WRA introduced the questionnaire [in 1943]. Once they did, though, even the most mellow camp was torn apart. People stopped speaking to each other; they terminated old friendships; many men were savagely beaten up.[21]

I'm referring now to the "no-no," "yes-yes" issue. Okay, you've heard about the 442nd and the wonderful job they did, making America more receptive to all of us because they shed their blood in Europe. They were the "Yes-Yes" boys. But have you heard of those who went to prison for us? Those were the "No-No" boys, who decided they would *not* bear arms for the United States until the United States returned their constitutional rights. They were our unsung heroes, as far as I'm concerned.[22] They were not threats. They would never have lifted a hand against the United States, nor would they have aided someone else lifting a hand against the United States. They went to prison to emphasize we did not have our constitutional rights, and they've been reviled and ostracized in our community ever since. Some of them today are still so fearful [of criticism], they will not divulge their names.

I went on record in their behalf in 1978, because when the national JACL convention was held in Salt Lake City that year, a local JACL leader wrote a series of articles welcoming the delegation and lauding the strong points of Japanese-Americans. He emphasized how wonderful the 442nd was. At the same time—thirty-five years after the war—he made a slur about the "No-No" boys, calling them "the unthinking camp rabble-rousers." So I wrote a rebuttal.

I said, I remember no individual who was "unthinking" during that crucial period. In my perception, those who protested [the draft] were no less devoted to this country than those who volunteered. Consistent with American tradition, the "No-No" boys were willing to test the strength of the United States Constitution by going to prison. They were saying equal rights for equal responsibility, that people who are pent up and deprived of their constitutional rights should *not* be asked to bear arms.

The piece caused a furor. I didn't mind. [Despite the JACL's insistence] I don't think we can decide who among us was "most" American. What can be agreed upon is that we were all victims of a grave injustice. In the article, I recall[ed] a woman in our camp who went mad during the administering of the loyalty questionnaire. I still remember her name. She stood outside our barrack one day and just started screaming. It was during lunch hour, and it was well over a hundred degrees. But I remember shivering because I had never heard such an anguished sound before. Her scream wasn't quite human or quite animal. It was something in between. That's the only way I can describe it. I remember she just stood on her barrack's step and screamed, and no one tried to stop her, because all of us felt like doing that. Internally, we were all screaming [at the time]. But she was doing it for us.

And to me, this is the real legacy of the camps! It is not just the discomfort and dislocation caused by the evacuation. And, hopefully, the time is arriving when we in the [Japanese] community can realize this and start to heal this pain. We can begin, I believe, by showing some understanding or appreciation for those who fought and paid for American convictions in differing ways. They, too, are entitled to the human dignity we profess to be the right of every individual.[23]

EPILOGUE

TOARU ISHIYAMA, 62, SUPERINTENDENT, OHIO DEPARTMENT OF MENTAL HEALTH RESEARCH CENTER

A passionate, ebullient man, Dr. Ishiyama sat for our interview after delivering a paper at the National Redress Conference held at the University of Utah in 1983. The conference was held in Salt Lake City, the conference organizers wrote, because the city was "an important crossroad in the history of relocation: the wartime home of the National Japanese American Citizens League, the site of a small community of Japanese-Americans, and a point of transition for many who were held at . . . Topaz."[24]

Dr. Ishiyama was invited to present his recollections of Topaz at the conference and to lead a group of evacuees on a pilgrimage to the site of the camp. "The major experience I had at the conference was going to the camp," he confided to us. "I was supposed to say a few words by the small monument they erected [at the camp's entrance]. I started to say, 'We lived here for two years,' and that's all I could get out. I just broke down [and wept]. The moment freed me, though. I could see it moved the others as well. It was a public catharsis for us."

One of four children, Dr. Ishiyama was a freshman attending the University of California when his family was evacuated. After spending two years in Topaz, he served in the medical corps of the U.S. Army attached to the 349th Regiment of the Eighty-eighth Division in Italy. Upon his release, he enrolled at Western Reserve

University in Cleveland, Ohio, where he completed his doctoral course work in clinical psychology in 1958. Between 1952 and 1972, he was chief psychologist and chief program developer at the Cleveland State Hospital. He later also served as special assistant to the state director of mental health and the regional director of mental health for the City of Cleveland.

My name is Toaru Ishiyama, which literally means "rock mountain" or, as they say in German, "Steinburg." I was born in Stockton, California, on July 1, 1921, and I now live in Parma, Ohio, which is a suburb of Cleveland. [Before we get under way] I'm going to give you a qualifying statement. All the controversy about who did what to whom and when—like what the JACL did or didn't do—may have been an important issue [for others]. It wasn't for me. My experience is personal.

When the war broke out on December 7 [1941], we were living in Alameda, and it quickly became a scary time [for us], because we had blackouts at night, and newspapers talked about submarines shelling the Monterey coast and the Japanese sending bombers over. My chronology is fuzzy here, but I think in February 1942 the military indicated [California would be divided into military] Zones A and B. We were in Zone A, which meant [that by a certain date] all noncitizen Japanese had to voluntarily leave the zone.[25] So my mother left for a place called Centerville, about thirty to forty miles southeast of Alameda, just outside the restricted zone.

I was a citizen. I had just started going to the University of California, so my feeling—before they shipped us [to the assembly center]—was hopeful: they're not going to do anything like this to me. My mother, she was an alien—so I understood [asking her to move]. It was dumb, but at least it was legal. But they can't do it to me, I thought. So when, some months later, the decision was made to put *everybody*—citizen and noncitizen—into assembly centers, it felt just like rape. And the correct analogy *is* rape, because when it happened, I couldn't believe it. I said to myself, "Why is this happening to me? It *shouldn't happen*," and all that.

Then, in order to survive, you realize you've got to accommodate. I didn't see myself picking up a gun and going after the United States government, so I did [accommodate]. You can use all kinds of words like repression to describe [accommodation], but the point is [that] you decrease the power of that emotion. You numb it out.

Generally speaking, the Issei did the same thing using the old Japanese attitude *"shikata ga nai,"* which means "it can't be helped." When you're poor, when you're oppressed, there's the saying, "You can't fight fate." And this is what happened. [I remember] my mother relayed that one of the community elders said, "We've got to go. It's a matter of survival." So we packed and went.

Don't forget, too, most of the older Japanese were Issei, and back in the old country, they were the peasants, the oppressed. The survival of the peasant has been a [popular] theme in recent Japanese movies. But there's no question they *were* survivors. And they were survivors not because they got all excited about what son of a bitch [landowner] was going to come and cut off their hands. They were survivors because they were like the soil—they were strong, and they didn't strike back. I'm not suggesting that was characteristic of everybody, but that was the *gombaru*, the mode. It meant, "Dish out everything you can. I'll beat you by taking it. One day you're going to find out you can't beat me. Even if you thought you beat me, [you'll realize] you ain't got me beat, because I'm still here." And that's the victory. So there was little resistance.

We reported to Tanforan Assembly Center in May 1942. Then, four months later, we were one of the first groups shipped to Topaz. By the way, physically, Tanforan was much worse than Topaz. [In Tanforan] four of us lived in a horse stall. Everybody did, and everybody joked about it. We said, "This is where Sea Biscuit [a legendary race horse] stayed." We all claimed his stall was our stall. Then funny things happened. Like there used to be a bright light that floated up [from the ground]. My mother called it a fireball, which in the old Japanese culture meant ghost. But it turned out simply to be the phosphorus in the manure. So that was a miserable place. Topaz was better, because at least you didn't have the stench of manure.

Curiously, people talk about the onslaught of feeling upon seeing the [concentration] camps. But for me, after the initial onslaught [of Tanforan], everything else followed. I mean, you have all kinds of reactions to an event like this, but [in time] they all become an extension of the first rape. I remember, on the train [to Topaz], the shades were drawn. They told us, "You've got to leave the shades down." Well, we were traveling through the Sierra Nevadas with their beautiful pine trees. And I'd never seen the Sierra Nevadas before! [I thought] what beautiful scenery with the snow and all! But we *had* to keep the shades down.

Then, it occurred to me: This is a death train, a funeral train. That's what it is. We are all in the hearse. We are not going to die, but we are dead. And anything after that is nothing. So entering Topaz is nothing. It's like jumping into [cold] water. The first time you jump in is dramatic. But [afterward], you simply move from one part of the water to another, and it's all water. In other words, once you establish the milieu, that you're a prisoner, going from one jail cell to another cell is not a big thing. It's another cell. It may be dirty, so you clean it up. And you've got to find out where the sink is—that sort of practical coping. But it's no big deal. It really isn't.

I'm saying, for me, the first time I was put in jail, *that* was a trauma. After that, being transferred from one jail to another and the mode of transfer were all consistent with the original definition: *You're no damn good.* So, for me, the camp was just another obstacle I had to deal with. There's sand—okay, there's sand. There's lots of wind—okay, there's lots of wind. It's hotter than hell—okay, it's hotter than hell. Once the original definition is made and it doesn't kill you, then everything else is consistent. And you adapt.

We see this in our society even now. When somebody defines you as worthless, you kind of stop looking ahead. The definition closes you up, and you go, "What the hell, I'll enjoy myself. Screw the others." What you do [especially if you're young] is become pleasure seeking. You go with whatever is. You drift. You don't say. "I've got to do these things in order to get there." That's gone. You don't know whether there is a "there."

It's too bad nobody ever did a systematic study of what happened to the camp kids. I reviewed the psychological and sociological literature from the 1940s and found practically nothing, except for a piece in an educational journal written by a Caucasian teacher who taught in camp for a couple of years. She observed that the kids progressively [learned] not to look forward to anything. In the early months, they still had a lot of drive to do well. But, later, they no longer had "ambition." That's the word she used. You hear the same thing about the ghetto.

Now, [the big question is] how do you come to terms with all this? I'll tell you what happened to me. I was in the service, and because of the GI Bill, I started back to school [after the war]. Originally, I wanted to go into medicine. But I thought, "That's going to take too long." So I decided to go into business. I spent three years as an accounting major, in fact. Then it occurred to me, "First, I hate this; second, what am I doing in business?" We're talking about the '50s now. "What company is going to hire me? They want white dudes." Thirty years ago, it wasn't popular to hire minorities.

So I looked at psychology. I was taking it as a minor, and the people [in it] seemed liberal. So I decided *that's* what I'm going to do! All right, one of the things that happened with clinical psychology was you need [to go into] didactic therapy. That's part of your course work. The whole notion was that unless you are involved in therapy yourself, you can't adequately treat others. If you don't understand yourself, you begin to project your problems onto the client. My therapist was Jewish. He understood the whole dynamic of incarceration from the Jewish [war] experience. So the whole atmosphere of this program encouraged me to become introspective.

Well, what happened was that I had a psychotic break. It wasn't a typical psychotic break. I call it "my psychotic break." I couldn't sleep. Free-floating anxiety was coming up. That's what I called it. I thought, "My nerves are just shaky." My mind was clear. At night, I'd say to myself, "Boy, if only I could sleep, I'd feel so much better." But my mind kept working, working.

What emerged, what the therapist said was coming out, was anger. So we worked on [understanding] this anger. And, after a month, I started sleeping in fits and starts. Then [the anxiety] subsided. It subsided because I gained some control of what "it" was. What it was was crying. I would cry, for no [apparent] reason. I mean, I'd just be there just crying away [saying], "Oh, my god! Oh, my god!" Whether I had any concept or idea tied to the crying didn't make any difference—I just cried.

By the way, I grew up believing "Boys don't cry." I got smashed in the head, got beat up, I never cried. My mother would say, "See, our son never cries." The old warrior bit. Anyway, there I was, crying. Then it occurred to me: When you get assaulted as a kid, you cry. If you stop crying, you're in trouble. So I recognized my anger [over the evacuation], but I realized it was anger combined with anguish. It was kind of—*God, damn it, you betrayed me!* The anger was really tied to what I call a tear. I learned if you handle your tear, then you can handle your anger. If you don't, you can't. This is why we have so many [Japanese-American] people who are [still] angry. Simply expressing their anger does not get them over it. Because behind the anger is a tear.

Now, you might ask what am I doing at this conference? Well, [to effect social change] you've got to tie your head and your emotions together. So when I say [to myself], "You sons of bitches, you really screwed us and I just can't passively take it anymore," my head responds with, "All right, let's do something about it." So I feel good getting involved in this kind of thing, even though I know it doesn't really work here [in the heart]. Some of us are deluded into thinking once we get some redress money, we'll feel cleansed. I don't think that; I don't expect any money from the government. It really doesn't matter anyway. The money is the icing on the cake. I want to get the cake itself.

What is the cake? The cake is the admission on the part of our government—that elusive entity—that what happened in 1942 was an abomination, and there is an increasing understanding that it should never . . . that, perhaps, I say this tongue in cheek, it will never happen again.

Postscript: In the winter of 1982, the Commission on Wartime Relocation and Internment of Civilians published the results of its congressionally mandated two-year study into "the facts and circumstances surrounding Executive Order 9066" and the impact of the executive order on American citizens and permanent resident aliens.

The commission found that "the promulgation of Executive Order 9066 . . . and the decisions which followed from it were not driven by analysis of military conditions. The broad historical causes that shaped these decisions were race prejudice, war hysteria, and a failure of political leadership." The commission concluded that "a grave injustice was done to American citizens and resident aliens of Japanese ancestry, who, without individual review or any . . . evidence against them, were excluded, removed and detained by the United States during World War II." It recommended a presidential apology and reparations.

Six months after issuing this initial report the commission reconvened and clarified what it meant by an apology and reparations. In addition to calling for "a formal apology by Congress" and "presidential pardons for persons who had run afoul of the law while resisting the wartime restraints placed upon Japanese Americans," the commission recommended "a one time, tax free payment of $20,000 to each Japanese American survivor who had been incarcerated during World War II." Although Congress regarded the recommendations favorably, it took five years of legislative maneuvering to pass a bill that both houses approved by veto-proof margins. On August 10, 1988, "in a signing ceremony in the Old Executive Office Building in Washington D.C.," President Ronald Reagan made the bill the law of the land.[26]

NOTES

1. This and the other Issei interviews were conducted in Japanese and were translated into English by Dorcas Nakao.

2. "Ken" is a state or prefecture in Japan, and "Gun" is a county or a rural district within the state.

3. "Go" is a Japanese game that most closely resembles chess.

4. Immigrants from Japan are called Issei, from the combination of the Japanese words for "one" and "generation"; their children, the American-born second generation, are Nisei.

5. Japanese emigrating to the United States after 1885 were prevented from becoming citizens by the Naturalization Act of 1870. This act restricted eligibility for citizenship to "free white persons" and "aliens of African Nativity and persons of African descent." The Chinese Exclusion Act of 1882, believed to apply to all Oriental groups, reinforced the stricture.

Ozawa Takao, a veteran of World War I, contested the restriction by filing for naturalization in 1914. "Though the Japanese were definitely not of African descent," wrote historian Yuji Ichioka, "the question of whether they might be classified as so-called free white persons remained an open one."

Over eight long years, the case made its way to the U.S. Supreme Court. In 1922, the Court dispelled any doubt by ruling that Ozawa Takao was "neither a free white person nor an African by birth or descent" and consequently "was not eligible to citizenship." The verdict sealed the fate of the Issei until the McCarran-Walter Act of 1952 "abolished the category of aliens ineligible for citizenship," permitting Issei to become naturalized citizens of the United States. R. A. Easterlin, David Ward, Williams S. Bernard, and Reed Ueda, *Immigration: Dimensions of Ethnicity* (Cambridge, Mass.: The Belknap Press of the Harvard University Press, 1982), 87–103; also, Yuji Ichioka, *The Issei: The World of the First Generation Japanese Immigrants, 1885–1924* (New York: The Free Press, 1988), 210–226.

6. E. Daigoro Hashimoto (Dr. Hashimoto's father) was considered one of two "major [labor] contractors" who operated in the Rocky Mountain region at the turn of the twentieth century. An employee of the Oriental Trading Company in Seattle, Washington, he secured "an independent labor contract with the Denver and Rio Grande Railway [in 1900] and established himself in Salt Lake City," where he became the owner and operator of the E. D. Hashimoto Company. He subsequently supplied Japanese track labor to the San Pedro, Los Angeles, and Salt Lake City railways. He also provided food and clothing to Utah section hands.

The "Labor-Contracting System," as historians have called it, thrived until the 1908 Gentlemen's Agreement barred the further entry of Japanese laborers into the United States. At the height of the system (1900–1907), when thirteen to fourteen thousand men were working as section hands in the western states, major contractors like Hashimoto, "whose income came from fees assessed on the wages of laborers," earned several thousand dollars a month. Japanese immigrant sources have commonly referred to the contractors as "kings" who were the objects of envy of common laborers. Ichioka, *The Issei*, 57–82.

7. In the two decades following the passage of the Chinese Exclusion Act of 1882, West Coast "exclusionists" directed their lobbying efforts at eradicating the growing "Japanese menace." Their initial activities resulted in the 1908 Gentlemen's Agreement with Japan by which Japanese laborers were barred from entering the United States and "the Japanese government pledged to issue passports [only] to . . . parents, wives, and children of . . . residents."

Assuming this agreement would halt all Japanese emigration, the exclusionists felt "betrayed" by the steadily growing Issei population. In 1919, consequently, they "attacked the picture-bride practice," alleging it violated the Gentlemen's Agreement because "female laborers were entering the United States under the guise of being 'homemakers.'" Fearing an ugly incident, the Japanese Foreign Ministry capitulated and unilaterally decided to "cease issuing passports to picture brides effective March 1, 1920." In 1924, the U.S. Congress also capitulated to West Coast pressure, passing the Immigration Act of 1924, which barred from entry all "aliens ineligible for citizenship." Ichioka, *The Issei*, 173–175.

8. The Japanese Association of America was established in 1908 by the Japanese consulate and Issei community leaders for two reasons: (1) to fight the growth of anti-Japanese sentiment in the United States and (2) to help the Japanese government fulfill its obligation under the Gentleman's Agreement by issuing "residency certificates" to Issei already settled in the country, allowing them to journey to Japan and return "alone or accompanied by spouse, children, and/or parents." Over time, as Issei women arrived and started families, local association activities broadened to support Issei settlement and community development. Associations typically provided translators and legal counsel and sponsored annual festivals, picnics, and youth programs. Following the bombing of Pearl Harbor, the FBI arrested the organization's leaders, effectively dismantling the association. Most of those leaders, men in their fifties and sixties at the time, were confined in special internment camps for the duration of the war. Ichioka, *The Issei*, 156–184.

9. Sociologist Harry Kitano suggested that the Japanese American Citizens League can be thought of "as a second-generation counterpart to the Japanese Associations." He noted, "It was first begun early in the 1920s by Nisei, who felt their interests were not served by the Japanese Association." Local groups, such as the Loyalty League in Fresno and the Rei Nei Kwai in Utah, were established, and by 1930, these local groups had consolidated into a national organization (the JACL) supported by local chapters.

The primary importance of the JACL, Kitano explained, was its role in accelerating the "acculturation" of the Nisei. The organization was modeled after American groups rather than traditional Issei groups. Compared to organizations representing other minority groups, the JACL appears especially similar to the NAACP. Both organizations "stand ready to protect and aid" their respective ethnic groups and both rely on "predominantly accommodative strategies." Harry H.L. Kitano, *Japanese Americans: The Evolution of a Subculture* (Englewood Cliffs, N.J.: Prentice Hall, 1969), 82–84.

10. Like its national model, the Salt Lake chapter of the JACL emerged out of the desire of the Nisei to form an organization that articulated their concerns. "What happened," recounted Shake Ushio, one of the founding members of the Utah chapter, "is that in the late 1920s the Nisei on the coast, who were older than us, became aware of discrimination and prejudice as they became adults. They also became aware of the fact that America and Japan were running on a dangerous confrontation course, which was going to affect us. There were many [Nisei] organizations on the coast, but by 1930 all Nisei energies went into JACL because the overriding necessity was to organize to meet the threat of a further diminishing of our rights." Personal interview, Shake Ushio, Oral History Institute, June 21, 1984.

The national JACL held its founding convention in Seattle in the summer of 1930. In 1935, a Utah chapter was formed. Organizational minutes list Inouye as a founding chapter member. His board membership and involvement have continued throughout his adult life.

11. On December 7, 1941, President Franklin D. Roosevelt issued Proclamation No. 2525 giving law enforcement personnel the authority to secure areas by restrain-

ing "alien enemies." The proclamation also stated that "no alien enemy shall have" weapons, short-wave radios, signal devices, cameras, or documents intended for use in combat against the United States. On March 24, 1942, a curfew was added, requiring all alien Japanese and all persons of Japanese ancestry to be in their homes between eight P.M. and six A.M. Roger Daniels, *The Decision to Relocate the Japanese Americans* (New York: Lippincott, 1975), 61-64, 124-126.

12. The Sweetheart Celery, or white celery, was introduced to the Utah market by the Japanese farmers. "And it was a very touchy crop to grow," explained Jim Matsumori. "You'd plant early from seed and harvest late. It took a lot of risk and a lot of patience, and it finally didn't make economic sense. But, at one time, Utah used to have what they called a celery week, and, for promotion, ZCMI would gift wrap two or three bunches in a box and send [them] all over the world. White celery was only grown here, and the reason it was so unique is that it took the cold, freezing weather to make the white celery crisp and tasty and sweet." Personal interview, Jim Matsumori, Murray, Utah, Oral History Institute, August 14, 1984.

13. The *Rocky Mountain Times* began a triweekly publication in Salt Lake City in 1907. Seven years later the *Utah Nippo* (the *Utah Daily*) began to be published. It later supplanted the *Rocky Mountain Times* and was published until 1991.

14. The all-Nisei 442nd Regimental Combat Team (also known as the "Go for Broke" outfit) was established on January 1, 1943, after a prolonged struggle within the War Department. The Western Defense Command, which engineered the evacuation of Japanese from the West Coast, fought against the combat team, claiming that Nisei soldiers would undermine West Coast security. But Assistant Secretary of War John L. McCloy and the commander of armed forces in Hawaii, Lieutenant General Delos C. Emmons, believed the majority of the Nisei were loyal and deserved the opportunity to prove it.

On February 1, 1943, consequently, the Selective Service Board, which had classified all Nisei IV-C, or "Enemy Alien," after Pearl Harbor, received orders to rescind that classification. In the following months, approximately three thousand Hawaiian and fifteen hundred mainland Nisei (most from the camps) volunteered for the 442nd Combat Team. The valor and fighting spirit of these soldiers are today legendary. The 442nd fought in seven major campaigns in Italy, France, and Germany. In addition to being the most decorated unit in army history, it suffered more casualties than any other unit of its size during the war.

15. Chester Tanaka, *Go for Broke: A Pictorial History of the Japanese American 100th Infantry Battalion and the 442nd Regimental Combat Team* (Richmond, Calif.: Go for Broke Inc., 1982), 90–99.

16. "The Army's decision [to form the 442nd Combat Team and] to use Japanese-Americans as combat troops," wrote historian Roger Daniels, "marks a turning point in the history of the relocation and of Japanese Americans. From the time of Pearl Harbor until September 1943, repression was generally intensified; from September 1943 on, although there were many setbacks, a general liberalization took place." Roger Daniels, *Concentration Camps USA: Japanese-Americans and World War II* (Hinsdale, Ill.: The Dryden Press, 1971), 151.

17. The "loyalty review program," or loyalty questionnaire, was initially created by the War Department in February 1943 as a vehicle by which Nisei could leave the camps and join the armed forces. Searching for a politically responsible way to release evacuees, the War Relocation Authority (WRA) requested that the questionnaire be given to all internees "over seventeen years of age" as a "first step" in their eventual resettlement.

Offering a way out of the camps, it is a bitter irony, one historian noted, that the program "instead became one of the most divisive, wrenching episodes of the captivity." The division in the camps arose over two questions. The first asked if a person were "willing to serve in the armed forces of the United States"; the second, if he or she would "forswear any form of allegiance to the Japanese emperor, or any other foreign government."

These questions caused confusion, division, and bitterness. Some Issei, for instance, would not answer "yes-yes" because, barred from becoming American citizens, they didn't want to renounce Japanese citizenship and become stateless. Some Nisei believed a "yes-yes" answer would demonstrate that they once were loyal to the emperor. The most violent clashes, though, were between JACL followers who believed in the critical importance of forming the 442nd Combat Team and "demonstrating loyalty" and camp "protesters," who felt a "no-no" vote was the only way to voice their anger over the evacuation and the questionnaire. Though the army, at the time, considered a "no-no" vote a sure sign of disloyalty, the verdict of historians is that most such votes were expressions of "outrage" at the injustice of the evacuation. Macbeth, *Personal Justice Denied*, 185–197.

18. "In seven major campaigns, the 442nd took 9,486 casualties—more than 300 percent of its original infantry strength, including 600 killed. More than 18,000 men served with the unit. . . . The 442 was [also] one of the war's most decorated combat teams, receiving seven Presidential Distinguished Unit Citations and earning 18,143 individual decorations—including one Congressional Medal of Honor, 47 Distinguished Service Crosses, 350 Silver Stars, 810 Bronze Stars and more than 3,600 Purple Hearts. As President Truman told members of the 442nd as he fastened the Presidential Unit banner to their Regimental colors, these Nisei fought 'not only the enemy, but prejudice.' " Macbeth, *Personal Justice Denied*, 258–259.

19. In the first stage of the evacuation of Japanese-Americans from the coast, people were housed in one of fifteen "assembly centers" erected by the Western Defense Command. There were twelve centers in California and one each in Oregon, Washington, and Arizona. Tulare was opened on April 30, 1942, and remained occupied until September 4, 1942. The average period of time people spent in assembly centers before being moved inland was three and a half months.

20. A month after issuing Executive Order 9066, President Roosevelt issued another executive order establishing the War Relocation Authority, which was responsible for administering the relocation camps and for subsequently placing Japanese-Americans back into American life. The WRA took over the responsibility for the evacuees from the Western Defense Command (WDC) and built ten relocation centers during the summer of 1942. It erected two centers each in Arizona, California, and Arkansas and one each in Wyoming, Idaho, Utah, and Colorado.

21. The violent conflicts Ms. Seko referred to were clashes between JACL leaders who adamantly supported WRA policy and army objectives and camp dissidents who believed the loyalty questionnaire and the charge of disloyalty against the Japanese population were monstrous mistakes that had to be publicly exposed. The conflicts, thus, were clashes of competing perceptions and strategies that were suddenly brought into the open by the questionnaire.

22. Ms. Seko's "No-No" boys are not the ones who answered negatively to the key questions in the original loyalty questionnaire. The men who refused induction and who were imprisoned were a different, although connected, group.

In December 1943, nine months after establishing the 442nd Regimental Combat Team and creating the vehicle through which Nisei could volunteer, the government announced that the Selective Service would begin to draft Nisei again. The men deemed available had passed the initial loyalty review, and, indeed, most of them "welcomed" a draft because "it reinstated their rights" and allowed an "escape from the debilitating idleness and confinement of camp." About three hundred Nisei, however, "refused to report for physicals or induction on the grounds that their citizenship rights should be fully restored before they were compelled to serve in the armed forces." Of these, 263 were "tried, convicted, and sentenced to three years in federal prison." Macbeth, *Personal Justice Denied*, 246–247.

23. In this regard, author Michi Weglyn wrote, "Within the community [today], the silence over the camps reflects continuing deep divisions, wounds that still fester. A cleavage, even now, divides the proestablishment patriots of the period and those stigmatized as 'troublemakers'—the . . . camp dissidents who failed to live up to the standard of being 'good' and 'respectable' members of their ethnic group. One senses, too, a lingering resentment against the JACL, though it is rarely given . . . expression." Michi Weglyn, *Years of Infamy: The Untold Story of America's Concentration Camps* (New York: William Morrow and Company, 1976), 279.

24. At an emergency meeting convened in San Francisco in March 1942, JACL leaders from the West Coast and the intermountain states decided that the JACL "would be of greater service" outside the region that was evacuated. So, they voted "to move headquarters to Salt Lake City, safely out of the evacuation zone." JACL headquarters remained in Utah until the end of the war. Financial support for the organization was provided by the Salt Lake City JACL and other chapters in the Intermountain District. Bill Hosokawa, *Nisei: The Quiet Americans* (New York: William and Morrow Company, 1969), 311.

25. In a press release dated January 24, 1942, the attorney general of the United States designated eighty-six "Category A," or prohibited, zones in California plus eight "Category B" zones. All enemy aliens were encouraged to voluntarily evacuate from Zone A sites ("around airports, dams, power plants, pumping stations, harbor areas, and military installations") to Zone B sites or beyond by February 24. Mandatory evacuation plans had not been crystallized at that point. Macbeth, *Personal Justice Denied*, 72–73.

26. Angus Macbeth, *Personal Justice Denied: Report of the Commission on Wartime Relocation and Internment of Civilians* Washington, D.C.; U.S. Government Printing Office, December 1982, 18, and Roger Daniels, *Prisoners Without Trial: Japanese Americans in World War II* (New York: Hill and Wang, 1993), 97–103.

BOOK SEVEN
GREEK COMMUNITY

PREFACE

Helen Papanikolas

Two Greeks came to Utah before the 1900s: One was Nicholas Kastro, who told later-arriving compatriots he had known Brigham Young; the other was Leonidas Skliris, who arrived in 1897 and established himself as the leading labor agent not only in Utah but throughout the West and Midwest. Although contract labor had been outlawed in the United States after the deluge of Irish immigration in the 1850s, Skliris was able to bring covertly a contingent of Greeks to work on the Lucin Cut-off, a railroad line built to cut across the Great Salt Lake, in 1902 and another group of twenty-five to break the Carbon County coal strike of 1903. The boys and young men left "for exile," as they called living in strange lands, and embarked to fulfill the destiny decreed by their people's culture for males: providing sisters with dowries and helping impoverished parents. They intended to return to Greece with enough money to set themselves up in business or become moneylenders. Ten who lived the immigrant experience—two Greek born and eight American born—tell us about their life in America in the interviews that follow.

Most of the young Greeks who immigrated to America had been villagers in their homeland, one fourth of them illiterate in their own language. Their daily life had been a dawn-to-dusk tilling of rocky earth. They came to America with barely enough "show money," usually about twenty dollars, to convince immigration officials that they would not become a burden to the government. They knew hunger.

In his late nineties, Peter Condas, born in central Greece, recalled his father working all day with a hoe, then sitting down to dinner—a bowl of vinegar, cut-up garlic, and dried corn bread. The bread, he remembered was so hard "you couldn't put a bullet through it."

Peter Condas's older brothers, like others, had listened to the American myth brought to Greece by Skliris's men and other padrones. These labor and steamship agents rode donkeys through valley and mountain villages with stories of America's wealth. Parents mortgaged their ancestral land at exorbitant rates to provide passage for their sons to the mythical land. Standing before family icons, the sons crossed themselves and swore oaths: They would go, quickly make the needed money, and return.

After three weeks or more on steamships and four days and three nights sitting in dusty, foul-smelling trains, the men came to Salt Lake City, to a fledgling Greek neighborhood near the Denver and Rio Grande Western and the Union Pacific railyards. The labor agent's office was situated within the neighborhood, and the men went there to secure employment in coal mines, the subsidiaries of the railroads, and on rail gangs.

An ever-increasing number of Greeks came into the city, some already with work promised by labor agents, others riding freights on hearing of Utah's industrial expansion: Coal and metal mines were rapidly opening, railroad lines were being extended, and rails were being changed from narrow to standard gauge. Mormon church authorities counseled their members to continue to work the land, and industrialists were forced to bring in immigrant labor to fill their needs.

The Greek neighborhood grew into what was called Greek Town by the Americans. By 1910, as the Greek population in Utah neared five thousand, Greek Town in Salt Lake City became a self-contained island of coffeehouses, restaurants, hotels, boardinghouses, bakeries, a Greek-language newspaper, and a small, domed church. Wherever Greek laborers were sent by the padrones, a Greek Town sprang up. Greek laborers on Denver and Rio Grande Western, Union Pacific, and Oregon Short Line railroad gangs were separated from American workers and given the poorest accommodations. In Carbon County coal camps, in the Magna mill, in the Garfield, Murray, Midvale, and Tooele smelter towns, and in Bingham Canyon's copper district, they lived in segregated areas in tents or in shacks they built themselves with neither water nor privies. To keep their jobs, all were forced to pay bribes, not only to their own padrones but also to the bosses.[1]

After a few years in America, the Greek workers realized they could strike against their employers. The first strike was called by the Greeks in 1909 in the Murray smelter. Because a recession occurred at the same time a priest gathered the illiterate strikers in the church basement and taught them to read and write Greek.[2] A more serious Greek-led strike took place in Kenilworth, Carbon County, in 1911. During the strike, a deputy was killed. Company guards set up machine-gun nests among boulders and junipers on the mountain slopes.[3] For the most part, the Greek strikers were uninterested in the Western Federation of Labor's ideology they heard in miners' halls. In the devastating Bingham Strike of 1912, however, twelve hundred Greek miners heeded the call of the Western Federation, mainly to free themselves from their labor agent, the powerful Leonidas Skliris.

In the first three decades of the twentieth century, the labor strikes inspired a vociferous hostility. Newspapers, public officials, and members of the middle and upper classes railed against this, to them, un-American radicalism. The participation of Greeks, Italians, and South Slavs in the strikes, together with their nationalism, increased the already fomenting anger against all southern and eastern European immigrants.

Greek nationalism, forged under four hundred years of Turkish occupation, had inspired a passion among Greeks for their poor country. In America the Greek immigrants did not foresee that their nationalism would bring trouble for them and misery for their children. They were pulled on the one hand by a consuming nationalism and on the other by the steady work in America that put money into their pockets for the first time in their lives. Notwithstanding the attempted lynchings, burnings, rampages through Greek Towns, and deaths in mines and on railroads, America had spellbound them. Folksongs of immigration like the following, evoked this spell.

> I've come to this strange land and I'll not return.
> I've taken a witch for a wife, her mother also is a witch.
> She casts spells on ships, on the ocean.
> She has bewitched me too and I can not return.[4]

In time, having saved small amounts of money, many Greeks left the coal and metal mines, smelters, mills, and rail gangs and established grocery stores, shoe shine parlors, and the ubiquitous restaurants. A number went back to the very work they had come to America to avoid: farming, sheepherding, and goatherding. In America, though, they could begin with a flock of fifty or a hundred sheep. In Greece, a man with more than ten sheep was considered fortunate. This almost-forgotten way of life is detailed for us in the interview with John Sampinos, the son of an immigrant from the mountains of central Greece.

Although most of the men still expected to return to Greece, they sent for village brides with only an exchange of pictures to identify themselves. These marriages signaled the beginning of a new generation in America to whom eight respondents in this chapter belong. In their interviews, they recall the mingling of their and their parents' experiences. At communal festivities, while men turned lambs on spits, while mothers baked bread and pastries in outdoor earth ovens, the children heard stories of village life in Greece and of their parents' precarious first years in America. In their remembrances they also recall details from their own lives that help to illuminate the Greek immigrant experience in Utah.

The homes, they learned, were the mothers' domain. In the Greek Towns, most often situated near railroad yards, the small houses were decorated with the women's weavings, crochet, and embroideries they had worked on since childhood. Icon lights glowed in the dark. Gardens flourished with plentiful irrigation water.

Midwives and folk practitioners were called upon in preference to the mine and mill doctors.[5] "We used all the old Greek customs: garlic around the neck and the various cold cures," Walker Diamanti, the son of Carbon County's foremost folk healer, recalled. Another immigrant son, Andy Katsanevas, described his mother's village superstitions, many of which are still a part of his life today.

Mothers strictly observed the fasts that preceded the great feast days of the Eastern Orthodox church: Christmas, Easter, and the Dormition of the Virgin. The children sat and stood through the three-hour-long liturgies in Salt Lake City's Holy Trinity Church, built in 1905, and in Price's Hellenic Orthodox Assumption, erected in 1916. Both churches were built in traditional Byzantine style, and robed priests wearing the *kalimafkioin,* a rimless, cylindrical black hat, performed the ancient mysteries of marriage, baptism, and burial. The most important event of the year was Holy Week, which culminated in the Resurrection, symbolized by a lighted candle appearing in the darkened church.

The mothers renewed the customs the fathers had let fall away. Children listened to women keening laments over the open casket of their husbands, killed in industrial accidents, and of the children, dead of illnesses that had defied folk medicine. The unmarried dead and children lay dressed as for marriage, with wedding crowns on their heads and gold bands on their ring fingers. Children watched the women prepare the funeral dinners and the sweetened memorial wheat that was eaten forty days after a death.[6]

In the Greek Towns, the ancient law of hospitality was paramount. The word *xenos* had a double meaning—"stranger" and "guest." The respondents remember that their houses were "open to all." Their parents had been forced to accommodate to the American way of life to survive, yet their traditions of hospitality and mutual help gave color to long days of hard work. These traditions helped them face the nativist attacks on them. Outcries against Mediterranean and Balkan immigrants increased with the advent of World War I and reached hysteria when the United States entered the war on the side of the Allies. The Greeks in Utah rallied to save two of their compatriots who were about to be lynched: one in Price, who had been jailed for taking an American girl for a ride in his new Buick; the second in Salt Lake City, where a Greek, accosted by a group of teenage American boys, shot and killed the brother of Jack Dempsey, the noted boxer.

By 1920, the Greek immigrants in Utah had formed solid communities, with churches, lodges, and networks of relatives, countrymen and godparents. The mothers had little need to leave their neighborhoods for the hostile unknown beyond. They felt safe in their enclaves. Their children, however—as the respondents recall—felt the effect of two competing cultures into their old age. When mothers did venture into American stores, they took their children with them as interpreters. The children were beset with shame for their mothers' inability to speak English. Yet it was uncommon for the first immigrant children to begin school knowing English.

Greek was spoken inside and outside the houses in the Greek Towns. The experience of Ted Speros was typical. "When I first started going to public school," he said, "I spoke no English, so it was rough for me." He did not even know the words to ask permission to go to the washroom.

The most common epithet shouted at Greek-American children by Americans was "dirty Greek," as one respondent told us. Another spoke of the anxiety of having schoolmates come to her home, hear her mother speak Greek, and know she was different from them. Mary Kannes Diamant said: "American kids steered clear of us. . . . If we'd walk into the cafeteria, for instance, . . . and look for a table . . . they would get up and walk away." Stan Diamanti recalled, "Regardless of where we went, whether it was among other ethnic groups or people that referred to themselves as Americans, we had to be ready to fight." Most Greek immigrant children feared going to school.

The labor activity of their parents only increased the hostility against them. In Carbon County, not only did the Greeks become leaders in the coal strike of 1922 after a countryman was killed by a deputy sheriff, but the World War I anger at immigrants had never abated. The striking Greeks and their children became the target of extreme animosity. The Price *Sun* called the Greeks, "a vicious element . . . unfit for citizenship."[7] The Ku Klux Klan marches and cross burnings of 1923–1924 left indelible, hurtful memories. Adding to the trauma for the Greeks, forty-nine of their men were killed in the Castle Gate Number 2 Mine explosion of 1924 that left ten widows, seven of them Greek, and forty-one orphans. The Greek widows wore black until their deaths; their sons, black-dyed shirts, and their daughters, black dresses and braids tied with black ribbons for at least a year after the explosion.

Although the children of the immigrant Greeks had been born in the United States, the judgment of Americans continued to be that the Greeks were "unassimilable," a word often found in newspapers of the period. Americans resented the money orders the immigrant families sent back to Greece, the coffeehouses, the Greek-language newspapers, and the Greek schools held after public school. All were evidence to them that the Greeks could never be Americanized.

The immigrant children attended Greek schools with feelings that ranged from pride to rebellion. This attendance was the most glaring symbol of how different they were from their schoolmates, one respondent recalled.

While children played and fought in Greek Towns, they experienced the security of their people's nearness. When the Greeks shared in the 1920s prosperity, however, and moved into more affluent neighborhoods, the children became isolated from their former friends. It was not unusual for a child to find that he or she was the only Greek immigrant child in the new school. The children lost the comradeship and feelings of safety they had known, and they became more vulnerable to American prejudices. Boys were able to sublimate some of the hostility by competing in sports and playing in school bands. Girls could do neither. They were forbidden to take part in after-school activities and had no say about whether they would or would not go to Greek school, which sons often refused to attend.

This pattern of leniency toward sons and strictness toward daughters permeated the upbringing of Greek children. Sons would be sent to universities; for daughters, a high school education was deemed sufficient. "I was an excellent student," Ellen Vidalakis Furgis said, "but I gave in to my father. I guess I decided to be an obedient person within our culture." During the Depression years of 1930–1940, sisters often worked to send brothers to universities.

Daughters were also prohibited from dating, an immoral characteristic of American mores to the immigrants. Of dating, Mary Lines recalled, "Of course, she [her mother] knew only one pattern, a Greek pattern with expectations based on the lifestyle she had left behind in 1911. . . . It was very hard."

Although Greek-American men dated "American" girls, their parents naively believed that when the time came for marriage, they would marry "good Greek-American" girls. The young men, though, often married the young women they escorted to school dances and movies. The oldest daughters of the Greek immigrants married immigrant men through arrangements made by parents and other relatives. Parents often took their younger daughters to lodge conventions with hopes of finding husbands for them.

To help keep their children within their Greek culture, parents formed boys' and girls' auxiliaries to their lodges. During the Depression decade, the activities of these clubs provided the children with their only bright moments. Their families' carefully accumulated savings exhausted, some fathers had to resort to working with the WPA, cleaning streets and canals. Sheepmen, once among the most prosperous of the Greeks in America, lost everything; the price of lambs had fallen from eighteen dollars to three dollars a head, and often there were no buyers. Not until World War II did the Greeks, like most Americans, know security again. By then, they no longer made toasts to the native soil for which they had once pined. Nor did they sing songs about America as a bewitched land. A clear picture emerges from the interviews in this chapter: The Greeks' successful accommodation to American life led many to climb out of the anxiety and poverty of the early years and the Depression into the middle class.

World War II brought the immigrant era to a close for the Greek-American population. Young Greek-Americans, some of them women, entered the armed services. Marriages escalated, and a third generation began to appear. The sons and daughters of immigrants were not so insistent as their parents were that their own children attend Greek schools; they stressed instead Greek Orthodoxy. Many customs that were naturally a part of village life, especially funeral customs, were considered inappropriate in America and were dropped. Family cohesiveness remains, however, and is celebrated on the feast days of the Greek church and on American holidays. Now, almost one hundred years after the first Greek immigrants arrived in Utah, their great-grandchildren live a completely American life, yet most retain their Greek Orthodox ties.

Several of the second-generation immigrants whose voices we hear in this chapter have become wealthy through the sale of coal and mineral rights on their fathers' homesteads and others through land development. Most important, for the Greek immigrants, America's promise was not a myth; it was real in ways beyond the financial. Walker Diamanti, who became a diplomat in the

U.S. State Department, said, "I feel only in America could the son of illiterate, immigrant parents rise in one generation to a position of trust and honor and be accredited to serve in the country of his father's origin."

From these interviews, one learns more than the events of each respondent's life. We read of respect for fathers and of a great love and devotion for the illiterate mothers. We sense the deep need of the sons and daughters of those early forebears to acknowledge their Greekness in this America, their birthright. Incidents, perceptions, conversations, the details of life, have become a legacy for them and live on in these pages for us.

NOTES

1. Additional information on the historical events mentioned in this preface can be found in Helen Papanikolas, *Toil and Rage in a New Land: The Greek Immigrants in Utah,* 2nd ed., rev., reprinted from *Utah Historical Quarterly* 38 (Spring 1970), 121–133.

2. Maria Takis gave this explanation for her husband's learning to read and write Greek during the strike. Interview, Salt Lake City, August 1977.

3. Alan Kent Powell, "A History of Labor Union Activity in the Eastern Utah Coal Fields: 1900–1934" (Ph.D. diss., University of Utah), 1976, 121.

4. Georgios S. Spyridakis and Spyros D. Peristeris, *Ellinika Dhimotika Traghoudhia* ("Greek Demotic songs"), Vol. C (Athens, 1968), 340.

5. Helen Papanikolas, "Greek Folklore of Carbon County," in Thomas E. Cheney, ed., *Lore of Faith and Folly* (Salt Lake City: University of Utah Press, 1971), 76–77: "Magerou: The Greek Midwife," *Utah Historical Quarterly* 38 (Winter 1970): 50–60.

6. Helen Papanikolas, "Wrestling with Death: Greek Immigrant Funeral Customs in Utah," *Utah Historical Quarterly* 52 (Winter 1984): 29–49.

7. Price *Sun* (June 30, 1922).

Ted Speros. *Kent Miles*

Peter Condas. *Kent Miles*

PROLOGUE:
SALT LAKE CITY, 1924

PETER GEORGE CONDAS, 90, SHEPHERD, MINER, BUSINESSMAN

George and Peter Condas were part of the final wave of Greek immigrants to reach the United States in the 1880–1920 era. Traveling "fourth class" from the port of Piraeus, the father and son arrived at Ellis Island on December 19, 1916. Immigration officials, however, prohibited their entry until Peter's brothers in Bingham posted a thousand-dollar bond. Peter explained to us that his passport age had been reduced from eighteen to fourteen so that he could avoid conscription. But the authorities wouldn't allow in a sixty-five-year-old man who "couldn't work" and a minor who "had to go to school" without assurance that they wouldn't become public charges.

Peter worked for six months at his brothers' slaughterhouse, then became a miner at Utah Copper and, later, Apex Mine. In the 1930s, he joined his brothers in the sheep business. The Condases successfully homesteaded thousands of acres of land in Park City for sheep grazing and still owned the land at the time of this interview. Rising property values in the 1970s and 1980s had made them quite well-to-do.

A small, portly man, Peter Condas unfolded the story of his life in great detail. One particular "fact" he could not forget, or, apparently, forgive, was that the "immigrant pioneers" had to endure inhuman conditions to survive in their adopted land. He described those conditions with unconcealed indignation.

My name is Peter George Condas. I'm born on April 15, 1897. So I'm a pretty old man. I was born in a little village by the name of Strome, ninety miles west from Athens. My father, he was a farmer's son. He didn't have no education. He married a village girl named Helen Charchalis. They had eight children—four boys and four girls. The girls, they died when they were young. The boys, they grow up and die old. In our town, we didn't have no doctor, no hospital. To get a doctor, you had to go thirty-two miles. And by the time the doctor come, the person was dead. [The villagers] didn't have anything. Let me tell you, they was living a pretty bad life.

In the year 1904, my oldest brother, John, left for the United States. He was about eighteen. I tell you what make him leave. Rumors were going around town: If you can only get into the United States, that's all it takes. You can live a rich and happy life. You don't have to work hard. All you got to do [is] go out in the fields, pick up flowers, especial[ly] roses, sit down in one of the big streets in a corner, [and] a man with his wife or girlfriend will buy your flowers. That's what they heard. So my mother started crying day and night: She won't be able to see her son anymore. She died on account of that [in 1908].

Then, my two other brothers come to Utah. I stayed back with my father.

My father had two pieces of land. He was raising potatoes, corn, and wheat. He also had grapevines and thirty or forty goats. But, I might as well tell you, it was a poor existence. He worked all day with a hoe. And when dinner came, he had a bowl, a bottle of vinegar, and garlic. He cut the garlic up, put it in the bowl, added the vinegar, and put in dry bread to soak it up. He had to put the bread in [the vinegar], 'cause when that damn corn bread gets dry, you can't put a bullet through it. But that's the kind of life it was. Furthermore, he worked all his life and he didn't have anything to amount to anything, except the land and the goats he got from his father.

So, in 1916, when my brothers wrote "We're sending $200; sell everything, and come over," my father sold everything. Well, he gave it away. We [only] got eleven hundred dollars for everything, because the people who lived there were poor; and we came to America.

We arrived [in Utah] on December 29, 1916. And, as far as I remember, when we come to Bingham, the first Sunday, my brothers give us a party. It was nice: roast lamb, and as many as seventy-five [Greek] people came from the surrounding towns. We were living in the lower part of Bingham, Lead Mine. That's where they had their meat market and the slaughterhouse. And we had a nice time. A couple of days later, my brothers, who had almost seven hundred head of lamb, told me, "Pete, you might as well help us kill the lambs from now on."

Well, in the old country, we were taught to obey our father, mother, and [older] brothers. So I worked with them. With Spero or John, we killed as many as twenty-six lambs a day. We could kill, clean, hang them up ready to go, in two hours. We was that fast. I helped for about six months. During that time, I didn't ask for money, and they didn't give me any. But after six months, I figured it was time to look after myself. So I found a job with the D & R. G. [Railroad], which was a quarter mile up above where we lived. I laid and replaced rail for two dollars a day. Then I moved up to Copperfield and went to work at Kennecott.[1] Now, in 1917, there were [approximately] two thousand Greeks working in Bingham's copper mines. And, you might as well say, Bingham was all men. There were no women [around] in those days.[2] And the job was so bad, so dangerous, only Greek, Mexican, and Japanese would work in the mines. Others didn't want the job. There were times they killed two or three people in twenty-four hours because there was no protection. The banks were 145 feet high; and when the steam shovels loaded the dirt, rocks came down on people working at the bottom—just knocked them down. If you got killed, the [company] carpenter built a box, put you in, took you down to Bingham Cemetery, and threw you in the lot. That's all there was to it.[3]

They didn't pay nothing to nobody in those days. There was no unions. There was only a company-run carpenters' union, which spied for the company—told the bosses what working people think about their jobs. So the working man didn't have nothing. And if you didn't like it, there was always three or four hundred people outside wanting your job. That's where you were. It was rough times. Life was cheap.

After a couple of years, I went up to Apex Mine and stayed there until it closed in 1924. Then I moved to Greek Town, which was around Second South, between West Temple and Sixth West [in Salt Lake City]. It had restaurants, barbershops, and coffeehouses.⁴ Almost all the Greek people in the city lived in or were scattered around that area. Well, let's put it this way, they was *trying* to live, because it wasn't a time for making money. It was a time for survival.

For example, when people came from the old country, everyone had to show twenty-five dollars so they could come into the United States. The ones who wanted to come to Utah either went to Bingham or to Carbon County. That's where the jobs were. And many of the people either [had] their father or brother or somebody here they relied on for help. You know what I mean? So when people came to Bingham Canyon, they had that twenty-five dollars but no job. Furthermore, they couldn't speak the language. Do you know what that mean[s]? That mean[s] even [for] the ones who had someone when they come here, the odyssey just begins. [It] just begins.

Often, the person they were relying on for help was out of work, or he was sick at home, or was hurt on the job and was in as bad shape as that man was. You know what that means? Means there was no help, for anybody. The state, the county, the city, the Red Cross, the church, nobody cared. And people here didn't have any respect for us. That broke me up. There were a lot of good Greek people here. They were smart and successful, and them others still don't think nothing of them. So it was very hard.

When I come to Salt Lake City, I was twenty-eight years old. I walked around town, but I can only see picture shows and theaters from the outside. I never step inside, because I could not afford to spend the money to see what's inside. The other fellows was the same. I'm telling you, things were so bad, people were living in fear. They were desperate and scared. They don't know what tomorrow will bring.

That's the time a few of us decided to do something. Up in Bingham Canyon, in a company house in Copperfield, we got together and figured out something has to be done to protect the man who comes here from Greece or another part of the United States and get[s] in a situation where he has nothing to eat, no place to stay. We figure instead of having one or two men trying to help somebody, [we would] get everybody behind him, form a [fraternal] lodge.

So, on the 11th day of March, the year of 1926, twenty-six of us got together in a little house, below the Bingham terminal, to form something to protect everybody. The day was cold. I remember [there] was snow on the ground. We went inside; we sit down. We start article-by-article, read it, and put it up to vote. Whenever everybody was in favor, it would go in the book. If there was any rejection, we correct that or drop it. And we formed the Athanasios Diahos lodge.

After that, when somebody [new] came to Bingham, he [would go] to our [lodge] committee. The committee knew where everyone was living. They took the man, buy him working clothes, working shoes, and introduce him to other Greek people. Everybody was glad to help, because they all could have been in his position. Therefore, if they had room, that man moved in. They fed him. But he had to get up every morning to look for work. They told him where to go; they told him what to do. If he can get a job, all right. Otherwise, he was coming back, bringing up the coal and the water and cooking; so, when people come home, they would have their supper ready to eat [and] hot water to wash [in]. He was doing that until he gets a job.

The lodge worked wonderfully. It help[ed] anybody either coming from the old country or anywhere from the United States. That's why I want to make this remark. I thank the following people and their children for their efforts: Jack Talas, George Metris, Sam Charchalis, John Condas, Harry Metos, Chris Metos, Alke Diamant, Gus Skedros, Mike Saltos, Helen Papanikolas, the Malkogiannis family (several were involved), and a lot of other good people. I thank them for their help, because, Christ, nobody had anything in those days. We had only each other to count on.

Postscript: Peter Condas passed away on July 24, 1994.

ANTHONY "TONY" KONTGAS, 81, BUSINESSMAN

The Kontgases (mother, sisters, Tony, and Tony's younger brother) arrived in Price, Utah, in 1920 to reunite their family. Tony's father had settled in the area a decade earlier. "When we arrived, Price was not a progressive place," Tony recalled. "The streets were nothing but mud. There were no roads. Telephone and light poles were in the middle of the street; and when it rained, you got stuck in mud clear up to your knees. It was horrible. But that's all we knew, so we accepted it."

Tony washed dishes, sheared sheep, worked as a telegraph operator, and served in the Pacific during World War II—where he learned, he noted, "to grit my teeth tight and hold myself together"—before returning to Price to build a successful grocery business. In 1952, he developed a mysterious "heart condition" that incapacitated him over the next twenty years. Although deeply shaken by his failing health, he seemed neither angry nor bitter. In fact, the tragedy instilled in Tony a keen appreciation for the transience of beauty and youth. "I've accomplished what I wanted to," he said, with an edge of fatalism in his voice. "I came over here. I've got a home. I had a business. I've got a family. How much more do I want? I've accomplished my desires."

My full name in Greek is Antonios Kontzanpasakis. My father, who was a mail carrier in Crete, arrived here in 1910 and later shortened our name. From what I understand, he came, like many of the youth, because they were in their prime, heard work was available, got together, and immigrated. Lots of the Cretans came in groups. My father came directly to Utah and first resided up at Sunnyside, where he operated a boardinghouse. Afterwards, he moved into Price and opened a candy store. They were popular in those days because they made all kinds of sweets by hand. He operated the store until we came to Utah on May 5, 1920.

When we arrived, there were about four thousand young Greeks in Carbon County, and most of them worked in the coal mines. Every camp you went into, you saw Greek men in the prime of their youth. There was hardly anybody over thirty years old. And I would say about ninety to ninety-five percent were Cretans. The remaining five percent were from other parts of Greece. They were a beautiful group of young people. And I got to know many of them very well. After we arrived, you see, my father converted the candy store into a restaurant. Then, in 1922, he sold it and opened a coffeehouse; and I worked there every day after school.

In 1924, forty-nine [of these] people got killed in the Castle Gate mine explosion. And every one of them I knew very well. The day it happened, I was in the Echo Theatre. I was interested in movies, and Mr. Stringham, who ran the projector, would let me go up to the projection room. Well, Mr. Stringham was in the office that morning, and he asked me to take some letters to the post office across the street. It was about nine o'clock. I still didn't understand English too well. But the clerk in the post office knew me, and he said, "Hey, Tony, come here. Do you savvy?" "What?" I said. "Castle Gate mine, you savvy, coal mine? Boom. Mine boom."

Right away, I realized what he meant. I ran across the street and told Mr. Stringham. He said, "My God, are you sure?" I repeated what the clerk told me: "Coal mine, at Castle Gate, boom." Well, he did some checking and said, "That's right." So I ran and I found the Greek priest. He was a fine, outstanding man. I told him what I learned, and he got a hold of a Greek who owned a Cadillac. He was a politico; nobody else could afford such a car. And he drove us up to Castle Gate.

We zig-zagged up, I remember. Oh, God, we had a heck of a time making it. We went up to Number 2 Mine. It was way up on top of the hill. And I never saw anything like that in my life. Women were standing by the entrance screaming, yelling, hollering, crying. I saw a pile of dirt, timber, tracks, coal, and everything else—bigger than this living room—sitting right across the wash, hundreds of feet from the mine entrance. The explosion just blew it all out. And the poor women were screaming and hollering and yelling. I had never seen anything like it before.

I watched the fire departments from both Price and Helper come and pull out their fire hoses and try to pump water into the mine. But that was just an absolute waste of time; it didn't do any good at all. So we got back in the car and came back. Later, after they picked up all the bodies and brought them out, they started having funerals. This one particular time we had nineteen Greek caskets. Me and the priest, you know, we were always peeking in the coffins. We opened up this one casket a little, but we couldn't tell what it was. We knew it was a human being. But we couldn't tell who it was. That's how badly many of the bodies were burned. We just hoped we were burying the right individuals—I mean, Greeks.

One hundred seventy-two people died in the explosion. Almost one third were Greeks. And it was very bad for our entire community. All these nationalities had someone in there.[5] I know some Greek families [of the men killed] stayed afterward, but most moved out. I don't know where they went; I don't know whether the women remarried. But there weren't many Greek families here at that time. Maybe ten, fifteen, something like that. Most of these young men were single and in the prime of their life.

Postscript: Tony Kontgas died at his home on December 4, 1995.

SECOND GENERATION

WALKER A. DIAMANTI, 62, DIPLOMAT

Brash and eloquent, Walker A. Diamanti was the only one of seven Diamanti boys to live his adult life outside Utah. A graduate of Wasatch Academy, an exclusive, local, Presbyterian boarding school, he attended the University of Utah School of Law and the Hague Institute, from which he received a Ph.D., before embarking on a successful career with the U.S. State Department in 1954.

"In hindsight, I see I was fortunate," he told us. "When I came of age, about thirteen, I went off to boarding school. At that point, my father and brothers were in the coal business. They started out lowly in the Depression, scratching on a coal outcropping on someone else's land; yet they eventually did well. And by the time they sold their mine in the 1970s, they were wealthy and were great coal producers.

"But this is the point I'm making: My brothers did well, and they stayed put. Theirs is the story of ethnic success in Utah. I'm proud of them. But I never wanted to join them. I had the service bug from a young age: I wanted to serve my country. It's hard to identify the germination of my desire. But if I had to, I would trace it back to those wonderful, old missionaries who taught me in high school. They instilled in me the sense of service to my fellow man.

"As I look back, in fact, attending the Wasatch Academy was the watershed event of my life. That was the difference. I ceased to be a [typical] Greek after that, except by volition. I never spoke Greek, except on visits home; I didn't hear the Greek stories; I didn't live Greek. It's true, I'd come back in the summers. But I was not one of the tribe anymore. I was the white sheep. The others were the black sheep. I was the white sheep who broke out of the herd."

At the present time, Walker resides in Washington, D.C. The interview with him was conducted in Salt Lake City at the home of his relative, Penelope Koulouris.

I am Walker A. Diamanti. The middle initial "A" stands for my true name, Alkiviadis. But as a youth I found my baptismal name awkward and didn't use

Walker Diamanti. *Kent Miles*

it. The last name is Diamanti. It's often taken for Italian because it lost a terminal "s" crossing the Atlantic. My Greek name is Diamantis. I was born in Helper, Utah, in my maternal home on October 19, 1921. At the time of my birth, I was the seventh living son of my mother. A daughter had been born in Greece in 1904. She lived for four years and died in Utah in 1908. There were two other live [female] births, one in 1913, then one later. But when I was born, I was the seventh living son of my parents.

My earliest recollections are all Greek. I was baptized and raised Greek; and my first memories are of Greek religious festivals. The [Greek] Orthodox ceremony is a dismal one for a young child standing in church all those long hours. As I get older, [the ceremonies] get sweeter. But I have to admit, at the time, I thought it was a rather barbarous custom. I especially objected to the many candles and the incense used during the ceremony. The church was filled with candles, and it was frightfully hot and intoxicating with such overpowering smells. As I say, I take with it equanimity today, but as a child I found it somewhat repulsive.

Being the seventh son, I remember siblings buzzing all around the house. Interestingly enough, the language at home was Greek, but only to a point.

When we spoke to our parents, we spoke Greek; amongst each other, we spoke English. Around the [dining-room] table, the conversation was "eye" focused. When I looked at my parents, Greek came out. When I looked at my brothers, American came out. I won't call it English, because we spoke American. [*Laughs*]

I'll tell you the story of my father, John Diamanti, first. He came from a little village in central Greece called Mavrolithari. Literally translated, it means "black rock." He was the oldest of five boys and dropped out of school at age eleven to herd sheep. He did that until he emigrated to the United States. As is the story with many immigrants, he begged and borrowed a few dollars [to pay for passage]. In those days, it took seventy dollars for a boat to Naples and [for passage] from Naples to New York, with still enough head money to get you in when you arrived. I always thought you had to have ten dollars; my brother tells me it was fifteen dollars. It could have been twenty-five dollars. But, whatever it was, my father indebted himself to get to America.

He arrived with the flood of immigrants coming at the time. I don't know if you're familiar with the statistics. But over a million people were coming [annually] in those years. This is before the immigration acts [of 1921 and 1924].[6] He was picked up by a Greek labor organizer in New York and immediately put on a railroad labor gang, where he punched tunnels for $1.35 a ten-hour shift. This must have been foreign to him and very hard. But he saved money and ended up in Chicago as a butcher, which is closer to his line of work, because all Greeks know how to butcher and skin animals. From there, he received letters from his friends in Carbon County, who were working in the coal mines. They bade him to come where they said work was plentiful and wages were good.

He came to Carbon County in 1904 or 1905. It was an active coal mining area. But he never [seriously] mined coal. He went to Helper and went into the sheep business with an older Greek, who soon after departed. He was one of those Greek men who came to make it and go back, and [he] went back. They were all bachelors at the time. They didn't bring wives. . . . They were going to the land of "golden streets," [and] I suppose most of them intended to work for five years and then set themselves up in business in Greece. But whatever my father's intentions were, his naturalization dates from 1912, which means he must have filed his first papers no later than 1907. So, it's quite clear he had no intention of returning to Greece.

My mother came to Carbon County in about 1906. She was the first Greek woman in the [Helper] area, and she had a unique experience. Since a lot of young [single] Greek men came to Carbon County as coal miners, she was sort of "Mother Nature" to them. Our home was an open door, with people always visiting. Mother fed and cared for a lot of them, including some orphans. The Greeks called all children who lost their mothers orphans. Chris Jouflas (who later was mayor of our little city) was orphaned as a young boy, and Mother just took him in and raised him until his father remarried.

My father was also an incorrigible bringer home of strangers, unannounced—and at any time. Once, the Greek archbishop came to town, and Dad dragged him and his whole entourage down to the house. Mother [supposedly] had the washing machine up in the middle of the kitchen, and here Father arrived with an entourage of fifteen to twenty eminent Greeks. But she was unflappable. She pushed the machine out of the way, went out in the backyard, slaughtered a few chickens, scalded and plucked them, and while the men were sitting around drinking wine and eating cheese, she whipped up a meal worthy of the occasion. She was a fantastically generous and warmhearted person.

Our home was typically ethnic. We had a garden; we ate lots of vegetables, including, I recall, corn for breakfast; and we had an outdoor oven where mother baked bread once a week. We were a healthy family. We used all the old Greek customs: garlic around the neck and the various cold cures. When someone had a cold, they would lie him on his stomach, put a ball of cotton dipped in alcohol on his back, light the alcohol, then put a little whiskey glass over it. As the alcohol burned, it created a vacuum. These were terrible torture instruments. They'd put eight or nine glasses on someone's back, each with this lighted alcohol. When they removed the glasses, there would be great welts on the person's back. But this was the way of drawing out the illness. Surprisingly, few people died, and many lived. [*Chuckles*]

My early memories also include a lot of Greek get-togethers. Greeks were great celebrators. Certainly, Easters were memorable, with elaborate ceremonies. [In preparation] people like my mother fasted for forty days. She took nothing but water and boiled vegetables; she ate no meat or animal products. But most Greeks fasted from Good Friday through midnight mass on Saturday, when they had a moving ceremony. At first, all the candles were out; the church was dark. At the stroke of midnight, the priest came out with one lit candle and said, "*Christos Anesti*" [Christ is risen]. The young men then rushed forward and lit their tapers from the priest's taper. And the lights flowing back through the church were a spectacular sight. When I was vice-consul in Greece, I saw such a ceremony on a hill just east of Athens. You could actually see the lights snaking down the hill.

On Easter morning, the Greeks broke their fast. We used to do it with great barbecues, which were joint affairs. Greeks from throughout Carbon County and sometimes from Salt Lake would meet in a flat of lovely springs and groves just before Scofield. Earlier, in the middle of the night, young men would have gone up to start the lambs roasting. Then, after church let out, everyone headed for this rendezvous. Of course, there was much eating, drinking, and celebrating, including a sort of Junior Olympics.

The Greeks were always competitive in the athletic sense. Every year they would put a handful of money in a hat, and place the hat a hundred or two hundred yards away. Then they'd line up all the little guys—the children—and the first one to reach the hat got the money. Later [in the day], they had a boulder-throwing contest. The older boys had a large boulder; the younger boys had a small boulder. You could compare it to shot putting. Then they had what amounted to a broad jump. They'd draw a line, and guys jumped to see who jumped the furthest. There was always great pride in athletic prowess.

Another recollection, a mixed one for me, is our parents' great pride in their ethnic origin. They wanted us to learn Greek. This became a great source of difficulty, because they would import tutors, Greek teachers, some all the way from Greece—not just for us, but for the community of young [second-generation] Greeks. And this was a time—the '20s—when, I daresay, Americanization was heavily emphasized in our schools. Carbon County had many first-generation Americans. Due to the mines, we had Greeks, Italians, Yugoslavs, Hungarians, Bulgarians, Romanians, Germans, Chinese, Japanese, English, and Scots. So the schools emphasized *Americanization*. As a consequence, to my regret, I resisted learning Greek. I mean, I spoke it—it was my mother tongue. But I did not want to go to Greek school.

Added to our parents' problems was the fact that [Greek] *had* to be taught after regular school. So we would go to public school, then when the other kids were out playing, we had to be in a classroom. I daresay, no teacher lasted long with us; we were all hellions. Some of the girls learned. I have one brother who writes Greek elegantly. But the rest of us were "anti" learning. We didn't mind being Greek, but we didn't want to go to Greek school. So we did dreadful things to tutors. One day, we would put snakes in a teacher's desk; the next day, frogs; the next day, mice. A fourth day, we might put carbide in the inkwells or dip spitballs in the inkwells and shoot them up to the ceiling, so they would drip down on the teacher. We were just hellions. I regret it now. I'm an illiterate Greek. But at the time, it seemed much more important to be American—with a capital "A."

Of course, my mother was brokenhearted. She'd say, "It'll never hurt you. *Anything* you learn will be good for you." I'd say, "No!" It was a source of strife and unhappiness between us. My father was never demonstrative. He was easygoing and silent. But my mother was bombastic. She would deplore my negation of our cultural heritage. Of course, she forgave me; but the next day, it was the same act all over again, trying to get me to Greek school.

At the school, everything was in Greek. As a matter of fact, I don't think these Greek teachers knew English; or, if they did, they didn't know it well. Anyway, from the moment you walked in until the time you left, everything was in Greek. And they [really] tried to teach us a good Greek, because, let's face it, though we spoke [in Greek] to our parents, their Greek was peasant Greek. Their tribe migrated from Albania and settled in central Greece, a rugged, mountainous area. So they were actually hillbillies—Greek hillbillies. Not an "elite" group, but a remarkable people with unusual talents.

One of my father's talents, and a tradition recorded in stories of our area, was his alleged ability to predict the sex of unborn children. At Easter celebrations, when a husband brought his pregnant wife around, my father would put his hand on her stomach and predict the sex of the unborn child. His accuracy is said to have been good.

Another skill was his ability to foretell the future by reading the shoulder blade of the Easter lamb. When a barbecue was pretty well advanced, someone would hand him a shoulder blade, or he'd extract it from the lamb. After it was cleaned up, he would hold it up to the light and read from the tracery of the veins whether it was going to be a good or a bad year. This never failed to happen. Anytime there was a barbecue, father "read" the shoulder blade of the lamb. I can still picture him holding the shoulder blade—five, maybe six, inches long—with a rapt audience listening to him foretell that "the rains will be sufficient; the sheep will have multiple twins." All his friends were sheepmen.

Another of his skills was interpreting dreams. Father had a marvelous old book called *Onirokitis*, which literally translated means "Interpretation of Dreams." Every morning at breakfast, mother would recount her dream, and he'd thumb through the book. It was topically organized. She might dream a bear was chasing her down the mountain—well, that would be my dream—or one of the children fell down a well. Father was never at a loss to find the topic and read the interpretation. People took great stock by these. I recall sheepmen sitting around our house, having a few drinks, waiting for the meal to begin. Someone would speak of a dream, and father would reach for his dream book, scan it until he found the subject, then read out the interpretation.

He was very impressive. So was my mother. Completely illiterate—she couldn't read or write in *any* language—she was a remarkable woman. Generous, moral, smart. Whenever we were doing something she thought improper, she would say, "*Estima filotimo.*" She would grind it into us. A few days ago, I asked some of the older Greek women in Price to translate that phrase. [They said it was] essentially untranslatable [but] somehow "self-explanatory." "*Estima*" has to do with gauging one's self-worth, one's estimation of one's self. And "*filotimo*" has to do with self-respect, honor, or propriety. So I was raised in a home where, I daresay, there was a moral standard. Mother had high expectations and required us to toe the line.

She was also an accomplished storyteller and would enthrall me as a child. I could just sit and listen to her for hours telling stories from the old Greek myths. That's what she heard as a child and that's what she passed on. Now that I'm older and have read some of the literature, I realize Greeks have been passing on these stories, mouth to ear, for generations.

Mother also doted on me. Being, as I call myself, her seventh failure to have a girl, we were close, particularly in those impressionable years when I was too young to go to school. She used to speak to me about the past, the present, and her hopes for the future. She had great expectations for us and great confidence in me. I must say, she gave me the feeling I was destined for something.

My father was [completely] different. I heard him say "damn" once in all the years I knew him, and he lived to be eighty-nine. He was a nonemotional person. Absolutely. But mother was known for her bombast and often chewed him out. She'd say, "You old rascal!" She didn't mean it, of course. He'd walk out, let her cool off, and come back in. He never said a word. He didn't ignore her; he just stood there; and her remarks flowed off his back like water off a duck. Five minutes later, my mother would be smiling and saying, "Ah, he's impossible," and that was that.

But Mother often recalled for me that everyone was poor in the village, and that it was a great act on the part of my father to have come to America, and that they had done well here, having seven sons who were all growing up. She was proud to have borne her sons and particularly proud of me. I may be ego-centric, but I always felt she expected the most of me. It's perhaps because she had me alone after the others went to school and doted more on me, and I worked more [at home] with her. I used to dust and clean around the house until she would say, "Ah, if only you were a girl"—at which point, I used to strip off the apron [she'd given me] and run out of the house in a fury. Silly things like that. I remember it happening more than once.

Yet I always felt warm and pleased when she spoke about where we had come from, where we were now, and where she expected us to go. My father was always gone. He was off with the sheep; or, if he was in town, he was likely to be at the coffeehouse with the older Greek men. Greek men didn't stay at home and help with the housework or raise the children. They were people that came home at mealtime and at bedtime. The home was the woman's domain. As a result, I'm my mother's product. I knew my father very little. I admired him. I was a great admirer of my father. But I had no intimacies with him.

As a postscript, I have a story to tell which I call "America, America." The title belongs to Elia Kazantzakis in his marvelous movie about Greek immigrants coming to America [at the turn of the twentieth century]. The reason I call it "America, America" and tell it with pride is because I find it not only complimentary, but accurate.

This is my story: My father, a modestly literate Greek peasant, left Greece in 1904 to come to America. My mother, who was totally illiterate, followed two years later. They raised a large family here, of which I'm the seventh son. In January 1954, I returned to Greece as a diplomatic representative of the United States. And I feel only in America could the son of illiterate, immigrant parents rise in one generation to a position of trust and honor and be accredited to serve in the country of his father's origin. I think only in America could that happen. I love this story, and I often tell it to my rather uppity diplomatic colleagues, because to me that is America. It doesn't make a damn bit of difference where you came from. It's what you put into it and what you get out of it [that counts].

Ellen Furgis with her family.
George Janecek

ELLEN VIDALAKIS FURGIS, 60, SOCIAL ACTIVIST, HOUSEWIFE, WRITER

The oldest of five children, Ellen V. Furgis was born in Bingham, Utah, on June 3, 1926. When she was eight years old, her mother died of spinal meningitis. "I was orphaned at a young age," she explained to us, "and I grew up from that. I once talked to a psychiatrist. He said the thing that saved me from being unable to cope was the fact that I was thrust into a role of responsibility for my family, and I assumed the role."

Fortunately for the people of Utah, over the years Ms. Furgis also assumed responsibility for enriching other families, both within and without the Greek community. She started a kindergarten in the Jordan School District; she helped introduce multicultural subject matter into the state's public schools; she published several popular Greek cookbooks; and, as the chairperson of the annual Greek festival, she broadened and solidified an important community event.

The subject closest to her heart, though, has been the neglect of women in the Greek community. "I've been angry about this for years," she confided, "because when I was growing up, women in our culture were treated as second-class citizens. Most men worked in the mines, and they worked hard. But the women worked twice as hard. And they were never acknowledged. They were taken for granted. When the women's movement started, many people said, 'They're going too far!' I said, 'They are not. Women have been suffering injustice for eons; and it's been festering. Someone just finally had the nerve to say, Enough!' "

My parents were both from the western end of the island of Crete. My father, Spiro George Vidalakis, was from the small town of Moustako. My mother, Karko Mavrogenis, was from Lakos, a village in the mountains. Life in Moustako was difficult for my father. His father was an alcoholic, and his mother was very concerned that he, too, would become one if he stayed there. So, as soon as she could, she scrounged enough money to send him to America; and when he was eighteen, in 1913, he came to America alone, not knowing a word of English or how he was going to make a living.

He was classified as an unskilled laborer, as many Greek immigrants were, and sent to Utah to work in the mines. He wound up at Bingham's U.S. Mine and worked as an underground miner on the night shift, probably the worst possible assignment he could have had. He put in ten-hour days for a two-dollar-a-day paycheck. But my dad was hardworking and had a great personality. People seemed to like him, and he did well.

My mother came to America under somewhat different circumstances. There were six girls and one boy in her family; and she was the baby. In Lakos, they lived in a tiny one-room shack with spare furnishings. A great big curtain in the center of the cabin marked off their living quarters. During winters, domestic animals were sheltered on one side, while the family lived on the other. There were no indoor cooking facilities. A brick or rock kiln oven was outdoors, and every day my mother's family would carry fagots of wood to light the kiln and heat a heavy cooking pot. They made their living gathering olives. It was a poor life, but it was not as bad as our urban ghettos. With a few sheep, some goats, a smokehouse, and a garden, they were able to live off the land.

My mother was talented and bright, brighter than my father. Tall and statuesque, she was a pretty woman with hazel eyes and chestnut hair—unusual since most Greek women have black or thick, dark brown hair and are short in stature. A lot of Cretan men asked for her hand in marriage. But her sister, Argero Leventis, who was a picture bride and lived in Bingham, knew life in Crete would always be hard for her. So she brought both my mother and her [own] husband's sister, a pretty woman, too, to work at their boardinghouse in Bingham.

My uncle, John Leventis, was into mining. He had a gold mine in Virginia City and was making quite a lot of money. He also ran a coffeehouse in Copperfield and was very involved in workers' rights. He was the first person to organize the Greek miners in Copperfield and was in the first major strike made against Utah Copper. Promised a raise, which they never received, the miners met with my uncle at his coffeehouse to discuss their next move. He suggested they stay out of the mines until they were paid right. "Let them get the ore out of the mine themselves, if they think they can do it! But you know damn well they're not going to do it!" He was a tiny guy, extremely vociferous, and an effective leader; he was really nice, but you wouldn't ever want to push him around.[7]

My father took his evening meal at my aunt's boardinghouse, and it didn't take long before Mother met him. During the days, she was a chambermaid; in the evenings, she would waitress. As I understand, my mother already had three marriage proposals from people in fairly good economic standing, but she turned them down and eventually accepted my father. I guess his looks and his personality won her over.

In those days, women in the community relied on each other more than we do today, which helped my mother and the other Greek women feel more secure about living in—what was to them—foreign land. My mother was a marvelous cook and very hospitable. All the neighbors loved visiting her. They would bring homemade goods, and she would send them off with a plate full of Greek cookies or pastry.

My mother also sewed beautifully. One Christmas, my father bought her an old treadle-type Singer sewing machine that I think he won by gambling. Anyway, she was so excited, she made almost everything we wore. She crocheted bedspreads and tablecloths. She was a multitalented person, and I often wonder what she could have done if she had been literate. I remember, Mrs. Pappasideris, her friend, wrote letters for her to send to Greece because she couldn't write them herself. In return, my mother gave her a pair of hand-embroidered pillowcases. It was a trade-off. But it took my mother a whole month to prepare those pillowcases, whereas it took Mrs. Pappasideris a half an hour to write the letter.

My mother also was extremely frugal and always got the optimum possibilities out of a dollar. I remember, whatever we had left over from dinner automatically became our breakfast. If it was lima beans without meat or boiled dandelion greens seasoned with lemon juice and oil, that's what we had. We literally lived on thirty dollars a month and lived, I think, quite well. At the time, I resented her frugality. I mean, we couldn't even have an ice cream cone because the price of a cone would pay for a quart of milk. But she made good decisions. Even as a child, I could see that. My father was the person in the forefront, always. As in most Greek households, women were in the background. Yet my mother was far more visionary than my dad could ever have been. She wanted him out of the mines, so she told him they would save enough money to buy a car and run a taxi service. Now, at that time, women were not supposed to make such decisions, but she used her brains, saved enough money, and got him out of the mines.

We lived in a little courtyard [that had] wooden houses that, by today's standards, would be considered shacks. About a block or two away was the heart of the little town of Copperfield. On one side of the street, Louis DePray sold

Italian foods. Next to his place was a Greek coffeehouse; further down the street was an independent grocery. There was also a huge mercantile store, just like you'd find in any mining town. Every two years, we'd go there to buy shoes, and Mother would purchase enough material to sew all our clothes. Many Copperfield merchants lived in the Burns apartment [house], which was right on that street. Next to it was the Panhellenic Grocery, owned by two families, then the Lendaris Mercantile, which was owned by two people. Almost every Greek business was a partnership venture in those days.

A huge cement building with more apartments was on the other side of the street. At one end of its main floor was a coffeehouse; at the other, a butcher shop. Kennecott [Utah Copper] was at the end of the street, and, as you walked toward it, you could see the boardinghouse where my parents met. In those days, lots of bachelors still lived in that boardinghouse. I remember, we always had two or three bachelors at our house for dinner. During the warm weather, my mother sat on the front porch crocheting, and they would walk by, stop, and visit until dinnertime. She'd invite them in. Money was scarce, but she always had extra food for them. Afterwards, everyone sat around, played cards, and talked late into the night.

In those days, like most minorities, Greeks kept to themselves. There was not the reaching out [across cultures] that there is today or would be if Greeks came to America now. There was also an intimidating force in Bingham: the Ku Klux Klan. They burnt crosses up in Dinkeyville, which was the Mexican community. The burning crosses could be seen from all over, and people were just terrified. I remember, blacks worked in Bingham, but a town ordinance prohibited them from staying overnight. I watched them leave every day at about four thirty. In the late 1920s, I believe, the Klan became especially active.[8] In fact, the grand master was one of the town's practicing physicians. My father drove his taxi by then. Employed by the superintendent of the U.S. Mine, he took children from the mining camp to the public schools. On the way, he often saw the Klan prepare for their rituals and would come home to warn us. These people would put on their robes, burn crosses, raid coffeehouses, and actually axe down all the furniture. They would get away with doing an inordinate amount of damage. No one, as far as I know, stopped them. I recall a Klan raid took place a little ways from our house. It was really frightening. The next day, there was a hushed network of gossip, because you never knew who was a Klan member and who wasn't.

My mother died of spinal meningitis on August 26, 1934. She was running a 106-degree temperature that just fried her brains, and they couldn't do anything for her. They packed her in ice, but the physicians didn't have any antibiotics. I think it was just a matter of months before penicillin was introduced. It would have saved her life. At the time, though, when my dad went to the hospital, the doctors told him they couldn't bring the fever down.

We think she got sick from the canal that ran under our front porch. We called it a canal, but it was an open sewer with boards over it and rats as big as cats. At first, we kids thought they *were* cats. We'd sit on the front porch, eat bread, and watch them come up through holes in the wood and grab pieces of fallen bread. Mother would drag us back into the house, lock the door, and tell us not to get near them. She was afraid we'd pet them and get sick. I've always wondered if that's how she got sick—if somehow the bacteria of that place did her in.

While my mother was in the hospital, we stayed with my aunt at her boarding-house. When they visited my mother, I was the only child allowed to see her. We couldn't go too near the bed, and we had to put on a robe and a mask. I remember, on August 25th, my father decided I had better stay home and put the other children to bed. When they returned, I heard them saying that she ate all of her dinner and seemed so calm. My aunt said she ate a little cluster of grapes with such enthusiasm she knew it was a bad omen. After she had finished eating, she laid back, and that was it. She died that night.

The following night, at ten or ten thirty, they brought her home, and we all stayed up. It was strange. I had never seen a coffin or a dead person, and here she was in the living room lying on all these satin pillows. I kept waiting for her to wake up. It wasn't until the next day when we rode in my dad's car to the Salt Lake City cemetery that it dawned on all of us that she was never going to wake up. That was hard for us children. It changed all our lives, because we were all very young. I was eight; my sister was six; my brother was five; and our baby sister was only six months old.

I don't think my father ever got over it. Certainly, he never remarried. In those days, many men married by proxy. I think they respected their wives and maybe learned to love them. But I think my mother and father were *in love* from the time they met, and I don't think he felt there was anyone who could take her place.

After my mother died, we were too young to assume my father's household responsibilities, so we stayed with my aunt. During that time, my father moved two miles away, to a place called Lead Mine, where he opened up a bar and gas station combination called Moonlight Gardens. We thought it was a wonderful name for that type of establishment. It had a dance floor, a nick-elodeon for dancing during the week, and an orchestra for weekends. This was something new for a Greek immigrant—to be involved in a restaurant but not offer food.

We were living with my aunt, and for a while it was all right. But when it seemed like it was going to become a permanent situation, my aunt became angry with us and we . . . we became afraid of her. I didn't understand then, but as I've grown and come to understand personalities more, I realize my aunt was a very organized woman with only one child. Four children were sud-denly thrust upon her. What must she have thought? [Because I was] the old-est, she said I should be able to do things without being told. In order for me to escape—and I mean literally—whippings, I had to be one step ahead of her all the time. At eight years old, I was terribly frightened—petrified, really.

After a while, my father thought it would be better if the family moved down [to Lead Mine] so he could be closer to us. My Uncle John bought one house, for use as a boardinghouse, and my dad put three hundred dollars down for a house near the bar. Though we lived with my dad, we still had our meals at my aunt's and were still expected to do all the chores. I was a good student but with little opportunity to study. From school, I went right to her house, and she would make me iron the entire family's clothes, scrub the floors, or clean the bathroom. With ten people in the house to care for, even washing dishes took a lot of time.

We lived this way for about two years, then it just got too much for both of us. One day, after I cleaned the sink with a toothbrush, I was putting some Chamberlain lotion on my hands. I guess I didn't clean the sink as well as I should have, and my aunt, angry about the work I had done, became so incensed she grabbed the bottle and whacked me on the head with it. It broke and cut my head open, and the blood started running. I said, "This is it! I'm never coming back here!" And I never went back.

It was a stormy parting, and my father thought, "Well, I'll just let her cool down; she'll go back." But I swore I would eat bologna sandwiches until I learned how to cook. I went to school, worked as my father's bookkeeper, took over the entire household, and learned how to cook while maintaining straight A's at school. Soon my two sisters and my brother quit going up to my aunt's house for meals. I took over caring for my family, which made me a more responsible person and probably led to my career in cooking. It's interesting, too. In my aunt's later years, I was the one who took care of her. Before she died, she wanted me to know she really regretted her treatment of me. I felt sorry for her.

My father never attended [the Greek Orthodox] church and never took us, so we virtually grew up without ties to our community. I had few Greek friends, which was probably my fault, because I worried about having them in my home. I never thought it was good enough for them. You have to understand, since we didn't have a mother, our home had a "bachelor atmosphere"—linoleum floors instead of carpeting, handmade furniture with two-by-fours for legs instead of lovely store-bought styles.

I was accepted by the elite in school, though, because I was academically ahead of the norm. I had my heart set on going into engineering, too, because of my math skills, but my father wouldn't hear of it. He was a chauvinist who believed girls didn't need to go to college. His attitude was prevalent among the Greeks. In those days, it was assumed women didn't need to go on to college. In fact, in most cases, they were second-class citizens from birth and shortchanged by the attitudes that prevailed throughout our history. Yet, when I think back to my formative years, women were the real strengths in families. They were better able to cope with crisis. In fact, they met all crises: houses burning down, deaths, illnesses, accidents. Men seemed more like witnesses than participants. My father worked hard. But after work, he was done for the day. Not my mother. She got up at five thirty each morning and went to bed long after dark. She bottled the fruit, cured the meat, raised the chickens, made the wine, packed our lunches, cleaned the house, washed our clothes—by hand, with washboards—and managed the household accounts.

My father was a "Dapper Dan" [fun-loving] type. After driving his taxi, he liked stopping by the coffeehouse and gambling on *barbout* [a game of dice]. He would come home with three dollars—much less than what he had earned that day—and my mother would absolutely fall apart. She'd say, "How am I going to pay the rent? How am I going to buy food?" He would not listen to her. He would take me—I was about four or five at the time—into the car, and we'd go for a ride and buy an ice cream cone. When we'd get home, they would argue, and I would think how great my dad was for buying me an ice cream cone. But then I would have an intuitive feeling she was right.

As for my attending the University of Utah, my father disagreed. He said all I needed to learn was typing and shorthand, and he drove me straight from Bingham to the LDS Business College in Salt Lake. I was an excellent student . . . could have gone far in a university . . . but I gave in to my father. I guess I decided to be an obedient person within our culture. I did finish LDS Business College, [and] then I thought, Maybe he'll let me go to the university. I went home again, and he said no. So, I rebelled. Within a short time, I left home and moved in with three other Greek girls, worked part-time at KALL radio station and at the USO [United Service Organization], and enrolled at the University of Utah. Of course, my father had no use for my aspirations, so I did it on my own.

I can't tell you how much university life meant to me. I took English, history, and the humanities. I read Faulkner and Chekhov. For a few years, I was the happiest I had ever been. It was like having chocolate cake and coffee every time I went to class. But the situation was short-lived. As the Second World War neared its end—and I remember the euphoric day it ended—I didn't have enough money to continue schooling and pay for rent, food, and bus fare. So I had to give up a university education and work full-time.

I was twenty-seven years old when I got married. I suppose, once again, my cultural attitudes prevailed. Marriage was expected of me. Now, don't get me wrong, I wanted to marry. But it was an adjustment on my part, because I was independent, working, making more money than my husband, and still followed "custom" by taking my paycheck home and giving it to him. I resented that. I also understood that George was the firstborn in a Greek family and never made to do anything in the home. According to custom, that was [the women's] role. In marriage, he was to be a good provider; and he was.

After I had my first child, my husband would not let me go back to work, because he found it demeaning. I'm not sorry he felt that way. After all, it is part of our tradition. And I don't think you should be sorry for your decisions. But had I been born at another time, I probably would have *not* given up my work. I'm not bitter, though. Like many other women, I have found my way. My philosophy is pretty straightforward. I think we're put on this earth for a purpose, and if one's talents and skills can somehow improve or enhance another's life, that's the ultimate achievement. Believing this, I became a volunteer and a social activist, and have stayed involved all my life. My friends say I was born at the wrong time; I could have been a leader for the women's movement. But I consider myself the lady with the running shoes who sits in the back row of the theater—one foot restrained by tradition, the other ready to tackle what I believe must be done.

STAN JOHN DIAMANTI, 72, MINING ENGINEER

Stan Diamanti (the older brother of Walker Diamanti) seemed like an enigma to us. He was a lifelong miner who did not like mining, the quintessential blue-collar man who believed life should not be defined by work. He romanticized the past, yet he portrayed it, instinctively, warts and all. He was modest, homespun, diffident; he was also outspoken, eloquent, direct—a natural and effective storyteller. All of his life he labored to build up the Carbon Fuel Company, which was owned by his two older brothers; yet when one of his older brothers (Jim Diamanti) started slipping Stan extra funds to help him after he retired, he returned the money.

The interview with Stan Diamanti was conducted in his living room shortly after Jim Diamanti's death. He was visibly distressed throughout our conversation but spoke without explaining or concealing his grief. His voice was soft, deep, unaffected; occasionally, it broke.

My parents were wonderful people, and they were both well loved because they took care of people in this town. When relatives and immigrants were sent here from the old country with a tag around their neck, they were usually sent to "John Diamanti, Helper, Utah."[9] From there, Dad would find work for them or send them on to relatives who had come before. And Mother always took care of neighborhood kids. She didn't want us to be a burden to anyone, but it was all right for everybody else to live in our front yard. When she baked fresh bread once a week, all of us gathered round. The kids would call her "Chief," because they said anybody who can control a tribe like that had to be at least a chief.

Our younger days were happy days, because there was always enough room at our table for one or two more. From where we lived, you could look up the road and see halfway to town. Every now and then, we'd spot Dad—[God] rest his soul—walking home with two or three friends. We'd see him and run in and tell mother. He'd never call. He'd just bring them home. But in fifteen minutes, my mother could put a banquet on the table. I never figured out how she did it. We'd go to church, come home, and in ten minutes there'd be everything your little heart desired sitting on the table. I guess that's where my brothers learned to cook. Everybody learned but me. I was just too impatient, too mischievous.

Stan Diamanti. *Kent Miles*

When I was eight years old, mother [nick]named me Ligla. That's Greek for "greasy." That will be your life, she said. Because whether it was a bicycle, an ice skate, or anything else, I could either fix it or fix it so nobody else could. "You'll never have much, because money doesn't mean much to you. But you'll never be without or go hungry." That's how she put it; and that's how it's been.

As for an education, I never got one. I went to school because everyone else did and because it was fun. Kids don't play in this day and age like we did. [*Chuckles*] When we played tag, that mountain over there and this mountain over here were our boundaries. The same way with marbles. We played marbles and I wore out the front of my shoes and the knees of my overalls. We also played hockey, and we never had any trouble getting hockey sticks, because the old cars were made with hardwood bows. You could find an old car and cut you a beautiful hockey stick. So we had a lot of fun; and we didn't get in any trouble with the law.

What we did get into was plenty of discrimination. We were [constantly] called "dirty little Greeks." That may not sound right [today]. But that's the way [Americans] referred to us. The Italian kids were called Dagos or Wops. They didn't so much mind being called Dagos. But Wop was a dirty word. So we all fought. There was only one rule: Big guys didn't pick on little guys. If I had an argument with a big guy, he'd find somebody my size to do his fighting. The big guys didn't whip the little guys just because they could. In other words, [there was] fairness; something we don't have much today.

Now, it's horrible to say, but the people who were the big wheels in the coal mines and in other industries treated anyone who was a little smarter and didn't want to be a slave or a serf as a dirty Greek or a dirty Dago. There was a lot of that in my day. We tried to not let it bother us, because we were proud of being Greeks and Americans. But it sometimes did. So we'd fight back; we fought a lot, actually. But after a while, you didn't mind. I used to fight for fun, for the hell of it, or for a nickel. I don't know how to explain it to you. It was just a different day and age.

I saw the Ku Klux Klan burn their crosses over on the hill here. They'd burn their cross to show they had power. But it didn't faze us much. We didn't think it was a big deal, because if you had any problems in those days there were always neighbors and the town behind you. Helper used to have every nationality, race, creed, color; you name it, we had it. So if you had a death in the family or anything, the neighbors were right there to do for you in any way they could. Greek people are jealous of each other's [financial] success. But when it was necessary, they would band together and do whatever needed doing. And not only the Greeks. When there was a crisis, the Italians, Slavs, Czechs, and everybody else banded together and said, "You touch one and you have the rest of us to contend with."[10]

My father originally came into Carbon County in 1905 as a strikebreaker. The coal companies were having labor problems, and they brought quite a few Greeks in from back East. But once he got here, he didn't go along with it. He got into slaughtering. He'd go to Sanpete County—what we called Mormon country—and buy cattle. He'd drive them over, slaughter them, then furnish meat to the mines. He later owned [one of] the first automobiles, a Model T, and went around delivering meat.

Unfortunately, like me, he wasn't much of a businessman. He went into business three times, and three times [he] lost it all. Right before World War I ended, he went into the cattle business. Of course, you know what happened after the war; the bottom fell out of everything. The same thing happened twice more in the sheep business. They finally took the sheep away from us [for the last time] in 1931 or '32. We had a beautiful herd—three thousand sheep. We were grazing them in New Mexico at the time, and the bank came and took them because of five thousand dollars that he owed. It was a rough proposition [too], because we only got three and a half cents a pound for wool, and I can remember after the warehouse sold the wool, they sent Dad a bill for eighty-six dollars for the balance of the storage.

But Dad didn't take it hard; he was easygoing. And, in 1935, he borrowed a couple of hundred dollars from a friend, and we started the Hardscrabble Coal Mine. All of us started working up there, except Dad. [*Chuckles*] He'd come around, but he never did mine coal. He went back to being a hillside chemist. Do you know what a hillside chemist is? That's a bootlegger. Between going broke and starting up again, that's what Dad did—that's how he kept the family together.

Dad was known for being the best bootlegger in Carbon County. In those days, people weren't too careful about how they made whiskey. You'd get what they called fusal oil in it.[11] You could get deathly sick if you drank it. But you never had to worry about John Diamanti's whiskey, because he knew how to take care of it, and he always did. That's why we were never [dirt] poor, I guess, because there was always alcohol around to sell. And there was always people around to buy it.

When I got older, I used to deliver [it]. The whiskey cost fifteen dollars a gallon. Lots of times, I remember delivering to the cathouses. I'd give them the whiskey, and they'd give me a dollar for delivering. The prostitutes would always want to kiss me and give me candy, which upset me. I guess it wouldn't make any difference in this day and age, but when I was a kid I can remember [there were] twenty-one saloons and eighteen houses of ill repute in Helper. On Saturday nights, Helper was like Mecca. Guys would shower, come down, and go to the coffeehouses. But they'd always wind up going to the houses of ill repute, spending their money, then going back again.

It was a pretty raw existence. A lot of people lived in dugouts. Some, to save money, dug rock houses on the hillside and lived in that. Some had lights, most didn't. They'd haul water and use candles. The company houses had electricity. 'Course, the companies built them because that's how they kept people. I don't know if you've ever been up Spring Canyon, but they had company houses all through there. Usually, it would be a four-room house: two rooms for one family on one side, two for the other family on the other side. If you happened to have a big family, you'd get all four rooms.

But it was rough living. You were up in the canyon; you had no refrigeration; and you lived out of cans. Most fellows had to furnish their own picks, shovels, and [blasting] powder. And the worst part was that there was no compensation for accidents. If you got hurt at the mine, you didn't get paid wages, or if you did, it was a minimal amount. And, well, the rich got richer; the poor got poorer. Like Floyd Adams told me the other day, when his father got killed up in Hiawatha, his mother got twelve dollars a month. Can you imagine a woman and four children living on twelve dollars a month? If they didn't have friends and neighbors to help them, they just couldn't get along. You'd be surprised how many young boys—fourteen, fifteen—went to work in the mines because their fathers were killed or maimed, and they became the head of the family and had to earn a living. That's just how it was.

That's why I've always said it was a good thing when the unions came in. I won't say it's *still* a good thing. But it *was* then, because the companies would push you around and literally work you to death for the God Almighty

American dollar. So unions were important. They wanted to see to it [that] the companies didn't take advantage of us—or [the unions tried] to, anyway. Companies were all looking out for number one. The more they made, the more they wanted. I won't say they made vast fortunes. They made enough money, though, to where they could have taken better care of their people. But they wouldn't do it.

Some of the stories I heard about mine bosses could make your hair stand on end. Like one I heard—I can't remember which mine it was now. One of the entries started to cave in. The boss told a guy to go get a horse [from inside]. The guy said, "The hell with the horse." The boss said, "That horse is more important than you are. Either you go get it or go down the road." When the unions came in, they actually tried to protect their members from being harassed like that. And they tried to get them a decent wage. When John L. Lewis became head of the UMW, he said, "A day's work for a day's pay"—which, I still think, is wonderful.[12]

Now, I worked in and around mines my whole life; but, personally, I never got used to being a miner. So I couldn't recommend it. I [also] lost my fingers in the mine. I got my hand caught under the conveyor belt outside. It happened on October 10, 1956, right before quitting time on payday. I was running the tipple that day, because the operator didn't show up. And I saw where there was a piece of coal cutting the [conveyor] belt. I was going up the ramp, and there was a bar lying [on it]. My brother Jim was always preaching safety, so I picked up the bar. I thought I'd put it where it belonged. But instead of taking a hammer that we used to knock coal out when a piece got stuck, I had the bar in my hand and stuck it [in the conveyor belt] and got my hand caught between the bar and the belt.

Right as it happened, I looked around to see if I could call someone over. But I heard the welder running and I knew Harry couldn't hear me. Harry Draper and I worked together at the machine shop. Down below, they had the conveyors running, loading trucks, and I knew they couldn't hear me. So I just got a hold [of the bar] with my left hand and braced my feet and waited. There was a piece of iron underneath the belt—a plate—and it took 'em out [my fingers], one at a time. The only thing I was afraid of was passing out because of the pain. But there wasn't much as it happened. When it first hit, I felt pain; but after that I hardly felt anything.

Afterward, I wrapped my hand in a handkerchief and started coming down. Actually, I hollered a few times, but the fellow on the bottom of the tipple, loading the coal, never heard me. But my brother, standing at the watchman's house, must have, because by the time I got back off the tipple, he was standing right there and asked me what happened. "I cut my hand off," I said. So we run and jumped in his pickup. Then, when we got about halfway down the canyon, that's when I started to get pain. But it might surprise you—there just wasn't that pain like when you burn or cut your hand. Jim had more trouble than I did. I thought he might have a heart attack, because, well, tears were welling in his eyes and he looked at me with the hand gone, feeling [terribly] sorry.

When I went to the doctor, I remember he asked me if I had the fingers, and I said, "No, they went to Japan with the rest of the coal." [*Chuckles*] But it was bad. I spent twenty-five days in the hospital. When I came out, I had recurring nightmares of putting my hand through the belt. My wife used to tell me I'd wake in the middle of the night shaking with fear. Strangely, I could never remember the dreams in the morning. After a couple of months, I was back to work. I wasn't repairing locomotives and generators like I done before, but I was back because of the old work ethic. I worked for another twenty-two years, until my brother Jim sold out to Brasta, [and] then I retired.

After that, it's kind of funny, Jim started sending me a [monthly] check for this or that. I don't know if it was out of guilt or what. But I had my retirement, my Social Security, my few investments, and I was all right. I mean, what was I going to do with it? So I got him to knock it off. I said, "I don't need it. We don't have any use for it." I guess you're supposed to try to get more [money] all the time. I guess that's the whole point for most people. But that isn't what makes life worth living. I'll give you a Greek proverb [I like]. It loses a lot in translation, but it says: "By the time money comes, wisdom is lost." What it means [to me] is, How you live and what you get out of your life is what matters. That's what I believe.

Postscript: Stan Damanti died in Helper, Utah, on December 7, 1989.

MARY KANNES DIAMANT, 61, HOMEMAKER

Mary Kannes Diamant was born in Bingham Canyon, Utah, on November 25, 1922. "I grew up in Bingham," she told us, "and there was no doubt about it: [Lower] Bingham was [like] a Greek village. We knew everybody and everybody knew us." Families celebrated name days, holidays, church and national festivals; and marriages continued to be arranged by proxy, even among the second generation.

"They had men who knew where children of marriageable age were. They made arrangements with the parents, and the kids generally didn't know anything about it. They didn't even know each other until they put the rings on their fingers. I know this," she said, "because my parents tried it on me, and it didn't work. I made up my mind I was not going to get married that way."

Mary Kannes married Alke Diamant, one of the first attorneys from the Greek community of Salt Lake City, in 1944. The couple settled in Salt Lake City, where they became intensely involved with the city's Greek community and, in particular, with the Greek Orthodox church. At present, Mary Diamant, a widow, is one of the volunteer coordinators for the annual Greek festival.

My father, Anastasio Kannes, came here in 1913 as a youngster from the village of Skotene. My mother, Helen Iounnou, was from Argos, a larger town nearby. Although they met and married here, I must say theirs was one of the first elopements that took place in this valley.

Mother was seventeen years old when she arrived. Her mother, who wanted to bring her family to America, had died of pneumonia in 1918; and, after living with aunts and uncles, [my mother] and her sister finally came to America in 1921. Interestingly, it was my stepgrandmother who influenced my grandfather into sending for them. She insisted he bring them over. But after they got here, for some reason, some kind of antagonism or enmity developed between the girls and my grandparents. I don't know how it started. But life was not all honey and roses. My mother recalls trouble because Grandma—an American lady—couldn't speak Greek, and Grandfather [who could interpret] was always in his café. He was one of the proprietors of the old Stadium Café on West Temple and Second South. Anyway, Granny got exasperated; and the girls got twice as exasperated, because they had been uprooted from their home and had come to a strange land. So it was hard; it was quite an upheaval for them.

My parents met at a wedding at the old Lagoon [resort] in Farmington, because the church had no reception center then. They didn't have big and glamorous receptions like we had later. They'd get together and have dinner and dance and sing, and everybody who was Greek, regardless of whether they were invited, went. And, evidently, my mother caught my dad's eye; and she figured, right there and then, she'd like to marry him.

In those days, wherever there were eligible young ladies, marriage proxies came in. She had several proposals, but she kept saying no. Finally, one of my father's uncles got smart enough to go to my grandfather and ask for Mother's hand in marriage for Dad. So they got engaged. But then another fellow offered my grandfather more money, and he tried to break off their engagement. That was when the kids decided they weren't having any of this. "We decided we're going to get married whether he liked it or not," Mother said.[13]

And that's when they eloped. They honeymooned in Salt Lake, then settled in Bingham. My mother said they had to go wherever my father made his living, and there was no way he was going to make a living in Salt Lake. They rented a house owned by Mr. Praggastis for several years until Dad decided to build his own. And that he did. With the help of some cousins and compatriots, he built a concrete house, four rooms, with a full basement and a bathroom, which was a novelty at the time. And that's where we grew up.

I'll add this: As far as Bingham was concerned, the LDS were in the minority. At one point, almost two thousand Greeks worked in what they used to call old Utah Copper. An awful lot of Czechs, Slavs, Italians, and Yugoslavs were there, too, especially when you'd go up into canyon offshoots such as Copperfield and Highland Boy. If you went beyond Copperfield, into what they called Boston Khan, you'd find Orientals. A group of Japanese and Chinese used to live at the very tip-top of the mountain.

Now, the most perfect description of Bingham [Canyon] I ever heard was made by Shirley Temple after she visited. She said the dogs in Bingham had to wag their tails up and down rather than sideways, because the mountains were too close. And that's exactly how it was. The mountains were pressed together. On one side was the [Utah] Copper mine; on the other side was the D&RG railroad. In between, there was this one little, crooked street and above it all these houses climbing the sides of the mountains. All the way up Main Street, business and houses were intermixed. And when the snowslides came, the houses came down [because they had no foundations].

I'll tell you, everybody who lived in that canyon lived by sirens and whistles. We had no [paid] fire department, only a volunteer force. So, if there was a blast on the whistle, the guys would wait to see what it was. A certain number of blasts meant a fire; another meant a slide, grab your shovels and run. I remember we really dreaded August, because it was our rainy month; and when it rained, slides of rocks and silt came down off the mountain and flooded our homes. Many's the time we had to shovel out the back of our house because there was nothing to hold back the rocks during flood month. There was nothing to stop it. The people up in Highland Boy and Copperfield had it worst. They were in the most precarious position. Some of their houses were built along the mountainside and hung on the edge, supported by stilts.

Utah Copper Company was also constantly "regrading" levels, deepening its pit. The levels passed above the houses; and every time they'd blast, boulders came rolling down the hill, several times right through our house. Dad reconcreted and mended our house until he got wise enough to build a concrete retaining wall to protect it. But it was rough on everyone at the time, 'cause most houses were little tinderboxes, poorly built. We got to a point during winter or summer that when Utah Copper was going to blast, they'd give us three shrill whistles; and we knew that meant to get out of the house, because no one knew what was going to come down [the hill].

We lived in Lower Bingham, or Frogtown; and, in Frogtown, there were the Praggastis, Speros, Drossos, and Warris families. I mean, we were just one big [Greek] family. We celebrated name days and birthdays by going from house to house. For instance, St. John's was the 7th of January. So, as a family, we'd go see anybody whose name was John. We'd start at the top of the canyon and end up at the bottom. I remember people danced through houses and wound up outside, [still] dancing. They prepared food like you wouldn't believe. Everybody celebrated. Many a night I slept on a bed covered with coats and stuff as a kid, because [the older] people were having fun, and we [kids] had to go to sleep someplace.

Frogtown also had a large number of Greek businessmen. Greeks were the type who wanted to be independent. They never liked taking orders from anybody, which is why those who could save money started a business. There were a lot of American businessmen in the canyon; but of all the minorities in business, Greeks dominated. We had ice cream shops, coffeehouses, restaurants; we also had shoemakers, pharmacists, grocery stores, barbershops. We even had Greek taxi drivers. They had their own cars, and they would taxi people from Lower to Upper Bingham, from Copperfield to Boston Khan.

My favorite was Mr. Praggastis. He had the only general mercantile store in town. On one side of the store, he had groceries, fresh bread, and fresh doughnuts. On the other side, he had mercantile merchandise, such as ladies' hair nets and those fancy combs women used to put in buns on the back of their hair. Mr. Praggastis tried to have a little bit of everything you needed. If he didn't have it, he'd get it. I used to go there all the time, because I really loved him. In the back of his store, he had a little glassed-in cage where he kept his books and safe. He'd sit there with his glasses tipped on the edge of his nose and wait to see who was coming through those doors. If he liked who it was, he'd come out and show them around. If he was upset with them, he'd send his son or one of his daughters to wait on the people. He was quite a character.

My father was independent for a while, too. He and my uncle leased a mine and dug out whatever ore they could. But it was a dog-eat-dog world, and they barely eked out a living. When Utah Copper decided to hire more men, they went to work there. Dad started on a track gang and worked himself up to a crane operator. He was a workaholic. Whatever he was capable of doing, he was willing to do. When he finished at Utah Copper, he'd do repairs for Mr. Praggastis, who [also] owned several wooden houses he rented [out]. Dad would do the painting, plumbing, and whatever needed to be done to earn more money, because we had a growing family by then.

My mother worked, too. The women did a tremendous amount of [house]work in those days. Mother washed on a scrubbing board, ironed by heating the iron on the old coal stove. And if there was a high holiday, name day, or anything, she did the laundry for her five kids *and* my three uncles. She baked bread, cleaned house, sewed our clothes, and did yard work. And if anybody came to our house—I don't care whether he was an adult or a child—they never left without eating. That was part of our hospitality. I don't care how poor times were—my parents would restrict themselves to make sure the guest had whatever we had.

Dad tried to help her by seeing to it that she got the first washing machine in Bingham, one of the old tongue-licking things. It had a huge copper tub with a tongue that worked back and forth. We also got the first radio in Bingham. We were fortunate about that. It was a Zenith; they delivered it to our house, and everybody got excited. My folks invited all of Frogtown, which was all our friends, to come and listen. I can still see it, plain as day. Here was everybody sitting around, and here's a big piece of furniture up against the wall, and everybody is staring at it as though something was going to come out of it. They listened and would call us to come out from the kitchen, where we were playing, to translate and explain what we heard.

Looking back, I can see we had some great times—and some awful ones. Between 1928 and 1932, for example, we had some exceptionally lean years. After the crash of 1929, Utah Copper laid off [a lot of] people. It got to the point where Dad only worked ten days a month—that's all. The other twenty days he'd scrounge what he could as a part-time plumber and carpenter to supplement the family income.

Being his firstborn, his "fair-haired little girl," I sometimes followed him around. When there wasn't enough coal or wood to cook or keep the house warm, we'd go up the hill, cut down trees, bring them home, and chop them into kindling. There were days we'd go out in the fields—if we could walk down the mountainside—and go into what they called Welby Flats, where the farmers were. And we'd gather dandelion greens and wild asparagus, cook them at home with a little oil and lemon and bread, and that would be our meal for the day. We would also walk the tracks with buckets, and whatever coal remnants fell off the D&RG we'd gather up, take home, and use for heating our stoves. A lot of us did that.

But the thing is, we shared. We were all in the same boat. And I think that's why we got so close, because we went through everything together. I remember people couldn't afford nurses, they couldn't afford medical care. So Mother and Dad took turns sitting overnight with the [sick] children of our friends so the parents could get some rest. At one point, when I became sick, they returned the favor. When I was nine and a half years old, I had a kidney problem, and I bloated from 58 to 106 pounds. The doctors wanted to send me to the hospital, and we couldn't afford it. So Mother and Dad had to boil these great big Hudson Bay blankets, wring them out by hand, and wrap me in them to force me to perspire to get rid of this water so it wouldn't affect my heart. And they did it. They did it for three solid weeks. Then Mrs. Chipian, our neighbor—God love her—she'd come and spell Mama so she could have some time off. Mrs. Praggastis, Mrs. Speros, Mrs. Drossos, Mrs. Lewis, all did the same thing. We were like one great big family. All the way from Lower Bingham to Highland Boy and Copperfield, if something happened to one, we'd all come running. That's how we got along.

We left Bingham in 1939; I was seventeen years old. We were one of the first families to leave, because my parents felt our educational opportunities were limited. So we moved to Salt Lake City to better our lives. Ironically, the opposite happened for a while. [In Bingham,] despite the Klan, we didn't know there was any clash between foreigners and Americans. My first awareness of [this] clash came in Salt Lake City in 1939, and that was quite startling.

We came down, and, as luck would have it, we ended up [living] at 759 Windsor Street, and I ended up going to East High for my senior year and [running into] the discrimination that was directed against minority groups at that point. And, let me tell you, it was pronounced. A couple of Greek kids, Goldie and Ardelle Francis, lived on Eighth East, and daily they would walk up and meet me in the middle of the block so we would walk to school together. In fact, Goldie and Ardelle took me on, more or less, to protect me and break me in to what was going on. I'm glad they did, because the American kids [in school] steered clear of us; they didn't want anything to do with Greeks.

I mean, if they saw you coming down the hall, they'd walk along the other side. If we'd walk into the cafeteria, for instance, the three of us would look for a table where there weren't many kids because we knew what was going to happen. They would get up and walk away, and we weren't about to let ourselves be hurt that way all the time. And I don't care how far we sat [from them]. Even if we sat at the other end of the table, people would get up and walk to another table. They'd just pick up their trays and go. I was never so unhappy in my life as I was that last year in high school.

In addition, I had a blatantly prejudiced teacher. One day—I'll never forget it—I was sitting in home living class. She knew I was Greek, and she said *to the class*: "You'll find *anything* down on the West Side [of the city], from a Negro to a Greek." I took exception to this, and I openly called her on it, which resulted in my being sent to the dean's office. There was blatant discrimination.

That Christmas, I went to ZCMI and applied for a job, because they used to take high school seniors and give them part-time employment during the holidays. Well, it seemed I had the job all sewed up until she looked down at my application. Where it said religion, I wrote "Orthodox." And she just looked at me and said, "You will not do in this store," and openly—*in front of my eyes*—tore up my application and dropped it in the wastebasket. I never did get the job. But that's the way it was. There was open hostility [in Salt Lake City], not against Greeks per se, but against [all] non-LDS [people]. And it became quite a thorn in my side as I was growing up. It really did. It became quite a thorn in my side.

ANDREW KATSANEVAS, 65, EIMCO PLANT SUPERINTENDENT

One of five children, Andy Katsanevas was born in Helper, Utah, on November 20, 1922. Following his father's death in the 1924 Castle Gate mine explosion, his family relocated to Salt Lake City, where he grew up on the city's West Side.

During World War II, Mr. Katsanevas served in the merchant marine, then, after the war, entered a four-year apprenticeship program at EIMCO and became a layout mechanic. "Layout mechanics were the carpenters in the steel trade," he said. "They laid out steel and made various shapes, sizes, and products." He worked for several years as a journeyman, then was promoted to shop foreman and, later, plant superintendent.

In his mid-forties, Andy Katsanevas also began assuming a leadership role in the Salt Lake City Greek Orthodox community. Beginning in 1968, he served two terms as president of the Holy Cross Church's Parish Council and, later, was instrumental in the planning and construction of the Hellenic Memorial Center, which presently houses the community's museum.

My parents are from Crete, Greece. My dad was from an area called Swaka, which is the "he-man" part of Crete. My mother was from Hanea, the capital of Crete. She followed her first husband to Sunnyside, Utah, where he worked in the mines. That's what most Greek men did at the beginning. Through one relative or another writing home, they found out where the jobs were. That's how it worked. My mother's first husband was killed in the mines. As close as I remember the story, he was digging for coal when a slab of rock dislodged and crushed him, leaving my mother a widow with children.

In those days, though, families didn't allow young Greek women to stay single. So, several years later, when relatives insisted she marry again, she married my dad. In 1922, I became their firstborn child. Two years later, my brother Mike was born. Five days after his birth, my dad, who was home because of the birth, returned to work. My mother tried to get him to stay, but he insisted on going back. At about eight o'clock that morning, the 8th of March, 1924, an explosion occurred which killed my dad and a number of other miners. Oh, it was very tragic. Families were left with seven, eight, nine children. There was no such thing as compensation, and while funds did exist, like the one set up by Governor Mabey, they were very minimal.[14]

I had some uncles who would have been killed, too, in that explosion. But they were trying to organize a union elsewhere and were involved in a strike-breaking situation that very day. So, they were lucky! Of course, my mother never got over it. From that day and for forty years, she wore black: cotton black hose, black shoes, and a black dress. As was the custom, she mourned all her life and raised all of us on her own.

While we were growing up, we were all expected to go to the Greek church—when [they held services]—and we were talked to about religion all the time. Our priests from the old country believed in exorcism. When a family moved into a home, a priest would be invited for dinner. After a meal, he would exorcise the home. He would walk into different rooms and read certain chapters out of the Bible. He'd bless the home with incense and sprinkle holy water throughout.

My mother took weekly confession; all the older ladies did. But the older men, no way. The male ego is an odd thing, and these Greek men were very stubborn people. They didn't feel they should reveal anything to anyone unless they wanted to. They attended church; we all did. But they would never confess. That's just the way it was. For us kids, though, it was a different story. Priests were always respected, and parents took no exception to how priests disciplined us. They could shake us, grab us by our ears, shove us out of the classroom door, and no one would ever say a word.

Most of our religious education was taught by the original immigrants and some of the old priests. They were full of superstition and stories about the supernatural. But, you know, if you're going to believe in God and life after death, then you've got to believe there are other things that can happen. So we believed it all. We were told to never whistle in the dark because the devil will appear. Don't look into a mirror at night, and don't sweep the house after dark. I don't know why [you shouldn't sweep after dark]. But even now, if my wife sweeps late at night, I'll tell her to stop. We were told to leave a house by the same door we went in. And, if you've been away from home on New Year's Day, don't be the first one back in. To be safe, toss a big rock through the door so the strength and health of that home will be as strong as that rock. Primping up in the mirror is also a bad omen. It has to do with the devil, but I don't know why.

Now, ever since I was a kid, I've had weird [supernatural] things happen to me. When I was around five and we were living in Castle Gate, my mother took me to visit a neighbor woman down the street. She was sick in bed and, for some reason, I don't know why, she had tried to kill herself. She had taken several big Sultan matches, chopped their heads off, dissolved [the match heads] in water, and drank the solution. The day we were visiting her, she screamed that the devil was at the foot of her bed, trying to take her.

Of course, we didn't see any devil; and after a little while, we left her and started out the back way, because that was the way we went in. All of a sudden, out from nowhere, I saw two huge, odd-looking people walking up the back stairs. I remember, a few seconds later, I heard the woman scream again; and my mother said she didn't understand because she never saw anyone pass by.

When I was about eleven, I had another incident. My uncle worked in a mining community clear back up in the mountains in Columbia, which is about twenty miles outside of Price. He used to visit us frequently—especially since my father died—and he'd always bring candy or give us money. This one night, around nine or ten o'clock, I heard a knock on the door. When I went over and peeked out a window, there stood my Uncle Gus on the porch. I yelled to my mother, "It's Uncle Gus!" And I opened the door, but there was nobody there. Nobody. About midnight, that same night, we got word that he was killed in the mines down there. He was dead exactly when I saw him on the porch. Modern civilization tells you these things don't exist or don't happen, but they do.

Greek people also know about the evil eye—and that some people give it and some people get it. Greeks believe somebody gives you the evil eye primarily because they are envious of you. They admire your looks, your physique, or the type of person you are. I used to get deathly ill with no particular visible evidence of any real sickness. My mother said it was the evil eye, and she'd take me to Mrs. Funtas up the street. As soon as this woman saw me, she put some drops of holy water into a shot glass filled with regular water and said a prayer. You never knew the words, because she'd say them inaudibly. Then she made the sign of the cross on the glass and took three or four big sighs, until it seemed she was ready to pass out. When I drank from the water, though, believe it or not, I got well.

Another time, when I had the evil eye, Mrs. Louris wound a white ribbon around my waist and made a cross in the bow. She, too, mumbled words on all four sides of the cross, and the ribbon stretched and loosened all by itself. Maybe it was psychological—I wouldn't know that; but it did draw the evil eye away.

I was still a kid when we moved from Castle Gate to Salt Lake City. I know we didn't bring many things with us; we never had a lot of things. We moved into Cliff Place, which is on 350 South West Temple, and paid ten dollars a month for rent. Cliff Place had three or four houses that looked into a courtyard. Behind it was Rigby Court, with probably another twenty homes occupied by Greeks, Italians, Swedes, and, of course, Americans. There were fences that divided the two complexes, but they didn't stay up long. Rather than walk clear around the block to play or visit, kids ran tires through the fence and opened up enough boards to pass through.

As a boy, certain things were expected of me. I was expected to bring the coal up from the basement, clean the yard, chop the wood, and go to the grocery store. My sisters were expected to do housework and help Mother with the dishes. Everyone tried to contribute. My sister Joanne contributed the most monetarily, because she had a high school education and worked at a bakery making about nine dollars a week. My older sister, who was born in Greece, wasn't allowed in school when she first came over. Then she had such difficulty picking up English, my mother pulled her out of school. Finding work outside the house was also difficult for her. But as I grew older, I didn't have any trouble getting a job. Most of my friends had no problem finding work. We weren't picky about what type of work we did, so we got jobs shining shoes, selling newspapers, or jerking sodas. Later, when I was at Weber College, I'd spend summers working on construction and give the money to my mother.

Living at Cliff Place wasn't harder than living at Castle Gate. The only thing I had to do was to stick up for myself. Regardless of where we went, whether it was among other ethnic groups or people that referred to themselves as Americans, we had to be ready to fight. If we were playing softball in Pioneer Park and another group of kids came over and wanted to take over the field, we'd have a war. And if we chickened out, if we refused to fight, we didn't play.

From where we lived, we could walk to the Growers Market, located where the [downtown] Hilton is today. It was an open market with stalls for selling produce. The Bamberger Railroad ran along the back of it. During the summer months, early in the mornings, farmers would truck their goods in, rent stalls, and sell fresh vegetables or fruit. Since all the traffic came in from the West Temple side, vendors who set up shop close to that side sold out quicker than others. People always dickered for the cheapest price. We'd go down there and work for those farmers. We'd be bag boys or sell vegetables; and they'd pay a nickel or a dime for five or six hours of work. I'd say probably a couple of hundred farmers came in each day and sold their goods.

Sweets Candy Company was also in that area. Sometimes, we'd go to the back of their factory and find boxes of defective candy they tossed out. You know, those that were smashed or a little deformed. We'd eat them—they were delicious. Sometimes, too, we'd watch crews unload railroad tank cars of syrup. They'd hose it into Sweets' basement, and after they'd leave, we'd find big gobs of corn syrup stuck in the coupling. We'd fill cups full of it. It was good. Heck, it was sweet, good stuff.

Though Greek people drank and I had access to liquor my whole life, drinking was the furthest thing from my mind. My buddies would go uptown and get into poolhalls, but that was something I didn't get into, either. My mother taught me they were evil places, so I swore I'd never get involved.

In 1938 or '39, Paramount Billiards as well as Stubecks, which was a pretty famous place that had customers from various social levels, were both located in our part of town. At that time, I was about sixteen and worked upstairs [above Stubecks] in an ice cream parlor called Politz. Stubecks was always busy. People spent a lot of time playing "The Game of Life" on a regular pool table. The object of the game wasn't to shoot the ball into the pockets, but to just nudge the other guy's ball a certain number of times until he was considered "dead." People could get into a game with one to five dollars. They'd play for hours, pick up forty or fifty dollars, or lose whatever they had. I never played, but some of my friends got good enough to be in tournaments. Stubeck was a loan shark. People who'd try to get out of paying him back would be seen, days later, with blackened eyes or broken bones.

Those were the Prohibition days, too. You'd see people strolling along the streets carrying milk bottles that were actually painted white and filled with whiskey. Bootleggers used all kinds of bottles, and there was a woman in the neighborhood who collected and sold them. Sometimes we'd scavenge bottles or swipe them from the back of her place, then go around to the front and sell them back to her.

There was probably a half a dozen Greek coffeehouses all over the city. They had names like Parthenon, Crete, Old Crete. When I delivered newspapers with my brother Steve, we'd go in, and they'd always treat us to an orange soda or some *loukoumi* [gelatin squares rolled in powdered sugar]. The walls in these places were plain, but they usually had a picture of the king of Greece or President Venizélos because the owner was a supporter of one or the other political faction. The floor was mainly wood. The tables were small and round, made from steel with plywood centers. The chairs were steel backed with plywood seats. They were sturdier than heck. The atmosphere was jovial.

Drinks were served in barrel-shaped glasses or demitasse cups made of heavy porcelain. The old-timers played cards, pinochle, or *Prefa* and sometimes a Greek game called *Koulitsina*. And they'd cuss. Oh, you can't imagine the cussing. An old-timer sometimes would get so irritated with losing a game, he'd storm out, cross the street to another coffeehouse, and find somebody else in there to play with. Of course, women weren't allowed inside. If they wanted their husbands, they'd stand by the door and signal or send somebody in to get them. They'd never go in themselves.

In our grade school and junior high years, we played athletics or chased around with the guys or got into beefs—things of this nature. We liked girls, we enjoyed being around them, but dating was considered "sissy." Of course, once we did start dating, Greek parents were strict. My mother was especially strict if I dated non-Greek girls.

In high school, we all went to the same church, the same Greek school, the same GOYG [Greek Orthodox Youth Group], and the same activities and dances. But I was a poor Cretan. Many of the other kids had parents who were from the mainland. They were into businesses and were more affluent. So I didn't socialize with them, and they didn't with me. That was all right; because, for the most part, all the [Cretan] guys stuck together and did things in groups. When I started dating non-Greek girls, though, I had to do that on the sly. I'd tell my mother I was going out with my buddies, you know.

In those days, a lot of the marriages were still being arranged by parents. My own sister's marriage was arranged. Trying to entice me, my mother would say, "This Greek girl has a lot of property. Her parents have a lot of money." But there was just no way I would marry anybody on a fixed situation like that.

I was seventeen years old when I joined the merchant marines and went into the Second World War. Right after the war, I met my future wife, Margaret, on my own. A year and a half later, we married. She was LDS. Yet we raised all our children as [Greek] Orthodox, and fifteen years after we married, she decided to join the Orthodox church. At the time we married, her parents reluctantly accepted our marriage; but there was never any formal acceptance from my family. My mother didn't even attend our wedding. Eventually, though, it worked out. When my mother finally deigned to come to our home for dinner and met Margaret, I remember [that] right after we ate, my wife got up and instinctively straightened the table—just like my mother would. My mother must have been struck by that, because she soon ended up acknowledging her. I guess all she really needed was common ground.

THEROS JOHN "TED" SPEROS, 70, RESTAURATEUR

Cofounder and proprietor of Lamb's, the oldest "continually operating" Greek restaurant in Utah, Ted Speros was born in Bingham Canyon, Utah, on December 26, 1914. His father, Theros John Speropoulos, was born in Akarta, Greece, a village between Athens and Athos. When his father was five years old, Ted Speros told us, his paternal grandparents passed away. The younger siblings were placed with different relatives, and Ted's father "drifted" into Athens to work. When he was sixteen or seventeen, he "heard" that people from his village were finding lucrative jobs out in the western portion of the United States. So he emigrated to America and wound up in Bingham Canyon, where he initially worked as a miner, then opened a small grocery store.

Following the outbreak of the Balkan War in 1913, Ted's father, like thousands of young, patriotic Greek men, gave up his safe haven and returned home to fight with the Greek armed forces. After serving his two years, he married Efstathia Apostolopoulos. The newlyweds returned to the United States in October 1914; that December or January, their first child (Ted) was born. "Actually," Ted quipped, "you could say I was started in Greece and completed in America."

I was born in Bingham Canyon and christened Theros John Speropoulos. I thought I arrived on December 26, 1914, but many years later, I discovered I was "legally" born January 13, 1915. My mother claims *she* knows when I was born. The discrepancy in dates could have occurred because doctors treating patients in small mining camps accumulated birth and death records before sending them on to the [State] Capitol building, or one of my birth dates might have been taken from the Gregorian calendar while the other from the Julian. It doesn't matter to me. I celebrate both.

I grew up in Bingham Canyon; and although I don't know about other mining towns, in Bingham, Greeks lived conservatively and it was important for them to own their homes. Our four-room house was small, but it was ours. We had a big kitchen and an old coal stove with a water tank on the side for circulating and heating the water, a bedroom for my parents, and one for my sister. My brother and I slept in the dining room. Every night, we made up our folding beds, and every morning, my mother closed [them] up.

We had a stove in the kitchen and one in the dining room. In the evening, my dad stoked the kitchen stove with paper, wood, and coal. When the alarm clock rang at five o'clock in the morning, my mother woke up, put a match to the paper, lit the stove, and put on the old coffee percolator. For several years, we had an outhouse. In the winter, you'd think twice if you woke at night and had to go to the bathroom. I remember the time when my dad put a toilet in one of our closets. It was cause for a celebration.

Getting it installed was easy, I remember. Those were the days when Greek people helped each other. . . . You could always count on two or three relatives showing up to help dig the trench and put the pipes in for plumbing. Of course, nowadays, with such strict regulations, you can't do that. Iceboxes, too, were luxuries few could afford. For a long time, we used an outside closet that was as cold as a deep freeze.

On Saturdays, my mother boiled water on top of the stove and filled up the number three tub for our baths. Every Monday, she put the same tub on the top of the stove, filled it with water, and washed our clothes on a scrub board. It was years before we had a real bathtub. In fact, the first time my godfather installed one in his home, my cousin and I raced to get into it! When my father installed one in our house, it was a sign of the [changing] times. All these innovations—the radio, the bathtub, the toilet, the indoor plumbing—came in during our lifetime.

Day-to-day living was fairly traditional for us. In the evenings, after dinner, we read in the living room. We always had Greek lessons. In addition, my dad paid for the newspaper and checked for any references to Greece. If he didn't find one word that mentioned Greece, he'd say, "Why am I spending all my money on newspapers?" So we carefully analyzed what we read. If we spotted anything with the word "Greece" or "Greeks," we brought it to him.

My father worked hard. He was out of the house by five thirty in the morning and back by four o'clock at night. My mother took care of the children. She did all the cooking, the baking, the washing, the cleaning, and worked very hard. I remember the house was always spotless and the table always set for dinner by the time my father came home from work. Occasionally, my father would make our school lunches, usually two sandwiches apiece. But my mother did everything else.

Our meals were cooked in the Greek tradition. Because of that, we saved a lot of money on food and rarely wasted anything. For instance, on Sunday morning, my mother would boil a chicken for Greek soup. For lunch, she'd use the broth and put rice and an egg in it and maybe a thigh and a leg. For dinner, she'd take the rest of the chicken, baste it with tomatoes and spices, and oven bake it with potatoes. There was never any waste. Other times, my dad would buy a soup bone—and, in those days, soup bones were different. They had enough meat on them to feed an entire family. My mother would make a nice soup by boiling beans with the bone. Oh, it was so delicious, I can taste it even now.

When I first started going to public school, I spoke no English, so it was rough for me. I remember, when I had to go to the washroom, I raised my hand. But when I was called on, I didn't have the words to explain what I wanted. So, I pointed. Everybody started laughing. Most of the teachers were sympathetic, though, and patient, not only with the Greek students but all the other ethnic groups. They knew what the problems were, because many of them were from the second generation, too, and had experienced these difficulties. In fact, there were so many minorities in Bingham [that] I didn't know I was living in a Mormon state until I was almost twelve years old.

My father was active in the Greek community and dedicated to giving us a religious as well as public school education. After the Greek community got permission from the school board to use Bingham High's classrooms for Greek lessons, they paid an instructor to teach all of us from Bingham, Highland Boy, Copperfield, and Lower Bingham. These teachers were tough. I remember one slapped our hands or hit us with the pointer or a ruler if he thought we weren't paying attention. If we weren't prepared, he'd make us stand on one foot. My brother Peter was a good student. I was a regular "stander-on-one-foot." If we really misbehaved, this man paid our fathers a visit. I hated that.

Yet, even my public school teachers were known to pay my father a visit. I guess I was a scrapper. Bingham Canyon had wooden sidewalks, and groups of kids would regularly call us names and try to push us off. So I fought back. There was also a girl at school who called me "Dirty Greek" whenever she passed me on the stairway. One day, I guess I had had enough. So when she said it again, I shoved her down the stairs. She wasn't hurt, and she never called me a dirty Greek again. But I had a problem with her older brother, who was bigger than I was, until he discovered I had a friend who was bigger than he was.

Oh, my mother! She would get so angry with me. "Ted! Ted! Don't fight!" she'd yell. But once, when I was beating up on a fellow who wouldn't stop calling me a dirty Greek, she ran out, shaking her fist and yelling at me, "Don't you stop or I'll start up with you!" [*Laughs*]

Describing life in Bingham, I want you to know I'm speaking about hard-working people. Those Greeks who left the mines opened up businesses such as shoe shine shops, hat cleaning parlors, grocery stores, bakeries, floral shops, restaurants, construction companies, and, later, automobile dealerships. And those who stayed with the mines were loyal to their companies and bosses. Their unity became one reason why it took years for Utah Copper to organize its union even though a lot of strikes took place. Another reason was because workers were already paying money to a company hiring agent.

See, each ethnic group [initially] had its [labor] leader. A man named Skliris worked with the Greeks, and every month, the miners paid him a dollar or two just to keep their jobs. They figured, why should they join a union when they were already paying for security? Of course, this Greek person was taking advantage of them. He dictated what they should do, who they should work for; and, at the same time, he declared his loyalty to them. He was of little real help to Greek workers. But this was the way it went for many years.

I didn't work at my dad's grocery store, because when he closed the business, I was young. I did work at my godfather's store and washed windows, cleaned the yard, and burned the tumbleweeds. I also worked at the soda fountain for the Royal Candy Company, another Greek-owned store. I went to school during the week and worked for them weekends and summers. All the time, I watched my uncles, my dad, and the other Greeks in Bingham. I saw them getting up at five thirty in the morning and walking to work every day, year in and year out. I saw them coming home with their empty lunch baskets, walking slowly, tired. There was no such thing as an eight-hour day. And I realized I just didn't want that type of life.

I had never been in the restaurant business. But when I was about seventeen, my dad's distant relative worked as the head waiter at Latches Shop in Salt Lake City. In the summer of 1933, I worked as a busboy, received a dollar a day for ten to twelve hours of work plus free board and room. Soon, I was given an apron, black trousers, black shoes, a white shirt, bow tie, and a tray for cleaning tables. I thought I was a hot shot!

This was a businessmen's restaurant, so there were lots of dimes, quarters, fifty-cent pieces—maybe even an occasional dollar—left on the table. Well, every time I cleaned a table, I pocketed this money. I was thrilled because I was making so much money. After two or three days, though, I was told I was taking the waitresses' tips, and I went right back to the dollar a day or ten cents an hour salary I started with.

I graduated from high school two or three months earlier than usual because we were still in the Depression and there wasn't enough money to keep the schools opened. I still worked at Latches, but now as a cook. In the meantime, Dad's work at Utah Copper was drastically reduced from thirty days a month to ten, then to five. He'd tell me the only thing he didn't want to see was a welfare truck stopping in front of our house. "I don't care," he'd say, "as long as we don't have to go on welfare." What a disappointment it was for my dad when, after working all his life and raising his family, the welfare truck did stop in front of our house. But we survived. My dad started working at Latches, too. And with our combined earnings, we got by.

Now, there was plenty of gambling in those bleak days. A lot of betting on horses, too. For half a block down on State Street and Second South, bookies had private offices at the Felt Building, the Boston Building, and other offices. Most of them, though, were located in the back rooms of restaurants and pool halls. A telegraph service from the track was hooked up to phones in these private suites. As information came along, it would be relayed: This horse was ahead, that horse was ahead. Then the information went to bookies, who would pay off—or not.

Gambling was supposed to be illegal; but whenever a place got raided, you'd be surprised by the number of people who were gambling—and *who* was gambling. Even after the federal government stepped in and cut the telegraphic services, gambling continued. Bookies went around town and picked up individual bets. I saw men gamble up to five thousand dollars at a time.

By this time, I was eighteen to nineteen years old, making under two dollars a day, and the gambling bug bit me, too. For a while, I'd call down and place a bet. If I made five or six dollars a day, I felt rich! I got carried away and started wearing white pants, white coat, and spats on my shoes! But I didn't stay in the business long. Between my dad's admonitions and seeing Latches lose his restaurant because of gambling debts, I stopped betting with my future.

Just before World War II broke out, an Ogdenite named George Lamb bought the Commercial Grille on Main Street [in Salt Lake City] and called me in to work for a week or two after he became ill and was hospitalized. He knew about me, and, by this time, I was married and making a living in the restaurant business. As it turned out, after those two weeks, I stayed on with Lamb. We changed the name to Lamb's Grill Café and worked as partners— on a handshake—for more than thirty-three years.

The war years were busy years. They changed the face and look of downtown Salt Lake City and changed our lives. On weekends, soldiers from Kearns, Hill Air Force Base, and Dugway came into the city. They went to shows, dances, restaurants, and crowded the streets and all the establishments. All they wanted was to be entertained and well fed. Lamb's became an American restaurant serving food with a Greek touch, and, boy, we were going like nobody's business!

At the same time, I was called into the service. Since Lamb was hospitalized again, I received a deferment and was sent to work as an operator on a crusher at Magna Mill. I worked afternoon and graveyard shifts for the duration of the war and an additional six months. At the same time, I worked at the café as host and cashier. I also made deposits, took care of the kitchen help, and ordered the food. Working both jobs and going back and forth, I averaged thirteen to fifteen hours a day. Sometimes, I thought I was asleep on my feet.

Since this was during the war, gas was rationed, and most of our food and scarcity items were obtained with red points. We had to tailor our menu to accommodate those allowances. As a result, chicken, fish, pasta, fruits, vegetables, and only two types of steaks (tenderloin and club) were highlighted on our menu. I learned all about these points—what to buy, what not to buy, and when to buy it. At one time, we accumulated enough points to order a head of cheese that weighed forty pounds and was about a foot thick. We sliced it and served it free to our customers. We made our soup from scratch—still do. And always, always, the backboard table was covered with fresh fruits—casabas, Persians, Crenshaws, watermelons, raspberries, and plump, ripe strawberries. Everything was delicious and beautifully displayed. The waitresses wore white uniforms; the tablecloths were white linen; and white linen napkins became our trademark. During the war years, we were so busy, we got our chef a deferment and handled more than seven hundred people daily.

Yet, from the time we opened, Lamb's meant more than food. Lamb and I were interested in the type of clientele we served. And since we were located right in the center of the business district, the café became *the* place for decision makers and talkers. Lawyers, bankers, judges, politicians, newspapermen, businesspeople, union men, miners—each [professional] group had its own table and were never seated anywhere else. Discussions on every imaginable topic took place; candidates were chosen; deals were made; stocks were bought; and privacy was maintained.

There were splendid people in this area. Ben Roe, a Jewish merchant, had a ladies clothing store. Every morning, Mr. Roe, Mr. Nebeker, and Mr. Cline met here for breakfast and talked politics. I remember, Mr. Roe loved raspberries. If you went up State Street, you'd see Shapiro's Luggage. Every day, Mr. Shapiro also walked into the café and sat at one of the first two tables. Businessmen such as Joe Rosenblatt, who founded EIMCO, had their table for sixteen in the back dining room, where the Masons also met.

Mr. Fitzpatrick, Mr. Fish, and a number of reporters from the [Salt Lake] *Tribune* established their own "press table," a big booth that is still kept for them. Very few *Deseret News* reporters came, although they gave us good publicity.

Mr. Orville Adam, president of Zions Bank, arrived and met with five or six colleagues. This was a daily ritual. They talked stocks. Then, when they got through eating, they'd match dollars. The odd man got the dollars.

The city was smaller [during the postwar years], but the issues were just as lively! The Republicans would be in one dining room, the Democrats in another. They'd arrive at the same time and go to their respective tables.

Once, when we decided to replace some of the well-worn chairs used by members of the exclusive Alta Club, they were up in arms. "We sit here every day, so we'll decide which chairs to use!" They did.

Another time, we added music for our lunch crowd! What a mistake! They were here to have lunch and conduct business, they said, not to be entertained! In the '40s and '50s, almost everyone smoked cigars. We had high ceilings in the café, and it was unbelievable how the smoke rose up to the ceiling. From the front entrance to the back rooms, by the time lunch was over, you couldn't see through the smoke. The walls were solid black—and every few months, we'd have to wash them down.

Lamb and I also made it a point to try to help some of our people. One fellow, William Gorden, an organizer of Burns Detective Association, retired in Utah and became one of our regulars. You could set your watch by him. A tall, strong, elderly man, when he died, he left a note for me to use his money to bury him and send the balance to his family. He left me his .38 pistol, with the bullets, and his brass knuckles. These were remarkable people. They gave this place such a feeling of permanence that if I close my eyes now, I can still see them sitting here, talking, arguing, debating, laughing. We knew when they would arrive, who they would meet, and what they liked to eat. When one of our regulars died, we would take away his chair and place his picture, a candle, and some flowers on his table until the funeral service was over.

As much as I say how well we knew our customers, I have to admit they knew us, too. Every morning at six thirty, Lamb would check in to see what we needed. By seven thirty, he'd place the order, then visit with his friends and customers. He'd be into some deep discussions when I'd walk in at nine o'clock. But, before I could even take ten steps, some customer would say, "Ted, don't order the ground round! George ordered it and bawled the hell out of them because there was too much fat the last time."

Lamb checked every order and sent back anything that wasn't okay. But he talked so loudly from his office upstairs, everyone throughout the restaurant, from the dining rooms to the counters, knew exactly what he was saying. I'd walk in, [and] they'd say, "Ted, you don't have to . . . " The customers loved the camaraderie.

Looking back at Lamb's Grille Café is like taking a nostalgic tour through Salt Lake's heritage. We are one of the oldest, continual, in-operation restaurants in the state. Our booths, tables, counters, light fixtures, and steam tables have remained unchanged since 1938. Our glass counter is one of the longest counters in the state. In the back room, George Washington's picture, given to Lamb and signed by Governor George H. Dern, who was later appointed by President Franklin D. Roosevelt to serve as secretary of defense, still hangs on the wall. On another wall, a "trout sign," one of the first signs made by Tom Young of Young Electric Sign Company, reads "Quality, Service and Sanitation"—the very qualities that we still strive towards.

In a way, I think we [second-generation] Greeks accomplished what the early immigrants only dreamed of. We established ourselves, raised families, and sent money home to help others. It's true my mother always wanted to return to Greece. But, after fighting in the Balkan War, my dad never did. He often told us that America was his country; it gave him the things he wanted in life. He said, "I want to be buried here, in America." As far as going home, I think like my dad. I *am* home.

MARY PAPPAS LINES, 66, SOCIAL WORKER

One of eight children, Mary Pappas Lines was born in Price, Utah, on January 10, 1921. Her father had arrived in Utah in 1904; her mother followed nine years later. Since their house was one of "the first established homes in Price," it was for many years, she recalled, the informal "center" of the community and the official welcoming post for newly arrived brides.

"When the bachelor miners from the mining camps would bring their wives over, they'd usually stay at our house [and mother would get them oriented]. So, I grew up— I don't think I liked it—always sleeping on the couch or on the floor. I have an ongoing childhood memory of people staying at our house."

Against the wishes of her parents and in contradistinction to the mores of her community, Ms. Lines married a non-Greek and, later in life, returned to school and became a social worker. Her interview, and her "journey," offer a lucid portrait of one woman's struggle to transcend ethnic and gender boundaries without sacrificing core beliefs and values.

My mother's maiden name was Jennie Jouflas. Actually, Jennie was a made-up [American] name. Her Greek name was Ionna, the female derivative of John. My father's name was Pappas. The Greek name was Gustav Constantine Pappageorge. But he never used his whole name in America. My father came here when he was about eighteen. And like most immigrants, he was recruited by the labor bosses who brought in young workers from the villages, then dispersed them in factories in the East or coal mines in the West. He didn't like to talk about the first years in this country, though, when he worked in the mines. What he did say was the mines were a trial he had to go through, then his life could begin.[15] He was the oldest son in his family, and it was his obligation to help raise a dowry for his sisters, which he did. So his first responsibility after he got here was to send whatever money he had back to his father to help his sisters marry. It was understood he would do that before he could marry.

My parents were both from Mavrolithari, a remote village in the province of Rumeli. Fortunately [for the kids in the family], they were both very verbal and talked a great deal about their [early] lives. In fact, when I was in my mother's village some years ago, I felt I had been there before, because she had described everything in such detail—where the houses were, where the [village] square was, and where the big pine grew in the middle of the square. She talked about it so much because she was homesick. They were both homesick.

Mary Lines. *George Janecek*

My father used to tell us how strange it was initially to be here. He told us about going out into the farmlands in Emery County, which were almost exclusively [occupied] by Mormon pioneer families, to buy stock from the farmers and bring it back to the slaughterhouse. The people were kind to him. That's how he always felt. But their customs were different. They would ask him to stay overnight, and he would, because the transportation at night, even over short distances, was difficult. They'd give him blankets and, as they got ready for the evening meal, ask him if he would like to eat. Out of propriety, he would always say no; and he would go to sleep hungry, not understanding why they asked. You see, a Greek hostess would have forced food on him. After his polite "No," she would have said, "You *must* eat," and put the food on his plate. But once he said no, they wouldn't ask again.

The other story he told always made me feel sad for him. He had gone over to Vernal for the same reason—to buy livestock and bring it back to sell. But after returning from one of the farms, he got lost. It was dark, and, he said, he did not allow himself to really express, even to himself, the despair he felt at being alone and getting lost. [But] he got off his horse and lay on the ground and wept. "What am I doing thousands of miles from home, a perfect stranger?" I always felt sorry for him when he told that story. But he was very religious. He prayed to overcome his despair. And when it was dawn, he got back on the horse and rode directly to where he needed to go. Today, we tend to think he overcame his despair, [and] then with a cooler mind was able to find his way back. But my father believed he was helped because he prayed.

My father was twenty-seven when he went back to Greece and married Mother, who became the first Greek woman to live in Price. Mrs. Diamanti was first in Helper. But Mother was first in Price, and this wasn't easy. She would get so homesick my father would put her on the train with one or two children, and she would ride to Helper and stay with Mrs. Diamanti for a few days. [I remember] when the second family moved into Price, my mother said she was ecstatic! At last, another Greek woman! She told us about visiting this newly arrived family and how they talked so long and she so hated to leave that she stayed too long. On the way home, it was evening. She was frantic that my father might beat her. But when she got home, my father was sitting at the kitchen table with olives, cheese, and a glass of wine. When she hurried into the kitchen, he said, "So how was Mrs. Dragatis today?" And mother told about the flood of relief that swept over her. What was amusing, when she told the story, was that she thought to herself, "Oh, that's the kind of man he is." I used to think, "It's too bad she ever found that out," because it seemed she took advantage of my dad. Having her tell the story was nice, though, because you thought from then on it was too bad for him.

My mother wasn't [formally] educated, but she was smart. She ran the house and ran our lives, and she wasn't a wilting violet. Though she spoke broken English, if there was a conflict at school, she'd put her hat and her good shoes on and march up to school to talk to the teacher [and] work it out. I saw her as powerful. To describe her to somebody, even after I was married, I would describe somebody in full tilt—like a schooner, you know—full speed ahead! That's how I saw her. She was a little over five feet tall, and after we were all grown (we were all tall like my father), there wasn't any of us that couldn't stand up and put our arm over her head. Yet, maybe the scariest thing you could imagine in your life was to oppose her. It wasn't easy.

I'm trying to recall when I first knew [my mother and I] were different. I must have known it as soon as I started school, when I was five or six years old. I didn't compare myself with the French family, who lived next door, but with the Americans. And I had some self-consciousness about having American kids come to our house. I can remember feeling embarrassed that we were different, that as soon as we stepped in the door my mother would talk Greek.

In the first place, the kids made fun of me. "Your mother says blah-blah-blah." Also, as soon as we got in a minor quarrel over "Run My Sheepy, Run," or whatever, in the [school] yard, then you were a "dirty Greek." I would go home with that, but my mother would always make short shrift of it. She would say, "Are you crying, you silly girl? Look at yourself. Are you dirty or are you clean?" I don't know what her [next] words would be, but she would infer it was too bad for them they weren't also Greek. Then they'd have something to be proud of.

Yet I was quite impatient with all that as a youngster—that somehow she thought we were *so* special and nobody else in the world knew all the stories we did. When I got into junior high and high school and found out other people knew about Plato and Socrates and Homer and the *Odyssey,* which I was bored and impatient with, her attitude seemed a waste of energy and not a well-founded belief. I remember thinking, "If it's so wonderful to be Greek, how come nobody else thinks so?"

So I rebelled. I think a lot of the young people did. I rebelled as much as I could, even over things that didn't matter much. I can remember rebelling about religion. During my teenage years, I called them "voodoo rites" to my mother. I wanted to impress her—shock her—[with the fact] that I didn't think the same things she thought and that I didn't believe. She would dramatize and gasp, "What if the priest heard what you said?" Later, after I married, I also felt good about not doing the typical Greek things in my home. I didn't cook Greek food, and I didn't wait on my husband. Well, I did, but not to the extent my brothers or other Greek men were waited on. My husband would press his shirts without thinking. My brothers didn't know where their shirts were.

But the most rebellious thing I did—*except* for my marriage to a non-Greek—was to leave home after graduating from high school and come to Salt Lake and take a job. Greek girls didn't leave home unless they got married, and my mother was really shocked at that. She fought me for a long time over it. But we had a pattern in our family. My mother would battle the children up to a point. She would try all of her tricks, and if they didn't work, then she would call in my father. Though he wouldn't oppose her, you could almost count on him at that point to help you do what you really wanted to do. So my father and I "compromised." The agreement was that I could come to Salt Lake if I moved in with the two French girls who had grown up next door.

Now, I can remember an important thing—wishing she hadn't given up [fighting me] when she did, because I was frightened. I was afraid of coming to Salt Lake [alone]; and it seemed the battle [with her] was the most important thing. The day I left, my mother and my brother got up about four in the morning, and I felt terrible. I kept thinking, "If she would just ask me [to stay] one more time, if she would [only] do something to make me stay." I was really afraid, and I felt guilty getting my brother up at four. The Price [Canyon] road was treacherous. It went to the top of the mountain—it wasn't down near the riverbed like now—and it was wintertime. And I can remember my brother [driving] with the window rolled down to make sure he could see the road because it was snowing, and the feeling I had [was] I caused all this trouble. . . .

When I was older, I realized my actions were my way of trying to separate myself from her. [But when I was nineteen] I just wanted to be free of her Greek ways. To me it was very hard to think that I couldn't have any independence or autonomy, that to get along at home, I needed to follow the pattern. It was hard for me, too, because I was emotionally dependent on my mother. I had grown up there. I was a good student. I had never done anything to disgrace or embarrass her. So why did she think she always *knew* what was better for me than I did?

Of course, she knew only one pattern, a Greek pattern with expectations based on the lifestyle she had left behind in 1911. Do you see what I mean? It wasn't only the difference between Greek and American cultures [that caused problems]; it was also the fact that she didn't progress beyond the world she left. Greece progressed. But we were all brought up with this picture of Greece in 1913, in the remote mountain village that Mother lived in. And she more or less wanted [us] to maintain that same cloistered, overprotected, and sheltered life she had lived. It was very hard.

I stayed in Salt Lake City two years, and, I remember, I was homesick the entire time I was there—*the entire time*. But after the two years, I thought, I've stayed long enough. I've proved a point. They won't throw it back at me. Yet, when I got off the train in Helper, and my mother was there with whomever in the family she brought to take me home, and they got all my clothes in the car, she said, "Now, young lady, you don't leave again until you get married." And I remember standing there thinking, "I wish she hadn't said that. Now, I *have* to leave again." And I did. After a year, I went to live with my married sister in California.

Mother and I got to know each other more as women once I was married and she would confide in me. [I remember] she was at my house one day when I was preparing a birthday party for one of my children: blowing balloons, fixing cupcakes, and getting ready. I noticed her getting quieter and quieter, and I thought, "She came to visit me; maybe she doesn't like it that all the little children are coming." I asked her, "Mama, is anything wrong?" She said, "Why do you call me Mama? If I were you, I wouldn't call me Mama. I didn't do any of these things for you. And I don't know if it was because I didn't know how or because I didn't have the time. You learned to walk on your first birthday. I put you down, and I don't think I picked you up after that."

After my mother died, I went through a severe personal crisis. I was in my early forties, I had three young children, and there was no longer anyone to battle. So I had to sort out what I wanted from my life. I decided I would go back to school. This is the one thing I had always wanted to do. You see, in our community, it was believed men should be more educated than women and that women did themselves proud, or did well, by marrying well. They gained status through a marriage; they couldn't do it on their own. Well, I always resented that [attitude] because I was the best student of all of the children and only finished two years of college in Price before marrying.

So I made up my mind to go back, get my undergraduate degree, and teach English. When my husband saw I was determined, he was very supportive. He initially felt it would be good if I taught. But, later, when I decided I didn't want to teach high school English the rest of my life because it was too confining, our marriage suddenly collapsed. I wanted to stay married. But he felt we were in a power struggle. Anyway, after I made the decision to go [on] to graduate school, we went our separate ways.

At that point, a chance meeting with a social worker changed the course of my life. I went up to see him at the University counseling center because it looked like I was going to fail physics. In the first place, to get anything but an "A" was a blow to my ego. Then, to realize I might fail physics because I had never done anything to prepare in that direction [was devastating]. But this man really helped me. We met throughout the year [in which my marriage was failing], and he didn't ask me to pay. He was caring, and he had time anytime I needed help. I associated this with social work, and I pretty much modeled [myself on his behavior]. So, when I realized I didn't want to be a teacher, that seemed to be the only thing I really wanted to do. I wanted to be a social worker. I wanted to do the things he was doing.

I remember thinking at time[s], "There must be something really wrong with me [for me] to keep going to school while my marriage was failing." There were times I thought, "If I could just stay home, [if I could] stop wanting to be anything else or do anything else, then maybe my husband and I would get back together and everything would be fine." But I couldn't. I literally couldn't [do it]. I had never thought of it until this minute, but it seemed as though my survival depended on it. It seemed that I was struggling for my life, my identity, my own personhood.

As a pretty young child, I can remember not wanting to be like my mother. Not because I didn't care about her, but because I wanted to be educated and

I had certain American role models. I remember, in grade school I thought my teacher epitomized what you should be like: American and educated. I remember in high school watching a girl and competing with her for [class] officership. We both belonged to the same girls' clubs, and it seemed we were always running against each other [in grades]. I'd get a little lax in class and she'd get a better grade, and that would put me in high gear again. I [remember I] would watch her when we went to banquets. I watched how she held her hand in her lap, and I mimicked her. That seems strange now. But, at the time, I singled her out because to me she was American. Her dad was a banker, and I was looking for models to help me make that transition [into the mainstream].

I didn't look for these models at home, because I wanted to be different from what I thought we were. When I say "we," I also think of the Italian, French, and Greek girls I knew. Somehow we weren't viewed as positively as I wanted to be [viewed]. [I mean,] we were part of this small mining community filled with foreign families, and we weren't totally acceptable. [We] didn't measure up. As long as you were from one of the immigrant families, you didn't measure up. I wasn't the only one [who felt it]. We talked about it often. The American girls were somehow viewed more positively than we were.

Of course, in hindsight, I *know* I should have stayed and fought this view. But when you keep thinking that if you go someplace else, leave all that behind you, life will be different, that's what you do. It was sad. Yet I really believed the drive to live my own life was to reach a place where I would be acceptable to *others*. As I know now, it was really a drive to be acceptable to myself. As I now see it, you're always striving to be acceptable to yourself. The sooner you can define what that needs to be and get there, the better off you'll be. You won't have to worry about pleasing everybody "out there."

So I feel good about myself now. I feel the way I live and the things I do and have done, my mother would approve of. She felt it was important to be dignified, to have respect, to be a good mother. She loved education, and somehow I know that for all of her protestation of my moving "ahead," she was probably a women's libber before her time. Somehow I know she really supported me even though she had to give lip service to the "woman's role." I've also accepted a lot of the restrictions she put on us, because in her heart she felt she was being the best mother she knew how to be.

Moving away was important. Losing my Greek name during my marriage allowed me to see that keeping up Greek customs is *my* choice, *my* decision. So I have come full circle. After all those years of struggling and rebelliousness, I have come right back to everything my mother would have wanted me to do. For a while, I felt cheated, that somehow a trick had been played on me. But I feel good about it now. My sister in California still laments that she wasn't allowed to date in high school. Her children were baptized in another church. [Yet] I called her last Sunday and she told me, "It's funny you would call. I've got the directory out in front of me, and I was looking to see if there's a Greek church around here. I thought maybe I would go today."

JOHN "JOHNNY" SAMPINOS, 58, RANCHER, SHEPHERD, BUSINESSMAN

Gregarious, impulsive, and fiercely independent, John Sampinos was molded by the ethos of the Greek mountain people and the American frontier. He was a cross between an Old World sheepman and a cowboy.

Born in Price, Utah, on March 5, 1929, Sampinos came of age in a world of narrowly defined gender roles. "All the boys in the family worked on the farm," he told us. "But our sisters never did. They were home all the time. Their place wasn't with the sheep. Even today, my sisters don't know where our property lines began or ended. I could take them to a completely different ranch, and they would say, 'Oh, okay.' The women just lived entirely different existences [than the men]."

After graduating from high school, Sampinos went to work full-time in the sheep business his father and uncle had started. He stayed in the business until deteriorating profits in 1964 compelled him to seek other ways of earning a livelihood. Over the next two decades, he said, he raised cattle, managed a private club, worked an oil rig, and helped rebuild the Castle Dale power plant. In 1982, after the family sold its twelve thousand acre ranch, he leased land and returned to raising cattle. He dreamed of reviving the sheep business as well until his unexpected death in Price on May 5, 1990.

My father, Sam Sampinos, came here in 1907 when he was twenty-seven years old. He was originally headed for Panama, he told me, to work on the canal. But that yellow fever epidemic was going pretty strong, and they brought him into Ellis Island. That's how he ended up in the United States. He worked in the Pittsburgh [area] for a while, then was recruited or talked into coming out to Utah to work on the railroads and in the coal mines.

To my knowledge, he came to Kenilworth on contract, but he didn't work contract long. He saved some money, then he and Harry Mahleres, my uncle, bought a little farm outside of Price, and they started running a few sheep. They were from neighboring villages, just three hours walking distance, and they knew the business from Greece. Dad had run sheep; my uncle ran horses. Anyway, they thought it was a good idea to get out of the mines and raise sheep. So they became partners, and they remained partners until my uncle passed away. Each had an undivided half interest in everything they owned, and they trusted each other implicitly. They had differences of opinion, but they always worked it out. It was a beautiful partnership.

Dad's sister eventually came from Greece and married my uncle; and they all lived at 281 South First West [in Price]. Then, in 1923, Dad went back to Greece and got married. When he returned with Mother, they expanded the house and lived in it together. It was a unique situation—being partners and brothers-in-law—but it worked out. That's where all [ten] of us were born, and we each had four parents. And it didn't matter if my dad or my uncle or my mother or my aunt scolded or spanked you. If you got in trouble, one or more gave you holy hell! And no one ever said anything. It was a very unusual situation, maybe one in a million, where you'd find four adults and ten children that can live in one home.

John Sampinos (in neckbrace)
with his family. *Kent Miles*

Now, the early years [in Price] were tough. The native Utahn was prejudiced. My father said they didn't like Greeks. They didn't want to have anything to do with them. I remember, he told me, they were going to [lynch a Greek] guy in town—Tony Michelog's brother. He was going with a little Anglo-Saxon girl from Huntington or Cleveland, a little town about fifteen miles south of here. They were going to get married, but her parents didn't want her "running around with a Greek." So they said he molested her and threw him in jail. They were going to lynch him. But word went out to Sunnyside, Hiawatha, Kenilworth, Moreland, Columbia, Castle Gate—to all the [mining] camps. Also, P. O. Silvagni gathered the Italian miners. And the two groups came into Price on a siege. They actually had Price under siege! On all the [street] corners, at every business establishment, [armed] Greeks and Italians congregated. There were three thousand Greeks in town—and [hundreds of] Italians. They said if they hung Michelog, there wouldn't be any [white] person breathing air the next day in Price. They would annihilate them. So Michelog was released, and the situation went back to normal. But that's what happened in about 1916 or 1917.[16] There was a lot of strife.

Yet there also was a lot of opportunity. Today, you have to buy an existing outfit, an existing ranch, to lease federal range. Then there was a lot of free, open range. People just bought sheep and started grazing them. They might have had a little base to begin with. But, in general, [the sheepmen would] just start grazing [their sheep] and they'd trespass on somebody else's land. Everybody was doing it. Everybody was trespassing.

My father and uncle started running a few sheep around Price; later, they leased summer range around Hill and Willow Creek in the Uintah Basin. They ranged sheep over there for maybe fifteen or sixteen years. Then, in 1936, the government expanded the Ute reservation, so they told people that were leasing ground they'd have to leave. They gave them a year or two years' notice; and that's when my dad and uncle moved back to Carbon County and bought the old Fisk ranch. It comprised twelve thousand acres of summer range. They also bought the Anderson brothers' farm down in Soldier Creek, where we had a winter permit from the government. That's one of those Bureau of Land Management grazing permits. By then, they were running thirty-five hundred head of sheep.

Now, you may not realize, but running sheep is year-round work. In the winter, you'd bring your sheep off the summer range to where they can forage before the snow got too deep. In the spring, right about the end of April, you'd pull them up to your lambing ground and shear them before lambing. Our crews were mostly Mexicans at the time—they'd come up and one man would shear 110 to 120 sheep a day. There was a good wool market in those days. The brokers bought according to grade, and if it was clean, fine wool, you'd get a better price. The wool would be put in bags, and it would go right straight to the woolen mills.

After lambing, say from about the 10th of May until June 1st, you'd wait till the lambs got about two weeks old, and you'd brand them and cut their tails off. We mixed paint, linseed oil, lamp black, some flour for a thickener, and we painted the sheep with it. It stayed on from six to eight months. We also had to get them earmarked. Someone in St. George, see, or a reasonable distance away, could use your [paint] brand, but not your earmark. That's why we had to use both. Some people notched, or cut the tip, and split the ear. Ours was an overbit and an underbit. Two cuts were taken out of one ear; the other ear was cropped, then split. That was our earmark. It was a registered mark with the state. They printed a brand inspector's book at the state capitol, and it showed all the Utah brands.

After branding, we cut the ewes' tails short, so the tails wouldn't prevent breeding. It also kept them cleaner when they gave birth. We left the male lambs' tails a little longer and castrated the buck line. If a lamb keeps his testicles, you see, it starts breeding, and it won't be as good a meat. Also, you don't want them breeding in the herd, because the offspring turn around and start breeding the mothers, brothers breed sisters—then you get throwbacks. They don't gain as much weight, and they get deformed. You get freaks coming up: six-legged lambs; two-headed, crippled sheep.

When the grass started getting good on the mountain, when the grass started coming green, we gave it a chance to grow. Then, around June 10th, we took [the sheep] from the spring permit to the summer range. We herded them all summer. And the sheep ranged and foraged until October. In October, we put them in a corral and separated the lambs from the ewes. Then, if we wanted to sell them, we separated the heavy male lambs and the ewes and took [the male and female lambs] to the market. We kept the [mature] females and our big males. If we kept some of the ewe lambs that were the bucks' offspring, then we changed rams; because you didn't want the father breeding the daughters. That's how it went.

My father was a smart sheepman. He brought a lot of the knowledge he gained from running sheep in Greece—for instance, how to dock, or castrate, the lambs. Now they're using emasculators and rubber bands that clamp off the testicles, stop the circulation, and in about a month the bag and testicles just fall off. Their method was faster and more humane. You'd take the bag, cut the tip off, push the testicals up, grab them with your teeth, and remove them. You grabbed them with your teeth because they were too slick, too small to grab with your fingers. That was the old way. They grabbed the testicles and just pulled them out. And it was fast. It pained the lamb for a couple of days, then it was over—whereas a rubber band hurts for a long time.

Dad also used a lot of old country remedies. Like when a lamb or sheep would get an eye infection—they call it pink eye or cancer eye on a cow—its eyes were red and ran all the time. My dad and uncle used to grab the sick sheep, force its eyelid open, and clean it up. We kids would be standing around, and they'd say, "Okay, pee in it." Well, whether you had pee or not, you'd better pee in that sheep's eye. I guess the urine cleaned it. The acid and chemicals in the urine cleaned it up.

If a ewe lost its newborn lamb while [another] newborn lost its mother, they'd skin the dead lamb, wrap its hide around the live one, and roll it good in that lamb scent. Then they'd tie the mother up and force her to take the [orphaned] lamb. And she'd claim it. She could tell it was her scent. When a ewe rejected her lamb, they'd just keep her tied up till she took it. They'd tie her to a post, a brush, anywhere. They'd tie up her front legs, and they'd go by every day. They'd ride past her, get off the horse, catch the ewe, and make sure the lamb nursed. After two or three days, she'd take the lamb. She'd accept it. They saved a lot of lambs that way.

I got into the business 'cause I grew up following my dad and uncle, working with them after school and during the summer. All our herders had tents, bedrolls, and stoves. And, in the spring, we kids packed the horses and mules, took the tents down and all the grub boxes, stoves, bedrolls, and helped them move from the spring to the summer range and set up camp there. That's how all of us boys got in the business—we started out moving the camps on horses and mules, then later we went to trucks.

Dad and Uncle moved them once in a while, but they weren't much for towing or driving the sheep wagons. They'd come up, though, [and] supervise us young guys, tell us what to do. Sometimes we young kids thought we already *knew* what to do. In fact, we knew it better than our dads did. That's when my dad used to say, "I wish I could get to be as smart as an eighteen-year-old boy." [*Chuckles*] Hell, he'd forgotten more than we would ever learn about the sheep business.

It also became our job to take salt to the herders so they'd put them out on the range. You put salt on the summer range because sheep crave salt and there's no natural salt on the mountain. There's saltbush on the winter range but nothing on the summer range. Then we'd go from camp to camp, take groceries to the men, count the sheep, and look for coyote, bear, or lion kills. We'd finally come back down to the farm, irrigate, and store the hay for the winter to feed the sheep and horses. You needed that to run the operation, 'cause we had a lot of horses. Before the trucks came in, we had thirty horses and mules. And they worked hard. During the summer, the herders used them every day, and we'd change horses each month. When we were lambing, we went through horses even faster. The herders were putting fifty miles a day on a horse going up and down the canyons, checking all the little frog herds, where your sheep have lambed. They checked them three or four times a day, so we'd change off every other day.

Now, I liked the business; I took to it; and I got along fine with my dad. We'd have our differences of opinion, but he was an honorable man. Yet I didn't get paid wages growing up. A lot of times I wished there would have been a wage. But there wasn't one until I got married. When I got married, my father bought my rings and said, "We'll help you get a car and a house. And now you're either going to work with us and get this much money or else you're going to get a job that pays more." So that's what I did.

And the sheep business was prosperous for many years, because my father and uncle made a good living and accumulated property. Almost up until my uncle died in 1968, they purchased sheep and property, because owning land was very important to Greeks. Land meant freedom—freedom and security. It was a place to call your own, and property you can leave your children. It was precious, too, because you couldn't get it in the old country. Property in Greece, since before Christ, was handed down from family to family. There was little extra or excess property anywhere in the country. But in America there was all this land. Because that was one of America's assets: It had endless land. That's why my dad and uncle and all the other sheepmen grabbed up what they could.

The ground they bought was paid off, too, because you could buy summer range for anywhere from one to three dollars an acre. And as the American population expanded, and land values went up, many sheep ranchers became well-to-do. Thirty years ago, in fact, there were quite a number of big sheep outfits here. There had to be at least fifty big outfits in the Carbon-Emery County area. By big, I mean outfits running six thousand to seven thousand head of sheep. I remember Moynier and Sons, Marsing Brothers, Bernard Iriart, Gus and Angelo Pappas, Tony Michelog, John Marakis, Chris Vataselmas, Joe Beltino, Falsone, to a name a few. They all raised sheep. In Carbon and Emery counties we used to shear over a million sheep [a year]. That was in our heyday.

After World War II, when synthetic fibers started coming in, it [all] began to go down. When they started making clothing out of polyester and nylon, the wool market started falling off. And as it fell and some old-timers died, their kids started pulling out. They didn't want to run sheep, because they didn't want all the work. Our parents weren't afraid of work. But the kids wanted to fish and hunt. They wanted to run a river during the summer. Well, during the summer, our parents put up hay and irrigated so they could feed the horses and the sheep in the winter. But the kids didn't want to be tied down like their parents were.

Then the government started cutting down on permits; the environmentalists came in and said you're overgrazing the range; and finally the coyote problem got bad. At one time, like I said, there were fifty herds here; then, five years later, there were thirty; five years later, twenty. Well, all the coyotes were still around. But now they weren't eating off fifty herds. They were eating off fifteen or twenty, and they started congregating on the herds left.

We'd always had a lot of coyotes, and we would poison them. We would put out baits; they'd eat off this poisoned dead meat; and they would die. Then the environmentalists stepped in [saying], "You can't kill that way." So we stopped using poison baits, and the coyotes started killing a lot of sheep. You could go out and range lamb and dock 130 percent, which is 130 lambs to every 100 ewes. But by the time you got ready to take them to the mountain [in summer], your percentage had dropped from coyote kills. Then after your bear and lion kills, you might come off that mountain with 80 percent. Well, we couldn't take such a loss. We couldn't afford it.

The last good-sized herd we had was in 1963, 1964. We got out of the sheep business after that and went into cows, because the coyotes were hitting us too hard. The other ranchers did the same. So there are few sheep outfits left today—about ten to fifteen percent of what it was at its height. The Marsings still run sheep. They've got range where the coyotes aren't bad, and they shed lamb. They control the lambing. And the wool prices are good now; the lamb market is up. I'd say it's as high as it's ever been. How long it will last I don't know. But if they control the coyotes and meat imports, a lot of people in this country will go back to the sheep business. But when you can't control predators and you can import cheaper meat than we can raise, it'll just keep going down. Eventually, your sheep and cow men will become a thing of the past.

In 1982, we sold our land. I didn't want to, but it seemed like we had no choice. And this happened to a lot of outfits. When I say outfits, I mean ranches. Where two people [originally] owned [the family ranch], these two had five children each and their children got married and each had four or five children. So, all of a sudden, instead of ten heirs, you've got twenty heirs on one side and twenty on the other. Now, what are forty heirs going to do with that property? They're not going to farm it; they're not going to run sheep. They may not even pay taxes on the property because pretty soon there are so many people but very little ground. Whereas in the beginning two owned a lot of ground, now forty own a bit of ground each; and they can't make a living there.

So we decided we'd sell that property, and each individual could do what he wanted with the money. Well, to make a long story short, when my father and uncle bought the land, the mineral rights were reserved by the government. In about 1980, a big coal deposit was found under our land, and the government leased the coal rights out to a power company. The power company, in order to drill down to that coal, had to get surface rights. Well, we owned the surface rights, and they came up with such an exorbitant offer (in excess of one hundred times its original value!) that we sold it. I still regret it, because I was very attached to the land. But we seemed to have no other choice. And I didn't want to see my family break up—like I've seen a lot of families in Price when the heirs began arguing about what to do with the land. It's not worth that, I thought. It's just not worth it. So we sold the land.

NOTES

1. In 1917, the corporation was still called Utah Copper. Kennecott Copper was incorporated as a holding company for all Guggenheim-affiliated copper properties on April 29, 1915, but it did not gain controlling stock interest in Utah Copper until 1923. Leonard Arrington and Gary B. Hansen, *The Richest Hole on Earth: A History of the Bingham Copper Mine* (Logan: Utah State University Press, 1963), 66–67.

2. According to American immigration figures, approximately 186,000 Greeks emigrated to the United States between 1881 and 1910 and "about 95 percent . . . were males." Theodore Saloutos, *The Greeks in the United States* (Cambridge, Mass.: Harvard University Press, 1964), 45.

3. Utah Copper began using steam shovels in 1906 "to strip the . . . overburden," or the soil covering the ore. In this process, it was not uncommon for the machines to dislodge boulders and roll them down on the unsuspecting men working in the quarry below. Industrial accidents were frequent. Monetary compensation was rarely, if ever, awarded. T. A. Rickard, *The Utah Copper Enterprise* (San Francisco: Mining and Scientific Press, 1918), 47.

4. Wherever Greek immigrants worked in substantial numbers in the early 1900s, Greek communities developed. As author Theodore Saloutos wrote, "The Greeks built churches; sponsored schools, social events, church programs, . . . musical productions; and the men continued that most ubiquitous and popular of all Greek institutions—the coffeehouse." Salt Lake's Greek Town was anchored by the Holy Trinity Church, located on Third South and Second West and dedicated on October 29, 1905. Until World War II, author Constantine Skedros noted, the blocks adjacent to the church held "well over a hundred Greek-owned businesses," including coffeehouses, restaurants, shoeshine parlors, grocery stores, and confectioneries. Saloutos, *The Greeks in the United States,* 71; and Constantine Skedros, "The Greek Orthodox Community of Salt Lake City, Utah," in *A Tribute to Our Heritage* (Salt Lake City, Utah, 1986), 1–2.

5. The committee appointed by Governor Mabey "to survey the situation of the widows and orphans" after the explosion reported the nationalities of the victims as follows: "74 Americans, 49 Greeks, 22 Italians, 8 Japanese, 7 English, 6 Austrians, 2 Scots, 2 Negroes, and 1 Belgian." Of these 171 dead men, "57 were single, 114 were married. They left 417 dependents, including 241 children and 25 expectant mothers." The committee did not consider boys aged sixteen and older and girls aged eighteen and older dependents. Michael Katsanevas, Jr., "The Emerging Social Worker and the Castle Gate Relief Fund," *Utah Historical Society Quarterly* 50(3): 241–254.

6. The U.S. Congress passed the Johnson Act in 1921 limiting the annual number of immigrants from southern and eastern Europe "to 3 percent of the foreign born of that nationality as recorded in the census of 1910." The Johnson-Reid Act, or the Immigration Act of 1924, further reduced the annual quota to "2 percent of the foreign born . . . as recorded by the 1890 census." As Richard Easterlin and his coauthors wrote, "The choice of the 1890 census . . . placed immigrants from Southern and Eastern Europe at a still greater disadvantage because few had come to the United States that early." Articulating the purpose of these restrictions, Senator Johnson, one of the sponsors of the bill, said, "The myth of the melting pot has been discredited. . . . The day of unalloyed welcome to all peoples, the day of indiscriminate welcome to all races, has definitely ended." Richard A. Easterlin, David Ward, William S. Bernard, and Reed Ueda, *Immigration* (Cambridge, Mass.: Harvard University Press, 1982), 94–97.

7. The Bingham strike of 1912 was initiated by the Western Federation of Labor, which was seeking a fifty-cent pay raise for the miners and recognition of the union from Utah Copper. Bingham's Cretan contingent joined the walkout primarily to liberate itself from the clutches of labor agent Leonidas Skliris. Called the "Czar of the Greeks," Skliris exacted monthly payments from Greek immigrants for locating employment for them throughout the state. One of the proprietors of the Acropolis coffeehouse in Bingham Canyon, John Leventis "was the acknowledged leader, the *Capitanios*" of the Greek strikers. "The strikers would doff their hats to their priest and community leader, but they followed only the orders of John Leventis." Although the three-month walkout failed to acquire recognition for the union, and the miners received only a twenty-five-cent raise, the action had great significance. The hated "padrone," or labor agent, system was brought out into the open and discredited; and Skliris was driven from the state. Helen Papanikolas, *Toil and Rage in a New Land: The Greek Immigrants in Utah,* reprinted from *Utah Historical Quarterly* 38 Spring 1970, 121–133.

8. According to author Larry Gerlach, the "heyday of the Ku Klux Klan" in Bingham and in Utah occurred between 1923 and 1926, with 1924 being "the year of peak organizational activity." By 1928, the invisible empire—as the Klan was known—in Utah was nearly moribund; by 1930, it was, effectively, disbanded. Larry Gerlach, *Blazing Crosses in Zion: The Ku Klux Klan in Utah* (Logan: Utah State University Press, 1982), Chapters 4 and 5.

9. Since the Greek immigrants at that time spoke no English, it was common to attach tags to their lapels bearing the name of a countryman and the immigrant's destination. The tags helped immigration and railroad personnel direct newcomers to the overland transportation they needed.

10. As an example of neighbors helping neighbors, "whenever the Knights of the Ku Klux Klan burned a cross in Helper or Price, the Knights of Columbus retaliated with a fiery circle as a symbol of unity and defiance. Although principally by . . . Catholics, such activities were supported by all nationalities as a means of demonstrating immigrant solidarity to the Nativist Klan." Gerlach, *Blazing Crosses in Zion*, 98.

11. Fusal oil is "an acrid oily liquid occurring in insufficiently distilled alcoholic liquors." *Webster's New Ninth Collegiate Dictionary* (Springfield, Mass.: A. Miriam Webster Inc., 1988).

12. The United Mine Workers (UMW) union was officially recognized as a bargaining agent by Utah's mine officials in 1934. Richard D. Poll, ed., *Utah's History* (Provo, Utah: Brigham Young University, 1978), 489–490.

13. As a rule, the parents of Greek women in the United States at the turn of the twentieth century were spared the need of providing a dowry when the women married. "The scarcity of women . . . elevated their status and weakened all efforts to introduce the dowry system in this country. . . . For all practical purposes . . . , the tables were reversed in favor of the women." Saloutos, *The Greeks in the United States*, 86–87.

14. Following the March 8, 1924, explosion at the Number 2 Mine at Castle Gate, Governor Mabey appointed a committee to survey the situation. The committee concluded that "the . . . relief required by law . . . would be insufficient in most cases because of the gravity of the disaster" and recommended that "an effort be made to raise a fund by public donations to add to the sum legally due . . . dependents." This fund—totaling $132,445—was raised in a month and a half; and Ms. Annie Palmer, a "social worker," was retained and placed in charge of distributing monies on a monthly basis. Records indicate Ms. Palmer maintained close contact with dependant families and disbursed the fund over a twelve-year period. Although the relief measures by today's values would be judged substandard, the fund apparently served "a large number of people" and kept most families from sinking into abject poverty. Katsanevas, "The Emerging Social Worker," 241–254.

15. Most Greek immigrant men worked in the coal mines "just long enough to get a stake," then went into a small business or sheepherding. In the case of Mary's father, it was sheepherding.

16. The incident actually occurred in Price in 1918, just before the Armistice. As described in *Toil and Rage in a New Land,* "a Greek was brought to court to face charges of contributing to the delinquency of a minor. He had given a [white] girl, just under age, a ride in his car and neighbors had seen him 'flirting' with her. A crowd gathered outside of the Price

courthouse where the Greek had been taken. . . . A clamor began to lynch him.

"Greeks of Price sent calls to their countrymen in all the coal camps. P. O. Silvagni rallied the Italians saying, 'If it's a Greek this time, it'll be an Italian next. The streets of Price [soon] swarmed with gun- and knife-carrying Greeks and Italians." The lynch mob quickly dispersed. Papanikolas, *Toil and Rage in a New Land,* 156.

BOOK EIGHT
CHICANO-HISPANO COMMUNITY

PREFACE

Edward H. Mayer

The first Europeans to travel across the North American continent were Spaniards interested in claiming land for Spain. Although they never succeeded in finding the fabled cities of gold, they explored and settled vast regions of the continent in the name of the Spanish crown. One of the areas they explored was the northern frontier of New Spain, now the southwestern United States, which included Utah. Their exploration of this area began in 1540, when Francisco Vasquez de Coronado led the first European expedition to reach Utah territory. Over two hundred years later (in 1776), the next Spaniards arrived. While searching for a route to California, Fathers Dominguez and Escalante arrived on the shores of Utah Lake, where they came in contact with and taught Christianity to the Laguna Indians. The two men explored and mapped out much of southeastern Utah, giving many features, such as the La Sal and Abajo mountains, Spanish names.

During the 1800s Spaniards on the Old Spanish Trail traded in Indian slaves, furs, and other commodities. However, by 1821 the Sante Fe–Saint Louis Trail had become an important trading route for American fur trappers and traders, and the continuing Anglo trade, settlement, and colonization threatened the northern Spanish frontier. At the same time, Mexico's fight for independence from Spain, which Mexico won in 1821, brought internal turmoil that made the northern frontier more vulnerable to Anglo colonization. Mexico lost the Texas territory in 1836, and twelve years later it lost half of its remaining land with the signing of the Treaty of Guadalupe-Hidalgo, which ended the Mexican-American War of 1846–1848.

The treaty ceded the northern half of Mexico, which included the areas that are now California, Arizona, New Mexico, Colorado, Nevada, and Utah, to the United States. Although the treaty also guaranteed the rights of Mexicans in U.S. territory, that aspect of the treaty was flagrantly disregarded: For Mexicans, equal treatment under the law, recognition of land titles, and the preservation of culture, including language and religious rites, were ignored.

The Spanish-speaking people became "strangers" in their own land. For the thousands caught in this situation, life became uncertain, bewildering. Many were unable to adjust. Dahlia Cordova, one of the respondents in this chapter, described her father's experience: "Like many others, my father is a descendant of farmers who decided to remain in this country [after 1848] and become citizens rather than go back to Mexico and lose their land. Ironically, they lost their land anyway because of the impositions of taxes they couldn't afford to pay."

After 1850, few Spanish-surnamed people made Utah territory their permanent residence. At the turn of the twentieth century, however, with the passage of the new Homesteading Act, a number of Spanish-speaking families from southern Colorado and northern New Mexico settled in and around the small Utah town of Monticello. As U.S. citizens, they were eligible for homesteading claims, and they became farmers, cattle ranchers, and sheepherders. Their experience in sheep raising was legendary. In fact, Mormon pioneers in the Bluff area learned the skills of the sheep industry from them. Because of the growing number of Hispanos, in Monticello, the city soon became a gateway to Utah for those coming from New Mexico.[1] The Hispano migrants received a warm welcome from the earlier Spanish-speaking settlers.[2]

In the twentieth century, significant numbers of Mexicans began settling in Utah. The first large movement of immigrants from Mexico occurred shortly after 1910, following the start of the Mexican Revolution. The Mexicans were fleeing from the economic, social, and political conditions that gripped their homeland during the Revolution. In Utah, these Mexican immigrants found work on the railroads, in the mines, and on farms along the Wasatch front. Many became migrant workers. The experience of Guadalupe Gonzalez Rodriguez was typical. "During the Revolution," his son recalled, "my father left Mexico and went up to California as a migrant worker. He followed the migrant path that went through California, Oregon, Washington, Idaho, and Utah. He just followed the seasons."

Most of these first immigrants were single young men who came north to earn money for their families, then return to Mexico. Many of them arrived in Utah by chance. However, as the Revolution in Mexico intensified and conditions became desperate, many brought their families to Utah. These family groups soon made up the backbone of the Mexican *colonias* (communities). The majority of the families settled in and around the larger cities because there were more opportunities and jobs in those areas. The major settlements along the Wasatch front were in Salt Lake, Ogden, and Bingham, but other Mexicans were drawn to farming communities, such as Garland, and to the coal towns in Carbon County. Mexican immigration to Utah, and the rest of the nation, was further stimulated by the increasing need for labor in agriculture and industry. By 1920, some twenty-three hundred people who had been born in Mexico were living in Utah. By 1930 this population had increased to more than four thousand.

The development of the economy in the Southwest, which was based on agriculture, mining, and the railroad, owed much to the labor of the Hispanics, in general, and the newly arrived Mexican immigrants, in particular. The continued need for cheap labor in the 1920s brought further immigration directly to Utah from Mexico. As other immigrant groups gradually left the lower paying, mostly menial jobs and moved into other, better positions, the Mexicans quickly replaced them.

The Denver and Rio Grande Western and the Union Pacific railroads were the chief employers of Mexicans and other Hispanics. They worked as track laborers, keeping the railroad lines in good condition. In 1923, twenty percent of the workers listed as track laborers on the payroll of the Union Pacific between Los Angeles and Salt Lake City had Spanish surnames. This percentage kept increasing and, at one point between 1920 and 1930, reached thirty-five percent.

Like their Asian and southern European immigrant predecessors, the Mexicans found life in the United States dreary and exhaustive at best, and exploitative and violent at worst. The Mexicans faced deep-rooted prejudice and stereotypes that had been instilled in Americans from the time of the Alamo and the annexation of Texas. They were thought of as being devoid of moral and intellectual worth and as being members of an inferior culture. Still, for most Mexicans, America remained the land of promise and opportunity.

In Utah's *colonias*, life was little different from life in Mexico. Like the Hispanos who had settled in Monticello, the Mexican immigrants founded communities in which they could speak their language and celebrate their traditions. The nearness of their native country to Utah and the increase in the number of Mexican laborers at harvest time allowed for a continued replenishing of their culture.

As with most Hispanics, the importance of the traditional family ran deep. The father was the dominant personage, but the mother figured strongly in every segment of family life. She created a spiritual retreat in the small railroad section house or, in some cases, in the cramped railroad car the family called home. The mother was also important in passing along the native culture. John Florez expressed warm thoughts about his mother. "In the evenings," he said, "after she got supper, my mother would pray with us and tell us stories. She knew a lot of what they called *Cuentos,* traditional Mexican folktales." For the Mexican fathers and children, it was a pleasure to return home, after a day in the new environment, to a sanctuary in which the language was familiar and the smell of tortillas and beans welcomed them.

The chaperoning of unmarried daughters was another family tradition that continued in Utah. It was commonplace to see an older brother accompanying his younger sister on dates. And when a young man felt interest in a girl, he would ask permission from her parents to continue the courtship. If they wished to marry, the young man would inform his father, who would then visit with the girl's parents and ask for her hand in marriage. The marriage ceremony was also a family affair, as it was the parents who selected the *patrón y madrina,* the sponsors of the newlyweds.[3]

Extended family and kinship ties in the early Hispanic community functioned to reinforce traditional, emotional, financial, and spiritual needs. Celebrations such as baptisms, confirmations, weddings, and other Hispanic fiestas were family affairs that included not only the immediate members of the family but also all uncles, aunts, cousins, and grandparents.

Another important support to the family was the *compadrazgo,* the spiritual relationship between godparents, a child, and the child's parents. In the Hispanic community, the responsibility of the godparents was greater than in most Christian groups: They were responsible for establishing an influential bond not only with the child but also with the parents. The two couples became *compadres* and *comadres,* thus forming a bond as strong as family members.

With the growth of the Hispanic community, organizations and activities emerged that supported the worship and celebration of its traditions and customs. Religion had always played an important role in the lives of the Hispanic people, and its importance did not diminish for the immigrants in Utah. Father Reyes Rodriguez remembered, "In our home, religion was not formal. We didn't have family prayers. My mother was not one to burn candles before pictures of the saints. But whenever we got up from the table, we always had to say, '*Gracias a Dios*' (Thanks to God)."

Mexican and other Spanish-speaking Catholics found an active Catholic church in the state. The Catholic Mission, which had served the Italian community on Salt Lake City's West Side, changed its focus to the Spanish-speaking Catholics in the 1920s when Padre Perfecto Arellano from Mexico was given charge of the mission. With the assistance of three Mexican priests, he served the Mexican community, ministering to their spiritual needs. In 1930, with the help of Mexican nuns from the Order of Perpetual Adoration, he established Our Lady of Guadalupe Parish and placed it under the able direction of Father James Collins. The parish became a center for worship, a sanctuary where mass was given in Spanish, and a hub for Mexican cultural activities and celebration. Other parishes, like St. Joseph's in Monticello, also recognized the importance of meeting the needs of the Hispanic community and began to give mass in Spanish.

Religious ceremony was not limited to the church. Many families built small altars in their homes where family members could say their personal prayers. Many fathers and mothers would also lead the children in family devotion or in the recitation of the rosary. One of the most beautiful religious traditions of the Hispanos was the placing of the *luminarias,* or small fires, in the front yards of the homes at Christmastime. The *luminarias* were placed in the yards to help the three kings on their journey to find the Christ child.[4]

The organizations developed in the 1920s, however, were not only religious ones. The Comisión Honorífica Mexicana, a nationwide organization, was established in Bingham in 1927 by Jesús Avila to assist Mexican nationals until direct consular aid could be obtained. At the same time, La Cruz Azúl, the Blue Cross, was founded in Salt Lake City to help the sick, unemployed, and otherwise needy members of the state's Hispanic community. The Hispanic people prided themselves in their sense of unity. Whether they had a financial or spiritual need, the Hispanics would first seek assistance from the family, then from the extended family, and finally from *compadres* or neighbors. They felt it humiliating to go outside the community for help.

In both Bingham and Salt Lake City, Spanish language and literature classes were held for adults and children. Families also taught their children traditional music and dance. Within the Mexican community, celebrations including song and dance were organized for Cinco de Mayo (May 5), Independence Day (September 16), and other holidays.

During the Great Depression of 1930–1940, the growth that had occurred in the 1920s in the Hispanic community—indeed, in many U.S. communities—was abruptly halted. The Depression was a difficult period for all workers in America, but Hispanics were especially hard hit and were among the first to lose their jobs. Many Anglo-Americans displaced Mexicans in jobs they had earlier scorned. Dan Maldonado described what life was like for the Hispanic children at the time: "Every once in a while I'll see people going up and down the railroad tracks with sacks, picking up aluminum cans, and it'll remind me of [the Depression] days and what we [kids] were doing. . . . I remember a group of us, all about eight or nine years old, started going junking. We'd take our gunnysacks and pick up bottles, scraps of metal, copper wire, aluminum, anything we could sell. . . . Those were rough times."

Throughout the country, displaced Mexicans were repatriated. Between 1931 and 1934, more than three hundred thousand Mexicans were sent back to Mexico. Of those repatriated, about sixty percent were children who had been born in the United States and thus were citizens.

World War II ended the Great depression and greatly stimulated agriculture and industry in the Southwest. The sudden labor shortage impelled the United States to initiate the Emergency Labor Program of 1942 (the Bracero program) and to once again look to Mexico for agricultural workers. This influx of workers revitalized many Mexican communities throughout the United States. But the Mexican laborers were unable to meet all of Utah's wartime needs in agriculture and industry, and a large migration of Hispanos from northern New Mexico and Colorado began in the 1940s. These descendants of the Spanish explorers who settled the Southwest left the villages they had inhabited for more than three hundred years to work in war industries. They, like Norbert Martinez's grandfather, were recruited to work in the mines, on the railroads, and in the defense plants in Tooele and Ogden. Martinez recalled, "My father's father was a rancher, a sheep and cattle man. He was one of the old Spaniards. Our culture is more Spanish than Mexican, and we were part of the Spanish families of northern New Mexico. . . . It wasn't until 1943 or '45, when I was about six or seven years old, that we all left New Mexico and settled in Bingham Canyon [to work in the mines]."

The war had another significant impact on persons of Hispanic descent in the United States. Wartime labor needs caused unprecedented numbers to enlist in the U.S. armed forces. More than three hundred thousand Hispanics served in the European and the Pacific theaters. Their loyalty and valor helped them to gain more military honors than any other ethnic group. Seventeen Hispanics earned the Medal of Honor by the end of the war.[5]

After the war, these Hispanics returned home with new dreams and aspirations. They were eager to participate in the society they had fought to preserve. The GI Bill provided them with many opportunities in the areas of education, job training, and home loans. But the veterans found that deep prejudices and discrimination still prevailed. In Salt Lake City, for example, when Epiefanio Gonzales attempted to purchase a home on the city's East Side, he was told by the realtor it would be better if he stayed with his own kind. A veteran of the U.S. Corps of Combat Engineers, he was devastated. "I mean, how would you feel," he said, "if you came home decorated, you fought your heart out in the war, you said to yourself, 'Now, I'm and American; I'm just as good as anyone,' [and] then all of sudden you're [made to feel] like a second-rate citizen with no privileges? That can have a terrible effect on a person. . . . It can really take the starch out of you."

The negative attitudes of the majority population toward the Hispanics were especially destructive to the youth, who were caught between two cultures, the Hispanic and Anglo-American. The prejudice and discrimination they faced in the schools caused many first- and second-generation Mexican-Americans to reject their culture. One of the most important, and most easily measured, cultural traits lost was language. The use of Spanish was discouraged on school playgrounds, and the demands placed on the students to speak English without an accent gave the bilingual Hispanics the wrong message— that Spanish was of no value. The need many of them felt in the late 1940s and 1950s to acculturate also separated them from the traditions that they had grown up with. As adults, these Mexican-Americans abandoned the *colonias*.

In the decade after World War II, a cultural awakening occurred among the Mexican community congruent with a movement to bring about political and social reform. Organizations like El Centro Cívico Mexicano, in Salt Lake City, the Sociedad Mexicana de Cuahotemoc, established in Helper in 1949, the Sociedad Fraternal Benito Juárez, started in Ogden in 1952, and the Comisión Honorífica Mexicana planned social and cultural activities for the Mexican community to help maintain the Hispanic culture and language. Groups such as the GI Forum (a Mexican-American organization) were not only concerned with cultural pride; they also took an active role in fighting discrimination and related problems. The first chapter of the GI Forum in Utah was established in Ogden in 1954 under the leadership of Abel Medina. The following year, a Salt Lake City chapter was organized.[6]

The activism brought on throughout the country by the civil rights movement and the Vietnam War also brought renewed activism to Utah's Hispanic community. A group of young Hispanos and Mexican-Americans, who preferred to be called "Chicano," said *Basta!* ("Enough!").[7] In December 1967, these young leaders met in Salt Lake City and set goals for demanding a rightful place for Chicanos in society. Under the leadership of Jorge Arce-Laretta, John Florez, Rey Florez, Father Jerald Merrill, and Ricardo Barbero, they established SOCIO (Spanish speaking Organization for Community. Integrity, and Opportunity), an organization that would deal with the economic and social problems of the Spanish-speaking people of Utah. Within six years, the membership of SOCIO had grown from four hundred to nearly twenty-seven thousand. SOCIO provided a voice for the forty-three thousand Hispanics then living in Utah and created a vehicle through which Chicanos could unify to meet community needs.

An effective organization, SOCIO formed the Utah Migrant Council, founded the Chicano Studies Program at the University of Utah, and lobbied to create the Chicano ombudsman position for the state. The importance of these developments cannot be overestimated. They engendered a different attitude among the state's Hispanic population. Young people began envisioning careers that previously appeared out of their grasp. At the same time, a pride in heritage and language reappeared (something that had all but been lost in the 1940s and 1950s) as well as a willingness to confront the problems of discrimination head on.

Though SOCIO has not survived as a statewide organization, its fruits and victories are evident in all aspects of Utah society. The children and grandchildren of its members have become doctors, judges, attorneys, educators, and artists who are changing the face of Utah. The American dream has become an obtainable reality for many Hispanics because of the members of SOCIO, and others who sought to create a just society. In 1995, it was estimated that there were more than 110,000 Hispanics in Utah. This number is made up of Hispanos, Mexican-Americans, and immigrants from almost all the Spanish-speaking countries. All have benefited from the forward-thinking members of earlier generations.

In the following interviews, we enter the Hispanic experience through the testimonies of those who struggled to succeed and to prove the Mexican stereotype false. We learn how the Hispanos from New Mexico and Colorado and the children of the Mexican immigrants fought to maintain their culture while contributing to the richness of Utah life. Although their dream of creating a society with equal opportunity for its diverse members is far from realized, measurable change has come about. Professor William Gonzalez spoke for many Hispanics when he stated at the end of his moving interview, "There [still] isn't full equality, because you can't undo the history of a nation overnight. But we are going in that direction. We *are* moving forward."

NOTES

1. Although "Latino" has recently begun to replace "Hispanic" as the generic label for Spanish-speaking people in the United States, the older, more familiar term is used

in this preface. In addition, "Hispano" is used to refer to the people who migrated to Utah from New Mexico and Colorado, and "Mexican" and "Mexican-American" are used to refer to immigrants from Mexico and their descendants.

2. William H. González and Genaro Padilla, "Monticello, the Hispanic Cultural Gateway to Utah." *Utah Historical Quarterly* 52 (1): 9–28.

3. González and Padilla, "Monticello," 16, 17.

4. González and Padilla, "Monticello," 23.

5. Matt Meier and Feliciano Ribera, *Mexican Americans/American Mexicans* (New York: Hills and Wang, 1972).

6. Vincente V. Mayer, "After Escalante: The Spanish-speaking People of Utah," in Helen Z. Papanikolas, ed., *The Peoples of Utah* (Salt Lake City: Utah State Historical Society, 1976), 437–438.

7. Until the mid-1960s, "Chicano" was considered a derogatory epithet, suggesting a low-class, uneducated, uncouth person. Many young Hispanos and Mexican-Americans, however, named themselves "Chicanos" to dramatize their allegiance with poor Hispanics struggling to eliminate injustice in American society.

John Florez. *George Janecek*

PROLOGUE

EPIEFANIO GONZALES, 64, FARM LABORER, ARTIST, SIGN PAINTER

Epiefanio "Epie" Gonzales views his life through the lens of the "religious experiences" that taught him the power of faith and forgiveness. "People like me cannot afford to go to a psychiatrist," he told us. "Your rich people can visit psychiatrists daily. It's almost like visiting a hairdresser for them. Poor people like me have to turn to religion. But we have found out that we can do this, and it can cure us even from [physical] illness. So we believe in healing. Everything can be healed by forgiving people."

One of nine children, Epiefanio "Epie" Gonzales was born in Carlton, California, in 1921. From the age of eight, he attended school sporadically because his work was needed to supplement the family income. At nineteen, he enlisted in the U.S. Army and served for five years with the Combat Engineers in Africa and Europe. In 1944, in the week-long battle at Monte Cassino, Italy, he was awarded the Silver Star for his bravery.

Following the war, he returned to Salt Lake City, where he soon abandoned his dream of becoming a graphic artist. "At that time," he said, "it seemed impossible for me to dedicate myself totally [to my art]. I mean, an artist has to sacrifice; that's why they call them starving artists. [Laughs] But you can't do those things with the responsibility [of a family]. Getting married made it impossible [to realize] my dream. But, you know, I don't blame myself. If you want it badly enough, you do it. My drive wasn't there. I wanted a family more. I suppose it's partly cultural. I don't know how to explain it. But my children make me feel rich. For me, they are my posterity."

My stepfather was a laborer for the Santa Fe Railroad [in San Bernadino, California]. They were [called] gandy dancers. Have you ever heard that expression? What they [really] were is stoop labor. [They did] hard work, hard labor. That's about it. He worked on the railroad until the Depression hit. Then we went as farmworkers into Montana. And that was a big change for us.

We [had been] living in a barrio in San Bernadino, right across the viaduct. It was a happy environment for me. It was mostly Chicanos, and we played, had a lot of fun, and done a lot of mischievous things. There was no winter. We run around barefoot. So it was a paradise. It was beautiful. From there we went to Montana. And that was like a change between day and night. I mean, we went from a warm country to a cold country. Montana was as cold as Alaska would have been. And we went from fitting in our environment to being curiosities. We were the only kids [there] speaking Spanish. It's like we were from another planet.

And there was a lot of suffering in Montana because we all had to work. As a family, we all had to contribute. I started working at the age of eight in the beet fields. I didn't attend school until truant officers forced my stepfather to get me little bits of schooling. So it was hard. We were all providing, working, the whole family. Nowadays, kids tell you how beautiful summer is, how lucky you are to be out on a farm! Well, summer [for us] meant work from sunup to sundown, [including] weekends. It wasn't much fun at all.

We weren't exactly migrant workers. This sugar factory, which contracted with us in California, wanted Mexican laborers to harvest their fields [in Montana]. So each summer they would place us on a different farm. The farms were scattered throughout the state. It'd be like working one summer in Bountiful, then moving up to Ogden, then down to Moab. That's how they shoved us around.

Once on a farm, we lived in dwellings the farmers provided. Some of them were good. I remember a couple, maybe two or three, that were nice homes with good front yards and a lot of shade. But the rest of them were just shacks. That's all they were. In fact, we could often look at the stars right through a knothole. So I would say conditions were not very human. But that was it. Things were tough during the Depression. You swallowed a lot of pride, you suffered a lot and took whatever you could [get].

My parents took it badly. They took it hard. It's like if you suddenly get sick, you have the tendency [to say], "Why am I sick and he's not?" They took their poverty out on each other. My stepfather was a drinker. He was a drunkard. In order to excuse himself, he would beat my mama, or he would blame God. I remember, he would look at God as a whip. You know: You're responsible. You don't like me. And the doubled fist. And monkey see, monkey do, we [kids] grew up with an idea of God being a punishing God, a God that didn't like us.

I can see now that the Italians came to this country and worked hard to make something out of themselves. The Jewish people came here and did the same. The difference between them and us is they had trades they could pass on to their children. But my folks were peons in the old country with no trade at all. [They were] just laborers. So what could they do? They had no education. My mother was illiterate. I don't know if my stepfather could read or write. I know he spoke terrible English. Just terrible. So it was a bad environment. It made you very insecure.

When times got worse, we had an influx of Filipino labor. They didn't have families. They were mostly unmarried people who ganged together and worked for half the wages we needed to support each other. They were [also] very unified, and they ate a lot of rice. That was their staple. And we couldn't compete with that. I remember, it got so bad we decided to go back to California, and this is as far as we got. Our little vehicle, our little Chevy, broke down right in front of Pioneer Park, and that was that. There was welfare here, so we went onto welfare. My stepfather went on to California. He came back, but I think he was only here a week before he abandoned my mother with the rest of the kids. . . .

Now, one thing about my mother, she was a proud person. [She didn't want] to go asking for welfare; she wasn't lazy. We didn't have much, but she would always iron and patch us. I remember she used to have a saying, "Poverty is not angry with soap." So she'd scrub us. She'd whip us to be clean. Yet she showed little love for us, for so many kids, because she was always pre-occupied just taking care of us.

You know, psychologists say you have to spend thirty minutes of quality time [a day] with each child. But where can a mother like that [find the time] to counsel you, to help you? She never had the opportunities to cuddle us. And that can have a terrible effect on a person. It can make you feel loveless. They say we react to love at six months. If you have that omitted from your life, that can cause a problem. That can cause a very serious problem unless somebody tells you along the way [how] to heal yourself from this.

I happen[ed] to go through this. So I know it wasn't my mother's fault. She was a loving person in a different way. She had a different kind of love. And it must've been tough on her. She probably went through a lot of frustration when we started going astray, sloughing school. But it wasn't her fault. It was a jungle here during the Depression. *A jungle.* There was a lot of thievery going on. It was bad. Not only for us Chicanos, but on the whole. It was rough. Bread lines and all. I remember, we used to go to school, then ask for permission to go out and work. The Union Pacific paid twenty-five cents an hour for snow removal. So we'd go out and shovel snow till dark.

I [also] remember, we couldn't go swimming as kids; we were not allowed in certain places. And when I returned from the service, it wasn't much better. I tried buying a home up in the avenues, and the real estate man told me, "The area is restricted. No Mexicans are allowed." He said, "If you want to fight it, you could take it to court, and I'm pretty sure [in the end] they'll let you live there. But I wouldn't want to live in a place where people don't want me." That's what he said. And that's what we grew up in, and it hurts.

I mean, how would you feel if you came home decorated, you fought your heart out in the war, you said to yourself, "Now, I'm an American; I'm just as good as anyone," [and] then all of a sudden you're [made to feel] like a second-rate citizen with no privileges? That can have a terrible effect on a person. It can make you bitter. It can really take the starch out of you.

A lot of people believed that I'm dark complected because of a sin I was supposed to have committed as an Indian. You've probably heard of the Lamanite Chastisement.[1] Well, there were a lot of people that believed that stuff, and they looked at you [strangely] and excluded you from their life. You felt a strong discrimination [at work] against you, and this can also have a terrible effect.

I'd go into a department store, for instance. I could be standing in line in front of you, you could be in back of me, and the cashier would turn to you and ignore me. In a restaurant, I'd sit down, and the waitress would bypass me and go to someone else. I finally got to the point that I would take my wife shopping because she's lighter skinned. I would say to her, "You pay, so I don't have to feel this hurt all the time," because it got to hurt a lot. I said to her, "I don't want to feel the trauma of being rejected, being overlooked." Not that it happened all the time, but it occurred often enough, because it was imbedded in [Mormon] people that I am dark because I have sinned. The second failure, of course, came when they found out I was a Catholic. To Mormons, if you were a Catholic, you belonged to the Church of the Devil. So all this can have a terrible effect on your life if you let it, if you don't get it straightened out.

I just happened to be one of those that did straighten it out. I found out that I'm something special, that this God of ours is a God that has no favorites. He loves us all. It's in the scriptures—"I can show my mercy to whom I please. I love whom I please and I have no favorites." So I found out that I'm very special, that I am dark because of an act of love. When God created the black man in Africa, he gave him knitted hair to protect him from the sun. Where my ancestors came from in Mexico, they also had to be protected. I happen to have more oil in my skin to protect me from that environment. When you start putting it all together, you realize this is an act of love, not of hate or condemnation. And you discover that you are a special person. You learn to love and respect yourself.

I also thank God I found out I had to forgive people for all this [abuse]. I even had to go back and forgive my parents for not giving me an education, not pushing me into school, not saying, "Look, I'll bust my butt so you can get an education and better yourself." I thank God I learned to get rid of all this stuff, to empty myself from all this resentment. This way, my kids have never been denied. I worked my butt off to provide for them. I have a son who is a successful graphic artist. I still have two in high school, and I have four who have graduated from the University [of Utah] and business college. So I thank God I was able to turn it around. I *had* to do something different.

But I feel frustrated, because the same conditions [I grew up in] exist yet at this date—1985—among [many of] our people. A lot of us are still in that rut. I suppose what really hurts [me] is seeing so few Chicano college graduates coming back into the barrio and saying, "Hey, come on, let's do something about this." Whereas, I see a great percentage [acting like,] "I wish I could change my blood. I wish I could change my color." A few say, "I'm Chicano and I'm going to help," and that's beautiful. But there aren't enough to reach out to our people and tell them, "We got to get out of this rut. We've got to help ourselves."

My wife has a nephew who's an attorney. The other day he called my son, who'll be finishing his college studies in April, and said, "If you can pass the test for the law studies, we'll help you. They want more Chicanos in this field." I said, "What are you going to do?" He said, "I'll take it." I thought, that's four more years [of support]. But I don't care. I'll sacrifice, I'll do without, just to get him a fair shake. But after he gets into this [field], I would like to see him help his own people—I mean, his own race, *La Raza*.

I want to see him do that. Because I've been up to the [Utah State] Prison with our parish to play [soft]ball. And when they say, "Will the Chicano populace fall out to play ball?" it hurts to see practically all of them [coming forward]. So many of our young people. I get very emotional seeing a lot of our young kids that should have been in colleges, finishing high schools, wasting their time there. Because that's a waste of time. You don't come out of there right. There's nothing educational there at all. You come out worse.

I suppose a lot of people say—God help them—"Why don't they learn to help themselves?" But I don't believe that. I believe *we* should help each other, that we must bear each other's burdens.

We're all pilgrims in this life, and we all need somebody that leaves us a little better for having met them. When I returned to Utah after the war, ran into discrimination, and started lashing out at my family and others, Father Collins got me involved in my church and parish. He kept after me to help him. I remember one time he told me, "Epie, please come in early in the morning to help me with a ladder." I went in, and that man—I don't know if you're familiar with our old [Our Lady of Guadalupe] Parish—lived in a tiny apartment, cooked on a little hot plate, his pants' seat was shiny, and he had holes in his shoes. Yet he knew four languages, including Spanish, and he had left behind the luxuries of life to dedicate himself to taking care of people—*all* people.

And what I thought I was doing—helping him—had a reverse effect. It helped me. A conversion started in me. I rediscovered this faith of ours that took me through the war, and I started enjoying my life again. And this little priest was the instrument. So I look at [life] as if we're all out in the desert. We're thirsty, and if we meet a guy with water, he can refresh us. *Father refreshed me.* He gave me a new sense of direction. He channeled me into the way I turned out to be. So I believe we *must* do this for each other. It's our only hope—our only way out.

JOHN FLOREZ, 64, SOCIAL WORKER, COMMUNITY ACTIVIST, FIELD DIRECTOR FOR THE NATIONAL URBAN COALITION, DIRECTOR OF EQUAL EMPLOYMENT OPPORTUNITY AT THE UNIVERSITY OF UTAH

Passionate, independent, controversial, John Florez, a former civil rights activist and a leader in the Chicano movement of the 1960s, astonished friends and foes alike by joining the Republican party in 1980 and, subsequently, serving on Senator Orrin Hatch's professional staff and in the administration of Ronald Reagan.

One of three children born in a barrio on Salt Lake City's West Side, Florez was one of Utah's earliest and most effective Chicano civil rights activists and community organizers. Working through Salt Lake City's initial Community Action Program (CAP), he obtained the funds to build the Central City Community Center and was one of the founders of SOCIO in 1967 and of the Utah Migrant Council in 1968. In 1969, he accepted a position as assistant director for field operations with the National

Urban Coalition and for five years "traveled," he told us, "through the major cities of the Southwest organizing citizens coalitions to solve urban problems."

In 1980, he made the move that shocked Utah's Chicano community—joining the Republican party. But Florez says he did not betray his principles by opting to work with the Republicans. He was "just sick and tired" of asking Utah Democrats to fulfill their promises to minorities. "To me, their attitude was condescending. It was demeaning," he said. The Republicans gave him the opportunity to find out "how things get done in this country." But, even more important to him, "In the [Utah] Republican party, there isn't this condescending attitude [toward minorities]. You're treated as an equal. And when you're treated as an equal, people are saying that 'I have expectations of you.' And what a great thing that is for one human being to have of another: the belief in you that you can do it."

John Florez was the director of the Office of Equal Employment Opportunity at the University of Utah at the time of this interview. In 1989, he became deputy assistant secretary for the U.S. Department of Labor. In 1991, he was appointed executive director for the White House Initiative in Excellence in Education for Hispanic Americans.

My parents were born in the state of Zacatecas, which is in the central part of Mexico. I don't know how they crossed the border [into the United States]. But they ended up in San Antonio, Texas, [in 1916] and from there my dad said they were recruited to go to Idaho as farmworkers. They were put in a boxcar, given a piece of bologna and bread, and brought up North. They ended up living in tents here. To this day, my dad has a little nick on his ear where the rats gnawed away at him while he was sleeping in a tent.[2]

In Idaho, they followed the crops. Then, in about 1920, they came down to Utah, and my father became a laborer on a track gang with the Denver and Rio Grande Railroad. That's what he ended up doing most of his life. He was a hard and loyal worker. I don't remember him missing a day of work in his life. In the summer, he worked all day over iron rails, oiled black ties, and cement-like clay dirt. Being a laborer on the track gang entailed hauling ten- to twenty-feet-long rails and pulling out old ties and replacing them with new ones. Each worker had to replace eight ties a day, which usually wore out two picks a day.

In the winter, he had to be out there at all times because the tracks were always breaking down and the switches were constantly freezing and had to be cleaned. It was nothing for his [crew] boss to stop by in the middle of the night and tell him to get out and work. It also wasn't uncommon, when a train ran off the track, to work a twenty-four-hour shift. During the Depression, he worked whenever they asked him, because there were always four or five people waiting to take over his job if he ever failed to show up. So he came out of that environment where wages were low (he said twenty-five cents a day), unemployment was high, and you took whatever work you could get.

As a four-year-old boy, I remember waiting by the tracks for my dad to come home from work. We had a little game going. He would always have something left over in his lunch bucket for me. One day, I remember sitting and waiting on a pile of railroad ties, and my dad yelled at me *not* to move. He had spotted a rattlesnake that was ready to bite me. He picked up a railroad metal flange, threw it at the snake, and killed it with one blow.

We lived on Eighth South and about Sixth West, right by Portland Cement. We were no farther than twenty feet from the tracks. We lived in an old boxcar—the wooden type they used for passenger cars in the olden days. There were six cars, and Mexican and white families lived in them. They were quite narrow, but long, so we divided ours in half. One half was a kitchen, with an old potbelly stove and a table. The other half was our bedroom. An outhouse was way down—far from us. There was no running water. But we had hot water. What my father did was get an old metal water tank, cut off the top, and hook it up to the stove. The water tower where the trains got water was half a block away. When he'd come home, sweaty and black with grease, we'd take our buckets to the tower, fill them with water, then go home and fill the tank. So we were the only family in the neighborhood that had hot water. He was an ingenious little guy, always tinkering with things.

In winter, we heated our place with old railroad ties. We had a two-man saw, and we'd cut ties in one-foot[-long] blocks. Then, before going to bed, we would put a block and a piece of coal in the stove, and it would last a good part of the night. You'd wake in the morning, of course, and you'd be freezing your buns off. [*Laughs*] But in the mornings—and this is important—my father would get up before any of us and get the stove warm. He'd make sure the house was heated. He didn't show much emotion. He didn't show any overt love. But he was our provider. There wasn't any question about it.

Then picture this: On both sides of us we had old steam engines which spewed out black cinder. All around us nothing grew. The ground was all black—cinder-covered. It was finely ground stuff, as I recall, almost like volcanic ash. Yet around our porch, around the edge of our railroad car, my mother always had nasturtiums. She had a green thumb, and that was a very important part of our lives, being able to see something grow and flower. I also remember my mother scrubbing the wood floor with soap and lye. So our little house was clean.

I was thinking about [my parents] this morning and about the question of integrity and values that stick with you. My father taught us that a man only has his word. If you don't have that, you don't have anything. If you apply this to politics and how people make promises, you realize that if you only bullshit people, then only that comes back at you. My mother emphasized giving—giving for the sake of giving. Keep in mind, this was during the Depression. My mother would make a large stack of tortillas and a pot of beans. It was [always] more than the family could consume. But since we lived on the main railroad run, what would happen is that tramps would come through. They would stop by, and they would always barter. "Can we cut wood? Can we bring in coal for food?" When they'd stop at our house, she'd say, "If you're hungry, eat." She wouldn't ask them to do anything.

And you know what? A year later, in the fall, some of the same tramps would come back. And they would come back with cheese, with eggs, and with linen and silverware [stolen] from Utah hotels. [*Laughs*] But it's not what they brought that counts. It's her principles and values that are so much a part of me. That is, you give for the sake of giving, without the intent or expectation of receiving anything back. But, in fact, the more you give, the more comes back to you. That's a very important value that I learned—that love of giving.

My mother also was a special person—always in control, always a leader. She was a *curandera* in the community.[3] She had mystical powers, and so people would come to her from Colorado, Nevada, New Mexico, even Texas, for counseling or to ask her to cure their cancer, their paralysis. They'd come, and somehow she was able to give them an answer they could accept or understand. A lot of it was in the manner in which she put her thoughts across. She was very reassuring. Whatever the problem, she was there to give the right answer.

She spoke with a lot of authority, and she was intensely religious. She did a lot of praying; she would say her rosary and pray throughout the day. Medical folk practice in the Mexican community, the whole business of curing people, is related to Catholicism. So when people came to her to be cured, she would start out saying, "*I* will not cure you. But the grace of God and your faith in God will cure you."

In many instances, people came to my mother after going to the county hospital and not receiving help. If you look at that from a cultural standpoint, [you'd say] the culture defines the illness and the culture prescribes the cure. The Anglo culture, for example, did not have anything called *empacho* or *susto*.[4] My mother used to say the center of the nervous system is in the stomach. So when you're frightened, it means the nervous system has spread all over. The *ventosa*, the logical remedy, then, is to bring it back together.[5]

She'd start by putting a person on his or her stomach. Then she would get a piece of bread, put a matchstick in it, put it [on] the small of the back, light the match, and invert a glass over it. The vacuum created by the glass sucked up a part of the skin. She also rubbed the person with oil. She rubbed oil into the arms and legs; and she kept moving, rubbing and praying, and before you knew it you were cured of *susto*. But there's an important principle here. The person's faith that he or she will get well was part of the cure. Freud said you can't separate the soul from the body. So what my mother involved was the individual's total psychology and support system. In essence, she became the medium for this to happen.

She also read cards for people and counseled them on matters of love. If you wanted somebody attracted to you, she gave you certain things. If you wanted to repel a love, she gave you other things. She had little silk satchels, and it was my sister's job to make them. I call them satchels, but they were square bags, about one and a half inch by one inch. She would fill them with rose petals, hair, animal teeth, bones, rusty nails. She gave them to women. They would pin them inside their dresses if they wanted to get rid of a lover or to have a lover come to them. The beauty of magic is you can use it for anything you want. [*Laughs*]

In the evenings, after she got supper, my mother would pray with us and tell us stories. She knew a lot of what they call *Cuentos*, traditional Mexican folktales. In every culture, you have what they call the *Llorona*, the legend of the crying one. According to ours, it's a nun that fell in the well or in a mine shaft. At nighttime, you can hear her crying. When you hear this wailing in the wind, it's usually a *Llorona*. So I grew up with these stories and her accounts of Aztec culture. She taught us about Guatemoc and Xochimilko.[6] She talked about the pyramids, the Aztec calendar that to date has not been replicated, and how Cortez conquered the Aztecs. And I got to feeling very proud of my roots, that I came from this tremendous culture. And that helped me. Because when I started public school, I immediately entered another world—a world where I was [labeled] "different."

You see, I came from this mystical world where my mother cured people and we ate tortillas [and] *bapas* [potatoes], and we ate with our hands and drank *cocaleche* [coffee with a little milk]. Then I went to school, where I was immediately bombarded with the idea of "nutrition." That is, you have to have eggs, bacon, toast, and jam. As a matter of fact, [in elementary school] we'd go around the room and the teacher would ask each of us what we had [for breakfast]. Everybody would say, "I had cereal," or "I had Cream of Wheat," or "I had bacon and eggs." Well, I had some beans and a tortilla. No milk, because we couldn't afford it. We had just a bit of milk on top of coffee.

Then the school started teaching "manners": how to eat with a knife, fork, and spoon. And I was immediately labeled a savage because I ate with my hands. Well, with a tortilla, you just scoop it up. But [they said] you're not supposed to use your hands. So, all of a sudden I started thinking, "My parents are savages because they don't eat with a knife, fork, and spoon." As a matter of fact, we didn't have any in the house—except for the ones the tramps brought, which we stored in the mason jar in the middle of the table in case there was a piece of meat we had to cut.

But those kinds of experiences quickly told me I was different and I was bad. I mean, I was taught one thing at school, and six hours later I went back home and saw my parents eating with their hands. So a resentment began developing in me, a hostility towards my world. That's a very destructive process. The stability and the love of a family have to be there to overcome that. I thank God I had that stability in my family, plus the richness of our culture. So no matter what I was bombarded with, I could come back to my home and community where I could get my battery recharged as an individual, as a worthwhile human being.

While I was growing up, the old Mexican families congregated in an enclave by Sixth South between Fifth and Sixth West. Most of the men worked on the railroad; yet Purity Biscuit Company was there, about a block from the Guadalupe Mission. The ice company and the macaroni factory were there. They all hired Mexicans. So that was my world.

On the weekends, we [the Mexican families] would come together. We would have dances at each other's homes. We'd start Saturday afternoon and go till three or four o'clock the next morning. The musicians would play until their fingers were bleeding. There was no baby-sitting. We kids were all part of the milieu, part of the package. My godfather, Julio Lemos, was always there. He had a great handlebar moustache. And after eating, we kids would go to bed. In the middle of the night, though, he would come and pick me up. He was usually drunk. And he'd dance all around with me. And if you think about significant others, the extended family, it was there. There was a hell of a lot of love there. And those ties were terribly important. They gave me a sense of community, a sense of belonging.

Stop and think of those children who didn't have that. They got blasted at school without being replenished at home. I came back [from school] *hating* what I was because I wanted so much to be like everyone else. But I was one of those who survived. What happened to me was I got angry, and I got into a lot of fights, because I felt I was being dumped on a lot because I was Mexican. And, in fact, I was. I remember Old Lady Fiddlesticks. That's what we called her. I had a difficult time with her because she openly favored the white kids. So I mouthed off a lot [in her class], and I fought back. I mean, if you think about it, it was either get the shit knocked out of you or survive. And I wouldn't take the shit, and I'd fight anybody regardless of their size. I think I still would. Yeah—it's pretty much the way it was.

Eventually, I did get peer recognition. As a matter of fact, in high school, I was a class officer and an all-state quarterback. Two years in a row. It's interesting. I was at a dinner meeting the other night, and this person, an administrator at the University [of Utah], said, "I'm amazed you were an all-state quarterback." A lot of people still know me as one of the best passing [high school] quarterbacks around. He said, "It's unusual for someone of your build to even end up being a quarterback." But that pretty well characterizes the things I've been able to do.

You see, I learned [that] if you want to do something and you *need* to compensate, you compensate. As a quarterback, I knew I was shorter than anybody else who played that position. So when everybody else was playing softball, tennis, basketball, I just played football—all year long. I trained for it. While the basketball team practiced in the spring, I ran up and down the bleachers. So that was the whole idea: If you want it badly enough, you work at it. And this goes back to the idea of being a survivor. I mean, you can sit back and take it, or you can get tough enough to deal with it and [even] dish it out.

You know, in the Anglo community, I'm *always* asked the question: "What is it that made you 'make it,' you know, get an education and do all the good things you've done?" I tell them, the *key* was the love my parents had for us [kids] and the love they had for their country. I came out of a Mexican world with a powerful sense of nationalism. Though my parents fled their country because of oppression, because of killings, because of the Revolution, there was always that sense of one day we'll go back. I mean, my father to this day is *not* a U.S. citizen. His country is still Mexico. And my mother was always reluctant to learn English, because she never wanted to give up her language. So the key was this sense of identity my parents gave me. A feeling for my roots, a sense of belonging, a sense of history. When I think about it, that was the difference. My home was a very comforting place. Going back there each night gave me the strength to face the shit again the next day.

FATHER REYES GARCIA RODRIGUEZ, 60,
CATHOLIC PRIEST,
THE GUADALUPE CHURCH, SALT LAKE CITY

A small, round-faced man with a pleasant voice, Father Reyes Rodriguez did not look or sound like an unconventional priest. Born in Salt Lake City on May 21, 1934, he was raised in the Mexican community that lived and worked in the vicinity of the Guadalupe Mission. After attending high school, he served a four-year tour in the U.S. Air Force, where he discovered his growing interest in Catholicism and the religion's salutary impact on his life. Upon returning to Utah, he enrolled at the University of Utah, began his religious studies in earnest, and soon thereafter made the decision to become a priest.

In the fall of 1960, the Salt Lake Diocese sent him to study at the Mount Angel Seminary in Oregon, where he immediately ran into conflict with the institutional demands of the church. "They had an ideal of what a priest should be like, and I found I did not fit that mold," he said. "My religious feeling was shaped by my parents' sort of self-expression, their lack of dependence on the formalized faith, and that did not fit [the church's] authoritarian model. Fortunately for me, things changed tremendously over the years. The church made a 180-degree turn. And now they encourage priests to be more creatively engaged with their congregations, which suits me better."

After he was ordained in 1967, Father Rodriguez returned to Utah and, for most of the next thirteen years, was "a gypsy priest," traveling and ministering to the needs of the state's small Catholic enclaves. In 1981, he became pastor of the Guadalupe Church and found that he had come full circle. The interview with him was conducted in his church office. He spoke at length of his parents and seemed haunted, almost stricken, by the painful changes that occurred in their marriage.

Maria Hinijosa Garcia de Rodriguez—my mother—was from Fresnillos [in] Zacatecas, Mexico; Guadalupe Gonzalez Rodriguez—my father—was born in Bolanos, a mining town off the beaten track in Jalisco. I'm not sure what his father's livelihood was, except Bolanos was a poor area with a few mines. My father had a sister and two brothers. His older brother had a carpenter's shop; his younger brother ran a little dry goods store. I don't know if the family was religious. My dad wasn't oriented to the institutional church. He had his own sense of religion, and he was actually very anticlerical—*extremely* anticlerical. I have my own opinions of why he was the way he was. But deep down in his heart, he was a religious person. He believed in God, and he lived his life according to those beliefs.

My mother was actually born in Rio de Medina. I said Fresnillos, but these were little ranches, small communities. They call them *ranchos*. There were two [children] in her family: her brother and herself. Her mother died either giving birth to her brother or shortly thereafter. So they were raised by her father, until the time of the [Mexican] Revolution. In the Revolution, her father was killed; at which time, they were taken in by grandparents. When [the grandparents] became too old to take care of them, their godparents took over. And when [the godparents] got too old, about 1920, they were sent to live with an aunt in Salt Lake City.

My mother told me it was [all] very hard because they were very poor. Her grandparents just had their little farm where they raised corn and beans. They had a few animals, and life was very simple and plain. When they moved in with their godparents, they were asked, "What do you want—good clothes or full bellies?" That was the choice they had to make. They naturally chose to be able to eat.

I remember my mother [also] telling me, several times, about her grand-father's or godfather's values. The values they *insisted* on. They were really very rigid, very stern about people being truthful. If they were ever caught in lies, they were treated very firmly. Almost sternly. She distinctly remembered that.

The people on these ranches lived far away from churches. So their religion was a religion of the home, a religion of the family. It wasn't oriented towards going to church. When those opportunities were available, they would [go]. But when they came from the *ranchos* into the churches, it was on special occasions such as baptisms or first communions. So Mother wasn't a person whose religion was oriented to the church. Yet she was deeply religious in terms of her love of God, her recognition of God as the creator of all things.

In our home, religion was not formal. We didn't have family prayers. My mother was not one to burn candles before pictures of saints. But whenever we got up from the table, we always had to say, "*Gracias a Dios*" (Thanks to God). And whenever my mother would undertake something, whether it was cooking or sewing, she would say, "*En el nombre de Dios*" (I dedicate this to God). It was almost like a prayer. They began each day with, "*En el nombre de Dios*, in the name of the Lord, I present myself this day to God." That was how simply they approached things. There was always the recognition that God is in control. That everything is ultimately oriented toward God.

During the Revolution, my father left Mexico and went up to California as a migrant worker. He followed the migrant path that went through California, Oregon, Washington, Idaho, and Utah. He just followed the seasons. Wherever there was work, he would move. At that time, Utah [and Idaho] were large producers of sugar beets, and that was something he worked in.

He was married before he met my mother, but his first wife died. He met my mother at a community gathering. That's where he saw her. Of course, it was difficult to get together [with her] because young girls were never let out of sight. They were never allowed to go anywhere unaccompanied. He said you had to be pretty sneaky to even get across your interest in someone who was always guarded by relatives—because my mother was very tightly held by her aunt, as they held all the girls at the time. In fact, to this day it remains a mystery to me how people ever got married. [*Chuckles*] I guess they just went on hunches, because they never really got to know each other well.

My parents were married in '28 or '29, at the Guadalupe Mission, which was [located] on Fourth South between Fourth and Fifth West. Then they moved to Layton [Utah], because Dad worked the fields there. And that was rough. They were totally dependent on the seasons. And it was back-breaking work because you had to either stoop or crawl to harvest beets.

I remember, as a kid, thinking my father was very strong. His arms were big—massive—from work. His triceps were huge. And he was very hairy. His arms and chest were covered with hair. In fact, we used to call him *La Oso*, the bear. But he was a quiet man. [He] didn't speak much. At home he was almost withdrawn and [evoked] a mixture of tenderness and fear. Being a person who wasn't very intimate with his children, he could just look at you and scare you to death. I remember being very much afraid of him. He wasn't a person to hug us. That wasn't his style. But his affection was there in other ways: in terms of presence, in terms of support, taking care of his family.

He was also a creative person. He taught himself to repair cars. As a matter of fact, he fixed cars for friends and made a little money on the side. He taught himself how to read English. He read the paper. And he was thrifty, financially *very* conservative. And in many ways, [he was] extremely humble. Because he had to take care of his family, it didn't matter to him what he did for work. He could wash dishes, he could do anything—it didn't hurt his pride. I remember [that] when he later worked at [American] Smelter and they'd go on strike, he'd find work in a restaurant, mopping floors or washing dishes. He would just do anything. Interestingly enough, he never thought of going to the [Catholic] church for help. He was his own man. He wasn't influenced by anyone I know of [except] by my mother, [and even then it was] in ways that maybe even he didn't understand.

My mother was a *very* sensitive, very tenderhearted person. She could easily be injured and take it deeply. I recall she was in constant conflict with the aunt she'd lived with, who was folksy and very gutsy. When Mother lived with her, her aunt didn't let her be. So if she said something [negative] to Mother about the family, my mother would cut off the relationship. She wouldn't speak to her or go to her house. It took her a long while to get over such a slight. She took things deeply, and was sort of thin skinned, even in the neighborhood.

We lived in a three-room duplex directly across the street from the Rio Grande Depot. The Guadalupe Mission was almost in our backyard. So our neighbors were mostly Mexican-Americans. But [across] our backyard, there was an LDS family. The man was Norwegian, and he was very hotheaded.

We'd fight with his kids. You know how kids are; we'd bop each other on the head and make each other cry. He'd come storming out of his house, cussing and calling us "damn Mexican kids" or "dirty Mexicans." If my mother heard, Ai!, right away she'd get angry and insulted, and her hair would stand on end.

Yet she was a very capable woman. She sewed for people in the neighborhood—not on a regular basis, but she got some money for that. She also made my sisters' clothes, particularly when they got older. I remember her going to rummage sales, secondhand stores. She'd buy clothes, tear them apart, and redo them. She also used to get a Sears catalog and make clothes by copying them. They were both extremely creative people.

My mother also was an excellent cook. To me her Mexican food was the best in town. And she would go to great lengths to make it just as authentically as she did in Mexico when she was a little girl. She used to soak her corn in lime. Then it had to be rinsed and ground. Out in the garage we had one of those hand grinders. It was a little stone tray with four legs: two high ones in the back, two short ones in the front, so it angled down. Using a metate—a stone hand piece—she'd grind [the corn], making it finer and finer. We'd all take turns, because you had to get down on your knees and put your whole body into the grinding.

She'd make corn patties and stuff them with meat or with beans. They were delicious! And with the same dough she'd make tamales, spreading the batter on the corn husks. In Mexico, the corn batter of the tamale is softened or mixed with the stew of the pork. In fact, they used to kill a pig and use its head for the meat in tamales. Usually they take the broth from the meat and mix it with the batter, along with the fat, until it's a paste and doesn't stick to your hands. Then you spread the batter on your corn husks, which have been softened, add stew meat with chili and spices, fold the leaves over, and cook it with steam. [Since it was a long process] we didn't have it often. But, I remember, the thing you looked forward to at Christmastime was going to midnight mass, coming home, and having tamales and *atole*, a sweet, creamy drink made from corn. That was our Christmas gift.

Now, growing up, I remember our home being a happy home, [with] the security of two people who loved each other and cared for each other. My parents were never very demonstrative. But their love was there; you knew it. Yet when my [older] brother reached the seventh grade, their relationship became strained, partly because he became extremely rebellious. He started associating with different guys in the neighborhood—you know, pachucos—and staying out late, not coming home, then getting disciplined.[7] Severely sometimes. I can still hear him calling us when my father was beating him. My [two] sisters and I would be just crying our eyes out because he was being beaten so badly. My dad didn't spare . . . I don't think he spared his energy when he beat him.

In the eighth grade, my brother ran away from home. He hitched on a train and went to California. There he began stealing bikes, tearing them apart, and selling the parts. I don't recall him stealing cars. He was just incorrigible. I mean, there was no real criminal activity. But he so angered my dad that one time [after he returned to Utah my dad] got a rope, about as thick as my index finger, wet it, and drove all around the neighborhood until he found him, brought him home, and beat him—beat him terribly with that rope.

My brother promised to behave, but the promises didn't last long. When he was finally sent to the state industrial school in Ogden, it was a painful experience for my parents. We used to go and visit him on Sundays, and they were heartbroken. Then, I don't know if my dad encouraged him or he decided [on his own], but he went into the service at the age of seventeen. He was in the Korean War. [But when] he came home, he still stayed out at night with friends, carousing and drinking. And my dad was just beside himself; he couldn't stand seeing a grown man who wasn't responsible. And this, coupled with other things, finally created a deep conflict between my mother and dad. Their relationship began to go through a very straining time.

My mother's downfall, I think, was that she protected my older brother. I mean, when he was in Korea, he sent us his [monthly] allotment check. I think it was ninety dollars a month for the entire time he was in the service. All of it came home and went for home needs or went into the bank. So when my brother came home and was living irresponsibly, my mother had no problems if he wanted ten bucks. She'd give it to him because, hey, all the years he was in he was sending us money.

In addition, while my brother was in the service, we moved from our rented house down to Redwood Road and Eleventh South. And the money he sent us helped pay for that house. It wasn't an elaborate place. In fact, I couldn't stand this about my dad—he was too stingy. He bought this little house, almost like a shack. It was out in that part of town where the water level is low, and it was a little crackerbox of a place with three rooms and an outhouse. He saw us fixing this place up and making it [habitable]. I thought, "My God, we're going from bad to worse." [*Laughs*]

In town, we at least had an inside toilet. This one [on Redwood Road] was built right on the ground and had an outhouse and a dinky yard. [But] my father dreamt of fixing it up, which we did the following spring. We lifted it off the ground and put a foundation under it. Dad added a bathroom and extended the kitchen. But the point is, my brother's allotment checks went into the needs of the [new] home. So it seemed out of kilter to my mother to make such a big deal. But for my dad, it *was* a big deal. Because she catered to him, she was encouraging him to be irresponsible. My father was unable to put things in another perspective.

So this grew into a terrible conflict. My sister and I talked about it, and we couldn't understand it. While we grew up, my mother managed the house. My dad would bring her his check. She'd buy the groceries, she'd buy our clothes, and she would save money. At some point, for some reason, he didn't think things were being managed right. He began to say, "I'll buy the groceries; I'll pay the bills." And that was just really crushing for her. In fact, it got to the point where there was no communication between them. They talked about a divorce, but it was resolved by her death.

For me, it was so traumatic to see my parents go through this that I left home and went into the service. Because it was just too sad—the conflict, the anger, the harsh words. It was a big heartbreak, and I *couldn't* understand it. Where was it coming from? Why was it happening? Before my dad died, I had the opportunity to ask him about it. But he couldn't understand it, either. He attributed it to *her* change of life. He couldn't see his own role. But I could see it was him. Suddenly, he started questioning her competence. That was a complete reversal [of his earlier attitude]. Yet he couldn't understand it. He was saddened and bewildered by it.

My mother died in '55. I was in Greenland at the time. I was able to come home just to see her buried. About two years after her death, my dad remarried. [He] married a Mexican woman, and following his retirement from American Smelter in 1967, he sold the house and moved to Mexico. He retired there. He was a naturalized citizen [of the United States], so he'd come back every six months to renew his visa. He'd come to Salt Lake, of course, see us, then return to Guadalajara. But to the very end he was an insecure man. Because he grew up poor and lived through the Depression, he was always insecure monetarily. He never had enough money in the bank. The Depression, you see, was a terrible time [for Mexican people]. You had to be out begging for food, doing anything just to survive. He already had two children, so he was trying to raise a family during those difficult years. And, I think, it left such a deep impression on him that he never got over it. All his life, he was fearful of being poor and hungry.

DANIEL MALDONADO, 65, SHOEMAKER

Gentle and introspective, Dan Maldonado expressed sadness during his interview that he had never recorded the history of his parents, who fled Mexico during the Revolution and traversed the intermountain states before settling in Utah. Those precious stories, family and community legacies, were "buried" with his parents when they died. As if determined not to repeat the mistake, he related his own experiences with great care and vivid detail.

The fourth of five children of Rosario Garcia and David Maldonado, Dan Maldonado was born in Salt Lake City on January 13, 1929, and grew up "just this side" of the Rio Grande Depot. "Throughout all the years of my life [as a boy]," he recalled, "it was the same people in the same areas. All the time. We saw the same people in [the Guadalupe] Church as at Pioneer Park. For years, in fact, it was a neighborhood that didn't get any bigger. How would you word it? It was close-knit. Then, I guess, about the time the war [World War II] started, people started moving out and moving away. This is when I noticed the breaking up of the Mexican neighborhood I

Dan Maldonado. *Kent Miles*

knew real well. They started tearing down buildings and factories. The area started changing."

In 1944, Maldonado withdrew from high school during his junior year and went to work as a full-time shoemaker. For the next twenty-one years he worked as an employee for or junior partner with other shoemakers. In 1965, he opened his own shop in the Glendale Shopping Plaza and has been self-employed ever since.

It's funny how things happen. Every once in a while I'll see people going up and down the railroad tracks with sacks, picking up aluminum cans, and it'll remind me of [the Depression] days and what we [kids] were doing. I guess we picked up ideas from the older people [in the neighborhood]. I remember a group of us, all about eight or nine years old, started going junking. We'd take our gunnysacks and pick up bottles, scraps of metal, copper wire, aluminum, anything we could sell. Copper was easy to recognize because of its color; aluminum and lead, because of their weight. Iron was the only one we had trouble with. Because if we picked up some spikes by the railroad, we couldn't sell it. It was against the law to buy or sell railroad property.

We collected lead foil from cigarette packs. We'd see packs laying in the street and get our hands stepped on, 'cause the older guys sometimes took them from us. But we'd collect twenty-five or thirty [empty] packs, throw them into a bucket of water, and let them sit till the glue dissolved. Then we'd peel off the lead foil and roll it in a ball.

We'd collect all week, and on Saturday we'd walk down to Utah Junk or Pepper's and sell our stuff. They had great big scales where guys would dump barrels and trucks full; then they had these little scales that went up to one hundred pounds where we'd come in with our gunnysacks hoping we'd hit ten cents. I remember, we also took old toy soldiers. Fifty years ago, they were made of lead, and we'd melt them down. We took pieces of insulated copper wire. We burned off the insulation, because the junk yard wouldn't weigh it with insulation.

We lived across the street from Utah Ice and Storage, where they made ice and filled refrigerated cars. So [selling] ice was our other business. They'd bring the cars in and fill in the top load. But as soon as a car came in, everybody grabbed their wagons because we knew there'd be some breakage, and we'd pick up some good-sized chunks.

North of us between Fourth and Fifth West, there was a block with three cafés and five or six beer joints. They all had open ice coolers. So whenever we'd get ice, we'd run over and sell it for a dime, fifteen cents. We knew the back doors to all them places. A couple had swinging doors, and we'd peek under them to see who was in there, because it was always somebody's dad or mother. We'd like to sneak looks, too, because they were real rowdy places, and this was where a lot of the Mexican and Italian people got to know each other.

But, see, we did it for money. Because at the time you didn't go ask your folks for money because there wasn't any. There just wasn't any money around. Once in a great while the folks would give us a dime. But that was big money to them: the price of two loaves of bread. Those were rough times. I remember, some of our neighbors who had always talked about returning to Mexico became American citizens so they could get WPA jobs. Then they were always having discussions; the older folks were always saying they gave up their citizenship "for a lousy pick-and-shovel job."

I also remember everybody in the neighborhood fixed their own shoes. *Everybody* had a little shoe last. Dad did our fixing, and, I guess, I got fascinated watching him work. He had a box of nails and a little hammer. Pretty soon, I was asking him to let me hammer on a heel, put on a sole, or cut around it, because he had a linoleum knife he'd trim the soles with. After that, I just took over his job, because I enjoyed it. Then I started doing it for everybody in the neighborhood, anyone who had soles and heels and wanted it done.

One day, when we were out at Lagoon [resort], Dad ran into an old friend of his, an Italian shoemaker, and told him what I was doing in the neighborhood. And this fellow, John Nacarratto, said, "Well, bring him down. If he's got it in him, I'll get it out." And that's how I started working in a shoe shop. I was twelve years old. I'd go down there [after school], get two bits for cleaning, and watch him work.

My first days in the shop, I remember, I just stood around and ogled everything. I had never been close to large machines, so John just explained everything or tried to. Then he started letting me do simple stuff—you know, pull a heel, put one on. Something I couldn't get hurt on. Maybe smash my fingers. I remember he put a crate [there] so I could reach the jack, because they were floor models and I was used to the little one I sat down with at home.

Now, on the West Side, we always had a big conglomeration of [ethnic] people. It was always Mexicans, Italians, Greeks, Syrians, and everybody was poor to the point where there were no distinctions. Yet, when I started working at the shop, which was between Seventh and Eighth South on Main Street, about where Sears is now, this black fellow come in. He was carrying a pair of shoes and wanted to know if we worked on "colored people's shoes." I said, "Sure, we work on anybody's shoes." See, the black kids I knew went to all the places I went. So I didn't know there was any such thing as a shoe place that wouldn't [serve them]. Later on, as I got into my teenage years, I started finding out about restrictions.

Anyway, after about a year with John, I got promoted. I graduated. [*Laughs*] I had started out at two bits a day. Then, once I started [high school], I went down on Saturdays, made fifty cents a day, and John started teaching me more of the work. It was so different from what I had learned, because that do-it-yourself kit was strictly amateur stuff compared to working in a modern shop. He did nice work, too, for the type he was getting. He got mostly work shoes, cruder work. But one thing he believed in was giving people their money's worth. He'd make the repairs as tough as possible. He would instill in me: This guy works on the railroad, so give him something that wears longer. This guy is a mailman, so he doesn't need such heavy stuff.

He tried to accommodate everyone, and he was a real sympathetic person. There was a lot of older people for whom ten or fifteen cents was a hell of a lot of money. He'd cut back as much as he possibly could for them. If it was a fifteen-cent job, he'd cut it down to ten. Things like that. He taught me to be patient and conscientious. He was never out to make a pile of money, and he kind of impressed this on me, because I've never been that way either. I've just enjoyed what I've been doing. Because that's all I've done since I was twelve years old is fix shoes. I have never been, how would you say, ambitious. There were plenty of opportunities for me to expand my operation. But I never wanted to be any more than one person doing the job. So I just did as much as I could and turned down what I couldn't handle. That's why I'm still a poor shoemaker. [*Laughs*]

I stayed with John for two years, finished my apprenticeship. At that time—1943—businesses started feeling the bite on the labor force because everyone was being drafted. Help was needed everyplace. So I went to a downtown shop, and they hired me right off the bat. Gave me eighteen dollars a week—which was big money.

About the same time, the zoot suits and the pachuco cuts came in from California, where it all started. The pachuco haircut was the duck tail—hair that came square down in the back. I had it . . . but I didn't grease mine. I just used oil and combed it back. But, man, there were some guys who looked [like they had] patent leather hair. We also wore the zoot suits. High-waisted pants, no belts, baggy down to the knee and tight around the ankles. Our jackets were big shouldered and long. They came almost to the knee, and we had wide-brimmed hats. You must've seen the pictures. It was like the *chollos* [street gangs] of today.

And—oh, man—my mother hated it! She hated it because the zoot-suiters got a [bad] reputation right off the bat, and she didn't want her kids stereotyped. See, there was so much trouble down in LA [Los Angeles] with gang wars that the minute people [in Utah] saw zoot-suiters—especially a bunch of us—they figured there'd be trouble. And there was, because the style was a badge, an emblem, a kind of [substitute for the] Mexican flag. And whenever you got a bunch of guys like that together, they were intimidating. So what happened down [on] the coast happened here—though in a smaller way.

Like if a fight broke out in a theater and a Mexican was involved, it was immediate: "No more Mexicans allowed." This swept through *all* the theaters. That's when I began recognizing the problem of prejudice. Usually, [the fight] was over a small matter, like somebody mouthing off to an usher or somebody lighting a cigarette in the theater, which was against the law. They'd tell the guy to get out, and he'd say, "Who's going to make me?" Stuff like that. But then the cops would come in and kick all the Mexicans out.

There were a lot of confrontations like that. I remember, one time, there was a fight *outside* a theater involving a Mexican and an American kid. The cops come out. We were inside; we weren't aware of the fight. But the cops came down, took us up to the front of the theater, right in front of the screen, and put their lights on us. They said, "All right, let's have your knives." We said, "What the hell are you talking about?" They said, "[We] hear all you guys carry knives." Somewhere along the line, they may have picked up a thirteen- or fourteen-year-old kid with a knife. So [now] we all carried knives! [*Laughs*] [Well,] they searched us. Nobody had a knife. So they just threw us out. There was a lot of that prejudice.

Once, three of us were walking to Pioneer Park, and we were confronted by several white guys—adult men. We were about fifteen. They came up and said, "What the hell are you doing here?" We said, "We're going to the park." They said, "We don't want no Mexicans around here! We're going to kick you out and keep you out. And we're kicking out anybody else that's Mexican that comes in here!"

Man, we couldn't imagine what the hell this was all about! So we went back down to the Rio Grande Depot. Right across the street, there was a Mexican café. We went there 'cause all the guys used to hang out there, and we told them what happened. They asked, "Are they still there?" "I think so," I said. "They're trying to kick all the Mexicans out of the park."

Well, the older guys said, "Let's go," and they jumped in this guy's car, and we all went over to where they were sitting in their car, drinking. Our guys walked over to them, and I heard them say, "What the hell's wrong with you?" Then, before I knew it, I saw fists flying in and out of the windows. One of our guys started kicking out their headlights—those old cars had big headlights—and another guy was around the back smashing their taillights. And the guys on the sides were with their fists going in and out of the windows.

Suddenly the car took off, and I heard someone [in the group of Mexican youth] yell, "Where's Buddy?" Pretty soon, the car got about thirty feet down the road and the back door flew open, and here's this kid hanging onto the window and his feet just kicking [at the ground] to beat hell. But it was an older car. It couldn't pick up much speed. So he let go, and he dropped there on the street. We ran over to him and he was okay. But nobody noticed he had opened the door and had gotten in the back.

Afterward, we went back to the café. Everybody was there, talking about it and so forth. Forty minutes or an hour later, here come their car down the street. We all started coming outside to see if there was going to be more action. Everybody was lining up. But all of a sudden, a rifle stuck out of the window. Somebody yelled, "Jesus, they've got a gun!" And everybody ran inside. I guess they had a .22, and that thing went ping, ping, ping, ping down the wall [of the building]. No one was hurt, but, man, we were real nervous going home that night. We went through the alleys and everything. So that's how it was . . . for a while.

All in all, though, I'd have to say it's been a good life. And today, ninety percent of the people I know treat me well. There are a few, though, that have to remind me I am—what would you call it?—a minority. It's not [overt] discrimination. It's that feeling you get when people patronize you—when they start building you up, telling you how good you are, how nice you are. This, that, and the other. But you know darn well they would *never* take you home or have you marry their sister. It's *that* feeling—that whatever it is you're good at, you're good [at], and that's it. I've known a lot of [white] guys throughout the years that thought I was a really good shoemaker. But that was my place. I am a person who serves them. You know what I mean? They can praise me, [saying] that I am as good as anybody at whatever I am doing. They can praise my abilities as a craftsman. But they believe there's a line as far as I can go as a person, as a human being. They want me to know *there's still a line.*

Francisca Yannez. *Kent Miles*

FRANCISCA "PANCHA" GONZALES, 79,
MIGRANT WORKER,
HOMEMAKER, WAITRESS

"A lot of Anglos say, 'Here in the United States, you Mexicans never suffered that much.' I say, 'The heck we didn't.' I know I did, 'cause we went through the Depression when we couldn't afford to buy anything. We couldn't afford chairs or beds. I remember my dad made us benches. Oh, he was a good little carpenter, and he taught the boys, too. But that's about the hardest life we had. We had our good times, but we had our bad times, too."

One of eight children of Donaciano Gomez and Augusta Negrete Gomez—who crossed the border together, a step ahead of the Mexican Revolution—Pancha Gonzales was born in Amarillo, Texas, in 1918 and brought to Utah at the age of three months. She grew up in a barrio on Salt Lake City's West Side, where her father worked as a track laborer for the Union Pacific Railroad. When she was nine, her father was laid off, and the family began working "in the beet fields" in Idaho. They returned to Utah for the winters, and she told us how she and her brothers stole coal to keep their house heated.

In 1930, her father was hospitalized with a mysterious kidney ailment. He died the following year at the Salt Lake County Hospital. Two years later, she married for the first time. She was fourteen years old. The marriage lasted thirteen years and ended in divorce. Her second marriage lasted thirteen years and also ended in divorce. Her third marriage, however, was the charm that transformed her life. Tough, feisty, outspoken, Pancha Gonzales related her experiences as part cautionary tale for the innocent and part redemption fable for the strong at heart.

I got married at the age of fourteen. If my dad had lived, I don't think I would have gotten married, 'cause he was strict. . . . But he died in December 1930, and I got married the following May. You see how stupid I was? I mean, I was just a kid. I didn't know anything. I thought, oh, I'm going to wear flowers, a veil, and a big long train on my dress. That's how I thought.

I didn't think I was going to get up early in the morning, make tortillas, feed my husband, and what have you. That's how they raised most of us: women in the kitchen and men outside. But [in my family] it was different. My father taught all of us to chop wood. He told me, "If you ever marry a lazy man, at least you can do something for yourself." He taught my brothers to sew and cook so if they marry a lazy woman "they won't sit there, cry, and starve to death." We'd get up in the morning, and he's the one who taught me how to make tortillas. He'd say, "Pancha, make me a tortilla." I was just a little kid. Imagine how little I was. He made me a little bench and a little board and a little rolling pin because I could barely reach the table. I didn't make good tortillas. But he taught me right then and there.

He knew everything. If my mother got sick, he'd get the family in there and we'd all get out [and work] like ants. Everybody done work. One thing he did, too: He was the cleanest man. You could eat off the damn floor. We didn't have no linoleum. We just had wooden floors. But those damn wooden floors had to be washed once a week with lye. I don't know if you know what lye is. But that damn thing will eat your hand if you don't watch yourself. And I don't care what kind of mattress you had. If it was out of the cheapest damn straw, you had to get out once a week and clean that damn thing.

I think I got tired of doing the same things over and over. I think that's why I didn't have any brains. I think I just wanted to get out of the house and to see what the world was like, and I [thought I] wasn't going to get out any other way but get married. I remember this fellow went and asked for my hand. And my mom said, "I don't think she wants to get married. Her dad just passed away." In those days you'd mourn for a long time. But I wasn't in the mourning situation. I was all mixed up. I thought, if I don't say yes to him, I'll lose him and I'll never get married.

My husband was eighteen, and it was a sad marriage—a sad thirteen years. We moved up to Idaho. My husband and his family leased a beet farm up there. And it was hard. He used to like to drink and be merry, as they say. Drink and be merry. But I only had one baby. Wasn't I lucky? I think God looked on me with pity and said, "This girl, this baby, is getting married and she doesn't know nothing." I didn't. I went in there just as if I were blind. [In those days] you never thought about nothing. My mother never sat me down and said, "Look before you leap. Look who you're going to get married to."

But I had the best sister-in-law. She was two years younger than me, and, oh, we loved each other. We'd get together, we'd cry, we'd wish for this or that, and we'd keep each other going. There wasn't a thing I needed she wouldn't help me with. To this day she is still like a member of my family. She calls me up and says, "Pancha, do you remember how we used to work in those days?" We worked more hours than I did with my family [growing up]. We'd put in fifteen hours a day and think nothing of it. I'd come home all beat from the beets and still have to pitch hay and go after the pigs and cows that got out of the pen. And I couldn't get used to the shacks we lived in because that's all the farmers gave us. They didn't give us good places. I mean, honest to God, when I'd wake up in the morning, I could see the icicles on the edges of our blankets. Can you believe it? It's a wonder we didn't die.

It was sad, too, because we were both so uneducated about sex and married life. We were too young to be married. Yet I didn't know any better, and he didn't either. Because we were raised that way. If I could have waited until I was eighteen, it might have been a different story. This way, it wasn't. It wasn't that kind of story; it was a sad story. And I didn't know how to get out. I mean, my brain wouldn't help me make up my mind. My mom brought us up to stick it out. When you get married, you've made your bed. Now you sleep in it. You work out the marriage the best you can. People didn't get divorced. They just went through life. So I didn't tell her my husband beat me. 'Cause we seen a lot of love in our house. But sometimes he'd beat me so hard on the floor I couldn't even get up. He'd switch me with a willow stick. It's a wonder I didn't go crazy.

But, you know, my way was a happy one. When he wasn't around, I listened to music. I'd put on my Mexican [radio] programs, and I'd sing and dance to myself. When he'd come in, it was all hush-hush because he drank a lot. See, that's what got him crazy. I finally did divorce him when he came back from the army. At first, he threatened me. "If you don't come back, I'm going to kill you." But I survived the threats—even another bad marriage.

After I divorced Tony, I married right away. Do you know why? Because he was much older, and I was looking for a father. I was looking for a daddy because I missed my dad so much. Anyway, I married Dario Yannez. He had two kids, and his wife left him for a *cubachi* [white man]. And, for a while, boy, I was really happy. He treated me nice. He was a good guy. But he was a gambler. That was the only thing. And he never showed me his check. He said, "That's my money. I'm going to buy you whatever you need, but you can't have my money." Then he got to be such a big gambler, he didn't come home anymore. But I loved him. Isn't that funny? I'd never had anyone treat me nicely, say they loved me, take me out. *Never.* That's why [I loved him]. Because I was a green hornet. Because I didn't know my butt from a hole in the ground, as they say.

I stayed for thirteen years hoping he would change. My brothers and sister kept wanting to know if I was going to divorce him. But they didn't know what I was going through. There's a saying that means "Nobody knows what you have. The only one that knows is you, because you have it in your pocket." In other words, you have it in your heart. That's how they say it in Mexico. Nobody knows [your life] but you. So I begged him, [and] I told him over and over, "Why do you want to live this kind of life? You don't come home anymore. You are gone three, four, five days at a time. Your kids are asking for you. I'm asking for you. What's the matter with you?"

He wouldn't change. So we got divorced. But you want to know something? I never gave up. I always wanted a man. Even though they gave me hell, I knew some day I'd find somebody that would appreciate me and we would love each other, and I finally did. Me and Pilar [Gonzales] got married in 1961, and we really *do* love each other—and we do communicate. He always tells me, "Don't go be sick on me, Pancha. If you get sick, I'll die without you. I don't want to be living without you." I say, "I'm too damn mean, Pilar; I won't die. I'm too damn much of a big mouth." He's just the opposite. He's one of them mushy Mexicans, always pulling my ears, hugging me, pulling my hair.

But for the last twenty-six years he's been my life. I'm telling you, that guy's been everything to me. Yet I made things different with him from the start, because the other guys opened my eyes. When we dated, he wanted to stay overnight. He told me, "It's okay. You've been married before." I said, "I don't give a damn if I've been married before. I have my kids in my house, and I don't want you there." "So what are we going to do?" I said, "We'll go dance, eat, then everybody will go home." He didn't believe it, but I proved it to him. Then he wanted to get married right away. I said, "Show me how long you've worked for the Union Pacific? How much do you make?" He said to me, "How can you be so cold?" I said, "I want to know the kind of life you're leading."

I spoke to his cousins who lived here. I found out he wasn't a woman beater and he wasn't fussy. Then I told him, "It looks like we can make it. But don't ever try anything with me. Don't ever mistreat me and don't abuse me. Not even once, 'cause I will not take it. I don't give a damn how old I am; I don't need you that bad. And if you're tired of living with me and want to go on your own, tell me like a man, 'Hey, this is it.' But don't ever come back—because I don't care how much I love you, I will not take you back." And you know what? We've made it work.

I've been to Mexico with him. We've gone on trips in our motor home and just had a ball. He loves mariachi; so do I. We love the same foods. And we loved Mexico; we loved the music. I never saw anybody have as much damn fun as those Mexicans. When we came back, this state reminded me of someone mourning. You know, like after a president died or something like that. I think that's what makes [Anglos] so unhappy. I tell them, "You people are cold." They get mad. But when these *gabachos* [Anglos] come back from

Mexico, they always say, "Oh, Mexicans are the most friendly people. We love their dances and music." I say, "Yeah, they're never dead. You people are the dead ones."

My brothers and sister tease me. They'll say, "Oh, Pancha's our new Mexican Council." But with Pilar I've become a real Mexican. He's the one—the poor guy—he's taken me all over. He's got me happy. And what makes me feel real good is that I tell people I'm a Mexican. You're more respected when you do that. All these kids nowadays, even from New Mexico, they'll never tell you, "We're Mexicans." They say, "We're Spanish-Americans," 'cause they know the Spaniards came in and overtook New Mexico. I say, "What the hell do you think they first did with Mexico? And where do you think your ancestors come from? Aren't they from Mexico?" I tell them, "Hell, the Spaniard won't even look at you. He'll call you dirty Mexican. He won't even call you Mexican."

Hell, I've heard that [from our own people] so many goddamn times it's not even funny. I once told a guy down at the Mexican Civic Center, "Don't ever say dirty Mexican around me again, 'cause I'm going to turn around and kick you in the butt. I'm no dirty Mexican. I know how to take a bath. I know how to comb my hair. You call me a Mexican. That's what I am."

NORBERT ANDRES MARTINEZ, 55, MINER, HAIRDRESSER, RESTAURATEUR, BUSINESSMAN

One of eleven children, Norbert Andres Martinez was born on November 20, 1939, in Dixon, "a suburb of Taos, New Mexico," and was raised in Bingham, Utah. After he graduated from high school, it became his trademark to work the "graveyard shift" at Kennecott while taking daytime jobs elsewhere in the city. While sleeping his customary "three to five hours a night," he was, in succession, manager of the Alpine Ski Chalet, produce manager at Warshaw's Grocery, manager of the Red Barn restaurants, and proprietor (with his wife) of a hair salon called Andres'.

In the early 1970s, using his mother's New Mexican style recipes for burritos, tortillas, and soft shell tacos, he and his wife started a mobile food service called Senior Tacos, and their lives changed. Their products were in such demand that Norbert left Kennecott and opened his own factory specializing in mass-produced "home-style" New Mexican tortillas. The renamed business was called Mama Maria's Tortillas (after his mother) and was profitable from the start. Today, Mama Maria's makes over thirty Mexican food products and distributes to major food chains throughout Utah as well as to areas in Wyoming, Idaho, and Nevada.

"Of course," Norbert quipped, "my dad will tell you I was a born a wheeler-dealer because I sold ore to the tourists as a six-year-old kid in Bingham. But I always wanted a business of my own because I saw my family in business in New Mexico. My uncle, Joe Madrid, had a huge country store, where he had groceries and farm implements. I'd

Lorna and Norbert Martinez.
George Janecek

go on buying trips with him to Santa Fe, and I loved the wheeling and dealing. My great-grandfather, Ruben Martinez, also did this on his ranch. He traded grain and livestock. I liked seeing them cut a deal. It excited me because it seemed everyone always came out a winner. No one lost out."

My father's father was a rancher, a sheep and cattle man. He was one of the old Spaniards. Our culture is more Spanish than Mexican, and we were part of the Spanish families of northern New Mexico. It seems that some of the Spanish families came up from Guadalajara to El Paso and split up there. Some went to Louisiana and others came through San Diego. They went up the Santa Fe Trail, and since these were sheep and cattle men, they saw the beautiful mountains and settled in all the little surrounding valleys. Then some of these men spread north through Colorado and into the Taos area. The land is beautiful and unique where we come from. You know what Heber is like? Well, it's like that, only bigger. And it has the most crystal clear water running through it—one big, vigorous river and two small creeks.

My father was raised with his [maternal] grandparents, who lived in the area of Panasco. In those days, parents sent one of their sons to live with grand-parents—usually the oldest. But my Uncle Luciano was very sick as a young child and the next child was a girl, so my father was sent. From the time he was a year old until he was eighteen, my dad lived with the Madrids and, in fact, was considered a Madrid by name until he filed for a social security number. His grandmother became his mom; the Madrid children—two brothers and the rest sisters—became his family. For many years he thought his older brother and sisters were cousins. I won't say he was the black sheep of the family, but he was a little on the wild side, living with his grandparents and not being under his father's heavy-handed ruling.

Now, Dad attended school until the sixth grade. Then [his family] gave him a choice: Either continue with school or work on the ranch. He chose to stay with his grandparents and help them because they were getting old.

My father's paternal grandfather, Ruben Martinez, raised sheep and cattle and grew grain. He sold alfalfa that was so rich in protein it was high in demand by places like Santa Fe Downs. He also had so many crops that he kept his [extended] family in food; and he had enough to trade off with others. He was always helping people out. But what I found interesting about his life was the fact that no matter where he went, no matter what town we went to in the area, he was looked up to as a leader. As kids, we felt power walking with him into stores and seeing the respect he'd receive. We received special treatment just because we were his [great-]grandkids. He reminded me of the old cattlemen who settled the country. People called him "Don Ruben." I called him "Mi Rubito."

My father was married when he was twenty-one; my mother was four years younger. They met in the little village of Llano, where my dad's uncle, Virgil Trujillo, owned a general store. This uncle owned property, had one of the only cars in the whole valley, and was quite a politician. Over the years, he had been the acting sheriff and acting mayor and wrote out wills. Before that, in his younger years, he did a lot of traveling and was kind of like a liaison for everyone; he was one of the first men to work in the Bingham mines and to bring New Mexicans here.

Dad used to ride his horse from his grandfather's ranch and spend his spare time at my uncle's store. My mother and her aunt, who was a Romero, shopped and picked up their mail in there. So that's how they met.

Their wedding was a traditional New Mexican affair. It lasted three days and occurred after the *emprendo* [the dinner at which the two families formally endorse the marriage] took place. From what I was told, on the first day, my grandfather and his entire family on my dad's side asked for my mother's hand in marriage. On the second day, my grandfather on my mother's side invited my dad's side to a dinner. A long table was set up with food and drinks. Everyone sat around it, and the families mingled. Of course, the bride sat with her family on one side, the groom with his on the other. They married on the third day. The families of each side blessed the couple, and they had a big feast and lots of music. My grandfather, who killed the sheep and beef for this party, always said my dad cost him about four sheep and a beef. [*Laughs*]

At the wedding party, a ballad, or *entrega,* was sung. It had a beautiful melody that brought tears to everybody's eyes. It explained the responsibilities of married life. While the musicians played continuously, another musician would call the name of members of both families, who would throw coins into a little suitcase, or onto a blanket, to give the bride and groom a helping hand. This could go on for an hour and a half or until no one was left to call and everyone had given his blessing.

After they married, they bought a house and lived in Penasco. Actually, my mother built the house with the help of relatives while my father was working. My mother's uncle put up the tin roof. Most of the houses there had tin roofs. I was about four years old at the time, and my grandfather gave me an Appalousa that I used to ride in the pasture. No harness, no bridge ring, nothing. I'd just jump on his bare back and ride him all over. But my parents didn't have any money to pay my uncle for putting up the roof. So they gave him my horse as payment. I still see that uncle and I tell him, "Hey, you're the guy who took my horse!" [*Laughs*]

During the winter, when my father wasn't doing sheep work for my grandfather or herding sheep for the Covey Ranch in Wyoming, he would leave the rest of us behind and join his cousin in Bingham to work in the mines. It wasn't until 1943 or '45, when I was about six or seven years old, that we all left New Mexico and settled in Bingham Canyon. Each summer, though, we would go back to Penasco to visit my grandparents and help with the harvest. My folks also returned two or three times a year to pick up maybe a mutton or half a beef, or a pork, horse beans, and Indian *chicos* [dried corn]. But in the summer I would stay longer than my parents because there was always a lot to do. And I loved being there. I remember my grandmother separated the grain from the straw by shaking a screen. She was also in charge of preparing medicines like sagebrush tea and homemade yogurt.

And since I was the oldest of the grandsons, I got to know a lot about my grandparents and great-aunts, which was really fortunate for me. They didn't do a lot of traveling, but I remember they spoke about subsidizing their living by working on railroad ties. They would go down to New Mexico and drive through a place called Chama, where they make a lot of western movies, and make railroad ties the rough way, with axes, and sell them to the railroad. My grandfather, of course, always took advantage of these trips to sell his sheep and wool.

Because it snowed a lot in the mountains during the winter, my grandfather would take the sheep towards the desert, towards what they call Los Cerros, which means "little mountains." There was a lot of cactus, sagebrush, and wild grasses in that area, so they didn't have to feed with so much hay. But my grandfather would have to burn the thorns off the cactus so the sheep could eat it. They would do it at night, so the sheep could eat during the day.

Apparently, that's why my grandfather had trouble with his eyes later on. They thought it was from staring into the flames.

Grandfather had a lot of land. Some he acquired with Spanish grants, and some he accessed through BLM [Bureau of Land Management] permits. When I was a kid, we would take the sheep from corrals down in the valley and go up into the highlands. The sheep would spread out, covering the land. Sometimes it felt like the whole mountain was moving.

In May, after the lambing, we sheared the sheep. My grandfather had a couple of relatives who worked for him. They used old rough-hand clippers, and some of them were very fast at shearing! I remember one man in particular, Julian. He was kind of crippled, but, boy, talk about a man who could shear sheep! Our job was to pick up the wool and throw it into big sacks. We'd be full of ticks and all, but when you're a kid, it doesn't bother you.

I recall, each day, part of the herd was left behind to shear and the rest were taken to pasture. My Uncle Leo and I would go up one side of the mountain (Llana la Yewah) and come down around the other. I remember my grandfather was very fussy about getting the sheep back just before the sun was setting. He wanted them to graze the full time of daylight. Once, I remember, we got back too early, and he made us go back up to the pasture until it was dusk.

What was really unique for us boys, though, was seeing the workers docking (castrating) the new lambs. They did it the old way: They'd cut the bags and pull out the "oysters" with their teeth, because they were too slippery to grasp with their fingers. By the time they were finished, their faces were all bloodied up. Then they'd take these Rocky Mountain oysters—you know what I'm talking about—and fry them for eating. As a kid I thought it was gross, but as we grew older, we got the taste for it.

The last time I returned to New Mexico was in 1953, when my grandmother passed away. After that, I stayed in Bingham. We lived in a little town called Dinkeyville at the top of the canyon. They called it that because regular trains couldn't get up above us, but Kennecott had small locomotives called Dinkeys that could. They used to park them near us, and that's how our place got its name. Dinkeyville was the highest residential site in the whole canyon and was predominantly Mexican with a few Japanese, Filipinos, Greeks, Italians, and Anglos. From Dinkeyville, we moved to Terrace Heights, back to Dinkeyville, and then, when we got notice that Kennecott had bought the apartment building my father was managing, we moved to Lark. We didn't live there long. And I didn't like it. It was [like] a camp to me, and I didn't stay around there. Some people, like my cousin Mike, who's an attorney, will tell you different. He loved Lark. I just slept there and left as soon as I could.

When I was young, I went to school in Copperfield. As a matter of fact, I tell my kids, I walked a good mile and a half down the canyon every day to get to school. I'd walk home for lunch and then back down to school again. If we needed milk or eggs, the walk to the grocery store was about a mile away, too. But we had fun in those days. There were a lot of things kids could do. Kennecott provided us with the Gemmel Club—a gymnasium. It was a beautiful facility. Our parents paid for membership, and we played basketball, pool, set pins for bowling, and boxed. The civic center in Lower Bingham also had a swimming pool that was as hot as a bathtub. We had to walk a mile and a quarter to get there, but it was worth it. I think every kid in Bingham learned to swim there.

In winter, there were enormous amounts of snow and great blizzards. One winter, to get from one house to another, we dug trails and tunnels underneath the snow. In the city, every kid had a bike; but up here, most kids had a sled. Some kids made their own by taking the metal strips off old wooden barrels. They used the wood for the sled and the strips for runners. We also learned to ski by drilling holes in these barrel boards, tying strings through, and strapping [the strings] around our boots. Then we'd go up the steep mountains and ski straight down as far and as fast as we could. I don't remember anyone getting hurt.

We were a tough, tight little bunch. When we got to be high school age, we discovered mining kids had this reputation with people in the valley as being mean and brutes. The girls from the valley loved the Bingham boys, but their parents weren't crazy about us. I remember dating my first valley girl. As soon as her dad found out where I was from, he slammed the door in my face. He wouldn't even let me talk to her. We had a reputation for fighting, I guess. We weren't mean. We could get along. Yet, if it came to a fistfight, why, you learned to do your best. If you didn't fight hard, the big boys in our group would beat you up. So you learned to give it all. It was crazy, but it was part of growing up.

In Bingham, we intermingled a lot, so there was no real segregation. It was just a matter of walking farther or not. I had a girlfriend in the seventh grade who lived in Lower Bingham, in Frogtown. I had to walk her halfway down there, then walk all the way back, through the tunnel, past Copperfield, and up a mountain to get home. I tell my kids, "You complain today if you walk a half a block!" [*Laughs*] There was a friendliness in Bingham, though, that's kind of hard to describe. But if you talk to Bingham people, they'll tell you the same thing. Up there, if a neighbor moved in, everybody helped him. My dad is very open, very liberal. He'd go out and introduce himself to people, whether they liked him or not or whether he liked them or not. He was that type of guy.

But as far as work was concerned, in those early days at Kennecott, the Mexicans, Italians, and Greeks basically had the same menial jobs: first on the tracks, then to the powder department. Most of them didn't get skilled jobs like running trains or working the big shovels. When my dad was there, it was unheard of. In fact, it wasn't until the early '60s, when I was working at Kennecott, that I became the fourth or fifth Hispanic that even got into the shovel department.

Like many Hispanics, my dad was a powder monkey. They're the ones who would hang down from the top level on ropes. Banks were fifty feet high, and they would scale down with sticks to dislodge loose rocks or debris, so when they blasted nothing would fall on the men below. I remember, when they were preparing to blast, you'd hear the warning whistle: four shorts, four longs, then two longs. If you were working in the area, you'd look for a place to hide. If you didn't, you were crazy. Mine traffic would stop, and flagmen would be warning everybody to take cover. The blasting I saw scattered debris everywhere. It shook every level and buried an entire next level. Depending on how heavy the blast was, it could knock down power lines. It was dangerous work.

Now, every two or three years, when the union contracts were up and everyone was looking for benefits and raises, we'd have the possibility of a strike. So you could also say all our lives we were a "strike family." In 1948, I was pretty young, but I remember when everyone went on strike for something like nine or ten months. We stayed in Copperfield, but my dad went to Wyoming to work with my grandfather for the Union Pacific. This eventually became a way of life. When I married, I told Lorna, "Well, this is the way we do strikes. You save so much money for three years, and if you strike, you live with it. If you don't strike, well, you're three thousand dollars—or whatever you've saved—ahead."

I don't remember violence and fighting in the early days, but after I was hired, there were a few incidents. I remember, an uncle of mine, Fidel Martinez, a tough, little guy, got into a row with a couple of deputy sheriffs. We were carrying picket signs, were told to move back, and a deputy sheriff pushed him. So he hit him and kept on swinging. It took fifteen cops to control and get him in the car. They even had him on national news. That's the same year I made flippers [slingshots] to pass out on picket duty to harass the strikebreakers. On another strike, Lorna was six months pregnant and we didn't want to spend any of our savings, so we hired on to pick cherries, made about three hundred dollars, and then had a vacation. I climbed the ladder to get into the trees to shake them down, and she stayed on the ground and picked off the bottom of the tree. We were a great team.

In 1961, I got in the electric shovel department. It was a real unique time for me. A lot of guys that were older than me in seniority had taken a bid on this shift and got it. But then there was a reduction in the labor force, and they were sent back to their [old] departments within thirty days. By the time another bid opened on the shovels, these guys were cautious and didn't bid on it. I had nothing to lose. So even though there was about twenty-five other guys ahead of me in seniority, I bid on it and got it. From then on, I stayed in the shovel department as an oiler, which is a helper to the shovel engineer, until my turn and seniority came around. Then I became an electric-shovel engineer and changed from Grade 12 to Grade 20—which brought a big jump in pay.

I felt good about that, too, because the old-time shovel operators out there—the big honchos—were mostly Anglos. A few of them, I guess, were grouchy to see me come in. But most of them were all right. I worked day shift at first, then I got on the graveyard shift. For most people, graveyard is not meant for working. Everybody gets tired. About two o'clock in the morning, you feel like you've got icicles on your eyes. You can't stay awake. But I worked graveyard for twenty-three years and loved it. It was easy for me. There weren't that many bosses around, so I was kind of my own boss. I made my own judgments, and if something happened or something had to be done, I only had one boss to deal with instead of an entire company. That was a calming thing. And it worked out really good for our [family] business and whatever I wanted to do on the side. So I can't criticize Kennecott like a lot of guys have done. They can say what they want. But my folks made a good living and managed to raise ten of us brothers and one sister. And for twenty-eight years, I made a good living there and supported my wife and three children. So I won't complain. My only regret is that the mine grew and devoured all the little towns we lived in. The only thing I have left are these images in my own mind.

ROBERT "ARCHIE" ARCHULETA, 64, TEACHER, COORDINATOR OF THE WORK INCENTIVE PROGRAM, MINORITY SPECIALIST, CURRICULUM SPECIALIST

The quintessential grassroots-style activist, Robert "Archie" Archuleta moved to Salt Lake City in the autumn of 1953, right after completing his student teacher training in northern Idaho. From the outset, he became active in all phases of the Chicano community's struggle for civil rights.

While teaching full-time, he lobbied for civil rights legislation with the NAACP; helped develop "a chapter of the GI Forum"; supported the creation of SOCIO; and, in general, participated in what he called "the big push" in the 1960s and 1970s to open the doors of employment for minorities. "You see, it was almost all white until then," he told us. "There were few blacks, Native-Americans, Asians, and Chicanos in the professions. So it became pretty clear there was an awful amount of unfairness and injustice which needed to be remedied."

The "first Hispanic" to be hired in the Salt Lake City School District, Archuleta taught elementary school for fifteen years, then became coordinator of the district's newly developed "alternate daytime high school." For five years, he worked to help adult dropouts, including alcoholics, drug addicts, and ex-convicts, graduate high school. In 1975, he became a minority consultant at the district's central office. Then, several years later, he became a curriculum specialist, a position that he filled until his retirement in 1987.

Robert Archuleta.
George Janecek

My name is Robert Archuleta. People call me Archie. I was born in Grand Junction, Colorado, in 1930. My father's family and my father were all born in New Mexico, in a little place called Chaperito, which I understand no longer exists. My mother was born in Higbee, a tiny little spot between La Junta and Raton, New Mexico, and raised on a cattle ranch. They both came from typical New Mexican villages. If you are unacquainted with [northern] New Mexico, the little towns were divided and each person had a small plot beside his home for subsistence farming. The surrounding land was communal. It belonged to everybody, and on it they grazed sheep, cut firewood. They came out of that [environment].

Shortly after 1850, when a lot of the Anglo-Americans began to come in, there was a move on the part of the *Ricos*—the rich Hispanics—and Anglos to systematically plunder those communal lands with the collusion of the state and federal government. The history of New Mexico follows the same pattern as Texas, Arizona, [and] California. Our people were systematically stripped of their lands. One of the ways it happened was through taxation. When the Mexican government was in control, you were taxed according to subsistence. In other words, if you had a good year, you paid a good tax. If you had a poor year, you paid a poor tax. Most of it was in-kind. When the Anglo-Americans came in, they began to demand cash, and that was hard to come by. So in order to keep their land, people would mortgage it, and they would lose it.

By the late 1800s, almost all of our people were forced to do work for other people, like going onto cattle and sheep ranches, [and] then they would come back to their own land. My grandfather used to take my uncle and dad out sheepherding, so [my dad] went through this time of transition and upheaval. This was also when the cattle wars took place, like the Lincoln County wars. All they were, were basically landgrabs where larger farmers took our people's land. A number of people hung on to their places. But my parents' land was sold. So this is one of the things they both lived through.

My parents met in Colorado in 1918; they were married the same year. My father worked for the railroad in Pueblo, Colorado. He started during the First World War. Then, in the late '20s, the big layoffs came, so we moved to Grand Junction. Dad figured there was more work there, and he went to work for a farmer. He became his man, I guess. He took care of the dairy cattle and helped with the hay and all. We stayed there until the Depression hit and wiped this guy out. Then we moved into a little barrio [in] Grand Junction, where I was born.

It's funny—the first thing I remember about my father is that he was gray. I was the last one born, and he would have been forty-four [years old] at the time. So I remember him as really gray. My mother always had really black hair. It was very dark. My father was light skinned, too, and had funny eyes, neither green nor gray. My mother was very Indian looking—dark hair, dark eyes. He was about five feet six inches. She was just under five feet. My dad spoke English with a very heavy accent. All of my mother's family spoke English without accents. So they were an interesting combination. Very interesting.

But my mother was unusual. Everyone could talk to her. She was easy to talk to, and she was kind of a counselor. She had begun to fool around with herbs. She was not a *curandera,* but she was getting close to it. See, just before she married my dad in 1918, she took some classes in nursing because she was thinking of joining the [military] nursing corp and going overseas. She never finished the course, but she became a midwife. She had no license, but I remember nights [in Grand Junction], we would all be in bed, and all of a sudden [there would] come a knock on the door. "Lencha!" My mother's nickname was Lencha. "Lencha, come! The baby's coming."

My brother and father called her Dr. Rags because she demanded that everybody who threw away sheets or pillowcases give them to her. She'd boil them, wrap them, and put them in a bag in the closet. So when somebody was going to have a baby, she'd just reach up and have them. She always had a damned enema bottle [too] with the long tube. So I called her Dr. Enema. [*Laughs*] But she'd put all her stuff together and off she'd go. She'd be back the next day [saying], "Another little baby was born."

I remember there was a partial epidemic of diphtheria. A lot of the little kids in our barrio were dying. She'd go sit with them and try to help, because it was very hard to get doctors to come out. Very few doctors would come out for Chicanos. There was a fellow who came out when I had pneumonia. He came out until he got real old. But he was one of the few. The others wouldn't come because we didn't have any money and because, I guess, it was a form of discrimination. At any rate, my mother would do what she could. Her big thing was mustard plasters, coal oil, herbs, and teas.

In [early] 1942, we heard there were a lot of beets in Oregon, so a *Renganche* [group contract] was formed. I don't know who did it, but a whole bunch of people from our neighborhood were contracted to a beet grower in Oregon, right on the Snake River, across the border from Idaho. That was big beet country. We went up in April, and we followed the crops in that area for the whole summer—well, from spring until October. Afterwards, we sat around and talked about where are we going to go? Nobody wanted to go to Grand Junction, because there was no work there. Dad said, "We can either go to Portland, where they're hiring people in the shipyards, or we can go to Pocatello, Idaho, where they'll hire on the railroad." Everybody voted for Pocatello, because it was closer to Grand Junction. So we went there. And that's where I grew up.

Now, Pocatello was quite a bit different from Grand Junction. As far as discrimination against Chicanos, Grand Junction was, if you'll pardon the expression, the asshole of the world. It was terrible. When I was in the third grade, I fought almost daily with my Anglo schoolmates. I was constantly fighting, because they were always calling me "You dirty little Mexican," "You dirty little greaser," or "Hey, grease spot!" And at the drop of a hat, God, we were at it. In nothing flat, you'd flatten someone that gave you that stuff.

In 1940, when I was ten, just before the war began, I remember the draft started, and they had a little party in our barrio for a friend of the family who had just been drafted. Everybody was celebrating. I was only ten, but we [kids] used to hang out [with the adults] because people would play their guitars, violins, sing, and dance, and if you were lucky, the good guitar players "crapped out" and you got to play on the guitar. So we were always hanging around and waiting, because they wouldn't let us touch their guitars if they were sober. Toward the end of the night, this guy got kind of quiet and started crying, and everybody had their arms around him. And in Spanish, he said, "I don't mind going to serve my country. I was born here and this is my country. What I don't like is putting my belly out there in front of the enemy's bullets to save the gringo. I hate that!" He was really upset. He said, "Throughout my life, those sons of bitches have never done anything for me. I've been the lowest rat on the totem pole." And the thing I always remember, that has stuck in my head, is [that] he said, "I'm not afraid to die. I can be as brave as the next guy. But I hate to put my guts between the enemy and these fuckers."

I [also] remember there was just no money. We Mexicans were poorer than hell. We were living right next to the coal chute. [The railroad] stored coal there. It went up on pullies, and they loaded the trains with it. So we kids used to go down by the tracks and get the coal that fell off. Most of the time, there was none, so you climbed on the cars and stole it. The detectives were always chasing us, screaming, "You dirty, filthy, thieving little Mexicans!" Kids on the street would call us similar names, so you just grew up with this.

But, comparatively speaking, Idaho was different; so was Oregon. The farmer and his wife we contracted with took us in like part of their family. There was no discrimination at all. Yet [after all we'd been through], my mother and father were both very race conscious and imbued us with it. When we'd sit at nights, they always talked about "them and us." My mother's caution was always, "Wear socks, wear clean underwear, carry a hankie, because gringos think we're dirty Mexicans. So we have to show them we're not." And she was always saying, "Remember, we're as good as they are! No matter what is going on, we are as good as they are!" She pushed that constantly.

In Pocatello, there was a little movie house called "The Crumb." In Spanish, we called it *Piojo*, the flea; but in English it was "The Crumb" because that was in the early '40s when everything was "crummy." [*Laughs*] It was a neat little movie house. The real name was the Rialto. And it was beside the tracks where most of the blacks, Chicanos, and Native-Americans lived. See, Pocatello was a strange town. The further east and west you went, the more high-toned it was. But right in the middle, around the railroad tracks, is where most blacks, Chicanos, and Native-Americans lived. There were a lot of Native-Americans [too] because the reservation, Fort Hall, was about thirteen miles north of Pocatello.

But the man who ran this movie theater was a cold sort of a guy. When people came in on Saturdays and Sundays (those were the big days), he had the Anglos go to the right and the rest of us (Chicanos, Indians, and blacks) go to the left. Nobody ever said anything. People just accepted it.

One day, when I was in high school . . . It was at the time I was feeling a little ambivalent about my parents. You know, you're a little ashamed of them because they don't talk English real well, and my mother was real dark and my dad had this horrible accent. You know how that is. You think, first, they're not very smart and, second, they have these faults. [*Chuckles*] Well, that's how it was. Anyway, I'd gone to work in the spuds, and I had gotten some money and I was going to take my dad and mother to the show. That was the big thing. But my dad didn't want to go. So I took my mom and my sister, and we walked in. My mother was not in the greatest mood, and this sucker says to her, "You go to the left." She started to go, stopped, and said, "Aren't there any seats on the right?" "Oh, yeah," he says, "there's plenty of them." "Then why do we have to go to the left?" He looked around to see if anybody was listening [to their conversation]. There was a whole line of people waiting behind us. And my mom says, "I want to know why you want me to go to the left?" "Well," he says, "we've always done it that way." She says, "I think we'll go to the right today. I like to sit on the left, but today we're going to sit on the right." Everyone was standing real still, real quiet. And here he took our tickets, and off we marched to the right. After that, everybody started spreading out. It was spontaneous.

But I learned a big lesson that day. First, when you confront people who are doing something which is unfair, oftentimes they don't even know why they're doing it. If they do [know], they're ashamed of it. Second, when you confront them, you have the opportunity to break it open, and it's very uncomfortable. [*Laughs*] *It is*. I'm not much of a person for confrontations. Yet [over the years] I've been known to stick my neck out for unpopular causes and take the consequences. And I think that's where it comes from—my mother. I still remember, after seeing the movie *The Grapes of Wrath*, I thought, She's like the film's strong mother figure. She didn't take a lot of crap from people. Fair was fair, and unfair was unfair.

Now, my mother and father also valued education. Most Chicano-Hispano families I know today value education very highly. Most of us have come to the realization that it's probably our last frontier. It was important back then, but I think less so. See, in the old days, the frontier extended everywhere, and if you couldn't make it in a certain place or you were having a hard time, you just picked up and you moved your whole family to Oregon, California, or Utah. Chicanos generally went through that. We always had something we could look forward to moving into. There was always a greener pasture. No job in Grand Junction, we'll go to Oregon. No jobs in Oregon, we'll go to Idaho, or we'll go to Utah. So there was always this movement.

But in the past twenty to twenty-five years, a fundamental realization came to us that there are no more physical frontiers. So we have to go to education. In our family, my dad always wanted my two older brothers to go on to school. They didn't. They both dropped out in the seventh grade. My sister dropped out in the tenth grade. Somebody's got to go on, though, he felt.

Well, I had an accident in '46, and I lost part of my leg. I was playing football. I got hit by a big guy, snapped my leg in a real bad spot, and I got gangrene from it. At first, it wasn't noticed. When they did the X ray, everything seemed okay. But it went bad from there. I developed gangrene, and they had to take off my toes. As a result, from the time when I was a freshman in high school to my first year in college, I was on crutches. And my dad said, "You can't go to the railroad like the rest of us. You're going to have to do something different."

His highest aspiration for me, along with my mom, was for me to become a kind of secretary. They thought that really was a move up. He even played around with the idea of me being a barber. But a barber friend of his said, "We don't really make that much money, and there's a lot of standing." See, I was on crutches for years, and it looked like that was the way I would always have to be. So he kept saying to me, "You're going to have to do something different."

When I graduated from high school, we went and bought a whole series of materials for taking the post office merit exam. They thought, well, we ought to go in that direction. In the meantime, a friend of mine who had graduated [high school] with me and was hearing impaired was [going to college] on a vocational rehabilitation scholarship. The counselor said, "Do you know anybody else [who needs this]?" And he gave him my name. I was sitting out there in front of the [neighborhood grocery] store. Every morning I would go out there, study these tests, then mail them off. This guy came to see me one day, and he said, "Would you like to go [on] to school?" I said, "You're putting me on. What are you, some sort of a nut?" I thought he was really goofy. Then he started talking and said, "I'm serious." I said, "No kidding?" My eyes got big. I had never thought of going to college. *Never.* None of us thought of it.

See, in 1949, only about half of the guys I palled around with—we were called "The Dirty Dozen"—graduated from high school. I was one of them. The rest dropped out or went into the service. So going to college was not even a remote possibility. It didn't even enter our minds. Yet when this guy came up and said, "Would you like to go?" I said, "Sure! . . . Do you think I can do it?" "Of course," he said. "You can do it." So he filled out all the papers, and we walked back to my house. I told my parents, and they were pleased. I think they always used to pinch themselves, saying, "We never expected that—to have a teacher in the family." I think I was the first Chicano college graduate from our hometown. There were others taking courses here and there. But I think I was the first to graduate.

Now, I won't kid you. It wasn't easy, because I had doubts about whether I could succeed or not. When I was going through college, I kept saying to myself, "God, I'm going to be a teacher!" Then, in my senior year, I did my student teaching in a little farming community in northern Idaho, close to Montana. I stayed there for eleven weeks, and I taught elementary school in the morning, high school in the afternoon.

At first, I was awed by the realization that these little people were looking to me for leadership. Suddenly, all my self-doubts, all my weaknesses, became starker in my mind. I said, "Jesus, what am I doing teaching these little [Anglo] kids? Who am I?" But [teaching] is a kind of revolving wheel. As you see children progress, as they come to depend on you for their progress, it builds you up. So you're building right along with them. I grew with them and realized that I had a lot of potential to teach—and [it turned out] I did. I became a good teacher.

But after a few years in the Salt Lake City system, I quickly learned there are limits to what education can accomplish. Let me put it this way: Philosophically, I'm not a believer that education wags the body politic or the body economic. There are other factors that are far more important than education in this country, and the first one is economics. You see, even though I see education as the last frontier for most of us minorities, as a way of upward mobility within the system, education does not *make* jobs. We educate for jobs that exist out there, or we do not educate for jobs that exist out there.

What I'm basically saying is that in order for Hispanic, Chicano, black, and Native-American kids to do better in school, they have to have [access to] jobs that have dignity, some wherewithal that allows them to build their lives. You ask any minority if they really prize education, and they'll say, "You're damn right we do." I don't think one would say no. In the old days, that would've been different, because you could go right out and work. But, now, if you graduate high school and we send you out to McDonald's or an assembly line for $3.50 an hour, what have we prepared you for? So, you see, unless the economic opportunities are there, educational opportunities will only allow a few of us to filter to the top.

Where does that leave educators? Well, it means in the classroom we must do everything we can to help children learn as much as they can; we must give them all the skills we are capable of so they can confront their society—their environment—and cope with it. But outside the classroom, as a human being, it tells me I must also constantly struggle for better paying jobs, safer jobs, cleaner jobs, that can be done with a modicum of dignity for the good work people do and enough pay to feed, clothe, and house them. Without that, everything else is futile.

So, personally, I've been an activist. I was a member of the NAACP for many years and also helped establish a chapter of the GI Forum in Salt Lake. That was in the '50s. About when our momentum petered out, and we realized we were too few in number to take on the system, SOCIO came about.

SOCIO was the largest organization we've ever had in this state and the first real Chicano organization that purported to and *did* fight battles for our people here. John Florez along with his brother Rey and Father Merrill were instrumental in getting it going. But everybody that got involved—Hispanic activists—knew we needed something to bring us together. SOCIO did that and then went right to bat for us. And it did a whole variety of things. They picketed the community action centers because they refused to hire Chicanos and began attacking the educational system in ways we could not do from within.

For instance, there were an inordinate number of Hispanic kids in Special Education. They were not there because they were retarded or had brain damage, but rather because they didn't do well in school or in English testing. This was in the days before [public schools] had Resource. In Resource, if a child is not learning, they'll test him and find out the problem and help him with that particular skill. In those days, kids that had reading problems or were emotionally struggling were shunted into Special Education. Those were classes for kids who couldn't learn or were deemed brain damaged. And this was a national pattern, not only for us but for blacks as well.

Of course, a lot of that was changed when the Handicapped Education Law was passed, and everybody had to shape up. But before it was passed, SOCIO took on the Salt Lake City School District and told them to cut that out. And they began to clear that up. Then once the federal law was passed, it stipulated that if you thought there was something wrong with a child and wanted to test him, you had to get written permission from the parents. After the testing, parents and teachers sat down and *together* decided what was best for the child. And the child could *not* be placed in a Special Education class until the parents okayed it. That was a far cry from the days when parents weren't even told about it. The kids were just shoved in there.

SOCIO also put pressure on the district to open up new positions for Hispanics. They had no Hispanic or black administrators. When I came in, in 1953, as far as I could tell, I was their first Hispanic teacher. So SOCIO began negotiating with the district and got them to open up and offer administrative positions to minorities. As a result of that, Joe Sandoval, the first district representative for Hispanics, was hired. I eventually succeeded him.

I also became a member of the board of the Crossroads Urban Center, which has a food pantry, feeds many of the down and out, and does a lot of advocacy work. I stayed with them because the social service bureaucracy plays games with people's dignity, enforces foolish rules, or overreacts to rules. For instance, when the Food Stamp emergency law was passed, it said there would be times when people could be given emergency stamps. It meant they were to be given the stamps *now*, not in ten days. Well, we found out, our people were often being forced to come back over and over again, for as long as a week. In the meantime, what could they eat? What do they eat?

Well, advocacy permits you to go in and shake those turkeys up. So we did that. We did that with Mountain Fuel as well. Before a moratorium was placed on Mountain Fuel to prevent them from turning fuel off in the winter, they had the nasty habit of cutting off people's utilities if they couldn't pay their bills. It didn't matter to them if a pregnant woman, or children, or an invalid was in there. What was important was profit and at the cost of human dignity. So we went to bat for them. We wrote letters, we negotiated, we telephoned. When all that failed, we took Channel 4 News down with their TV cameras. They broadcast it on the five o'clock news, and those buggers turned the gas on within two hours, which shows you the lesson that it was more important for them to save face, continue their profits, than to take care of people. People came last.

Now, I never had any great aspirations in the 1960s and 1970s. I didn't believe we could instantly revamp the system. But I believed that the resolution of many of our problems was not entirely educational. Education was important. But it was not our main problem. Poverty and employment were our main problems. And we needed to spend as much effort in doing something about them as we did about education. Education does not create our society. The society develops in other ways and includes education.

So, I *am* an educator, and as an educator, I love what I do. But I recognize it for what it is, I hope. [*Laughs*] I recognize what it can and cannot do. At least, I'm striving for that. And I think it's important that our people—Chicano-Hispanos—have it. We've got to have it. It's our last frontier. The other frontier for us is gone. People who come here today no longer can go and get land. They must now get an education. But even getting an education won't assure them that they'll make it in the system. For that, we need jobs—better, safer, cleaner jobs. Hopefully, as a people, we're getting smarter about that.

SILAS EPHRAIM LOBATO, 73, BARBER, MUSICIAN

Small, slender, soft-voiced, Silas "Si" Lobato was apologetic during his interview with us about his lack of participation in Chicano civil rights efforts. He said he had not "taken up" any causes, political or religious. In his business—cutting hair—you had to learn to get along with everyone.

Si's family left Las Tablas, New Mexico, in 1924, when he was three, in search of work. "My father had things to barter with, but no money," he explained. "So he went out to seek a job for wages. I think he was the first one of the family to leave. But the rest of my uncles and aunts followed afterward. The big exodus came on the eve of World War II. All my relatives, just about in mass, moved out to Utah to find jobs."

While seeking year-round work, the Lobatos shuttled between Colorado beet farms and Utah's Bingham mine. In 1931, they settled on a farm in Centerville, Utah, and his parents separated. His father moved to Chicago but returned to Utah several years later to give his youngest son the option of living with him. "I wanted to go with my dad," Si recalled. "But when he gave me the choice of 'your mother or me,' I reluctantly told him I'd stay, because in my own mind I knew I'd be better off with the rest of the family. So I stayed, and from the fourth grade through high school, we lived on one farm in Farmington. It wasn't easy. We were the only Hispanic family there. But we were able to blend in and put down roots."

Si Lobato operated several barber shops in Salt Lake City before opening two hair salons in the Main and Western terminals at the Salt Lake City International Airport.

When I was in high school, I kind of thought of taking up being a chef. That was in my mind as a career. But I think the navy took that out of me, because they put me in the kitchen, made me a ship's cook, second class.

That's nothing like gourmet cooking, believe me. [*Laughs*] See, I was in the Seabees during the war [World War II]. My outfit was a construction battalion. They recruited skilled workers like riggers, welders, masons, carpenters, and a certain amount of unskilled people like myself who were laborers. So I just worked in the kitchen and stayed there. That was my job. But, like I say, I didn't want any part of the kitchen after being in the service.

I thought maybe I'd go back to the railroad. They offered me a job I used to do before, working as a track hand; and they gave me living quarters. But I didn't like the prospect of going back to the railroad. So that's when I decided to take up barbering. I actually started in the barracks, in Camp Shoemaker, California, waiting for my discharge papers to be processed. Guys wanted to go on liberty. They hadn't time to go to a barbershop, so I started cutting their hair. They said, "Hey, you're pretty good. Why don't you take that as a trade?" And that's what gave me the idea—that and the war ending.

I was home on leave when the war ended, you see, and all of a sudden the whole country was on a great high. In fact, the day Japan surrendered, it was [broadcast] on all the radios, in all the media. I was in the movies, and it came on the public address system. And you wouldn't believe the reaction! It was just one big celebration—like a New Year's party throughout the country which lasted for days. People were out in the streets snake-dancing. You know, grabbing hands and just snake-dancing all over. Everybody was in light spirits. [It was] like a big Mardi Gras, and the feeling lasted for months.

The war ended in August [1945], and even when I came back in October, you could still sense people were happy. Their sons [and husbands] didn't have to go to war, or they could come home from war. It was sheer happiness. There were "Welcome Home Sailors," "Welcome Home Marines" signs all over. Servicemen were welcomed with open arms. [It was] nothing like Vietnam.

So I'd say that [atmosphere] had a lot to do with my deciding to become a barber, [and to] follow music. They always went hand in hand for me. Plus, I knew this barber in Salt Lake. He was, beyond any doubt, the best barber I had ever known. He was very fine, very artistic. My idea was to work for him and play in his band, which eventually came to be. See, I'd known Sam Garcia—Samuel H. Garcia—when I was a boy in Bingham. He used to be a barber in Bingham Canyon, and he was an unusual guy. He was [a Mexican who was] fluent in Spanish, English, and Greek. He had worked for many years in a Greek barbershop. Also he got along with the Croat, Slav, and Serbian people. So when I came back, that was in my mind. And I stopped in, talked to him, and he said, "Yes, when you get ready, we may find a place for you."

I was discharged on October 17, 1945, and, well, I immediately started school at the barbers' union. At the time, school lasted two thousand hours, or the better part of a year. We studied anatomy—thoroughly. We did extensive physiological study with regards to the anatomy of the cranium and the face. We learned all the parts of the body connected with barbering and cosmetology. It came easily to me because I had taken biology and physiology, related courses, in high school. So the terminology was easy to pick up. It was a breeze; I enjoyed it.

My family felt good, too. In Hispanic circles, a barber is looked up to. At one time, you see, the barber and the surgeon were one profession. I don't know in what century, but they practiced bloodletting. Letting of the blood [was symbolized] by the red part of the barber pole; the cleanliness—trimming the beard, cutting the hair—was the white part. In fact, [in our community] they call a barber a maestro, just like we call a conductor maestro, because he's the master of a skill. Even today I have Spanish-speaking people calling me maestro. So, yes, there's a certain pride that goes with being a skilled barber.

At the end of my student days, I became an apprentice, and I arranged to be placed with Sammy, because it was the logical thing for me to do. When I went to work for him, I was the fourth barber in a four-chair shop, and I enjoyed my work there very much. There was an old barber who worked right next to me. He was one of these rough barbers, the opposite of Sam Garcia. He used to nick about everybody over the ear with his razor. He'd really give them a chop job. He was one of those fast barbers [too]. I guess he made more money than anybody, 'cause he got people in and out. But he was a bit unethical. He used to go to the head of the stairs [outside the shop] and wait for customers to start down. He'd be talking to them and take them right into his chair while the other barbers were waiting for business. So he would kind of cheat [them] this way. Well, one day, he was up there waiting. He was standing there, and all of a sudden we seen him coming down, mumbling to himself. As he walked into the shop, went to the back room, we heard him say, "Out of eighty thousand people [in the city], that damn pigeon chose to crap on me!" [*Laughs*] I guess that was his payment for cheating.

I finished my apprenticeship in 1947 and started my barbering career. At first, I stayed on with Sam, then about a year later I decided to branch out into music. Sam and I talked about it and I told him I wanted to go on the road. He advised me against it because I had a pretty good following in the shop. But I really had an urge to perform. You've heard the phrase "going on the road." Well, that's what I wanted to do.

Now, Sammy had a six-piece combo—piano, drums, bass, guitar, sax, and trumpet—called Sammy G's, and I played guitar in it for a while. For bigger jobs, he also had a twelve-piece band, and I played bass violin there. We played dance halls like Lagoon and the Avalon ballroom. We'd also go up to the Bingham dances regularly, because he was well known there.

I remember there was a time when I was playing with Sammy G's on weekends and at the old La Conga Room on the corner of Second South and Regent Street three weeknights. Those were good times for dance music and clubs. There was a lot of left-over excitement from the big bands [like] Glenn Miller, Tommy Dorsey, which were prevalent during the war. So there were clubs all up and down Main and State Street. There was the Chi-Chi, the Hut

Set, the Casbah, the Glenwood, the Windsor, and the Convertible, which was an after-hours club. At one time we were the Convertible's house band. We'd start maybe twelve thirty or one o'clock A.M. and play until daylight. People that danced to us at one club would follow us to the other.

Salt Lake was altogether different then. There was a nightlife, and old buildings like the Templeton were still around. That type of architecture was prevalent throughout the city. Now they have these modern glass cubicles which have no feeling. In fact, Salt Lake is not at all what it used to be. [Back then] I could go down the street and walk past a bakery and smell fresh bread baking, or past a shoe shop and smell the pungent odor of leather, or [past] different [ethnic] restaurants with their fragrances. The city was an overgrown small town. That's how I would describe it. But with character! Picture walking past a barbershop, seeing a barber with one of those visors they used to shade their eyes swinging a towel over a man's face to dry it. This was a typical Salt Lake scene.

I remember the old businesses, too, and the people—mostly the people. At one time I couldn't walk a block without meeting half a dozen people I knew well enough to stop, shake hands with, or visit for a moment. A familiar face was always there. Now, it's a city of strangers.

I left to go on the road in '48 and was gone three years, playing nightclubs. We formed a group called The Three Dons (guitar, bass, and guitar-vocalist), and we traveled in the intermountain area. The furthest we traveled was to Pueblo, Colorado. Mostly we went to Rock Springs, Green River, Plaindale, Jackson, all through Wyoming, southern Idaho, and Nevada. There was a time we had an agent, who'd book us for different occasions. He also had a traveling show with a chorus line; some of these people were friendly with us, so we often appeared together.

And I liked it: I liked the people; I liked the music; and I liked the atmosphere of the clubs. They were places to have a good time and to beat up on each other. [*Laughs*] That was part of the scene, I guess. But mainly I wanted to play my music and get away from the pressures of day-to-day living. Maybe I wasn't mature, I don't know. I was fresh back from overseas, I had tried making it in barbering, I was doing all right. But I still wanted to perform. My wife didn't care for it. She wanted me home. So we had a big conflict. I guess I rebelled. Instead of going to the choir, as she wanted, I went to the nightclub. I suppose that's a good way to put it. It was quite traumatic, because while I was away, my divorce became final. So once I left, I was gone.

But I was determined to stay on the road, get it out my system. And I had some good experiences. One of the most pleasant associations I had was with radio station KBRS in Rock Springs, Wyoming. They broadcast us live. It wasn't dubbed or transmitted later. We'd get calls at the studio for various requests, and we'd fill them as best as we could. We got quite a following through this program; I remember they called it "El Rancho Grande." We played a lot of Mexican and Spanish music for the coal mining audience around Rock Springs and Green River. But we even got fan mail from way back in Ohio, I recall. So that was one of the highlights of being away.

We stayed in Rock Springs the better part of a year, playing for the station and at this club—the Rock Springs Bar. Some of the people who heard us on radio would come and listen to us in person. So we packed the house. Some of the Anglos liked us, too; we played country western music for them. But our trade was the Spanish-speaking people. We had a thing going between us. We really enjoyed each other. And to me, this is what it was all about.

We were on the road till 1951. Then I saw we weren't going anywhere. We had lots of jobs, but we weren't going to the top. We weren't recording. So I came back to Salt Lake and got a job at the Chesapeake. It was a billiard hall with a barbershop in the back. I went to work for Vern Little, another excellent barber. From there, about the time of the Korean conflict, I went to the old Greyhound station, which also housed the Bamberger Depot. We had a lot of servicemen in and out of that shop. That was one of the busiest shops I'd ever worked in.

Later I moved across to the Temple Square Hotel because I had a problem with the boss. He came back from lunch one day, and I was working on a black fellow, a soldier. I was cutting his hair. And right away I could tell [the boss] was displeased. When I finished, he called me aside and said, "Hey, we don't do black people here." I said, "What's wrong with them? Isn't their money any good?" He said, "If you want to keep this job, you'll turn them down." I said okay, but at that moment I decided that wasn't the place for me.

I was also starting to get a following of Spanish-speaking people. You know how they are. They're friendly, they speak their language regardless of who's around, and he resented it. The next thing he told me was, "Don't speak that Spanish language in this shop. It doesn't sound good, and my customers don't like it." I said okay, and [right then] I told the fellow sitting in my chair, "Come on, let's finish this haircut somewhere else." I had already seen a job available across the street at the Temple Square Hotel, which was a Trailways station, so I took him across the street, sat him in the new chair, set up my tools, and started barbering there. I kind of hated to do it because of the [brisk] business [we'd had], but I didn't like the idea of discrimination. I didn't like it back then, and I still don't.

I'll tell you of another incident; it happened shortly after that. By then, I had my own shop down on 162 West South Temple. I had finished working at Temple Square and gone into my own shop. I was [standing in my doorway], watching the people go by, and a fellow down the street, a black man, got out of a station wagon. I looked at him, and he looked so familiar as he came up the street with that bounce, that really jolly-type walk. As he got closer, I said, "Aren't you Louis Armstrong?" He said, "Yeah, man, how did you know?" I said, "Everybody knows Satchmo." "Are you a barber?" he asked. I said, "Yeah, come on in."

He had been at the Hotel Utah; he had [just] played there. But they wouldn't serve him [in the hotel barbershop]. So he went looking for a shop, and mine was the first one he came to. All right. He was a real gentleman. Beautiful. He had the trumpet player's callus on the side of his lip. I noticed it because he was one of my idols as a musician. I gave him a haircut, a shave, a facial, and my son, Mike, who was seven or eight years old, gave him a shoe shine.

Let me tell you what happened after that. After that incident, a movie came to the Capitol Theater called *High Society*. I knew my boy had been impressed by this man, so I took him to see this movie without telling him that Louis Armstrong was playing in the movie. He also had a speaking part. As he came on the screen, my little boy got up in the theater and shouted, "There's the man whose shoes I shined!" [*Laughs*] I said, "Yeah, son, that's Louis Armstrong." [*Chuckles*] That's an incident in my boy's life he'll never forget; nor will I, incidentally. It was an honor to meet that man.

WILLIAM HERMAN GONZALEZ, 60, ASSISTANT PROFESSOR OF LANGUAGES, UNIVERSITY OF UTAH

Six feet tall, broad shouldered, with dark pigmentation and a chiseled, almost severe countenance, Dr. Gonzalez has the classic combination of Native-American and Spanish features. The youngest of ten children, he was born in Monticello, Utah, on April 7, 1935.

Ramon Gonzalez, his paternal grandfather, had arrived in Monticello on March 7, 1900, and homesteaded land in the vicinity of Indian Creek. Several "Anglo" families resided in Monticello at the time, but his was the first Hispanic family to homestead in Utah. "I asked my mother about this a couple of times," Dr. Gonzalez told us. "Her family came fifteen years after Dad's. I said, 'Why did you pick Utah? Why didn't you pick California, where it's warm?' She said, 'The land was free then. You just came out and homesteaded.' So that was it; I guess it was as good a reason as any."

Dr. Gonzalez grew up in Monticello, but not on his grandfather's homestead. The family lost that farm in 1902 when his grandfather died and his father was compelled to "work for wages" to support the family. The eighty-acre farm on which he was raised and to which he is deeply attached was willed to his father by "Old Man Jim Hicks," an old-time cowboy his father met while working for the S&S Cattle Company. "That's the place I grew up on," Dr. Gonzalez said. "And now we're the only Hispanics left with land in Monticello. The rest moved or sold out to Anglos or gave it up because of taxes. It was just hard to make a living out there."

A graduate of San Jose State College, Dr. Gonzalez concluded his graduate studies in Spain, where he received three master's degrees and completed his doctoral course work. He began his teaching career at the University of Utah in 1970, just as SOCIO was becoming an agent of change in the Chicano community. A passionate civil rights advocate, he was an active member of the Salt Lake City chapter of SOCIO and was

William Gonzalez. *George Janecek*

instrumental in its effort to diversify the university's faculty. "My father was a fighter,"
he explained. "He didn't get angry often. But when he did, he was frightening. So my
oldest sister and I are both fighters. We'll speak our minds when we have to."

In 1970, Dr. Gonzalez was one of four Chicano instructors at the University of
Utah. "Today [in 1987]," he noted, "the university has more than eighty-three
instructors of Hispanic background."

One of my earliest childhood memories is going out to the farm. . . . It was
just six miles [out of town], but it seemed an eternity to go out and come back.
I remember the irrigation ditches carrying water—*beautiful*. I can remember
long, cold winters—those were *awful*. I can remember coming into town, and
there were still hitching posts on the streets. And I vividly remember the CCC
[Civilian Conservation Corps] boys [in our area]. Their camps were up on the
mountain, and you'd hear them coming down the mountainside.[8] [Their
singing was] like something out of Europe, kind of an operetta. They spoke a
different Spanish than ours.

Sometimes a few of them [became] part of the family, because there would be twenty of us at the table. There was always plenty of food, plenty of deer meat, potatoes, tortillas. They would also go down to the farm and help us put up the hay. I was always glad to see them coming, because we'd get the work done in one-fourth the time. I can remember cutting five acres of hay with a scythe and stacking it to dry. I was the littlest, so I had to stack it into shocks [groups of sheaves of grain placed on end]. I remember spending the days in the wagon; it had a big hayrack. We'd load the hay and bring it up to the barn. I can also remember lots of cows, [lots of] milking. In 1941 all these kids disappeared. Yet when I'd meet [any of] them later, they said some of the most beautiful experiences they had ever known were working with us on the farm. Because most of these kids were Puerto Ricans out of New York City. They had come out here and stumbled over this Hispanic section of our state. It's a beautiful chapter in the history of that era.

Oh, I can recall a lot of things. I remember going to school on my first day, understanding English but not speaking it, because we couldn't ever speak English [at home]. My dad wouldn't allow it. He spoke fluent English yet considered speaking English at home an insult. So we only spoke Spanish. My mother would get upset. She said the only way she could learn English was if we [kids] spoke it to her. She was very upset about that.

I remember going out and chopping wood. In the summer and fall, we had to go out with the wagon and bring in wood for the winter. We didn't have running water, and our lot didn't have water access. So we would go down to the corner where a water main had broken. A lot of people would get water out of a hole by that main. It was a natural spring. They would go down with their buckets and carry water home. Our life was basically the [old] farm life of New Mexico. [Only] it was [taking place] farther north.

[My] dad was very Catholic, extremely Catholic—but not an extreme Catholic. He was very severe, very strict. He had been forged in New Mexico. Kids there, I think, didn't have childhoods. They were supposed to act like men at twelve years of age. Sometimes he was just like one of the Puritan fathers we talk about, an orthodox Puritan. He sometimes reminded me of that. With him it was always "Yes, sir. No, sir." That was it. He was a good man, though. Often he'd go downtown by the post office, and he'd come back with a couple of Navajos. There was always [extra] coffee and bread at the table for the Navajos. They'd ride their horses in, and he'd take [the Navajos] to the house and feed them.

[He was] a solid New Mexico–type Christian, in the sense [that] whoever came to your door, you had to feed them, you had to give them something. My mom was more practical; she was his second wife. His first wife died in the flu epidemic of 1917. They had five children. He married my mother, Carolina Belarde, in 1924. Her family had left Gallina, New Mexico, in 1915 and come north on a wagon. They settled about six miles north of town, [a place] called Carlisle. They homesteaded there, and her brothers tended sheep. Since her mother had died [in New Mexico], she brought up her nine brothers and sisters. So she was definitely more practical.

In fact, I see Dad as being idealistic and Mom as the practical one. She had to know what to buy. She had to make sure there was [enough] food on the table. Sometimes there wasn't much. Dad could go without; he'd been a cowboy, and they'd sometimes go two and three days without eating. I guess he thought the rest of us could do that [too].

I remember, when I was eight or nine and my brother was ten or eleven, we'd stay at the farm. If my father was working [elsewhere], somebody had to be down there. So my brother and I would go and stay a week at a time. We would milk the cows and make cheese, and on Saturday afternoon we'd let the cows and calves out and we'd ride [back to town]. On Sunday night we'd go back again. We'd spend all summer doing this. Mother used to worry about rattlesnakes or the horses stepping on us. But then she realized this was life in our part of the country. She'd come out of the same thing in New Mexico, yet she seemed to think we shouldn't go through that.

I remember making cheese—getting big pans of milk with my brother and putting the rennet in to curdle the milk. We'd put it in big flour sacks and hang it off a tree to drain, so by week's end we had a load of cheese to take back to town. Then my mother would sell it. I remember that—clearly.

My mother was a very practical, very hardworking woman, yet she never learned English. She could understand it, but she never spoke it. I remember, she'd go to high school PTA [Parent Teacher Association] meetings and she'd feel embarrassed. She was always embarrassed because she thought the gringos ate much better than we did.

I remember one time, when I was a freshman in high school, we had a class dance and we had to take cookies. I said, "Mom, I have to take two dozen cookies to the dance." She said, "Well, you have to buy them at the store." I said, "Oh, no, these can't be store cookies. They have to be homemade." She was very embarrassed about it, but she made this pan of very thick New Mexico cookies, called *bizcochitos*. And I took them to the dance. She came up with my sister later, and she didn't see her cookies. The next day she said, "What happened to my cookies? Were you too embarrassed to put them out on the table?" I said, "No, Mom, it wasn't that. Someone grabbed one of them out back, bit into it, and said, 'Who made these cookies?' I said, 'My mom.' The guy said, 'God, these are good.' And everyone grabbed them, so they didn't even get to the dance floor. They never made it out to the table. They ate them all in the back." She felt pretty good after that. She stopped hiding her tortillas [from my Anglo friends].

But she was a very humble woman, unsure of herself. She was very intelligent, but for many years she had a tremendous [inferiority] complex.

Now, Monticello was divided into three [Hispanic] sections. The eastern part of town had a few families; then down south there was a big section of Hispanics; and in our area there were a few families. So we had these little pockets of Hispanic families in town. As a matter of fact, we had nicknames for each area. The eastern part had an irrigation ditch running by it and was called Blue Lake, because people there were thought to be snooty. The place where everyone lived was called Chihuahua. They called our area New Jerusalem because we were very Catholic. So every barrio had its special name, which is typical.

I've done a history of Durango, and old Durango was divided [the same way]. Each area had its nickname. Yet if there was a tragedy or anything like that, people really came together. If someone was sick, the whole town of Hispanics was there. Among the men there were always petty falling-outs. But when someone was dying, people would come together in prayer to console the family. And if a person passed away, all the families would gather to take food. The men would be in charge of digging the grave. The women would be in charge of the food, and they would cry together. All the women would get together—sometimes there'd be some men, but mainly the women—so there was a cleansing, a catharsis.

I recall the wakes [too]. Everyone had to go. And there were certain ballads they brought from New Mexico. They would sing [these] ballads. They'd start with the rosary for the person who passed away, and the chanting [of ballads] would last all night. It was kind of a brotherhood chant, these ballads. [Those who chanted] were called the Brotherhood of our Father, Jesus the Nazarene. The [chanting] practice had been handed down through our oral tradition, and it was very compelling, very powerful. In New Mexico during Lent and Holy Week, the men [in the brotherhood] would meet in a building outside of town called the Morada, the dwelling place. The men would [stay there] and chant and observe Holy Week very strictly. This was also carried on in the homes.

Though my father didn't live long enough in New Mexico to belong to the brotherhood, whenever there was a death, he and the men would take over and chant. They had a rosary and they'd chant these ballads.

The [ballad about the] Virgin's search for the child Jesus was a famous one. You find it everywhere in South American countries. [In it] the Virgin follows the trail of Jesus' blood. It is early in the morning; the bells of Jerusalem ring [in] the morning prayers. Mary meets a woman and asks her, "Have you seen my son go by here?" The woman answers, "Yes, he went by here. He's carrying a heavy cross. He has nails in one hand, a hammer in the other, and a rope around his neck. And with every few steps, every time they pull on the rope, he falls to the ground." Hearing this, Mary faints. Then John and the Magdalene take her by the hand. Yet no matter how much they hurry, they always crucify [Jesus]. This [ballad] is sung to a mixture of Gregorian and Saeta [Indian] melodies. It's very beautiful.

Of my parents' ten children, I was the closest to my father. A lot of my older siblings just kind of stood apart from his brand of Catholicism because they thought it severe. Well, it was [severe], but I guess I didn't mind. I remember a lot of times my dad would just drag me down to church and have me pray with him. Being the youngest and the favorite, I had a lot of trust in him. I remember he'd say, "Just go with me," and there wasn't much I could do. We'd go to church, clean the snow off the steps, then go inside and say the rosary.

The New Mexican rosary is very long. It has fifty beads. He'd begin with a profession of faith, then he'd say three Hail Marys, then start the rosary. He'd start the meditation on different aspects of Jesus' life, then he'd say Our Father and ten Hail Marys. When he finished, he started the Second Mystery. Then he offered prayers for family members, for the dead, for rain, for wind. In August there was no wind, so we said the rosary to see if He would send wind so we could thresh the wheat. By the time he got through, remembering everyone and their parents and relatives who had died, it seemed it had gone on for hours.

We prayed for everything. We always had prayers before meals—*always*—then after. If someone had an accident on the road and died, you'd stop and say prayers there. I remember one of Dad's godchildren was killed in a car accident. The car turned over between Monticello and Verdure. When Dad found the place, he put up a cross there, then a monument. When we'd go by, we'd always stop and pray for the soul. Sometimes we'd be driving by and see [other] people out there praying. It was kind of idyllic. The simplicity of the faith was unbelievable. But this was the legacy of Franciscan spirituality. The devotion in the family was strong. Everything was touched by religion.

And that's the [key] to the New Mexico Hispanic. He's totally Franciscan in his outlook. The Franciscans came in through there, and they brought the faith, intermarriage, everything. So everything [in our life] is Franciscan oriented—including the vow of poverty, absolute poverty. The reason Hispanics have never [completely] acclimated in this society is this Franciscan principle of poverty. It's part of the whole heritage, and you can't undo it just by throwing it overboard. It's very strong. It's almost genetic. You can see it—they give away everything. You're not supposed to collect anything. You're not supposed to have it. Some of the older [Franciscan] Brothers have done away with this [now]. But for the most part, they'd give you the clothes off their back. My dad was similar. Even the little we had he was [always] willing to share.

I remember, when I went back to Spain to study in 1962, I saw it there, too. It was like coming home. I could really see my culture. When I'd visit five homes in the village, I'd have to have five cups of coffee or beer. I couldn't refuse.

I went to Spain after graduating from San Jose State and doing my army stint. I received a scholarship from the Spanish government, and I went over to get a master's in Spanish. But after a year I entered theological school and studied philosophy, theology, dogmatic theology. I finished with master's degrees in philosophy, theology, and Hispanic culture. I also concluded my doctoral course work. It took me eight years.

I came back in 1970, and, let me tell you, that transition was extremely difficult. The culture shock was just unbelievable. What was hard was seeing the discrimination, because I was seeing it *for the first time* [after coming] from a place where I had lived as a part of a group. You see, I had become totally Hispanic. No one questioned where I was from [in Spain]. I was just a human being, a part of the whole.

Then I came back, and people started labeling and classifying me, putting me here and putting me there. That was very hard to accept. And the patronizing attitude toward minorities, which is so prevalent in Utah, was annoying. I had ten times the education of most [white] people, but they'd still look down their nose at me. I couldn't get over that. And seeing the situation of the Hispanic was shocking. When I arrived, there was one, or possibly two, Hispanic schoolteachers in the *entire* valley. Most Hispanics students at the university couldn't find jobs. There was just nothing, nothing [for them]. They'd come to a barren land.

So that's where we started. Then I joined SOCIO. It was an organization that was just getting off the ground [in 1970]. It needed a lot of dedication. We worked on it for six years, day and night, establishing chapters all over the state. Our goal was to give the [Utah] Hispanic his identity, not only in the Anglo civil structure but also within our church. Because our [Catholic] church was just as racist as anything out there. [The priests] thought that by making us Anglos, by making us ashamed of our heritage, we'd be more easily accepted. I said, "There is no way we are going to be ashamed of our heritage. We have a very rich heritage."

So we fought within civil institutions; we fought within the church; and we made changes. When I think about it now, I see our progress has been tremendous. I see lawyers, doctors, professors, [and] teachers with Hispanic names, and they are a product of our efforts. At our first university faculty meeting, there were three Hispanics; all of them were TAs [teaching assistants]. We now have full-fledged, tenured faculty, people in important positions. So the confrontations paid off. We wanted equal representation, especially at the university, because it was a *totally* white institution. One of the reasons minorities didn't want to go there [to teach] was because it meant you had to leave everything. You'd be completely whitewashed. You gave up your identity. You tried to assimilate. Some people gave up their religion and everything else so they could fit. But there was no way I was going to do that.

So when I look back, I see it's been a long, intense journey. I remember confrontations with [the state] Welfare [Department], the Tooele School District—tremendous confrontations. A couple of Hispanic kids were killed out there [in Tooele], and there was blatant racism. They wouldn't accept Hispanics, and Hispanics had been living there since 1945. Yet once they saw we weren't [just] antagonists but were honestly trying to create a more equitable system, their attitude to us changed. Tooele was exemplary in this.

One school [in the Salt Lake area] wound up hiring a Hispanic principal; there were Hispanic valedictorians and student body presidents. And all of a sudden there was this tremendous crop of [Hispanic] kids coming out. We'd see them come to the University [of Utah] for scholarships. So we were productive. No one had examined the system or set up an opposition [to it] before

[SOCIO]. Of course, people called us troublemakers, even within our church. I was [labeled] a troublemaker, a rabble-rouser, but I didn't care. Christianity means commitment. If you profess Christianity, you have a moral obligation to change bad situations. There is a very strong moral obligation to act. I believe in that very firmly, even if acting means going against your own church or your own group. And it *has* paid off. Change has come about. There [still] isn't full equality, because you can't undo the history of a nation overnight. But we're going in that direction. We *are* moving forward.

EPILOGUE

DAHLIA CORDOVA, 40, ASSISTANT PRINCIPAL, GLENDALE INTERMEDIATE SCHOOL

In between classes, while hordes of seventh- and eighth-grade students race through the hallways, Dahlia Cordova is barely discernible above their heads. Yet, at five feet two inches, the assistant principal at Glendale Intermediate walks tall with her strong principles and dedication toward educating the young and supporting ethnic awareness.

The daughter of a schoolteacher, Lorenzo Jaramillo, Dahlia has followed in her father's footsteps. After graduating from Menaul High School in Albuquerque, New Mexico, she continued her education at the College of Eastern Utah, Utah State University, the University of Utah, and the University of Alaska. Throughout, she maintained a 4.0 grade point average even though, at times, she was the only "person of color" in an environment still tempered with racial stereotypes. But learning how to "reject rejection," as Dahlia put it, she persevered and has become well known in the Salt Lake community for fostering ethnic awareness.

Voicing her belief that "people of color need to have their story told and heard by others," Dahlia wrote The Navajo Way of Life *and* Nuestra Herenia Cultural *(Our Hispanic Heritage), two monographs to be included in the curriculum material for junior high school students in the Salt Lake City School District. She told us that she will not be satisfied with any level of public education until it has risen to embrace the diversity of all people.*

My father was born in Truchas, New Mexico. Do you remember the film *The Milagro Beanfield War*? That took place on his family's land in Truchas. Wide and expansive, it is really beautiful land, part of the vast territory the United States acquired after the Treaty of Guadalupe-Hidalgo was signed in 1848. Like many others, my father is a descendant of farmers who decided to remain in this country [after 1848] and become citizens rather than go back to Mexico and lose their land. Ironically, they lost their land anyway because of the imposition of taxes they couldn't afford to pay.

Dahlia Cordova. *Kent Miles*

My father was seven years old when his family moved to Helper, Utah. His father worked for the railroad. I believe he used to water the trains to make sure they had sufficient fluid to run. Eventually, my grandfather saved enough money to buy a small house on a street that fronted the Price River. But no matter how long he lived there, he couldn't read, write, or speak English. When he'd sign a legal document, which he did for their home, he made an X on the paper. It was enough for him, and he got along; but he wanted more for his son. So by the time my father was ready to go to junior high school, his parents had the foresight to send him to Allison and James, a Presbyterian boarding school in New Mexico.

There, my father received a fellowship and met a teacher who very much believed in what he could do . . . and what he could become. Mrs. Womsley—who [early on] taught at Allison and James—was influential in guiding my father's academic life. She was a mentor, a guardian angel who inspired him. She encouraged him to pursue an education, and she wrote letters to his parents [urging them] to allow him that opportunity. Later, when she transferred to Menaul, the Presbyterian high school, she took him with her.

At Menaul, they used to say my father was like a walking dictionary. He knew the spelling and definition of any word asked him. Although Spanish was his [native] language, he spoke English flawlessly. He was also very bright in terms of his mathematical ability, and [he] was the first person in our family's history to go to college. Eventually, he became one of the first people of color to teach in a Utah school.

After my father graduated from Menaul and married my mother, he was drafted into the army and sent to Korea. There, he got sick and caught rheumatic fever, which caused incredible damage to his heart and threatened his life. He received a medical discharge and was sent home. Growing up, I remember he would get very ill, deathly ill. I often watched my mother put him in the car and drive from our house in Carbon County all the way to Salt Lake, to the VA Hospital. She'd stay with him until he could come home. Then she'd be gone again, taking him to physical therapy treatments and doctor appointments.

When this happened in my early years, we children stayed with neighbors. As I got older, though, I took on more responsibilities. By the time I was eight years old, I was cooking, cleaning house, and taking care of my brothers and sister. Often my mother had to take my father to the doctors, to the hospital, or to physical therapy. Sometimes we worried that my father wouldn't come back.

But my father was a fighter. He was the first person in the country to have open-heart surgery, a three-valve transplant, and live through it. He fought to live. And no matter how many times he was told his future was slim, he wouldn't let it deter him from his dream of teaching. In pursuit of his education, he went to Westminster College, to the University of Utah, and even to Stanford. All this time, he struggled with his illness. Yet he completed his college education and got a job teaching junior high school first in Draggerton, Utah, then in Price. Within his short career, he had a way of teaching that children remembered for years. And he had such a love for teaching and for children that even when he suffered a stroke, which temporarily took away his ability to speak and write, he still didn't allow it to stop him from giving.

Paralyzed on his right side, [he dragged] himself up and down our long hallway all through the night [before an important meeting]. Slowly, he walked back and forth, back and forth. It hurt to watch him. No matter how painful it was, he refused to let anyone take him to the hospital. By morning, he was able to walk normally; and when the teachers held their annual meeting that day to discuss the school year, he was there. My family had to virtually pry him out of there to get him to the hospital, where he stayed for three months.

My father loved learning, and he believed in education as a means of making changes, breaking through stereotypes, and opening doors. When he first started teaching in Utah, people like him couldn't get a job anywhere else but in Draggerton. He became known as an excellent teacher and was instrumental in helping [other people of color] find employment. In Price, he initiated the nationally known GI Forum, a predecessor to SOCIO. Lawrence Gonzales, who later became a principal in the Salt Lake School District, credits my father with helping him get his first teaching job. In those days, people of color worked in the mines or for the railroad. They weren't teachers.

During our last Christmas season together, when he knew he was dying, my father called each of us into his room. He told me he wanted me to help my brothers and sisters to go to school and [wanted me] to continue my education, because that was the only thing that was going to help me be successful in life. He said that was what he had worked for in his life and that's what he wanted for me and what he was leaving for me. At the time, I was sixteen years old and was attending Manuel, just like my parents. They had just picked my brother and me up for Christmas vacation, and we were no sooner home when he got sick. That night, he was taken to the hospital, and within three days he died. He had no time to open his Christmas presents. He was thirty-nine years old.

My father always believed that neither ethnicity nor the color of one's skin should hold a person back from accomplishing his or her dreams and aspirations. Growing up in Carbon County, I attended elementary school, junior high, and one year of high school [there], and I always felt I was excluded socially and academically from all the activities. People of color were put down, taunted, and told—even without words—that we would never amount to anything. Our survival relied on our sticking together. That was our reality. Black, Native-American, Chicano—we never went outside our group. I never participated in any of the extracurricular activities. There was nobody like me in the Pep Club or in cheerleading. There was nobody like me on the student council. None of us were a part of that. We were never invited to join in, nor did we get any type of encouragement from anyone on the faculty.

Nothing was said. It was just understood which kids would experience those kinds of opportunities.

Think for a moment about what happens to kids who aren't encouraged to participate in school. When I look back at all of the friends I grew up with, the Hispanic women, I see that many of them didn't complete their high school education. A lot of them ended up getting pregnant, married at a young age, and locked into a day-to-day existence with little financial means to make any kind of change. But then, what were the expectations? At Manuel, expectations and opportunities existed threefold; and it was there that my life changed academically, socially, and emotionally. Fifty percent of the students were people of color from not only the United States but from other countries throughout the world. As a private religious school, the emphasis was on reflection, academic excellence, and self-worth. The environment was a multicultural experience in which everyone embraced their differences and looked into their history. Like my parents, I was encouraged to challenge myself and to succeed. I was commonly placed on the dean's list for my grades. I got a chance to run for student body officer and was nominated to be on the Queen's Court. The world opened up to me.

In traditional mainstream public schools, these opportunities were rare and hard to come by. In traditional schools, as part of a curriculum, you would think by now that everyone's culture, their history, and experiences would be explored. But it isn't so. In this country, people of color have not had the opportunity to have their story told. We've been discriminated against by non-inclusion. If you look at textbooks, you'll see nothing about people of color and their perspective on history. There are so many people even today who don't realize that the southwestern territories were part of Mexico before they were acquired by the United States as a result of the Mexican-American War. So many people don't know that. Yet they will tell us—people who have a different language—to go back to where we came from, not realizing that we have always been here, many of us before their ancestors arrived.

So it's all a part of ignorance. And the only way we're going to stop prejudice and discrimination is to stand up and correct the misconceptions that exist; to not allow the ethnic jokes that exploit people—all kinds of people— to occur within our circles; to acquire more education and knowledge that explains the contributions ethnic groups have made to this country; and to give voice to our stories so that others may understand and learn.

In my family, I'm the first female to acquire a graduate education. Throughout my college experience, there was not another Hispanic female in any of my classes. There was not even another person of color. I felt different and knew, just like my father did, that I would have to work hard to achieve my goals. All through college, I maintained a 4.0 average. I also believe I have broken the stereotype that has hindered Hispanic women and am moving forward with other Hispanic women into careers and professions that were once denied us.

My mother did it, too. She is a woman I truly admire. When my father realized that his health was failing, he encouraged her to pursue some type of training, so she could be prepared if he were to die. So while my father went to school, my mother completed her GED [high school equivalency work] and enrolled in the College of Eastern Utah. When my father went to BYU [Brigham Young University] for speech therapy after his stroke, she continued at Provo Community College and graduated with an associate degree in social work. Her desire to learn was nurtured by my father, and, in the end, she did what my father had hoped.

After his death, she picked herself up and carried on. She overcame obstacles, racial stereotypes, and traditional gender roles. To take care of us, she broke with tradition and for the last twenty years has been working in the mental health field.

Like my father, she taught me to strive for what I believe in. She helped us confront the negativism that came because we are people of color. She had a soft, calm voice—still does—and could soothe us with the sound of her voice and her words. She counseled us and made us feel better.

But I think my father is the person I've tried to emulate. I wanted to become a nurse because I loved taking care of him. I'd rub him with alcohol and then powder his legs, and he'd always say, "You're my little nurse." Most likely, the reason I got into education, too, is because it was his dream. But I've earned what I have. I've been told that my education and my job were given to me because I'm a minority, a woman, and [affirmative action] quotas had to be met. I've been told that and I resent it. My father gave me the impetus to get an education. No one gave me my grades—I earned them. And no one gave me this job—I earned it.

No one gave me my work because of my culture or my gender, although my culture and gender were often the cause of discrimination. I remember having to redo a test because my nursing instructor couldn't believe that a person "of my kind" could score a hundred percent on a test. When I scored a hundred percent on the second test, it was still painful, because this teacher was expecting me to fail because of my culture. It was humiliating, but her bigoted nature strengthened my desire to prove her—and others like her—wrong.

In Anchorage, when my department and I worked to balance an educational curriculum with representation of women, ethnic groups, and handicapped individuals, other administrators did not remark about the effectiveness of the program but [remarked about] our culture. "You mean those people are going to be selecting our new curriculum?" they said. "Those people" were two Hispanics and a black.

When my family moved back to Utah from Alaska, my daughter went to her first day of elementary school and was told by another student that Mexican people stink. That stereotype still exists, as well as the notion that Hispanics are lazy, dirty, smelly people who won't amount to anything and are here in the States illegally.

Well, we're not here illegally. If you understood your history, you'd know my family didn't immigrate recently to the States. They were already here. My people are Chicanos. People don't understand that. They don't know the difference between the terms Chicano, Mexican-American, and Hispanic, and they use the words loosely. Hispanic is a general term the United States government has used to categorize all Spanish-speaking people no matter where they come from. People who come in from Mexico and become citizens are called Mexican-American. But people of Mexican descent are not necessarily Mexican-Americans. I am of Mexican heritage because I have a mixture of Spanish and Indian blood. But as far as my identity and my placement in this world are concerned, I am a Chicano—an American from the southwestern territory of the United States.

When my children come home from school, upset with the discrimination and taunting that still occurs in this day and age, I tell them this and I teach them what my parents taught me. I teach them how to "reject rejection" and embrace the future. You can't change people's attitudes. You are only in control of who you are and how you feel. If you can learn to reject rejection by knowing that you are a good person, that you come from a strong cultural and ethnic background, that you can be educated, and that you have a lot to contribute to yourself, your family, and to your world, you will no longer be obligated to the rejection and you will succeed with whatever you attempt to do.

NOTES

1. The Mormons held that Indians ("Lamanites") were the progeny of Laman, a Book of Mormon profligate. As explained by author Joseph Jorgensen, "Laman and his progeny were cursed by God with dark skins and slovenly ways because of Laman's behavior." Joseph G. Jorgensen, *The Sun Dance Religion* (Chicago: The University of Chicago Press, 1972), 171–173.

2. Our four interviews with John Florez were conducted between May 10, 1984, and October 24, 1984, at which time his father was still living. Reyes Florez passed away on November 25, 1986.

3. In the traditional Indian societies of Middle America, a *curandero,* a medicine man, or a *curandera,* a medicine woman, was called to diagnose and determine how an individual lost his or her soul and to take the necessary steps to regain it.

4. *Empacho* means a heaviness in the stomach or in the bowels, a sense of being impacted. *Susto* literally translates to mean "fright."

5. Although several remedies were used to cure people of *susto, ventosa* (or cupping) was a common one. John Florez describes it in the next paragraph.

6. Guatemoc was one of the ancient gods of the Aztecs; Xochimilko is a lake near present-day Mexico City known for its floating gardenias and gondolas with serenading musicians.

7. During World War II, members of Los Angeles's large second-generation Mexican population formed loosely structured street gangs. Gang members adopted a distinctive dress style known as the zoot suit, or pachuco. As described by Matt Meier and Feliciano Rivera, it consisted of "a broad-rimmed, flat hat, a long draped coat;

. . . high-waisted baggy-legged trousers with tight fitting pegged cuffs . . . ; a long duck-tailed, squared-off hair style, and a lengthy elaborate key chain."

In the spring of 1943, following the death of Jose Diaz, a young Mexican man who was severely beaten and left to die on a rural road in Los Angeles, a series of street fights spontaneously erupted between zoot-suiters and soldiers stationed in the Los Angeles area. These skirmishes soon developed into full-fledged riots, in which Mexican youth even suspected of being zoot-suiters were pulled off buses and trolleys and assaulted by sailors.

The volatile situation abated over the ensuing months, but not before the racial conflict spread to midwestern and even intermountain cities such as Chicago, Detroit, Denver, and Salt Lake City. Matt S. Meier and Feliciano Rivera, *The Chicanos: A History of Mexican Americans* (New York: Hill and Wang, 1972), 192–196.

8. The Civilian Conservation Corps was a creation of President Franklin D. Roosevelt and the New Deal. The basic idea of the program, as described in the *Almanac of American History,* was twofold: "It would provide healthy work for unemployed young men and it would do necessary work in protecting, improving and increasing the nation's natural resources." By June 1933, CCC camps were built in forests and fields throughout the country, and by August of that year "some 300,000 youths between the ages of 18–25 were living and working in these camps." Wages were low, but all the men (many from urban areas) received food, clothing, shelter, transportation, medical care, and training. The length of employment was "a minimum of six months . . . up to a maximum of two years."

By the time the CCC was phased out in 1941–1942, "Over 2,500,000 young men had passed through some 1500 camps. They had . . . worked on projects that helped check soil erosion and control floods; they had built miles of roads and trail in remote areas and had constructed cabins and campgrounds still enjoyed 50 years later. . . . One of the indirect results of the CCC was to bring the national parks and forests into the consciousness of millions of Americans." Arthur M. Schlesinger, Jr., ed., *The Almanac of American History* (New York: G. P. Putnam's Sons, 1983), 462.

AFTERWORD: PROJECT NOTES

Leslie G. Kelen and Eileen Hallet Stone

SELECTION OF GROUPS

The eight groups included in this book reflect our desire to create a *representative* documentary portrait of Utah's oldest, largest, and most culturally viable non-Mormon communities. To select groups suitable for such an enterprise, we relied on a combination of historical, cultural, and demographic considerations and used the following three-step process: First, to obtain narratives recounting earliest settlement, we identified communities that were indigenous to the area or that arrived prior to Utah's statehood or during the 1880–1920 immigrant era. Second, to investigate and portray their long-term social accommodation, we narrowed this pool to groups that had sizable populations and had developed and maintained viable cultural institutions. Then, third, to convey the state's racial and cultural heterogeneity, we selected those groups that were emblematic, we believed, of the experiences of native peoples, racial minorities, and ethnic minorities.

These same considerations compelled us, regrettably, to omit a number of significant non-Mormon communities. For example, although the Navajos in San Juan County constitute a sizable native group, they were not included because their history and development are less central to, and revelatory of, Utah life than is the history of the Utes. And although Irish-, Finnish-, Lebanese-, Basque-, Yugoslav-, and Hungarian-Americans arrived early and were central to Utah's development, their descendants either had not maintained cultural institutions or were too few in number for our study. Finally, we opted not to interview members of the state's growing Korean, Tongan, and Vietnamese communities because they arrived in Utah, by and large, after World War II and thus form a new wave of non-Mormon immigrants.

SELECTION OF INFORMANTS

Informants were selected through a two-step process. First, we asked community leaders (pastors, priests, rabbis, educators, historians, and lay leaders) to help us compile lists of informants. Our desire was to interview senior citizens from all social strata and to place the interview transcripts in an archive for the use of future generations. We explained that some interviews might be used in book form and that, consequently, we were looking for people who *wanted* to talk about themselves, their families, and their community. Our first series of interviews were drawn from these lists.

Our second and third series of interviews were selected after we examined the initial body of information we had collected, established our own contacts, and could identify areas of community life omitted from earlier interviews. Although this method was time-consuming (we interviewed on the Northern Ute Reservation, for example, in 1982, 1985, 1986, and 1987), it enabled us to locate key additional informants, document complex intragroup dynamics, and develop comprehensive community profiles.

For interviews with Ute, Chinese, Japanese, and Mexican-Hispanic informants who could not speak English, we solicited help from their children and grandchildren. They graciously arranged the interview sessions for us and acted as translators. In the Japanese community, three professional translators volunteered their services, and one of them was present at each interview. Another volunteer translated each Issei interview into English, in longhand, and then typed it.

THE INTERVIEW PROCESS

The oral histories were generally recorded in people's homes and places of work; occasionally, however, an informant asked to be interviewed in our office. We approached each interview with a chronologically oriented questionnaire, based on published accounts of each community's history, to be used as a starting point and rough guide. Each interview session, however, was permitted to take its own course, depending on what informants wanted to relate or were capable of relating. The key to obtaining a quality oral history, we found, was to sufficiently structure an interview to secure needed historical information while allowing an informant the freedom to explore the experiences that moved him or her. A successful interview, consequently, was a collaboration in which informant and interviewer jointly participated in creating a narrative of personal and communal worth. Such interviews invariably had something miraculous about them; they arose out of a specific ethnic context and transcended its confines, becoming, in the process, universal accounts of human growth and truth seeking.

Interview sessions often blurred, and occasionally erased, the boundary between informant and interviewer. Lasting friendships sometimes developed. Informants invited us back to their homes, and in Greek and Japanese households, as an example, informants served us elaborate meals followed by ouzo or heated saki. Photo albums were ceremoniously removed from bookcases, family photos were lifted from walls, and we were taken on intimate, multi-generational journeys through a number of families' trials and tribulations. It is difficult to convey the impact of such encounters. We felt as if the doors of an inner sanctuary had opened and we could suddenly walk off a Salt Lake City sidewalk into a village in Mavrolithari or Hiroshima. We offered, or attempted to offer, the informants the gift of our devoted attention, and they, in turn, graced us with access to worlds we had not known existed.

Although the bulk of our interviews were with senior citizens, during the project's final phase we recorded interviews with younger informants to "flesh out" community profiles. In the Ute and African-American communities, these oral histories proved critical. In the Ute community, the younger informants had witnessed the painful and continuing erosion of traditional spiritual values, and they explained to us its staggering psychosocial impact. In the African-American community, the younger informants described the acceleration of the civil rights movement, recalled participation in local and national activities, and narrated the drama of confronting de facto and de jure segregation practices throughout the state. In both instances, the stories did not merely supplement community history; they transmitted core aspects of community experience.

REPOSITORY

In January 1990, we concluded negotiations with Chase Peterson, president of the University of Utah, and Gregory Thompson, director of the Special Collections Center at the university's Marriott Library, to establish an ethnic archive from our oral histories and documentary photographs. Over the following year, we deposited 689 interviews, fourteen thousand black-and-white negatives, and two hundred forty 16" × 20" master prints in the archive for the use of students, scholars, and the community at large. In addition, we deposited another forty interviews that were conducted between 1985 and 1989 with politicians, community leaders, and historians from the "mainstream" Utah culture whose work and experiences shed light on the history of the communities we studied. Among these informants were four former Utah governors, a state supreme court judge, three state legislators, and several university professors who had conducted in-depth field research in Utah's ethnic and minority communities. Although these interviews do not appear in this book, their content corroborates the stories told here.

In all, from the initial contacts we made in the Jewish community in the spring of 1982 to the conclusion of the book in the winter of 1995, we recorded and transcribed 729 oral history interviews. The twelve years we invested in the project were times of intense engagement with the lives of individuals and communities. Conducting oral histories, documenting history from the bottom up, and then editing the contents of the interviews into a book is akin to participating in a series of fiercely demanding personal relationships. Given each community's history and experience, the dynamics of each cultural encounter were unique. Of course, no one seeking to conduct ethnic oral history interviews can expect a different scenario. Yet no one should underestimate the impact of the aggregate experience. It transformed us. We were—*we are*—amazed, shaken, privileged, and grateful.

We must add that this project is neither definitive nor comprehensive. Limited by scope—the number of communities included—and by focus—the specific people interviewed, the project represents the visions and the experiences of the people with whom we spoke, at the time we spoke with them, and is neither a summation of their lives nor an account of their community's *total* Utah experience. The interviews (and the book) can best be likened to windows and doorways that open into the lives of individuals and families while suggesting the evolving multigenerational complex that comprises the groups themselves.

Authors and Contributors

LESLIE G. KELEN was born in Budapest, Hungary and emigrated to the United States with his family in 1959. He grew up in New York City and has been a resident of Utah since 1976. In 1983, he co-founded the Oral History Institute, an independent, non-profit organization dedicated to portraying contemporary life through the documentary medium. He is the author of *This Is A Peace I Never Asked For* and co-author of *The Other Utahns: A Photographic Portfolio* and *Sacred Images: A Vision of Native American Rock Art*. He is presently executive director of the Oral History Institute and an adjunct instructor in the Humanities department at the Salt Lake Community College.

EILEEN HALLET STONE, transplanted from New England, is a Utah-based journalistic writer who for the past seventeen years has been recognized for her work in projects as diverse as nineteenth century architecture, populations in crisis, child care, and ethnic histories. She has published in excess of 300 articles to date. Currently the editor of the *Graphic Arts Journal* and a tri-state religious periodical, this is her first book. She resides in Salt Lake City with her son Daniel Ian Gittins Stone.

GEORGE JANECEK began as a fine art photographer in New York City and switched to photodocumentary work after settling in Utah and working with the Oral History Institute. In 1990 he moved to Czechoslovakia (his country of origin) and now resides and photographs in Pilsen in the Czech Republic.

KENT MILES was born and raised in Salt Lake City. Since 1979 he has worked as a free-lance photographer specializing in editorial, corporate, and documentary photography. His most recent work includes the exhibit, "The Class of 94: Photographs from the Salt Lake Community High School" and *Wonderfully Worth Doing*, portraits of artists for the Art Access Gallery.

HELEN PAPANIKOLAS, whose parents emigrated from Greece in the early 1900s, has been frequently honored for her research and writing. For over forty years, she has published essays and monographs on Utah labor, immigration, and ethnic history, and within the past decade has published a book on her parents' migration, *Emily-George*, and two collections of short stories, *Small Bird, Tell Me* and *The Apple Falls from the Apple Tree*.

KATHRYN L. MACKAY is an associate professor of history and the coordinator of the teaching and learning forum at Weber State University in Ogden, Utah. She has written and published extensively on Ute history and is a contributor to the recently published *Utah History Encyclopedia*.

LARRY CESSPOOCH is the founder of the Ute Audio Visual department, the editor of the *Ute Bulletin*, and the director of public relations for the Northern Ute Tribe. Over the past decade, he has contributed to numerous publications and consulted with many local and regional organizations working to depict Ute culture.

RONALD G. COLEMAN is associate professor of history and ethnic studies and associate vice president for diversity and faculty development at the University of Utah. He researches and teaches African-American history with a special emphasis on western Black history.

JACK GOODMAN, a native of New York, came to Utah in 1945. During his long career in journalism, he worked for the *Salt Lake Tribune*, KALL RADIO, Channel Two and Channel Four and was area correspondent for the *New York Times* and *Newsweek*. Since his retirement, he has written a weekly column for the *Salt Lake Tribune* called "Cityview."

MICHAEL T. WALTON has a doctorate in history from the University of Chicago and has published extensively in the history of science and in 16th century Jewish history.

ANAND A. YANG, professor of history at the University of Utah, is the author of numerous publications on Asian social and political history and has substantive research interests in Asian-American studies. He is also active in Utah's Asian-American community.

PHILIP F. NOTARIANNI is the coordinator of public programs for the Utah State Historical Society and an adjunct instructor in the Department of Ethnic Studies at the University of Utah. He has published numerous articles on Utah immigration, ethnic, labor, and mining history.

NANCY J. TANIGUCHI is associate professor of history at California State University in Stanislaus. Her first book, *Necessary Fraud: Progressive Reform and Utah Coal*, was published by the University of Oklahoma Press in 1996 as part of their legal history of North America series.

EDWARD H. MAYER is professor of Spanish American literature and culture and director of Chicano studies at the University of Utah. He has published numerous essays on Spanish American drama and Mexican American life in Utah.